ANOTHER WAY, ANOTHER TIME

JUDAISM AND JEWISH LIFE

ANOTHER WAY, ANOTHER TIME

Religious Inclusivism and the
Sacks Chief Rabbinate

MEIR PERSOFF

ACADEMIC STUDIES PRESS
Boston
2010

First published in 2010 by Academic Studies Press

28 Montfern Avenue
Brighton, MA 02135
United States of America

press@academicstudiespress.com
www.academicstudiespress.com

Library of Congress Cataloging-in-Publication Data:
Persoff, Meir.
Another way, another time : religious inclusivism and the
Sacks Chief Rabbinate / Meir Persoff.
p. cm. -- (Judaism and Jewish life)
Includes bibliographical references and index.
ISBN 978-1-934843-90-1 (hardback) -- ISBN 978-1-936235-10-0 (pbk.)
1. Judaism--21st century. 2. Sacks, Jonathan, 1948- 3. British Chief Rabbinate-
-History. 4. Religious pluralism--Judaism. 5. Postmodernism--Religious
aspects--Judaism. 6. Orthodox Judaism--Relations--Nontraditional Jews. I. Title.

BM45.P475 2010
296.0941'090511--dc22
2010009562

ISBN 978-1-934843-90-1 (cloth)
ISBN 978-1-936235-10-0 (paper)

Book design by Adell Medovoy
Cover photo credit: John Nathan, Jewish Chronicle
Typeset in Joanna MT 11/13

For Klal Yisrael

'If Orthodox Jews are to mend the Jewish world, they must rise beyond sectarian thinking to a position where they can recognise alternatives within the tradition ... The tradition of argument calls for respect for positions with which one does not agree. It leads one to admire stances one does not seek to imitate. These are values powerfully implicit in the rabbinic texts. And not accidentally. For Rabbinic Judaism emerged from the ruins of one disastrous division within the Jewish world. We face another. What mended divisions then has the power to do so now. For whether the future translates into convergence or schism depends less on the chimera of Jewish unity than on how conflict is handled.'

Jonathan Sacks, *Traditional Alternatives: Orthodoxy and the Future of the Jewish People*, 1989

'Chief Rabbi Jonathan Sacks is extremely talented, a brilliant speaker and quick with a pen. He is very successful and represents the community both within and vis-à-vis the outside world ... On the other hand, he sometimes encounters difficulties in his relations with other rabbis.'

Lord Jakobovits in Conversation, 1999

'Only do those things by which you would not be embarrassed if they were published on the front page of tomorrow's newspaper.'

Chief Rabbi Lord Sacks, *Daf Hashavua*, 2009

Contents

Foreword, by Geoffrey Alderman   xi

Preface   xv

1. *With Open Arms*   1

2. *Beyond the Limits*   33

3. *Leading by Example*   45

4. *The Culture of Contempt*   67

5. *The Search for Survival*   91

6. *The Stanmore Accords*   125

Interlude. *From First to Second*   145

7. *The Indignity of Difference*   167

8. *The Crucible of Judaism*   187

9. *The Dynamic of Renewal*   221

10. *Rites and Wrongs*   237

11. *The Stanmore Discords*   257

12. *The Mirage of Unity*   281

13. *The Pull of Pluralism*   293

Notes   317

Bibliography   359

Index   367

Chief Rabbi Jonathan Sacks with Prince Philip, Duke of Edinburgh (left), and Rabbi Hugo Gryn at a 1993 communal gathering in London

The Chief Rabbi with Jackie Gryn and Rabbi Tony Bayfield at the 1997 memorial meeting for West London Synagogue's Rabbi Hugo Gryn

Foreword

The British 'Chief Rabbinate' is a peculiar institution. Ordained neither by British law nor by Jewish religious precept, it evolved during the eighteenth century and matured during the nineteenth. Though not unknown, the institution of a 'chief' rabbinate was rare among the Jewish communities of the diaspora; and where it did exist, its existence was as likely to have been decreed by the Gentile authorities as by the Jewish – if not more so. To be sure, the largely self-governing Jewish communities of Central and Eastern Europe commonly appointed rabbis, but not 'chief' rabbis.

In normative terms, a rabbi, so appointed, enjoyed powers equal to that of his rabbinical colleague in the next village or town. But the British 'Chief Rabbinate,' as fashioned by Nathan Marcus Adler and his son Hermann in the nineteenth and early twentieth centuries, was an altogether different institution. It was Nathan who elevated the office, historically based on the Great Synagogue in the City of London, into a highly centralised instrument of social as well as religious control. It was Hermann who built into these foundations a fierce and unashamed British patriotism, enabling him to walk the corridors of power with ease.

Not for nothing had the King-Emperor Edward VII referred to Hermann as 'my Chief Rabbi.' When Joseph Hertz succeeded Hermann Adler in 1913, he could claim to be – and indeed was – the ultimate religious authority of the Ashkenazi Jews throughout the British Empire. Even those Jews, to the right and to the left, who did not share Hertz's belief in a centrist Orthodoxy nonetheless bowed (some less willingly than others, it is true) before the majesty of his office.

In the second half of the twentieth century, this edifice began to crumble. The British Empire was dissolved. The Nazi Holocaust had destroyed the great reservoir of talmudic scholarship that had nurtured and nourished Ashkenazi rabbinical learning hitherto. But it had also undermined Jewish faith in liberal values. As I have written elsewhere, 'Before (say) 1933, modernity had something to offer the Jew: equality before the law; the opportunity to benefit from a secular education and to advance into the professions; freedom of worship. After 1945, for many of the Jewish survivors, modernity had little if any attraction. Emancipation had promised much, but had instead delivered destruction and death on a massive scale.'[1]

---

[1] Geoffrey Alderman, 'Orthodox Judaism and Chief Rabbis in Britain,' in *Jewish Journal of Sociology*, Vol. 49 (2007), p.81, on which this and the following two paragraphs are based.

So it was that 'ultra'-Orthodoxy – hallmarked by an unbridled arrogance and an unthinking and (frankly) vindictive intolerance, and grounded much less in authentic Judaism than in a bogus refusal to engage with modernity – received a new lease of life. In the days of the Adlers, 'ultra'-Orthodoxy was scarcely known among the Jews over whom they ruled. Hertz had his differences with the sectarians, but weathered a number of storms without conceding for one moment his belief in, and practice of, the 'Progressive Conservatism' (his phrase) that he preached.

But in the post-Holocaust world, the centre ground that had sustained successive Chief Rabbis for a century and more began to disappear. British Jewry became pluralised and polarised. Only a Chief Rabbi of great wisdom and learning could have sought a new accommodation between the multiple Orthodoxies that the Jewish world now presented.

Israel Brodie (Chief Rabbi, 1948–65) was neither. An intellectual lightweight with no claim whatever to talmudic scholarship, Brodie owed his appointment to his Oxford education and his thoroughly English manners. Desperate though he was to build and rebuild the bridges between the various forms of Orthodoxy over which he now reigned (but did not rule), he proved spectacularly unequal to the task. And in his comprehensive mishandling of the 'Jacobs Affair,' he succeeded only in pouring yet more fat on to the fire.

The man who did have the intellect, and the claim to talmudic learning, was Brodie's successor, Immanuel Jakobovits (Chief Rabbi, 1967–91). In his previous volume, *Faith Against Reason*, Meir Persoff laid out and analysed for us the manner in which this refugee scholar tried, and failed, to heal the wounds caused by that affair. On the one hand, Jakobovits laboured unsuccessfully to build new bridges between the various denominations and sub-denominations into which British Jewry had fractured. On the other, he actually destroyed, or severely weakened, the bridges that had existed hitherto. So it was that he bequeathed to his successor, Jonathan Sacks, an office weaker than it had ever been.

Sacks is an enigma. On an academic level, he is without doubt the most accomplished holder of the office of British Chief Rabbi. But, in many respects, he lacks perspicacity, and (among other things) any sense of the political. Palpably, moreover, he lacks the courage of his own convictions.

He came into office waving the banner of 'inclusivism.' But did he really believe it would work? In January 1995, following an outcry from the right over the certification of Masorti (Conservative) marriages, he saw fit to publish an article in the *Jewish Tribune* – the mouthpiece of the sectarian ultras – condemning adherents of Masorti for having 'severed their links with the faith of their ancestors.' A week later, after a predictable counter-outcry from the left, he published a 'clarification' in the *Jewish Chronicle* stressing his belief in an Orthodoxy 'uncompromising in its tolerance, its compassion, its warmth.' Did he really believe that the readers of one article would not also read the other?

In February 1997, he wrote a letter – surely the most ill-considered letter ever to fall from the pen of a Chief Rabbi – to the rabbinical head of the Union of Orthodox Hebrew Congregations, declaring that the praise it pained him to lavish on the late Reform rabbi and Auschwitz survivor Hugo Gryn was 'due recognition for the good deeds that he did ... not as a Jew, but simply as a person,' one whom he then proceeded to describe as 'among those who destroy the faith.' Its contents aside, it apparently never occurred to Sacks that the letter might be made public.

Five years later, in order to placate the ultras, he agreed to rewrite passages in his book, The Dignity of Difference, claiming that the volume had been meant for a non-Jewish audience. Did it never occur to him that Jews, too, might read it?

In the summer of 2009, he buckled under pressure from the English judiciary and agreed that the prestigious JFS (Jews' Free School) in North-West London might, after all, admit children on the basis of a superficial test of religious practice, having previously declared that only those whom he and his Beth Din recognised as Jewish – subject to strict and unbending halachic criteria – might enrol as pupils there.

In short, under Professor Lord Sacks, the office of Chief Rabbi has become an object of scorn across much of the Jewish world. But both he and the office survive – and, to some extent, thrive. This is partly because not a few of those who are, in private, his fiercest critics are also among the most zealous defenders of the institution. It is also because he and his office have developed over time close, and mutually beneficial, contacts with the non-Jewish world. The life peerage conferred on him in 2009 reflects and demonstrates his standing in the eyes of 'the establishment.' He is – now – virtually untouchable.

But that does not mean that he is beyond critical scrutiny. And there can be few observers better qualified than Meir Persoff to carry out this most necessary assessment.

I say this not because – or merely because – Persoff was my doctoral student. Nor do I say it simply because he has negotiated access to sensitive archives still in private hands. I say it because this former research student has been able to deploy his material against the background of an extensive knowledge of the inner world of British Jewry, gathered over a lifetime reporting and commenting upon it without fear and without favour.

Another Way, Another Time will certainly not be the last word on Jonathan Sacks. But all who write on this subject hereafter will need to measure their efforts against the yardstick Dr Persoff has fashioned, and which he now sets before us.

GEOFFREY ALDERMAN
Michael Gross Professor of Politics and Contemporary History at the University of Buckingham

*The newly installed Chief Rabbi Jonathan Sacks delivering his inaugural address
at the St John's Wood Synagogue, London, 1 September, 1991*

Preface

'Thirteen years ago, almost exactly to the day, I began a journey as rabbi of the Golders Green Synagogue, and today, on my barmitzvah in the rabbinate, you have bestowed on me the honour of one of the great positions of leadership in the Jewish world.' [1]

The prequel to this study, *Faith Against Reason: Religious Reform and the British Chief Rabbinate, 1840–1990*, [2] concluded with a 1992 declaration by Jonathan Sacks in response to a damning report [3] on the state of Britain's centrist-Orthodox United Synagogue, which the recently installed Chief Rabbi of the United Hebrew Congregations of the Commonwealth had been elected to head. 'Now,' he affirmed, 'is a time for leadership if ever there was one; and we must not be found wanting.' [4] Along with 'financial malaise,' the report had identified radical failings at the heart of the organisation, including 'a loss of morale at every tier, confused and conflicting approaches to the United Synagogue's objectives, lack of role definition at both a lay and a professional level, and, above all, a deep dissatisfaction with the centre.' [5]

In May 1991, just four months before Sacks assumed office, Isi Leibler, one of world Jewry's (and centrist-Orthodoxy's) most prominent and outspoken public figures, [6] had discussed the failure of his camp's rabbinical leadership – a key component of 'the centre' – to confront the 'burning issue' of Jewish religious extremism traversing the globe. [7] While applauding the 'unprecedented resurgence' of Orthodoxy in recent years, he had warned against 'the dangers I see arising as a consequence of inadequate spiritual leadership, and an increasing domination of that leadership by extremist elements who are displacing their moderate counterparts and denying legitimacy to viewpoints other than their own.' [8] Twenty years on, with little or no lessening of the extremist stance, Leibler's seven-point 'solution' – which he admitted to sounding like 'a somewhat utopian fantasy' [9] – bears repeating. In encapsulated form, it called for

> • 'a breed of enlightened Orthodox rabbis who are *yir'ei shamayim* – God-fearing Jews – *and* who are willing to stand up and be counted and, if necessary, condemn the growing extremism and bigotry which have permeated sections of the yeshivah world and alienated many Jews from Judaism. In other words, we need rabbis with courage to resist the "halachic blackmail" so frequently employed by their extremist colleagues.'

• 'rabbis who are willing to denounce behaviour which is incompatible with Jewish ethics and morality.'

• 'rabbis who recognise the importance of moderation without compromising the observance of mitzvot or commitment to a life of faith; rabbis who will have the courage to proclaim publicly that, within the framework of halachah, there is scope for different interpretations; rabbis who will stand up and repudiate the zealots.'

• 'rabbis who have the courage to stand up and fight against those who, under the banner of halachah, fight against the tradition of Torah and Reason.'

• 'rabbis who combine intellectual openness with a commitment to *Torah min hashamayim* [Torah from Heaven].'

• 'rabbis who realise that the entire people of Israel is not comprised of observant Jews alone, but that the non-observant Jewish masses are also part of the people whom God has chosen (a well-known talmudic dictum [tractate Sanhedrin 44a] states: *af al pi shechata Yisrael hu*, "even if a Jew transgresses, he remains a Jew"). Our rabbis must regard themselves as spiritual leaders for *all* Jews, and not merely for those who observe the ritual mitzvot.'

• 'rabbis who acknowledge that *ahavat Torah* [love of Torah] and *ahavat Yisrael* [love of all Jews] are inseparable, and who recognise their obligation to act as a bridge between the committed minority and the uncommitted majority who are in danger of losing their identity as Jews ... To do this, our rabbis must be sensitive to human suffering and should be righteous without exuding an aura of religious superiority or self-righteousness.'[10]

Remarking at the time that 'the entire Jewish tradition reflects a tolerance for differing viewpoints,' Leibler added, however: 'Sadly, this tolerance is noticeably absent today. Rabbi Jonathan Sacks, the Chief Rabbi-elect of the British Commonwealth, who does not regard himself as an adherent of the Modern Orthodox stream, nevertheless warns against the prevailing intolerance and the public brawls between Orthodox groups, which he describes as the antithesis of "arguments for the sake of Heaven." He maintains that, despite Orthodoxy's emergence and its increasing influence over the past decade, it is still inclining towards confrontation rather than reconciliation when resolving its inner problems, and seeks to impose authority rather than indulge in dialogue.'[11]

The relevance of Leibler's remarks to the role of the British Chief Rabbinate and the United Synagogue in the wider communal arena, and to their ambiguous relationship with the London Beth Din, will become clear as this volume unfolds. Alongside my previous book, a number of recent studies[12] have discussed the rightward swing within British centrist Orthodoxy and the attenuating influence, size and structure of the moderate camp.

Faith Against Reason – for the first time in the historiography of Anglo-Jewry – traced the increasingly stormy relationship between the Chief Rabbinate and an increasingly polarising community, from the founding of the West London Synagogue of British Jews in the 1840s to the end of the incumbency of Immanuel Jakobovits, five Chief Rabbis and 150 years later. It examined the causes and consequences of the Reform 'modifications' and of the opposition to them; the genesis and spread of the subsequent secessionist movements, Liberal and Conservative (Masorti); the reasons for the growing divisions and dissension within the community; and the results of internal and external influences on all parties to the disputes.

Within that framework, Another Way, Another Time – which, it should be stressed, is neither a biography nor an overview – probes the Chief Rabbinate of Jonathan Sacks, now Baron Sacks of Aldgate,[13] who launched his tenure with the aim of an inclusivist 'Decade of Jewish Renewal.' Seeking to reach out, as he put it in his installation address, 'to every Jew, with open arms and an open heart,' within a few years he was attracting calls, from opponents and supporters, for his resignation and for the abolition of his office. As will be seen, however, similar calls date back to the election of Hermann Adler, exactly a century before Sacks' accession, and pursued each Chief Rabbi from that time on, as his authority and constituency continued to diminish. This study concludes that the Chief Rabbinate has indeed reached the end of the road and explores other paths to the leadership of a pluralistic and – ideally – inclusivist community.

First reviewing Sacks' early writings and pronouncements on the theme of inclusivism (the term he employs in preference to 'inclusiveness' or 'inclusivity'), it then demonstrates how, repeatedly, he said 'irreconcilable things to different audiences'[14] and how, in the process, he induced Stanley Kalms, his 'kingmaker' and foremost patron, to declare of Anglo-Jewry: 'We are in a time warp, and fast becoming an irrelevance in terms of world Jewry,'[15] and to assert – in a contribution to this book – that 'there has been no initiative towards inclusivism.'[16] Given the opportunity to comment in these pages on why, in the opinion of many – including some of his most fervent supporters – his early espousal of, and numerous statements on, inclusivism in Anglo-Jewry had failed to materialise, the Chief Rabbi declined to do so, saying, through his office, that 'as he does not accept the premise, he is unable to respond to it.'[17]

In his introduction to Faith Against Reason, the eminent historian of Anglo-Jewry, Todd M. Endelman,[18] raised the question 'whether intra-communal religious strife was more common in Britain than elsewhere, consuming time, energy and resources in unparalleled ways decade after decade.' This, he wrote,

> is difficult to answer. Jews are a fractious people ... Religious conflicts, tensions, squabbles and breakaways were common in other Western Jewish communities, especially in Germany, Hungary and the United States. Moreover, comparing peaks and troughs of quarrelsomeness is no easy task. An alternative, more fruitful approach is to ask, instead, whether the institution of the Chief Rabbinate (not its incumbents or its ideology but its very existence and structure) in some way facilitated or encouraged religious strife.[19]

My composite studies set out to answer his point, to question assertions of Chief Rabbinical supremacy on the ecclesiastical stage, and to consider the extent to which the lay leaders – the president of the Board of Deputies (under Adler) and of the United Synagogue (until Hertz) – and the Beth Din and right-wingers thereafter, influenced the Chief Rabbis in the bitter struggle against the non-Orthodox movements.

As my earlier preface pointed out, the *modi operandi* of each of these rabbis revealed much about their backgrounds, personalities, authority and effectiveness, and helped shape the verdict of history on their leadership record. These elements were successively weighed in relation to the progressive sectarianism that gathered pace at crucial, and contrasting, stages in the onward march of Anglo-Jewry, and in determining the degree to which each Chief Rabbi was responsible for the diminution or perpetuation of internecine strife. In describing the 'how' as well as the 'why,' both works afford the protagonists generous leeway to speak for themselves, incorporating into the narrative significant passages from their correspondence, addresses, broadsides and disputations, as well as – particularly in this volume – broadcasts, interviews and articles.

An abundance of source material appears through exclusive access to the private papers of three prominent (and now deceased) figures in the later years covered by the survey – Jakobovits, Louis Jacobs and Sidney Brichto, the last two, respectively, former leaders of the Conservative (Masorti) and Liberal movements in Britain – and through patient trawling of London Metropolitan Archives and the collections of Yeshiva University and the Jewish Theological Seminary of America, New York. These papers, in particular, shed light on the tempestuous relationships between the opposing forces, and on the shifts in direction and emphases of the – ultimately unsuccessful – campaigns to quash the secessionists in more recent times. The narrative and analysis benefit also from my close association with the three rabbis named above and, in both a professional and a personal capacity, with many other leading players across the Anglo-Jewish spectrum in the convulsive events of the past several decades.

Delivering the keynote address[20] at a 2008 conference on 'British-Jewish historical, cultural and literary studies, past, present and future,'[21] Endelman discussed the frames of reference within which the community's religious orientation moved rightwards during the tenures of Hertz and Brodie, and, citing an appraisal of this question in relation to their theological outlooks and personal characteristics,[22] criticised what he regards as the trend in Britain to 'divorce the history of Anglo-Jewry from the mainstream of Jewish historical writing' and thus to 'look inward rather than outward.'[23]

Recognising that tendency, both *Faith Against Reason* and *Another Way, Another Time* set the domestic crises and controversies against a backdrop of contrasting schisms in Europe and the United States, helping them to achieve Endelman's ideal of 'a coherent, unified, transnational Jewish historical framework, or core, into which Anglo-Jewish history can be integrated.'[24] The perilous situation facing 21st-century British Jewry, particularly in the fields of conversion and marriage, is replicated, without compunction, in the courts and political corridors of the State of Israel, where, in matters of personal status, lives and families are being shattered almost daily at the drop of a black hat.

Across the continuing drama of division and divisiveness, the role and relevance of the Chief Rabbinate – whether in Britain or in Israel (the United States is free of Chief Rabbis and until 2008 managed to handle such affairs, with far greater success, on a local level[25]) – assume vital importance. It is worth noting how the historical and contemporary parallels between the religious authorities in both countries make this study a valuable resource in unravelling the practical application of inclusivism and rejection.

In today's troubled Jewish world, the 'one people' agenda, focusing on personal status, has largely superseded theological complexities in the hearts and minds of both leaders and led. A landmark case before the English courts[26] – the ramifications of which were set to continue long after this book went to press – heard tangentially of a woman converted by Israel's Special Rabbinical Court for Conversion (established by the Chief Rabbinate) who was married by an Orthodox rabbi in an Orthodox synagogue in New York and whose Jewish status was later unilaterally rejected by the London Beth Din, on the grounds that, knowing she intended to contract a forbidden marriage with a Cohen [male of priestly descent], 'at the moment of her conversion she did not accept all the tenets of Orthodox Judaism.'[27]

In Israel, where similar cases frequently arise, a three-man panel of ultra-Orthodox rabbis, set up by the Chief Rabbinate's High Rabbinical Court, published a ruling in May 2008 that *every* conversion performed since 1999 by Rabbi Chaim Druckman and his fellow religious-Zionist judges in courts established by an earlier Chief Rabbinate was to be retroactively annulled, on grounds not unlike the English case. Responding to their edict, a Conservative (Masorti) rabbi and professor of Jewish law commented: 'I hope and pray that the Supreme Court will overturn this mistaken and destructive ruling. I hope and pray that the State of Israel will start to appoint modern-Orthodox and other qualified rabbis as *dayanim* [judges]. If not, the Chief Rabbinate will have to be abolished, because it will have cut itself off from most of the Jewish people.'[28]

As indicated earlier, the abolition of the Chief Rabbinate – the British version – is a theme running through much of this study, with questions of Jewish status and ecclesiastical authority following close behind. The 'cataclysmic split' which (as we shall see) some have predicted, and which Sacks suggested may have 'to some extent already occurred,' is unquestionably the most crucial issue facing today's Jewish world. *Another Way, Another Time*, and its prequel, go some way towards explaining why.

* * *   * * *   * * *

I once again offer thanks to the families of the late Rabbi Dr Sidney Brichto, Rabbi Dr Louis Jacobs and Emeritus Chief Rabbi Lord Jakobovits for the unprecedented access afforded me to their personal papers during the writing of *Another Way, Another Time* and *Faith Against Reason*, and to sources (both public and private) from within the various synagogue streams who opened their files and shared their experiences. Renewed acknowledgement is made to the many others who proffered help, hospitality, friendship and information – among them, in the preparation of this latest study, Rabbi Dr Raymond Apple, Julian Baggini, Benjamin Balint, Judy Lash Balint, Rabbi Dr Tony Bayfield, Dr Steven Bayme, John Belknap, Rabbi Dr Jeffrey M. Cohen, Dr Benjamin J. Elton, Professor Todd M. Endelman, Rabbi Dr Lawrence A. Englander, Dr Joel Fishman, Professor Lloyd P. Gartner, Rabbi Dr David Goldberg, Sue Greenberg, Dr Rona Hart, Emeritus Professor Colin Holmes, David Jacobs, Gerald Jacobs, Dr Keith D. Kahn-Harris, Lord Kalms, Christa Kling, Candice Krieger, Elkan Levy, Dr Igor Nemirovsky, Kira Nemirovsky, Jackie Persoff, Stephen Pollard, Rabbi Danny Rich, Sara Libby Robinson, Simon Rocker, Karen Silver, Dr Gabriel

Sivan, Rabbi Jackie Tabick, Daniel Vulkan, Paul Vallely, and Professor Leslie Wagner. I am again indebted to the *Jewish Chronicle* – my professional home for forty years – for the use of photographs from its historic collection; to the archives, institutions, libraries and journals listed in *Faith Against Reason* for their ongoing and unfailing co-operation; and particularly, this time round, to London Metropolitan Archives for the exceptional assistance rendered by its staff. An earlier, and shorter, version of *Another Way, Another Time* formed part of my submission for the degree of Doctor of Philosophy from Middlesex University, London, and I express warmest appreciation to my director of studies, Professor Francis Mulhern, and my supervisor, Emeritus Professor Geoffrey Alderman (together with their administration officer, Charmain Alleyne), for their support and advice at all stages of that process. Additionally, I thank Professor Alderman – currently holder of the Michael Gross Chair in Politics and Contemporary History at the University of Buckingham, acclaimed author of *Modern British Jewry*[29] and *Controversy and Crisis*,[30] and regular JC columnist – for contributing the foreword to this book.

* * *   * * *   * * *

Another Way, Another Time was completed soon after the passing, on 14 December, 2009/27 Kislev, 5770 (third day of Chanukkah), of my dear brother, Dr David Asher Persoff. This volume pays tribute to his indomitable spirit, in the footsteps of the Hasmoneans, and – in the words of another of my siblings – to his majesty, his high-principled nature, his perseverance, and his dedication to family, community and faith. He served as a model of what he confronted in life, turning problems into challenges, and building a home based on traditional values. May his memory be for a blessing.

MEIR PERSOFF

Jerusalem

January 2010, Shevat 5770

Chief Rabbi Baron Sacks of Aldgate, with his House of Lords sponsors, Baron Winston of Hammersmith (left) and Baron Carey of Clifton, 27 October, 2009

With Open Arms

'The greatest leader the Jewish people has ever known, Moses, trembled when he contemplated the burden of leadership, and said: "Mi anochi, who am I?" What, then, shall I say who, until the age of twenty-five, never dreamed of becoming a rabbi, let alone a Chief Rabbi?' [1]

Five years into the Chief Rabbinate of Jonathan Sacks, his principal backer, Sir Stanley Kalms – the former chairman of Jews' College, which Sacks had headed before taking up the post – publicly called for his protégé's resignation, and for the virtual abolition of Anglo-Jewry's highest ecclesiastical office. Surveying the Chief Rabbi's record, Kalms wrote:

> He was the arch-proponent of 'inclusivism,' the widening of Jewish involvement in the issues that affect all Jews, the imperative necessity to share our culture, rather than the methodology of recording one's religious virtuosity. On the major issue of inclusivism, as soon as he was installed he decided that, as he had twenty-five years in office ahead of him, his plans – whatever they were – should be paced over that period.
>
> Sadly, in an age of extremely fast-moving events, of single-issue movements that carry clout, and of uninhibited pluralistic influences, this was, to my mind, both an unacceptable and a dangerous policy. Leadership is about firm convictions, clean strategy and a clear, communicable action plan. Popularism and survival are not on the agenda of a true leader. They are merely the consequences, or rewards, of that commitment …
>
> Rabbi Sacks has great oratorical skills, but, inhibited in his outpourings, the words hardly fill the appetites of Anglo-Jewry. We are in a time warp, and fast becoming an irrelevance in terms of world Jewry … In fairness to himself, the Chief Rabbi should consider retiring from office. He is an academic by nature, and his talents could be immeasurably better used.
>
> The United Synagogue [US] should be happier, relieved of the heavy burden of maintaining his office on a declining membership basis. For practical purposes, the US should set up the rabbinical council on a rotation basis. Every six or twelve months, a rabbinical member would become president and be the titular religious head of the community. [2]

In an interview the previous fortnight, marking Kalms' knighthood in the 1996 New Year Honours, Sir Stanley had declared: 'I'm a great supporter of the Chief Rabbi's abilities but not of the Chief Rabbi's achievements … One of the great roles of the Chief Rabbi was to advance inclusivism. I don't think inclusivism has budged one inch … If he had a base, he might be more powerful. But the United Synagogue refuses to give the Chief Rabbi the power and authority to be a Chief Rabbi.'[3] Expanding on these views, some twelve years later, Kalms argued that

> the Chief Rabbi, as an appointed employee of the United Synagogue, is under the tight discipline and jurisdiction of the honorary officers. He deals with halachic matters under the auspices of the Beth Din, plus inconsequential communal issues, and is prescribed to the line which that organisation sets.
>
> It is an established fact that the Beth Din has always been to the right of the community. Again, the members of the Beth Din are employees of the United Synagogue. The United Synagogue is extremely jealous of its control over its officials and allows virtually no discretion or initiative; the powers of the Chief Rabbi are therefore narrowly limited to matters of communal Orthodoxy and conventions.
>
> If one looks back to the previous Chief Rabbi, Lord Jakobovits, he suffered similar restrictions and was denied the authority even to instigate educational initiatives outside the narrow focus of the United Synagogue's honorary officers. He was fortunate in that he gathered around him a group of wealthy Jewish philanthropists who funded his educational programme and gave him a certain degree of independence and a wider platform to express his views.
>
> However, in his case, as in the case of the present Chief Rabbi, there has been no initiative towards inclusivism, which I interpret as widening the appeal of the United Synagogue as a communal organisation, to embrace those members of Anglo-Jewry who are more challenging in their approach to the Jewish faith.
>
> In giving this explanation of the limitations of power of the Chief Rabbi, I am not suggesting that there are easy solutions – or, indeed, any solutions – but the fact is that Sir Jonathan Sacks is perforce locked into a static cage representing, in this modern world, an excessively narrow view of Jewish religious identity and attitude.
>
> It is well known that the vast majority of the members of the United Synagogue do not fully practise the Orthodox lines of their synagogue, and there are many who work together with other groupings to face the crisis in the growth of Islamism and anti-Zionism/anti-Semitism that is

endemic today. These facts nullify the argument that the system is not broken and should be left as it is, albeit ignoring the sticking-plaster that holds the community together.

This is not the forum to go into more serious differences that lie barely beneath the surface, but I can say with some conviction that the Chief Rabbi is under-utilised and made substantially ineffective by the narrowness of his mission statement, and by the intellectual inadequacies and visionless focus of the United Synagogue's honorary officers.[4]

At the outset of Sacks' tenure, in 1992, the Kalms review on 'The Role of the United Synagogue in the Years Ahead' had referred to the organisational and management structure of the Chief Rabbinate in these terms:

> There is broad support for the idea of trying to bring greater clarity and coherence to the Chief Rabbi's role within the United Synagogue, within the wider Jewish community, and within the wider UK community. For historical reasons, there is an ambiguity, in practice, in terms of the 'ownership' of the Chief Rabbinate. This stems from the role of the Chief Rabbi as the spiritual head of the United Synagogue and of the United Hebrew Congregations …
>
> The ambiguity remains for two reasons. The senior lay leader in the Chief Rabbinate structure is the president of the United Synagogue. This is not unreasonable in a situation in which the vast majority of the funding comes from the United Synagogue, but it does blur the sense of independent identity that might come from a separation of roles. The United Synagogue is also ultimately responsible for the Office of the Chief Rabbi, including salaries …
>
> The way forward must be to develop the existing organisational structure towards a more national concept of the Chief Rabbinate … encompass[ing] the full range of its responsibilities and reflect[ing] the relationship of the Chief Rabbi with the constituent organisations who recognise and support his office.[5]

Of his relationship with one such constituent organisation, the London Beth Din – under whose auspices, Kalms pointed out, the Chief Rabbi deals with halachic matters – the United Synagogue notes: 'The title of Av ["father" (nominally head) of the] Beth Din is formally held by the Chief Rabbi, Lord Sacks, whose high profile as an international religious leader and author and lecturer of renown has done so much to enhance the stature of Orthodoxy both nationally and internationally. By dint of his extensive workload, as well as the convention of his office, the Chief Rabbi is not generally personally involved in day-to-day Beth Din work, but remains in constant contact with the dayanim.'[6]

The Kalms review, appraising the dayanim's role, reflected widespread concerns regarding the association between the Chief Rabbinate and the London Beth Din:

> In our view, it is essential that, within the parameters set by halachah [Jewish law], the Beth Din represents the religious ethos of the United Synagogue as a whole. It is answerable in this respect to the Chief Rabbi as Av Beth Din, and the Chief Rabbi himself is charged with the responsibility of ensuring that the religious policy of the United Synagogue continues to be one of Orthodox inclusivism … The Chief Rabbi should ensure that regular and meaningful consultations are held between the Beth Din and the rabbinate, as well as the Beth Din and lay representatives, to ensure that there is continual communication regarding the reasoning behind individual matters of religious policy, and so that the Beth Din is informed of the reactions and sentiments of the United Synagogue membership as a whole.[7]

The relationship between Sacks and his Beth Din – and with other ultra-Orthodox rabbis outside his sphere of authority – lies at the heart of his Chief Rabbinate and is crucial to an understanding of the shift in United Synagogue orientation, and its ambivalent stand on the issues of pluralism and inclusivism, both before and within 21st-century Anglo-Jewry.

* * *   * * *   * * *

Jonathan Henry Sacks entered this world, in March 1948, weeks before another Jewish stripling was making its debut – or, rather, its revival – on the international stage. As events were to demonstrate, the State of Israel was to have a profound influence on him over the ensuing decades.

The eldest of the four sons – all academically gifted – of Louis and Louise (Libby) Sacks, he was born near London's strictly Orthodox Stamford Hill neighbourhood, into an eminent rabbinical, medical and political family of Lithuanian origin, and with strong Zionist leanings on both sides[8] – his maternal great-grandfather, Arye Leib Frumkin (1845–1917), was one of the founders of Petach Tikva.

The Frumkin pedigree was to feature prominently in later life when, as Chief Rabbi, Sir Jonathan Sacks adopted the title Baron Sacks, of Aldgate in the City of London, following his elevation to the peerage in 2009. Explaining why he had chosen to nominate Aldgate, in London's East End, he said: 'My late father sold cloth in Commercial Road, and my grandmother ran Frumkin's wine shop. I wanted not to forget my roots. That's where I used to help out when I was a child and where my earliest memories are.'[9] Aldgate was also associated with his predecessors when the Great Synagogue, Duke's Place – destroyed in the Second World War – was the seat of the Chief Rabbinate.

Of his parents, Sacks was to declare in his Chief Rabbinical installation address: 'Most of all, on this day of days, I thank my parents, who gave me a *Yiddisher neshomo*, a Jewish soul, and who made me realise that the greatest love parents can have for a child is to want him always to grow.'[10] Later, he amplified his gratitude:

> I was once asked by an interviewer who the formative influences on my life were. I replied, 'My late father, who was always prepared to lose a friend rather than compromise a principle, and my mother, who kept all the friends my father lost.' By her example, she taught me and my brothers what other, more overly religious people sometimes forget: that having faith in God means having faith in other people, and that the measure of our righteousness lies in how many people we value, not in how many we condemn.[11]

And of his father:

> He came to this country at the age of five as a refugee from Poland. At fourteen, he had to leave school to support the rest of the family. As a result, he never had a proper formal education.
>
> I vividly remember the conversations we used to have when I was a child. On our walks back from the synagogue, I used to ask him questions. His reply was always the same. He used to say: '*Mein kind*, I never had a Jewish education, so I do not know. But one day you will have the education I missed, and you will teach me the answers.'
>
> Can you imagine the effect those words had on a five-year-old child? I was a grasshopper, but I felt like a giant. My father wanted to learn from *me*. He wanted us, his sons, to go on ahead of him. He gave us two extraordinary gifts: the pride to want to grow as Jews, and the space in which to do so.[12]

Jonathan was just two when the family moved to the suburbs of North-West London from the 'other-worldly' home of his maternal grandfather,

Eliyahu Ephraim Frumkin, in whose personally-owned 'little shul a few doors away ... I developed a taste that has never diminished for small houses of prayer, in which physical proximity seemed to create a mood of spiritual intimacy.'[13]

The future head of the United Synagogue admits that, not having grown up within its orbit, 'it was many years before I became convinced of its importance.' In a touching and telling autobiographical passage, he relates how he rebelled against his father's desire to have him worship at the local US house of prayer, describing the building as 'too forbidding,' and its congregants as 'too prosperous and self-preoccupied ... If this was the United Synagogue, I wanted nothing to do with it.'

A nearby *shtiebl* (conventicle) was more to his taste and, while 'over the next twenty years I had occasion to pray in many synagogues, they were all of this kind – small, unpretentious and without formality.' Occasional visits to United Synagogue congregations provided no spiritual satisfaction. 'The synagogues were too large, the atmosphere too anonymous, and the services less a participatory activity than a performance in which the rabbi and chazan played the major roles, and we, the congregation, were often reduced to spectators. No one welcomed us, we felt like outsiders, and we risked constant embarrassment by finding that we were sitting on someone else's seat. In short, I did not like the United Synagogue.'[14]

During those formative twenty years, Sacks attended St Mary's Primary School, Christ's College[15] in Finchley, and Gonville and Caius College, Cambridge (gaining first-class honours in philosophy), before proceeding to New College, Oxford, and King's College, London. Perhaps it was at Oxbridge that he acquired his reputation – alluded to by Kalms, and summed up by the author and communal commentator Chaim Bermant – as 'a slight, donnish figure, giving an impression of cold aloofness, never completely at ease in company and much happier in his study than in the drawing-room.'[16]

Reminiscing, years later, with a British philosophical journal about his induction into the world of philosophy, Sacks recalled his adolescent home as 'a house where there was a television in every room, where we took the *Daily Express* and the *Daily Mirror*, and where there weren't many books.

'My teenage rebellion was into books. We lived in Finchley and that was close enough to wander around Hampstead in the second-hand bookshops, and what you found was Locke and Hume. Both were engaging writers. That was a feature of British philosophical writing: not only was it quite empiricist, it was down-to-earth linguistically as well.'

Sacks turned to philosophy, he said, because 'I just wanted to make sense of it all.' That was, however, 'destined to come crashing against the limits of linguistic philosophy at the end of the '60s, which really just didn't claim to answer that kind of question at all.' The crash occurred at Cambridge, where Sacks read moral sciences (as philosophy was then called). Nevertheless, 'I still got a great deal out of my undergraduate studies – number one, this rigid insistence on clarity of thought and validity of argumentation: you could see that that was universally applicable, just to think straight.' Number two was the personal encounter with a range of tutors, most notably Roger Scruton and Bernard Williams, his first doctoral supervisor.

'I was going through a hugely religious phase. After I had finished my undergraduate career, I went to Israel and got involved with some Jewish mystics – and Bernard Williams was not only a lapsed Catholic, he was also an atheist.' Williams, however, was the epitome of 'academic openness and rigour – he never attacked my views, he just wanted me to express them clearly. I think that was a lasting lesson.'

By the early '70s, Sacks had committed to writing a doctorate on the concepts of sincerity and authenticity, but that plan was abandoned, partly because of 'the aridity of Oxbridge philosophy at that particular point,' but also because Lionel Trilling had published his book, *Sincerity and Authenticity*, in 1971. 'I read it and said, "That's done, forget it."'[17] Instead, he went on to gain his PhD, on rabbinic jurisprudence, at King's in London.[18]

It was at Cambridge that Sacks first came into contact with Louis Jacobs – a major player in the following chapters – when the budding Chief Rabbi, as external secretary of the University Jewish Society, thanked the Masorti (Conservative) rabbi for addressing the inaugural meeting of its discussion group. 'I think that the meeting was a great success,' wrote Sacks to Jacobs, 'for it precisely set out what is to be our task, and validated its appropriateness. Everyone I have spoken to enjoyed the meeting very much, and it has served to stimulate interest in the group's future activities … We hope it will not be the last time that you honour Cambridge with your presence.'[19]

While still a student, Sacks recalls of this period,

> I met one of the great rabbis of the twentieth century. At that time, I was at the crossroads in my own religious development, and I asked him the following question: 'I would like to become a more committed Jew, but I also value the world outside – the great music, art and literature whose inspiration is often drawn from quite unJewish sources. Must I make this sacrifice? Is religious commitment exclusive?'
>
> He replied with a parable: 'There were once two men who spent their lives transporting stones. One carried rocks, the other diamonds. One

day, they were given emeralds to carry. The man who had spent his days carrying rocks saw emeralds as just another heavy weight, a burden of no intrinsic value. The one who had carried diamonds recognised emeralds as another form of precious stone, different but with their own distinctive beauty. So it is with faith. If your own faith is nothing more than a burden, you will not value the faith of others. But if you cherish your faith, you will value other people's faith also, even though it is different from your own. You will know that faiths are like jewels. One is especially your own, but all are precious.'

It was a wise answer, and I have tried to live by it ever since ...'[20]

Discussing this theme in another context, and at another time – in a chapter entitled, significantly, 'Why I Am a Jew' – Sacks wrote: 'I cannot hide my sense that something is wrong with Jewish life today. I see it in almost every direction I look.

'It is not only that young Jews are disengaging from Judaism at a rate virtually unprecedented in history. Nor is it the grievous and unnecessary fractiousness that injures the relationships between the various Jewish groups, religious and secular, orthodox and liberal, and the different strands within Orthodoxy itself. It is, rather, an inescapable feeling that we have somehow lost the script of the Jewish story, that breathtaking attempt to build, out of simple acts and ordinary lives, a fragment of heaven on earth, a society of human dignity under the sovereignty of God, a home for the Divine presence ...'[21] He added, a few paragraphs later:

One of the most profound religious truths Judaism ever articulated was that God loves diversity; He does not ask us all to serve Him in the same way. To each people He has set a challenge, and with the Jewish people He made a covenant, knowing that it takes time, centuries, millennia, to overcome the conflicts and injustices of the human situation, and that therefore each generation must hand on its ideals to the next, so that there will also be a Jewish people conveying its particular vision to humanity and moving, however haltingly, to a more gracious world. The most eloquent words God spoke to Abraham, Jacob, Moses and the prophets was to call their name. Their reply was simply *hineni*, 'Here I am.' That is the call Jewish history makes to us: to continue the story and to write our letter in the scroll.[22]

The 1967 Six-Day War, coinciding with Sacks' spiritual quest, proved a watershed in his journey as a Jew. 'War,' he wrote later, 'was imminent, and its aim was the destruction of Israel ... There were fears of a second

Holocaust.' He had begun his studies at Cambridge and, in the run-up to the war, the city's 'little synagogue was full of students who had not been there before, praying for a miracle. For many of us, those days evoked feelings we did not know we had. As the Holocaust had been for a previous generation, so the Six-Day War was to ours: the birth of the realisation that Jews are an *am*, a community of fate.'

That realisation led to another, based on a question Sacks asked of himself and of his 'fellow Jewish students who were simply drifting away: If I was joined by a bond of fate with Jews in Israel, was I not also joined with *them*?' That question 'came back to haunt me over the next few years and was eventually to change the direction of my life.'

The answer, in turn, led Sacks to re-evaluate his view of the United Synagogue, and to seek a place in the community which would 'connect those who were observant with those who were not, which was motivated by a sense of responsibility towards Jewry as a whole, and which might address those who felt left out, excluded, uncomprehending, unwelcome and ill-at-ease.' It was this spiritual re-evaluation, he concluded, 'that led me, slowly but inexorably, to the United Synagogue.'[23]

Feeling a consequent swing to an ecclesiastical path, the burgeoning rabbi found himself propelled towards the London-based Jews' College and Etz Chaim yeshivah, resulting, in 1976, in his receiving *semichah* (ordination) at both institutions – first from Rabbi Nosson Ordman (on *Yoreh Deah*)[24] at Etz Chaim, and then from Rabbi Nachum Rabinovitch (on *Orach Chaim*)[25] at Jews' College.

Noting the latter occasion, Sacks wrote to the *Jewish Chronicle*: 'Mr Frank Levine, of Jews' College, mentioned to me that he was writing to you with a brief account of Ya'akov Grunewald and myself obtaining *semichah* from Jews' College.[26] He asked me to send you a curriculum vitae and a photograph. I enclose both. I am afraid the photograph is the usual-convict variety, with the hunted look invariably evoked by having to say cheese to a picture-taking robot.'

Outlining his academic record, Sacks concluded with references to his Jewish Society presidency and Hillel student counsellorship at Cambridge, and to his doctoral work 'on the philosophy of action.' He added: 'It is my intention' to enter the ministry once an opportunity becomes available.'[27]

On Jews' College, Sacks was later to comment – pointedly, in light of the Jacobs Affair[28] that, in 1962, had engulfed the College, the Chief Rabbinate and, indeed, Anglo-Jewry itself:

> Jews' College is the oldest extant rabbinical training seminary in the world [established by Chief Rabbi Nathan Marcus Adler in 1855]. It is a centre

for advanced Jewish studies, and for rabbinical and teacher training ... It
does not represent right-wing, left-wing or 'centrist' Orthodoxy. It does
not align itself with *charedi* or *dati*, traditionalist or modern Orthodox.
These adjectives and their associated ideologies are neither helpful nor
warranted by rabbinic tradition.

The task of the College, intellectually and spiritually, is to approach
questions through the guidance of Torah and its contemporary sages. The
attachment to one particular outlook or sage is a necessary decision of
individuals. It is not a function of institutions, least of all of an institution
convinced of the power of Torah to unite, and of the imperative force of
the rabbinic tradition of exploring all sides of the argument – rejected as
well as accepted opinions – before reaching a conclusion.[29]

In 1973, relevant to these remarks though predating them by several
years, a second encounter with Jacobs followed the latter's review of a book
by the Israeli Bible scholar Nehama Leibowitz.[30] Describing the volume as
'excellent devotional literature,' Jacobs had qualified his faint praise with
the view that 'in no way can [it] be considered a work of scholarship as
this is nowadays understood. It is impossible to believe that the Professor
of Bible at Tel Aviv University confines her lectures to the kind of material
here presented. Perhaps she believes that what is suitable for university
students is unsuitable for the ordinary reader.'

It was one thing, declared Jacobs, to reject the Documentary Hypothesis;[31]
it was quite another 'to ignore completely all the achievements of modern
biblical criticism. Thus there are no references to the writings of non-
Jewish scholars, no historical investigation of any kind, no discussion of
authorship or dates, while there is everywhere implicit a glib dismissal
of any evidence for compositeness in the Pentateuchal record. No textual
problem is even looked at, and no untraditional view even considered
except for the purposes of disavowal.'[32]

'I am very interested,' Sacks wrote immediately to Jacobs, 'by the
problem of modes of biblical interpretation that you raised in your review
... You stressed the need for an assimilation of the findings of modern
biblical criticism, but you did not give an account of what a symbiosis
of "objectivity" and "faith" would be like – what additional significance
such a commentary would have for a religious understanding of the text.

I am deeply interested to know how you envisage such an enterprise. Clearly,
there is no univocal meaning of 'the meaning of a text.' Contemporary
philosophy of language stresses the need for locating a communication
within the context of the whole system of beliefs of the community in

which it is to be understood. One could understand Genesis – or the Bible generally – as a quasi-historical account in which questions of authorship and authenticity would be significant and answerable only in scientifically 'objective' terms. One could conceive it, as Buber did, as saga attempting to excavate from the text alone the significance of the events to those who experienced them and those who later recorded them. But neither of these methods would do justice to the centrality of the text in Jewish thought.

Discussing 'how revolutionary changes in thought have occurred within Judaism without corresponding institutional or ritual revolutions,' Sacks wrote further:

> The doctrines which have allowed this treatment of the text have been such as the idea of an infinity of meanings which a Divine (as opposed to human) communication may bear: a mysticism of the word according to which, at one extreme, the whole of the Five Books is one of the Divine Names; and the consequent significance which is granted to the text even as a collection of letters rather than a series of discrete words.
>
> One would have thought, then, that Nehama Leibowitz's enterprise (which I have not seen) was an intellectually legitimate one vindicated by a theory of meaning which has considerable contemporary support. And that a proper contemporary Jewish reading of the text would not be one which directed itself to critical datings and attestations of authorship, but one which re-excavated its meaning through concepts which were set within the context of modes of thought accessible to Jews today.
>
> The apparatus most likely to be able to do this would seem to be, perhaps, a reworked and systematic version of Chasidic ideas which, say, in their Chabad form, come close to the ideal of existential phenomenology in which modern Christian theologians, following Kierkegaard, find their own most congenial device.

Sacks told Jacobs that he 'would be extremely grateful if you were able to spare a moment to explain to me your views on the question, which I would value highly. Your review whetted my appetite to know more of what lay behind your criticism.'[33]

Subsequent correspondence led Sacks to question 'the exaggerated claims currently being made by the critical school on the basis of unsophisticated use of statistical techniques and (as I understand it) a quite unjustified emphasis on the Syriac and Greek translations of the Masoretic text … as well as a disposition towards erroneous inference based on a neglect of grammar on the part of the Traditionalists …

The possibilities of pursuing a middle course [Sacks told Jacobs] still seem paradoxical to me. One might conceive a place for, say, mystical exegesis while handing over empirical questions to the biblical critic. But the assumptions which have allowed the *sod* to co-exist with the *p'shat* in Judaism (Divine authorship and letter-by-letter sanctity of the text) are incompatible with critical presuppositions. It looks more like an either/or choice than a field for compromise ...

Faced with the choice, even aware of all recent scholarly developments, a Jew might, without wilful oblivion, still say something like

(1) Criteria of meaning depend on the light in which the text is viewed (one would read *Titus Andronicus* differently, if still coherently, if one viewed it as a political tract rather than as a tragedy) and the authorship which is attributed to it ...

(2) The issue of authorship, when one of the candidates is G-d (not Moses), is not an empirical question.

(3) The issue of the light in which the text is to be viewed (qua revelation, qua history, qua saga, qua myth) is not an empirical question either, any text being able to bear a number of coherent but mutually incompatible readings. Or if you say, the proper reading is discoverable on an investigation of the author's intentions, then this becomes an empirical question only if authorship is, in the particular case, also an empirical question.

(4) Therefore, if (1), (2) and (3) are true, there is a *choice* between alternative interpretive schema, so long as each is internally consistent.

(5) Therefore a Jew may choose a traditional reading of the text without laying himself open to a justified charge of 'lack of objectivity.'

Sacks closed the exchange by admitting to Jacobs that 'what few ideas I have are solely methodological' and that he would 'attempt to mitigate my shameful ignorance of contemporary critical studies.'[34]

His attempt bore fruit, and a decade later the two crossed swords in a classic (and classical) case of the biter bit. This time Jacobs was the author, and Sacks the critic, and the volume under review was *A Tree of Life: Diversity, Flexibility and Creativity in Jewish Law*,[35] demonstrating (according to its jacket) 'how the halachists [codifiers of Jewish law], influenced by their diverse cultural backgrounds, sought throughout the ages to maintain the flexibility of the law ... The halachists acknowledged the role of the human mind not only in understanding the Torah but in creating Torah, so that the divine shoot planted in the past is nurtured to become "a tree of life."'

'For the first time in these columns since the "Jacobs Affair" broke twenty years ago, a rabbinical response to the non-fundamentalist views of Rabbi Louis Jacobs' was how the *Jewish Chronicle* trumpeted Sacks' review, which spanned two full pages[36] and spawned several more in spirited argument,[37] including a page-long rebuttal from Jacobs himself.[38]

Commenting that 'the worst controversy hits the nicest people,' Sacks described Jacobs as 'a man of quiet detachment, courteous, softly spoken, urbane. Add the gift of fastidious and exhaustive scholarship, and a pen from which falls, like fruit from a tree, book after book of strenuous research. The perfect ingredients ...

'We owe Louis Jacobs and his book a considerable debt: for demonstrating the creativity, range and relevance of Jewish law; for proving that its timelessness did not inhibit its flexibility; for showing that, within its unity of method, diversity was possible. The sheer weight of evidence he has accumulated to refute his own conclusions speaks volumes for his integrity. But in taking too rough a hold on the Tree of Life, he has pulled it, roots and all, from the soil in which it grows.'

Between these opening and closing paragraphs, Sacks dissected the evidence and conclusions, noting that 'the book's argument, as to be expected, is that the halachah has changed in response to historical and social development and ought to continue to do so. The Torah was not, after all, revealed once and for all at Sinai. It grew slowly as the accretion of documents and decisions: the work of men intermittently inspired. It is sometimes right and sometimes wrong; and where wrong we have the right and duty to amend it.

'Provocative thoughts,' declared Sacks, 'that have lost none of their defiance since they first appeared, in rudimentary form, in *We Have Reason to Believe*, back in 1957. Yet, for all that, not original thoughts, for, as Jacobs himself points out, they have a long lineage ...'

After tracing the lineage across fifteen decades, Sacks returned to the book in hand 'and to the long argument of which it is the latest expression. And to the inescapable question: is it, after all, correct? To which the answer must be an unequivocal and final "No." And not just in the self-evident sense that it conflicts with Orthodoxy. But in the prior sense that, in the last analysis, it just doesn't add up.

> For fifteen of the book's sixteen chapters, Jacobs shows that Jewish law, in the hands of its sages, was diverse, flexible and creative. This despite (or because of) the fact that its exponents believed the Torah to be Divine, and its laws eternal.
>
> In the final chapter, Jacobs argues that creativity is now only to be had by believing the Torah to be human, and its laws subject to repeal. A

proposition of which the rest of the book is an elegant refutation. Why the *volte face*?

Jacobs clearly believes that contemporary halachic authorities have not addressed themselves to the issues of our time. This is an error of the same logical form as the man who complained to his rabbi: 'Rabbi, I prayed and prayed for a new car, and my prayer wasn't answered.' To which the rabbi, a sharp mind, replied: 'Your prayer *was* answered. The answer was "No."'

Confusing 'No reply' with 'The reply is "No"' is yet another fallacy of the book. The sages of our time *have* addressed every issue on Jacobs' agenda. It is just that they have given answers other than he would have wished. Why?

Sadly, Jacobs takes flight from his own methodology at the very point at which it would have been most revealing. If at every other time halachah responded, as he argues and documents, to the 'social, economic, theological and political conditions that occur,' why should the same analysis not be given of Jewish law in the nineteenth and twentieth centuries?

Jacobs, in turn, charged Sacks with 'sens[ing] a contradiction between my acceptance on faith of divine revelation and my being impressed with biblical criticism. There is no contradiction whatsoever. Revelation is an event or a series of events in which there is a meeting between God and man. That such meetings occurred is, indeed, a matter of faith.

Criticism examines the record of these meetings in the Bible. It is, in fact, a mighty attempt to discover what this record says about itself: how it came about, who wrote it down, and when and whether our present texts are completely accurate in all their details. Of course, if by revelation one understands verbal inspiration, that the very words of Scripture were conveyed by God ... there can be no biblical scholarship. But that is the issue at stake – does scholarly investigation render the doctrine of verbal inspiration untenable?

To take a simple example: Abraham Ibn Ezra – a forerunner of biblical criticism – averred that the final section of Deuteronomy, describing Moses' ascent on the mountain to die there, could not have been written by Moses. If this is countered by an affirmation that, despite appearances, on grounds of faith, it is believed that Moses did write it, the question to be asked is: on what is such faith based, and why should it be preferred to what the texts seem to be saying?

To invoke faith regarding matters that can be determined by investigation is to believe it possible for God to plant false clues. It is on grounds of faith that I reject such a perverse notion.

Nor was Jacobs the only London rabbi to proffer a rejection. Nearer home – within Sacks' own Jews' College, no less – Holocaust-survivor Simche Bunim Lieberman, its lecturer in Talmud and Codes and a leading halachist responsible for the semichah programme, incurred his principal's displeasure first by urging him not to write the review, and then by circulating among their colleagues a two-page critique of it, couched in rabbinic Hebrew – a device later to be used by Sacks himself.

Addressed to 'My beloved and honourable friend, Rabbi Aharon (may he live), in answer to your request,' the critique – which mentioned neither Jacobs nor Sacks by name – opened with a series of biblical, halachic and talmudic sources prohibiting responses to, and the dissemination of, the statements and writings of an *apikoros* (heretic).

'Of a man who is afflicted with a disordered mind and the leprosy of heresy,' wrote Lieberman, 'and heresy shines forth from his forehead, and he is assumed to be a heretic in his book, if he writes another book of philosophy or opinions, even if it bears no explicit signs of heresy, it is forbidden to read it or to bring it to the house of Israel ... And certainly it is forbidden to receive his book for the purposes of review, especially if one knows that it is an heretical book.

'To conclude [the review] by suggesting that we ought to praise the heretic author for his great work, etc., is disgusting – that a God-fearing Jew should write such strange things instead of warning the nation that the books are like venomous cancer [liable] to kill pure souls, and that it is prohibited to bring them into the house of Israel.'

Of particular severity, cautioned Lieberman, was 'publicity in a newspaper whose policy is to humiliate and denigrate charedim, and whose sole objective is to give a platform to that man, whom the heart has already forgotten and in whom the world is no longer interested ... And it is already known that this paper will not publish anything good that a charedi has written. "Silence is adornment to the wise" – and all the more so to fools.'[39]

While their talmudic and halachic expertise bore no comparison, Lieberman and Sacks had one experience in common: both had studied at Etz Chaim yeshivah, to which Lieberman was sent by Dayan Yechezkel Abramsky, head of the London Beth Din, after arriving at a Windermere (Lake District) hostel from Theresienstadt as a post-war DP.[40]

Spurning an opportunity to move to America, following subsequent study at Gateshead yeshivah – where he was recognised as an *illuy* (genius) – Lieberman worked for several years as a private teacher and halachic consultant, before being appointed to Jews' College in 1971, succeeding the renowned talmudist Rabbi Kopel Kahana, 'one of the foremost rabbinic scholars in the world.'[41] Lieberman, highly recommended by Jakobovits, was regarded in the Orthodox domain as a fitting choice.

Lieberman's cousin, the historian Lloyd P. Gartner, remarks of the appointment: 'Jews' College had long held a place within the Anglo-Jewish religious establishment, but was seen as weak and insufficiently supported. Nor were its graduates considered conspicuously learned or pious. It was hoped that Rabbi Lieberman would provide a counter-attraction to the magnet of Gateshead.

'For his part, Simche felt that he needed the approval of the Rebbe of Ger [Gur] – the Chasidic sect to which he belonged – before teaching there. The Rebbe assured him that he would remain a Ger Chasid in good standing, though he did not endorse Jews' College itself.'[42]

Weeks after writing his critique, Lieberman was dismissed from the College on grounds of redundancy. Kalms, as chairman, informed his council colleagues that 'structural changes are needed to incorporate Rabbi Jonathan Sacks – the new principal – in a teaching capacity,' and that 'the number of new students at the College does not justify Rabbi Lieberman's retention.'[43]

In an interview with the *Jewish Chronicle*, Kalms stated that the College was 'not looking for a replacement' for Lieberman, since Sacks was 'now taking his class in rabbinics. But we are looking into the possibility of extending our range of courses, which could mean an additional appointment, though we have no one lined up at the moment.'[44]

Reacting to this statement, Sutton minister Geoffrey Hyman, a former student of Lieberman's, said that he was 'shocked and bewildered' at the turn of events. 'I fail to understand how the College can find no room for such a scholar, who has won the acclaim of other leading rabbinical scholars, yet at the same time appoint several part-time lecturers. When I took semichah in 1982, there were only three of us in Rabbi Lieberman's class, yet the question of redundancy never arose then.'[45]

Taking issue with both Kalms and Sacks, the College's dean, Rabbi Dr Irving Jacobs, declared: 'Jews' College cannot afford to lose such a man, who has an international reputation as a scholar.' Asserting that he was 'concerned not only with the fact of the dismissal, but also with the manner of it,' he added: 'All academic institutions have disagreements, but I would never have thought this redundancy, or dismissal, could ever happen here. I will be behind Rabbi Lieberman in whatever action is necessary for him to get justice.'[46]

In its report to the council in 1972, Jews' College had announced: 'We welcome as a permanent member of our staff Rabbi S. Lieberman, a talmudic scholar of stature.'[47] And, lauding Lieberman's 'rare talents' and 'nobility of mind and heart,' Jakobovits – the College's president – had later apprised him of 'exciting new opportunities for significant growth and development about to open up.' But after his sudden and summary dismissal, sanctioned (unwillingly, as will become evident) by Jakobovits, and the 'unbearable tensions on both sides,'[48] the Chief Rabbi could do little more than express his earnest hope that 'this unfortunate situation will be resolved in an amicable manner.'[49] Jakobovits' sentiment was echoed by Sacks, who said that 'we are united in working towards an amicable solution.'[50]

As the search for an 'amicable solution' continued, Lieberman addressed a *cri de coeur* to one of his advisers. 'I really have no words to express my gratitude to you,' he wrote, 'especially at such a crucial time to me, being oppressed by the so-called "power" of the Chief and by a man of the City.

> I felt broken hearing the remarks of Mr S. Kalms stating that they can't reinstate me as my image does not fit Jews' College. In fact, I have previously heard that he made such remarks about me in the College library. In his eyes, a teacher or Rabbi is just like putting a model in one of his shop windows. It is unbelievable that one Jew should discriminate against another Jew.
>
> Maybe it would be right to bring the matter to the Board of Deputies. I am also disturbed that the Chairman and the Principle [*sic*] should discuss my private affairs with the students, and we need to protest about it to the Chairman and the President. From all the matters discussed at the meeting [between the parties, held the previous week at the home of Dayan Chanoch Ehrentreu, the Rosh Beth Din], the only thing that I could associate with is that Mr Kalms agreed that I was grossly underpaid.
>
> Besides the Chief consulting the Dayanim (which is also unheard of, as Dayanim should not decide on something without hearing the other side first), the Principal is saying that he consulted Dayan Ehrentreu about throwing me out, and he claims he agreed. If I had known of this previously, I would never have agreed to meet at his house.[51]

Following further negotiations, Lieberman's redundancy settlement was increased from an initial offer of £4,072.68 to 'a far greater sum' than the reported £45,000.[52]

Later that summer – when, according to the JC, 'the clouds that gathered around Jews' College in the wake of the Lieberman affair look finally to have passed'[53] – Sacks told the annual meeting of governors and subscribers: 'The purpose of the College is to bring a Torah of life and not a Torah of strife into the community.'

Writing in the annual report, Jakobovits observed: 'This has been a momentous year in the time-honoured annals of Jews' College. Operating very much in brand-new premises [the College had moved from London's West End to Hendon, via temporary accommodation at Finchley Synagogue] and "under new management" – academically as well as administratively – it has undergone not merely a face-lift but a faith-lift.

'The obvious gratification with this long-awaited turn of fortunes is tinged with sadness and regret at the departure, for diverse reasons, of some long-familiar and widely respected seniors of the College family. It is clearly easier and quicker to erect a new edifice – and ours is a model of functional and ascetic effectiveness – than to construct new programmes, new priorities, and altogether new visions. The encouraging beginning that has been made is a challenge rather than a fulfilment.'[54]

Kalms referred to 'our dispute with Rabbi Lieberman' in more laconic terms. Noting that a settlement had been reached, he added: 'The affair has given rise to some exceedingly unpleasant publicity and has revealed certain extreme communal attitudes.

> At times, it seems the community divides itself between those who are totally unbending in their perception of tradition and whose horizons are the edge of their particular ghetto, and those with a wider concern, whose vision extends at least to the periphery of our Jewish society. It has been interesting to read and hear some of the current stream of criticism, particularly that often directed at myself and my lay colleagues by those who do not wish us to remain in office until we are 120.
>
> One unendearing piece of snide is that the College is run as a big business. May I respond? Every decision made by my lay colleagues and myself, while it may well be expressed in the language of our trade, is uniquely arrived at by our upbringing in the tenets of our faith. Our actions based on this concept are to strengthen our cause.
>
> There is no remit within Judaism against efficiency, achieving objectives, modern technology, developing skills in communication, and good marketing of one's product. Judaism uniquely can absorb the blend of total tradition and modern times. And I believe we are increasingly successful. Indeed, wearing another hat, I would certainly be doubling the dividend ...
>
> We have much to do, and our ambitions at times exceed our capacity. But we have a vast programme of additional projects and a determination to improve everything we attempt. I am unashamedly bullish![55]

The 'new management,' in the form of Sacks, eschewed any direct mention of Lieberman in his written report as principal. 'It happened,' he began. 'We moved. Moved, but not only to a new site. Within the past year, we have welcomed new staff, gained a renewed mandate from the Council for National Academic Awards, introduced new courses, planned a new degree [a BA programme to which, the *Jewish Chronicle* had reported,[56] Lieberman was opposed]. Above all, we sensed *panim chadashot*, an emergent fresh identity.

After two years of exile and many more of uncertainty, we have had to do more than bless *shehecheyanu* over being able to carry on. We have had to go through pains and pleasures of *mechayeh metim*: piecing together the fragments of recollection of what we once were for Anglo-Jewry, and giving them new life.

It is worth saying clearly what those fragments spelled out. They read: that the Torah taught at Jews' College should be communicable Torah – not the property of an elite. That it should be living Torah, as compelling today as it was when it was given in letters of fire at Sinai. That it should be confident Torah, unintimidated by the challenge of being 'your wisdom and understanding in the eyes of the nation.' That it should be *Torat chesed*, a Torah that never forgets its moral imperative.

Our task has been to give life to these components of an identity in institutional form. It has been controversial. Some would prefer Torah to be incommunicable; others would like to study it as a phenomenon of the past; some would prefer it walled and shaded from the eyes of the world; others would house it in fear rather than *chesed*. These have been the pains of rebirth. Like all birth-pains, they are to be lived through rather than reacted to.

The strength of the College was, and always will be, the Torah we teach, a Torah coextensive with life, always contemporary and, above all, never afraid of life. The assets we have – in staff, students, books, buildings – are assets only because of what they ultimately represent for the life of Torah in the Anglo-Jewish community.

So long as our priority was survival rather than revival, we existed but did not ask why we exist. Now that we have been privileged to make the blessing of *mechayeh metim*, all of us – staff and students and honorary officers – have shared in the process of piecing together our purpose. And that has been the most significant undercurrent of perhaps the most eventful year in the history of the College.

Remarking that he had 'enjoyed the closest of working relationships with our chairman, Stanley Kalms, in the process of transforming ideas into reality,' Sacks concluded: 'The single adjective that sums up the year is — breathless. In a succession of rapid challenges and changes, the foundations have been laid for the College's academic future, for a renewal of its presence in Anglo-Jewish life, and for a great harvest of teachers and rabbis in the next few years.'[57]

Over the next few years, however, spanning the emergent Chief Rabbi's Decade of Jewish Renewal, the College suffered a near-fatal seizure, the name 'Jews' College' ceased to exist, and the harvest of rabbis sown within its precincts dried up altogether.[58]

Harking back to the affair, following Lieberman's death in 2009,[59] *The Times* recorded of his dismissal and its outcome:

> Rabbi Simche Lieberman provided a last link between Jewish Orthodoxy in the United Kingdom and the lost world of traditional rabbinic scholarship which had flourished for centuries in Eastern Europe, and which the Holocaust destroyed. The manner of his departure from Jews' College became a cause célèbre within Anglo-Jewry, a defining moment that symbolised the ever-widening rift between Orthodoxy and ultra-Orthodoxy within Britain's Jewish community.
>
> In 1971, Lieberman joined the academic staff of Jews' College, the rabbinical training academy established in London in 1855. His appointment was a coup for the institution, then an associate college of the University of London, and he attracted many students who would otherwise have gone to study at more traditional yeshivot.
>
> But among Lieberman's colleagues at the College was Dr Jonathan Sacks, the protégé of the College's then chairman, Stanley (now Lord) Kalms. Sacks' and Kalms' vision for the College was not shared by Lieberman — in particular, the widening of the rabbinical training curriculum. The College's president, Chief Rabbi Immanuel Jakobovits, kept aloof from these simmering differences.
>
> In 1984, Sacks became principal of the College. The following year, with Jakobovits' approval, Lieberman was summarily dismissed. The 'Lieberman Affair' divided Anglo-Jewry, but in the wider rabbinical world, the support was more on Lieberman's side. He had powerful and wealthy friends (most of them his former students), and they saw to it that he had the best legal advice money could buy.
>
> In May 1985, Kalms, Sacks and Jakobovits agreed to have the matter decided by a Beth Din specially constituted for this purpose, the first time a British Chief Rabbi had consented to have his authority challenged in

this way.[60] But the Beth Din never convened. An out-of-court settlement was reached the night before it was due to sit.

Lieberman retired to the northern Israeli city of Safed, where he continued to teach and to publish. His funeral, on the Mount of Olives in Jerusalem, was attended by some of the greatest living talmudic authorities.[61]

* * *　* * *　* * *

Coincident with these earlier events, Sacks had assumed the position of minister at central London's prestigious Marble Arch Synagogue, having briefly (1978–82) served another United Synagogue constituent, the suburban Golders Green congregation at Dunstan Road.[62] 'Eventually, after many detours,' he wrote of his U-turn, 'I entered the United Synagogue as a rabbi, and I was not disappointed.

'The communities I encountered were remarkable in their range and breadth. In few other places in the world would Jews so different in their background and levels of observance have gathered in a single congregation to pray together and relate to one another … More than most other Orthodox bodies, the United Synagogue extended the boundaries of belonging.'[63]

* * *　* * *　* * *

The first moves in the search for a successor to Jakobovits as Chief Rabbi came in October 1988, when the United Synagogue council set in motion the complex machinery. Sidney Frosh, then newly elected as president of the US and chairman of the Chief Rabbinate Council, announced: 'We are starting with an empty piece of paper. We have no particular candidate in mind.' Of the 'kind of person' he would be looking for, he added: 'He has to be a man of learning and of stature, and a man for this day.'

Jakobovits similarly called for his successor to be a 'man who is in tune with the times.' In a radio interview, he affirmed: 'I am not looking for a repeat performance of my twenty-two years. Every age needs its own unique response.' He avoided naming names, but laid down some guidelines for his successor. They included 'giving priority to Jewish education, strengthening the bonds between Israel and the diaspora, and searching for issues that unite the Jewish people, transcending what are, alas, and to our bitter distress, major religious divisions.'[64]

Three former presidents of the United Synagogue, in addition to

Frosh, were among the thirty-six communal figures (all men) nominated
to select the new Chief Rabbi – George Gee and Victor Lucas, two of the
fifteen US representatives on the Chief Rabbinate Conference committee,
and Salmond S. Levin, president of the National Council of Shechitah
Boards. On the advice of its rabbinical hierarchy, the Federation of
Synagogues pulled out of the process.[65] 'The Federation wishes to keep its
independence and could not work under a constitution where it would
have to accept the authority of the Chief Rabbi,' asserted its president,
Arnold Cohen.

In February 1990 came a report that 41-year-old Sacks, whose name had
been openly and widely canvassed, had moved 'a step closer' to becoming
Chief Rabbi.[66] The selection committee had unanimously endorsed
Frosh's recommendation that Sacks' nomination be placed before the 200
members of the Chief Rabbinate Conference and that a 'call' be made to
him to take up the post. 'It would be unprecedented,' declared the national
press,[67] 'if the recommendation were overturned.'

A statement from the Chief Rabbinate Council quoted Sacks as saying
that he would be 'honoured to accept the call and the high responsibilities
of leadership that go with it.' The new incumbent, who had been chosen
to deliver the 1990 Reith lectures, had indicated that he would wish to
take up office in September of the following year. 'Rabbi Sacks has a great
intellect,' said Frosh. 'He is one of the young group of modern philosophers
in the Jewish community.'

Days later, Sacks announced that he would spend a year of study in
Israel before assuming the post, adding: 'I want to come to the position
having immersed myself in the atmosphere of Torah learning.' An official
statement noted that he had asked to take up the appointment in September
1991 'in order to disengage himself from commitments.' It also paid
tribute to Jakobovits for 'having agreed to waive his insistence on retiring
in February 1991.'[68]

Several years after accepting the 'call,' Sacks was asked: 'Looking back
at 1990, when you were appointed Chief Rabbi, do you think you really
wanted to become Chief Rabbi, or did it just "happen"? Is it something
you aspired to?' 'Did I really want to?' he shot back. 'I didn't even want to
become a rabbi.

> I lived through that very critical period around the Six-Day War which
> made a huge impact on my generation. It made many of us much more
> religious than we were, in a curious way. I found that my Cambridge
> contemporaries were suddenly becoming religious and I was struck by
> the fact, after a few years, that none of them went into the rabbinate. I

thought they would all have made wonderful rabbis. So I became a rabbi on the principle that if no one else is willing to do it, maybe you have to.

'And what,' Sacks was asked, 'makes a wonderful rabbi?' He replied: 'I am the ideal person.' He added, some minutes later: 'On one occasion, I did ask the question – what is a Chief Rabbi? Most people think of a Chief Rabbi in the following terms: everyone has a rabbi, but who do the rabbis have? The answer is: they have a Chief Rabbi. The Chief Rabbi is the rabbi of the rabbis. But that's not my definition of the Chief Rabbi. I think that some people have rabbis, and I'm the rabbi for the people who don't have rabbis.'[69]

* * *   * * *   * * *

In the run-up to Sacks' election, Kalms had bankrolled a raft of activities aimed at securing his candidate's success. The most prominent was an international conference, styled 'Traditional Alternatives: Orthodoxy and the Future of the Jewish People,' a primary task of which was to address, in Sacks' words, 'the growing rift between Orthodoxy and Reform – my attempt to set the scene for the tense and intense drama that is Judaism's contemporary dialogue between its commanding past and its as-yet uncharted future.'[70]

The gathering, modelled in many ways on a New York literary symposium held some years earlier,[71] accorded with Kalms' aspirations – as he told Jakobovits at the time[72] – 'to enhance leadership, inspiration and vision within British Jewry. I have said to you that I thought the community was apathetic and that I was extremely uncomfortable with the direction of Anglo-Jewry. You well know my oft-repeated concerns regarding pluralistic influences, which you have asked me to refer to as "diverse influences."

'I have discussed with you my plans for a major conference next year in London, bringing together all the principal modern Jewish philosophers and leaders, under the auspices of Jews' College, to stimulate the type of discussion which is so urgently needed and, at the same time, to put the College on the map. You expressed unambivalent enthusiasm for the idea. I propose to personally finance the entire project.'

In a publication introducing the event, the aspiring Chief Rabbi quoted the warning of another perceived candidate for the post, Reuven Bulka, of Ottawa's Congregation Machzikei Hadas,[73] that 'if present trends remain unchecked, the policies which prevail within Reform Judaism, and the commensurate reactions which they will surely evoke within the

Orthodox camp, may well result in a cataclysmic split within the North American Jewish community.' To some extent, Sacks commented – with British Jewry clearly in mind – 'this has already occurred.'[74]

At the conference itself, held in London in May 1989, Bulka – a nephew by marriage of Jakobovits[75] – opined that 'modern Orthodoxy should not become a movement but act as an internal lobby. It should be positive and take the bull by the horns in trying to find solutions within Jewish law to such issues as the plight of the *agunah*, a woman unable to marry because her husband refuses her a *get* (religious divorce).'

Kalms, however, it was reported, 'appeared to favour a more aggressive stand. He referred to the United Synagogue as a "movement" whose centrist philosophy stood in contrast to "Jewish fundamentalists."'[76] For his part, Sacks told the thousand-strong audience, gathered from across the communal divide:

> Links between religious and secular, Orthodox and Reform, have grown increasingly fragile in the last few years, to the point where only crisis brings us together. Thus a formidable responsibility lies with Orthodoxy, a responsibility of leadership towards the entire Jewish people ... The Orthodox world has been too preoccupied with small details of ritual observance, at the expense of larger issues.
>
> The laws of Torah are compassion and kindness and peace in the world. Where is that Torah today? This conference is not about right, left or centre, but about smallness and greatness. Will Orthodoxy see itself threatened by assimilation and secularisation? Will it retreat yet further into its protected enclaves, while the rest of the Jewish world falls to pieces? Will it build an ark for itself, while the rest of the Jewish world drowns? Or will it see itself challenged by this unique moment to lead the Jewish world?

Warm and sustained applause greeted Sacks' address. 'It was overwhelming,' said Reform rabbi and Jewish studies don Nicholas de Lange.[77]

Four months after the conference, Kalms 'stunned his colleagues by announcing his resignation from his communal posts' – the chairmanship of Jews' College and of the Chief Rabbi's Jewish Educational Development Trust – claiming that he had 'been involved in communal leadership long enough.'[78]

While rumours abounded as to his motives, including reasons of health and lack of support, Jakobovits was nearest the mark when revealing that 'relations between us were not always of the best ... He was [however] an exceptional and valued partner, despite our occasional differences.'[79] These differences were never publicly aired, but they were wide-ranging and included fundamental disagreement over the role and future of the Chief Rabbinate, and the headship of rabbinics at Jews' College.

Shrewd observers, with their fingers on the pulse of internal politics and their minds still focused on the Lieberman affair, may have spotted hints, however, in the College's reports of the previous two sessions. While acknowledging what he described as 'welcome advances,' Jakobovits had nevertheless cautioned: 'I am by no means complacent about aspects which call for determined attention if the College is to fulfil all the expectations of the community as well as of its leaders.

> For instance, we must still pursue the search for personalities of world renown, particularly in the sphere of rabbinic scholarship, to attract the best of the kind of students we want to be the leaders of tomorrow's communities. A sense of realism is also required to recognise that some of our finest and most committed young people now turn increasingly to the 'yeshivah world' for intensive instruction and inspiration. While most of our present rabbinical students now have some yeshivah experience, we have yet to build firmer bridges and promote greater mutual confidence and co-operation between the College and the resurgent centres of Torah learning here and in Israel.[80]

Kalms' vision of the College's future followed a different route. 'Thus far,' he declared, 'Jews' College has become pre-eminent in the field of Jewish academia, and while certain problems will always remain with us, particularly recruitment and funding, there are other even more vital issues to be faced.

> The current euphoria must not conceal the warning signals emitted by the velocity of diaspora life. With Israel constantly under criticism both by the media and by those Jews who seek to exorcise their concerns, however genuine, by speaking in alien forums; with Jewish fundamentalism offering a nest of introversion; and with seductive pluralistic influences constantly beckoning – and, indeed, succeeding with those who might reasonably have been expected to resist – our task is to ferment both the curriculum and the right technique to create a resistant ideology. Those whom we seek to influence and teach as future leaders of our community are being unreasonably and unexpectedly exposed to the latent and destructive elements in our community. It is a challenging task to formulate, but one in which we must succeed.[81]

A year later ('as my own tenancy starts to expire,' he cryptically forewarned), Kalms delineated his vision in even starker terms. 'Anglo-Jewry,' he wrote, 'presents a different perspective in the eyes of individual beholders. To some, it is a lost cause, intellectually lazy, religiously indifferent. A classic case of pluralistic submission with only a narrow enclave of fundamentalists holding the line. To others, Anglo-Jewry is a bastion of crumbling traditions, drifting nowhere downstream.

'Many of us at Jews' College share a more positive view. Anglo-Jewry is in sound health, but is deficient in important ingredients – self-confidence and imaginative thinking. Anglo-Jewry needs a clearer philosophy, a commitment by its leadership to face contemporary realities. It will not be deflected by historical platitudes. If our community – particularly our youth – is not with us, not Jewishly orientated, that is our fault, not theirs.'[82]

Debating these points in their wider context, and in relation to Sacks vis-à-vis the Chief Rabbinical succession, Kalms wrote to Jakobovits on one occasion: 'It is a tragedy and sad reflection on rabbinical disharmony that you never grasped his talents and developed him into your heir-apparent. You must take more than half the blame for that.'[83] The Chief Rabbi responded:

> On Jonathan S., I will not be so insensitive as to reverse the call for 'taking half the blame.' I share your disillusionment, as well as your acclaim, of his talents. He knows, even if you do not, that the failure to strike up proper bonds between us is certainly not due to any lack of trying on my part – and is definitely not a 'reflection on rabbinical disharmony.'
>
> As you well know, I for one do not think we are doing him any favours, or promoting his professional prospects, by supporting his every whim, however irrational – whether a sabbatical after two years' tenure, or agreeing to be his agent in dismissing Lieberman (which costs me heavily to this day in exposure to ceaseless public slander), or support for his refusal to take over rabbinic responsibility for the Jews' College minyan – at an ongoing cost to the College and the community which cannot be calculated.
>
> In all these cases, my views firmly opposed yours, but out of friendship as well as respect for your chairmanship [of the College], I did not demur. But Jonathan, sadly, did not benefit, and missed out on any number of essential opportunities for development into an heir-apparent, which can only be gained the hard way.
>
> As you will confirm, I had even offered him regular experiences by delegation – at inductions, top-level representation, and other 'development' occasions – but all to no avail. If you knew all the facts on

this objectively, you would certainly revise and retract the relevant remarks in your last letter.[84]

On this, Kalms conceded: 'It was unnecessary for me to talk about responsibility for Jonathan in percentage terms. I certainly agree that I have been indulgent, perhaps excessively. You know I have a soft spot for rabbis – and you, of course, know their minds better and are much less simpatico.

> Maybe you subconsciously saw him as an intellectual competitor. Perhaps I was frightened of losing his unique talents to the community. A critic might say I bought his friendship and loyalty. I will be proved right or wrong within the next one or two years. But you, typically, asked me to retract without asking yourself some key questions. Why was your relationship a failure? Was it entirely Jonathan's fault? A little critical self-analysis is demanded.[85]

Reverting some weeks later to the Sacks issues, Kalms wrote to Jakobovits: 'We have agreed to disagree regarding Jonathan.' And on a replacement for Lieberman (whom he did not mention by name), he added: 'You passionately feel the need for a world scholar to be head of rabbinics at Jews' College. I understand this view and do not feel that I am personally in a position to argue the finer points of your argument.

'It seems to me sufficient that so long as we provide a stream of high-quality rabbis to our community with a suitable philosophy, it matters not where they come from. However, I have to be influenced by alternative choices which have been proposed by serious, responsible, leading members of the community.'

But, he told the Chief Rabbi, referring to other matters, 'notwithstanding the counter-aggression of this letter, there is more in which we are in agreement than disagreement. We have to work together, and it will be my intention to endeavour to do so.

'I have always enjoyed that part of our relationship which has been challenging. I have derived much pleasure from our discussions and your company over the years ... You will have to accept that we are a double act and that one without the other would be less than half. But it won't be the same – it could actually be better. In all equity, I have to say that my locker of constructive criticism and challenges is still brimming and in future will be brandished like a flaming sword!'[86]

The correspondence concluded with Kalms' expression of hope that they might 'exorcise the issues of disagreement, open the door to discussions about the future of the organisations we lead, and see whether we can bring back our dialogue to both a pragmatic and a philosophical level.'[87] 'I too,' replied Jakobovits, 'equally look forward to restoring our friendly partnership.'[88]

Despite the apparent warmth of these sentiments, however, the 'flaming sword' was soon to be extinguished. 'Few years in the long history of Jews' College,' Jakobovits wrote publicly some twenty months later, 'can have witnessed more dramatic changes in its leadership than the one just concluded. First, the chairman of the council resigned unexpectedly ...'[89]

* * *   * * *   * * *

Overriding the differences between himself and Kalms, the Chief Rabbi in due course openly welcomed the announcement of Sacks' appointment. 'I greet his election with particular delight,' he declared, adding that his successor's 'record of leadership and scholarship provides every promise of a richly blessed incumbency.'[90]

Anticipating the outcome, Bermant wrote: 'Kalms, who has a gift for picking winners, had alighted on Sacks as the next Chief Rabbi not only because of his intrinsic ability, but because he thought that Sacks might redress the rightward shift which had been inspired by Lord Jakobovits. The very title "Traditional Alternatives" reads like a proof of Sacks' intentions.'[91]

Another commentator, historian David Englander, asserted of the 'rightward shift' and of Sacks' possible influence on it: 'Divisive and painful, the return to tradition [under Brodie and Jakobovits] exerted a profound effect upon the character of Anglo-Jewry.

'Reform and Liberal Judaism were not crushed in the Orthodox offensive; nor did Progressive Conservatives succumb. Nevertheless, the centre of gravity shifted. Progressive Judaism, like the post-Thatcherite Labour Party, looked very different at the close of the Orthodox attack than at the beginning. Its transformation was such that Dr Jonathan Sacks felt able to look beyond the rhetoric towards a process, albeit a very protracted one, of reconciliation.'[92]

These intentions Sacks made clear – or so his constituents believed – when he was inducted into office by his predecessor some eighteen months later. As the installation drew near, the *Jewish Chronicle* had contrasted the challenges faced by the outgoing Chief Rabbi with those of his successor, remarking that 'an era is drawing to a close.'

On Sunday, Rabbi Immanuel Jakobovits will end nearly a quarter-century as British Jewry's most prominent religious leader, and Dr Jonathan Sacks will assume the office of Chief Rabbi. When Lord Jakobovits assumed office, he inherited deep divisions within mainstream Orthodoxy. He can rightly claim to have helped narrow that rift; to have helped the religious centre to hold; and, despite an overall shrinkage of the identifying Jewish community, to have planted seeds for the future through his unflagging commitment to Jewish education.

At least as important, he has exercised the prerogative – indeed, the duty – of a Chief Rabbi in raising his voice on issues of compelling social, and moral, concern. If he has erred on occasion – and what leader worthy of the title, during twenty-four years at the centre of influence, decision and controversy, would not have? – it is perhaps in a tendency to overstep the blurry boundary between moral and temporal power; between the political and the partisan. Far better this, however, than to have made of his pulpit an ivory tower, or to have shied away from issues because they were not explicitly 'Jewish,' much less strictly Judaic.

His successor inherits new challenges. Although he will be called upon to turn his own erudition and leadership skills to many of the same national and international issues as Lord Jakobovits, the communal imperatives have changed. Far more pressing than the halachic debate that gripped United Synagogue Orthodoxy in the 1960s is the divide between it and the more strictly Orthodox on the one hand, and the degree to which increasing numbers of Jews, especially the young and the secular, feel little or no sense of communal involvement, on the other.

Chief Rabbi Sacks may be tested less by what he says about the inner city, Israeli politics, or even the inherited question of Paula Cohen's conversion,[93] than about the recent stain of mob intimidation in Stamford Hill. Among the young or secular, he will be challenged less by the tendency to marry out than to opt out altogether. He will have to listen as often as preach, and to apply his Orthodox Judaism to unorthodox questions. It is a tall order – but one to which Rabbi Sacks' background and talents seem especially well suited, as were Lord Jakobovits' to the challenges he inherited twenty-four years ago.[94]

Addressing, 'with affection, my dear and revered successor,' Jakobovits drew on these challenges in the course of his induction address two days later:

If you were to pose the questions, 'How can I, as the newly installed Chief Rabbi, triumph over the lurking dangers, pitfalls and challenges, how can I assert myself to leave the distinctive mark of my leadership upon this great community, and how can I be certain that I will enter *b'li pega*, without mishap, and emerge without mishap, to celebrate a yomtov at the end of my career?', then the two words *chazak ve'ematz*, addressed to Joshua, say it all: 'Be strong and of good courage.'

Our sages in the Talmud interpreted this phrase to have two distinct meanings: *chazak batorah ve'ematz bema'asim tovim*, 'Be strong in Torah, and courageous in good deeds.' In your new exalted office, your first task will be to preserve the Torah, to keep intact our traditions, to interpret Jewish teachings as you find and understand them. *Chazak* – for this 'be strong!' If you will sometimes encounter enormous pressures, to bend a little here, to modify there; if some will seek to subject you to their dictates, telling you what you may say and what you may do, then 'be strong.'

In matters of principle and conviction, resist at all costs, assert your freedom of action and of speech to ensure that you are never deflected from what you deem to be right. Thus you will be respected. Your task will be, above all, to become, as our illustrious predecessor, Chief Rabbi Hertz, said of his charge in his installation address in 1913, 'Defender of the Faith.' His biography, written some thirty years later by Philip Paneth to mark his seventieth birthday, was entitled *Guardian of the Law.*

Secondly, *ve'ematz*, 'be of good courage,' *bema'asim tovim*, regarding good deeds in the community. Anglo-Jewry has a peculiar penchant for self-denigration. It delights in running itself down, stressing failings, magnifying scandals, while ignoring or belittling successes and achievements. A community that does not believe in itself cannot flourish. It will not attract its best sons and daughters to community service – for who wants to invest in failure? *Ve'ematz* – 'be of good courage.'

Highlight *ma'asim tovim*, the many wonderful good deeds to be found in the community, and confound the prophets of doom. Generate courage through self-esteem, and success through confidence. Through such good courage, Joshua managed to conquer the Promised Land, and through such indomitable courage, this great community under your leadership will prosper spiritually.

I recall that on one of my last visits in Jerusalem to Rabbi Abramsky, of sainted memory – one of the greatest Torah sages ever to have graced our shores – he showed me the passage in the first chapter of Joshua: 'Be strong and of good courage, for you shall cause this people to inherit the Land which I swore to their fathers to give to them.' Then it states: 'Only be strong and very courageous to observe, and to do according to all the law which Moses My servant commanded you.' You see, commented Dayan Abramsky, 'for the conquest of the Land, you need to be "strong and of good courage"; but for the conquest of the Torah, you require to be "strong and very courageous."'

After two thousand years of exile, and the catastrophe of the Holocaust, our generation has two supreme priorities: to consolidate our national rebirth in the Land of Israel given to our Fathers; and to restore our people to its timeless assignment given at Sinai. Of these two, said the dayan, the second is the more difficult and demands even greater courage.

This is indeed manifest in our time. Harder still than to generate concern to advance peace with security is the even greater challenge to excite Jews the world over to resume our destiny as a 'light unto the nations,' as spiritual pathfinders and moral pioneers, fulfilling the purpose for which we wondrously survived all our tribulations over the millennia. We, the rabbis, must help to restore the balance between the yearning for our physical homeland and the commitment to our spiritual heritage, as commanded to Joshua.

My dear colleague, you enter this venerable office with a higher public profile than any of your predecessors. Your notable achievements, in reviving the fortunes of Jews' College, in blazing new trails through your Traditional Alternatives, and in winning fame and acclaim through your outstanding Reith lectures – all these testify to the exceptional endowments you bring to this high office, and the good will within and beyond the community on which you can count for support and response to your leadership.

Sustained by your wife, your parents and family, and your many friends, may you be blessed with robust health and the gift of wisdom to write a new volume, a *shirah chadashah,* to the glory of our community and our people, earning the reverence for our faith by this promise of Moses when he laid down his office: 'And all the peoples of the earth shall see that the Name of the Lord is called upon you, and they shall have respect for you.'[95]

Responding, Sacks called on his flock

to join with me in renewing our *ahavat Yisrael,* our categorical commitment to the love of every Jew. We must reach out to every Jew, with open arms and an open heart. If we must disagree, and sometimes we must, let us do so with love and dignity and respect. We can prove the Torah's greatness only by inspiration, not by negation. We are a divided community. But let us work to lessen those divisions by coming closer to one another and to God. We have suffered enough from anti-Semitism. Let us practise philo-Semitism. We have suffered enough from the assaults of others. Let us never inflict them on ourselves.[96]

Before exploring Sacks' own successes – or failures – in his professed attempts to 'lessen those divisions,' it is necessary to re-examine his predecessors' records along the paths that led to such divisions – and, most especially, to their perpetuation and escalation.

2

Beyond the Limits

'We have an unparalleled capacity to travel hopefully ... But do we have the capacity to arrive? That is the single most crucial question facing Jewry today.' [1]

Faith Against Reason tracked the last 150 years of Anglo-Jewry's 'hopeful' travels. It suggested, however, that the hoped-for destination – unity without uniformity – is as distant as ever, is possibly little more than an unattainable dream. As Sacks has noted,[2] the concept of inclusivism was endorsed in the very title of the United Synagogue when, at its foundation in 1870, it adopted the Hebrew name *Knesset Yisrael* ('Congregation of Israel'). The title – which, its founders observed,

> was felicitously chosen for the Amalgamated Body – is one fraught with great and solemn reminiscences. It embodies aspirations for unity, harmony, and concord in the future, together with recollections of a great, glorious, and imperishable past. May it typify results commensurate with the feelings of which it is the symbol![3]

Two of its earliest constituents – the Hambro' and New Synagogues – were both offshoots of the Great Synagogue, 'but their interests were considered to be so divergent that originally they declined to be governed, even in spiritual affairs, by the same ecclesiastical authorities. Each Synagogue had its own Rabbinical Chief, exercising authority over his own congregants, and enjoying independent jurisdiction. The first advance towards conjoint action was effected in 5518–1758, when the Great and Hambro' Synagogues appointed one Chief Rabbi [Hart Lyon], with ecclesiastical jurisdiction over both congregations.'[4]

On the death of his successor, David Tevele Schiff, in 1792, the Hambro' decided that it was 'unnecessary' to perpetuate the position, but 'the highly gifted and worthy'[5] Solomon Hirschell, Lyon's son, was nevertheless elected. Following the 1842 imposition of the *cherem* (excommunication, or 'caution,' as the rabbinate called it) against the Reform seceders,[6] and Hirschell's subsequent demise, the Hambro' added a significant rider to its schedule of laws:

Concord, which is the foundation of social happiness, is only to be preserved by the adoption of such regulations as are conducive to the general welfare. Laws are therefore necessary for the establishment of good order; and that the same may be preserved, it is necessary that we implicitly observe such Laws framed for the support and benefit of the Congregation. The inefficiency of Laws to regulate our Congregation has been long felt by those who have had the management of its affairs; for although all those laid down for religious observances are clearly deduced from sacred sources, yet the government of Assemblies for the worship of God requires certain rules and orders to be followed, in order that the eccentricity of individuals may not disturb the general harmony.[7]

Thus it was, on the publication of Nathan Adler's *Laws and Regulations*[8] three years later, that general approbation greeted his recommendations; and that, in 1863, the Great Synagogue was moved to declare: '... it is a source of the highest gratification at the present time to testify how much the Congregation and the Jewish community at large are indebted for their spiritual welfare to the learning, zeal and ability of the present Chief Rabbi ...'[9]

These sentiments were consolidated within the 1870 Jewish United Synagogues Act in its undertaking to contribute 'with other Jewish bodies to the maintenance of a Chief Rabbi and of other ecclesiastical persons.'[10]

* * *   * * *   * * *

The emergence of Reform Judaism in Britain came in the wake of, though was largely distinct from, the progressive approach adopted by Israel Jacobsohn at Seesen in Hanover, and Gotthold Salomon in Hamburg, 'to whom the old-fashioned synagogue service, with its lack of grace and dignity, was utterly distasteful, but who could see no alternative except in the church, which was even more distasteful.'[11]

Largely untouched by the *haskalah* ('Enlightenment') movement sweeping across Europe, the Judaism of Reform's proponents in England 'remained completely of the old type.'[12] 'Not a breath of criticism of the Jewish theology underpinning the synagogue service'[13] was seen to emanate from their ranks.

Politically, Britain's 25,000 Jews were well off compared to their Continental counterparts, able to settle where they pleased, to engage in business, lease land, and vote in parliamentary elections. In the decades leading up to the 1842 secession, calls for change had centred almost exclusively on issues of congregational decorum and administration.

Dismissing the minority view expressed in an earlier petition for 'such alterations and modifications as were in line with the changes introduced in the Reform synagogues in Hamburg and other places,'[14] the service at the West London Synagogue initially retained considerably more Hebrew, as well as prayers for the return to Zion and the coming of the Messiah – though not for the restoration of the sacrificial cult.[15] The format followed the wording of a resolution adopted in April 1840 at the inaugural meeting of the proposed congregation: 'That a revised service be there performed in the Hebrew language in conformity with the principles of the Jewish Religion, and in the manner best calculated to excite feelings of devotion.'[16]

'It must be clear to everyone,' wrote the West London's senior minister, Morris Joseph, some seventy years later,

> that if our founders had adopted the radical standpoint of German Reform, their movement would have been very short-lived. The Anglo-Jewish community of their day was not prepared for any save the most moderate changes, and the original programme of my synagogue represented the limits of the outlook and the needs of the average Liberal Jew in England at that time. Had it gone beyond those limits, the West London Synagogue would probably not have come into existence. German Reform was notoriously far more drastic than English Reform has ever been. I have before me the original Prayer-Book of the Hamburg Temple, issued in 1819, and it contains a large proportion of hymns and prayers in the vernacular. At this very day, on the other hand, the service in my synagogue includes only one English prayer – the prayer for the King.[17]

As in Germany, however, the essence of reform was a repudiation of rabbinical authority, with a rejection of the mishnaic and talmudic laws on a level with those contained in the Torah. Nor, suggested a future Chief Rabbi, was this 'rabbinical authority' any less contemporary than it was historical:

> In contrast to the situation in other countries, Britain's Chief Rabbi was never *primus inter pares*. He was neither a chief minister nor a chief rabbi presiding over colleagues of equal qualifications or rank, however locally limited their jurisdiction. In fact, he was – or sought to be – the only recognised rabbi in his realm, with the Beth Din serving as ecclesiastical 'assessors' to 'advise' him on matters of Jewish law … This was obviously conducive to the disproportionate influence of the British Chief Rabbinate, in the absence of rivals or a diffusion of power.

But inevitably there was also an obverse side to this rigid system of centralised control and the suppression of challenges to authority within the Establishment. The system encouraged centrifugal forces of dissent and secession. In Anglo-Jewry, the separatist congregations – whether of the Reform and Liberal on the left, or the *Austritt* variety on the right – arose primarily against the monolithic power structure of the officially 'authorised' community. Disaffection was generated by repulsion from the centre rather than by attraction to the extremes; the factors leading to secession were institutional rather than ideological.[18]

Discussing the results of schism and reform during Adler's incumbency, Sacks has argued:

What made Anglo-Jewry different is that, by the time crisis occurred, strong communal leadership was already in place ... The existence of a Chief Rabbinate in Britain was a vital force for restraint in a period when, throughout most of Europe and America, the citadels of tradition had been overrun by radical secularism or reform ...

Anglo-Jewry was fortunate in being led by a figure of the stature of Adler ... [H]e brought to his leadership not only the unimpeachable authority of his scholarship but also a robust and far-sighted approach to communal organisation.[19]

Whether it was the good fortune of conditions in England or the wisdom of his leadership, he made the decision to create in Britain a Jewish community that would resist the twin temptations of being Orthodox but exclusive, or inclusive but non-Orthodox, but would instead be faithful to one of Judaism's most majestic ideas, *Knesset Yisrael*, the community of all Jews standing before God.

It took an unlikely combination of skills and circumstances for him to succeed, and naturally he did not do so completely. But he and Commonwealth Jewry did so more effectively than anywhere else, and their achievement has lasted for more than a hundred years ...

Modern Orthodoxy is concerned with ideas, Inclusivism with people. Modern Orthodoxy is about content, Inclusivism about constituency. Modern Orthodoxy, like Maimonides' *Guide for the Perplexed*, is an answer to the problems of an intellectual élite. Inclusivism is concerned with Jews as a whole, learned and unlearned alike.

When Modern Orthodoxy succeeds, it creates a philosophy. When Inclusivism succeeds, it creates a community. That is what Nathan Marcus Adler did, and it makes his contribution to modern Jewry no less significant than that of [Samson Raphael] Hirsch.[20]

Faith Against Reason highlighted the fallacies in this argument, the weaknesses in both Adler's character and approach, the damaging effects of his frequent ambivalence, and the slow but steady erosion of Chief Rabbinical authority and influence over the wider community. It demonstrated, in particular, that the 'tepid, slight and limited'[21] advance of British Reform had little to do with Adler's 'skill' or 'wisdom,' and even less with claims of Adlerian 'Inclusivism.' As the historian Cecil Roth put it, with half an eye on future battles:

> Surveying the schism after a long interval of years, it seems in some ways rather insubstantial. The Reformers, though they did not reject the Oral Law as drastically as their critics alleged, were impatient of the Rabbinic development of Judaism and tended to omit much that was poetic in Jewish worship and beautiful in Jewish ceremonial, simply because it had no biblical authority.
>
> They could not realise that the intellectual world was entering upon a phase when, precisely in their own advanced religious circles, the attitude towards the Bible would change and they would be driven back to a conception of an ever-developing evolutionary Judaism, interpreted in each era by its religious leaders – 'every generation and its seekers, every generation and its teachers' – a conception nearer by far to that of the rabbis of the talmudic age than of the Reformers of 1840.
>
> As for the minutiæ of worship and the manner of conducting divine service, which a century ago seemed to be the crux of the dispute, improvements were easily and insensibly incorporated, little by little, in the usage of most English congregations, the Great Synagogue generally leading the way. Within a very few years, some of the revolutionary proposals of the secessionists had become almost a commonplace. A little more patience, a little more imagination, and the schism would have been unnecessary.[22]

Adler's contemporary, the chronicler James Picciotto, similarly averred: 'What is certain,' he wrote in 1875, 'is that most of the reforms asked for by the so-called seceders have been introduced in our days into the Orthodox congregations.' The Reformers, he pointed out, had said that they would have returned to 'the ancient Synagogue,' even after their own place of worship had been opened, if 'very moderate concessions' had been made to them, 'and if certain acts which they had characterised as harsh and unjustifiable had not been perpetrated.'

Of the wider conflict, Picciotto added: 'Time, the great healer of wounds, has meanwhile effected its work. Calm reflection could not fail in the end to remind all parties that discord, with its train of evil consequences, has caused great national disasters, and that Israel, at the present age, needs more than ever union and concord in its onward march towards its glorious future destinies.'[23]

Arthur Barnett, one-time minister of the 'benevolently neutral' Western Synagogue,[24] wrote:

> Looking back impartially, one may justifiably assert that what was happening was, in no sense, a revolution in Jewish theology but merely an adventure in Jewish aesthetics. Within a very few years after the establishment of the Reform Synagogue in West London, practically all the changes sought by the seceders had become the common practice of the congregations under the ecclesiastical authority of the Chief Rabbi. What was really a storm in a teacup only later developed into a raging conflict of angers and resentments.[25]

Today's historians broadly share these views, and have found few actions to commend in Adler's record. 'There is little evidence,' asserts Aubrey Newman, the United Synagogue's official chronicler, 'of any independent authority being exercised by Nathan Adler ... On occasion he did intervene, either to be very firmly put in his place or else to find that others were already doing what he would have wished on his behalf.'[26]

In sum, contended Israel Finestein, '[Adler] managed to satisfy no party entirely, and still less himself. There is a touch of tragedy about his Chief Rabbinate (from which he was happy to retire in 1880), a recovery from whose effects was to await the twentieth century.[27] His vision was not matched by his power; his notional authority exceeded the resources which were made available for its full exercise.'[28]

In a double-edged summation of Adler's tenure, Todd Endelman comments:

> By centralising religious authority and preventing the emergence of an independent, native-born rabbinate, Adler and his lay supporters helped to guarantee the institutional hegemony of Orthodox Judaism in Britain ... However, this achievement was not without its downside. The stifling of religious innovation robbed communal life of the intellectual ferment that accompanied the debate about Reform in more open, pluralistic communities and that stimulated the creation of scholarship and religious thought across the denominational spectrum.[29]

It was the growth of such scholarship and religious thought – as well as of pluralism – during the ensuing decades that was to help change the face of the increasingly fragile and fragmented Anglo-Orthodox community, and of the Chief Rabbinate at its core, and to hasten the 'revolution in Jewish theology' that threatened to tear them both asunder.

* * *   * * *   * * *

Another factor accelerating this change, and coinciding with the closing years of Adler's (by then ineffectual) rabbinate – and the even less respected incumbency of his son, Hermann – was the migration of Jews 'who set forth from their lands and homes to other countries and continents [and who] decisively changed the probable course of Jewish history.'[30]

As far as Britain was concerned, 'the peaceful calm of Anglo-Jewry was shattered … by the immigration of thousands of Russian and Polish Jews. They outnumbered the existing small community, which, in consequence, underwent a profound change both in structure and in character,'[31] leaving 'a Jewry – or, more accurately now, a series of Jewries – quite different from that which had existed but a quarter-century before. These differences were not merely religious and social; they were also cultural, political and idealistic. In London, moreover, an entirely new synagogal body had been called into existence, which gave expression to these differences, and articulated them both internally and to the wider world. In response, as it were, the already established community erected mechanisms of its own to preserve an identity and an outlook suddenly under attack.'[32]

United Synagogue opposition followed the establishment of this body, the Federation of Synagogues, in 1887, and of the Chevrat Machzike Hadath ('Society of Upholders of the Religion') four years later. Questioning their *raison d'être*, the US council declared: 'At a time when the desire of the community is to unite as much as possible its various organisations, and to make further provision for the religious requirements of the poor in the East of London, it surely seems inopportune to create and extend a body whose policy must inevitably tend to disunion and disintegration.'[33]

But disenchantment with the younger Adler's 'inability to resist the growing encroachments on Orthodox custom that were constantly being demanded and introduced'[34] – as well as with the 'near absolutism of the Chief Rabbinate,' the 'wholly decorative' powers of the Beth Din, and the 'sorry status' of the immigrant rabbi[35] – led in time to the election as a full-time dayan of the Federation's Moshe Avigdor Chaikin, a product of some of the greatest yeshivot in the Pale of Settlement and the first of a succession of East European rabbis (another was Shmuel Yitzchak

Hillman) who would exert a growing hold on the Chief Rabbinate and its court.[36] Chaikin's appointment, however, was destined to await the death of Hermann Adler, who, on his election as Chief Rabbi, had 'made it clear that he was not prepared to accept any limitation' on his powers, nor 'even be bound to consult the Beth Din.'[37]

The passing of the years, and the establishment of the Union of Orthodox Hebrew Congregations (Adath)[38] – an attraction to those even within United Synagogue ranks

> wishing to intensify Orthodoxy – [led to] a cry commonly heard that the Chief Rabbi and the Beth Din had fallen into the hands of the 'Ultras' who were exerting in consequence an influence that their numbers alone did not warrant. In some respects, of course, this was true ... All this was an aspect of the Chief Rabbinate with which the honorary officers could not deal, and the result was to make any differences between them the more difficult to heal. He [the Chief Rabbi] could legitimately turn to other Jewish organisations for support, even when, paradoxically, they did not recognise his official status, whereas the honorary officers could turn for support only to the customs and traditions of the United Synagogue itself.[39]

Anxious to uphold those traditions – and despite an increasing tendency by Adler's successor, Joseph Herman Hertz, to lean on his Adath son-in-law Solomon Schonfeld – the honorary officers made much of the term 'progressive conservatism,' coined by Hertz himself in 1923.[40] In their preface to the by-laws of the United Synagogue published thirteen years later, they wrote of their 'acceptance of Tradition as a living force and not as a dead weight' in the following terms:

> The spirit which imbues the whole code of by-laws is that of the Progressive Conservatism which the United Synagogue itself exemplifies, rejecting on the one hand the clamour of those who, in the desire for constant change, would recklessly cast aside Tradition; and on the other, the invitation of those who regard all things as settled, deluding themselves with the pretence that time and environment and circumstances are factors of no account, as though our lives and our mutual relationships are not susceptible to change.[41]

When change came, however, it tended to diverge from that envisaged. A year earlier, Abramsky, spiritual head of the Machzike Hadath and a 'fierce fighter in the wars of Hashem [God],'[42] had assumed the leadership of the London Beth Din. His appointment was greatly to advance the shift to the

'Ultras' begun by Chaikin – 'his towering personality and commanding influence [wrote Jakobovits of Abramsky] extended primarily to … moving the Beth Din's previous "middle-of-the-road" course strongly and irrevocably to the right'[43] – and was a major factor in the creation of the Reform Beth Din in 1948, particularly in light of the progressives' independent action in the fields of marriage, divorce and conversion.[44] 'It was Abramsky above all,' declares the United Synagogue, 'who established the policies and customs that are followed by the London Beth Din to this day.'[45]

* * *   * * *   * * *

The founding of the Jewish Religious Union in the opening years of the twentieth century introduced a radical and polarising element into the battle between the forces of tradition and reform. Questions began to be raised – and challenges thrown out – regarding core concepts of Judaism that had hitherto remained untouched in the study halls and synagogues of Anglo-Jewry, precipitating the theological controversies that have embroiled it ever since.

The initial successes of the Jewish Reformers in early nineteenth-century Germany were soon hampered by the refusal of the Prussian government to recognise them if they broke away from established form. One result was the emigration of a number of potential leaders to the United States, German Jews whose religious views were as liberal as their politics.

In the synagogues and institutions (most notably the Union of American Congregations and Hebrew Union College) established by such men, these rabbis easily obtained positions commensurate with their abilities and, before long, transplanted there a Reform Judaism with a distinctly American flavour.

Among them was the charismatic Isaac Mayer Wise (1819–1900), whose arrival in Cincinnati – a city with a large and cultured Teutonic community – presaged the declarations of 1855 (Cleveland), 1869 (Philadelphia), 1885 (Pittsburgh) and 1889 (Detroit) as the recognised platforms of Reform in America,[46] instituting what they termed 'the mission of Israel' to disseminate the theology of their movement among the Jews of their adopted land. Across the Atlantic, this missionary zeal was to find its foremost exponent in Claude Montefiore, a scion of the West London Synagogue and the creator, with Lily Montagu, of the Jewish Religious Union's godchild, Liberal Judaism. 'If,' he was to declare in 1912, we differ from Conservative[47] Judaism as regards the miracles recorded in the Bible, as regards the doctrine of inspiration, as regards the perpetual validity and authority of the ceremonial law, this is because of, or this has led up to, positive doctrines, no less important and definite, and (as we believe) nobler and truer, than the doctrines held by our Conservative opponents. Indeed, Liberal Jews are, on the whole, more disposed than Conservative Jews to regard a consistent body of doctrine – a systematic theology – as necessary and important. Liberal Judaism is, therefore, quite as positive and affirmative as Conservative Judaism; its own affirmations are as essential to it as other affirmations are essential to Conservative Judaism, its rival.[48]

A decade earlier, following his spiritual and physical journey from Finsbury Square[49] to Berkeley Street, Morris Joseph had been more circumspect on the subject:

Apart from a few leading ideas, the Jewish Creed has always been in a fluid condition, and Judaism leaves us free to construct our own theology, so long as we do not trench upon certain easily recognised principles which, because they are wrought into the very fabric of the religion, could not be discarded without destroying the religion itself ... We must not take our Religion wholly on trust; we must satisfy ourselves of its truth by bringing it to the test of reason. 'How do I know that there is a God?' is a question that is not only natural but commendable. It is the glory of Judaism that it encourages such questions, that it invites us to free inquiry into the grounds of our religious belief.[50]

Treading in the academic footsteps of Montefiore, Joseph and the maverick New West End minister Joseph Hochman[51] – and, indeed, of the Adlers, Hertz and Israel Brodie (emulated, in time, by Sacks) – the yeshivah-trained Louis Jacobs[52] was but one of many clerical figures in Anglo-Jewry whose exposure to 'the wisdom of objective scholarship' resulted in a meeting of the 'two worlds'[53] of traditional Torah studies and Higher and Lower Criticism of the Pentateuch.[54] Unlike his Chief Rabbinical colleagues, however – at least in their publicly declared stance – Jacobs arrived at the conclusion, 'eschewing obscurantism, religious schizophrenia and intellectual dishonesty ... that a synthesis is possible between the permanent values and truth of tradition and the best thought of the day.'[55]

Towards the end of his life, enlarging on this thesis in relation to the concept of *Torah min hashamayim* ('Torah from Heaven'), Jacobs wrote:

... modern knowledge and scholarship have made it impossible to accept the traditional view that God 'dictated' to Moses, word for word and letter by letter, the whole of the Pentateuch (the Torah). My argument runs that, while such a doctrine of verbal inspiration is now untenable, the traditional doctrine that the Torah is from Heaven can and should still be maintained.

To put this in different words, God is the author of the Torah (conceived of as the sum total not of the Pentateuch alone but of Jewish religious thought through the ages), but, as in His creativity of the world, He co-operated with His creatures in producing the Torah, through human beings reaching out to Him. There is thus a human element, as well as a divine element, in what we call the Torah.[56]

In refutation of this argument, Brodie forty years earlier had cited the view of former Jews' College principal Isidore Epstein when justifying Jacobs' exclusion from the ministry of the New West End Synagogue.[57] Referring to 'the kind of halachah which has begun to make its appearance of late in certain quarters which do not recognise the divine origin of the Bible,' Epstein had declared:

By favourite tricks they play with the Bible, which they regard as partly divine and partly human − it being left to individual judgment to disentangle the divine elements from the human − they rob life's pilgrimage of the sole reliable signpost pointing the way wherein sojourners must walk 'when turning to the right and when turning to the left,' and thus render life pathless.

In other words, by rejecting the absolute authority of the Bible, without being able to replace it by anything else, they encourage the most reckless individualism in religion, an individualism full of contradictions and vagaries, leading as often away from God as it does to God.

Thus we come to the real divergence of, for want of any other name, we may call the Orthodox halachah from any other kind of halachah, such as that emanating from the Conservative no less than Reform schools − the question of authority. The difference of attitude with regard to authority goes further than the mere difference in matters of ritual, practice and so forth.

The fatal and inherent weakness of those who deny the divine origin of the Bible, even if their personal religious behaviour conforms to the highest standard, lies in the lack of any valid objective authority for what they teach or affirm. Apart from private judgment and individual opinion, they have no objective criterion or authority for what they tell people to do or believe, thus depriving their halachic pronouncements of all validity.[58]

This charge of 'reckless individualism in religion' underpins the controversies that have wracked Anglo-Jewry from the 1840s secession to the Sacks Chief Rabbinate – upon whose unfinished business the spotlight again falls.

3

Leading by Example

'I want to encourage leadership in others; to be a catalyst for creativity;
to open closed doors and let in the fresh air of initiative and imagination.' [1]

No stranger to controversy himself, Sacks has addressed the topic in much
of his writings; indeed, one of his books (in its American incarnation) is
entitled *Arguments for the Sake of Heaven*.[2] In it, he asserts:

> ... when there is no immediate solution to problems facing the Jewish
> people, the most important religious imperative is to engage in what the
> sages called 'arguments for the sake of Heaven.' One of the themes of the
> present study is a plea for recovery of what I call 'tradition as argument'[3]
> ... The question that has become suddenly urgent is whether the current
> conflicts within Jewry can be incorporated within this model of 'argument
> for the sake of Heaven.' If so, there can be dialogue. If not, there can only
> be confrontation. The one creates community, the other destroys it. Why,
> then, has dialogue between Jews become so difficult in the twentieth
> century? Why is it so often replaced by mutual delegitimation? If even
> Reform and secular Jews have turned, in recent years, towards tradition,
> why has there not been a revival of rabbinic Judaism's greatest tradition:
> the tradition of argument, tradition *as* argument?

Because, Sacks believes, 'the brit yi'ud, the covenant of Torah, has not yet
been renewed.

> Jewish attitudes have become more 'traditional' without yet returning
> to tradition. The inability of Jews to communicate across the ideological
> divide is a measure of the extent to which Jews still stand 'between two
> covenants.'[4] ... If [argument] proceeds through a debate informed by text,
> precedent and interpretation, it becomes part of Torah. It becomes part of
> the commentary each generation of Jews writes to the covenant. But if it
> proceeds through political pressure, mutual delegitimation and violent
> confrontation, there is no real argument. There is a search for victory,
> not truth. The clash of opinions becomes secularised. Judaism, instead

of providing the means for handling conflict, fuels the flames of conflict into conflagration. The great tradition of 'argument for the sake of Heaven' comes to an end. That has happened in our time. It is a process that must be reversed.[5]

* * *   * * *   * * *

Following the Traditional Alternatives conference, and his subsequent election, Sacks posed the fundamental question: 'How shall Orthodox Jews relate to Jews who do not share their commitment to halachah or the classic terms of Jewish faith? Liberal, Reconstructionist, Reform and Conservative Judaisms represent significant challenges – not perhaps to Orthodoxy itself, but to its claim to be the one valid interpretation of Judaism.'[6] Writing years earlier, he had discussed the question in these terms:

> It has been part of the ongoing obligations of Orthodoxy in the last two hundreds years to defend itself not merely against scepticism, apathy and the attractions of other cultures, but also to validate its claims against other supposed 'varieties' of Judaism – against the movements we have come to know as Liberal, Reform and Conservative Judaism ...
>
> We do not need a Freud to tell us that when a person or movement commits itself to an ideology which lacks coherence, then to understand such an action we should look less at the stated reasons than at the unstated motives which brought it forth ...
>
> In defending Judaism from Reform, the Orthodox world may have paid a price, in losing the sense of self-criticism, forgetting the tensions of a life of faith, becoming unpractised in speaking to the inner dilemmas of the spiritually striving. This it must now recover, for the ground of the struggle has changed.
>
> The person whom we are in danger of losing is no longer he who wants to be a 'man in the street,' but one who wants to be a 'Jew at home.' If, and only if, we recognise his difficulties, and set them in their context as a legitimate Jewish experience, will we be able to guide him back to his spiritual home.[7]

In several of his early works, Sacks had attempted to answer the question in the context of inclusivism. 'The most urgent task of Orthodoxy in modernity,' he wrote before becoming Chief Rabbi, 'is to think a way forward to recovering the substantive reality of *Knesset Yisrael*, the Jewish people as a single entity standing before God ...

'If Orthodoxy is to act responsibly toward the whole Jewish world and not simply toward its own immediate constituency, there are deep dilemmas to be faced about its relationship with secular and non-Orthodox Jews. It cannot embrace pluralism, the view that a secular or non-halachic reading of tradition is legitimate. But it cannot withdraw altogether into segregation without abdicating the responsibilities of religious leadership.'[8]

Sacks' definitive study of pluralism, inclusivism and Jewish unity came in his classic work, One People?, published two years into office. Orthodoxy, he wrote, did not recognise the possibility of denominational pluralism: it could not concede legitimacy to Jewish interpretations 'that deny or secularise the fundamentals of faith …

> Orthodoxy cannot subscribe to pluralism in the contemporary sense, for Orthodoxy is the decision to continue to understand tradition in the traditional way, as objective truth and external authority. Pluralism arises when a movement initially conceived in opposition to a tradition seeks to reaffirm its links with that tradition within the framework of a non-traditional consciousness. It involves a revisionary translation of the tradition into new terms of reference.
>
> Jewish pluralism, as an argumentative strategy, consists in recategorising issues that had hitherto been grounds for schism into one or other of the areas where the tradition had allowed for more than one interpretation. It involves seeing debates that had previously been central to the definition of Judaism as in fact marginal …
>
> Halachic pluralism is, in short, a symptom of the secularisation of religious behaviour. This is why it is self-evidently plausible to modern consciousness and at the same time necessarily incompatible with Orthodoxy. For Orthodoxy is the refusal to transform Jewish law from the revealed constitution of the covenant into a self-defined code of personal autonomy or an evolving historical process.[9]

Pluralism succeeded, wrote Sacks, only if the terms of Orthodoxy were false; but it failed within the terms it set itself, for it sought to accommodate liberal and Orthodox Judaisms within the same universe of discourse. They were variant interpretations of the same covenantal truth. 'Orthodoxy cannot be so accommodated. Only an Orthodoxy misconceived as an ultra-traditional liberalism can. Orthodoxy is defined in terms of truth and authority, not interpretation and option. This fact cannot be translated into pluralism.' So, Sacks concluded, 'we are left with the traditional alternative – inclusivism.'[10]

My reading of the Jewish sources, which may of course be faulty, suggests that God, in choosing Israel, made a covenant with an entire people ... Inclusivism is the belief that the covenant was made with a people, not with righteous individuals alone. One may leave or enter the people by apostasy on the one hand, conversion on the other. But the normal mode of faith is through birth, community, and the transmission of tradition across the generations ... Inclusivism involves a denial of truth to secular and liberal Judaisms (much as these Judaisms involve a denial of truth to Orthodoxy). But it insists that secular and liberal Jews are part of the covenant, participants in Judaism's bonds of collective responsibility, to be related to with love, dignity and respect.[11]

What, Sacks asked, would an inclusivist advocate? 'Firstly, a deep sensitivity to the language in which we speak of other Jews. The Jewish tradition attached the highest significance to speech. God spoke, and the universe was: the world was created with words. Human beings, too, create or destroy social worlds with words ... We may not speak of other Jews except in the language of love and respect. Rabbinic tradition taught collective solidarity and the prophetic obligation to speak well (*lelamed zechut*) of the congregation of Israel.'[12]

The inclusivist, moreover, 'attaches positive significance to the fact that liberal Judaisms have played their part in keeping alive for many Jews the values of Jewish identity, faith and practice ... movements which have served to retain Jews within Jewry who might otherwise have drifted into another faith or no faith at all ...

'Every Jew today who, after the tragedy of the Holocaust, the attacks on the State of Israel, and the ravages of assimilation, chooses to stay a Jew and have Jewish children is making a momentous affirmation that may not be dishonoured. Even if we must sometimes reject the beliefs and deeds of an individual Jew, none the less he or she is a fragment of the *Shechinah*, the divine presence which dwells in the midst of Jews wherever and whatever they are. For the inclusivist believes with perfect faith that the covenant binds all Jews to one another, and that a Jew who remains attached to the chosen people cannot be unchosen.'[13]

* * *   * * *   * * *

At both ends of the religious spectrum, *One People?* had a mixed reception, with, in Orthodox circles, one critic unmasking 'Dr Jonathan and Rabbi Sacks,'[14] and another spotting 'the Cambridge don beneath the *kippah!*'[15] Perhaps the most warm-hearted of the communal reviews came from the

Liberals' Rabbi Sidney Brichto, who had figured prominently over the years in many a Chief Rabbinical clash.

In 1987, following an extended period of manoeuvring across the spiritual divide over issues of personal status in Jewish law – notably, a joint approach on conversion – Brichto had proffered 'revolutionary proposals for Progressive acceptance of the halachic authority of an Orthodox Beth Din.'[16] Earlier discussions between Jakobovits and Reform representatives, opposed by the London dayanim, had been inconclusive, even though conducted – as the then Chief Rabbi put it – 'with great discretion and in a sense of responsibility on all sides for what was at stake.'[17]

Brichto's formula had opened with a fervent appeal. 'It would be an act of abhorrent and unforgivable self-destruction,' he wrote, 'were we not to find the means of agreeing on a unified halachah in those areas which divide Jew from Jew and lead to enmity and internecine strife.

'In view of the seriousness of the situation, the time has come to put forward a solution – which will, however, in the present climate, most likely be rejected by both the Progressives and the Orthodox. Yet I do this now because now is the time for responsible Jews to have the courage to go out on a limb. When the future of the Jewish people is at stake, organisational and personal considerations are of secondary importance …

'For the preservation of Klal Yisrael, I am prepared to entrust the halachah to the Orthodox. Why? Because there is no one else. Because the Orthodox have retained the structure of halachah for the sake of Klal Yisrael, I am prepared to accord them the responsibility of finding the means to enable all religious sections to achieve a standard practice in the important areas of Jewish status, marriage and divorce. They must appreciate, however, that we Liberals and Progressives have a great interest in the matter. Orthodox rabbis entrusted by us to administer the halachah must do so with humility, compassion, ingenuity, creativity and, above all, a love for Klal Yisrael.'[18]

In the event, as he had predicted, Brichto's plea was dismissed even by his own side. But Sacks, in a personal message following his appointment as Chief Rabbi, had acclaimed the proposals as 'the most courageous statement by a non-Orthodox Jew this century,' prompting him to tell Brichto: 'I felt it was a genuine way forward. Others turned out not to share my view. It will be a while – eighteen months – before I take up office. But I believe we can still explore that way forward together. For if we do not move forward, I fear greatly for our community and for Am Yisrael.'[19]

Five years later, having received no sign from Sacks of any 'move forward,' Brichto vented his frustrations via a Masorti platform. 'I was very hopeful,' he wrote, 'that Jonathan Sacks as Chief Rabbi would take an initiative to explore my proposals. I did not question his sincerity when, in response to my letter congratulating him on his appointment, he informed me of his positive response to the "Brichto Proposals."

> I received his letter on 5 March, 1990. I do not think that he has changed his mind, as he very recently remarked jocularly to me and others in reference to the problems of Jewish status: 'Sidney and I agree on this subject. The problem is that we are the only two who do.' Why, then, has the Chief Rabbi in the interim five years not taken steps to 'explore that way forward,' in view of the importance he attached to the proposals?
>
> Over that period, his initiatives in launching his Decade of Jewish Renewal were demanding all his energies. The attempt to be inclusivist without offending that section which believed – as he did – that it alone represented authentic Judaism required skills of diplomacy neither he nor anyone else possessed. One has also to acknowledge that the lack of support from my own movement would have made him think, once he sat in the hot seat of the Chief Rabbinate, that in pursuing a resolution to the problems of Jewish status, he was on a hiding to nothing.
>
> Will my proposals ever again be considered, or will they be viewed as one more abortive attempt at compromise, doomed to failure, and the consequence of political naiveté on the part of the proposer? I must confess, both in sorrow and in anger, that I believe the latter to be the case.[20]

Thirty months before unleashing this plaint, and in clear reciprocation of Sacks' earlier comments, Brichto described *One People?* as 'a tour de force. Brilliantly documented and skilfully presented, it looks honestly at the Jewish experience of the past in order to find a resolution to the problems that today threaten the Jewish people with dissolution.

> Rabbi Sacks asserts in the preface that, 'in writing about Liberal, Reform, Conservative and Reconstructionist Judaisms, I have tried to come to terms with positions that are fundamentally not my own.' He is, I believe, the first Orthodox rabbi in a position of authority ever to do so, and for this he deserves our praise ...
>
> While Progressive Judaism, in view of its openness, may not be happy with his approach [on pluralism], it has no alternative but to accept it if it wishes to establish a working relationship with those Orthodox leaders who are prepared to talk with representatives of non-Orthodox groups.
>
> The only way forward is for Progressive Jews to cease demanding 'legitimisation' from the Orthodox. They, after all, do not seek ours ... What is essential is that we seek to establish relationships with those who agree that we are all part of a single Jewish people, with a common fate

and a common destiny – praying and striving for the messianic age.

If we reject each other's ideologies but still love each other as Jews, and if we set aside once and for all the rhetoric which we all too frequently use, we may begin to resolve those issues which could yet divide us into two Jewries – primarily, our differing approaches to divorce and conversion ...

The challenge of Progressive conversions – the question of patrilineal descent, in particular – does not lend itself so easily to halachic solutions. While making tentative suggestions, Rabbi Sacks recognises that the problem may be insoluble. Yet, if his inclusivist attitude were to become the basis for discussions, everything is possible.

Whatever conclusions are reached, *One People?* is essential reading for all who wish to establish the basis for a constructive dialogue between the various religious sections in Jewry. Just as Rabbi Sacks was kind enough to welcome my own proposals – in which I supported an exclusive, though more flexible, Orthodox handling of halachic issues – I can write of his programme for unity: for those who truly love *Klal Yisrael*, his is the only reasonable way forward.[21]

Far less accommodating was Dow Marmur who, while minister of London's North Western Reform Synagogue, had initiated the status discussions with Jakobovits. Writing now as senior rabbi of Holy Blossom Temple, Toronto, he observed: 'This excellent, erudite, informative and important book wants to reach out to all non-Orthodox Jews by describing each of us with the talmudic term *tinok shenishbah*, a child raised among Gentiles and thus not really knowing what he or she is doing. As much as we may appreciate the argument, we cannot accept the conclusion.

If I understand Rabbi Sacks, every non-Orthodox synagogue is an institution for Jews who have had a disturbed spiritual background, caused by modernity, out of which they have not yet managed to grow. This is the non-Orthodox synagogue's good point, as far as he is concerned. But it is also bad because, by seeking to legitimise the spiritual orientation of its members, such synagogues impede their progress towards the religious maturity and Jewish authenticity that only Orthodox Judaism can offer.

This seemingly patronising contention is the cornerstone of Rabbi Sacks' philosophy of 'inclusivism.' It is the only way in which Reform Judaism, for example, can be viewed from an Orthodox perspective. The alternative is to see it as heresy, or as another religion altogether. Religious pluralism has no place in the Orthodox scheme of things ...

For Liberal and Reform Jews, the most controversial aspect of the book is its attitude to non-Orthodox Judaism. Since the author largely sympathises with the exclusivists on his 'right,' he is not troubled by their separatism. But by rejecting pluralism he asserts that the only way in which those 'left' of him can be integrated is if they are prepared to regard their liberalism as an interim stage on their spiritual journey, a temporary station on the way to the Orthodox destination. His only hope for us – misguided children raised among Gentiles, victims of modernity – is that we will grow up and become part of his mature world of Jewish Orthodoxy.

'This then,' Marmur declared, 'is the gist of the manifesto on Jewish unity of a Chief Rabbi who wants to represent all Jews while legitimising only Orthodox Jews ... The author of this well-written and well-argued book refuses to acknowledge Reform, Liberal and Conservative Judaism as legitimate partners in the historic enterprise of preserving Jewish continuity in the modern world.

'Bearing in mind his brilliant intellect, his high-profile office and his urbane style, non-Orthodox Jews living in the countries he seeks to represent might have expected more. But perhaps that is unrealistic. Orthodoxy, even with a very human face, is ultimately incapable of being humane. That would put individuals before the collective.'[22]

Discussing Sacks' inclusivist approach as outlined in the book, Cambridge academic Stefan Reif commented: 'It is admirable that an Orthodox Chief Rabbi should be searching – with halachic backing – for ways of uniting all Jewish factions; and it would be equally admirable if the politics inherent in the attitudes of various Jewish groups could be abandoned long enough for some frank and open discussion of this "inclusivist" solution, as well as other possible solutions to the problems of Jews who can no longer marry each other.'[23]

Glasgow philosopher Ephraim Borowski wrote of *One People?*: 'Although he denies that [it] is a polemical work, Rabbi Sacks is right only in the pejorative sense of "polemic." It takes sides, it intimates the triumph of aspiration over analysis, and, as he tacitly admits in contrasting his position with the pessimism of [Israeli historian] David Vital, it is not dispassionately reasoned, but is an expression of a devout commitment to the cause of unity. In the last resort, he himself succumbs to "the continuing power over the Jewish imagination of the idea of 'one people,'" and allows his optimism – and his Orthodoxy – to outstretch his reason and his realism.'[24]

* * *   * * *   * * *

In his early bid to 'bind all Jews to one another,' Sacks frequently called on the community to observe the courtesies of civility and tolerance. 'It would be wrong,' he asserted in 1986, 'to say that today's Jewish religious circles are ones in which lashon hara [slander, calumny] occurs, is tolerated, passes without notice. Wrong because it would be the most perverse understatement.

> Lashon hara, far from being an occasional forgivable lapse, has become part of the very texture of a certain kind of Jewish life. We have evolved a culture, an apotheosis, of lashon hara. It has become almost impossible in certain circles to gain religious credence or acceptability without 'talking disparagingly' of someone. Lashon hara has become a ritual of initiation and group membership.
>
> Character assassination, condemnation, heresy-hunting, baseless denigration, the rush to judgment on a spider's-web of gossip: these have become the normal conversational modalities in at least some Jewish groups, not least those to whom the Mishnah Berurah and its author, the Chafetz Chaim, are held in esteem.
>
> In such a culture, words are not words but weapons; stature is measured by the exhaustiveness of one's condemnations; verbal terrorism reigns. The violence done to Jewish law and values is insane and obscene. This the Chafetz Chaim saw, understood and said. Few listened.

'No reader of Jewish news, no observer of religious life over these past few years,' wrote Sacks, 'can have failed to recognise this escalating culture of condemnation ... It has even penetrated, sadly, to the normally judicious ranks of mainstream Anglo-Jewish Orthodoxy, where attacks have begun to be heard on the so-called "Right" – the yeshivah and Chasidic worlds.

'It would be a tragedy indeed if the mainstream were to cut itself off from the energies, enthusiasm and sheer flow of Torah that come from these worlds. That the mainstream has a wider constituency and a different challenge to face in maintaining the allegiance of its members should not need to be defended by denigrating others.'[25]

'"Argument for the sake of Heaven,"' Sacks declared on the eve of Traditional Alternatives, 'does not imply pluralism. But it does imply a willingness to engage in reasoned dialogue with views with which one disagrees.'[26] And, at the conference itself: 'If Torah is, God forbid, ideologised, politicised, used to delegitimate other Jews who also care for Torah, then it will bring not peace but conflict to the world.'[27] Months later, he declared:

The religious voice that has sounded loudest, and most often, has been that of one group of Jews denouncing the faith and practice of another. Who benefits? Neither Jews nor Judaism. No movement was ever given strength by castigating the rest of the Jewish world as heretics, on the one hand, and fanatics, on the other.

We need not be religious pluralists in order to treat other Jews with respect. In the end, we must realise that there is more at stake than institutional rivalries. There is the honour of Judaism itself which must, if it is to command respect, speak with a voice that transcends the politics and personalities of its human representatives. We must never use the language of our enemies in speaking of other Jews.[28]

In his first interview as Chief Rabbi-elect, Sacks affirmed his aim 'to heal some of the rifts that have divided Anglo-Jewry, to encourage debate, and not shy away from communicating Jewish values to the wider community. I am determined as far as possible to emphasise what unites Jews and to encourage an atmosphere of mutual respect. The Jewish people have suffered too tragically and too often from internal divisions, and I hope that divisive words will be at a minimum from all sectors of the community.'

Asserting that he would 'run a very open Chief Rabbinate,' he added: 'The sages had great faith in the concept of "argument for the sake of Heaven." By that they meant that not even the greatest sage in history could get it completely right all the time. But if he listened to constructive criticism, he was more likely to do so.'[29]

* * *   * * *   * * *

'After a period of overlap far too long to be helpful to anyone' – Reform's journal, *Manna*, declared, on behalf of its leadership – 'Rabbi Dr Jonathan Sacks has finally been installed as Chief Rabbi of the United Hebrew Congregations. As the spiritual leader of the largest synagogal grouping in Britain, he will be a significant figure in shaping the future pattern of relationships within a community hampered by painful divisions.'

Noting that the new Chief Rabbi was bringing to the job 'remarkable qualities,' Reform's leaders called on him to 'acknowledge a reality –

namely, that a significant percentage of the Jewish world identifies with Progressive Judaism; that Progressive Judaism enables such Jews to remain within the Jewish world; that Progressive Judaism is clearly committed to certain values, such as education, which are vital to Judaism as Orthodoxy understands it. Given these undeniable facts, and given an obligation to the Jewish world as a whole, Orthodoxy has to find a positive way of relating to the non-Orthodox groupings without compromising its own beliefs.

We sincerely hope that Jonathan Sacks will move the United Synagogue towards [this] stance. We recognise the fact that it will not be easy for him and it will not happen overnight. Rabbi Sacks must be given time and support, but a process of change must soon become evident. Anglo-Jewry is too small and poorly resourced for unproductive infighting, endless jockeying for position, and senseless duplication of effort.

The leaders pointed out that 'Progressive Judaism does not seek legitimation from Orthodoxy because it does not need it … If Progressive Jews have insecurities, they must deal with them in an appropriate manner and not seek to make capital out of contacts with Orthodoxy.' But the Orthodox establishment, for its part, had to end 'the strange and uncomfortable situation whereby there are contacts between the leadership of the various groupings within Anglo-Jewry, but they must not be spoken about or exposed to public light.'

Signs of progress would be 'the sight, and not merely the rumour,' of the Chief Rabbi in dialogue with Progressive Jews; a growing public acceptance of the many areas in which the various communities, 'from top to bottom, work together for the good of Jewry and Britain'; and 'the acceptance of Progressive representation in the leadership of *all* communal institutions rather than *most*, as at present.'

Rabbi Sacks, the Reformers concluded, was 'uniquely qualified' to lead Anglo-Jewry forward into 'a more rational, sensible and mutually respectful era. We wish him well and offer both our prayers and such practical support as we can muster. We recognise that, if Rome was not built in a day, Anglo-Jewry cannot be rebuilt in a week. But we will be looking anxiously for signs of movement in the right direction.'[30]

Signs of movement (as Brichto had later discovered) were not, however, notably – or, indeed, noticeably – 'in the right direction.' Despite his best endeavours to encourage debate, unity and 'an atmosphere of mutual respect,' internal divisions and divisive words dogged Sacks from the very beginning. Launching his Chief Rabbinate on a self-styled platform of inclusivism, he soon found himself called upon to respond to Kalms' review on the future of the United Synagogue:

The most powerful plea to emerge from the research [wrote Sacks] is 'for the United Synagogue to reject religious exclusivism and *welcome the non-observant, less observant or middle-of-the-road Jew*.'[31] Almost exactly the same

plea was made eight centuries ago by no less an authority than Moses
Maimonides, at the end of his *Epistle on Martyrdom*.

The passage is so crucial to what must be the ethos of the United
Synagogue that I quote it in full: 'It is not right to alienate, scorn and hate
people who desecrate the Sabbath. It is our duty to befriend them and
encourage them to fulfil the commandments. The rabbis regulate explicitly
that when an evildoer who sinned by choice comes to the synagogue, he
is to be welcomed and not insulted.'

Something is badly wrong with the spiritual state of Anglo-Jewry
if these points, honestly made and honestly responded to, are taken to
signal a movement away from Torah and halachah. Against such facile
misinterpretations, the simplest answer is the one given long ago by
Hillel: 'Do not criticise Jews; even if they are not prophets, they are the
children of prophets.' There is an authentic echo in these contemporary
Anglo-Jewish voices of one of the most powerful of our prayers: 'Do not
cast us away from Your presence.'

Those interviewed did not ask for an abandonment of halachah.
They asked for sympathetic rabbis, welcoming synagogues, and a
compassionate application of Jewish law. Those are legitimate demands,
spiritual demands. Those who dismiss them or turn a deaf ear to them have
either not understood Torah or do not have the spiritual qualities needed
to lead a congregation.[32]

Between the lines, in these early strictures, was a sideswipe at the strictly
Orthodox whose influence had seeped into Hertz's twilight years and had
increased steadily, in the Beth Din and beyond, during Brodie's tenure.
Sacks, with his Oxbridge background, had still to confront the wrath of
his dayanim and their Adath colleagues, whose world was 'notoriously
suspicious of outsiders' and to whom the new Chief Rabbi's credentials
were 'open to question.'[33] At this stage, *they* were the unsympathetic,
their hearts hardened – or so it was suggested – against a 'compassionate
application of Jewish law.' Sacks had yet to face similar accusations from
those to his left – or, at the very least, claims that he was under pressure,
from those to his right, to 'turn a deaf ear.'

The first test of his authority, and of his inclusivist platform, came
with 'stage two'[34] of his Decade of Jewish Renewal – the creation of a
community-wide organisation known as Jewish Continuity. Laying out his
stall,[35] Sacks wrote that he sought

to establish the Chief Rabbinate as a proactive force in the community, not
merely encouraging others to create projects of renewal, but leading by

example. Beyond the parameters of synagogue and school life, the Chief Rabbinate has in the past led by influence and exhortation. These are no small things. Through them over the past two centuries my predecessors have helped shape the direction of the community as it has met the challenges of changing times.

As I read the mood of the age, however, I doubted whether influence and encouragement alone were enough. I suspected – and that suspicion has since hardened to certainty – that we were living at a time unprecedentedly sceptical of authority. Few people today in secular democratic societies can exercise influence in virtue of position. That applies not only to religious leaders but to politicians and heads of other institutions also.

We respect not the position but the person, and we judge the person less by what he says than by what he does. Therefore I had to create a doing Chief Rabbinate. And since the battle for Jewish commitment today extends beyond the synagogue and Jewish school, I had to extend the field of doing as well.[36]

Asserting that 'as an established community we are out of touch with the realities of contemporary Jewish life,' and drawing attention to the 'great institution-builders – most notably Chief Rabbi Nathan Marcus Adler and Sir Moses Montefiore, who created in the Victorian age many of the communal structures we still inherit today' – Sacks added: 'There is a danger that what is old can become aged. And that, I believed, is what had begun to happen to at least some of our institutions. I therefore encouraged a process of self-examination which has yielded, thus far, an unexpectedly rich harvest … Individually, these have brought gusts of fresh air into our communal thinking, even if they have created occasional squalls and storms.'[37]

The biggest 'gust of fresh air' blew in Jewish Continuity – 'a challenge, an idea and a project, the most ambitious but the most urgently necessary project Anglo-Jewry has been called on to create in the last twenty years. Everything I have done in the Chief Rabbinate so far,' declared Sacks, 'has been mere preparation for this, the structural and spiritual heart of renewal.' There was, he wrote later,

one widely held view which I call Jewish Darwinism. It says that 'throughout the generations, only the fittest Jews survive … What is happening today has always happened: when Jews were free to leave, they left. Only the most dedicated remain. On this view, it is futile to speak of continuity as a programme for all Jews. Instead, one should concentrate on the committed. They are Jewry's survivalists.' This view is cogent and persuasive, but I reject it absolutely … I reject it because it identifies fact with value; it confuses what happens with what we are right to let happen. I reject it because the covenant at the heart of Judaism links us in bonds of obligation to all Jews, not just the righteous few.

The new organisation, Sacks pledged,

> will be aimed at all Jews in the unshakeable belief that every Jew is precious … Jewish Continuity will provide vision. Its aim is to secure the future of Anglo-Jewry by creating a community in which every Jew is given the opportunity to learn about and experience Jewish living. It recognises that this vision must be the subject of a dialogue between Jewish Continuity and the Anglo-Jewish community as a whole.
>
> Through its consultative processes and through the forums it creates, or encourages others to create, it will encourage that dialogue so that the many individuals and organisations concerned with the Anglo-Jewish future feel that they or their representatives had a voice in formulating strategy and subjecting it to scrutiny and evaluation … Though it will be supportive of all ventures that create continuity, it will embody a bias towards those institutions and projects which most affect Jews whose involvement in Jewish life is marginal … In short, Jewish Continuity will have a bias towards outreach and innovation.[38]

* * *   * * *   * * *

Launched in September 1993, Jewish Continuity was virtually wiped out within its first two years. When funding was finally in place, it quickly became evident that its outreach bias had to win the approval of the Chief Rabbi and his Beth Din. Paragraph 11 of its Memorandum of Association stipulated that 'all matters concerning the construction and interpretation of the objects of the Trust shall be determined by the Chief Rabbi.'[39] Before long, 'it found itself confronting the issue which has been ever-present since – its religious complexion. The first attempt to resolve the issue was to insist that, while all organisations were eligible for funding, Jewish Continuity would not support activities which involved participants breaking the laws of Shabbat and kashrut.'[40]

'It should not surprise anyone,' its chairman of trustees, Michael Sinclair, was later to remark, 'that since Jewish Continuity is an initiative of the Chief Rabbi, the outreach we are going to run will represent normative Judaism.' To which its treasurer, Clive Marks – whose Ashdown Trust was a central funder from the outset – responded: 'To insist that the sole form of Jewish education must be religious and halachic is, at this stage – I repeat, at this stage – unrealistic and self-defeating.'[41]

As a result of this and similar objections, Continuity in 1994 acknowledged the 'unsatisfactory'[42] nature of the halachic proviso and announced a reorganisation of funding, through the establishment of a separate – and 'entirely independent' – allocations board, to ensure support for non-Orthodox institutions. Professor Leslie Wagner, vice-chancellor of Leeds Metropolitan University and a member of the Chief Rabbinate Trust, was invited to set up the board, comprising 'individuals in the community whose capacity to make objective decisions will secure the confidence of the whole community that their ideas and proposals are being fairly considered.'[43] Wagner's deputy was named as Sir Peter Millett, president of the West London Synagogue and a Lord Justice of Appeal.

The allocations board, with seven members from across the religious spectrum, was 'designed to ensure that proposals from across this spectrum were treated fairly and objectively.' The board received funding through Jewish Continuity, but was 'independent as far as its decision-taking was concerned. A distinction was made between the pro-active programmes of Jewish Continuity itself and the allocations board reacting to bids received from organisations.'[44]

In mid-1994, Continuity and the Joint Israel Appeal entered into a partnership though which the JIA would extend its fund-raising campaign to assist both Israel and Continuity. Plans for the latter envisaged raising £3 million in 1995, with £1 million increments in each of the following two years. But difficulties arose in 1995 when (as detailed in the next chapter) the Chief Rabbi placed an article in the right-wing *Jewish Tribune* attacking the Masorti movement. Continuity's involvement with non-Orthodox institutions, albeit via the allocations board, had provoked outrage among the strictly Orthodox, and Sacks' attempted appeasement led, in large part, to the dying beats of his 'heart of renewal.'

Referring to the separation of Continuity and the board, he wrote in the *Tribune*:

Programmes of Jewish continuity based on a rejection of Torah are a contradiction in terms. They are bound to fail, and they deserve to fail. But because the vast majority of Anglo-Jewry identifies with Orthodoxy, it is still possible to launch, as I have done, a fund to resource programmes for Jewish Continuity which will be based solely on Torah and *mitzvos*, a fund administered, distributed and kept entirely separate from the independent Jewish Community Allocations Board. What will emerge in the coming years is a strengthening of Jewish communities through programmes of outreach such as those pioneered by Seed and other Torah-based groups, through a yeshivah-trained university chaplaincy, and other similar initiatives. There is no other way of securing continuity than through true Torah teaching and the power of genuine Jewish experience. Of that, I have no doubt.[45]

Responding to widespread criticism of these remarks the following week, Sacks wrote of Jewish Continuity: 'It will be inclusive. It will work for all Jews, especially marginal Jews, and for the totality of Jewish life. But because it wants us to be able to work for continuity together, it will observe standards we can all respect, even if we do not personally subscribe to them. Its programmes, where they have a religious content, will be consistent with Torah and mitzvot, for these have always formed the overarching canopy of Jewish unity and continuity.'[46]

The original remarks, Wagner later wrote, were 'highly controversial in suggesting to a number of people and organisations that the Orthodox were intolerant of non-Orthodox movements. That was claimed to be a significant factor in the reluctance of some donors to the JIA to agree to donations to Jewish Continuity. That, in turn, resulted in an actual 1995 out-turn of JIA allocations to the organisation substantially less than had been anticipated when the two organisations had planned the funding arrangements for the first three-year period. Some claimed that a majority of the JIA's donors were from the Progressives and the less religiously committed section of the community, and that those donors were bound to be disaffected if Jewish Continuity was not seen to operate on a broad front.'[47]

Before the impact of the Chief Rabbi's comments could be accurately assessed, the allocations board made the first of a number of major grants to Masorti and Progressive programmes[48] – 'especially significant,' wrote the *Jewish Chronicle*, 'in the light of the recent controversy surrounding Jewish Continuity ...

> Inevitably, however, political significance will be seen in favouring a movement only recently criticised by the Chief Rabbi as 'dangerous' to Anglo-Jewry. Continuity, still a young organisation, has many issues yet to work out if it is to fulfil its potential – among them the relationship between the core organisation and the allocations board. But the board's action this week could provide a starting-point for a new and united effort to redeem the vision of community-wide renewal which the Chief Rabbi himself has so eloquently proclaimed, in no way diminishing the importance of encouraging Orthodox outreach or education, but also recognising the value of efforts to enrich Jewish life and learning by those affiliated to other synagogal groups, or to none.[49]

Welcoming the establishment of the allocations board, but questioning its effectiveness – 'the danger in the long term is a division between those who drink the soup and those who are given money to buy it elsewhere' – *Manna* declared: 'Jewish Continuity is a visionary initiative of the utmost importance. It is now vital that, as an institution, it continues its progress towards being a fully independent, collaborative organisation which is truly for, of and by the entire community.

'The first courageous steps through the minefield of communal disharmony have already been taken. It is the community itself which is the greatest threat to Jewish Continuity's reaching the other side.'[50]

Weeks later, addressing a board meeting of the Reform Synagogues of Great Britain, chief executive Rabbi Tony Bayfield reported that a group representing non-Orthodox interests had met 'to look at the establishment of an alternative to Jewish Continuity should the present organisation not metamorphose into a truly pluralistic organisation.'[51] At a subsequent meeting, while expressing 'absolute delight' with Wagner's review, he signalled a further word of caution. 'I think it is of the utmost importance,' he declared, 'that we avoid sounding over-enthusiastic. Sometimes proclaiming a victory is the only way of turning a victory into a defeat … I have a hunch that the journey from the review to its acceptance and implementation will be far from straightforward.'[52]

His hunch proved prescient. The dispute over Sacks' *Tribune* article, involving wide sections of the community, led to a speedy dissipation of support for Continuity, while the threat to communal cohesion became increasingly apparent. 'The ability of the JIA, traditionally a cross-communal organisation, to raise funds for Jewish Continuity dried up almost overnight,' said one insider.[53]

Shortly afterwards, Marks resigned as Continuity's treasurer, after declining to ratify its budget, and Wagner was commissioned by the trustees to produce a report on the organisation's future. 'The inspiring vision of the Chief Rabbi in creating Jewish Continuity,' he later concluded, 'was unanimously praised, but the resulting ambiguity over its religious complexion was identified as a key problem.'[54]

* * *　* * *　* * *

'The questions are simply put, their resolution less so,' wrote Wagner. 'They are in essence: "Can Jewish Continuity operate across the spectrum of religious organisations in the community?" and "What is the role of the Chief Rabbi in relation to Jewish Continuity?" To some these are the same question. In fact, they are not.

Jewish Continuity has been a source of great difficulty for the Chief Rabbi. The roots of this difficulty lie in the role of the Chief Rabbi within British Jewry. He is first and foremost the Chief Rabbi of the United Hebrew Congregations, the organisation of mainstream Orthodoxy in the United Kingdom and, indeed, in parts of the Commonwealth. His base is the United Synagogue in London, but provincial Orthodox synagogues also recognise his authority and look to him for guidance. Other Orthodox synagogal organisations such as the Federation of Synagogues and the Adath, while having their own religious authorities, work together with the Chief Rabbi on common religious problems, and all subscribe to the same principles of the foundations of Jewish law.

The United Hebrew Congregations contains by far the largest number of members among synagogal groups in Britain. This, together with custom and tradition, has allowed the person holding the position of Chief Rabbi to be recognised as the major spiritual leader of the community, both inside the community and outside. In large part, the role of the Chief Rabbi in this capacity has been symbolic and presidential and has not been judged to conflict with his role as the leader of mainstream Orthodoxy. The qualities of the present Chief Rabbi have enhanced this representative function. His values, intellect, knowledge, leadership and communication skills are recognised both inside and outside the community.

However, continued the report, the Chief Rabbi's active involvement with Jewish Continuity 'has blurred and confused these two roles. Even before he was appointed Chief Rabbi, he committed himself with great enthusiasm and energy to the principle and practice of inclusivity – openness to every Jew whatever their faith or practice, or lack of it … [But] problems soon began to emerge. While there was no difficulty with Jewish Continuity dealing with non-Orthodox individuals – this, after all, is the purpose of inclusivity – the same could not be said for non-Orthodox organisations.

'Non-religious organisations such as community representative councils or Spiro[55] were acceptable ("*parev,*" to use a colloquial expression); non-Orthodox religious organisations were not. Indeed, the criticism came from both sides. From the Orthodox-camp perspective, the Chief Rabbi was perceived to be encouraging organisations which promoted and practised a form of Judaism which he did not recognise and could not support. From the Masorti and Progressive synagogue camps, there was a suspicion that, by receiving funds from Jewish Continuity, they were in some way being forced into de facto recognition of his authority and leadership on religious matters.'

Discussing the role of the allocations board, created to circumvent the problem, Wagner wrote: 'The fact that the board, while making its own decisions, is serviced by Jewish Continuity professionals and shares the same office has led many Orthodox religious leaders to conclude that the allocations-board mechanism does not separate the Chief Rabbi sufficiently from its decisions, and that he remains compromised by allocations made to Progressive organisations ... As Jewish Continuity moves into the second phase of its development as a result of this review, it is appropriate for the Chief Rabbi to consider his active leadership of the organisation.

> His current involvement creates significant difficulties for both him and Jewish Continuity. The Chief Rabbi suffers because, while he has no day-to-day involvement with Jewish Continuity's activities, he is held responsible by Orthodox religious leaders for its decisions. This applies even more so to decisions of the allocations board. Guilt by association and responsibility without power are uncomfortable positions, and the Chief Rabbi experiences them both.
>
> Jewish Continuity also experiences difficulties as a result of its present close association with the Chief Rabbi. The religious organisations of the community are engaged in a continuing competitive tension for supremacy and recognition. Partly but not wholly as a result of the Chief Rabbi's involvement, Jewish Continuity has become a proxy battleground where this competition occurs, finding itself caught in the crossfire between the different camps.
>
> A Jewish Continuity which was exclusively oriented towards Orthodox organisations would obviously not pose any difficulties for the Chief Rabbi. Even in an organisation acting across the religious spectrum, it might be possible to find a role which did not harm either him or Jewish Continuity and which reflected his representational role in the community similar to his role, for example, in the JIA. Many will feel that it would be a great loss for the Chief Rabbi not to be involved with the organisation. A mentoring or consultative role has been mentioned. It will require agreement by all concerned if these are to be regarded as non-controversial.

However, wrote Wagner, the religious-complexion issue was not automatically solved if the Chief Rabbi was less actively involved in Continuity. 'Orthodox participation and involvement in Jewish Continuity go beyond the question of the Chief Rabbi's leadership. Most Orthodox religious leaders would find it difficult to be directly involved in decisions funding Masorti or Progressive activities. Their decisions not to work with the organisation would also influence some Orthodox lay leaders not to participate. As a result, a Jewish Continuity which ostensibly was cross-community might in practice find itself dealing only with secular or non-Orthodox organisations.

> The Orthodox aversion to working with non-Orthodox religious organisations on religious or educational issues is regretted by many, but is a fact of life at present. The issues which divide the Orthodox and the Progressives are serious, not trivial, and have to be recognised. They go to the heart of the deepest concerns of how to lead our lives as individuals and as a Jewish community.
>
> Religious leaders and lay members on both sides are deeply committed to the ideologies and practices of their version of Judaism. Each side believes it represents the truth of Judaism as it should be practised at the end of the twentieth century. Most have shown a willingness and ability to work together on non-religious issues and, in general, to behave with civility to each other. But politeness should not be misunderstood for agreement. On religious issues there is a fundamental divide which inevitably spills over into communal politics.

Discussing the way forward, the report declared: 'Appropriate language is a necessary but not sufficient condition for re-establishing Jewish Continuity as an organisation that can operate across the religious spectrum with the support of all groups. An appropriate structure is also required which does not ignore or wish away religious sensibilities but instead recognises and tries to accommodate them. One of the contributors to the review put it neatly: "The issue is not who gets the funds but who gives them."

'In other words, the fact that the Progressives receive funds from a community-wide organisation may be accepted as a fact of life by most Orthodox leaders. But no Orthodox leader or organisation – not just the Chief Rabbi – will wish to be directly involved or associated with the allocation of such funds. The task is to create an organisational framework which enables Jewish Continuity to maintain its community-wide approach with Orthodox participation … The Chief Rabbi should be less directly involved in the second phase of Jewish Continuity which will follow this review. Any new role – as mentor, consultant or more symbolic – as in other communal organisations, must be accepted by all parties as non-controversial.

> A less active role for the Chief Rabbi would not on its own resolve the religious-complexion issue. Most Orthodox religious leaders will not participate in decision-making forums which directly fund non-Orthodox religious organisations. It may be possible for Jewish Continuity to operate

across the religious spectrum with the participation and support of the mainstream Orthodox communities – if there are changes to the language used and the structures within which it operates.

The language of pluralism should not be used as it can imply not just recognition of factual existence but legitimisation and approval. The language of diplomacy and international relations is more appropriate, with its use of terms such as 'co-existence' and 'peaceful co-existence.' These are words which both Orthodox and non-Orthodox can use without discomfort. In this report, the term 'cross-community' is used to refer to a Jewish Continuity which deals with all groups.

A structure is required which accommodates religious sensibilities. The key issue here is not who gets the money but the process by which it is given. However, there needs to be a will to succeed. Wise people can make the worst structures work, and foolish people can wreck the most sublime of structures. Diplomatic behaviour must accompany diplomatic language to enable Jewish Continuity to operate across the religious spectrum.[56]

In terms of funding, Wagner's report stated, Continuity had the option of either collecting its own funds or working in partnership with the Joint Israel Appeal. It noted, however, that the JIA 'could only participate in a cross-community Jewish Continuity: an organisation which restricted itself to the Orthodox community would have to raise its own funds either inside Jewish Continuity or outside. A JIA-funded organisation offers both greater opportunity and challenge. A closer symbiotic relationship between Jewish Continuity and the JIA would benefit both organisations and will require the lessons of their difficult relationship over the past eighteen months to be learned.'

Following publication of the report, in March 1996, crisis talks between the two organisations resulted in plans to merge them, with the creation of a new body the following year. The merger, said JIA chairman Brian Kerner, was being put in place 'in the realisation that Jewish Continuity by itself is not going to have a secure future.' Wagner commented: 'The biggest challenge remains the religious one,' adding that 'it is important to guard against the religious communities setting up their own bodies outside the new single organisation.'[57]

Earlier, telling a Board of Deputies' meeting that 'the moment is approaching' for him to step down from active involvement in Jewish Continuity, the Chief Rabbi welcomed Wagner's report. 'It should,' he said, 'begin to lower the by-now unacceptable levels of tension within Anglo-Jewry. It is time to fight apathy and indifference and not waste energy fighting one another. We need to include the uninvolved and the unaffiliated and to extend the boundaries of belonging.'

Likening himself to 'a parent for whom the time has come to let go,' he added: 'I took the greatest risk of my Chief Rabbinate when I created Jewish Continuity. It was an undertaking fraught with controversy. Sometimes I have been forced to take difficult positions on complex religious or communal questions. Those who criticise, injure only themselves. A rabbi whom they don't want to get rid of is not a rabbi, and a rabbi they succeed in getting rid of is not a real man.'[58]

* * *   * * *   * * *

At its launch, in September 1997, Kerner remarked of the re-formed United Jewish Israel Appeal: 'Our new name reflects the balance between our ongoing rescue work, our partnership with Israel, and our new mission, which is the renewal of Jewish life in Britain. It also reflects our determination to enhance a sense of harmony and mutual respect across the community.'[59]

When, a week later, the new organisation made its synagogue debut through the annual Kol Nidre appeal, instead of the familiar logo of the JIA came an enlarged set of initials – UJIA. 'With a new name, new leaders and a new mission,' reported the *Jewish Chronicle*, 'the transformation of the JIA is complete. Not only has the word "Continuity" now gone from the title of the merged organisation, it appears neither in the new mission statement nor in the launch brochure. "It's not the name, it's what's in the product, that counts," commented UJIA vice-chairman Michael Ziff.'[60]

As for 'the product,' the UJIA in due course reported 'steady rather than spectacular progress.' A year into its activities came confirmation that 'not least of its achievements is to have negotiated the religious politics which brought about Continuity's downfall.

'Regarded as neutral, it is working happily with both Progressives and Orthodox groups, its beneficiaries ranging from the Liberal Zionist group ULPSNYC to the right-of-centre Encounter outreach initiative. Whereas Continuity was criticised for trying to do too much by itself, the UJIA's policy is to work in harness with other bodies like the United Synagogue's community development department or the Reform and Liberals' Centre for Jewish Education.'

'There has been a real learning of lessons,' commented Bayfield. 'They have begun to succeed where Jewish Continuity failed. There's a real understanding of what partnership means.'[61]

4

The Culture of Contempt

'There is more than one way of building a shul, or conducting a service,
or teaching Torah, or constructing a communal institution.' [1]

Concurrently with his difficulties at Jewish Continuity, Sacks faced
opposition from 'the righteous few' over the certification of Masorti
marriages. Years earlier, within weeks of assuming office in 1967,
Jakobovits had granted Rabbi Louis Jacobs' New London congregation a
certificate, testifying that it constituted 'a synagogue of persons professing
the Jewish religion.' [2]

Anxious to end the bitterness that had resulted from the Jacobs Affair,
the newly installed Chief Rabbi had 'reached a concordat with him by
giving formal recognition to his congregation as part of the Orthodox fold,
after Dr Jacobs agreed to perform no marriages which could not be held in
an Orthodox synagogue.' [3] Asked to explain his recognition, Jakobovits had
later told the Chief Rabbinate Council that the New London was 'neither
Reform nor Liberal and generally not in breach of our principles, as it
recognises the guidelines of halachic law.' [4]

Jacobs' status was challenged, however, in 1983, when Marcus Carr,
the clerk to the London Beth Din, announced on behalf of the dayanim
that 'marriages performed by Dr Jacobs (the minister of the New London
Synagogue), even in cases where both parties are eligible for marriage
according to Jewish law, have no more halachic validity than marriages
contracted in a register office in civil law.' [5] His statement followed the Beth
Din's concern over conversions which Masorti rabbis had begun to perform,
and over the marriages of their converts in Masorti synagogues. [6]

Irate lay leaders of the New London immediately responded by
pointing out that the statement, as originally issued, 'gave no ground for
challenging the halachic authority of Rabbi Dr Jacobs ... It was not until
the Beth Din was specifically asked to state the grounds upon which they
based their "judgment" that Dayan [Isaac] Berger said that, with regard to
the marriage issue, it was because "the halachic requirement of the status
of the witnesses is not being complied with in all cases" ...

'Rabbi Jacobs has said that he and the reader of the New London

Synagogue are the witnesses to every marriage. If the Beth Din was referring to these two gentlemen, which of them is sometimes kosher and sometimes non-kosher? And on what grounds does their status change?'[7]

In an unexpected intervention, Ewen Montagu – who, as president of the United Synagogue at the time of Jacobs' exclusion from the principalship of Jews' College, had come to blows with then Chief Rabbi Brodie's dayanim – commented of this latest controversy:

> When I was in Jerusalem some twenty years ago, I called on that great scholar and beloved and respected man, Dayan Abramsky, who had not long retired, both to pay my respects and for the pleasure of seeing him again. The then recent tragic troubles caused by the rulings of the Beth Din over Rabbi Dr Louis Jacobs naturally came into our talk.
>
> Dayan Abramsky summed things up by saying firmly: 'What a pity that I was no longer in England. This need never have happened.' He then turned to look out of the window and said quietly: 'They are little men, and they are frightened of him [Jacobs] – and Rabbi Brodie alone is not strong enough to fight them.'
>
> I have never been sure whether I was meant to hear those spoken thoughts and have kept them confidential ever since. But with the danger of history repeating itself, I feel sure that they should be on record.[8]

'The timing of the Beth Din's latest attack on Rabbi Louis Jacobs,' asserted Dr Stanley Solomons, of London, 'as well as its oblique and personally offensive innuendo, together suggest a motive other than the defence of Judaism from an imagined heresy. After all, this same Beth Din has always been fully aware of the many marriages, as well as the conversions, that Rabbi Jacobs has conducted over many years.

'So why this sudden display – and why, if such marriages and conversions are really without the halachah, has the Beth Din not done its duty long ago, instead of waiting twenty years before speaking out? ... Is there the added snide suggestion that somehow, on going into the shul in Abbey Road, Jewish men automatically become less Jewish? Has the Chief Rabbi anything to say on this subject?'[9]

Eulogising Morris Swift, the former Av Beth Din, who had died the previous month, Berger declared of the dispute: 'Dayan Swift was portrayed in the press as high-handed, insensitive and harsh. We, who witnessed his activities, can state that he was the most compassionate and the most sensitive of men. But no amount of compassion is going to move a dayan to endorse a conversion which is patently invalid.

'We shall not allow various self-proclaimed compassion-mongers to deflect us, and we shall not be deflected from what we consider as the sacred halachic duty. We would like to erase the hateful phrase, "If it's good enough for Anglo-Jewry, it's good enough for the United Synagogue." Nothing but the best is good enough for Anglo-Jewry.'[10]

Jakobovits, who also paid tribute to Swift's memory, was silent on the subject, and remained so thereafter. But an insight into his dealings – and possibly into his silence – was provided many years later by Jacobs' son, Ivor, a senior figure in the Masorti movement:

> In the 1970s and '80s, problems involving children of non-Orthodox conversions were occasionally addressed by Chief Rabbi Jakobovits. He could see what a tremendous wrong would have been perpetrated in forcing such people to go through maybe years of difficulty to be converted under Orthodox auspices.
>
> He approached my father, Rabbi Jacobs (who was still seen as Orthodox but of the non-fundamentalist type), in secret, but on compassionate grounds, to convert and marry youngsters. My father did as requested, since those in question had absolutely no idea that they were not considered properly Jewish.
>
> It must be noted that Reform conversions were not always carried out halachically, so my father had to convert the people involved as he wouldn't have married those who were technically non-Jews.[11]

In January 1994, Sacks granted a certificate to the St Albans Masorti Synagogue, affirming that it 'constitutes a congregation of persons professing the Jewish religion,' but omitting two qualifying sentences added by his predecessor when certifying another Masorti congregation, the New Highgate and North London (subsequently New North London) Synagogue, some thirteen years earlier. 'This statement is made,' Jakobovits had written then, 'on the basis of the understanding that all marriages performed there shall be strictly in accord with Jewish law and tradition – kedat Moshe veYisrael. Furthermore, this letter and statement relate only to membership of the Board of Deputies and the appointment of a Secretary for Marriages.'[12]

Sacks' certificate to the St Albans congregation followed accusations from the Assembly of Masorti Synagogues that his office was employing 'unfair tactics' in attempting to discourage young couples from being married under Masorti auspices, and in warning that the children of such marriages might encounter practical difficulties in later life. 'There has been a handful of incidents in the past few months,' Jacobs claimed. 'It's very upsetting for the families involved. The Chief Rabbi's office seems to be saying that our marriages are in some ways not kosher.'

Referring to 'two recent cases' where young women from the Masorti community had wished to marry United Synagogue congregants, Jacobs said: 'In each case, the Chief Rabbi's office suggested that if the ceremony were held at a Masorti synagogue, the children of those marriages might not be able to attend Jewish schools or marry in Orthodox synagogues.' Both ceremonies were eventually held in United synagogues.

Jacobs added that he himself had been refused permission to participate in United Synagogue wedding ceremonies, 'something I have done many times in the past. Without giving any clear grounds for its actions, the Chief Rabbi's office is throwing obstacles in my path.' The office's executive director, Jonathan Kestenbaum, retorted: 'As far as we are concerned, there is definitely no dirty-tricks campaign.'[13]

Jacobs' claims were supported by JC columnist Chaim Bermant, who cited two cases from personal knowledge of marriage difficulties involving the Masorti rabbi. 'There was never any formal declaration that Jacobs wasn't acceptable,' wrote Bermant, 'only private intimations.' In one case, 'a young man who belonged to Muswell Hill [United] Synagogue, and was about to marry in the Masorti New North London Synagogue, was refused an aliyah on the Shabbat before his wedding. The rabbi of Muswell Hill is Dr Julian Shindler, director of the Chief Rabbi's marriage authorisation office. His wardens demurred but did not rebel, which shows what stuff the lay leaders of the United Synagogue are made of.'[14]

Disputing Bermant's claim, a former Muswell Hill warden – who had been in office during the period of which Bermant wrote – responded: 'I am aware of no incident of the type described by Mr Bermant during the past twenty-one months' – adding, however, that 'one factor common to the US and Masorti is that each vests halachic authority in its rabbis. Mr Bermant expects lay leaders to "rebel," and entire congregations to vote with their feet, if they disagree with decisions made by the rabbis they have appointed.'[15]

Describing the second case, Bermant asserted: 'The Sephardi community, too, which had been favourably disposed to Dr Jacobs and his followers, but which is now anxious to show that it is not a whit less holy than anyone else, has imposed a similar ban. There was a moment of farce about six months ago when some friends of mine invited Dr Jacobs to participate in their wedding ceremony at the Bevis Marks Synagogue. Rabbi Dr Abraham Levy, spiritual head of the Sephardi community, agreed that he could do so. A few weeks later, on pressure from higher – or at least different – authority, he said that he couldn't.'[16]

Of both incidents, and the attitude of the Beth Din and Chief Rabbi's office to Masorti marriages, the New North London's Rabbi Jonathan Wittenberg declared: 'Feuds of this kind do none of us any good. The purpose of the agreement between the previous Chief Rabbi, Lord Jakobovits, and Rabbi Dr Louis Jacobs was precisely to prevent them.'[17]

As the year progressed, Sacks found himself caught between a spirited membership drive by Masorti, aimed at extending its power base to Manchester, and a counter-attack by the strictly Orthodox that included allegations of a 'secret deal' between the Chief Rabbinate and Masorti.

Members of the Orthodox community in both London and Manchester expressed concern at this latter suggestion, one of them describing Masorti as 'being against the basic fundamental of Judaism, Torah min hashomayim. And the pity of it is that Chief Rabbi Dr Sacks appears to be engaged in a policy of appeasing them. His failure to publicly oppose them is causing unnecessary drift and confusion among our fellow Jews. It is imperative that the Chief Rabbi should pledge himself now not to co-operate with Masorti, in any shape or form, as their policy is to destroy Judaism.'[18]

As Manchester supporters of Masorti announced plans to establish a branch there, leading members of the city's Orthodox rabbinate pledged their 'absolute determination' to prevent it from gaining a foothold. 'The dayanim and all the main Orthodox synagogue rabbis will be setting out what we see as the dangers of the Masorti movement,' declared Manchester Beth Din registrar Yehuda Brodie. Masorti follower Sidney Huller, president of the Prestwich United Synagogue, retorted: 'There are many people belonging to Orthodox congregations who are attracted to Masorti. I have been disenchanted with mainstream Orthodox Judaism for some time and believe it has been hijacked by fundamentalists.'[19]

At a subsequent meeting organised by the city's Orthodox clergy, 'packed with well over three hundred people, and with standing-room only for latecomers,' Whitefield's Rabbi Jonathan Guttentag asserted that leaflets abounded 'purporting to show that their [Masorti] marriages are recognised by the Chief Rabbi's office.' He quoted from a letter written by the London Beth Din registrar denying any such recognition.[20] Dayan Osher Westheim warned that 'if people adopt the Masorti path, future generations could face difficulties in matters of divorce, conversion and marriage.' And Project Seed's Rabbi Yehuda Silver stressed that 'any Jew not ethically and morally committed to Torah is just as irreligious as those who don't keep Shabbat.'[21]

Confirmation that the leaflets were circulating came from a local resident, who referred in the press to 'recent claims from the Masorti movement that the Chief Rabbi has given his approval to their marriages. The document in question has been widely distributed by them in the Prestwich, Bury and Whitefield areas, and many people have been misled into thinking that there really has been some sort of deal and that Masorti is really not so very *treif*. Can the Chief Rabbi please give us a definite ruling on the matter so that they cannot twist his words to suit their purposes?'[22]

For the moment, Sacks avoided comment, but a statement from his office 'made clear that it does not accept as halachically valid any conversion or marriage conducted under the auspices of the Masorti movement … but also confirmed that the status of children of such a marriage is not affected by the fact that a couple were married in a Masorti synagogue, provided they were eligible to marry in an Orthodox synagogue.'

Explaining the directive, Shindler stated that the policy 'has never changed and no deals have been struck with Masorti.' He was issuing the clarification, he said, 'because of claims to the contrary' in the news magazine *Masortimatters*, which had referred, under the heading 'Masorti Marriages Win *Hechsher* [sanction],' to a letter from Jacobs to the Chief Rabbi on the Jewish status of children born to couples married in a Masorti synagogue. Many people, said Shindler, 'have misinterpreted the letter and the accompanying comment in the newsletter – "Yes, it's official, our marriages are kosher and we really are Jewish!"'[23] In his letter to Sacks, Jacobs wrote:

> Thank you for your telephone call yesterday, in which you repeated what we both and everyone else know to be true: that the Jewish status of their children is in no way affected by the fact that a couple were married in the New London Synagogue or in any other Masorti synagogue. I am especially gratified to learn that you have issued instructions to those under your jurisdiction that they must not make any statements to imply, even by hint, that the above is not the case.
>
> That we disagree on some theological matters does no harm. Indeed, I would say, it is all to the good. But I know that you do not wish to have a rift created where there are no grounds for it whatsoever, and it is greatly appreciated by all of us that, thanks to your efforts, the innuendoes will now stop, to the great benefit of the whole community.[24]

Writing as 'a Senior Rabbi within the United Synagogue,' Borehamwood and Elstree's Alan Plancey advised the strictly Orthodox community that 'at no time has any instruction been issued to muzzle the Rabbinate in their fight against the Masorti. The *psak* [ruling] from the London Beth Din has not been altered in any way to recognise Masorti weddings. We have always been encouraged to use our initiative in the preservation of *Torah min hashomayim*.

'The title "Masorti Marriages Win *Hechsher*" was a mischievous heading of the Masorti magazine editor and not a ruling from either the Chief Rabbi or the London Beth Din. A statement has been issued by the Chief Rabbi supporting the Manchester Rabbonim and their Synagogue Council in their task of exposing the Masorti for what it truly represents. Please rest assured that the United Synagogue Rabbinate will always stand for *Torah im derech eretz*.'[25]

Following Shindler's 'clarification,' and affirming its own 'commitment to traditional Jewish practice and an open approach to the study of Jewish sources,' Masorti's rabbinate issued a separate denial of a 'secret deal':

> We are not part of the United Synagogue, and our synagogues are not affiliated with the Office of the Chief Rabbi of the United Synagogue. We do not accept the authority of the Chief Rabbi, we do not receive guidance from him, nor do we seek it. Marriages conducted under our auspices are in accordance with Jewish Law. It is our understanding that the Office of the Chief Rabbi does not recognise our marriages, as it does not recognise any marriage that has not taken place under Orthodox auspices.
>
> There is no 'secret deal' between the Chief Rabbi and Masorti regarding recognition of our marriages. There has never been such a deal, nor has it ever been our intention to imply that there was. The Chief Rabbi has made clear on several occasions that a marriage under Masorti auspices does not disadvantage the status of children of that marriage, if the parents could have married in an Orthodox synagogue.
>
> Any future children are regarded as Jewish by the Office of the Chief Rabbi. These children may attend schools under the authority of the Chief Rabbi and may marry in an Orthodox synagogue if they so wish.[26]

While the halachic status of the children appeared to have been settled – at least for the moment – that of Masorti marriages remained a disputed issue.   Eighteen months after Shindler's statement, the New London's chairman, Eleanor Lind, corresponded with the Chief Rabbi, seeking further clarification following a meeting at his home attended also by Jacobs and by Hampstead Garden Suburb minister Edward Jackson.

'At the meeting,' Lind wrote to Sacks, 'I expressed considerable concern about the continued insinuations that there is an inherent invalidity in our marriages, despite your efforts on an ad hoc basis, and notwithstanding the letter we have from your office indicating that, provided the marriage could have taken place under the auspices of the United Synagogue, the status of the children is not in doubt. If we could have a statement from you to the effect that our marriages are valid/not invalid provided that the parties could have married under US auspices, this would go a very long way to resolving the anxiety of those who do not fully understand the issues.'[27]

Three months later, Sacks replied: 'I want to take this opportunity to assure you that over the coming months I will ask my office to address the issues which we discussed at our meeting in June. These are matters which require extremely careful consideration, and I am grateful to you for your understanding.'[28]

Dissatisfied with this assurance, Lind wrote further to Sacks: 'Frankly, I fail to understand ... why so much time has been wasted ... Please express to us in writing and publicly the view you have expressed in private – that the New London and other Masorti marriages are valid/not invalid provided that the parties could have married under United Synagogue auspices. Nothing less will really do now.'[29]

'On the status of children of Masorti marriages,' his office responded, 'the position of the Office of the Chief Rabbi is as expressed in the letter of Rabbi Dr Louis Jacobs of 23 February, 1994. The Chief Rabbi understood from your conversation that attempts would be made to end the attacks on Orthodoxy by members of your movement. That has not yet taken place ... As soon as you feel able to provide an assurance that provocations will cease, we can meet to explore the possibility of further conversations.'[30]

* * *   * * *   * * *

In December 1994, at the height of the Manchester and marriage disputes, the *Jewish Chronicle* editorialised that 'criticism – vigorous, strongly expressed, forcefully argued – is not only appropriate across the many different shades of Jewish practice and belief in our community. It is the lifeblood of vigorous communal debate.

> All too often, such criticism has been artificially stymied by a misplaced fear that debate, and the genuine doctrinal or other differences that provoke it, is by definition dangerous. The alternative – the pretence that all Jews are alike, that all Jews do or should agree, and that to act otherwise somehow imperils us all – is a far greater threat to the 'renewal' and 'continuity' now at the top of the communal agenda. But there is a corollary: the need for fundamental respect for fellow Jews, for a fabric of communication within which diversity can be accepted, encouraged, celebrated.
>
> The argument brewing between established Orthodox shuls and a nascent Masorti movement in Manchester, to take but one example, should in itself be no cause for concern. With one big 'if' – if, on all

sides, the inevitably sharp differences and debate among rabbis and their supporters are underpinned with a respect and tolerance by individual Jews for one another, from which both sides, and the community as a whole, can surely benefit.[31]

The plea, however, fell not just on deaf ears but on hearts and minds determined to expunge the Masorti 'danger.' Writing days later in the strictly Orthodox *Jewish Tribune*, Sacks denounced Masorti's campaigns as 'dishonest, disreputable and unforgivable,' and its adherents as 'intellectual thieves.' His article was widely reported in the national press, notably *The Times* ('Chief Rabbi attacks "disreputable" group') and the *Evening Standard*, which described it as 'a declaration of open war.' While the Chief Rabbi had a policy of 'avoiding criticism of other organisations,' his office explained, he was prompted to speak out by an 'exceptionally mischievous campaign' by Masorti.'[32]

Circulating his article in advance to members of his own rabbinate,[33] Sacks indirectly provided the *Jewish Chronicle* with the information on which it based both its front-page story and its inside editorial, 'Politics of Contempt.'[34] Relying on the circulated version – the printed article had not surfaced by the time the JC went to press – the paper reported: 'He [Sacks] coupled his attack on the Masorti (Conservative) movement with a condemnation of recent right-wing Orthodox attempts to "discredit" the United Synagogue, saying that the criticism was an unacceptable departure from "the politics of politeness [to] the culture of contempt."'[35]

Later in the report, the JC added: 'While calling Masorti moves to expand outside London a "danger," the Chief Rabbi also hit out at another danger – the attempt "by irresponsible voices within the Torah world to discredit mainstream Orthodoxy in this country." Right-wing criticism of various rulings made by Rabbi Sacks, especially on the status of women, has risen to a crescendo. The head of the Federation of Synagogues' Beth Din, Dayan Yisroel Lichtenstein, told the JC that there was "an uneasy feeling throughout the Orthodox rabbinate that the US is taking a left-wing turn."'[36]

In the event, none of the Chief Rabbi's references to 'the culture of contempt,' 'right-wing Orthodox attempts,' and 'irresponsible voices within the Torah world' appeared in the published piece. Two years later, during another Chief Rabbinical dispute, the spectre of censorship – with the tables turned – was to rise again.

In his *Tribune* article as printed,[37] the Chief Rabbi wrote:

An individual who does not believe in *Torah min haShomayim* has cut himself off from living connection with *Shomayim*. He has severed his links with the faith of his ancestors. He has cut himself off from what Rav Saadia Gaon declared made us a nation – our Torah, which alone unites the Jewish people across centuries and continents …

Undeniably, Anglo-Jewry faces a danger. The Masorti movement is currently engaged in a country-wide campaign to start new branches, particularly in the provinces. The specific danger is that it is being conducted with what seems to be a genuine attempt to mislead. Unlike its American counterpart, the Masorti movement in Britain has claimed to be 'orthodox,' 'traditional,' 'halachic,' and the true heir to *minhag Anglia* ['the English tradition']. It has even claimed that the late Chief Rabbi J. H. Hertz, *ztl* [of blessed memory], one of the most forthright defenders of Orthodoxy Anglo-Jewry has known,[38] was a Conservative Jew.

Chazal [the sages] said that there are seven kinds of *ganovim* [thieves], but the worst of all is *gonev daas habriyos*: the worst kind of dishonesty is intellectual dishonesty. None of these Masorti claims is true, and over the past ten years I have devoted, through my writings and speeches, more effort than any other Orthodox writer known to me to showing in detail how and why they are untrue.

The attempt to mislead Anglo-Jewry into thinking that a movement can abandon its faith in *Torah min haShomayim*, adjust Jewish law to the secular fashion of the times, and still be counted within Orthodoxy is disreputable and unforgivable. I have said this consistently and publicly. Masorti know this, which is why I have always been attacked by their spokesmen. Alone among Orthodox rabbis, I published a detailed refutation of the Masorti position in the Jewish press ten years ago.[39] Since then I have continued to publish extensive critiques of the Masorti position, alongside expositions of Orthodoxy, which can be drawn on by all those who are called on to defend our faith.

Let me say explicitly that there has been no covert 'deal' between the Chief Rabbinate and Masorti: none discussed, none proposed, none formulated, none contemplated. The position of the Court of the Chief Rabbi (London Beth Din) on Masorti marriages and conversions has been a matter of public record since the early 1980s, and there has been no change, nor will there be.

Neither marriages nor conversions performed under non-Orthodox auspices are valid in Jewish law. Any suggestion to the contrary is pure fiction, put forward by Masorti spokesmen, presumably with the intention of misleading Masorti members and potential members that theirs is a credible alternative to Orthodoxy. It is not, as I have made repeatedly clear.

For those who seek clarity, let me make my position absolutely clear. My task is at all times to strengthen *emunah* [faith], to increase the fulfilment of the *mitzvos* [commandments], to articulate in all contexts and constituencies the values of Torah, to oppose those views which are in contradiction with it, and to maintain as far as lies within my power, and with *siyata diShmaya* [God's help], the position of Orthodoxy as the affiliation of the majority of the community.

Now is not the time to defeat ourselves by self-inflicted injuries and internal dissension. Instead, it is a time to strengthen one another, each in our particular challenge, each according to our particular contribution.

Representatives of movements and institutions from across the community sought immediately to distance themselves from Sacks' attack. Describing the article as 'depressing reading,' Reform leaders declared that it 'must call into question the leadership position of the Chief Rabbi and his expressed concern for the whole of Anglo-Jewry ... The article and certain assertions within it are not consistent with the Chief Rabbi's previous statements and writings. We hope therefore that his words are not to be taken literally and that his position has not changed, despite appearances to the contrary.'[40]

The Board of Deputies, though under the ecclesiastical authority of the Chief Rabbi,[41] stressed that its members 'have a wide range of religious issues' and pointed to its 'central role as the bridge between all sections of the community. We seek to find and enlarge common ground between all groups in our community and to represent the views and aspirations of all sections of our community on matters of common concern.'[42]

Even Jewish Continuity emphasised, 'in order to ensure that there is no misunderstanding regarding our approach,' that it was 'a community-wide initiative and "inclusivist." This means that, in carrying out our mission to make Jewish life more meaningful and relevant, we are addressing, and seek to engage, all Jews, irrespective of background or belief.'[43] The Joint Israel Appeal, Continuity's fund-raising arm, stated that it would 'continue, as always, to work with all sections of the community, whatever their political or religious affiliations.'

Masorti initially limited its response to a JC feature delineating 'the meaning and the message' of the movement, without direct reference to the Chief Rabbi's article.[44] But in a subsequent item in its news magazine, it set out its case in stark, if subdued, tones:

The events of the past few months have reminded us how uncomfortable the Orthodox establishment feels about the Masorti presence. Our rabbis have responded with dignity. Without seeking to grab the headlines, they have quietly but firmly expressed sadness at the communal rift. They have stressed our integrity, emphasised what we stand for, and asserted our pluralistic belief that Masorti is one of many paths which lead to the practices and truths of Judaism ...

The controversy we are witnessing is not really about Masorti. It has far more to do with the struggle for authority within establishment Orthodoxy – a struggle which is being fought in the right-wing press over a number of issues ... Opposition to Masorti is the one area in which the right wing and the centre can unite; hence the message from the centre to the right wing is: 'Look how vehemently we oppose Masorti. Please don't doubt our Orthodox credentials.'

But whether Masorti is central or tangential to the debate in Orthodoxy, we have been publicly drawn in. We do not need to join battle; our opponents are condemning themselves far better than we can. But we do need to affirm our credentials ...

At a recent Board of Deputies meeting, following the Chief Rabbi's article in the *Jewish Tribune* and the ensuing howls of protests from all sectors of the community, our synagogue representatives – who, when they rise to speak, normally announce themselves by name and synagogue – stressed on this occasion their Masorti affiliation. This small gesture had the effect of reminding the Board of the significant number of Masorti members at the meeting. Sometimes we need only small, often unnoticeable, gestures like this to enable Masorti to grow into an establishment role ...

We stand in the centre of the Anglo-Jewish spectrum. We can use this position either to push the wings apart or to try and draw them together. We owe it to the future of Anglo-Jewry to act as a bridge, to bring the community together, and to rally around a banner that promotes tolerance and integrity without becoming a pain in the neck by continually looking over its right shoulder.[45]

Judging by its unprecedented postbag, representing 'virtually unanimous opposition,'[46] the *Jewish Chronicle* spoke for many in asserting that 'this week the Chief Rabbinate of Dr Jonathan Sacks took an extraordinary, and perhaps definitive, turn:

Barely had he moved into Adler House than the rhetoric of renewal ran into the roadblocks of realpolitik. The urge to be a Chief Rabbi to all Anglo-Jews bumped against his central, institutional role as the standard-bearer of established Orthodoxy. On issue after issue – the question of letting the Jewish Gay and Lesbian Helpline participate in a 'community-wide' walkabout; women-only prayer groups; and Jewish Continuity – the instinct to include all Jews, and to question old communal assumptions, ran up against the need to demonstrate a primary loyalty to the concerns of his primary constituency, and to his core faith, Orthodoxy ...

On one level, the Chief Rabbi's article written this week for the Orthodox *Jewish Tribune* – and distributed to his own rabbinate – is merely a factual rebuttal of an erroneous interpretation in a Masorti magazine of an assurance regarding marriages given to the movement's leader, Rabbi Dr Louis Jacobs ... [But] in tone, he has gone far beyond his office's businesslike rejection of [that] interpretation ... by calling the movement the worst sort of '*ganovim*,' thieves, and declaring that they pose a danger to the future of Anglo-Jewry. 'Nothing permits us to abandon the politics of politeness and embrace the culture of contempt,' he writes of his right-wing critics. Surely, this applies equally to the most important Orthodox Jewish office in the land.

The substantive implications of his message are stark. Rabbi Sacks' article is a forceful and eloquent battle-cry for Orthodoxy. Perhaps that is all any Chief Rabbi can, or should, reasonably provide. But it also suggests a hugely different agenda from that with which Rabbi Sacks assumed office barely three years ago.[47]

Once again, however, 'the urge to be a Chief Rabbi to all Anglo-Jews' got the better of Sacks. Within eight days of his arrows came his 'olive branch,'[48] published in the JC as a 'restatement' to his wider constituency. Declaring that 'it is not easy to be a leader within Jewry, and it never was,' he wrote:

The role of Chief Rabbi is peculiarly fraught with conflict, for he may be called on to do incompatible things. He is charged with being a leader of Orthodoxy. He is the head of the United Hebrew Congregations of the Commonwealth, the majority presence in Britain, Australia and elsewhere. He also feels a sense of responsibility for the Jewish people as a whole, and must strive to speak and act in ways that will address the community as a whole, including those who reject the beliefs for which he stands.

That sense of wider responsibility is particularly important to me for reasons set out at length in my book, *One People?* The covenant that binds us together as a people, sharing a collective fate and destiny, links all Jews from the most to the least observant ...

To me, every Jew is precious, as is every development, every human gesture, that leads us to treat our identity with pride, our religious heritage with respect, and grow closer to our Father in heaven. But this means that I have accepted a role laden with potential conflict. For I must

speak for the great tradition of the Jewish faith. And I must speak for
Jews some of whom disavow that faith.

How has that conflict been resolved until now? For the communities
under my authority, I have advocated an Orthodoxy uncompromising in its
faith and practice, but uncompromising also in its tolerance, compassion,
warmth, intellectual openness and challenge to spiritual growth. At the
same time, I have reached out beyond the Orthodox community, through
a whole range of community-wide initiatives … My principle has been:
let us act together where we can; and where we cannot, let us respect one
another. The effect, I believe, has been to enhance our sense of community,
and the regard in which we are held by others.

But this has rested on a tacit understanding, namely, that though a
Chief Rabbi does not speak for every Jew, he articulates ideals that we
collectively respect. The views a Chief Rabbi expresses are not just his own.
They are those of Jewish faith and law as interpreted by the sages of Israel
in an unbroken, millennial chain of continuity. Not everyone accepts those
standards as authoritative. Those who do are called Orthodox Jews. But
almost all Jews take them as reference points, some adapting them to the
spirit of the age, some giving them 'a vote but not a veto,' some seeing
them not as religious imperatives but as the 'evolving civilisation' of the
Jewish people.

That tacit understanding, wrote Sacks, had been broken 'by a number
of individuals and groups who have forced the Chief Rabbinate into an
either/or choice: either Orthodoxy or the whole community, but not
both. One campaign, in particular, I found unacceptable.

'The Masorti movement (though not its leader) has publicly suggested
that it has Chief Rabbinical support. It has argued that a former Chief Rabbi,
Dr Hertz, was a Conservative Jew, and that I had given my recognition to
Masorti weddings. Neither is true. Under such circumstances, no Chief
Rabbi could have done other than what I did: publicly to disavow these
claims in the strongest possible terms. But nothing I have done has given
me greater pain, for it threatens the entire fabric of communal unity which
I and my predecessors have worked so hard to weave …

Anglo-Jewry stands at a critical juncture. For more than a century, it has
set an example, rivalled by few others, of a Judaism that is faithful but
tolerant, respected by those who do not share its views and respectful to
them in turn. As a result, it has been able to put together, in a single year, a
framework for its future that no Jewry in the world can rival. That is now
at risk because of a few irresponsible individuals who would rather see the

initiative fail than respect a system in which we can all live. I give warning to them now that I will fight them all the way.

I will fight them because I refuse to compromise my Judaism, and I refuse to compromise my commitment to every single Jew. I ask no one to share my views, but I ask them not to ask me to compromise mine.

I will continue to hold fast to the twin pillars of our existence, Torah and the indivisibility of the Jewish people, even as they threaten to split apart. Jews are precious, and so is Judaism, and I will fight to defend either when it comes under attack. That task, the challenge of Jewish leadership through the ages, has never been easy or free of conflict. But it cannot be abdicated if we are to remain a community of faith.[49]

Sacks later declared, in another context: 'I've been constantly under pressure to do things that I may not do, that no Orthodox rabbi may do. I have been under pressure to recognise marriages and conversions that I cannot recognise, that no Orthodox rabbi would recognise …

'Let me explain. If a couple could have been married in an Orthodox ceremony, then the Jewish status of both partners is clear and their children will be halachically Jewish, regardless of where the marriage took place. Therefore, neither I nor the Beth Din have even raised the issue of the validity of marriages except reactively, because a campaign was mounted by a non-Orthodox group which said, "Our marriages are valid as far as the Orthodoxy is concerned."

The issue is not the validity of the marriage but the Jewish status in particular of the mother. There was therefore an attempt to shift the ground from the Jewish status of children to the validity of marriage, which I felt was malicious. It was misleading.

And the reason we had to react is that some marriages take place in some non-Orthodox synagogues when one or the other party, and in particular the woman, has had a conversion which would not be acceptable to an Orthodox Beth Din. The fact that they got married in a synagogue is not in and of itself proof of the Jewish status of the children.

That is why when we ask about the Jewish status of the children, we don't look at where the marriage took place. We look at the Jewish identity of the mother. If a marriage takes place in any synagogue under my auspices in Britain or the Commonwealth, the Jewish status of the mother has been independently established.

The fact that they got married under our auspices means that the marriage contract is a sign of the Jewishness of their children, because we did the research and performed the wedding. We can't have the same

confidence about people who don't exercise the same standards. The
reason that we hold firm to a common standard of Jewish law is so that
there can be one Jewish people.

Referring to the Masorti controversy, the Chief Rabbi commented: 'I
thought, and still think, these were deliberate attempts to foster a climate
of unrest. Those who mounted these campaigns knew that they were
asking me, or anyone in my position, to do something which could not
be done. My definition of a *mensch* is somebody who does not embarrass
somebody else for failing to do what he cannot in good conscience do.'[50]

Twelve years on – despite hints to Lind of 'further conversations,'
and subsequent statements on the children of non-Orthodox unions[51] –
the validity of Masorti marriages was still unresolved. As a result, many
couples from mixed United Synagogue–Masorti backgrounds felt coerced
into holding dual ceremonies. Two Masorti families described their
experiences. 'In 2009,' related the first,

> our daughter was married in a Masorti synagogue, according to the law
> of Moses and of Israel, by Rabbi Jonathan Wittenberg, before Shabbat-
> observant witnesses. The following day, she stood under a tallit in our sitting-
> room with her new husband for a shadow ceremony which apparently
> fulfilled the law of Jonathan Sacks and of the United Synagogue.
>
> We had joined our Masorti synagogue as newly-weds many years
> ago, and it had become our communal home. Although our son-in-law
> had for many years been closely connected to the Masorti community,
> his parents were equally committed to their shul, which operates under
> the United Synagogue, and he naturally wanted his *aufruf* [pre-marriage
> call-up] there. Its rabbi was delighted to oblige, subject to one condition
> upon which he and the synagogue remained adamant: that the couple
> held a wedding ceremony under US auspices.
>
> While painfully aware that this stipulation was an insult to us, to our
> community and, more significantly, to our rabbi, we were inclined to go
> along with it for the sake of *shalom bayit* [domestic harmony]. We took the
> view that our in-laws were as much victims of this bizarre demand as we
> and the children were, and that there was no point in making them feel
> any more uncomfortable than they already were.
>
> We decided that a solution lay in our children going through
> two ceremonies. They, however, strenuously rejected a proposal that the
> US wedding should be held first, believing that any so-called wedding
> ceremony between a couple already married would only be a sham.
>
> There was no question about anyone's religious status, as the US

was prepared to marry the couple; and no question that they had been properly married before witnesses – the hapless US rabbi who performed the subsequent ceremony had no doubt about that.

He expressed his personal respect for Rabbi Wittenberg, and even mentioned that he had driven past the previous day and had spotted the wedding party after the ceremony. And, to give him credit, he pointed out that the ring our daughter had then received under the chuppah could not be returned to her husband to be given again. He instructed the bridegroom to buy another item of jewellery – not a ring – which could be used instead. Nor were any of the other elements of the ceremony questioned. As for the witnesses, no direct aspersions were cast on their eligibility.

But extraordinarily, on the morning of the United Synagogue procedure, our son-in-law received a call from the rabbi that his co-witness was unable to attend, but would participate via speakerphone and, provided he (the groom) gave his consent to the marriage down the line, that would suffice. Since no one involved was taking the ceremony seriously, this made no difference – and the telephone witness took part, remaining silent throughout.[52]

Describing a similar experience, another London family spoke of 'media fear-mongering and lack of clarity surrounding Masorti marriages.' Long-standing members of the Masorti movement, they attended synagogue regularly and the father was formerly chairman of his congregation.

'Our son became engaged to the daughter of United Synagogue members. Initially, they wanted their rabbi and ours to officiate jointly at the wedding. We knew, however, that under present circumstances it would be impossible for their rabbi to participate and that he could potentially lose his job if he did so.

'Conventional thinking within the wider community is that the children of Masorti marriages might not be recognised as halachically Jewish. The girl's family suggested that the couple marry first under the United Synagogue and then have a bigger wedding under Masorti auspices. Our son was reluctant to do this and insisted on holding the Masorti marriage first.

'Both sides agreed to go through the motions of a "quickie" United Synagogue ceremony to take place within a week of the Masorti wedding. This second full ceremony was held under the chuppah in a small library room at a United synagogue, attended by some twenty guests. The entire marriage procedure was followed, even though the couple were already married. There were, however, two specific requests: a new ring had to be provided, and the bride was required to cover her head.'[53]

* * *   * * *   * * *

The Chief Rabbi's 'twin-pillars' approach, in the wake of the *Tribune* dispute, did little to reassure a torn and troubled community. Rejecting his defence, leaders of the Union of Liberal and Progressive Synagogues declared: 'If he claims to be the leader of the community, he cannot allow himself to be pressured into using intemperate language or exclusivist thinking about any sectors of that community.

'No one who professes leadership of British Jewry has the right to declare that we, or others, "have severed links with the faith of (our) ancestors." Indeed, in a modern society, the continuity of the Jewish people is ensured by those who choose Judaism in a positive manner. In our view, no individual could reconcile this conflict of interest. So let us leave the president of the Board of Deputies to speak to the non-Jewish world on our behalf, and let the religious leaders of the various synagogue movements speak according to their consciences on matters of belief, where relevant.'[54]

Appealing for tolerance, on behalf of Anglo-Jewry's foremost lay institutions, five prominent communal leaders – heads of the Board of Deputies, Joint Israel Appeal, Jewish Care, Jewish Continuity and the Central Council for Jewish Community Service – voiced their belief that 'the cohesion and co-operation of the community are essential to its strength and viability.

'Religious issues, where there are deeply held differences, should be discussed in a spirit of candour and in language which is balanced and restrained. In the spirit of the Chief Rabbi's appeal for tolerance, now is surely the time for the community to reassert its wish for mutual respect and common sense to prevail. We support all positive and constructive initiatives by the Chief Rabbi and other leaders to revitalise our community and to secure a vibrant future for all Jews.'[55]

Reviewing the controversy and its consequences, the JC described it as 'ferocious,' suggesting that it had 'dramatically underscored the difficulty of reconciling [the Chief Rabbi's] position as standard-bearer for Anglo-Jewry's largest Orthodox movement with his hopes of enlisting united communal support for, and participation in, programmes that can transcend intramural divisions and differences.

But the groundswell of anger at the narrower and less tolerant vision implied in his *Jewish Tribune* article conveys a no less important message. The centre of gravity of Anglo-Jewry remains one of moderation and tolerance.

Amid the pressures to be ruled by political and religious extremes, Anglo-Jewry's leaders would do well to remain mindful of that often-silent majority. It remains our community's greatest strength ...

The delicacy with which Continuity has felt impelled to negotiate the [religious] divisions suggests a belief that, where they arise, they can at best be skirted, with an 'agreement to disagree.' That is no bad thing, perhaps, particularly if the alternative is the kind of discord evident in the past week. But it also represents a squandering of the potential energy and strength that lies in the very diversity of our community.

'Chief Rabbi Sacks is absolutely correct,' affirmed the JC, 'in asserting that a strong and growing Orthodox Judaism will crucially help to guarantee the Jewish continuity which he so passionately seeks. But a strong Orthodoxy should also imply a self-confidence in its own beliefs and practice – a self-confidence that need not feel threatened by a far more open dialogue, and partnership, with other movements in pursuit of Anglo-Jewry's future.'[56]

Taking this caution on board, representatives of the divergent religious streams found early opportunities to advance 'a far more open dialogue.' The 'first small step'[57] followed a declaration by Simon Harris, then rabbi of the Orthodox (and independent) Yakar synagogue in Hendon, North-West London, that 'contact between ... the rabbis of United Synagogue-type congregations and those to their theological left is, I believe, a moral and spiritual imperative.'

To that end, Harris invited Reform's Tony Bayfield and Masorti's Chaim Weiner to explore with him the establishment of 'a cross-movement group.' Acknowledging what he described as 'the risk in such a move,' he added: 'I accept that criticism may follow, but I put the unity of our community above all.'[58]

After the meeting, foreshadowed by a guest sermon from Harris at the St John's Wood (United) Synagogue – where he proclaimed that 'if modern centrist Orthodoxy does not assert itself, it will be steamrollered' – the three rabbis announced that they intended to continue their dialogue and 'to find ways of creating public platforms.' Describing the meeting as 'positive,' Bayfield said: 'If Rabbi Harris spoke for a significant number of people, the prospects for a higher degree of co-operation, less back-biting and more sharing and planning would be considerable. Whether he has a constituency is a major question.'[59]

Answering Bayfield's question, *Manna* praised Harris's 'splendid article calling for dialogue and respect between the various sections of the community,' but added: 'As rabbi of the Yakar study centre, he has no obvious constituency, and it is far from clear that the 90 per cent of Anglo-Jewry which might endorse those sentiments will make its voice heard.

'Rabbi Harris needs to know that, as far as the platform advanced by him is concerned, he has a real constituency. If people agree with him, they must take the trouble to write to him and say so. It is time for the 90 per cent to stand up publicly and be counted, to demand and refuse to take "no" for an answer.'

On the specific issue of Sacks' attack on Masorti, the journal declared: 'It could be that the recent painful episode precipitated by the Chief Rabbi's article in the *Jewish Tribune* will prove to be a turning-point. It has made abundantly clear that the overwhelming majority of the community does not wish to see the fabric of Anglo-Jewry destroyed by doctrinal quarrels and would much prefer to highlight the considerable areas of common ground.'[60]

A larger constituency than Harris's was represented some weeks later when Anthony Ansell, joint vice-president of the United Synagogue, shared a platform with Raymond Goldman and Harry Freedman – senior figures, respectively, in the Reform and Masorti movements – and the Oxford L'Chaim Society's Rabbi Shmuel Boteach, to discuss 'Religious pluralism: a challenge to the Jewish community?'

While the two Orthodox speakers staunchly defended the Chief Rabbi's role – 'The non-Jewish world,' said Ansell, 'assumes that he [Sacks] is the spokesman for all Jews, and I believe it to our advantage that he is seen in that light' – Freedman called for 'an end to recognising the Chief Rabbi as the head of Anglo-Jewry,' and Goldman warned that 'unless we stand together and stop trying to delegitimise each other, the community will collapse.'[61]

Arguably the most revealing development in the march towards dialogue came, however, from an unlikely source. Responding that week to Manchester's first Masorti service, which attracted some forty congregants from Whitefield, Prestwich and Bury, Yehuda Brodie – who had earlier warned of 'the dangers of the Masorti movement' – now advised: 'Orthodoxy has to become more willing to allow discussion of its basic dogma.

'Masorti is appealing to the intellectual section of the community and allowing it to question. We have to dispel the notion that Orthodoxy does not allow intellectual freedom. The opportunity may not have been there previously, but we have to cater for that need, and that might mean a slightly different agenda.'

Malcolm Simon, chairman of the Manchester Council of Synagogues, took a similar line. 'Orthodoxy should have confidence in what it is doing, encouraging by example and inspiration. If people are tempted to join Masorti, it's because we have failed – and that's a lesson we have to take on board. We mustn't be scared of them. Just as the community has learned to live with Reform, so it can learn to live with Masorti.'[62]

Of these various approaches, the JC declared: 'Merely by meeting and talking, they recaptured a spirit of openness and tolerance too often absent among the religious leadership of Anglo-Jewry during the past few decades. They deserve praise for having done so.

'Others who truly seek the "Jewish continuity" of which so much is said these days should build on their example. The aim must be to make communication across our religious divisions unexceptional. The benefit, ultimately, will be to encourage the growth of a community that, rather than belittled by petty partisanship, is greater than the sum of its parts.'[63]

* * *   * * *   * * *

Among the 'others who truly seek the "Jewish continuity" of which so much is said these days,' Sacks himself took an immediate step towards 'recapturing the spirit of openness and tolerance.' In what the JC described as 'an apparent move to defuse the controversy sparked by his public attack on the Masorti movement,'[64] he used the United Synagogue's 125th anniversary to 'extend the hand of friendship to every Jew, whatever their private beliefs or levels of commitment.'

Reaffirming 'my personal commitment to the values which have inspired me, and which constitute the historic mainstream of Jewish life,' the Chief Rabbi declared:

> I believe in a Judaism which is true to itself and a blessing to others; which treats every Jew with dignity and respect; and which welcomes all seeking to enter its doors. I believe in a Judaism which, in its public expressions, is loyal to the traditions of our ancestors, whatever doubts and hesitations anyone may have at the level of private introspection.
>
> I believe that every Jew who identifies as a Jew and seeks to hand on our heritage to the next generation has made a momentous declaration of faith: faith in the covenant that has made us a singular people, and in the moral vision that has driven us to seek liberty, justice and compassion in our lives, valuing right above might, and principle above the politically correct icons of the age ...
>
> *Kehillah*, or overarching community, is a central value in Judaism. It means that we are prepared to put aside our private differences in order to work for the good of the community as a whole.[65]

Disputing the JC's suggestion that Sacks' remarks were 'an apparent move to defuse the controversy,' Jacobs responded: 'It is in no way apparent to me. There is not the slightest attempt by the Chief Rabbi to retract his unfortunate statement that we of the Masorti movement have severed our links with the faith of our ancestors on the grounds that we are supposed to have rejected the doctrine of *Torah min hashamayim*.

'I have repeatedly requested the Chief Rabbi to say what he means by this doctrine and have said, *ad nauseam*, that I do believe in the doctrine, which I understand as a declaration of faith that Judaism is a revealed religion and that the issue depends on the connotation of "from." If the Chief Rabbi believes, with his Orthodox colleagues, that the doctrine means that God conveyed the Torah to Moses, word by word, at a particular period of time, why does he not say so, in order to avoid confusion?

> And when he declares that he 'extends the hand of friendship to every Jew, whatever their private beliefs or levels of commitment,' he refers in the context of his article to his role as Chief Rabbi to the whole community, which he seems to identify with the United Synagogue. On this, it has to be said that he is not, in fact, the Chief Rabbi of Anglo-Jewry, but only of those who recognise him as such. The real issue is whether the office of Chief Rabbi, in the way Rabbi Sacks interprets it, is a force for communal cohesion and unity, or whether it frustrates these laudable aims.
>
> The Chief Rabbi's Orthodoxy, as he has stated in his writings, is 'inclusivist,' but does not – and cannot – recognise pluralism. Since we live in a Jewishly pluralistic society, it is no use asking us all – Masorti, Reform, Liberal, Adath, Federation, Sephardi, Manchester rabbis, and the rabbi of Southport – to pretend to be other than we are, so as not to rock the boat. It is the Chief Rabbi who is doing the rocking.
>
> We are all mature human beings who can agree to differ on theological matters and who, for precisely that reason, can – and, on the whole, do – work together. The whole fuss over Masorti has been useful both in making people think more seriously and honestly about what they believe, and in helping us to appreciate that communal harmony cannot be imposed – however gently, not to say patronisingly – from above.[66]

Before 'the whole fuss' was allowed to subside – it was never extinguished – the right-wing and centrist Orthodox, with a little support from Reform, had a few further words of discomfort for the Chief Rabbi's constituency. In an outspoken attack on the United Synagogue, and with some bemusing praise for the Progressives, British Mizrachi's *Jewish Review*

– 'The Voice of Religious Zionism' – declared: 'What is lacking [within the United Synagogue] – and this has gone from bad to worse – is life, spirit, ideological commitment (*Weltanschauung*) and, in consequence, the best of our young people …

'Looking at the organisation from the outside – and even the inside – one gets the impression that mainstream Orthodoxy in this country is old, outdated, without spirit … While we allow the impression to be created that right-wing Orthodoxy represents the only framework with a clear ideological background, and while Reform and, recently, Masorti appear to be making inroads into centrist Orthodoxy, the United Synagogue members, and even its spiritual leaders, are developing a fortress, defensive mentality …

'The Progressive movement of the whole country meets once a year, not necessarily in London, to discuss their problems, choosing directions. Mainstream Orthodoxy is divided by iron curtains between London, Manchester, Liverpool, Glasgow, and even within London. We should admire – not just envy – the success the Reform movement has made.'[67]

'For too long,' agreed the *Jewish Tribune*, 'the Orthodox Jewish community has been losing out to the glib-tongued spokesmen of the Reform, Masorti, Liberal and assorted movements which claim to speak on behalf of *Klal Yisroel*. This has resulted in a distorted image of Judaism and Jewry being presented to the world at large, and in a massive imbalance in representation.'[68]

For its part, while extolling the Chief Rabbi's 'initiative, vision and courage' in tackling the problems facing Judaism and Jewish survival in the diaspora, *Manna* wrote of Jewish Continuity: 'Given the importance of the subject matter, the source of funding, and almost any other criteria one cares to name, Continuity has to be an organisation which is not only for the community but of the community and by the community. What it seeks to do falls little short of social engineering. Not only will it be ineffective unless the community has a sense of ownership and consent, but there is something morally unacceptable about a paternalistic approach, however well-meaning and frustrating all forms of democracy may appear.'[69]

* * *   * * *   * * *

As the Jewish year 5755 wound down, and Yom Kippur drew near, events in the community took an unexpected turn. The Chief Rabbi, reported the JC, 'made a personal apology to the spiritual mentor of Masorti, Rabbi Dr Louis Jacobs, for the harsh public attack on Masorti earlier this year. Rabbi Sacks' show of remorse for the "intemperate" tone of his criticism came in a telephone call on the eve of Yom Kippur, and was disclosed by Rabbi Jacobs during a High Holy-day sermon.'

Jacobs, however, told his congregation that 'while it was nice of the Chief Rabbi to have made the call, it did not mean very much in practical terms. What we are concerned about is that there should be a clear statement from his office that our marriages are in order – which they are. I don't need an apology. While I don't want to start up a new controversy, neither do I wish to let the matter be swept under the carpet.'[70]

An indirect reference to the controversy appeared to come from Sacks himself during his Yom Kippur sermon at the St John's Wood Synagogue. While mentioning neither Jacobs nor Masorti by name during his address, on the theme of 'division,' he took the opportunity, said his spokesman, 'to reaffirm the extension of the hand of friendship to every Jew. The Chief Rabbi traditionally uses the occasion of Yom Kippur for making apologies.'

Mizrachi president Arieh Handler, a congregant at St John's Wood and also editor of the *Jewish Review*, remarked: 'I and many others understood that the apology was directed towards Masorti, even though the Chief Rabbi made it clear that he had not changed his views. He just felt he had not expressed himself in the best possible manner. He said it was not right to attack people for holding different views.'[71]

Many years later, in a Yom Kippur-eve 'Thought for the Day' on BBC Radio, Sacks admitted: 'We all make mistakes.'[72] And as the 5770 penitential period commenced, he was to add: 'Never think that being a religious Jew entitles you to look down on non-religious Jews. It doesn't ... The single most important lesson of Yom Kippur is that it's never too late to change, start again, and live differently from the way we've done in the past. God forgives every mistake we've made, so long as we are honest in regretting it and doing our best to put it right.'[73]

He may well have been thinking back to the commission, not long after his Masorti apology, of another – far more challenging – mistake that was to rock the Chief Rabbinate to its very foundations.

The Search for Survival

On Monday, 10 February, 1997, at 9.59 a.m., a four-page document – typed exclusively in Hebrew, on the letterhead of the Office of the Chief Rabbi – was faxed to the *Jewish Chronicle*, for the attention of this writer. Dated 12 Shevat, 5757 [20 January, 1997], the letter was marked by its author 'Not for Publication,' was addressed to 'His Honour the Rabbi and Gaon, Dayan Chenoch Dov Padwa, *shlita*, Av Beth Din of the Union of Orthodox Hebrew Congregations,' and was signed *harav hakollel r'Yaakov Tsvi Zaks*. A month later, following the lifting of a High Court injunction obtained against the JC and its editor by lawyers for the Chief Rabbinate, the letter was published, with brief omissions, unleashing the fiercest and most far-reaching controversy in the institution's history – ironically, despite (or, rather, because of) its incumbent's declared wish, during the same episode, 'to follow the paths of peace.'

Six months before these seismic events, Hugo Gryn, senior minister of the West London Synagogue – described by *The Independent* as 'probably the most beloved rabbi in Great Britain'[2] – died after a brief illness, aged 66. Born in Berehova, Czechoslovakia, the young Gryn was in 1944 deported to Auschwitz with his family, of whom he and his mother were the only survivors. Reaching Britain through the Central British Fund for World Jewish Relief, he was sent to a boys' hostel in rural Scotland, won a science scholarship to King's College, Cambridge, and later read Semitics at University College, London, under Leo Baeck – himself (like Simche Bunim Lieberman) a survivor of Theresienstadt.

Although from Orthodox stock, Gryn was persuaded by Baeck, and by the British Liberals' co-founder, Lily Montagu, to study for the Reform rabbinate at Hebrew Union College, Cincinnati, where he was ordained in 1957. Seven years later, he was appointed assistant to Werner van der Zyl at Upper Berkeley Street, succeeding him as senior minister in 1968.

Gryn's place in the community – and vis-à-vis the Chief Rabbinate –
was well caught by the *New Statesman* at the time of his death:

> While some see the 150-year-old post of Chief Rabbi as at best a PR
> mechanism, irrelevant to the modern world, others believe it to be a vital
> fulcrum that can harmonise and inspire both Jews and non-Jews ...
>
> The one place where the Chief Rabbi is seen to speak for the entire
> Jewish community is in the non-Jewish world. Jonathan Sacks' enormous
> success in this area has in part been because of his eloquence; and in part
> because of the fact that the outside world was untouched by any turmoil
> within the Jewish community. Until, that is, the death of Hugo Gryn.
>
> If Chief Rabbi Sacks ever had a serious rival as a Jewish religious
> broadcaster, it was Rabbi Gryn. Holocaust survivor, compelling and witty
> orator and a veteran of the BBC's 'The Moral Maze,' Gryn held a valued
> place in the hearts and minds of a large slice of the public. Although
> he was a Reform rabbi, he was widely respected within the majority –
> Orthodox – segment of the Jewish community, and was seen by some as
> a rallying-force for unity.[3]

From Gryn's funeral Sacks chose to be absent, or at least was reported
to have been 'out of town' and to have been 'represented by his honorary
consultant,' Alan Greenbat.[4] Commenting on Greenbat's presence, the
Chief Rabbi's spokesman, Jonathan Kestenbaum, said that 'any criticism
of Rabbi Sacks would be unfounded. He has been criticised in some
Orthodox circles for sending *any* representative to the funeral.'

While the United Synagogue assigned no formal delegate – an omission
former US president George Gee described as 'singularly painful'[5] – Sacks'
wife, Elaine, and Rabbi Dr Abraham Levy, spiritual head of the Sephardi
community, were at the Hoop Lane (Reform) cemetery, Golders Green,
where West London assistant minister Jackie Tabick eulogised Gryn as a
dreamer, 'guided by the tenets of prophetic Judaism, giving meaning and
direction and hope in this often-chaotic world.

> And what were the core elements of his dream? To create a world
> where peace would reign supreme, where racism, prejudice and any
> kind of entrenched bitterness – of *sinat chinam*, senseless hatred – would
> be consigned to the dustbin of history ... For the community here at
> home, he had dreams of a time when intra-communal wrangling and
> bitterness would cease, when *sinat chinam* would no longer plague the
> Jewish world, and when all branches of Judaism would acknowledge
> the validity and worth of each other. And he worked towards that goal,

smoothing out problems, reaching out always to others, extending the hand of reconciliation and respect. He was a natural harmoniser; he knew the harm that enmity brings; he valued conciliation and friendship.[6]

In the face of mounting criticism of Sacks' absence, the *Jewish Chronicle* reported that 'the Chief Rabbi, with his wife, visited Rabbi Gryn's widow, Jackie, at her home, [and] Lord and Lady Jakobovits also visited Mrs Gryn.'[7] Jakobovits had earlier written of Gryn: 'We were personally very good friends. I had a very high regard for him. He never put a foot wrong or said anything in public that could have contributed to widening the gap between Orthodoxy and the Progressives.'[8]

The absences brought a swift response from Reform chief executive Tony Bayfield: 'It is a great shame,' he declared, 'that anyone who could have been at Rabbi Gryn's funeral should have felt a moment's doubt about honouring a man who was one of the greatest examples in this or any other generation of what Judaism should stand for. That any Jew should feel compromised by participating in the mitzvah of *kibbud hamet* [honouring the dead] is difficult to comprehend.'[9]

Reacting to the nonappearances, the chairman of the Council of Reform and Liberal Rabbis, William Wolff, stated that he was pulling out of the Chief Rabbi's Consultative Committee.[10] And, in a letter to the JC, Sir Peter Millett – by then ex-president of the West London Synagogue – wrote: 'Rabbi Hugo Gryn would have been saddened, though not surprised, by the absence of Orthodox rabbis from his funeral service. Many of your readers appear to believe that, by deliberately absenting themselves, these rabbis both demeaned themselves and desecrated their office.'[11]

In a personal letter to Sacks, Westminster Synagogue's Rabbi Albert Friedlander – a leading figure in the Progressive movement – proposed a 'dramatic gesture' which, he suggested, the Chief Rabbi should have made. 'My dear Jonathan,' he wrote,

> This must be a difficult time for you, and I do want to express my sympathy and my concern. I was saddened by your absence at the funeral and the prayers, but do realise that you live within a structure which can be agonisingly tight on these occasions, and which does not permit you to follow your natural feelings ... We cannot judge others when we do not stand in their place.
>
> My own suggestion – too little and too late by now – would have sketched out a dramatic gesture. There were so many people who could not be accommodated at West London that they not only filled the social hall but also stood outside the building. I really think that if you had

stood outside the building during the prayers or at the funeral, both sides could have accepted this.[12]

Your traditional cadre would have acknowledged the friendship between you and Hugo and would have been pleased that you stayed within the ells of what they conceive to be 'the Law.' And the Progressive community could have received the comfort that you had stood alongside Hugo to the very end.

I know that David Gryn [the rabbi's son] hoped desperately that something of Hugo's vision of a united Jewish community could have been glimpsed at that point.

What of the future? I look at Israel, and I am torn apart by the enmity I sense towards my own community. Will this happen in the UK? In these days before the [High Holy-] Days, I long for reassurance.[13]

Sacks' 'reassurance' took the form of an explanation for his absence, and an expression of hope 'to set the record straight.'

I returned to my office this morning [he wrote to Friedlander in early September], having been away for the month of August, to find your fax. First, I am struck as always by your sentiments of friendship, encouragement and support. Those sentiments are deeply and eternally reciprocated, and I count myself privileged to count you as a friend and a guide.

It is to me a matter of great sadness that Hugo's funeral has become a moment of political speculation. We owe it to his vision not to perpetuate this. The precise facts of course are these. I have been out of town for the entire month of August. The moment news was given to me of Hugo's passing, I immediately made a decision which in many respects was a groundbreaking one. I sent the senior minister working in my office, the Reverend Alan Greenbat, to formally represent me at West London Synagogue, and I asked my wife Elaine to formally represent me at the Burial Grounds. In many ways, these two people are the closest representation of the Chief Rabbi that exists.

I am sure that there were many people like myself who were caught out of town in the month of August and will look to find another opportunity to pay tribute to Hugo. Indeed, immediately upon my return I went to visit Jackie [Gryn] and we both pledged that our families will remain in close contact.

I do hope that you will do what you can to set the record straight both in Hugo's memory and in the name of our collective vision.

Signing himself 'in friendship and admiration,' the Chief Rabbi added the handwritten sentiment, 'and praying that we always work together, in friendship, to promote peace and respect for one another's sometimes painful constraints.'[14]

Sacks' assertion that he had been 'out of town' for the month of August – repeated by him in subsequent letters to critics and supporters[15] – received short shrift from Bayfield. Addressing a board meeting of the Reform Synagogues of Great Britain a week later, he declared: 'I know I am not alone in finding the absence of Rabbi Dr Jonathan Sacks at Hugo Gryn's funeral utterly unacceptable and objectionable. Hugo was the great bridge-builder, and it was made quite clear to Rabbi Sacks how much his presence, if only at Hoop Lane, would be appreciated.

'He was not [Bayfield's emphasis] out of town – why is the Jewish Chronicle so selective in its probing? – and the absence of the leadership of the United Synagogue had at least as much to do with failures of communication between 85 Hamilton Terrace [the Chief Rabbi's residence] and the United Synagogue offices as it had to do with any policy emanating from them.

'In any event, I find it a very defining decision as far as any hopes for communal harmony are concerned. I believe that we should continue to be more and more assertive, more and more prepared to stand on our own, and stop looking over our right shoulders.'[16]

Having failed to appear at a West London memorial service days after the funeral, Sacks came under pressure to associate himself with other planned tributes to the departed minister, while United Synagogue president Elkan Levy – also under attack – confirmed that there would be 'a US presence at a future memorial meeting for Rabbi Gryn.'[17]

Bayfield told his council that he had had a meeting and 'several conversations' with Sacks 'arising out of the acrimony over Rabbi Gryn's funeral' and that the Chief Rabbi 'has suggested that he and I meet at least monthly and endeavour to build on common ground and avoid further tension.'[18] Bayfield's statement elicited discussion among Reform's leaders over 'not letting Rabbi Dr Sacks off the hook over recent behaviour surrounding Rabbi Hugo Gryn's funeral.'[19]

A more pragmatic approach to the Chief Rabbi's absence was offered by Tabick in her Kol Nidre sermon weeks after the funeral. 'Those of you who like to follow communal matters in the JC,' she told her congregation, 'may have noticed that I kept what I hope was perceived as a very dignified silence over the whole Sacks affair, and not a silence arising out of apathy or disinterest.

Partly, my lack of correspondence arose because I understand the position he [Sacks] is in politically and theologically. I never expected him to be able to come to Rabbi Gryn's funeral or memorial service, despite what his heart may have dictated – he has a good heart and feels for us and our loss – but also, and perhaps more pertinently, because I did not feel that I or this synagogue needed any validation from the Chief Rabbi's office of the uniqueness of Rabbi Gryn and the importance of his worth in the community, and for the continuity of our people. Or, indeed, Rabbi Sacks' *hechsher* – rabbinic seal of approval – for this great synagogue and the religious values we espouse. Which is perhaps good, because we could never receive his approval.

With a mixed choir, mixed seating, a reformed liturgy, and an affiliation to the Reform Synagogues of Great Britain and its theology, with or without a woman rabbi, there is no way, given the present climate, he could even set foot inside this building, let alone attend a service. It may be sad, and it is hurtful to feel that someone you love and esteem has been slighted, but that is the truth of the matter. He could not visit us when Hugo was alive, and it is unrealistic – perhaps even morally wrong – for us to place expectations upon him to do so now ...[20]

Announcing in early 1997 that he would be addressing a Board of Deputies-sponsored gathering – which, according to *Manna*, had been suggested by the Chief Rabbi himself, 'prompted by the continuing disquiet'[21] – Sacks provoked immediate calls for him to pull out of the engagement.

The Federation of Synagogues' Dayan Lichtenstein spoke of 'widespread dismay' at the decision and warned of 'a split with the Orthodox right' if the Chief Rabbi took part and, in so doing, 'gave a certain amount of respect to Hugo Gryn's position as a rabbi. This is a major theological issue, and there could be severe consequences. Rabbis all over the country are viewing the situation with alarm. There cannot be any credence of Reform or any sign of legitimacy for them.'[22]

The *Jewish Tribune* commented: 'How can an Orthodox rabbi "celebrate the life and work" of a man who denied authentic Judaism and caused others to do likewise?'[23] In a prominent report reflecting this widespread unease among the strictly Orthodox, *The Times* noted that the Chief Rabbi was 'facing increasing divisions within the Jewish community over his decision ... While Dr Sacks has no jurisdiction over Progressive Jewry, some Orthodox Jews fear his presence at the meeting will give authority to the Reform movement.'

The Times quoted the Chief Rabbi as saying: 'I will be paying tribute to Hugo Gryn as a Holocaust survivor ... There were profound religious differences between us, but it has been my principle – as it has been the principle of my predecessors – that we work together regardless of religious differences on all matters affecting our common humanity, and certainly in commemorating the Holocaust. It was on that basis that we worked together in life, and it is on that basis that I pay tribute to him after his death. As a Jew, as a human being, I can do no less.'[24]

Devoting a leading article to the dispute, *The Times* cited the estrangement – and reconciliation – of Jacob and Esau and suggested that the Chief Rabbi 'will perhaps take heart from [that] story when he contemplates the all-too-public conflict which has divided British Jewry ... Although this dispute may appear obscure and unedifying to Jews and Gentiles alike, it raises profound and unavoidable questions.

> Orthodox, Reform and Liberal Jews do not agree on the interpretation of God's law, and none of them takes theological differences lightly. The history of rabbinical Judaism is one of dialectical exegesis. God's purposes only become clear through debate; and sometimes honest and learned scholars will disagree. A small minority of Orthodox Jews rejects dialogue with other Jewish denominations, and for that matter other faiths, as conferring legitimacy on heresy and idolatry.
>
> But Dr Sacks surely represents the vast majority of his community in this unostentatious tribute to a man whose endurance in Auschwitz bore eloquent witness to Jewish survival. In life, they shared in commemorating the Holocaust; it would be absurd for that partnership of common humanity to be sundered in death.
>
> If the story of Jacob and Esau teaches us anything, it is that reconciliation is always possible between brothers; far more unites the Jews of this country than divides them. The great enemy of reconciliation is not hatred, but fear. The historian Bernard Wasserstein has warned of 'the withering away of Judaism as a spiritual presence in the lives of most Jews in Europe.'
>
> Some Orthodox Jews react to this danger by retreating into a spiritual ghetto. By reaching out to other members of the extended Jewish family, the Chief Rabbi has shown that he, at least, is ready to face European Judaism's greatest challenge. Before Jacob was reconciled with Esau, he had first to wrestle with the angel.[25]

Early signs of support for Sacks came from sections of the United Synagogue ministry, with Mill Hill's Yitzchok Schochet declaring that, while Reform and Orthodox rabbis 'cannot share a religious platform, the Board of Deputies meeting is not religiously focused. There is no compromise, and I stand behind the Chief Rabbi 100 per cent. This is more a matter of bullying tactics by some Orthodox rabbis.'[26]

Days later, however, the US Rabbinical Council declined to offer unqualified backing, limiting itself to the view that 'although the Council reflects a broad range of opinions on the issue, it nevertheless understands the Chief Rabbi's position in attending the Hugo Gryn memorial.'[27]

Meanwhile, the presiding rabbis of the Union of Orthodox Hebrew Congregations, headed by Padwa, entered the fray. In a letter to Sacks, written in Hebrew, describing him as 'the esteemed rabbi,' and sent 'in a private manner, without any publicity, and in the hope that there will be no need to bring this matter to public protest,' they referred to his 'plan to participate in a meeting in honour of a Reform rabbi who died recently and – together with another of their "rabbis" and a Christian minister – to eulogise him.

> We understand that there is great pressure upon the esteemed rabbi to fulfil this suggestion, and it is clear to us that his good heart has a conscience on this matter, that it is not really his desire, and that he has agreed to it simply due to 'ways of peace.' However, there is a duty incumbent upon us to tell him that the matter of chillul Hashem [desecration of God's name] – Heaven forbid – overrides the concerns of 'ways of peace'; and there is no greater chillul Hashem than for people to say that perushim, the rabbis, are esteeming the honour of a man whose main task was, Heaven forbid, the uprooting of fundamental principles and substance of the Torah, and matters concerning the sanctity of Israel, God preserve us. Therefore, the Rabbinate of the Union of Orthodox Hebrew Congregations requests, with all expressions of entreaty, that the esteemed rabbi cancel this plan and not participate in any form of gathering whose aim is to honour those who uproot the religion.

The UOHC Rabbinate urged Sacks 'to reply to us with his decision at the earliest possible opportunity, and by the very latest within two weeks. And may it be His [God's] will that the esteemed rabbi will merit to sanctify the name of Heaven, for one who sanctifies the name of Heaven increases the honour of Heaven, and his own honour is thereby increased.'[28]

Having received from the Chief Rabbi 'a four-page confidential letter' within that period, the Union rabbis – disillusioned by its contents – went public with a statement that they had 'pleaded with Rabbi Sacks to refrain from attending the meeting, as Hugo Gryn had undermined the very fabric of Torah Judaism, and this was tantamount to a chillul Hashem.' While 'understanding his predicament' and acknowledging 'his commitment to authentic Judaism,' they added: 'We are bound to condemn Rabbi Sacks' decision to grace a meeting in memory of a person who publicly flouted, and caused others to flout, commandments of our holy Torah, and who was responsible for the performance of many mixed marriages as well as invalid conversions.

'Rabbi Sacks' intended participation in the meeting is bound to send the wrong signals to the Anglo-Jewish community, which, at all times and under all circumstances, should be that adherence to the Jewish faith, as laid down in the Torah, and as interpreted by our sages, is the only guarantee for Jewish survival.'[29]

Responding both to their own ministers' statement and to that of the UOHC Rabbinate, the United Synagogue's lay leaders declared: 'The president and honorary officers of the US are fully supportive of the Chief Rabbi in his decision to be present at and address the commemorative meeting which the Board of Deputies is holding for Rabbi Hugo Gryn.

'The honorary officers of the United Synagogue welcome the statement issued by the Rabbinical Council of the US, which notes their understanding of the Chief Rabbi's decision to attend the commemorative meeting. While the honorary officers of the US can understand the UOHC's dissension from the Chief Rabbi's decision, they acknowledge the dignified manner in which it has been communicated.'[30]

A month later, at the Deputies-sponsored gathering – praising Gryn's 'honesty' and 'courage' and focusing his remarks on the deceased's experience as a Holocaust survivor, without once referring to him as 'Rabbi' – Sacks drew warm support from the 400-strong audience. He was standing there, he said, 'as a human being and as a Jew, to pay tribute to one who, more than most, knew the pain, the tragedy and the hope contained in those simple words: to be a human being, to be a Jew.

> How easy it should be, how uncomplicated, to pronounce the sentences: 'I am a human being' and 'I am a Jew.' But in the twentieth century, the century of Auschwitz, it has not been easy. At times, it was almost impossible. And six million Jews of Europe died in that impossibility: the impossibility which said that if you are a Jew, you cannot be a human being. If you are a human being, you cannot be a Jew.
>
> Hugo Gryn lived through that impossibility ... By chance, or by a miracle, he survived. And for the rest of his life, he dedicated himself to communicating a message of reconciliation and peace and mutual understanding between races and faiths, so that he became, through his message, his work and, above all, his person, a living symbol of hope ...

But, said Sacks, 'there is something else I have to say, perhaps the most fundamental of all. There have been those in our community who have sought to turn this evening into a controversy; and I want to convey our distress to Hugo's widow, Jackie, and their children, who have twice seen their private grief turned into public conflict. Throughout it all, they have behaved with immense dignity – and our hearts go out to them tonight …

What did we, as Jews, ever ask of ourselves and the world? Simply to make a distinction between humanity and faith. Whether we were in Egypt or Babylon, whether we were under Greek or Roman rule, whether we lived in Christian or Muslim lands, we never asked others to share our faith, nor did we accept when they asked us to share theirs. All we asked, for ourselves and for others, was the right to be different and yet human. A person can be human without being a Jew, and a Jew can be human without being a Christian or Muslim or Aryan or Arab. That is all we asked: the right to be loyal to the faith of our ancestors without being excluded from the universal dignity of mankind. Our ancestors lived by that truth, and not a few died for it as well.

That is why Hugo and I worked together regardless of our religious differences, for the sake of our common humanity which precedes our religious differences. Those differences between us were painful and intense. He knew it. I knew it. But … what brought us together was something even deeper than our religious differences: it was humanity itself and our role, as Jews, as witnesses to the sacred flame of life and against those in every generation who seek to extinguish it in the name of hatred.

It was not the fact that we agreed that made this possible. It was that fact that we disagreed that made it necessary. For if Jews cannot stand together for the cause of peace and understanding and tolerance and humanity, we would fail to learn the lesson of the Torah, fail to learn from the experience of history, fail to learn from centuries of suffering and pain. We have too much in common, we have been through much pain together as a people, to risk our future by fighting one another, or dishonour our heritage by hurling abuse at one another …

As you know, there has been deep controversy as to whether I should attend this gathering, and though I myself never doubted that I should be here, I did not want my presence yet further to aggravate the rifts that exist between different sections of our community. The Torah tells us, 'seek peace and pursue it,' and of all the mitzvot, this is the hardest to fulfil. Those who seek peace between opposing camps risk antagonising both sides, and there is no way of avoiding those risks if we genuinely seek peace …

The reason he 'knew all along' that he had to be at the meeting, said the Chief Rabbi, was that 'Yiddishkeit demands menschlichkeit. There is a principle in Judaism that "the Almighty does not withhold the reward of any creature." The good we do is worthy of honour, whatever else we do, whatever else we are, whatever the differences that exist between us.

'I do not minimise the tragedy of religious conflict within our community. It breaks my heart as a Jew; and it threatens our very coherence as a people. But one thing I will not do. Even amidst sharp discord and the most bitter criticism, I cannot forsake the principle that the Torah's ways are ways of pleasantness, and its paths are paths of peace ... That is the Torah I learned from my teachers. That is the Torah which inspired us as a people. That is the Torah we are called on to live.'

And that, said Sacks, 'is why tonight I pay tribute to Hugo Gryn, a man of courage and of peace, a man who saw hell on earth and who survived, not only in body but also in mind, to bring back a message of hope from the very gates of despair ... The most momentous epitaph we could write to his memory is simply this: This was a mensch. In the deepest sense, this was a man. We were privileged to have him among us and to count him as a friend.'

Describing his predicament, Sacks told the gathering that, in the months leading up to the meeting, he had tried 'in many ways, through private conversations and letters, to carry the various groups in our community with me, however difficult the task. With hindsight, I now know that I tried too hard. I made regrettable mistakes, and my attempts to bring peace failed. But I would rather let it be said of me that he tried and failed than that he lacked the courage to try.'[31]

The Jewish Chronicle's report of the meeting concluded: 'He did not go into detail about his "private conversations and letters," nor about the mistakes he said he had made.'[32] Three years were to pass before, albeit obliquely, he was to shed light on their background.

* * *   * * *   * * *

Behind the scenes, an altogether more quixotic drama was being enacted. Following receipt of his letter – written exactly a month before his tribute to Gryn – the JC informed Sacks of its intention to publish the document, and invited him to comment. The Chief Rabbi's response, through his solicitors Titmuss Sainer Dechert, was to seek – and obtain – a seven-page injunction against Jewish Chronicle Newspapers Ltd and its editor, Edward (Ned) Temko, stipulating that 'until after final judgment in this action, the defendant must not do, or authorise or enable or procure any other person to do, any of the following acts, that is to say: (a) use or disclose (other than to legal advisers) by themselves, their servants or agents, or in any other manner whatsoever, any of the information or statements contained in or derived from a letter written by the Plaintiff to Dayan Padwa on or about 20 January, 1997 ("the Letter"), or (b) disclose to any person (other than legal advisers) the existence or terms of this Order.'[33]

As legal wrangling continued in and outside the High Court, discussions were initiated between the parties, burning the midnight oil across the inns,[34] in an effort to reach a settlement 'in the public interest.' While the JC remained silent over the altercation, Fleet Street (or its contemporary equivalent) was abuzz with rumours, and vague accounts – as well as copies of the letter – began to circulate in various quarters.

Reporting later on this aspect of the affair, the *Jewish Tribune* remarked in a front-page report: 'There was some consternation in North London that it is being implied that the letter to Rabbi Padwa was leaked to the press from sources near the Rabbinate of the Union of Orthodox Hebrew Congregations. This led Mr A. Conrad, secretary to the Rabbinate, to make a categorical public statement that the letter was not leaked from the Union Rabbinate's office.

'It is being suggested in some quarters that the mole could well be someone in the Chief Rabbinate's circle with an axe to grind. Apart from this possibility, it is known that a number of copies of the "private and confidential" letter were sent to Rabbinic and lay people in different communities before the press got hold of it ... The consensus of opinion in the charedi communities of the UK seems to be that Chief Rabbi Dr Jonathan Sacks has brought all his troubles on his own head.'[35]

Most revealing, much to the consternation of the Chief Rabbi and his lawyers,[36] was *The Guardian*'s diarist, Matthew Norman, who wrote: 'One minute publishing a book [*The Politics of Hope*], the next coming out for Tony Blair, Chief Rabbi Jonathan Sacks is everywhere at the moment. I was particularly intrigued by the *Sunday Telegraph* interview in which he defined leadership as "taking risks for the sake of your beliefs." Stirring words, but how they apply to his part in the controversy over Hugo Gryn's memorial service is baffling ...

'When Dr Sacks learnt that his letter to the Adath had reached the *Jewish Chronicle*, he did what courageous leaders always do when faced with an almighty row. He issued an injunction for breach of copyright – one which both JC editor Ned Temko and Dr Sacks's office say forbids them from discussing it in any way. Nothing like taking risks for the sake of your beliefs, is there?'[37]

In a light-hearted – yet telling – column published on the same day,

'Londoner's Diary' in the *Evening Standard* went further by hinting at the letter's contents:

> As the *broigus* – to give the row between Dr Jonathan Sacks and Judaism's Reform movement its Yiddish name – rumbles on, perhaps this is a good time to congratulate the Chief Rabbi on his excuse for those contentious remarks about Hugo Gryn.
>
> It wasn't me, Guv, honest, says Dr Sacks; it was that bleedin' rabbinical Hebrew wot I wrote in me letter. That ancient tongue and its archaic idioms, he claims, allow no leeway for less understated phrases than 'amongst those who destroy the faith' (his description of Dr Gryn), or 'they have no enemy equal to the Chief Rabbi' (referring to Reform Jews).
>
> Dr Sacks is widely thought an immensely clever man. Insulting the intelligence of the rest of us with what rabbinical Hebrew would doubtless translate as 'this arrant cobblers' – the Magistrates' Court equivalent, if you will, of 'Well, yer Worship, I bought them 400 tellies off this geezer I met dahn the pub. Can't remember his name, no' – is, however, the behaviour of a 24-carat *schlemiel*.[38]

Two weeks after the dispute erupted, terms of settlement were drafted and sent to Sacks for his approval. 'On 7 March,' they stipulated, *inter alia*, 'the *Jewish Chronicle* will publish an article by the Chief Rabbi.[39] On 10 March, the injunction will be discharged by consent. On 14 March, the *Jewish Chronicle* will publish a shortened version of the Chief Rabbi's letter to Dayan Padwa; the Chief Rabbi will prepare a preliminary version for approval by the *Jewish Chronicle*. The defendants will not at any time disclose or refer to the proceedings or the injunction, unless references to them come into the public domain (other than by the default of the defendants). The *Jewish Chronicle* will not refer to the existence or contents of the letter to Dayan Padwa in its issues of 28 February or 7 March.'[40]

In essence, the JC announced later, the settlement allowed for the omission of 'three brief passages of a personal nature which were not central to the letter's contents';[41] for an introductory paragraph by Sacks explaining its 'rabbinic Hebrew' and phraseology; and for an accompanying article by him on 'the context in which it was written.'[42]

The letter itself, declared the paper in a front-page editorial, had engulfed the JC, Anglo-Jewry and the Chief Rabbinate – 'among the most venerable of its institutions' –

> by a conflict unprecedented in their history and which none, surely, would have wished … The letter dealt exclusively with an issue which

was already a matter of communal knowledge and debate: the Chief Rabbi's response to the death of Rabbi Gryn. It was also, in both tone and content, at odds with statements which the Chief Rabbi had made, and was making, publicly.

The JC felt that it had a duty to place the letter in the communal domain – a position which we pressed in what diplomats might call a 'full and frank exchange of views' with the Chief Rabbi and those close to him, who argued with equal passion that for the JC to publish would be both irresponsible and wrong. Our belief that *not* to publish would be irresponsible has only been strengthened by further leaks over the past few weeks, creating a situation in which rabbinical and lay leaders from all sections of the community were aware of the letter's contents, while ordinary Jews – their constituents – were left in the dark ...

The letter raises profound – and disturbing – questions about the Chief Rabbinate, Rabbi Sacks and the future of our community ... Rabbi Sacks appeared to be telling his right-wing critics that he did not publicly want to praise Hugo Gryn, but was doing so – with 'pain' – for tactical and political reasons. He was – as in his 1995 denunciation of Masorti Jews as 'intellectual thieves,' which provoked the last major crisis of the Chief Rabbinate – in effect prostrating himself before a strictly Orthodox community that has never paid serious heed to the institution of the Chief Rabbinate, and will certainly not do so as long as it is occupied by a Cambridge philosophy graduate whom they see as far more comfortable on BBC's 'Thought for the Day' than in one of their synagogues or yeshivot.

Rabbi Sacks has written in the JC of the difficulties inherent in being a Chief Rabbi. Sometimes, he has said, one may be called upon to 'do incompatible things.' The problem is that the present Chief Rabbi seems to have resolved that undeniable challenge by saying irreconcilable things to different audiences – which is why the JC felt a public-interest duty to publish his letter ...[43]

In publishing the letter as 'a public-interest duty,' the paper did so with this preamble: 'The Chief Rabbi has asked us to state the following: "This letter has been translated from rabbinic Hebrew, a language which uses hyperbole rather than understatement, which at times sounds archaic, and in which some words or phrases – notably those such as 'shame and falsehood' or 'false grouping,' as in the text below – are idioms that cannot be translated in such a way fairly to reflect the far milder language that would have been employed in modern English. This should be borne in mind when reading what follows."'

Asserting, in his reply to Padwa's 'invaluable letter' – for which, he wrote, he was 'deeply indebted' – that 'better is an open rebuke than pretended love, more sincere are wounds from a friend than an embrace from an enemy,'[44] Sacks declared:

The leaders of the Reform, Liberal and Masorti movements know that they have no enemy and opponent equal to the Chief Rabbi, who fights against them intelligently and defends the faith in our holy Torah in his writings, articles and broadcasts; that he has in this respect achieved considerable standing in non-Jewish eyes; and that he does not accord them any gesture of recognition.

Because of this they oppose me vehemently and write critical letters to the newspapers, etc., and exercise all kinds of pressure. But this does not help them at all because we may not submit to intimidation, and I know from the depths of my heart that a Jewish sage who does not show strength in standing up to pressure is not worthy of the mantle of leadership ...

[E]veryone knows, Jew and non-Jew, religious and non-religious, that our community is indeed a community of faith in which the voice that is heard is the voice of Jacob, and that the Reform and Liberal movements do not have a significant standing among us.

The Reform movement knows this clearly and well and has already for a number of years, quietly and cunningly, tried to change the situation and to persuade lay leaders of communal organisations and interfaith organisations, and also non-Jews in these organisations, to appoint a second person to represent non-Orthodox Jews. Our office has fought against this tactic with determination, a battle which, genuinely, is daily, because in my opinion it is the principal battlefield on which to fight against the false philosophy of pluralism in our community.

There would be no greater victory for Reform and for pluralism than that there should be two Chief Rabbis, one Orthodox and one Reform, at every ceremony and national or communal gathering. If such were to be the situation, then in the eyes of the whole community time after time the impression would emerge that there are two kinds of Torah, two kinds of faith, two kinds of rabbi, that they are equal in their standing in the eyes of non-Jews and the community, and there is no greater shame and falsehood than that. My sacred task is to prevent this absolutely, and thankfully we have succeeded thus far ...

Justifying his attendance at the memorial meeting, Sacks implored:

The principal point is this, that if it were impossible for a Chief Rabbi to pay due recognition to the good deeds that he [Gryn] did, not as a 'Reform rabbi' or indeed even as a Jew, but simply as a human being, to improve relations between faiths and to perpetuate the memory of the Holocaust – efforts in which we engage in partnership with all human beings, Jews or non-Jews alike – then I would have given to the Reform movement the victory that they seek.

They could then say to all organisations that engage in wider relationships, and to the government itself, that this would constitute clear proof that the Chief Rabbi does not represent them, since he refuses to recognise even the activities that they engage in together with the Orthodox, in which case we, the non-Orthodox, require a representative and president and Chief Rabbi of our own, together with full recognition from the government and other faiths.

Such, indeed, would be the case, because this is what they have aspired to for a number of years and have merely sought the opportunity to do so. If this would indeed transpire, there would be no greater disgrace done to Jewish values than this, and the result would be lasting damage to the religious nature of the community ...

Sacks wrote that his presence at the meeting was conditional on its 'being clear to all' that he was there as president of the Council of Christians and Jews (CCJ); that the gathering was 'dedicated to interfaith relations,' emphasised by the participation 'of the bishop who is chairman of the CCJ'; that it was not a religious ceremony, nor held in a synagogue – 'either of ours or of theirs'; and that the organisers 'would understand from the outset that I would speak only on his [Gryn's] work in interfaith relations, and that I would have to explicitly signal that my words did not constitute a recognition of Reform,[45] or his role in it.' All these conditions, the Chief Rabbi told Padwa, 'were agreed.'

As a result, the Reform 'have no cause to seek recognition from the government or the heads of other faiths or other communal organisations, and this will be a significant victory for the honour of the Torah in the public domain. No one, Jew or non-Jew, can make a mistake and say that this constitutes recognition for Reform. On the contrary, it precludes recognition, since I am willing to talk only about his contribution as a human being.'

There had been no pressure on him to participate in the gathering, wrote Sacks, nor had any member of the Reform community asked him to do so, 'because what would be the benefit to them from my doing so? Everyone knows that this is not religious recognition.

On the contrary, they would prefer that I should refuse to take part in such an interfaith gathering, and then they could claim that an Orthodox rabbi has no standing in matters which affect the entire community and that there is, instead, a need for a Reform Chief Rabbi who could speak for the community about the Holocaust, anti-Semitism and peace between faiths. From this would emerge the very recognition that they seek.

Each of us knows his own pain, and what would I give not to find myself in a situation in which it is damaging to speak, and damaging to be silent. However, there is a sacred responsibility which rests upon me, not merely not to give this false group recognition, but also not to be a cause of their receiving that recognition from the State, the government, and the heads of churches, which is a substantive recognition in the eyes of the majority of people.

I write these lines with great sorrow, and only your Honour can know what conflict I experience in praising a person who was among those who destroy the faith, even for the good human deeds which he did. Your Honour knows that there are difficult circumstances in which it is impossible to do the completely right thing, and one has to choose the way which is least harmful, and so it is in our present situation. And it is clear that I have done this in order to enhance the honour of God and that of our Torah.

There is a rare opportunity at this gathering to say in front of the leaders of our community that I do not recognise the concept of a 'Reform rabbi' or any Judaism except the Judaism of Torah; and that it is our holy Torah which is the protector of the sanctity of life and the light amidst the darkness of the Holocaust. And only Torah and its disciples can be the foundation not only of our private lives, but also of the Jewish community as a whole; and not only vis-à-vis its internal affairs, but also, and specifically, vis-à-vis the outside world, as it is written in the Bible that 'these statutes' are our 'wisdom and understanding in the eyes of the nations.'

As a result of this, a victory would be won against the attempt of the Reform movement to receive recognition from the outside, and also a raising of the stature of Torah in the future as the authoritative voice of spiritual leadership in the community vis-à-vis the outside world. There is no danger here of setting a precedent, because there is no other member of their community who is famous as a Holocaust survivor.

The Chief Rabbi concluded: 'I do not expect the blessing of your Honour, but merely your understanding, because there are great dangers to the situation of Torah among the wider community if I do not go, and every day I pray that I should not have to endure such trials and that I should not give misleading rulings on matters of Jewish law or faith.'[46]

In his subsequent article, expounding on the linguistic and contextual nature of the letter and denouncing its misuse, Sacks wrote: 'My letter was constructed from the perspective, and in the language, of the Dayan himself. It sought to address a single issue: his concern that, by my attendance, I would be conferring recognition on Reform.

> I explained that this was not so. I alerted him to the sustained attacks on Orthodoxy by the Progressive movements, and pointed out that these could only increase if I did not attend. We have always worked together in remembering the Holocaust, fighting anti-Semitism, and improving interfaith relations. In these matters, we have long agreed to put religious differences and questions of recognition aside.
>
> It is vital to understand what the letter was and what it was not. It was not a public declaration of principle. It was a letter requested and delivered in confidence, written in rabbinic Hebrew, and sent to the Dayan for his eyes only. It was an attempt to allay conflict by diplomatic means. All peace negotiations depend on the ability to conduct private communications which focus on the specific concerns of each side.
>
> The rabbinic literature mandates extreme measures in pursuit of peace. In this case, I used language I would not adopt in public, and set out arguments that I believed would speak from the Dayan's perspective, to his particular concerns. The letter was a private attempt to mitigate opposition to the public tribute I felt honour-bound to pay Hugo Gryn, and should be understood in that context alone.

In the event, wrote Sacks, the UOHC issued its protest. And in the meantime, 'a series of scandalous actions took place. The private letter to Dayan Padwa, a saintly and honourable man, fell into the hands of individuals neither saintly nor honourable, who proceeded to leak it to the press, seeking to stir up controversy yet again. The leak was a breach of confidence. It flouted the Jewish laws of privacy. It was intended to destroy relationships of trust essential to communal harmony. It was, in the clearest sense, a *chillul Hashem*, an attempt to bring Jews and Judaism into public disrepute.

'There comes a point in the life of an individual or a community when we have to say: this must stop. For five years, I have sought peace and actively pursued it. Whether in my speeches, articles, books or television programmes, my address at the Albert Hall after the assassination of

Yitzhak Rabin, or my tribute to the memory of Hugo Gryn, I have said this as boldly as any Jewish leader alive. That effort has been rewarded by disdain from both sides, and now by betrayal.

'I must now ask all of us: is this what we really want? A community which makes life unbearable for a widow in her time of grief, and for a Chief Rabbi trying to act honourably in difficult circumstances, is not one of which we can be proud. Do we wish to be enveloped yet again by bitterness and mutual recrimination? Or are we prepared to draw a line over the past, and work to re-establish the tolerance, decency, harmony and compassion which once marked Anglo-Jewry, and may yet do so again?'[47]

Aware of the letter's imminent publication, Reform's lay and rabbinic leaders alerted their pulpit colleagues to its 'extremely offensive' references to Gryn and to the fact that 'the episode will undoubtedly prolong the unseemly wrangling within the Orthodox community over Rabbi Sacks' role in Hugo's funeral, memorial service and memorial meeting … Underlying the whole sorry episode are far-reaching issues about the structure of the Anglo-Jewish community and representation. These issues need to be addressed, but in a way that is detached from Hugo and his memory.' The leaders added:

> The RSGB is a democratic institution. There are few values more important than the freedom of the pulpit and the right of synagogue leadership to express views. However, this is a time when we believe that restraint and forbearance are called for … We do not wish to feed mendacious suggestions that somehow this entire episode has been engineered by us. Accordingly, we would respectfully ask colleagues to be restrained in expressing justified anger and righteous indignation, particularly in the press and pulpit. We think that it is most appropriate and helpful for there to be a unified Reform response. Depending on the contents of the letter, we intend to make a short and formal statement in the following week's Jewish Chronicle. The underlying issues will be tackled in a place and at a time when they can be properly addressed independently of ad personam issues.[48]

No sooner had Sacks' letter appeared, however, than voices began clamouring for his resignation. Rabbi Jonathan Romain – described by The Independent as 'spokesman for the Reform Synagogues of Great Britain' – 'called on Dr Sacks to renounce his title. "Clearly, the Chief Rabbi no longer represents all Jews and speaks only for the Orthodox sector," he said. "He no more represents Reform and Liberal Jews than does the Archbishop of

Canterbury represent Catholics and Methodists."

'Last night [the paper reported] there was much speculation on the hidden agenda of the person responsible for the leaking.[49] Matthew Kalman,[50] editor of the *London Jewish News*, suggested that the leak was a deliberate "trap" laid for reformists, in order to re-open the divide in the Jewish community. Yesterday, the "trap" appeared to have worked. In a joint statement, the British leaders of Reform Judaism called for a rethink of the post of Chief Rabbi.'[51]

Referring to Romain's call 'for the creation of a separate Progressive chief rabbinate,' a leading article in *The Times* asserted that this 'would cause a formal, permanent and irrevocable split in the Jewish community, not just in Britain but throughout the Commonwealth. Though most Progressive rabbis have not echoed this divisive proposal, the impression has been given that the Chief Rabbi has sacrificed principle for "diplomacy." This is damaging, not just to Dr Sacks, but to the image of Anglo-Jewry.'

The Times noted that 'even before the offending letter was published, Dr Sacks in effect admitted [in his Gryn memorial address] that he had gone too far to appease the unappeasable. His end did not justify the means. The letter was indeed a mistake. But it was written for honourable motives. It should not be taken as a definitive statement. A Chief Rabbi must be big enough to learn from his mistakes. This one is.'[52]

In a statement released within hours of the letter's publication, and faxed to the Chief Rabbi at 1.27 p.m.,[53] the RSGB leadership declared: 'Although we had been made aware of the existence of "a letter" and been warned that its contents would give us pain, nothing could prepare us for the shock of reading Rabbi Dr Sacks' words to Dayan Padwa.

> We are saddened that Rabbi Sacks has been 'fighting a battle' against us, and disturbed by the fantasy that we have been plotting to establish a rival Chief Rabbinate.
>
> The Chief Rabbi of the United Hebrew Congregations says that his whole purpose is to 'gain a victory' over us and then calls for peace. Rabbi Dr Sacks declares himself to be our 'enemy and opponent' and call us 'those who destroy the faith,' yet asserts that he is the community's single religious representative, speaking for us all.
>
> It seems that, constantly, the Chief Rabbinate is forced into two conversations, embodying two sets of languages and two messages tailored to the respective recipients. This is simply not consonant with a community of trust and integrity.
>
> What pains us most, however, is the continuing denigration of a great Rabbi and compelling Jewish teacher, Hugo Gryn. However hurt the

Reform community feels, our overriding concern is not to occasion any further distress to the Gryn family and to end this episode as far as Rabbi Gryn is concerned.

Recent controversies have highlighted issues which have been of concern to us for some years. Much of the tension within the British Jewish community stems from the maintenance of structures which have long since failed to reflect reality, and the preservation of fictions and illusions about representation which do us all a grave disservice.

We wish to consider these matters at a place and time when they can be addressed without involving the good name of Rabbi Gryn. They will require careful consideration, but we are determined that the various segments of the community will come together to discuss these issues and find a more honest and effective structure and pattern of representation. Only then can we have confidence that peace and co-operation will characterise the Anglo-Jewish community.[54]

West London's Tabick declared: 'We regret and are appalled at the tarnishing of the memory of a great rabbi and are so upset that his family have to face such an unpleasant situation while they are in mourning. It is obvious that Rabbi Sacks has an impossible juggling act to perform, and we at the West London are anxious that the wider issue of the Chief Rabbi's role in Anglo-Jewry should be suspended from our memories of Rabbi Gryn.'[55]

At a plenary session of the Board of Deputies, held in Newcastle two days after the letter was published, the president, Eldred Tabachnik, told delegates: 'We must strive as hard as we can to ensure that this controversy does not cause permanent and lasting damage to our community, to its structure, and to its good will. We must be careful to solve this problem with maturity and with judgment. Such determination will test us very greatly in the future, and it is far from clear at the moment what the ultimate solution will be.'[56]

Writing from New York on the weekly Torah portion of Shemini (Leviticus 9:1–11:47), with its message that 'those who presume to speak for God must live beyond reproach,' Rabbi Ismar Schorsch, chancellor of the Conservative movement's Jewish Theological Seminary, referred to the fact that, 'currently, the Chief Rabbi of Great Britain, Jonathan Sacks, [is] rightly under attack for compromising behaviour.

'Rabbi Sacks would not attend the funeral of a prominent Reform rabbi and Holocaust survivor, Hugo Gryn. He did, however, agree to participate at a memorial for Rabbi Gryn, provided it was not held in a synagogue. Though he spoke forcefully against the rising tide of intolerance among

Jews, he did so as president of an interfaith Council of Christians and Jews and not as Chief Rabbi.

'Worse, in a private letter – now made public – to a vocal Orthodox critic of his participation, Dayan Chenoch Padwa, Rabbi Sacks spoke disparagingly of the man whose memory he honoured in public.' The dismay ignited by Rabbi Sacks' conduct, wrote Schorsch, 'could be enough to bring down the institution of the Chief Rabbinate itself.'[57]

On the day his letter appeared, Sacks circulated an appeal to his rabbinical colleagues in the United Synagogue, explaining why he had written to Padwa. After setting out his reasons, he told the rabbis: 'It proved impossible to prevent publication, and there can be no doubt that its appearance, especially in a literal English translation, will do great harm to relationships within the community ...

'I would have wished to have given you greater notice of these events, but it proved impossible to do. I am now asking all of us in Anglo-Jewry to think very seriously about the damage caused by the recent rifts within the community, and the manner in which we have conducted ourselves.

'The Chief Rabbinate will come under heavy criticism during the next few weeks. I would urge you, during this period, to give the Office [of the Chief Rabbi] your understanding and support, and to use your influence as a spiritual leader to temper dissension and help us progress to a more harmonious future.'[58]

Sacks' plea was accompanied by a series of questions and answers, 'prepared for the Chief Rabbi and spokesmen on his behalf, drafted for your general information following our discussions about the current situation.' To the question 'What will you do if you don't get support for your initiative?', the reply given was: 'It is essential that the silent majorities in this community express themselves through their leaders and ensure that the squabbling stops. I have already received widespread support (name) and expect this to grow.'

Question: 'You surely don't expect the Progressives to support you after this letter?' Answer: 'The leaking of the letter was surely calculated to disrupt any attempts at reconciliation. I hope that the Progressives will reject that and see that the principles I have outlined offer a better way for all of us.'

Question: 'Why is a Chief Rabbi needed?' Answer: '[In] the Jewish community's interface with the wider public , we are often called upon for moral/religious viewpoints and, indeed, leadership. A community of some 300,000 must speak with one voice on these occasions ... Public divisions are directly damaging to the Jewish community's ability to present its case in the public arena.'

Question: 'What right is invested in you to assume this responsibility when you represent a minority of Jews?' Answer: 'I represent at least 72 per cent of affiliated Jews. No other rabbi represents more than 16.9 per cent. I have no reason to believe that unaffiliated Jews would not wish to be represented by a Chief Rabbi.'[59]

Days later, in a face-to-face interview, Sacks was asked by *Jewish Quarterly* editor Elena Lappin: 'Why did you actually have to write the letter to Rabbi Padwa?' He replied: 'I needed to be able to go on 20 February to deliver a tribute to Hugo Gryn.' 'I must repeat the question,' said Lappin. 'Why did you have to write the letter?' 'That is the answer,' responded the Chief Rabbi.

'Why did you need his authorisation?' she asked. 'I made a very clear statement on that,' Sacks insisted. 'Even though I had decided all along that I would attend, the opposition to my attending was so intense at a certain point that it threatened a very serious rift in the community. So, in order to mitigate that rift, I engaged in private communications.'

Told by Lappin that 'I simply don't understand how such a heated debate could go on after a man's death,' Sacks was then asked: 'Why didn't an open discussion take place while he was still alive?'

> I also don't understand [he replied]. I think the whole episode has been shameful. We've had nine months of controversy. It was started by the left wing of our community, it was then taken up by the right wing, and I have held a simple line throughout. An Orthodox Chief Rabbi cannot participate in a Reform religious service; a Reform rabbi cannot participate in Orthodox religious services. We cannot have joint religious services, and that has been the case for the last 200 years, since the beginning of Reform in 1817.[60]
>
> What we can do is to find neutral space in which we can respect one another and pay tributes to one another. That is why, when the neutral space was created by the Board of Deputies, I said this is what I can do. And because I can do it, I must do it. Because I respected everything that Hugo Gryn did for the sake of better relations between faiths, for the sake of hope after the Holocaust.
>
> I had to pay tribute to that within the agreed parameters of Anglo-Jewry. Why this should have created nine months of controversy is beyond belief. Why private diplomatic correspondence should have been published, leaked to the press and published, is also beyond belief. Clearly that was a calculated attempt to destroy good relationships in the community.

'In hindsight,' asked Lappin, bringing the subject to a close, 'you don't think it was a good thing to have it out in the open?' The Chief Rabbi demurred. 'If having something out in the open causes pain and injury to many people, if it damages relationships which we've been working for years to improve, if it sets Jew against Jew, then no, in hindsight I think it was wrong.'[61]

* * *   * * *   * * *

A fortnight after Sacks' letter was published, the actress Maureen Lipman – a congregant of Gryn's at the West London Synagogue – penned one of her own:

It has never occurred to me to be anything other than proud that I am a Jew. My heritage has fuelled and defined my work and my life. Last week, reading the *Jewish Chronicle*, for the first time I felt thoroughly ashamed for all 300,000 of us.

Hugo was my rabbi, my teacher, my friend ... [He] brought me back to Judaism as a worshipper and a practitioner after years of lip-service brought about by the demagogic and distant rabbis of my childhood and the hypocrisy of small-time shul rivalries and meaningless services where men ranted and women talked through the services about the cost of their hats ...

'Let us practise tolerance, cherish humanity, and celebrate our differences,' said Hugo – and what he preached, he practised. Now I read that, because of him, I'm not really a Jew; that my son is not barmitzvah; that the holy place at which I worship is not recognised as a House of God. '*Hamakom*,' says the prayer-book; 'God is everywhere.' But not in Upper Berkeley Street, say the Orthodox.

My husband [the playwright Jack Rosenthal] and I have sat at the present Chief Rabbi's table in his home. I'm anxious to know now exactly what I was there *as*. Not as a Jew, it would seem, but like the bishop who was also attending – as a prominent citizen and a human being. A lost soul? Well, I say 'humbug' to these fundamentalists who will tell me that we are destroyers of the faith. I say I am what I am, and it is for me and my God to decide what that is ...

Call me naïve, but I always thought of the Chief Rabbi as my representative. It is because we are thinking people that Reform Judaism satisfies our intellectual curiosity and our dislike of hypocrisy. Non-Orthodox Jews do not wish to change anything which their Orthodox counterparts do, nor do they wish to proselytise. Why are these people so frightened of us? ...

Everything Hugo stood for in his life is being put on trial by his death.

A great chance of love and respect and reconciliation was lost at Hugo's funeral. In place of courage and honour came hypocrisy, fear and bigotry. It is truly, truly shameful. And it must stop now.[62]

Former JC editor Geoffrey Paul viewed the controversy in its wider perspective:

> The question now confronting the Chief Rabbi [he wrote] is not really whether he is sorry, but whether he can, with hand on heart, face the philosophical U-turn needed for him to represent the entire community of Anglo-Jewish believers. Can he now accept the fact that their ways of faith are not his ways, but that he should make a place under his umbrella for any Jew trying to reach for a deeper religious commitment, whatever his or her starting-point? If he cannot answer these questions in the affirmative, then there really is no cross-communal role for the Chief Rabbi, and we will have reached a major turning-point in the history of an institution which, on the whole, has served the community well.[63]

Reform's initial 'shock' and 'anger'[64] at the Chief Rabbi's letter, vented immediately it was published, soon gave way to a more measured approach. 'We don't want to act in the heat of the moment,' said Bayfield. Questioning Sacks' assertion that his attendance at the memorial meeting had been needed 'to stop Reform plans to set up its own Chief Rabbinate,' he added:

> The Chief Rabbinate might to be able to continue its representative function for the whole community if it accepts changes. It would have to disavow that it is at war with us, cease to be sectarian and, for example, use the title 'Rabbi' in referring to our rabbis. Otherwise the office will have to be seen as only for the Orthodox, while Reform, Liberals and Masorti will have to find their own methods of representation to wider society. How can you expect anybody to be represented by an institution which describes a major section of the community as 'destroyers of the faith' and which says it is your greatest enemy? It would appear that the Chief Rabbinate is at war with us.[65]

In his article explaining the letter's language and context, Sacks had concluded with a plea for 'an end to public bickering.' Since Anglo-Jewry's inception, he had argued, its 'greatest strength was that it presented a cohesive front to the public. There were rare exceptions. But, for the most part, our ability to speak with a single voice in defence of Jewish interests gave us an influence out of all proportion to our numbers – certainly greater than other minority groups larger than ourselves.

'That is now seriously in danger. All too often recently, we have appeared to the public as divided, fractious and unruly. This weakens us internally and externally.

At times, the attacks have focused not on issues but on institutions. The Board of Deputies and the United Synagogue have both been targets, but the most determined assaults have been on the Chief Rabbinate. Those attacks have been public, private, bitter and sustained.

Whenever I have initiated a programme for the benefit of the whole community, or sought to make peace between contending groups, I have been attacked by those on the left for not going far enough, and by those on the right for going too far. The aim, and sometimes the effect, has been to make leadership of the community almost impossible. The clamour reached a crescendo following the death of the Reform rabbi and Holocaust survivor, Hugo Gryn.

What might and should have happened? A brave man had died. His family was in a state of grief. The sense of national – not just Jewish – loss was palpable. Tributes would have been paid by each of us in our own way. A period of dignified mourning would have been observed. We would have been brought closer by his great humanitarian example. I myself paid three public tributes immediately after his death, then in a national radio broadcast on erev Rosh Hashanah, and again at the memorial gathering held on 20 February this year.

Of the 'two bitter controversies' that had erupted following Hugo Gryn's death, Sacks again pointed out, 'the first was initiated by the left wing of our community, the second by the right. The first objected to the fact that I had not attended religious services following his death, the second that I was prepared to participate in a secular gathering in his memory. Both sought to change the ground rules that have prevailed for the past fifty years ...

'As of today,' declared the Chief Rabbi, 'I am issuing a call to Anglo-Jewish leaders and organisations to join a Coalition for Peace in the Community. I will be asking them to subscribe to the following principles:

• We recognise a duty to the Jewish people as a whole, and we will act responsibly in the light of that duty.
• We will seek to promote peaceful relations throughout the community, exercising restraint to avoid confrontation.

• We will emphasise what unites us as a people – our common past, our shared fate, our mutual responsibility.

• We will work together, despite religious differences, on matters which affect us all regardless of religious differences.

• We owe one another a duty of mutual respect, and we will not attack other Jews in public.

• We will defend our beliefs without publicly denigrating others.

• We will state clearly that those who sow dissension and dishonour Jewish values do not represent the community.

If we can implement these principles, good may yet come out of months of unnecessary conflict and pain. We must now call a halt to the debate over Hugo Gryn. A brave man has died, a man of courage and deep humanity. May he be allowed to rest in peace – and may we, at last, learn to live in peace.[66]

Referring to this plea, Bayfield said: 'We desperately want peace and co-operation, and will work for it. But it has to be based on a real understanding of *Klal Yisrael*, and there needs to be consonance between private and public attitudes and language.' Tabachnik thought the Chief Rabbi's proposal 'may afford a basis for discussion. The point is to find a formula that will hold all sides.'[67]

Levy, supported by Yisroel Fine, chairman of the United Synagogue's Rabbinical Council, declared: 'We welcome and enthusiastically endorse the seven principles for "Peace in the Community" enunciated by the Chief Rabbi. There is a need to maintain a respectful and tolerant understanding between the various sections of the community, which should be the overriding atmosphere of intra-community relationships. We look forward to our membership, and all other communities, warmly embracing the Chief Rabbi's initiative.'[68]

The *Jewish Chronicle*, still in a fighting mood, asserted: 'We passionately reject the Chief Rabbi's suggestion that Anglo-Jewry's greatest strength is its ability to "present a cohesive front" to non-Jewish Britain.

> Real leadership – as Rabbi Sacks himself has told a variety of newspapers and broadcast reporters – is about making tough decisions. It must involve rejecting the notion of a mere 'front' of unity and, however difficult, taking the risk of seeking genuine points of agreement.
>
> However reassuring may be a Chief Rabbi's ability to win praise among non-Jews, surely the Jewish community in Britain is finally mature enough to insist that the most important role of the Chief Rabbinate must be to serve, represent and lead fellow Jews – no matter what wider society may think.

Finally, and most importantly, we reject a central notion in the Chief
Rabbi's seven-point plan for communal peace – an undertaking merely in
public to respect and honour fellow Jews.

Politicians may have the prerogative (though even that notion is
questionable) to exercise *menschlichkeit* in public and disrespect in private.
Religious leaders cease to be worthy of that name if they do so. Indeed,
the peace which Rabbi Sacks – no doubt genuinely – seeks will prove as
fraught as some of his other well-meaning initiatives if it is built upon
the premise that merely by marking a letter 'Not for Publication' can one
proceed to denigrate a fellow Jew whom one has praised in public.[69]

From the Assembly of Masorti Synagogues came an equally withering
attack. 'The Office of the Chief Rabbi,' it pronounced, 'has become
decidedly political. Initiating reforms could not be carried through
without annoying someone. Instead of taking radical and unilateral action
at the beginning of his term, Jonathan Sacks backed away in the hope
that consensual politics would ultimately solve all problems – and such a
consensus would be arrived at through diplomatic channels.

Given the great divide between the readers of the *Jewish Tribune* and the heirs
of Leo Baeck, it was a short step towards an espousal that a merited end
was justified by unprincipled means. A spiritual leader had to be adept at
wheeler-dealing. He had to speak in the languages that different groups
understood … Thus his caustic piece in the ultra-Orthodox press which
condemned Masorti was coated in a medieval veneer.

Again with the Hugo Gryn memorial meeting, he believed that if he
tuned in to the right wavelength then he could avoid censure and avert a
crisis. His trust in the charedim was misplaced. He believed that his letter
to Padwa would be dealt with according to the rules of the game – that it
was private and not for publication, as stated.

Despite the almost programmed support from some United Synagogue
stalwarts, the release of such a letter into the public domain will only
further weaken that organisation, further polarise Anglo-Jewry – and,
ultimately, the ultra-Orthodox will gain from this state of affairs.

The dismay provoked by the publication in the *Jewish Chronicle* was in
part due to the contradiction in the public mind between the saintliness
of rabbinical calling and the underhand nature of political in-fighting.
British Jews prefer to view their religious leaders as the lofty guardians of
the Torah and not as sleazy politicians with tarnished ideals.

Yet this, unfortunately, is the reality of the position to which Jonathan
Sacks has committed himself in 1997. The goal of *shalom bayit* is a worthy

one, but its attainment, given this scenario, involves the verbal acrobatics of a seasoned politician …

Rabbi Sacks attained office when a generational change took place in Anglo-Jewry – and this included the *Jewish Chronicle*. A new team pursued an independent investigative approach which distinguished it from its more subservient predecessors … One line of argument can place the decision to publish a private letter in this arena.

Its publication amidst all the frenzied handwringing certainly sold more newspapers – and created more interest for the *Jewish Chronicle* in the media generally. Yet the decision in the final analysis should be seen as a correct one. It followed the paper's line of challenging issues which would have been swept under the carpet in the past. Unlike Jonathan Sacks, the *Jewish Chronicle* kept to its radical agenda. The issue was not one of private morality, but one of public concern to the entire Jewish community.

Of the wider ramifications for the institution of the Chief Rabbinate, Masorti's leaders declared: 'Masorti, the Liberals and, in part, the Reform have ideologically never accepted the nature of the office. This incident has brought to the surface the impossibility of being Chief Rabbi of the United Hebrew Congregations and being a spiritual leader for Anglo-Jewry at one and the same time. It has also dispelled much of the mythology associated with the office in the public mind.

'Jonathan Sacks' motives may have been honourable, but the path he chose to realise them became tainted and unworthy, with the result that trust has now become a disposable commodity in the political game. When the public fury has abated, a restructuring of how Anglo-Jewry operates will become inevitable.

'It will be driven by the reality of a shrinking community and the fact that the sum of the whole is more than its antagonistic parts. And the necessity for a single spiritual leader will be quietly debated by those who have hitherto loyally supported the idea of an all-embracing Chief Rabbinate.'[70]

Clearly speaking for the entire Progressive movement, *Manna* took a global view of the affair. It was imperative, declared a leading article, 'that the issues raised by the episode are detached from the personalities involved.

The long-dragged-out saga has caused endless pain to Rabbi Gryn's widow and family. The slurs on the name of a great rabbi are unforgivable and bitterly ironic, given Rabbi Gryn's commitment to reconciliation and bridge-building. Sufficient time must be allowed to elapse for the name of Hugo Gryn to be detached from the discussion of underlying issues.

Nor is it helpful for the Progressive community to get involved in discussions about Rabbi Dr Sacks' conduct and personality. At its heart, the matter is not about the conduct of a Chief Rabbi but about the conduct of a Chief Rabbinate.

The real issues are all to do with the Chief Rabbinate and its future ... The Padwa-letter incident simply illustrates a reality that, sooner or later, the community would have been forced to face anyway. It is that an institution which cannot permit its office-holder to attend the funeral of a distinguished rabbi and friend, and which reveals itself to be at war with those sections of the community that do not share its ideology, cannot act as the representative and spiritual figurehead of the entire community.

What is to be done? First, the Chief Rabbinate could change. It could be transformed into a much more inclusivist body truly capable of representing all sections of the community. This would demand a renunciation of sectarian action, a preparedness to call all rabbis 'Rabbi,' and a willingness to cross thresholds even if attending synagogue services is not possible.

Above all, it would require an acknowledgement that, although there are fundamental differences of theology, and although Orthodoxy can never legitimise non-Orthodoxy, there is, nevertheless, a shared and mutually respected commitment to Jewish education and to Jewish continuity.

If this is not possible, then the second option is for the Chief Rabbinate to be clearly portrayed and seen for what it has always technically been – the Chief Rabbinate of the United Hebrew Congregations, the United Synagogue and others who elect and fund its incumbent.

The more limited representational role of the office would have to be made explicit, and appropriate means would have to be established (not, we hasten to add, by the creation of a rival Chief Rabbinate) for other sections of the community to be represented and speak. The Christian community in Britain has long since adopted this position and it is widely regarded as honestly reflecting the realities and pluralities of life.

The third alternative is to accept that a venerable institution has passed its sell-by date. That may, eventually, be the conclusion, but there are many who would be deeply saddened.

Whatever the outcome, it must honestly reflect the community as it is today. And it must be coupled with a genuine agreement, across the community, to maintain a consonance between private and public language and private and public deeds. If people seek to retain illusions, however venerable, and to preserve fictions, however impressive, sooner or later reality will intrude, with disastrous effect.

We cannot afford, as a community, more disasters like the Padwa-letter episode. Without structures which provide for honesty, integrity and fairness, only dissension will rule.[71]

An insight into the pain caused to the Gryns was provided many years later by the family's middle daughter (and second of four children), Naomi, who – as will shortly be seen – collaborated in the posthumous publication of the rabbi's memoirs. 'In 1996,' she revealed, 'when my father died and there was this bizarre rift in the community, I took shelter in Israel.

> Every now and then, when I was told there was something particularly ugly about the so-called 'Sacks Affair,' I would go out and buy a copy of the *Jewish Chronicle*. One Shabbat, I was carrying under my arm a JC with the whole story about the letter to Dayan Padwa having been leaked.
>
> I was sitting in the car that afternoon with two friends of mine, two women who run a women's theatre company, one of whom is called Rena Padwa. So I said to her: 'Rena' – who was a single mother and an actress – 'do you know anything about this chap?' And she said: 'Yes, he is my uncle.'
>
> It turns out that the dayan's brother, the father of this woman with whom I was about to go to the beach for the afternoon, had at one point shaved off his beard, become a Communist, and gone to live in Israel. This helped ameliorate for me the pain of the insult that was being thrown at my father's memory.[72]

* * * * * * * * *

Eighteen months elapsed before the 'Coalition for Peace in the Community' was shakily in place. Despite its formation and well-intentioned aims, emotions were still raw when, a further eighteen months later, Gryn's memoirs, *Chasing Shadows*[73] – co-authored by Naomi – hit the book stands.

The *New Statesman* hailed it as 'not only an important historical document and engrossing memoir, but the only convincing case for a belief in God that I have ever read.' The *Evening Standard* wrote: 'This book is an essential witness to the horrors of the twentieth century and to the resilience of the human spirit.' After five printings, and with the book soon selling out, a paperback edition appeared within the year.

The *Jerusalem Post* marked its publication with a lengthy interview, in which author and poet Aloma Halter wrote of Naomi Gryn: 'Her life is fuelled by great enthusiasms and passions ... Neither does she mince words about "anyone who disrespects my father" – such as Britain's Chief Rabbi

Jonathan Sacks, whom she describes as "abominably yellow-bellied."

'She is referring to Sacks' actions around the period of Gryn's death, when Sacks sought both to acknowledge a colleague and a rabbi that the rest of Britain was mourning with such open affection, and yet tried, with a backstabbing letter, to utterly dissociate himself from anything that smacked of the Reform movement. "But all this," says the younger Gryn cheerfully, "is nothing compared to my sentiments about some of the bigots and racists who call themselves rabbis in Israel."'

Of *Chasing Shadows*, Halter wrote: 'It wasn't easy for Naomi to deal with living with this material, with which she had such a close connection, day after day. "It was quite a dark period for me," she says, "a confusion of grief and anger. At times, I felt very distressed. In order to do this project, I had to extend myself to the personality of my father, and I enmeshed myself as much as I could in order to sympathise, and then afterwards it was a long process getting unmeshed, coming back to myself."'[74]

Reviewing the volume, the *Daily Telegraph* described Hugo Gryn as 'very much someone who might well have been one's next-door neighbour. Indeed, he was someone whom millions of people felt they knew the way one knows a next-door neighbour, thanks to his regular appearances on "The Moral Maze" and other radio programmes. So the voice in this book is a familiar voice, and the style is a familiar style: there are no literary tricks, just a simple, and extremely honest, recounting of events.

'The story is clearly told. It is also remarkable for its optimism. Gryn deeply believes that God, and the faith and love of his father, explain his survival. Although he does not write about his later life – his rabbinical training, his subsequent role as a gentle figure of moral reason – it is clear that his experience in the camps led him back to religion, unlike many others.

'In the conclusion to this book, he writes that he is often asked: "Where was God in Auschwitz?" But he doesn't give any of the expected answers. He writes that "God was there himself – violated and blasphemed. The real question is, where was man in Auschwitz?"'[75]

Discussing the outcome of her task, Naomi Gryn wrote some years later: 'I finished *Chasing Shadows*, my father's memoir, which we'd begun together ten years before, about an idyllic childhood in the Carpathian Mountains that was abruptly halted when he and his family were deported to Auschwitz in May 1944.

'The book was published by Viking in February 2000 and no one has ever needed a bestseller as much as me. I cycled around Regent's Park in the spring sunshine; there was an unfamiliar emotion stirring in my heart, and then I realised it was joy. As I filed away all the glowing reviews, I found I could once again face myself in the mirror and put the bad stuff behind me.'[76]

She had earlier told Halter: 'It was a very symbolic moment for me when I was first shown the cover of the hardback, off-white with gold writing. I immediately understood – it was just like the gold and off-white tallit that I'd once bought for my father and in which, when he died, I asked that he be wrapped for burial. For me, the cover of the book, like that tallit, represented closure and the final burial of my father.'

And the book's impact? 'There are such important issues at stake, particularly about the need for people to regard each other with mutual respect.'

This 'issue at stake' was reflected in Hugo Gryn's own last words. He had survived his experiences in the Holocaust – came his message from the grave – with the belief that 'the reason I had to spend much of my time working for better understanding between religious groups is partly because I know that you can only be safe and secure in a society that practises tolerance, cherishes harmony, and celebrates difference.'[77]

* * *   * * *   * * *

By a remarkable quirk of fate, the cathartic publication of Chasing Shadows coincided with a similarly therapeutic anthology by Sacks – Celebrating Life[78]– illustrating how (in the words of the jacket) the Chief Rabbi 'discovered where happiness lives, often in unexpected places, through family, community, friendship and responsibilities,' and how he 'also found it through a renewed relationship with God, who speaks to our deepest needs.'

In her foreword, The Times' religion correspondent, Ruth Gledhill, wrote that 'this book is about survival, and about faith that survival is possible. It is about human dignity and the possibility that happiness can be had by all, if only we can open our eyes and believe.' Referring indirectly – as does Sacks in the opening chapter[79] – to the Gryn Affair (what Jackie Tabick and Naomi Gryn called the Sacks Affair), Gledhill added:

> It is when writing about his personal difficulties that Dr Sacks is most moving. Figures at the head of institutions can easily become icons for some, while at the same time turning into easy targets for others, for the iconoclasts. Rarely can such occasions be isolated from their personal context, even if the individual concerned cannot at the time, for reasons of political and personal integrity, depict the full context which can shed light on events which appear otherwise inexplicable.

Dr Sacks has, during his time as Chief Rabbi, endured various struggles within his own community which have spilled over into the secular world. Here he writes obliquely of the background to one such conflict, a series of events that in fact provided the inspiration for this book. Badly affected by the death of his father, he says, he went through one of the most difficult periods of his life. 'I made mistakes and, being a public figure, I suffered for them. For two years, I felt as if I were drowning.'[80]

'My late father, of blessed memory,' – Sacks said in a radio broadcast some months later – 'was, you know, a Jewish father, he was a great man. He came over to this country at the age of five, never really had an education because he had to leave school at the age of fourteen to support the family. He was sort of self-educated, but fiercely proud of his Jewish heritage.

'He taught all of us, myself and my three brothers, to walk tall, to believe in what we believe in, to stand firm for our moral convictions. You know, what can I say, he was a very fine man. My mum, who is very much still alive and well and bouncing around in her eighties, bless her, was the perfect balance.

'I loved him, I took his loss very badly, but you know, in the end, the first thing that hits you is that he is not there anymore, but after a year or two you discover that in a certain sense he is still there.'[81]

In the third year, having surfaced from the conflict and found happiness in unexpected places,[82] the Chief Rabbi ended *Celebrating Life* with these thoughts:

Not by accident is Judaism a religion less of holy people and holy places than of holy words – the Divine speech, recorded in the Hebrew Bible and endlessly studied ever since. Language is the vehicle of meanings. It is also the primary way in which we form relationships of trust. I 'give my word,' meaning that I use language to create an obligation which I am thereby bound to honour. The Hebrew word for faith – *emunah* – really means honouring your word, and trusting others to honour theirs. Above all, language is where we frame our values, express our ideals, and thus create the possibility of a gracious society. It allows us to have a vision and communicate it. 'Without a vision,' says the proverb, 'a people perish.'[83]

6

The Stanmore Accords

'Let us be driven by our calling to reach out, bring close, enthuse and inspire. If there is only one great leader in Anglo-Jewry and it is the Chief Rabbi, I will have failed.' [1]

Following Sacks' call for a 'Coalition for Peace in the Community,' his office announced that it had begun a 'consultation process with various groups on ways of bringing greater harmony within our community,' while, for the United Synagogue, Elkan Levy declared that he and his colleagues were 'looking forward to implementing the plan.' Masorti's Harry Freedman warned, however, that his movement 'won't support anything unless it has the full backing of the whole community and is brokered by a neutral body.' [2]

The *Jewish Chronicle*, in a leading article, noted that 'relations within Anglo-Jewry (or at least between leaders of its main religious groupings) have been more openly strained than at any time in recent memory.' Discussing the 'calls from various sides of the community … for a renewed dedication to tolerance and respect across differences of belief and religious practice,' it added:

> How, and indeed whether, this proves possible will depend largely on the Chief Rabbi and other lay and religious leaders, Orthodox and non-Orthodox, within British Jewry. But all should be aware that – along with the undoubted damage done to relationships in the community by the Sacks-Padwa letter – its publication may yet prove to have had at least one positive effect. This is the fact that issues too long avoided, and too long obscured by rhetorical acrobatics, are now out in the open. While the short-term result may have been to weaken the office of the Chief Rabbinate, it has also provided an opportunity to define far better the role and constituency of the Chief Rabbinate of Jonathan Sacks.
>
> The view of many US rabbis would appear to be that this should involve a renewed focus on his core constituency, United Synagogue Orthodoxy. Progressive and Masorti leaders would seem inclined to agree, though for different reasons. The letter, they suggest, has exposed the difficulty, if not the impossibility, in any Chief Rabbi's properly

seeking to represent non-Orthodox sections of the community while remaining true to his own religious credo. Yet whatever the outcome of the inevitable debates that will now take place within, and between, the various religious groupings in British Jewry, the main shared lesson to be drawn from the controversy surrounding the letter is the need openly to acknowledge those issues which may divide one Jew from another, while still retaining on all sides, and in all forums, that fundamental sense of mutual respect without which all of us stand to suffer.[3]

Turning their backs on the Consultative and Liaison Committees that had operated, intermittently, between the United Synagogue and the non-Orthodox over a period of years,[4] leaders of the Reform, Liberal and Masorti movements called on the US to join in talks 'on co-operation and on how the community should be represented to the outside world.'

In a statement pointedly referring to 'the United Synagogue's Chief Rabbi,' they urged the establishment of representative structures 'that are fair, effective and a truthful reflection of our community.' Freedman added that Masorti 'would like Anglo-Jewry's figurehead to be the president of the Board of Deputies or some other figure, agreed by the denominations, who can represent the whole community.'[5]

'Disgust over the actions of Rabbi Jakobovits' successor, following the death of Rabbi Hugo Gryn,' claimed Progressive leaders, had 'caused the Liberal and Reform members to withdraw from the Consultative and Liaison Committees ... Out of this distasteful, unhappy and unnecessary situation came the determination of the Liberal, Reform and Masorti movements to work even more closely together.'[6]

The previous November, addressing the Reform movement's council, RSGB board members had reported that 'the past months [following Gryn's funeral] have been difficult for Reform–Orthodox relations.

> The bad feeling has been a matter of genuine concern on both sides, but points of connection and lines of communication exist and are currently being strengthened. Rabbi Bayfield and the Chief Rabbi of the United Hebrew Congregations are in regular contact. A meeting is taking place in late November between Neville Sassienie [the RSGB chairman] and Rabbi Bayfield and Elkan Levy, the new president of the United Synagogue, and its chief executive, Jonathan Lew. This is intended as a relationship-building exercise.
>
>   The Consultative Committee also meets in November, convened by Rabbi Jacqueline Tabick, and the Liaison Committee, which has not met for some months due to diary pressures, now has a firm date in

December. There are clearly limits to what can be achieved, but these various points of contact should, at the very least, be able to clarify the ground-rules and make clear both what is possible and what is not. Even that would lower tension, and there are signs that positive areas of co-operation can be nurtured.

What is clear is the de facto recognition of the Reform Movement for what it is: the second largest synagogal organisation in the UK and, with the United Synagogue, the most significant player.[7]

Whether are not de facto recognition was 'clear,' Sacks' attack on Reform made even clearer the unreality of de jure recognition, the perceived path to which, the Chief Rabbi claimed, had prompted his letter to Padwa. It also demolished the Consultative and Liaison Committees and, for the time being at least, any lingering hopes of a 'relationship-building exercise' among the parties.

Separating the issues of recognition and representation, Sassienie maintained that, 'although it caused us shock and pain, it was right and brave of the JC to publish the Chief Rabbi's letter ... Much of the tension within the British Jewish community stems from the maintenance of structures which have long since failed to reflect reality, and the preservation of fictions and illusions about representation that do us all a great disservice. These matters will require careful consideration, but we are determined that the various segments of the community will come together to discuss them and find a more honest and effective structure and pattern of representation.'[8]

For the Progressives, Rabbi Charles Middleburgh asserted that 'if the Chief Rabbinate is to represent the entire community, in all its rich, pluralistic diversity, it will have to conduct itself very differently from the way it has done until now. If it cannot, a redefining of role, responsibility and authority becomes necessary and vital.'[9]

Masorti's co-chairmen, Ivor Jacobs and Alex Sklan, contended that 'perhaps there is no good reason why Anglo-Jewry needs a religious figurehead. American Jewry is no less influential for not having a Chief Rabbi. Although widespread in contemporary Jewry, the concept is a recent innovation which owes nothing to Jewish tradition. Masorti synagogues have never accepted the authority of the Chief Rabbi of the United Hebrew Congregations, nor would we participate in a Progressive Chief Rabbinate.'[10]

Four days into the Sacks-Padwa controversy, Bayfield formulated a Reform position paper entitled *Preliminary Thoughts on the Present Crisis*, a far-reaching document circulated among a select few, and speedily adopted by the RSGB board. The dispute, he declared, 'has highlighted a significant historical change that has gathered pace over the last two decades.

> At one time, the United Synagogue was a broad church, and the Chief Rabbinate could be said to represent religiously the overwhelming majority of the community. The shift from being a broad church to a sect (this is sociological, not pejorative, language), coupled with the rise of non-Orthodoxy, has turned the reality into a fiction.
>
> Maintaining the fiction has become less and less helpful. The present episode is simply a graphic illustration. It is axiomatic that we cannot be represented religiously by an institution whose figurehead feels unable to attend the funeral of one of our most distinguished rabbis. Perhaps the most disturbing aspect of the episode was that the leaked letter portrayed the Chief Rabbinate as being at war with our section of the community. This is manifestly inconsistent with cross-community representation. The illusion must be scotched in the interests of all concerned.
>
> It is important that the entire episode is not seen as a personal matter – that is, about Jonathan Sacks' ability or integrity – but is seen for what it is: an institutional, structural, representational problem. By achieving a structural and representational pattern which reflects reality, people's expectations in certain circumstances will be less, and that should help to avoid episodes of such pain in the future. If the religious representative of the entire community declines to attend a funeral, that is one thing. If the spiritual leader of the central Orthodox block fails to attend, that is still significant – but of a lower order of significance.
>
> Peace and co-operation with a de facto pluralist community is our aim. The realisation of the aim is dependent upon a community structure which is honest and transparent, and in which public and private utterances are consonant.

Bayfield concluded with a five-point Reform/ULPS/Masorti 'action plan,' to be negotiated with the United Synagogue and the Chief Rabbinate. Its aims included 'genuine efforts to make clear that "the Chief Rabbi" is the Chief Rabbi of the United Hebrew Congregations; a clear process whereby all organisations having the Chief Rabbi as a president, trustee, etc, have parallel representation from the non-Orthodox community; the strengthening of the Board of Deputies, and the role of its president, as secular representative of the community; and the renaming of the Consultative Committee, with new venue and agreed terms of reference, to act as an across-the-community consultative and leadership forum.'

'None of this,' Bayfield stressed, 'precludes an agreement that, in certain circumstances, we are happy for Rabbi Sacks to represent us on a particular occasion. However, that might well be coupled with a demand for clarification of his relationship to Reform, and the withdrawal of certain of the more offensive terms, such as "destroyers of the faith."'[11]

Responding to Bayfield's 'thoughts,' Freedman expanded on the Masorti view. 'I am not sure at all,' he wrote, 'why the Jewish community needs any form of public representation. However, if such a role is required, this should be done through the president of the Board of Deputies.

> This is simply because I feel that a non-denominational figure is the only possible representative for as pluralist yet divided a community as we are. However, the Board cannot represent the community until its religious authority is redefined.
>
> At present, the Chief Rabbi of the United Synagogue is its religious authority, and the president and the Council of Reform and Liberal Rabbis, together with the leader of the Sephardi community, have a secondary consultative status. This is not adequate. Either the Board has to accept that the senior rabbi from each denomination has an equal standing, or it has no religious authority at all.
>
> Ultimately, the issue lies not with the Chief Rabbinate of the United Synagogue, but with the Board. Of course, the United Synagogue has an inbuilt majority at the Board, and we will not be able simply to have these proposals voted through. I think, however, that we will have to become sufficiently militant to require the Board either to recognise the plurality of this community or to cease to function as our 'representative body.'[12]

Sending a copy of his *Preliminary Thoughts* to Middleburgh, marked 'Not to be leaked to Dayan Padwa,' Bayfield wrote: 'Herewith the position paper that was agreed by the RSGB board last night ... We believe that the Consultative Committee meeting should be postponed until the RSGB and the ULPS – and, preferably, the Masorti – have had a chance to meet and agree policy.'[13]

To Peter Levy, a leading figure in the Reform movement, Bayfield confided: 'We are now putting together an RSGB/ULPS/Masorti coalition to agree a common position. It will take time, but I see no reason for haste. In fact, we asked for a postponement of a meeting of the Consultative Committee tonight because none of us feels ready to go back and have tea at Hamilton Terrace.'[14]

And to Freedman, Bayfield cautioned: 'The present crisis has presented us with a negotiating opportunity. Sacks has weakened his own position, but it is by no means as weak as one might have expected.

> There is a great deal of rallying to his support. A surprising number of people are blaming the JC and, when all is said and done, a significant number of people seem to agree with the sentiments he expressed, if not with the language in which they were couched.
>
> We can do one of two things. We can try to negotiate a position that is more honest and transparent and gives us a fairer crack of the whip ... The alternative is not to do a deal – or to couch our demands in terms which prove completely unacceptable. Given his [Sacks'] continuing support, and given that the United Synagogue still has a considerably larger membership than the rest of us – and given his skill in portraying himself as the spokesperson for Anglo-Jewry to the wider world – we might actually come out of this situation with nothing tangible.
>
> The Board [of Deputies] would remain as it is; his office would continue to perpetuate the myth that he is Anglo-Jewry's Chief Rabbi; and we would make no progress in terms of representation and public profile. I would like to avoid such an outcome. It is a real possibility if we don't 'play our cards right,' and I believe that 'playing our cards right' means negotiating a realistic amelioration of our position. I am glad we are going to meet, and I relish the possibility of us working together constructively.[15]

In May 1997, a tripartite group was established by the non-Orthodox movements, comprising the chairmen, senior professionals and rabbinic leaders of each grouping and designed to construct 'a new framework which dispensed with the Chief Rabbi's patronage and afforded us not recognition, which we knew we would never get from the United Synagogue, but de facto acceptance of different groups with different constituencies, and an end to bickering, for the sake of the community.'[16]

Somewhat belatedly, meanwhile, the JC reported that 'a member of an Orthodox–Progressive liaison group, Lionel Swift,[17] is understood to have made approaches to the Reform on behalf of the Chief Rabbi. Reform personalities such as Sir Sigmund Sternberg and Sir Trevor Chinn have also made bridge-building efforts.'[18]

Swift had been delegated to represent Sacks in the negotiations and, on 24 March, had held a meeting with Bayfield at Sternberg's home, prompting the Reform rabbi to tell Swift soon after: 'It was really good to meet you, and reassuring to know that someone as sensible and realistic as you is involved in trying to bring about a resolution of this extraordinarily difficult situation.'[19]

During their discussion, minuted by Bayfield,[20] Swift depicted the United Synagogue and the RSGB as 'parallel lines, which don't meet but which seek to deal with each other with decency and respect.' Utilising that imagery, the two men explored ways of moving forward, and Bayfield asked Swift whether the Chief Rabbinate could become a more inclusivist institution 'and act, if you like, as the sleeper between the parallel lines.' Swift replied that this was 'not immediately feasible. It may be something for the future, but not now.'

Bayfield perceived Swift making clear 'the concern felt by the Chief Rabbi and the leadership of the United Synagogue to avoid having their Orthodox credentials questioned from outside this country and, therefore, their limited scope for movement, particularly at this time.' Given the Chief Rabbinate's inability to bridge the gap between the two lines, Bayfield suggested that 'what is clearly needed is a greater degree of clarity and transparency with regard to how the two lines relate and are represented.' He told Swift:

> Much greater care needs to be taken with regard to how the Chief Rabbinate portrays itself and its representative function. If it is impossible for the language and sentiments of the infamous letter to be the subject of an apology or a withdrawal, it is absolutely essential that there is a real recognition that the Chief Rabbinate cannot represent spiritually our section of the community. This is especially important vis-à-vis the churches and the outside world. Nothing is more guaranteed to provoke fury and the continuing rumbling of this issue in the wider world than the fudge.
>
> We should seek a strengthening of the Board of Deputies as the secular representative of the entire Jewish community, and we may need to revisit the issue of 'ecclesiastical authorities.' The Board, in turn, needs to be discouraged from supporting impossible enterprises such as across-the-community services. Because clergy from the various denominations cannot share a *bimah*, such services are bound to give rise to dissension and objection.

'I want to make it clear,' Bayfield assured Swift, 'that the last thing we would wish to do is to belittle or even humiliate the Chief Rabbinate and, still less, its present incumbent. We would in no way want to be seen as being disrespectful to a time-honoured institution. Still less would we wish to belittle Anglo-Jewry's most distinguished and articulate spokesperson.

'What we have to do is create a situation of honesty and transparency, with clear ground-rules and structures, within which all sections of the community can both talk and maintain their self-respect. If any section of the community feels that it is being dealt with unfairly, or if confusions remain, we will never escape from the present totally unsatisfactory situation.'

Apprising his lay colleagues of his discussion with Swift, Bayfield related: 'Siggy [Sternberg] pressed me very hard to have a confidential meeting with himself and Lionel Swift. Siggy clarified that Lionel was congruent to the Chief Rabbi and was seeking to resolve the present crisis ... As it happens, the meeting did little more than provide me with an opportunity for articulating the principles in my paper to last week's RSGB board meeting.

'Siggy feels that, unless we move fast and win concessions now, our position will weaken as the days and weeks go by. He is convinced that the Chief Rabbi can just sit it out and leave us pretty much where we were before. He also suspects that this is the advice that the Chief Rabbi is being given ...

'My impression was that Lionel felt we were asking for a very great deal and that Sacks would be shocked ... Increasingly, I do agree with Siggy that delay – in the behind-the-scenes negotiations – is not going to help. We do have to move while there is insecurity and uncertainty. I, too, can envisage a scenario in which the whole episode leaks into the ether and we gain nothing of substance, except for a recollection that it was somehow all our fault.'[21]

Weeks later, addressing the Manchester Festival of Reform Judaism, Bayfield used the Sacks-Padwa letter as the basis for a lecture on 'Fundamentalism and Reform Judaism in the 1990s.' He concluded with the declaration: 'There is a rising tide of fundamentalism throughout the Jewish world, a remarkable resurgence of a medieval outlook on life ...

'All Orthodox eyes look anxiously over their right shoulders, and I fear for those who still seek to occupy the middle ground; I tremble for the heirs of Samson Raphael Hirsch. I worry deeply for the bridge-builders, among whom I include myself, who wish to see a harmonious, respectful and co-operative Jewish community. We must recognise fundamentalism for what it is, in all its "oppositionalism," its fearfulness, and its rejection of modernity.'[22]

In early May, following a series of exploratory meetings between Reform, Progressive and Masorti representatives, the chairmen of the three bodies wrote to Elkan Levy seeking 'to take the discussions forward and to work with the leadership of the United Synagogue on issues of structure, representation and co-operation.' In the belief that the Deputies had 'a vital representative and harmonising role to play,' they proposed holding a preliminary meeting at the Board's offices, and under the chairmanship of its president, as a 'helpful model for future working.'[23]

Levy's spokesman replied that he was 'out of the country until the end of the month' and that, on his return, he would have an opportunity 'to give consideration to the letter.'[24]

The non-Orthodox leaders wrote also to Tabachnik, telling him that the Padwa-letter affair 'has been extremely painful for many people in our community ... We are determined to build something better than at present, something more conducive to a peaceful and co-operative state of affairs. We have, accordingly, written to the president of the United Synagogue suggesting that we talk. We would like you to chair our meeting and support the process.'[25]

An 'aide memoir' accompanying the letter to Levy prepared the ground for negotiations over the ensuing months. Introducing the issues, it pointed out that 'there are aspects of the "Padwa-letter" affair which are personal and specific to the incident and the people concerned.

We do not wish to pursue these aspects. It may be helpful to discuss elsewhere issues of personal and rabbinic derech eretz, private and public language, boundaries, etc. But these are not for our meetings. There are aspects to the affair which are more general and relate to issues of representation, structure and co-operation which, perhaps, should have been addressed some time ago and, in any event, must be addressed now. We have two objectives:

1. To ensure that, both in perception and reality, the patterns of representation and the structures by which Anglo-Jewish organisations relate and talk are fair, effective and a truthful reflection of our community, and the reasonable aspirations of its constituent parts.

2. To help build a community in which there is organisational derech eretz and respect, and in which the component parts work together in all areas where active co-operation is possible, to ensure that Anglo-Jewry has a rich and vigorous future ...

We do not wish to demean or diminish the historic office of Chief Rabbi of the United Hebrew Congregations of the Commonwealth. We are fully aware that we do not fund the office, and you [the United Synagogue] are fully aware that the office holds no authority for us. There are, however, times when the very natural but loose use of the term 'Chief Rabbi' and 'Chief Rabbinate' fosters an illusion that causes us offence and gives rise to expectations which cause pain when the expectations cannot be met. It would be really helpful if the United Synagogue could use its good offices to ensure the use of the correct title – for instance, on headed notepaper, in the *Jewish Year Book*, and in public statements.

For many years, the Consultative Committee on Jewish–Christian Relations, set up for the very specific purposes indicated by its title, has served other purposes as well. We believe that there is enormous value in regular meetings of the lay and rabbinic leadership of the United Synagogue, the RSGB, the ULPS, Masorti, and perhaps others – and, of course, the Board.

It is now time for such a body to come fully into the open in the sense of no longer masquerading as an interfaith consultative group. Its composition needs some revision. It should meet on 'neutral territory,' probably at the Board, and needs new terms of reference to reflect its role in discussing matters of overall concern, and matters relating to the community's relationship with the wider world.[26]

Several weeks later, a meeting of the tripartite non-Orthodox leaders heard that 'there has been no formal response from Elkan Levy, and this is resented. However, there are indications that the US wishes to proceed by a different route.' The meeting proposed the establishment of a 'small group' to undertake preliminary work 'so that any summit meeting would have sufficient material prepared to have a reasonable chance of success. This is not our preferred way of doing things, but we agree to give it a chance.'[27]

Joining the group in the initial negotiations were Lew and Swift, the latter representing the Chief Rabbi. Their first meeting, at Swift's home on 7 July, also included Bayfield, Freedman, and the Liberals' Rosita Rosenberg. Apart from issues of internal (intra-communal) and external (national) representation, the discussion centred on the Jewish presidency of the Council of Christians and Jews;[28] the 'full and correct title' of the Chief Rabbi; university, hospital and prison chaplaincies; and matters of personal status – 'the most challenging area.'

Under the heading 'rabbinic issues,' the following points were specified:

1. The title 'Rabbi' can and should be used with reference to the rabbis of all the denominations.

2. United Synagogue rabbis may not attend services at non-Orthodox synagogues.

3. US rabbis and lay leaders may sit on panels with non-Orthodox rabbis and lay leaders provided that those panels were not held in Reform, Liberal or Masorti synagogue sanctuaries.

4. US rabbis and lay leaders may attend non-religious functions on premises owned by the Reform, Liberals or Masorti, provided that they did not involve entering the sanctuary.[29]

Describing the meeting as 'positive,' Freedman reported back to his Masorti co-chairmen that, 'as we feared, it was very much a negotiation between us and Lionel Swift as Sacks' representative, with the US chief executive taking almost a back seat.

'Swift repeated on numerous occasions that he was there as an "honest broker." It was also very clear, however, that he was acting for Jonathan Sacks and would be taking our proposals back to him for response. Both Swift and Lew were adamant that Elkan Levy was not going to attend any meetings other than to sign agreements at an historic occasion, and that if this group did not resolve all the issues, there was nothing more to discuss.'[30]

By mid-July, the non-Orthodox representatives had submitted to Swift their 'items for consideration.' These included 'a joint statement agreeing the need to establish patterns of co-operation; an agreed shorthand term in place of the unwieldy "Chief Rabbi of the United Hebrew Congregations of the Commonwealth," to be used in conversation and the media; US support for our proposal to establish a working party with the Board [of Deputies] to look at the issue of ecclesiastical authorities; a standing commission with the Board and the [Israeli] Embassy to plan future memorial services; cross-communal discussions with Hillel on student chaplaincy; cross-communal discussions on conversions and marriages; and agreement that non-US rabbis may speak at US funerals.'[31]

* * *   * * *   * * *

In April 1998, following a series of protracted, difficult and contentious meetings,[32] the negotiators drew up a draft *Statement to the Community*; three months later, a revised text was placed before the respective parties. 'Despite serious misgivings,' Sklan told his ecclesiastical and lay colleagues, 'the consensus [in April] was that we should sign the agreement. We then heard from the United Synagogue that they wished to make changes to the statement. The most significant was to alter "United Synagogue" in the three numbered conventions [on religious practice, as detailed below] to "Orthodox synagogues."

'We found this unacceptable because (a) the United Synagogue is in no position to speak for Orthodox synagogues to the right of their movement; (b) there are Modern Orthodox rabbis who would not follow the conventions and would be willing to speak in our synagogues and participate in our services; and (c) our negotiations were between four specific synagogues groups, not between different ideologies.'

Sklan reported a proposal to remove the conventions from the main statement and to allow the United Synagogue to issue them unilaterally – a suggestion rejected by the US. 'It has become clear,' he said, 'that the conventions are really all the United Synagogue wants. The proposed Consultative Committee does not interest them, and they will agree to it only if we sign the agreement with the conventions.

'It seems to me,' said Sklan, 'that the conventions provide a means of excusing Rabbi Sacks for his appalling behaviour following the death of Rabbi Hugo Gryn, and I do not see why we should sign up to conventions with which we do not agree. I am happy to acknowledge, by appending them to the agreement, that there are conventions to which the United Synagogue currently adheres.

'The agreement is proposed by Elkan Levy. I do not recommend that we sign it, for the reasons I have stated. However, I feel that I should consult with you first as I believe that this will mark the end of our negotiations. If you believe we should sign this agreement, please let me know by the end of August.'[33]

In a parallel discussion, more serious reservations were being expressed by rabbinical leaders within the Progressive movement. Concluding a lengthy correspondence with his colleague Sidney Brichto on the issues involved, John Rayner, emeritus minister of the St John's Wood Liberal Synagogue, declared: 'Communal unity is not attainable unless there is, in addition, a common acceptance of pluralism. You [Brichto] say: "The Orthodox cannot accept it; it goes against their deepest principle." But that is open to question – perhaps even de jure, certainly de facto. As a matter of fact, they *do* accept it de facto. How can they do otherwise?'

The problem is that, according to Jonathan Sacks, de facto acceptance of pluralism is not a sufficient basis for 'normal relations' – that is, sharing platforms, visiting each other's premises, attending each other's funerals, etc., and all those things that are taken for granted in any other religiously diverse community such as Christianity, or politically democratic institution such as Parliament.

Jonathan Sacks has persuaded himself that this step, from de facto pluralism to normal relations, is halachically forbidden; and I don't doubt that he believes it sincerely. But to any external observer it is transparently obvious that the stance is politically rather than halachically motivated. It is part of the war strategy which Orthodoxy has been conducting against Reform for the last 200 years, without success in terms of its purpose (rather, counter-productively) and with disastrous consequences for Jewish unity.

For instance, his standard line of defence – that to have normal relations would be to confer legitimacy on each other – is patently false, (a) by any logic known to me, and (b) by the common consent of the great bulk of Anglo-Jewry, who are nauseated (as non-Jews are mystified) by the constant invocation of that specious argument to disallow normal, civilised communal relations.

Because the Orthodox objection to normal relations with us is, in my view, primarily political rather than religious, I think it is legitimate and necessary – from time to time, and with all due politeness – to point that out to the Orthodox community, in the hope that in the course of time more and more of its lay people, even if not its rabbis, will come to recognise it, as many already do; will therefore realise that the discord it creates is unnecessary; and will demand a different policy.

I reiterate a point I have made many times. By all means, let us explore what can be done to diminish the gap that divides us over such matters as conversion. I am not less willing for compromise – provided that it does not violate anybody's integrity, and that it is mutual – than anybody else. Indeed, for any inch they are prepared to budge, I am prepared to budge two inches. But since all the indications so far have been that they are not prepared to budge half an inch, it does seem something of a wild goose chase.

And even if, improbably, we were to succeed in reducing the gap by a few inches, it would still remain, as I am sure you would agree, many yards wide. Therefore the basic problem – which is how to live harmoniously together in spite of that gap – would remain not only unsolved but untouched. Hence my insistence that we must learn to live with our differences – or, in other words, to practise the art of pluralism. Compared with that, so far as the quest for communal unity is concerned, everything else is almost completely irrelevant.[34]

* * *   * * *   * * *

Twenty-seven months after Hugo Gryn's funeral, the Chief Rabbi's 'Coalition for Peace in the Community' – renamed the Stanmore Accords after the area in which they were signed[35] – finally saw the light of day, drawn up by the lay leaders of the United Synagogue, Reform, Liberal and Masorti movements (the latter having rejected Sklan's recommendation) in an attempt 'to bring about a more harmonious and productive relationship between the various sections of the community.'

> Like many members of Anglo-Jewry [they declared], we have been perturbed and distressed by the divisions and dissension which have become the more apparent since the death of Rabbi Hugo Gryn, of blessed memory. It is inevitable that with different principles and practices there exist profound differences of belief calculated to stir deep emotions and impatience.
>
> These deep divisions within the Jewish community have existed for more than a century. It would be wrong to minimise or ignore them. They are not unique to our Anglo-Jewish community. We have seen them developing not only in Israel, but in many lands in the diaspora. It is not surprising, since fundamental concepts of Jewish life are in issue: divorce, conversion – indeed, the question itself as to who is a Jew.
>
> The Jewish community is damaged by in-fighting and mutual recrimination. It harms us internally and externally. Internally, the spectacle of Jew attacking Jew has a harmful effect on the community, its members and its morale. It tends to show Jews and Judaism in a negative light and to obscure the positive achievements of the community, our community, and the inspiring values of Judaism itself. Externally, it compromises the unity we have hitherto been able to bring to matters of great importance, the support of Israel, welfare and defence among them.
>
> It would be wrong to suppose that our differences and divisions preclude peaceful co-existence, mutual respect and a considerable measure of co-operation on matters which are not divisive. There is a distinction to be drawn between substantive matters of contention and the protocols of respect and mutual courtesy which can and should exist between those who hold profoundly different views.
>
> The substantive points of conflict within the community cannot be resolved quickly. That does not mean they should not be tackled. But to predicate harmonious relationships on their resolution is to defer indefinitely the quest of us all for communal peace. To that end, a set of understandings and conventions will reduce the level of acrimony now and in the foreseeable future.

With these considerations in mind, and with the approval of our religious leaders, there have been discussions between us with a view to establishing certain protocols of behaviour, reaching certain understandings and clarifying certain conventions, thereby avoiding misunderstandings, resentments and the suspicion of an offence when none may be intended. We commit ourselves unreservedly to the pursuit of communal peace and co-operation.

Let it be said that mutual respect and co-operation on matters which are not divisive will be achieved only if there is a recognition of the sincerity of one another's point of view, and an understanding that certain beliefs and traditions impose limits on conduct and beliefs which are to be regarded as acceptable. The absence of recognition does not entail the absence of respect.

No section of the community should ask or expect any other to act against its convictions, or embarrass it for being consistent with its principles; no group should seek to exploit difference for sectional ends; and when shared activity or common ground is sought, the search for it should be with due recognition for the sensitivities of the various participants. Any discussion should be conducted in a mutually respectful manner and tone. We therefore wish the annexed conventions of Orthodox communities which are adopted by the United Synagogue to be widely known and recognised.

This statement is but a step to bring about a more harmonious and productive relationship between the several sections of the community. Much remains for consideration, and we will seek to deal with problems when they arise, each of us consulting our own religious leaders. We have accordingly agreed to take early steps to renew and revise the Consultative Committee with a view to continuing to deal with the whole subject of communal relations. Terms of reference have been agreed and are annexed hereto.

We trust that this statement will lead to the diminution of dissension within an historic community.

The 'annexed conventions' stipulated the following:

Annexe 1:
Conventions of Orthodox communities as adopted by the United Synagogue

Membership of a Reform, Liberal or Masorti congregation does not *ipso facto* prevent a Jew regarded as halachically Jewish by the Chief Rabbi or Beth Din from being called up or receiving a mitzvah at an Orthodox service.

Orthodox authorities do not recognise Reform, Liberal or Masorti conversions.

Where a marriage could have been solemnised in an Orthodox synagogue but the parties marry under Reform, Liberal or Masorti auspices, that fact does not provide any impediment to the children of such a marriage being recognised by Orthodox authorities as being halachically Jewish, and does not prevent their being admitted to Orthodox schools or marrying in an Orthodox synagogue.

Orthodox rabbis and ministers do not speak at or participate in Reform, Liberal and Masorti services. Their attendance at such services is within their discretion.[*] Orthodox bodies do not invite Reform, Liberal and Masorti rabbis and ministers to speak at or participate in services under Orthodox auspices.

[*The sentence on attendance was subsequently deleted on the instructions of the London Beth Din.]

Annexe 2:
Consultative Committee – Terms of Reference

Purpose
The purpose of the Consultative Committee is to provide a forum at which the main synagogal organisations of British Jewry can meet to discuss all relevant issues, in the interests of communal harmony and communal development.

Auspices
The Committee is an independent body, 'owned' by its constituent organisations.

Composition
Each grouping is to be represented at meetings by lay, professional and rabbinic leaders. Initially, it is anticipated that four synagogal bodies will participate – Assembly of Masorti Synagogues, Reform Synagogues of Great Britain, Union of Liberal and Progressive Synagogues, and United Synagogue. Other synagogal bodies may be invited to join on an equal basis with the unanimous agreement of the 'founding four.' The President and Chief Executive of the Board of Deputies shall be invited to be in attendance.

Venue
The Committee will meet at a mutually acceptable venue.

Frequency of Meetings

The Committee itself will meet quarterly. It may set up sub-committees, strategy and project group which will take the work forward and which may meet at other times and other venues.

Chairing of Meetings

Participating bodies, in rotation, will nominate a chair for each meeting from their delegates.

The ink on the accords was barely dry before the London Beth Din ordered the removal of the reference to discretionary Orthodox attendance at Reform, Liberal and Masorti services. Voicing their opposition to the sentence, which Levy subsequently described as 'an infelicitous piece of drafting,'[36] the dayanim declared:

> While the Beth Din warmly welcomes measures that will defuse tensions and enhance mutual respect within the community, nevertheless the Beth Din's long-standing policy has been to withhold its support of interdenominational committees. While their intentions may be commendable, they ultimately sow confusion within Anglo-Jewry. Notwithstanding the above, the conventions set out therein, in the main, conform with our guidelines, with the exception of reference to Orthodox rabbis attending non-Orthodox services. It is the ruling of the Beth Din that rabbis may not attend any services held under non-Orthodox auspices.[37]

Before this retraction, Levy had hailed the agreement as 'a considerable achievement,' adding: 'I do not believe that Orthodox Judaism has anything to fear from a dialogue with non-Orthodox Jews.' Sassienie said that it marked 'a significant move forward in the search for communal harmony and development' and would 'alter the atmosphere in the community.'

While Middleburgh voiced hopes that intra-communal relations 'can finally move on to a more sensible, mature and rational footing,' Freedman saw the Consultative Committee – which the president and chief executive of the Board of Deputies would be invited to attend – as 'the most important thing to come out of the agreement.'[38]

Welcoming the accords as 'very significant,' Manna declared that the 'enthusiasm' with which they were received was not only 'a remarkable show of consensus in Anglo-Jewry, but it also indicates that the overwhelming majority of British Jews belong in the inclusivist camp.

> The real divide in British Jewry is not between Orthodoxy and non-
> Orthodoxy, or the United Synagogue and the Reform Synagogues of
> Great Britain. Rather is it between the vast preponderance of British
> Jews who are committed to living as Jews within the modern world and
> society at large, and the fundamentalist far-right. This latter group has
> much in common with fundamentalists across the post-war religious
> spectrum whose fear of and hostility to modernity and contemporary
> society are a driving force. The significance of the Stanmore Accords lies
> in the breadth of the recognition that we are, indeed, one people – and
> must remain so.[39]

The Beth Din's statement, however, provoked surprise and dismay in
equal measure. Sources close to the deal said that 'the rabbinical court
had been kept aware of the negotiations throughout' and that Sacks had
had 'at least one meeting with Reform leaders during the negotiating
process.' Levy told the United Synagogue council that the agreement
had been negotiated 'with the full knowledge of, and some input from,
the Chief Rabbi and the Beth Din, although they did not see the final
alterations.'[40] Middleburgh remarked that his initial 'measured euphoria'
was 'slipping into despondency. We signed on the understanding that
this had the full endorsement of the Chief Rabbi and the Beth Din.'

The Union of Orthodox Hebrew Congregations described the accords
as 'marking the beginning of the end of the United Synagogue as the
guardian of an Orthodox *kehillah* [community]'; and the Federation of
Synagogues asserted that they would 'blur the clear difference between
traditional Judaism and the various Reform movements.'[41]

The JC assessed the implications of the agreement, and of the Beth
Din's involvement, within their historical context:

> The blast of criticism from Orthodox voices to the right of the United
> Synagogue was only to be expected. And, given the pattern of recent
> communal politics, it was perhaps equally predicable that the Beth
> Din would move to counter any suggestion that it was somehow less
> Orthodox than the Adath or Federation critics. Predictable, too, was the
> evident reluctance of the Chief Rabbi – who has spent an unhappy past
> few years trying, and spectacularly failing, to please both left and right
> – to enter this latest fray.
>
> But both he and the United Synagogue president will inevitably
> come under pressure in the coming days, if not to answer a right wing

whose opposition they surely expected, at least to address the implicit rejection of the Orthodox–Progressive deal by a Beth Din which at least nominally works for them.

How, or indeed whether, they choose to do so will be a defining moment for a synagogal movement which for many decades was pre-eminent not only in British Orthodoxy but in British Jewry as a whole – but a movement whose role and identity have become increasingly blurred amid criticism from both right and left, and disaffection among many grassroots congregants.[42]

While not exactly 'entering this latest fray,' Sacks sought to diffuse the situation on behalf of those who, he declared, wanted 'a community at peace':

They are troubled, as I am, by the tone of acrimony that so often seems to mar our public life. That is why I welcome the agreement signed by the lay leaders of four communal bodies to promote more harmonious relationships in Anglo-Jewry.

The document, as amended and clarified this week, is a genuine attempt to move beyond the rancour which should have no place in a community of those whose task is to walk humbly with God. The statement has nothing to do with blurring religious differences. Indeed, it recognises that profound differences exist and will continue to do so, and asks: how then shall we behave?

The answer given by Jewish law is *darchei shalom*, the ways of peace. Maimonides rules in one of his great responsa that this applies to relationships between Jew and Jew even when there are fundamental divisions between them on matters of practice and faith. He adds that the ways of peace are reciprocal. They call on Orthodox Jews to be respectful of others, but they also call on others to be respectful of Jewish law and tradition. Reciprocity will be the test of the current agreement.

I wish, therefore, to make an appeal to all those who care for the future of the community and for the integrity of our faith as a code of compassion in human affairs. The following principles should guide us.

On matters which affect us regardless of our religious differences, we work together regardless of our religious differences. On matters which touch on religious differences, we agree to differ, but with courtesy. Absence of recognition does not imply absence of respect. Think twice before condemning a fellow Jew. Establish facts before making an accusation. Exercise charity in interpretation. Honour confidences and act so as to inspire trust. Choose public expression only when private representation has been tried and failed. In public debate, be civil as well as fair to those with whom you disagree.

These things will not make us less persuasive; they will make us more so. They will create *kiddush Hashem* where too often there has been *chillul Hashem*.[43]

INTERLUDE
From First to Second

'May God, who will not forsake His people,
cause His spirit to rest in the work of our hands' [1]

The Decade of Jewish Renewal [*the Chief Rabbi wrote in September* 2001] has come to a close. Eight years ago, as part of that programme, I launched Jewish Continuity with a series of pamphlets. Much has happened since then. The community has been reinvigorated, and I want to express my thanks to the many people and organisations who have helped to make that vision a reality.

I want also to outline my thoughts for the next phase of my Chief Rabbinate. I have called it Jewish Responsibility. To me, that phrase signals what is most challenging in Jewish life; not waiting for something to happen, but joining hands to make it happen …

As a people, we are hard on ourselves: quick to criticise, slow to praise. We notice failure; success all too often passes us unawares. Abba Eban once called us 'the people who can't take yes for an answer.'

This is not a Jewish response. To the contrary, one of the fundamental Jewish values is *hakarat hatov*, 'recognising the good.' To see the world through Jewish eyes is to search out the goodness in each person, every situation – to identify it, praise it, and thereby strengthen it. That is what I want to do here: to give thanks to the British Jewish community for all it has done these past ten years in making our ancient faith new again.

Ours is a small community, one-twentieth the size of the Jewish populations of Israel or the United States. Yet for the past ten years it has shown an exuberance, energy and creativity equal to any in the world. This has been the work of thousands of individuals, hundreds of communities and dozens of organisations. British Jewry is not perfect. There is much still to do. But one thing has happened. There has been genuine renewal. As the Decade of Jewish Renewal reaches its close, I want – without naming individuals or organisations – to say thanks to some of the groups who made it happen:

• To the people who helped build more Jewish schools in the past decade than at almost any previous time in our history.

• To the teachers who made Jewish schools models of academic excellence.

• To the parents who responded in such extraordinary numbers that, however fast we build Jewish day schools, we still cannot keep up with the demand.

• To those responsible for the adult education programmes that have drawn crowds in numbers unprecedented in Anglo-Jewry.

• To the many rabbis who have made synagogue services more participative and spiritually meaningful – through such innovations as beginners' *minyanim*, explanatory services and alternative services.

• To the chazanim and choirs who have given a new lease of life to liturgical music, bringing back some of the great cantorial traditions as well as creating superb new liturgical music.

• To the rabbis and lay leaders who, by developing social, educational programmes, have helped turn congregations into communities, and shuls into genuine *batei knesset* – homes of community life in all its forms.

• To our many youth groups, who have deepened the Jewish content of their programmes and continue to be our single greatest asset when it comes to capturing the imagination and commitment of the next generation.

• To our students, who have shaped outstanding educational programmes as well as taking a leading role in fighting racism on campus.

• To the many outreach organisations who have become an important presence in the community, bringing back hundreds of estranged or alienated young Jews into an active engagement with our faith.

• To the people who in the last ten years have helped create new forms of communication within our community and beyond, among them Jewish radio programmes and websites.

• To the many organisations who have given the cultural life of our community an unprecedented range and variety.

• To the outstanding Jewish welfare organisations throughout the country, who daily care for so many in our community, with such professionalism, dignity and sensitivity.

• To the professionals and many volunteers who, in difficult times, have ensured the safety of every major communal event and institution, enabling Jewish life to continue as normal.

And, of course, there are dozens, hundreds of others. My own special thanks must go to my late and revered predecessor, Lord Jakobovits, of blessed memory, who created so much on which we have been able to build. Thinking of him, I feel as did the medieval sages when they said, 'We may be dwarves, but we sit on the shoulders of giants.'

The result has been a series of measurable changes. There are more children at Jewish day schools. There are more adults engaging in life-long learning. The activity levels of the community have risen. The Jewish voice has been more prominent in national debates. Many of our leading organisations have emerged more efficient and professional than they were before. Jewish life has become more self-confident, more exuberant. These things really are good news.

They are all the more remarkable when we consider the backdrop against which they have taken place. British culture today is aggressively secular. The place of religion in public life has become more marginal. That the Jewish community has been able to re-energise itself in these circumstances is remarkable – all the more so given the demographic fact that we are an ageing and numerically declining community. We may be smaller but we are stronger, and better equipped to face the future.

For Elaine and myself, it has been a privilege merely to be part of such a community at such a time. These achievements were not ours but yours, and we want to say 'Thank you' – to you and, above all, to the Almighty …

But to be a Jew is not to stand still. Jewish time begins with two journeys: Abraham's from Mesopotamia, Moses' and the Israelites' from Egypt. The words that set our history in motion were *lech lecha*, 'Travel, go, move on.' The time has come to chart the next stage of the journey, to look at where we are and where we must go from here …

We live today in an untraditional, even anti-traditional, age, and that is both a challenge and an opportunity. It invites us to ask the question, 'Why?' and thus remind ourselves of what Judaism really is and what it calls on us to be …

I want us to raise our sights as a community. For ten years we have built Jewish schools, revived communities, enhanced adult education, and given British Jewish life a vibrancy it has rarely had. Those are wondrous achievements and they are yours.

It would be tempting to say that there is nothing more to say – that we should keep on doing what we are doing, only more so. But I fear that if this is all, we will fail to rise to the unique challenge presented by the existence of the State of Israel and the hearing given to the Jewish voice in the liberal democracies of the West.

We will survive. But Jews do not survive in order to survive. In the first words of God to Abraham – words that set our history into motion – He said two words that still reverberate across the centuries: *vehyeh berachah*, 'be a blessing.' There is a myriad of ways in which a life can be a blessing; no two are the same. Each of us has gifts, talents, abilities, opportunities that are shared by no one else, and we are called on to share them with others in ways only we can decide.

God gave us the raw materials – life, our situation in time and space, and free will – and it is up to us, under His tutelage, to turn them into a source of blessing. That is the challenge of Jewish responsibility.

We have done much to renew our community. Let us now turn Jewish renewal into Jewish responsibility … There is no one way of doing this. It may vary from community to community, from one organisation to another, from one individual to the next. But it means turning our Judaism outwards toward our fellow Jews and our fellow humans.

It means challenging young Jews to give service to the community. It means each synagogue strengthening its welfare services. It means that each of us should ask not 'What does the Jewish community do for me?' but 'What am I doing for the Jewish community?' These are the things that change our lives, because we have helped to make the world more gracious or less lonely for someone else …

If I have learned anything in the past ten years it has been this: that when Jews give, when they share, when they say, 'If this is wrong, let me be among the first to help put it right,' they create moments, lives of such moral beauty that they tower above anything else in the contemporary landscape.

Judaism is God's call to responsibility. May we, in the years to come, be able to say: we heard, we responded, we gave, we grew. By writing others we write ourselves into the Book of Life.[2]

* * *   * * *   * * *

'In fairness to himself,' wrote Stanley Kalms in the 1996 judgmental outburst with which this volume opened, 'the Chief Rabbi should consider retiring from office. He is an academic by nature, and his talents could be immeasurably better used.' This 'extraordinary' call, wrote the JC a week later, 'has caused a public storm unprecedented in recent Anglo-Jewish communal life.'[3]

Bursting at their seams, the paper's correspondence columns – as well as community corridors, synagogue sermons, and Jews in the pews – reverberated with anger, astonishment, disgust and dismay (and with not a little approval) as they discussed 'the important issues of substance which have been raised.'

The responses came from all sides, all shades of religious opinion, all ages, all manner of men – and women. As letters (and Judaism) editor of the JC at the time, this writer was overwhelmed both by the sheer volume – and emotionalism – of the postbag and by the quality and range of the views expressed. What follows is a small but significant sample of the letters received.[4]

From Seymour G. Saideman, London N12

As president of the United Synagogue, I state my wholehearted support – and that of my colleagues – for the Chief Rabbi. He has never wavered in his messages of a tolerant, welcoming, inclusivist Orthodoxy,[5] and his leadership has been the driving force behind the revival of the United Synagogue in this, its 125th-anniversary year.

There are those who only write reports, others who build for the future in practical ways. I chose to accept the challenge of the latter. So did the Chief Rabbi.

Chief Rabbi Sacks has achieved much in a short period of time – and there is much that he still plans for our community. It would be better, therefore, to reflect on his achievements at the end of the Decade of Renewal, when the long-term vision can be clearly seen.

Meanwhile, irresponsible attacks on the Chief Rabbi and his office undermine our entire community and fuel the flames of our enemies.

From Rabbi David J. Goldberg, Liberal Jewish Synagogue, London NW8

Bravo to Sir Stanley Kalms for daring to spell out loudly what an increasing number of us – of the left, right and centre – have been thinking privately for some time, but, with that obsequious reverence for title or position which is one of Anglo-Jewry's least attractive characteristics, have refrained from saying publicly.

The Chief Rabbi of the United Synagogue, a dwindling section of the community, can no longer pretend that he is the religious representative of all Anglo-Jewry.

In hoping to placate every section of the community, he has succeeded only in disappointing all. As a healthily pluralistic community, each branch with its own organisational and religious authorities, we no longer need a single 'court Jew' to act as our spokesperson to the wider public.

From *Joy Conway, London NW11*

The Chief Rabbi made it clear, at the beginning of his term of office, that he would make the aspirations of women one of his priorities – within the framework of halachah.

As one who was involved in the recommendations of both the Kalms Review and the Chief Rabbi's review of women in the community, I have no doubts that considerable progress has been made. Women now sit on the United Synagogue council, and a pre-nuptial agreement has been endorsed by the five batei din.

The women's review has acted as a catalyst, raising awareness in the community and encouraging many positive moves.[6] The Chief Rabbi deserves the support of those members of the community who wish to see mainstream Orthodoxy flourish in the modern world.

From *Julia Bard, David Rosenberg, London NW1*

Contrary to Sir Stanley Kalms' argument, Chief Rabbi Sacks was never progressive on women's – or any other – issues. Few Jews had any illusions that he would affect their lives in any way at all, nor do they care whether he resigns or not.

There is a great deal of life and creativity in our community, which makes an important contribution to British society as a whole. However, this is in spite of, rather than because of, the way the community is 'led.'

Anglo-Jewry is often cited as a role model for other, more recent, immigrant communities. If there is one lesson we can pass on, it is that minorities should fight hard to promote democracy, pluralism, equality and tolerance within their own communities as much as within the wider society, and to challenge leaders who claim to speak or act in their name.

From *Fred S. Worms, London N6*

Sir Stanley Kalms' letter, calling on Chief Rabbi Dr Jonathan Sacks to retire, suggests a negative response. The resolution of genuine grievances and different approaches to our communal problems cannot be achieved by confrontation in the media.

The Chief Rabbi is the first to admit that, among the many positive developments in Anglo-Jewry during the past three years, some mistakes were made. I know from personal experience that he is willing to listen.

I have worked with Stanley Kalms for many years, both in the Jewish Educational Development Trust and in the founding of Immanuel College.[7] He is a pragmatist and a supreme realist.

It is all the more surprising, therefore, that he makes a rhetorical request which he knows will not be fulfilled. Its only effect will be the weakening of the authority of the Chief Rabbinate and the standing of the community, which is at present held in high esteem by the government and the leaders of the various Christian denominations.

A rabbinical council whose president would change every six or twelve months would be not a movable feast but an ongoing disaster. Evolutionary changes are preferable to the guillotine.

From Lord Woolf of Barnes, Sidney Corob, Israel Finestein, QC, Sir Peter Millet, Clive Marks, London W1

We read Sir Stanley Kalms' letter with some astonishment. Dr Sacks has been our Chief Rabbi for less than five years. He became Chief Rabbi in his early forties, a remarkable young man, because he was then – and still is – the best-qualified person to be the holder of that office.

After his appointment, the Chief Rabbi articulated with eloquence the deep problems which were then facing the community, and which are still threatening its very survival. They are problems which he knew were immensely difficult to solve.

However, by his sermons, writings and lectures, he created a vision as to how this might be achieved. In addition, he personally was responsible for highly imaginative community-wide initiatives which could help to achieve the results that are so important for the community's well-being.

The combination of the Chief Rabbi's eloquence and initiatives did raise high expectations across the community. This was true even of those sections which traditionally have been distrustful of the Office of the Chief Rabbi. The expectations have not all been met. For some, events have moved too fast; for others, they have not moved fast enough.

Chief Rabbi Sacks has acknowledged that, with the wisdom of hindsight, it can be seen that mistakes have been made which should not have been made. The ambitious nature of his programme probably made this inevitable, and there were bound to be disappointments.

However, when they occurred, the Chief Rabbi, in view of all that he has striven to do, was entitled to receive the support and help of those who share his vision. This is especially true at a time when the leaders of the community, as well as the Chief Rabbi, are still struggling to find the best way of achieving the progress which we know the great majority of the community would like to see.

We would have preferred to express our support personally to the Chief Rabbi and not through the press. However, as Sir Stanley has made a public call for his resignation, we feel it should be known that the vast majority of the members of the community such as ourselves, who are engaged in a great many communal activities, strongly dissent from the views expressed in Sir Stanley's letter.

From Ronnie Landau, London N12[8]

It was a depressing, if predictable, experience to read the responses from some of Anglo-Jewry's notables to Sir Stanley Kalms' letter. It all added up to a classic Establishment defence of the status quo: a graphic illustration, rather than a serious refutation, of the central point Sir Stanley was making.

The responses seemed to concentrate on the more personal dimensions of Sir Stanley's attack, while choosing to ignore its most compelling message. This was that Anglo-Jewry is a deeply disappointing, inconsequential and − quite possibly − moribund community, whose unimaginative 'leaders' are squabbling and fiddling while we impale ourselves on territorialism, bigotry and a fixation on outmoded structures and leadership models.

I am not qualified to judge the extent to which Sir Stanley's views may be born of a personal agenda. The substance of a person's argument, it seems to me, is in any case far more important than any speculation about the psychological background to its composition. But one thing is clear: the only way forward for this community is a commitment to *real* inclusiveness and *genuine* pluralism.

A rampant and contemptuous secularism is as unacceptable as is an intolerant religiosity − or, indeed, as is any monolithic approach to the inescapably fragmented condition that is contemporary Jewishness. An 'inclusivism' that is merely a hidden code for denominational one-upmanship, and even proselytising, or for shoring up the same old power bases, is anathema to an inspirational, forward-thinking remedy for our ailment.

And that is why Jewish Continuity, as at present conceived, seems to be such a hopelessly unoriginal, misdirected and largely self-defeating enterprise.

We are now celebrating the centenary of Theodor Herzl's *Der Judenstaat* − and indeed, later this year, the 207th anniversary of the

French Revolution. We should perhaps remember, therefore, that, in contradistinction to Fred Worms' point, it is sometimes revolution and not evolution, or conservatism masquerading as 'continuity' – a bland, overused and, by now, thoroughly debased term – that has brought innovation, dynamism and, yes, complexity to modern Jewish existence, infusing it with fresh life.

The future – especially the educational future – of Anglo-Jewry lies in the hands of its grass roots, not of its self-proclaimed leaders. That is the revolution, the deep revolution, we should be trying to effect. To achieve it, we must somehow work around, or outside of, the overarching political and institutional structures that have frustrated even so well-intentioned and brilliant a thinker as Jonathan Sacks.

That is also why it is perfectly appropriate that such a debate should take place in the letters pages of the *Jewish Chronicle*.

From Gabrielle Bradfield (aged 15), London NW8

Finally, Judaism is gaining the respect it deserves. Our values are now recognised as those to which the rest of society aspires. But there is one problem: relaying our messages to those outside the Jewish community. The only way is to present a united front, and to show by example. To do this, we need a driving force, focusing attention on the job in hand.

Having had the privilege of hearing the Chief Rabbi, I feel that here lies our chance. How many other men with such charisma are dedicating their lives – and talents – to Anglo-Jewry? This is truly the face of modern Judaism.

So why do so many in the community deem it necessary to tear down the Chief Rabbi at every opportunity? Whatever their reasons, they are ripping apart Judaism at its seams.

The Jewish community has much to offer the world. But that can be achieved only if it comes together as one body, with one leader. And, in my view, that leader is Rabbi Sacks.

From Cyril M. Jacobs, Hove

Sir Stanley's views will be supported by middle-of-the-road Jewry – the vast majority – in this country and beyond. If only the Chief Rabbi and his dayanim would listen to the voice of that gathering swell, the drift from Orthodoxy would be slowed down, if not halted.

From the Rev Dr Norman Gale, chairman, Rabbinical Council of the United Synagogue;
Rabbi Yitzchok Rubin, chairman, Rabbinical Council of the Provinces, Manchester

We write on behalf of our colleagues in the Orthodox rabbinate to deplore the unprecedented and outrageous call for the retirement of our esteemed Chief Rabbi.

Since his installation, Chief Rabbi Sacks has embarked on a breathtaking series of inspirational pastoral visits throughout Britain and beyond. He has lifted all who have heard him both by virtue of his immense erudition and oratory and through his enthusiasm, vision and determination to strengthen and promote religious observance and spiritual values.

We look forward to many years of his guiding and inspiring Anglo-Jewry to the fulfilment of its undoubted religious and spiritual potential.

From Natan Tiefenbrun, London EC2

As a young member of the community, heavily involved in Jewish education, I share the frustrations voiced by Sir Stanley Kalms, and others, that the pace of change within the community is too slow. While I concur with the view that Chief Rabbi Sacks has been constrained by communal politics in achieving his vision for the renewal of British Jewry, I strongly disagree, however, with calls for his resignation.

The Chief Rabbi's vision for our community is one that inspires my generation. We should be ever-more vocal in our support of his leadership, conferring on him the authority to sweep aside the suffocating influence of vested political interests and to take bold decisions in our name.

There is no justification for the siege mentality among the Orthodox leadership at a time of such opportunity, and less justification still for the resignation and pessimism expressed by Sir Stanley. The Limmud conference, and the reception the young participants gave to dynamic Orthodox rabbis and teachers from Israel and the United States, proved that there is a bright future for Orthodoxy in Britain.[9]

The Chief Rabbi must be given the mandate and freedom to lead effectively.

From I. Fromson, president, Representative Council; S, Goldblatt, chairman, Synagogue
Council; J. Rowe, chairman, Joint Israel Appeal; A. Schwalbe, president, Kashrut Commission;
Joy Wolfe, president, Zionist Central Council; Sir Sidney Hamburger, Salford

Chief Rabbi Sacks, like his illustrious predecessor, has brought enormous
energy, eloquence and intellect to his office and is held in the highest
esteem by Jew and non-Jew in whichever circle he moves. The institution
of the Chief Rabbinate is the envy of diaspora communities elsewhere,
and its central unifying force in Anglo-Jewry is beyond question and
must be preserved.

The Chief Rabbi has his critics, and we acknowledge that, collectively
and individually, we do not necessarily agree with every detailed decision he
has made. But there is a right and proper way to deal with such situations,
and Sir Stanley Kalms knows the 'corridors of power' better than most.

Rabbi Sacks' undertaking to build bridges between different sectors
of our community has aroused the admiration and respect of all, and, in
his efforts to achieve the seemingly impossible, he is entitled to look for
support from those in positions of authority. This we offer him.

Although we are all elected officers of major institutions in the
Manchester community, we write this letter in our personal capacities.

From N. S. Roseman, Bournemouth

Sir Stanley Kalms has recognised what most of your correspondents refuse
to acknowledge: that Anglo-Jewry is in a state of terminal decline, and
that time is not on the Chief Rabbi's side. If they believe, as I do, that the
community is worth saving, they will surely see the extent to which it has
been let down by Rabbi Sacks.

His appointment was a last attempt to reverse the trend and to return to
a period of hope. But from the moment he backtracked on his support for
an inclusivist Jewish Continuity programme, the writing was on the wall.

From Sir Ian Gainsford, London SW1

The Chief Rabbi of the United Hebrew Congregations of the
Commonwealth is elected as a spiritual leader of the Jewish community.
His counsel is sought on a wide range of matters of public concern. The
need is for a leader who represents Jewish values to the wider world
and who, in a climate of divisiveness, can aim to promote a vision with

which the many conflicting groups within the community can identify. This role is bound to be less dramatic than that of the leader of a faction, but it is what our community needs if it is not to fall apart.

Chief Rabbi Sacks is a man of exceptional intellectual gifts, which he has used fully in discharging the duties of his office. At a time of difficulty in attracting the most able minds to communal leadership, it seems perverse to attempt to marginalise him by suggesting that his academic excellence could be better developed elsewhere. His place is at the centre, and not at the margins, of communal affairs.

From Alan K.Wall, London N12

Orthodox Jewry must change with the times. If the Chief Rabbi is unable, or unwilling, to acknowledge the growth of other factions, it is likely that, within a decade or two, the United Synagogue will be little more than a communal backwater.

From Dr Lionel Kopelowitz, past president, Board of Deputies, London W9

Sir Stanley refers to the Chief Rabbi's 'electoral pledge.' The Chief Rabbi is not a political leader putting a manifesto before the country in order to gain votes. He outlined his approach in his induction address, but, apart from referring to a decade of renewal, did not specify a time span.

The Chief Rabbi and the community have powers neither to legislate nor to raise money by taxation. Jewish leaders are limited to powers of persuasion, and thereby convince the community of a policy to be followed. That inevitably requires much time and debate.

Sir Stanley's advice smacks of gross impertinence. He is wrong – and his letter should never have been written.

From Michael Gross, London NW1

The community can breathe a huge sigh of relief in finding that the Chief Rabbi is his own man. Success in retailing does not bring with it theological competence. Sir Stanley should stick to what he understands and leave the Chief Rabbi to provide the spiritual leadership, which he is clearly better qualified to do.

From Jonathan Shack, London NW8

In his successful business career, Sir Stanley has always emphasised the long term and investing for the future. When his company was languishing a few years ago, he did not retire. Nor should Rabbi Sacks now.

From Professor Leslie Wagner, Leeds

Who is Stanley Kalms?

From John de Lange, London N12

I know who Stanley Kalms is, but what does Leslie Wagner profess?

* * *   * * *   * * *

'The central issue has remained constant,' declared the Jewish Chronicle in response to this clamour. 'Can, or should, United Synagogue Orthodoxy find a way within the limits of Jewish law and tradition to be more inclusive of those of its congregants, notably women, who feel excluded from Orthodox religious life – and more open in its dealings with non-Orthodox movements?

How, and whether, that issue is resolved will have a crucial effect on the future direction of the Chief Rabbinate, the United Synagogue and the Anglo-Jewish community as a whole. Despite Sir Stanley's letter, nothing suggests that doing away with the Chief Rabbinate would be likely to bring such a resolution any closer. Nor is there any figure within Anglo-Jewish Orthodoxy who seems remotely as well equipped – as an intellect, writer and communicator – as Rabbi Sacks to do so.

The rub, of course, is that since assuming office nearly four and a half years ago, Rabbi Sacks has seemed alternately torn between those on opposing ideological wings of the US. The moderniser in him has launched a series of ambitious initiatives – the women's review and Jewish Continuity, to name but two of the most important. The creature – some would say 'prisoner' – of the status quo in Rabbi Sacks has, meanwhile, moved with agonising slowness in implementing many of the recommendations of the women's review ...

Yet, amid the political storm clouds which have gathered in the past few weeks, there is also the proverbial silver lining. As reflected in the response on our letters pages to Sir Stanley's broadside, a sizeable portion of Anglo-Jewry – encompassing the Orthodox centre and those on its immediate left and right – does respect and support Rabbi Sacks. Those coming out against the suggestion that he retreat to academia share a vision of a community whose disparate religious and other groupings can combine an unflagging and self-confident attachment to their own beliefs with a respect for diversity, a willingness to discuss and debate – and a hope that by working together, Anglo-Jewry can become not a victim of partition, but a community that is greater than the sum of its parts.

No Chief Rabbi, least of all one coming to office at such a delicate time in our communal history, can hope to please everyone. But Rabbi Sacks brings extraordinary gifts to the office. If he can rise above the fear of displeasing those on the communal extremes – and move forward with a new sense of assurance and clarity to articulate the hopes of a broadly tolerant and forward-looking centre – he will find that he has far wider support than he appears to imagine.[10]

In a parallel comment, Chaim Bermant asserted: 'Were the Chief Rabbinate to be abolished, the Beth Din would step forward to fill the vacuum, and all the fears Sir Stanley has voiced about the future of the community would be fulfilled in every detail. The fractiousness, pettiness and bigotry he so rightly abhors would become its dominant features. In fact, it would not be long before Sir Stanley would join with the rest of us to cry with one voice: "Come back, Jonathan, all is forgiven!"'[11]

* * *   * * *   * * *

Five years after his first call on Sacks to resign, and two years before his second such call, Kalms heeded Bermant's cry with a declaration of support for his beleaguered Chief. Contributing to the *Jewish Chronicle* a 'personal view' – a headmaster's report, so to speak – on the Decade of Jewish Renewal, he began: '"It's not a job for a Yiddisher boy" is the classic reaction to the student who wanted to become a rabbi. I don't know what the riposte is to "even a Chief Rabbi," but the jibe seems *passé*, when the student has a first in philosophy from Cambridge.

Jonathan Sacks was the rabbi at Golders Green Synagogue when we first met in 1979. I was a new honorary officer at Stanmore and I invited him home for some community talk. Our first conversation was sharp as I probed him for signs of fresh thinking, and I struck gold.

Within a few weeks, we were friends and, for the next twelve years, we spoke, met or planned daily. It needed no insight to sense that the United Synagogue was heading towards the depths of decline. A traditional antagonism reigned between the lay leadership and their rabbis, employer/employee relations at their worst: the organisation was run with unrivalled inefficiency by a centralist administration and a stifling constitution and was bogged down in ideological battles that should have been ditched long ago.

This was the background to Jonathan Sacks' preparation for office. He saw the challenges, the problems and the opportunities. He saw some of the limitations of office and, not unreasonably, underestimated them. The office is, in reality, an appointment of the United Synagogue and demands the good will of the right, centre and left to give it purpose and effect. A Chief Rabbi needs to be a trained navigator. But unburdened by a rabbinical family background, he saw integrity and reason around every corner.

At the time, Lord Jakobovits was busy with changes which would increase the influence and reputation of the Chief Rabbinate. A man of deep self-confidence and rabbinic pedigree, with a unique home support system – Lady Jakobovits – he had the strength to break with the authoritarianism of his employers. Gathering around him substantial lay leaders from across the community, he formed the Jewish Educational Development Trust (JEDT) to reinvigorate Jewish education outside of the impoverished and bureaucratic hand of the United Synagogue.

I was privileged to be the JEDT's first chairman and, later on, chairman of Jews' College. We were a formidable team to inject some fresh thinking into Anglo-Jewish life, and one of our major sources of motivation was our hopes for the Chief Rabbi-to-be.

Jonathan Sacks hit the ground running. He became principal of Jews' College, and a coterie of new students started their career under his auspices. His years of preparation for his inevitable office were constructive. A prolific author, he proved an inspiring writer of manifestos, preaching his vision of an inclusivist Jewish society.

Our greatest success, perhaps, in establishing the eligibility of Jonathan Sacks as natural successor to Chief Rabbi Jakobovits was our first 'Traditional Alternatives' conference in 1989. It was an ambitious event – a full day of challenging seminars with world-famous participants – to set out an agenda for modern Orthodoxy.

Perhaps it was now that Rabbi Sacks should have heard the first early-warning sirens. Two of our guest speakers, Rabbi David Bleich and

Rabbi Emmanuel Feldman, would not share the platform with another important guest, Rabbi David Hartman – and they don't come more kosher – for reasons which, to the middle ground, were distinctly uncomfortable. So Rabbi Hartman held forth from the floor of the conference with powerful and persuasive arguments for open dialogue among all Jews. Sacks and Hartman lifted their audience that day.

But, for Sacks, there was still a long haul to office. During this period, it is not unique for candidates to express ideas which raise expectations by playing to the widest audiences. Opposition politicians do it all the time – it's the way the game is played.

He was duly appointed Chief Rabbi in 1990, a year before taking office on 1 September, 1991, at the age of 43. The appointment was until 65, compared with 70 for Lord Jakobovits. But it is worth reflecting whether it is wise to make a virtual lifetime appointment for any office. Excessive security can have an adverse effect. Gone are the uncertainties that are needed to counterbalance over-confidence and dogmatism.

Although Jonathan Sacks and I had remained as close as ever up to his induction, I had already predicted that our personal journey was soon to be at its end – rightly so. A new Chief Rabbi needs new advisers, fresh supporters and wider alliances.

Unfortunately, a new Chief Rabbi also enters an office without any administrative or executive back-up worth speaking of – no cluster of advisers, few buttons to press. Rather, he moves into little more than a vacuum which he speedily must fill, both practically and politically.

No Chief Rabbi has started so nobly. His induction speech announcing the Decade of Jewish Renewal was inspirational. The seeds had been sown by Lord Jakobovits and there was enthusiasm across the community: even the cynics kept a low profile. A good working relationship quickly developed with lay leaders and rabbis.

But soon the aspirations of the manifesto hit the rocks of the limitations of office. Attempting to bridge religious divisions, he strayed into treacherous waters. Reforms for women's rights were lobbed into the long grass.

The Chief Rabbi's tendency to play to his weakness – he can be excessively secretive – was exposed, and the community remained factionalised. He mislaid many of his old and trusted friends and, lacking communication and management skills, continued to trail too many expectations which fell at low hurdles.

He had come to office at a time when the United Synagogue itself was tottering. Its president, Sidney Frosh, sensing disaster ahead, had asked me to conduct a full review of the United Synagogue's activities and prospects. *A Time for Change*, the 300-page report published by a small team of us in 1992, revealed that the US was plunging into a financial black hole. But its theme was positive – in particular, recommending more freedom for individual synagogues from head office to manage their own affairs – and strongly supportive of Rabbi Sacks.

The process of implementing change has been slow: it is still going on. But it should have created greater possibilities for the Chief Rabbi. Without rational explanation, however, he got embroiled quite unnecessarily in a right-left internecine battle and, lacking mature advice or perhaps unwilling to share confidences, he retired, badly scorched, to the sidelines.

It has been a troubled decade. Always full of promise, he has searched, occasionally misrouted, stumbled, challenged. But even in his darkest moments, a bright light of integrity and aspiration always shows.

With the benefit of hindsight, the community must now take stock. We have, in the Chief Rabbi, an outstanding, articulate and gifted leader. His ability to translate the wealth of our heritage into contemporary language and practical application is inspirational. He has captured the minds of serious politicians, leading clerics from other faiths, community leaders, intellectuals throughout the world and, equally important, enjoys serious support in Israel.

He has leapt from the confines of being head of a modest Jewish organisation to being a leading spokesman on far wider issues of concern to society. He has the support and understanding of his honorary officers, men with wider vision than has been customary.

He is respected in the corridors of power for the sheer quality of his contribution to addressing the core problems of our confused, twenty-first-century society. This is reflected in his books. They humanise religion and remind us of its great potential. Perhaps they promise too much. Sacks has the tantalising tendency to hint that the next chapter will be a key to self-enlightenment, and the next chapter never quite arrives. But his willingness to explore new paths reflects his philosophical distinction.

In all our interests, the Chief Rabbi must be allowed to discard any surplus baggage of his first ten years. He must be free from censure on communal and religious controversies for which the solutions lie elsewhere.

Nevertheless, he must still clarify the inconsistencies of his first decade. Explanation is never an easy task, but we are in the soul-searching business and the exercise needs doing.

What and where are his boundaries to inclusivism, to tolerance? Have the fundamentalist threats of the right been exorcised or are they still a serious influence? Can their intolerance be accepted in modern Orthodoxy?

The office of Chief Rabbi has created a unique base for a gifted man, but the responsibility to his community for clarity would make the next decade a less ambivalent journey.

To give value to the community that employs him, he must be permitted to deploy his high intellectual talents. The Chief Rabbi has the drive and the opportunity to set the pace and influence the high ground of contemporary political thinking. He ought to be the chosen instrument for carrying Jewish tradition and Judeo–Christian philosophy into the vanguard of social policy.

The last ten years have certainly seen mixed fortunes, but so would ten years in anybody's life. Today, the Chief Rabbi is serene. He is blessed with an outstanding rebbetzen, Elaine, who is a rock of support, and a joyful family. He has listened to advice and reorganised his working life to play to his strengths.

He is supportive of all community endeavours that lead to Jewish continuity. He remains inclusivist by nature, but is now rather more aware that others have to want it equally. With his confidence restored, he must do more to cultivate the common ground. He, like all of us, agonises over Israel.

We could be in for an inspirational ride over the next ten years. But as I said, Jonathan Sacks hit the ground running. Is the Chief Rabbi a sprinter or a marathon runner? A great deal depends on the answer.[12]

* * *   * * *   * * *

Two months into his second decade, the Chief Rabbi – in the words of a JC editorial – 'undertook a change of course which would have been unthinkable during the interdenominational turbulence in the Jewish community which marked much of his first decade in office.'[13] The 'unthinkable' was that he had recommended the elevation of a Progressive rabbi to join him as the second full president of the Council of Christians and Jews (CCJ).

The Council, Britain's oldest national interfaith organisation, was established in 1942 to promote religious and cultural understanding between Christians and Jews, to seek the elimination of religious and racial prejudice, hatred and discrimination – particularly anti-Semitism – and to foster 'religious and racial harmony on the basis of ethical and social teachings common to Christianity and Judaism.' While maintaining these objectives, in later years it responded to Britain's demographic and ethnic revolution by working in a multifaith context – with, among others, Muslims and Hindus – as part of its overall programme.

The setting for Sacks' 'change of course' was described nearly three years earlier by Clifford Longley, then the *Daily Telegraph*'s religious affairs editor, in a column intriguingly headed 'Is this the end for the Chief Rabbi?' Should Britain have one Chief Rabbi, asked Longley, 'or one and a half, or even four,' to lead its 300,000-strong Jewish community into the next century?

> That is, in effect, the issue to be decided at a special meeting on Tuesday where, strangely, many of those entitled to vote will be not Jews but Christians. They will be debating an amendment to the constitution of the Council of Christians and Jews to allow the appointment of an associate president.
>
> This is the solution favoured by the present Chief Rabbi, Dr Jonathan Sacks, to a bitter dispute between Orthodox and Progressive Jews which has led some of the latter to reject his right to the title. Dr Sacks is the sole Jewish president of the Council, the five Christian presidents being the Archbishop of Canterbury, the Cardinal Archbishop of Westminster, the Greek Orthodox Archbishop of Great Britain, the Moderator of the General Assembly of the Church of Scotland, and the Moderator of the Free Church Federal Council.
>
> In helping to define the Jewish pecking order in Britain, the CCJ has taken on a significance rather outside its original function. Since the nineteenth century, the Chief Rabbinate has spoken for all British Jews in their relations with other faiths and with the secular world. The title goes with the leadership of the United Hebrew Congregations, the largest synagogue grouping in Britain, but its jurisdiction has never been accepted by non-Orthodox Jews in internal Jewish matters.[14]

Calls for a second Jewish presidency of the Council had been resisted by successive Chief Rabbis for more than twenty years, and diehard opposition remained within the Orthodox fold. The suggestion had most recently been made in May 1997, when the respective lay chairmen of the Reform, Liberal and Masorti synagogal bodies wrote to the Bishop of Oxford, Richard Harries – chairman of the CCJ's executive committee – requesting such an appointment.

'We represent,' they told the bishop, 'a very sizeable – and growing – proportion of the Jewish community. A second Jewish presidency would not only reflect truthfully and honestly the structure of the British community, just as the five Christian presidents reflect the main "building blocks" of the Christian community, but it would also recognise our particular interest in, and contribution to, interfaith dialogue and the work of the CCJ over many years ... It is our fervent hope that this proposal will be seen, not only as fair and reasonable, but as a strengthening of our commitment to the Council of Christians and Jews, and a positive step forward.'[15]

Even as the 1999 constitutional amendment was being put to the test, Chief Rabbinate Council ex-delegate and CCJ member Lionel Kopelowitz announced that he would vote against it. 'It will dilute the Chief Rabbi's role as the public religious representative of the whole community,' he declared.[16]

The amendment, which would be reviewed after two years, involved the appointment of a leading non-Orthodox rabbi as associate president of the CCJ, although, wrote Longley, 'Dr Sacks' most vehement Jewish critics want a full second Jewish president now and are using this to undermine his standing as the sole representative of the Jewish community in its external relations. The Chief Rabbi has let it be known that he would resign from the Council rather than allow this to happen.

'The compromise is opposed by the former Chief Rabbi, Lord Jakobovits, who fears that even a Jewish associate presidency would destroy the unique status of the Chief Rabbi. Indeed, some Progressive backers of the compromise hope that the word "associate" will be quietly dropped as time goes by. Complete parity with the Christians immediately, which some non-Orthodox Jews would prefer, would mean appointing additional presidents from each of the non-Orthodox elements – the Liberals, the Reform, and the Masorti.'[17]

Since its foundation, noted Longley, the Council had served as a neutral meeting ground where Orthodox and non-Orthodox Jewish leaders could meet discreetly to talk over their problems. But the dispute following Hugo Gryn's death had 'brought relations between the Chief Rabbi and the non-Orthodox to breaking point' and had demonstrated that the CCJ 'has manifestly failed in that purpose.'

After months of 'patient diplomacy,' the Council's executive committee believed that it had found an acceptable compromise. This entailed the appointment of Bayfield as the first associate president, but complaints from some Liberal leaders led him to withdraw his name 'for the time being.' The position was therefore to remain vacant until the non-Orthodox reached agreement on how to fill it.

Days after Longley's article appeared, the CCJ voted for the amendment, by eighty-four votes to sixteen, 'despite continued infighting within the Progressive movement over the deal.'[18] In a statement, John Rayner, the Liberals' life-president, claimed the arrangement had resulted from 'collusion' between Reform leaders and Sacks, 'who initially suggested the idea.' Middleburgh, as executive head of the Union of Liberal and Progressive Synagogues, said that the ULPS had not been kept informed of the talks, and that while he accepted the 'democratic vote,' the deal itself had not emerged from a 'democratic process.'

Reform leaders welcomed the vote as a 'long-overdue recognition of the prominent role the Progressive community has always played in interfaith work.' But Bayfield added: 'I will do nothing to endanger the unity of Progressive Judaism as it receives a long-sought and much-deserved place and profile in the Jewish and wider communities.'

The Rev Malcolm Weisman, representing the Chief Rabbi at the meeting, called the vote 'a sensible step forward, which could eventually lead to a full presidency.'[19] Before the year's end, Albert Friedlander, by then emeritus minister of the Westminster Synagogue, became associate president and, just two years later – as a result of the Chief Rabbi's 'change of course' – was appointed a full president alongside Sacks.

His elevation followed approval by the five Christian presidents, and was additionally made 'in specific recognition of his outstanding personal contribution to interfaith relations in Britain and abroad.' The appointment was welcomed by Middleburgh, who said that it gave 'the Reform and Liberal movements their own representation at the CCJ top table.' Friedlander commented: 'I feel honoured by the invitation from the Chief Rabbi and Archbishop of Canterbury. I did check with my Liberal colleagues and would not have accepted the post without their support.'[20]

Focusing on the wider implications, the *Jewish Chronicle* observed: 'The effect of the change will obviously go beyond Rabbi Friedlander, since it ends an effective Orthodox monopoly of top-level Jewish representation on the CCJ. Surely aware of this, Chief Rabbi Sacks deserves both praise and support for having backed up with action a frequent verbal commitment to the idea of widened Orthodox–Progressive co-operation in "non-halachic" areas. Mutual tolerance and co-operation within the community should take priority over interdenominational rivalry.'[21]

Referring to such rivalry that had resulted in the Progressive presidency, Longley had – nearly three years earlier – warned of other concerns:

> There are several dangers in the situation. The CCJ is still the first line of defence against the return of anti-Semitism in Britain or elsewhere. It is the senior member in an international network of such bodies, which

still have vital work to do. It must not be allowed to be fatally wounded by an internal Jewish quarrel.

The presidency of the CCJ is still the only official forum where the religious and moral leadership of the nation is gathered together. Dr Jonathan Sacks has given an outstanding moral lead to the nation, and his contribution must not be lost.

There is a further suggestion to be heard from Orthodox Jewish sources which, as a friend and admirer of Dr Sacks, I hardly dare to pass on. But if he were to find a pressing reason to continue his work of national moral leadership in another guise – such as an Oxbridge philosophy chair and a seat in the House of Lords – the way would be cleared for a more emollient successor to head the United Hebrew Congregations. The office and title of Chief Rabbi could then be removed from controversy once more. Perhaps.[22]

7

The Indignity of Difference

'*In each generation the* Shechinah, *the Divine Presence, rests with those who take our old faith and make it new again.*'[1]

In his letter to Dayan Chenoch Padwa, Sacks had noted that his writings, articles and broadcasts had gained for him 'considerable standing in non-Jewish eyes.' Others, too, had lauded the Chief Rabbi's achievements, though not always in totally uncritical terms.

'Dr Sacks,' wrote Chaim Bermant after the Masorti imbroglio, 'brings many qualities to his office, including wide curiosity and an amazing breadth of knowledge. There is hardly a major philosopher whom he has not studied, or a major writer – to say nothing of any number of minor ones – he has not read. He is, in that respect certainly, by far the most catholic Chief Rabbi we have had. Why, then, this attempt to ingratiate himself with people who define themselves by their narrowness, who regard his very qualities as a handicap, and who have never recognised, and will never recognise, his office?'[2]

'Almost from the moment of his elevation to the most prestigious religious post in Anglo-Jewry,' declared the *Jewish Chronicle* during the same period,

> Rabbi Sacks has seemed a leader of both immense promise and profound paradox. A Cambridge philosophy scholar, he has demonstrated in his speeches and, above all, his writings a rare combination of intellectual agility, academic rigour, and almost poetic eloquence. He has read widely – from Maimonides and Montesquieu to Pirkei Avot and Plato. Having solidified his own faith through a personal odyssey from Cambridge to Crown Heights, he has a keen sense of the interplay between committed, Orthodox Judaism and those many Jews on the margins of religious and communal life, or indeed outside them.
>
> Through his 'Traditional Alternatives' initiative, he set out to relate the age-old beauties of the Torah to the closing years of the twentieth century. His aim – in the spirit of openness, and inclusivism – was to reinvigorate and enrich Anglo-Jewish life. In his induction address as Chief Rabbi, he

lamented inter-communal divisions, reached out to the disaffected, and trumpeted 'renewal' ... Yet the paradoxes also emerged. In part, no doubt, they were due to the expectations raised by his Kennedyesque inaugural flourishes. Equally, they may have stemmed from a sense of vulnerability: having been schooled at Cambridge rather than yeshivah, his Judaic credentials on the right were clearly suspect ...[3]

Seeking the following week to resolve the 'paradoxes,' the paper concluded: 'Chief Rabbi Sacks is absolutely correct in asserting that a strong and growing Orthodox Judaism will crucially help to guarantee the Jewish continuity which he so passionately seeks. But a strong Orthodoxy should also imply a self-confidence in its own beliefs and practice – a self-confidence that need not feel threatened by a far more open dialogue, and partnership, with other movements in pursuit of Anglo-Jewry's future.'[4]

While the Masorti affair was still running, Sacks published *Faith in the Future*,[5] largely a reworking of earlier essays and broadcasts on 'major themes of our times.' Writing in his preface that 'as Chief Rabbi, I am usually called on to address Jewish audiences,' he added: 'But there are times when the audience is wider, and the message more universal in scope. The chapters gathered here are of the second kind. They form a composite picture of what I have tried to say, these past few years, as a Jew in a society of people of many faiths, and some of none.

'At first, I found this a difficult experience. It is so easy to speak with people who share your faith, and so hard to communicate with those who don't. But slowly I discovered that talking across the fences that divide us is important. Not only because it helps us understand each other and our differences, but also because it helps us understand ourselves. We find out what we share and also what we uniquely own ... This book, then, is a Jewish contribution to a conversation in which many voices deserve to be heard.'[6]

Introducing Sacks to his 'wider audience,' Clifford Longley – Gledhill's predecessor as religion correspondent of *The Times* – wrote in the book:

> Most of those who already know of him know him as the Chief Rabbi of
> Great Britain, the head man of the Orthodox Jewish community in Britain.
> But Orthodox Jews will forgive me for saying, at least in this context, that
> is by no means the most important thing about him.
>
> Even before his name became prominent in his own community, some
> of us had picked up rumours that there was a fresh face on the block, a new
> and exciting talent that had attached itself to one of the more conservative
> religious institutions in Britain, the United Hebrew Congregations. It was

his growing reputation for originality and sheer intelligence that quickly took him to the headship of Jews' College in London, which is responsible for training Britain's Orthodox rabbis, and eventually brought him to the attention of the BBC. It was by this means that he first became a national figure, when his series of radio Reith lectures in 1990 captured widespread attention, if a little puzzlement too, for his lucid and thoughtful warnings about the moral and spiritual state of Western society.

This was a voice we had not heard before … Jonathan Sacks is a next-door neighbour, a fellow Englishman, one of us. Even when he is boring, which is not very often, he is boring in an English sort of way. Yet that is still not quite the essential point about him. He has not invented a new message. What he has done is to understand an old one, but to understand it so well that he can see what it has to say to us, even to non-Jews who inhabit an utterly different world from that in which the message first took shape.[7]

Reviewing *Faith in the Future* in its broader dimension, Rabbi Norman Solomon, of the Oxford Centre for Hebrew and Jewish Studies, highlighted its 'current of optimism,' its 'interplay of tradition and modernity,' and 'the warmth of personal experience which shines through.' The book, he wrote, 'will enhance the public image of Judaism. It should also stimulate intelligent discussion within the Jewish community.' A few paragraphs on, widening this point, he added: 'I concur with Sacks' own pluralist outlook, but courage is needed to acknowledge that this arises from Enlightenment philosophy, not from normative Judaism. Further courage is needed to extend pluralism, as it should be extended, to non-Orthodox forms of Judaism.'[8]

The Chief Rabbi, commented the JC – taking up Solomon's remark – 'is especially eloquent in his recurrent use of the metaphor of Babel to make a point of Judaic "pluralism" towards other faiths. Judaism, he writes, is one of many expressions of truth, one of many moral "languages" – each equally important for those who speak it; each, ideally, enriching the whole by respecting and conversing with the others …

'Pointedly, Rabbi Sacks does not go so far as to suggest that this implies a pluralism *within* Judaism, much less a pluralism *of* Judaisms. To do so would be to contradict the very notion and defining tenet of Orthodoxy … In *Faith in the Future*, he has positioned himself as a voice of moral leadership in wider society. A no-less-important vocation lies in bringing the same Judaic self-confidence with which he seeks engagement with other faiths to the construction of a new, vibrant and open religious dialogue within Anglo-Jewry.'[9]

Answering some of these points in a later interview, Sacks referred to engagement and dialogue in the context of the ongoing controversies within Anglo-Jewry, which he described as 'a very unpleasant place because of the internal political campaigns that have been run, some from the right of our community and some from the left.

I have tried hard [he said] to do many things in my Chief Rabbinate: to initiate programmes for the community, to visit communities, to get involved. However, I've done one thing, albeit in my fragments of spare time, which has been far and away the most important thing I've tried to do – that is, to conduct a Chief Rabbinate of ideas. I published six books in the last five years, since becoming Chief Rabbi, and I've put on the table of Anglo-Jewry almost every major issue in the contemporary world. The most recent is *The Politics of Hope*, which is about Jewish social and political ethics.[10]

When I was young, when I was a student, what I most wanted to hear was Judaism expounded in a way that was rational, persuasive and intellectually challenging. I didn't see it. I couldn't find it. And that's what I wanted. A rational debate. Something that I welcome in this community. There has not been one serious response to any of those books from people who take a view different to mine. Nobody else in those five and a half years has published a book, or even a slim volume, or even a seriously reflective article with footnotes, on any of those issues.

This is the thing that has disappointed me most. I believed – given everything I know of my academic training and of my talmudic roots – that Judaism is a culture of mutually respectful argument. What I am not used to is the manipulative plotting which has characterised our community for the last several years. This is not an area in which I am an expert. And if you enter strange territory, you sometimes tread where you shouldn't tread.

No Chief Rabbi has done this before, no Orthodox leader in the twentieth century has put forward his faith in language which doesn't make presuppositions. I am very disappointed that people have not taken up that challenge.[11]

Of that challenge in the wider arena, Gordon Brown – later British Prime Minister – wrote: 'I was delighted to be asked to write a foreword to the paperback edition of *The Politics of Hope*, for it is a book that has had a profound influence on my own thinking about civic society and about politics more generally over the past few years. I find that I come back to its wisdom time and time again – and now that it is back in print, I shall happily resume my practice of recommending it to my friends.

'Not all will agree with Jonathan Sacks in every particular, but he would not expect us to do that. What he invites us to do is rather to join with him in a moral debate – a "national conversation," as he puts it. His book offers not only a superb frame for this debate, but an opening contribution that is – as befits the man – at once deep-thinking, humane, learned and immensely readable.

'His invitation is one that I urge you most forcefully to accept ... I am optimistic that from a million centres of energy and good will within our country, the politics of hope can lead us towards the good society of Jonathan Sacks' dreams.'[12]

* * *   * * *   * * *

Five years on from the Gryn affair came another manifestation of Sacks' propensity 'to ingratiate himself with people who define themselves by their narrowness.' In The Dignity of Difference,[13] written after the 9/11 atrocity to coincide with the United Nations Year of Dialogue between Civilisations, the Chief Rabbi addressed the question 'Can religion overcome its conflict-ridden past and become a force for peace?' by offering 'a radical proposal for reframing the terms of this important debate ... We must do more than search for common human values. We must also learn to make space for difference, even and especially at the heart of the monotheistic imagination.'[14]

Following the publication of extracts from the final chapter,[15] Sacks found himself once again embroiled in conflict with the Orthodox right. In a Rosh Hashanah sermon at Manchester's Holy Law South Broughton synagogue, Rabbi Yossi Chazan – who seemingly had not read (or had overlooked) similar thoughts in Faith in the Future – suggested that The Dignity of Difference had 'gone too far' in its plea for interfaith understanding and questioned whether its views on other religions might amount to 'heresy.'

In the work, said Chazan, the Chief Rabbi had written that 'God has spoken to mankind in many languages: through Judaism to Jews, Christianity to Christians, Islam to Muslims.' The book had also stated that 'no one creed has a monopoly on spiritual truths; no one civilisation encompasses all the spiritual, ethical and artistic expressions of mankind ... In heaven there is truth; on earth there are truths ... God is greater than religion; He is only partially comprehended by any faith.'

Chazan had secured 'private support' for his opinions on the book from 'a number of rabbis in Britain and abroad' and, as a result, the Chief Rabbi and his Rosh Beth Din, Dayan Chanoch Ehrentreu, flew to Manchester for a 'closed-door meeting' with some of the critics. After their discussion, Chazan declined to comment, citing an agreement that the participants would not speak to the press; but from Israel a prominent interfaith activist, Rabbi David Rosen – youngest son of a one-time candidate for the British Chief Rabbinate, the late Rabbi Dr Kopul Rosen – told journalists that he had found 'nothing objectionable' in the extracts published. They represented, he said, 'venerable Jewish ideas, wonderfully presented.'

Support for Rosen's view came from Friedlander – with Sacks (as we have seen) joint Jewish president of the Council of Christians and Jews – who said that the Chief Rabbi had made 'important and valid points which help us in interfaith work. I hope,' he added, 'that almost everything he has written will remain in future editions.'

In a subsequent statement, however, Sacks' office announced: 'The Chief Rabbi has heard of the concerns of Rabbi Chazan and others at the meeting that one or two sentences might be misunderstood and will make appropriate amendments in the next possible edition of the book.'[16]

Elaborating on the rabbis' concerns, Whitefield's Jonathan Guttentag – a vocal opponent of Masorti some eight years earlier, and another of the participants in the meeting with Sacks and Ehrentreu – declared from his pulpit:

> The Chief Rabbi argues that only in heaven is there 'absolute truth.' On earth there is only 'partial truth.' Faiths should understand that they do not possess the 'absolute truth.' Each faith only has a 'partial truth.' This appears to be the basis of the solution Chief Rabbi Professor Sacks would like to suggest to prevent the clash of civilisations ... There is, however, in my opinion, a major problem with the central thesis of the book. Is Chief Rabbi Sacks suggesting that Judaism also does not contain absolute truth? That is certainly one interpretation of what is being said.
>
> In the noble aim of preventing a clash of civilisations, our Chief Rabbi seems – in conversations with the Archbishop of Canterbury and the imam from Iran – to be prepared to contemplate negotiating away the unique status of Judaism. When we make a *berachah* [blessing] over the Sefer Torah, we say: *asher natan lanu Torat emet* – that God gave us a 'Torah of truth.' How am I now supposed to understand these words, *Torat emet*? Torah of truth? According to the new view being propounded, while Judaism has its 'truth,' other religions, too, have their 'truths.' Well, that indeed is something very radical and very new. But it does not sound like Judaism.[17]

In paid and prominent announcements the following month, sages from Gateshead and the Union of Orthodox Hebrew Congregations, as well as Sacks' own Beth Din, put him squarely in his place. 'The Chief Rabbi, Professor Jonathan Sacks,' declared the former, under the banner headline 'Statement of Rabbinical Leaders of Great Britain,'

> recently published a book, *The Dignity of Difference*. The aim of the book is certainly a noble one – to reduce world tension and to avoid a clash of civilisations. However, it is with great sadness that we observe that one of the basic contentions of the book is irreconcilable with traditional Jewish teachings. Any implication that Judaism does not contain absolute truth represents a grave deviation from the pathways of traditional and authentic Judaism. We urge Rabbi Sacks, upon reflection, to repudiate the thesis of the book, and to withdraw the book from circulation.
>
> – *Rabbi B. Rakow, Rav, Gateshead Hebrew Congregation;*
> *Rabbi J. H. Dunner, Union of Orthodox Hebrew Congregations, London.*[18]

A week later, the dayanim of the London Beth Din – the titular head of which was Sacks himself – added their collective voice:

> The Chief Rabbi has recently published a new book entitled *The Dignity of Difference*, in which he articulates Judaism's response to challenges generated by globalisation and the current turmoil in world affairs. The broad message of tolerance constitutes a valuable and insightful response to contemporary world issues. We have had concerns, however, that certain passages in the book lend themselves to an interpretation that is inconsistent with basic Jewish beliefs. We therefore welcome both our Chief Rabbi's clarification of his position and his statement that in future editions of the book he will use different phraseology to restate the ambiguous points in order to avoid misunderstanding.
>
> – *Dayan Ch. Ehrentreu, Dayan M. Gelley, Dayan I. Binstock, Dayan Y. Abraham.*[19]

The Chief Rabbi's 'clarification' took the form of a second, and widely circulated, statement dismissing the interpretations and inferences which, he claimed,

> are quite foreign to my intentions and beliefs. The problem lies in the use I make of words – such as 'truth,' 'faith,' 'language,' 'voice,' and 'speaks' – that can be ambiguous, especially when, as here, one is trying to communicate across boundaries between different cultures and languages.
>
> I believed I had guarded against this possibility by making it clear

in the Prologue (page 18) that I was writing as an Orthodox Jew.[20] That means one who believes in the absolute truth and divine authorship of the Torah and its completeness as the totality of revelation at Sinai – God's covenant with humanity (the 'covenant of Noah') and with the Jewish people (the 'covenant of Sinai') ...

Nothing I have written should be taken as implying that religious differences are inconsequential or unsubstantive, that all religions are equally true, or conversely that each is incomplete; or that it does not matter if one abandons or changes one's faith. I hold none of these views.[21]

No sooner had he issued this statement than Sacks was compelled to ask his publisher to cease promoting the book, following a pronouncement from one of the Orthodox world's most revered leaders. Parts of the book, ruled Rabbi Yosef Sholom Elyashiv of Jerusalem, 'contain views contrary to our faith in the Holy Torah and it is therefore forbidden to have it in the home.' His edict came in a letter to Rakow, who said that he had sought Elyashiv's intervention after his own public plea for the book's withdrawal had been 'ignored.'[22]

The United Synagogue, meanwhile, became engaged in the dispute. Addressing a meeting of the US council, its president, Peter Sheldon, hit out at the actions of 'certain Manchester rabbis and others' who had cast doubt on the Orthodoxy of the Chief Rabbi. 'I have never heard the Chief Rabbi, privately or publicly, denigrate those whose views are different from his own. Yet some people who claim to be the custodians of authentic Judaism seem to find nothing wrong in publicly disparaging a Chief Rabbi and casting aspersions on his religious beliefs. I totally condemn such behaviour.'

Earlier in the meeting, Sacks had made a brief appearance to laud the United Synagogue's ideals of 'openness,' 'intellectual rigour' and 'tolerance.' Following his departure, however, he came under fierce attack from council life member Michael Gross, who had supported him during the Kalms controversy but who now declared: 'All that remains is to give a dead Chief Rabbinate a decent and speedy burial. Given that the Orthodox establishment around the world is looking askance at what is happening, do you think we can continue like this for another ten years [at around which time Sacks would be due to retire]?'

Gross's remarks were branded as 'abhorrent' and 'disgraceful' by one of the younger council members, Lester Harris of Clayhall Synagogue, who sprang to the defence of the Chief Rabbi's 'inspirational' leadership.[23]

For its part, following Rakow and Dunner's statement, the UOHC

Rabbinate in Stamford Hill maintained an official silence over the affair. But in Golders Green, at the Beth Shmuel synagogue of Union life-president Rabbi Elchonon Halpern, a notice posted by prominent members again referred pointedly to 'Professor' Sacks, coupling it with the biblical curse, 'the name of the wicked shall rot.' It added: 'His iniquity will not be atoned for unless he repents and withdraws all these books, so that they may be destroyed as is the law regarding other sectarian and heretical works.'[24]

This attack prompted a bitter response from the Chief Rabbi's brother, Alan Sacks, a Tel Aviv-based corporate lawyer reputed to have 'a no-nonsense approach' and the 'ability to drill right down into the main issues.'[25] 'From afar,' he wrote to the *Jewish Chronicle*, 'I watch with sadness an example of the religious polarisation with which I am so familiar here in Israel.

> I have not yet read my brother's book, *The Dignity of Difference*, and therefore I am unable to judge in their proper context the quotes which have caused such a storm. What I can comment upon, however, is the manner in which an 'enlightened' Orthodox rabbi is vilified and abused by certain elements of the ultra-Orthodox community ...
>
> The problems arise when one camp seeks to delegitimise the other, not by reason and argument but by coercion. The intellectual and academic abilities of the Chief Rabbi are not in doubt. However, in some circles, his secular knowledge and his efforts to promote traditional Jewish values within the modern Jewish world undermine his credentials as a rabbinic authority.
>
> As I understand it, the Chief Rabbi wrote *The Dignity of Difference* with a specific purpose in mind. The book was aimed at a wide and largely non-Jewish (and certainly not ultra-Orthodox) audience. Does anyone stop and ask the Chief Rabbi: 'Are there any traditional sources which support your argument? Have you gone beyond what great rabbis of the past would have agreed with?' No, it is much easier and more effective to brand the Chief Rabbi a 'heretic' and to stick up posters including him among 'the wicked whose name will rot.'
>
> The question to be asked is whether the controversial passages are in keeping with *an* authentic line of Orthodox Jewish thinking – not *the* authentic line of Orthodox Jewish thinking because, fortunately, and despite the growing power of sectarian voices, differences of opinion are still respected within Jewish tradition, provided that the argument is 'for the sake of Heaven.'[26]

* * *   * * *   * * *

Perhaps the most potent contribution to the debate came from Irving Jacobs, Sacks' successor as principal of Jews' College.[27] 'The Chief Rabbi,' he wrote, 'has a right and a responsibility to communicate with both the Jewish and wider communities on issues affecting our society. Nevertheless, there is a need for caution, as there is a temptation to present our unique legacy of truth to non-Jews as being comparable with their concept of reality.

> This can only lead to a distortion of the truth. Consequently, when a rabbinic leader addresses the non-Jewish world, it must be as the authoritative spokesman for authentic Judaism, presenting a consistent, unambiguous point of view, which is compatible with the traditions of our faith. Undoubtedly, Chief Rabbi Sacks possesses the necessary qualities and skills to be an erudite and eloquent spokesman for authentic Judaism in any forum. However, he appears to aspire to an additional role, that of spokesman for Judeo–Christian traditions to the wider community. His current predicament would suggest that these two roles are incompatible, leaving him with the uneasy task of clarifying not only his latest pronouncements, but also his aims and objectives. The sooner he does this, the better, as the current situation harms us all.[28]

In 1991, some eleven years before this caution was sounded, another scholar had lent support to the plea for a clarification of the Chief Rabbi's role. 'This week,' wrote philosopher David Conway, a former colleague of Sacks at Middlesex Polytechnic,[29]

> Chief Rabbi Lord Jakobovits steps down from office in favour of his successor, Rabbi Dr Jonathan Sacks. It is a timely moment to ask precisely what a Chief Rabbi does, and how much it matters that he does it ...
>
> It is undoubtedly convenient for the British authorities and media for there to be a readily identifiable figure to whom they can turn when in need of some authoritative Jewish voice. The main disadvantage is that such a person can all too easily become vested with a degree of influence quite out of proportion to the degree of consensus that actually exists in the Anglo-Jewish community. Such disproportionate influence can in the long run do more harm than good. And he can actually be misrepresenting a great many British Jews.
>
> In professing to speak on behalf of the entire community when he does not – and in being taken by those to whom he is speaking as so doing – he will have effectively disenfranchised those sections of the community on whose behalf he unwarrantedly claims to speak and who might otherwise

have had a chance to have their opinions taken into account.

A similar sort of doubt can be raised about the value of the role of Chief Rabbi as the authentic voice of Judaism in its application to issues of general public concern. By virtue of being widely perceived outside the Jewish community as the spokesman for it, and by fostering this perception, the Chief Rabbi can cause his pronouncements about contemporary issues to acquire a kind of gravitas and aura of authority they may not, in themselves, strictly merit.

The value of the role of Chief Rabbi as spokesman for the community and authentic voice of Judaism turns, therefore, on two questions: first, does there exist within the Anglo-Jewish community a sufficiently high degree of consensus on issues of Jewish concern to enable a single person to identify and articulate it? Second, does his office give his pronouncements on matters of public concern a dimension of authoritativeness which their specific content does not warrant?

Evidently, Lord Jakobovits does think there is a sufficient degree of consensus to justify his seeking to express it, and that his pronouncements on contemporary moral issues are not given more weight than they deserve. By no means everyone else in the community agrees. Dissenters are invariably found among Progressive Jews and self-identifying Jews with no specifically religious affiliation for whom Judaism is more a matter of ethnicity and culture than religious observance and doctrine.[30]

The point was emphasised during the Sacks–Masorti controversy, when *Manna* brought up what it described as 'a matter of extreme delicacy':

The Chief Rabbi [it asserted] is clearly the most prominent and, in many ways, the most articulate and authoritative spokesman within Anglo-Jewry. He takes great pains, when speaking to the world at large, to avoid statements which all the religious groupings within Anglo-Jewry could not share.

But there is, almost inevitably, a widespread perception in Britain at large that he is not just an outstanding spokesperson, but the sole religious leader of a monolithic community. This is immensely frustrating for those outside the United Synagogue, damaging to their self-respect, and obscuring the reality of a vital, argumentative, religiously diverse community.

If we can begin to tackle this issue – avoiding an undignified and destructive battle, avoiding unwanted damage to a man of great substance and dignity, yet allowing for both the self-respect and diversity of a non-monolithic community – we will have taken a giant stride towards a better future.[31]

Of *The Dignity of Difference*, *Manna* was later to write: 'He [Sacks] ruffled Jewish fundamentalist feathers by granting other faiths their dignity and their perceptions of God. He seemed to suggest that the Torah might not be the truth, the whole truth and nothing but the truth. He withdrew the book and made changes.

> What is less well remembered is that the first major change was to delete a long paragraph accepting evolutionary theory. Evolution was endorsed back in 1930 by Sacks' predecessor, Chief Rabbi Hertz, in an essay still available for all to read in the current edition of the Hertz Chumash. The Sacks paragraph of 2002 was deleted in deference to creationism and the new militant fundamentalism.
>
> This is in no way an attack on Chief Rabbi Sacks. Many would have taken the same view that he did – namely, that to remove a paragraph not central to the main thrust of his argument, and thus maintain a highly articulate and persuasive contribution to the national debate on religion and society, was prudent and worthwhile.
>
> What was so significant was that charedi rabbis both inside and outside the United Synagogue could compel their own Chief Rabbi, in the full glare of national, public attention, to recant.[32]

One Progressive Jew who did find favour with the Chief Rabbi's pronouncements, though not with his subsequent action – psychotherapist and rabbi Howard Cooper[33] – wrote of the situation in which Sacks found himself: 'Of the many trials that Dr Jonathan Sacks has faced as Chief Rabbi, the current pressure he is under to withdraw his latest book, *The Dignity of Difference*, is the most significant yet. It is a defining moment in his rabbinical career, and an opportunity for him to help Anglo-Jewry to transcend its parochialism.

> The declarations that Judaism, Christianity and Islam are all 'religions of revelation,' that 'no one creed has a monopoly on spiritual truth,' and that 'In heaven there is truth; on earth there are truths,' are bold, wise and, in a world fractured by religious disputatiousness and hatred, important statements of contemporary religious thinking. They are particularly so when they come from a religious teacher wrestling with the dilemma of combining an adherence to Jewish tradition with an openness to modernity.
>
> Rabbi Sacks should have faced down his critics, adhered to his motif of 'dignity,' and agreed to disagree with those who wish to shape Judaism into a narrow-minded, obscurantist sect. If he can yet do so, he will have

the vast majority of Anglo-Jewry – even Reform rabbis like myself – behind him. Let the Chief Rabbi draw strength from the deep intuition of the *Akedah*, the binding of Isaac, that we are not allowed to sacrifice the future on the altar of the past.[34]

The Guardian, which had also serialised extracts from the book, took a similar line. 'Inside the Jewish community,' it told its readers, 'an argument is raging about Professor Sacks' book on a scale unseen in a generation ... At issue is a series of statements that would surely be platitudes in any other context. "In heaven there is truth; on earth there are truths," the Chief Rabbi writes. "No one creed has a monopoly on spiritual truth." His critics have taken exception to the idea that Judaism might not include every truth there is to be known and might instead have something to learn from other faiths.

This is a sad business, for at least three reasons. First, a melancholy irony arises when the people of the book start banning books. Second, it is similarly regrettable that a plea for tolerance between religions should provoke such dissension within one. But, third, there is a particular sadness at what this episode has done for the Chief Rabbi himself.

Far from stoutly defending his stance, he has promised to rewrite the offending passages in a new edition. That has disappointed moderates and hardly pleased enemies who have seized on it as a sign of weakness. There was another way. The incoming Archbishop of Canterbury, Rowan Williams,[35] has also been accused of heresy by his own hardliners. Far from changing his tune, he says he cannot retract what he has written and that his accusers will have to live with it. Dr Sacks should have done the same: that he has not is a loss to his own community and to a wider society which might have looked to him for a moral lead.[36]

Three months earlier, *The Guardian* had published a lengthy interview with the Chief Rabbi by Jonathan Freedland, which raised eyebrows less for Sacks' theological views than for remarks he had made about Israeli policy.[37] The following passage on *The Dignity of Difference* (expanded upon in a Carnegie lecture explored below) went largely unnoticed:

'Sacks looked at the first twelve chapters of Genesis, before Isaac and Ishmael part: the symbolic moment when Judaism and Islam begin their separate journeys. "The key narrative is the Tower of Babel," Sacks explains. "God splits up humanity into a multiplicity of cultures and a diversity of languages." God's message to Abraham is: "Be different, so as to teach humanity the dignity of difference."

'That may sound like a statement of the multicultural obvious, but the Chief Rabbi knows that, for the Orthodox faiths, such talk marks a profound shift. Instead of the familiar notion of "one God, one truth, one way," Sacks is claiming divine approval for human variety. And he believes that even religious fundamentalists will have to take notice of this message – because it's right there, within their own sacred texts. "Religious tolerance or pluralism have always been secular doctrines that could be dismissed as Western or decadent by fundamentalists. This idea they cannot dismiss."'[38]

Across the Atlantic, support for Sacks came from a number of rabbis and scholars, both Orthodox and Reform. 'A new flap involving England's Chief Rabbi,' reported the New York *Jewish Week*,[39] 'raises the question: what does Orthodox Judaism say about religious pluralism and the salvation powers of non-Jewish faiths?

'The issue arose this week after the controversial Rabbi Sacks, who is Orthodox, capitulated to other British Orthodox rabbis on his religious right who charged that his new book is heresy, apparently for saying that Judaism does not hold the only truth. Which leaves the questions: what was so bad about what Rabbi Sacks wrote? And what does traditional Judaism say about the validity of other faiths?'

David Ellenson, president of the Reform movement's Hebrew Union College and a scholar of Orthodox Jewish thought, said that the objections to Sacks' interfaith comments were 'actually contrary to Judaism's own traditions,' citing passages from the Talmud and other rabbinic sources. 'There is no notion within Judaism that salvation cannot be obtained outside the precinct of the Jewish religious tradition.'

So why the heresy charge? 'There is a conscious attempt at counter-modernisation among these forces. The tradition is fairly broad and open on such issues, but the fear by some that openness to the modern world will foster Jewish assimilation has led them to restrict the openness. In order to protect the tradition, there are stringencies in both the realm of practice and belief that represent a narrowing of the very tradition that is being defended.'

Joseph Ehrenkranz, an Orthodox rabbi heading Connecticut's Center for Christian–Jewish Understanding, supported the book's views on religious pluralism. 'I agree with the Chief Rabbi. We don't have the absolute truth all the time, and there is more than one truth. If God has conveyed to Christians another ethic, where do I get the chutzpah to claim that He never spoke to anyone else?'

* * *   * * *   * * *

Just five months after the first version, the amended edition hit the bookstands, with the publisher announcing: 'The Dignity of Difference is now available as a paperback with a new preface. If you've only heard what other people have said about it, perhaps it's time you read it for yourself.'[40]

Writing, in the preface, that his caveat [as contained in the prologue to the original edition] had 'proved insufficient,' and that certain passages 'were misunderstood,'[41] Sacks added: 'I therefore decided to restate them in less problematic terms. Since the core argument of the book is simple and, in Jewish terms, uncontroversial, I have redrafted it in such a way as to circumnavigate all debated issues unrelated to its main thesis.'[42]

Such 'circumnavigation,' however, left at least one of his critics more mystified than ever. Reviewing the revised edition in the week of its release, London University philosophy professor – and, briefly, Jews' College head – David-Hillel Ruben[43] was forced to declare:

> In the second edition, the idea of truth in spiritual matters has become even less clear than it was in the first. The Chief Rabbi's tinkering with the passages that raised so much controversy has not been buttressed by what it needed: a clear restatement of exactly what truth means in spiritual and religious matters, and how, if at all, it differs from scientific truth, on the one hand, and from other areas of human endeavour, like music and art, where it seems to have no obvious applicability. The Chief Rabbi has made a convincing case for respecting people of different faiths and creeds, but no case at all, as far as I can see, for necessarily respecting what they believe. The nicest people can believe the most preposterous things.[44]

Addressing a Christian educational gathering, some six years later, Reform's Tony Bayfield told his audience that, 'for the first time in public, I am going to disagree with Chief Rabbi Sacks, or one version of him, profoundly – I hope for the sake of heaven ...

'I want to make it quite clear that in no way should it be heard or interpreted as an attack on Lord Sacks. It inevitably reflects on the politics and tensions within the Orthodox Jewish world, though that's not my business and it doesn't interest me. For me, it's just that Sacks provides the perfect illustration of the different theological territory occupied by the absolutists and the pluralists.'

When the second edition of The Dignity of Difference was published, said Bayfield, he became aware of dozens upon dozens of changes ... every single quotation I have used this evening had either been deleted or heavily amended. The distinction between God and religion – God as eternal, religion as limited by human beings and provisional – has gone. So has the declaration that God is the author of diversity and that we find God in that diversity, in the many others. So, too, has the most courageous assertion of all: that no religion possesses, or has access to, a single Truth.

'First Sacks' is a marvellous statement of theological pluralism; 'Second Sacks' represents a retreat into elegantly phrased absolutism. It is elegantly phrased because no one could possibly strip away from Jonathan Sacks his vast knowledge of post-Enlightenment theology and philosophy and the brilliance of his language. But it is, nevertheless, a restatement of the absolutist position: 'We've got the Torah, not you. We are closer to God and the Truth than you are. Of course we're committed to the dignity of difference, to respect; but that doesn't mean that you are our equal, or that we have anything to learn from you about the Holy One, blessed be He.'

The book has, in fact, ceased to be a statement of the dignity of difference. It has become, instead, an elegant example of continuing in-difference to the heart of the other. Radical pluralism has given way to absolutist hubris and overweening certainty.[45]

* * *   * * *   * * *

Again across the Atlantic, at New York's prestigious Carnegie Council for Ethics in International Affairs, Sacks faced an influential audience when invited to defend *The Dignity of Difference*, within weeks of its revised appearance. Introducing the Chief Rabbi and his book, the Council's president, political scientist Joel H. Rosenthal, noted that he himself taught a course at New York University on ethics and international politics.

'All of my students,' he said, 'come to the course having read several key articles and books, one of which is the bane of all international-relations professors – Samuel Huntington's *Clash of Civilizations*. We are always looking for answers to that essay. Jonathan Sacks has written one of the very best, and I thank you – and my students thank you. Your book lives in the lives of many students ...'

In response, Sacks opened his address by remarking that 'it is the most difficult and presumptuous thing to try to say something new about one of the oldest – indeed, *the* oldest – of human problems: how to live peaceably together in an age of conflict, and how to prevent religious differences from turning into a source of strife. That's what I have tried to do in the book, and I cannot say how moved I have been by the wonderful response it has elicited from Christian and Muslim thinkers, and from those of other faiths …

> What do you do when the question is no longer how do you get different religious groups to live together in one country, but how do you get them to live peaceably together in the world, where you have no Leviathan of international government? … In *The Dignity of Difference* I look not at secular doctrines but at the origins of Abrahamic monotheism: can we find there a strong doctrine? One way or another, we have to recognise, as I put it in the book, that religion is like a fire. Fire warms but it also burns, and we are the guardians of the flame.
>
> Therefore, I went back and I thought to myself: what do Jews, Christians, Muslims share; what is our common text? The answer is the history of the world from Adam to Abraham. Once you get to Isaac and Ishmael, you have a problem. But if you confine yourself to the first twelve chapters of Genesis, you are in business, because all three faiths claim descent, literal or biological, from Abraham, and therefore that is common ground between us …
>
> You do not have to be Jewish to be a hero or a heroine in the Bible, a knight of faith. In other words, when the rabbis come along in the first century and say, 'The righteous of all nations have a share in the world to come,' they are not making up something new; they are saying something embedded in the text and texture of the Bible itself. And there it is: there is one God, but there is not one path, one religion, one religious group you have to belong to, in order to reach that one God. Therefore, the question is: Why? Why does God not say, 'There is only one God; therefore, there is only one path to My presence?'
>
> Here I want to make a radical suggestion. It is an interpretation which, when the book first appeared in Britain, caused controversy among some of my rabbinical colleagues who had not read the commentaries on which I base my comment – impeccable commentators like Samson Raphael Hirsch, a nineteenth-century German rabbi, and Rabbi Naftali Yehuda Zvi Berlin, of Volozhin yeshivah – so they thought I was making it up.[46]
>
> Why? The answer I hazard is: God saw that Babel was, for Hirsch and for Naftali Yehuda Zvi Berlin, the first totalitarianism, the first imperialism, the first attempt at fundamentalism. How am I defining fundamentalism here? I would say it is an attempt to impose a single truth on a plural world. And having seen the building of the tower as attempted fundamentalism, God confused the languages of humanity at Babel and said, 'From here on there will be many languages, many cultures, many civilisations, and I want you to live together in peace.'

Thus God calls on one man, one nation, to be different in order to teach all humanity the dignity of difference. God lives in difference, and the proof is that His people are given that mission to be different. So, as the rabbis put it so beautifully almost two thousand years ago in the Mishnah, when a human being mints many coins in the same mint, they all come out the same.

God makes every human being in the same image, His image, and we all come out different, and it is that difference which is the basis of the sanctity of life, because every life is unlike any other life … Therefore, no life is substitutable, no life can be made good by any other life – and therein lies the sanctity of life.

So the rabbis said: God made everyone in His image, and each one is different. And I ask: can we find God's image in one who is not in my image, in one whose colour is different from mine, whose culture is different from mine, who tells different stories from mine, who responds to a different music from mine, who worships God in a different way? That is the challenge God sent us at the very beginning of the Bible.

Now you will see how I have tried to address Huntington's warning of a clash of civilisations from the very heart of the monotheistic imagination itself. The thing that led to holy wars, crusades and jihad was the principle called in Christianity *Extra Ecclesiam Nulla Salus*, that there is no other way than ours to salvation. But I believe that we can hear God whispering to us, from those early pages, that maybe there are other ways, maybe God is just too big to be compassed by any religion. Or maybe it is because God is the absolute Other, He wants us to see His image in the human Other.

Even though *The Dignity of Difference* is just a book of ideas, I think we need ideas in our arsenal as well as high-precision weaponry. I believe that it is possible to be true to your faith without ever, ever denigrating the faith of others … You can admire the fact that there are wonderful other cultures, other civilisations, other faiths, but this is ours. Each one of us can say that. And if that is enough for us, we will bring peace to the world.

After his address, the Chief Rabbi was asked from within the audience: 'It occurs to me, as a Christian, that the great arguments about religion are taking place these days within each religion as well as between them … Is there anything from your experience which can help us to set some ground rules for the disputes that go on with our fellow religionists? How do we carry on that argument in such a way that we don't denigrate them?' Sacks replied:

Your question is deeply relevant and very powerful. You all know of those differences within Christianity; you will know that we are no slouches at internal arguments ourselves, and we all know about the fault lines within Islam. All I can tell you is the working rules that I established.

The position of a Chief Rabbi is exceptionally fraught. I don't particularly worry about that, because if you look in the Bible you will see the first recorded words ever said to Moses were by the two Israelites whom he tried to stop fighting with one another. One of them said: 'Who appointed you as leader and judge over us?' Now, he had never even thought of leadership, and already they were telling him to resign. So I know that arguments within the family can sometimes be even worse than those outside.

However, being Chief Rabbi is really fraught because I am an Orthodox Jew, and when I speak in public in Britain I am taken to represent the whole Jewish community, a significant number of whom are not Orthodox Jews. So I live with that tension every single day.

Here are my working rules. On those matters that affect us regardless of our religious differences, we will work together regardless of our religious differences. On matters which touch our religious differences, we will agree to differ, but with respect. Those two rules are actually quite practical rules of thumb. So we work together across the community on fighting anti-Semitism, on defending Israel, on welfare matters, on interfaith and so on, and those are the contexts in which we work together. That means that almost every Orthodox Jew in Britain finds himself or herself sitting around a table with, working together with, a non-Orthodox Jew on those specific matters. On other matters, like who is a rabbi or who is a convert, we agree to differ, with mutual respect.

There is one final provision that has to be added. On his deathbed, Heinrich Heine said: 'God will forgive me. C'est son métier — it's what He's good at.' There are some matters which are best left to God ... So who is right and who is wrong in this particular internal theological argument, I leave to the Almighty. C'est son métier.[47]

* * *   * * *   * * *

'The result of the row, and the nature of its resolution,' wrote the *Jewish Chronicle* in the closing stages of the controversy,

> has been further to weaken the office of the Chief Rabbinate. Sadly, it is also likely further to limit the likelihood of genuine, mutually respectable debate within British Orthodoxy for the foreseeable future. The hope must

be, therefore, that lessons will meanwhile be learned, not least because the causes of this latest crisis are similar to those of some of the earlier disputes during Rabbi Sacks' eleven-year tenure – above all, a tendency to try to speak in different voices to conflicting, sometimes irreconcilable, constituencies. Ultimately, it must be hoped that both Chief Rabbi Sacks and the wider community can find a way to move beyond the need for periodic damage-limitation exercises, and to focus on the undeniable intellectual and other strengths which he does bring to his office.[48]

Compounding the humiliation of such 'damage-limitation exercises,' within months Kalms found a way by calling, once again, on Sacks to stand down. Nor did his call defy precedent. Every Chief Rabbi from Hermann Adler on – as later chapters will demonstrate – faced opposition to his appointment, and growing demands for the abolition of his office.

The Crucible of Judaism

'Let us see how we can bring the school, the synagogue and the Jewish home closer so that they reinforce one another.' [1]

Tracing its origins back to 1732, when it started life as a Talmud Torah with fifteen pupils, the Free School for German Jews was officially inaugurated on 13 September, 1814, leased a plot of land several months later, and opened, on 13 April, 1817, with 102 boys aged seven and over.

Within a few months, its small schoolhouse was well oversubscribed, and in 1819 the freehold was acquired on a site in Bell Lane, Spitalfields, where once had stood the Constitutional Brewery. In January 1822, it reopened – now named the Jews' Free School – with 236 boys and 280 girls. Eighty years on, catering for 4,250 pupils, it was the largest school in Europe; since its auspicious beginning, more than 100,000 children have passed through its doors.

In 1851, Sir Moses Montefiore, as president of the Board of Deputies, approached the government with a request to include the JFS in its educational grant provisions. In reply, the Committee of Council for Education asked the Deputies to formulate a draft 'model deed' to be used by Parliament while considering the request during an upcoming debate. Additionally, it sought confirmation that the Board was 'invested with a representative character with regard to the interests of Jewish schools.'

After supplying acceptable evidence, the Board included in its draft deed a clause requiring religious instruction in Jewish schools to be under the control of 'an appointee of the Jewish ecclesiastical authorities,' who would be, if so nominated, Chief Rabbi Nathan Marcus Adler. A resolution approving the draft – which would assist Adler in his bid to counter the growing influence of Reform – was subsequently passed at a meeting of the Board.

Days later, six absentee deputies, among them Baron Lionel de Rothschild and Sir Anthony de Rothschild – the latter president of the Jews' Free School; the former a vocal campaigner for Reform representation on the Board of Deputies – requisitioned a meeting to reconsider the draft. In a letter to the Board, the JFS governors objected to its seeking 'a power of interference in the management of this School which this committee, regarding themselves as trustees and managers of an educational institution wholly independent of extraneous control, would reluctantly feel themselves bound to oppose.'

The Board, and Adler, thereupon retreated and accepted an amendment placing the choice of ecclesiastical authority in the hands of the individual schools, their governors and subscribers. A century was to pass before another, more successful, attempt was made to install the Chief Rabbi – with far-reaching ramifications – as the official ecclesiastical authority of the JFS.

In 1957, the Ministry of Education submitted draft articles of government to the school. The governors responded by inserting an amendment that offered a powerful role in its affairs to the then Chief Rabbi, Israel Brodie. 'The religious observance and instruction in the school,' they decreed, 'shall be in accordance with the practice, rites and doctrines of the Jewish faith, and for these purposes the decision of the Chief Rabbi of the United Hebrew Congregations of the British Commonwealth and Empire shall be final.'

Under the articles, the governors were invested with responsibility for the admission of pupils, and they introduced a condition that no child would be accepted unless deemed Jewish as defined by the Chief Rabbi. The school, they made clear, was for 'pupils recognised as Jewish by the Board of Religious Education of the United Synagogue, which is under the jurisdiction of the Chief Rabbi.' Other applications, they added later, 'will be refused.'

Applicants for admission were thereafter required to supply a statement of eligibility, signed by the parent or guardian, and a declaration that the child 'is of Jewish birth or is Jewish by conversion.' Both statements – with details of the parents' marriage – would be forwarded to the Chief Rabbi's office for approval. If a convert, the mother was required to show evidence that the procedure had been conducted 'under the auspices of the United Synagogue or a body recognised by it.'[2]

* * *   * * *   * * *

Some thirty years later, during Jakobovits' Chief Rabbinate, the Masorti Assembly of Synagogues was alerted by concerned parents to 'a matter regarding the JFS Comprehensive School which has practical application vis-à-vis the Jewish unity issue.' Jaclyn Chernett, Masorti's director, consulted with her Reform and Liberal counterparts, Raymond Goldman and Sidney Brichto, in a bid to determine 'whether the appropriate education authority is aware that the school is not open to all Jews and is therefore prejudicing the rights of a section of the Jewish community.'

'I have ascertained,' wrote Chernett, 'that the Inner London Education Authority (ILEA) has adopted the phrase "recognised as Jewish by the London Board of Jewish Religious Education" since the 1950s. It is only recently that the London Board has followed up ketubot [marriage certificates] because of cases where children of doubtful Jewish status are in dispute.

'This follows the normal United Synagogue line that this course of procedure saves them from misrepresentation, and saves parents from what they consider to be personal tragedy if, later on, they find out their children are "not kosher" or cannot get married in a United Synagogue, even though they have been to a Jewish school.'[3]

Chernett's alert was accompanied by a statement from the JFS that 'the School is for pupils who are recognised as Jewish by the London Board of Jewish Religious Education. Our pupils reflect the whole spectrum of Anglo-Jewry, but the outlook and practice of the School is Orthodox. Our religious policy is under the jurisdiction of the Chief Rabbi.'[4]

In letters to Jo Wagerman, head teacher of the JFS,[5] and to the London Board,[6] Chernett sought clarification of the issue. 'We have been approached,' she wrote, 'by parents of children who are potential pupils at your school, who have expressed – as we do – considerable concern at the apparent paradox in your published references that "our pupils reflect the whole spectrum of Anglo-Jewry" and a request to see a copy of the ketubah "as proof that the candidate for admission is Jewish." While we appreciate that a ketubah will indicate that a couple have been married under the auspices of a particular synagogue, we would like to ask how the ketubah proves that the candidate for admission is Jewish.'

The honorary correspondent of the JFS, Nathan Rubin – who was also secretary of the United Synagogue and the London Board – replied:

> The published criteria for the admission of pupils to this School state that the pupils seeking admission must be Jewish in accordance with the requirements of the London Board. The Head Teacher of the School has to have regard to this requirement.
>
> From lengthy experience over many years, it is known that sight of the ketubah at an interview is adequate in most instances to verify that the pupil concerned is Jewish according to the London Board. There are instances where, having seen the ketubah, further inquiries are necessary. There are also some instances where, for one reason or another, a ketubah cannot be produced or where the ketubah itself is not sufficient evidence; discreet inquiries are then made with the co-operation of the parents or guardians.
>
> If there are still doubts, then we seek the advice of the Chief Rabbi or the London Beth Din.[7]

In March 1986, while this exchange was in progress, doubts appeared to arise – and the Chief Rabbi's and Beth Din's advice was sought – over the application of one particular candidate for admission: Paula Jacobs, granddaughter of the New London Synagogue's Rabbi Louis Jacobs.

Following their application and the ensuing interview, Paula's parents, Ivor and Tirza Jacobs – who were married at the New London – were told by Wagerman: 'I regret I am not yet able to give you the results of your application for a place for Paula at JFS as we have not yet received confirmation from the Office of the Chief Rabbi that your child is eligible for admission to this school as a Jewish pupil. As soon as we receive such confirmation, we will inform you of the results of the interview.'[8]

After a lapse of several days, Ivor Jacobs wrote to Wagerman expressing his and his wife's 'distress' on receiving her letter, which had arrived on the day a decision had to be made regarding the choice of a school.

'Without the positive letter that we had hoped for from you,' he told Wagerman, 'we could not assume that JFS would be a definite option available. Therefore, the decision was made for us [to accept the offer of an alternative school]. We can only think that this tactic of the Chief Rabbi's office might have been pursued to make selected parents opt out of furthering their children's application.

> We are not writing to you because there is a doubt about the Jewish status of myself or my wife – I am sure you are aware that both our fathers are rabbis[9] – but because we are concerned by the anguish that could be caused to other parents if the Jewish status of their child had to be proved to the Chief Rabbi. Surely this attitude can only lead to further communal friction …
>
> We feel very sad that our hitherto total support for the JFS [their son Daniel had earlier been accepted without question] has now been diluted, and we trust in your judgment to continue the welcoming atmosphere that the school has for all shades of Anglo-Jewry, in spite of what it appears others are trying to do.[10]

Wagerman replied: 'I am sorry the system has come up against several delays which are causing irritation and distress. The foundation governors, the London Board of Jewish Religious Education, require this investigation of the schools. I had to meet deadlines set by the local education authorities which the Office of the Chief Rabbi could not meet.

'Questions of halachah are beyond my competence and have always been referred to the Chief Rabbi. Hopefully, in future, decisions will be known before dates for informing parents, to avoid irritating indecisions …

I am grateful for your declaration of continuing support for the School.'[11]

After the matter was decided to the Jacobs' dissatisfaction, and in response to a letter from Ivor Jacobs to Jakobovits – stating, inter alia, 'I'm afraid that it looks very much as if the London Board and your office will now be exercising their power and will favour children who have a background that matches a set profile'[12] – the Chief Rabbi's executive officer, Shimon Cohen, conceded: 'We share your misgivings and have given instructions for applications to be dealt with routinely in all cases where no doubts or irregularities of status are evident.' He had earlier told Jacobs – too late for Paula's admission to the JFS – that 'everything is fine, no need to send documents.'[13]

Ivor Jacobs' misgivings, and the Chief Rabbinate's response, were to be severely tested in a landmark case twenty years later.

* * *   * * *   * * *

In 2006, a parent – known initially in court proceedings as E – sought to have his son M educated at the JFS and was refused.[14] Another family, known as Mr L and Mrs L and described as 'interested parties,' joined with E in the hearings; their case will be considered later in this chapter. A third family, S, also featured in the initial hearing.[15]

E was told: 'Because the School has not received evidence of M's Jewish status, it would not be possible to consider M for a place unless and until all those applicants whose Jewish status has been confirmed have been offered places. It follows from this that, as the School is likely to remain heavily oversubscribed, M's position on the offer list will almost certainly be very low, and the likelihood of being able to offer a place is very small.'[16]

A member of the New London Synagogue – noted Mr Justice Munby two years later, when delivering his judgment on a judicial review – 'E considers himself to be, and doubtless many others who consider themselves to be Jews would also consider him to be, of Jewish ethnic origin; to be of the Jewish faith; and to be a practising Jew. His former wife, M's mother, is of Italian national and ethnic origin.

'Before she and E married, she was converted to Judaism under the auspices of the rabbi of an independent Progressive synagogue. M is therefore, in E's eyes – and doubtless in the eyes of many who would consider themselves Jews – of mixed Jewish and (through the maternal line) Italian ethnic origin.

'According to E, M is recognised as Jewish by the Reform Synagogues of Great Britain and the Assembly of Masorti Synagogues, practises his own Jewish faith, prays in Hebrew, and attends synagogue and a Jewish youth group. Because the OCR [Office of the Chief Rabbi] does not recognise the validity of conversions carried out by Progressive synagogues, it does not recognise M as Jewish.'[17]

> I have before me [said the judge] two applications for judicial review which raise important questions as to the relationship between religious law and secular law – in this particular instance, secular discrimination law as embodied in the Race Relations Act 1976. These questions arise in the context of a dispute within our Jewish community about the propriety and legality of the criteria governing admission to a well-known Jewish school in London, JFS, formerly the Jews' Free School. The issues and the outcome are therefore of great importance for the various sections of the Jewish community. But they are also important to people of all religions, not least because they impact potentially upon 'faith schools' of all faiths and denominations.[18]

The second application to which the judge referred sought to have the school's admissions policy declared unlawful in that 'it does not reflect JFS's designated religious character; it discriminates directly or indirectly on racial grounds against children who are not of ethnic Jewish descent through the maternal line; it unlawfully fetters the governing body's discretion and/or sub-delegates to the OCR decisions on the admission of pupils to JFS; it is contrary to the School Admissions Code 2007; and it includes provision for the admission of children who have enrolled upon a course of conversion to Judaism under the approval of the OCR (it is said that this provision in unfair and misleading because the OCR has stated that it would not in fact approve any such child until the course was complete or virtually compete – a process taking many years with which, for all practical purposes, a child cannot comply).'

E asked for 'a quashing order to quash the schools adjudicator's decision, and a declaration that JFS's admissions policy for 2008–09 is unlawful.'[19] The school's admissions policy for 2007–08 (identical for 2008–09) was set out in material part as follows:

'1.1 It is JFS ("the School") policy to admit up to the standard admissions number children who are recognised as being Jewish by the Office of the Chief Rabbi of the United Hebrew Congregation of the Commonwealth (OCR) *or who have already enrolled upon or who have undertaken, with the consent of their parents, to follow any course of conversion to Judaism under the approval of the OCR.'* (The words emphasised by the judge did not appear in the admissions policies for 2005–06 and 2006–07.)

'1.2 In the event that the School is oversubscribed, then only children who satisfy the provisions of paragraph 1.1 above will be considered for admission, in accordance with the oversubscription criteria set out in Section 2, below.'[20]

During the proceedings, representatives of four religious bodies within the Jewish community submitted witness statements on their respective approaches to conversion. For the London Beth Din, senior dayan Menachem Gelley wrote (26 February, 2008): 'A convert's state of mind at the moment of conversion (i.e., immersion in a mikveh) is absolutely vital to the validity of an Orthodox conversion.

'If, for example, the convert was prepared to accept some or even most of the laws of Orthodox Judaism, but was not prepared to accept certain laws or even one law (e.g., the laws concerning Sabbath observance or the dietary laws), the conversion would be invalid, because the convert was unwilling to accept the Orthodox Jewish faith in its entirety at the moment of conversion. Indeed, it is a well-established point of Jewish Law that if a Beth Din discovers new information relevant to the time of a conversion, it should consider whether the conversion was valid, even if the conversion was not recent or took place in a different jurisdiction.'[21]

Michael Gluckman, executive director of the Assembly of Masorti Synagogues, wrote (5 February, 2008): 'To be recognised, a conversion must have been in accordance with the standards of the Masorti Beth Din. We strive for inclusion wherever possible … our aim is to welcome and include people.'[22]

For the Movement for Reform Judaism, Tony Bayfield wrote (7 February, 2008): 'When it comes to matters of Jewish status, we are more liberal than the OCR and adopt a more inclusivist policy. This applies particularly in the area of conversion, where we are keen to count in as many people who wish to define themselves as Jews as possible … Our formal requirements for conversion are almost exactly the same as those of Orthodoxy, but we are less exacting and more "pluralistic" in the demands we make in terms of religious observance.'[23]

Danny Rich, chief executive of Liberal Judaism, wrote (31 January, 2008): 'Liberal Judaism is guided by the following principles: affording the benefit of the doubt where an individual affirms something to be true or where documentation or other evidence is difficult to obtain or unavailable; a wish to be inclusive, by which a person recognised as Jewish by one rabbinic authority (even if it differs from our own) should not in virtually all circumstances be rejected as Jewish by another authority; and the value of compassion coupled with common sense over excessive legalism.'[24]

Commenting on these statements, Munby said:

All the evidence I have seen is to the effect that *all* Jewish denominations treat being Jewish as a matter of status, not a matter of creed or religious observance. Again, all the evidence I have seen is to the effect that, as Rabbi Bayfield of the Movement for Reform Judaism puts it, the entire Jewish world, both in this country and globally, would say that Jewish identity is determined by either descent or conversion.

The evidence is likewise at one in indicating that, with the sole exception of Liberal Judaism, which regards as Jewish a child *either* of whose parents is Jewish, all Jewish denominations, including Reform and Masorti Jews, follow the matrilineal tradition. Rabbi Rich explains that Liberal Judaism 'affirms the absolute equality of men and women so that a Jewish father is equivalent for status purposes to a Jewish mother.' So, common to all Jewish denominations is a belief that being Jewish is a matter of status, defined in terms of descent or conversion, and not a matter of creed or religious observance.[25]

The judge drew attention to the JFS's present instrument of government, dated 18 October, 2005, which noted in clause 8 ('Statement of School Ethos') the following: 'Recognising its historic foundation, JFS will preserve and develop its religious character in accordance with the principles of Orthodox Judaism, under the guidance of the Chief Rabbi of the United Hebrew Congregations of the British Commonwealth. The School aims to serve its community by providing education of the highest quality within the context of Jewish belief and practice. It encourages the understanding of the meaning of the significance of faith and promotes Jewish values for the experience of all its pupils.'

Munby also pointed to the JFS's website, as accessed on 10 September, 2007, which contained the following under the heading 'The Jewish Dimension': 'The outlook and practice of the School is Orthodox. One of our aims is to ensure that Jewish values permeate the School.

'Our students reflect the very wide range of the religious spectrum of British Jewry. Whilst two-thirds or more of our students have attended Jewish primary schools, a significant number of our Year 7 intake has not attended Jewish schools and some enter the School with little or no Jewish education. Many come from families who are totally committed to Judaism and Israel; others are unaware of Jewish belief and practice. We welcome this diversity and embrace the opportunity to have such a broad range of young people developing Jewish values together ...'[26]

Referring to counsel for the JFS, the judge remarked: 'Mr [Peter] Oldham submits that the effect of E's claim, if successful, will be to destroy the right of Orthodox Jews to have access to schools which give admission priority to Orthodox Jews and the right of the State to provide such schools. Seemingly, E accepts that members of other religions have that right, so why not Orthodox Jews?

'The reason, says Mr Oldham, is that E's case is, whether he realises it or not, built upon a central misconception, namely that religion, on his view, is confined to those who believe in a deity or are observant, whereas Orthodox Judaism, which as Mr Oldham correctly submits is plainly a religion, happens to be characterised by the belief, not that observance is a necessary part of membership, but that membership is defined by a status – acquired either by conversion or automatically through the matrilineal line – that cannot be lost ...[27]

'But it is equally clear from the evidence [the judge said later] that different sections of the British Jewish community, regardless of their views as to the appropriateness of JFS's policy, are deeply troubled about this litigation. Unease about the implications of the litigation is expressed by both the Orthodox and Reform witnesses. Mr [David] Frei [registrar of the London Beth Din] says that the United Synagogue and the Chief Rabbi would be "greatly concerned" by any suggestion that Orthodox Jewish schools should not be permitted to select their pupils on the basis of the test for Jewish status under Orthodox Jewish religious law.

'Rabbi Bayfield, who regards the School's admissions policy as "excessively narrow and restrictive," nonetheless continues: "But that is an internal matter for the Jewish community. We would not want the law of the land to question the right of the OCR to define Jewish identity the way that it does. We do not think it is wise or right for the State to get involved. In any event, this has nothing to do with race or racism."

'He adds: "What would be absolutely ridiculous and unacceptable would be to require synagogue attendance or a defined level of religious practice ... We would be equally outraged" – that is, equally with Orthodox Judaism – "if a 'Christian' model of 'Church' membership and attendance were imposed. We would advise very strongly against government or legal intervention in the admissions criteria at JFS – even though our view of the needs of the Jewish world and our outlook on the best strategy to maintain and develop Jewish life are very different. In our view, the OCR policy with regard to admission to JFS is strategically wrong, 'politically' motivated, not in the interests either of the community or the family concerned and unjust. But we would not want the courts or the government to intervene or adjudicate, certainly not on grounds of racial discrimination."'[28]

Including an extensive consideration of the legal context – drawing on European law, aspects of racial discrimination (direct and indirect), ethnic origin, objections to the JFS admissions policy per se, and references to the Nuremberg Laws – the judge's 71-page ruling was sent to the parties on 23 June, 2008 – fifteen weeks after the four-day hearing – and handed down a fortnight later.

The school's policy, he declared, was 'entirely lawful and proportionate to the aims and objectives of the school.' Sitting in Cardiff, he said that Jewish status could be defined only by Jewish law and was not something to be determined by the secular courts. The JFS admissions policy was 'entirely legitimate' and there had been no direct or indirect unlawful discrimination.

Commenting on the judgment, JFS chairman of governors Russell Kett said: 'The school abhors all forms of discrimination and welcomes the judge's express finding that the JFS does not racially discriminate.'[29]

E, for his part, was granted eight days in which to seek leave to appeal. Within that period, Munby gave him permission to challenge the ruling and to take his fight to the Court of Appeal. In a written decision, the judge said there were 'respectable and serious arguments that I was wrong,' stressing, in particular, 'the general importance of the issues involved and the desirability that, whether I was right or wrong, there should be a definitive ruling on them by the Court of Appeal.'

The decision was welcomed by E, who said: 'The judge has rightly recognised the respectability of the key arguments. Contrary to what has been suggested by some, the JFS is not a private "club" free to set its own membership rules. It is a State school, funded by the taxpayer, and as such is subject to the laws of the land, laws which, I believe, require that my child – and all Jewish children – be treated fairly and equally to others.

'JFS was established to provide education to the whole Jewish community, not a particular section of it, and formerly admitted all Jewish children on an equal basis. Its admissions policies should reflect those founding principles.'[30]

* * *   * * *   * * *

'A legal battle over the right of Jewish schools to define who is a Jew is to be heard by the Court of Appeal,' the *Jewish Chronicle* announced seven months later.[31] 'The case pits individual human rights against the freedom of religious institutions and, if successful, could force Jewish schools to rewrite their admissions policies.'

Heard over three days in May 2009, before Lord Justice Sedley (Sir Stephen Sedley, a Jewish judge and a recognised advocate of human rights), Lady Justice Smith and Lord Justice Rimer, the case plunged Anglo-Jewry – and notably its educational sector – into its most serious crisis in living memory. The judgment, commented the Chief Rabbi on its release, eight weeks later, 'has effectively branded Judaism as "racist."'[32]

> It is E's case [said Lord Justice Sedley, delivering his court's unanimous finding][33] that being a Jew, whether by descent or by conversion, is a question of ethnicity, with the result that to refuse a child admission to a school because his mother is not Jewish constitutes direct race discrimination against him, on the ground both of his own and of his mother's ethnicity. If, however, the criterion is applied in such a way that the discrimination is indirect, it is E's alternative case that it has no legitimate aim, since the purpose is to make a purely ethnic distinction, and so is equally unlawful.
>
> In either case, it is argued that the religious motive for such discrimination makes it no less unlawful. JFS as respondent, the Secretary of State for Children, Schools and Families as an interested party, and the United Synagogue as an intervener, contest both claims. They say that the criterion itself is a purely religious, not a racial, one and that its admittedly disparate racial impact is justified by the lawful designation and ethos of the school as Jewish.[34]

For reasons set out in the judgment, said the judge, 'the conclusion of the court is that the requirement that if a pupil is to qualify for admission his mother must be Jewish, whether by descent or by conversion, is a test of ethnicity which contravenes the Race Relations Act 1976. If the discrimination is direct, as we consider it is, it cannot be justified. If, contrary to this finding, the discrimination is indirect, we consider its purpose to be selection on the basis of ethnicity and therefore not to constitute a legitimate aim.'[35]

Discussing the JFS's admissions criteria, Sedley stated: 'For the United Synagogue, Lord Pannick, QC, whose argument the school and, in large part, the Secretary of State adopt, submits that the criterion of choice is a religious and not a racial one.

> The Chief Rabbi is concerned only to elaborate and apply the law of the Torah, and only those whom the Torah does not recognise as Jews are excluded. This was the argument which Mr Justice Munby accepted.[36] For M's father, Ms Dinah Rose, QC, contends that this approach elides the grounds of an act with its motive, whereas what the legislation is concerned with is not its motive but its causation. A religious motive will not excuse discrimination on racial grounds.
>
> We entirely accept the theological origin and character of the OCR's

definition of Jewishness. But we also accept that, as Ms Rose submits, this is the beginning and not the end of the court's inquiry. What remains to be decided is whether a school whose admissions policy is based explicitly on it is discriminating on racial grounds …[37]

M was refused admission to JFS because his mother, and therefore he, was not regarded as Jewish. The school has been perfectly open in giving this as the ground of non-admission. There are, of course, theological reasons why M is not regarded as Jewish, but they are not the ground of non-admission: they are the motive for adopting it …

The reason why the refusal to admit M because he is not regarded as matrilineally Jewish constitutes discrimination on racial grounds emerges clearly from the decision of the House of Lords in Mandla v Dowell-Lee [1983]. That case, as is well known, concerned the refusal of a private school to admit a Sikh pupil whose religion and culture would not permit him to comply with the school's rules on uniform.[38]

Describing in some detail the ethnic, racial and religious factors involved in that case, and applying its reasoning to the present case, the judge then continued: 'It appears to us clear (a) that Jews constitute a racial group defined principally by ethnic origin and additionally by conversion; and (b) that to discriminate against a person on the ground that he or someone else either is or is not Jewish is therefore to discriminate against him on racial grounds.

'The motive for the discrimination, whether benign or malign, theological or supremacist, makes it no less and no more unlawful. Nor does the factuality of the ground. If, for theological reasons, a fully subscribed Christian faith school refused to admit a child on the ground that, albeit practising Christians, the child's family were of Jewish origin, it is hard to see what answer there could be to a claim for race discrimination.

'The refusal of JFS to admit M was accordingly, in our judgment, less favourable treatment of him on racial grounds. This does not mean, as Lord Pannick suggested it would mean, that no Jewish faith school can ever give preference to Jewish children. It means that, as one would expect, eligibility must depend on faith, however defined, and not on ethnicity … By expressly adopting the Chief Rabbi's criteria in its admission policy, the school made them part of the policy. If, as we consider to be the case, those criteria discriminated on racial grounds, the school is answerable …[39]

Taking it that the OCR's criterion is even-handedly applied, its disparate and adverse impact on any child who is accordingly not regarded as Jewish is manifest: such children, of whom M is one, cannot gain admission to the school. The facts therefore satisfy s.1(1A)(a) and (b) [of the Race Relations Act 1976].[40] So the question is whether the school can show it to be a proportionate means of achieving a legitimate aim.

What, then, is the school's aim in adopting this criterion? Stress has been laid upon the ethos described in its instrument of government and mentioned earlier in this judgment. But this, as can readily be seen, relates to how children are to be educated once admitted to the school. It has no direct bearing on who those children should be. Indeed, given the wide disparity of religious and cultural family backgrounds of those admitted, who may even come from atheist or Catholic or Muslim families, it has little appreciable indirect bearing either. It is a gate-keeping provision which operates entirely by asking whether a child is Jewish.

It appears to us in this situation that there is no answer to Ms Rose's submission that this element of the admission criteria is explicitly related to ethnicity and so incapable of constituting or forming part of a legitimate aim.

For the United Synagogue, Lord Pannick has candidly accepted that the criterion is linked to ethnicity. For the Secretary of State, Mr Tom Linden, QC, initially sought, surprisingly if we may say so, to argue that it was possible under s.1(1A) for a criterion related to ethnicity to be a proportionate means of achieving a legitimate aim. But he did not persist in the submission, and we limit ourselves to saying that it would be remarkable if an amendment designed to strengthen the Act had weakened it by making it possible for the first time to justify indirect discrimination by reliance on the very thing that made the test discriminatory.

In our judgment, an aim of which the purpose or inevitable effect is to make and enforce distinctions based on race or ethnicity cannot be legitimate. We do not intend this to be an exhaustive account of what 'legitimate' means in s.1(1A)(c), but we consider that it bears at least this meaning.[41]

Summarising the court's finding, the judge concluded: 'Our essential difference with Mr Justice Munby is that what he characterised as religious grounds are, in our judgment, racial grounds, notwithstanding their theological motivation. It also appears to us, with respect, that the judge has at a number of points allowed himself to be distracted by wider considerations than the law warrants.

'For example, in several places he makes comparisons with the admission criteria and practices adopted by schools of other faiths. Underlying this is an apparent assumption that, since these are legitimate, JFS must be entitled to adopt such criteria as are required by the faith it espouses if it is not itself to be differently treated by the law.

'This is not, in our respectful view, the right approach. No faith school is immune from the prohibition on race discrimination, and race discrimination is what the Race Relations Act 1976 says it is. An oversubscribed faith school which admitted only children whose parents came from a country where the school's faith was the official religion would, we would think, have a case to answer.'[42]

* * *   * * *   * * *

Family L, since identified as Lightman, was one of several 'interested parties' involved in the 2008 hearing before Mr Justice Munby.[43] Mrs L (Miss M as she then was) was converted in Israel in September 1987 by the Special Rabbinical Court for Conversion established by the Chief Rabbinate of Israel. In his ruling, the judge stated: 'I have seen both a copy of the original certificate, in Hebrew, of her conversion, certified by the rabbinical authorities in Israel, and an English translation.' Munby continued:

> Mr and Mrs L were married on 3 March, 1988, by an Orthodox rabbi in an Orthodox synagogue in New York. Again I have seen a copy of the original certificate, in both Hebrew and English, signed by the rabbi. Mr L is a Cohen, a descendant of the priests in the Temple. According to Dayan Gelley, 'Jewish law prohibits a marriage between a Cohen and a convert.' On 8 April, 1991, Mr L approached the London Beth Din concerning a brit or bris (ritual circumcision) for his son.
>
> Subsequently, both Mr and Mrs L were seen by a dayan and two rabbis. The file note of that meeting says: 'They were told that we shall have to decide whether, in view of her closeness to Mr L and his family before her conversion and her subsequent marriage to him soon after, knowing that he is a Cohen and the marriage therefore forbidden, she could be said to have accepted the Jewish faith without reservation.'
>
> The final decision was reserved, being communicated to Mr and Mrs L in a letter from the Beth Din dated 25 April, 1991: 'Due to the circumstances of Mrs L's contracting a forbidden marriage soon after her conversion, we very much regret that we are unable to recognise the validity of her conversion. Consequently, we cannot authorise a mohel [ritual circumciser] to perform a brit on your son.'
>
> The decision is explained by Dayan Gelley in his witness statement dated 26 February, 2008: 'It appeared to the LBD [London Beth Din] that ... at the time of conversion, Mrs L intended to marry Mr L, despite knowing that such a marriage was contrary to Jewish law. She therefore did not accept the tenets of the Orthodox Jewish faith at the time of her

conversion, and her conversion was accordingly held by the LBD to be invalid. Accordingly, Jewish status did not pass to Mrs L's children by matrilineal descent. It is important to note that it is not the marriage between Mr and Mrs L that is itself of concern. Although this was a breach of Orthodox Jewish law (in the same way as not keeping the Sabbath, or breaching dietary laws are a breach of Jewish law), it is the fact that at the moment of her conversion she did not accept all the tenets of Orthodox Judaism that invalidates the conversion.'

There matters rested until November 2004, when Mr and Mrs L sought their daughter's admission to JFS. On 17 November, 2004, JFS wrote to Mr and Mrs L enclosing a copy of a letter to JFS from the OCR dated 5 November, 2004. That letter said: 'Having followed up all the details ... and on the basis of the information at present available, I have to inform you that this child cannot be regarded as Jewish.'

The letter from JFS to Mr and Mrs L said: 'Given this information, in relation to the school's admissions policy, your daughter will only be considered for admission in the event that JFS is unable to fill its standard admissions number with children who are recognised as being Jewish by the Office of the Chief Rabbi. If you have any questions regarding your daughter's Jewish status, they should be addressed directly to [the OCR].'

Mr and Mrs L appealed to JFS's admissions appeal panel. Its decision, in a letter dated 19 July, 2005, was that JFS was to offer their daughter a place 'as soon as the Office of the Chief Rabbi in London confirms that they recognise [her] as halachically Jewish.' Mr and Mrs L wished to take legal action, but being of limited means reluctantly decided they could not. But they support the action being brought by E.

Mr and Mrs L are members of a Masorti synagogue. They are Orthodox in practice, attend synagogue every week, abide by the halachah, and have brought up their children in a strictly Jewish religious environment. In a witness statement dated 21 February, 2008, Mrs L describes her feelings: 'We have been fighting for justice for our family for many years now and to not be able to pursue justice is almost unbearable. The actions of the Beth Din in not accepting my Jewish status causes me immense hurt, distress and torment on a daily basis, both to me as a practising Jew of over twenty years and to me as a mother. The only thing worse than my pain is to see the pain of my daughter.'

The judge stated further: 'Mrs L has been teaching at JFS since 1991. She is now head of department in her subject. Mr L in a witness statement, also dated 21 February, 2008, added this: "It has been particularly difficult for my wife teaching at JFS, although she has had a great deal of support

from the staff and parents, for which we are grateful. My daughter ... leads
an active Jewish life and asks why she can't go to the school of her choice,
where her mother teaches and where I and my sisters were pupils.

'"I find this hard to explain to her, other than saying that there are
small-minded people stopping it from happening. I am desperately sorry
that we are unable to take our own proceedings, but we are a family of
average means against a large, well-financed establishment. ... I cannot
begin to express the pain and suffering that our whole family feels as a
consequence of the actions of the London Beth Din. It has now been with
us for many years without it diminishing or dimming. My wife has been
incredibly brave in going public about this matter and the distress will
only be over when our family is accepted as Jewish by the Beth Din and
when [our daughter] is given a place at JFS."'[44]

Writing in the *Jewish Chronicle* following the Court of Appeal judgment –
and disclosing his identity as David Lightman – the child's father declared:
'Twenty-two years ago, my wife, Kate, had an Orthodox conversion to
Judaism, in Israel. Later we fell in love and decided to marry, which we did
in an Orthodox ceremony. We built a kosher home, attended synagogue
weekly and enjoyed a full Jewish life.

> After three years, we had our first child and wanted to arrange the brit.
> The shul told us to contact the Beth Din, as we were married outside
> the United Kingdom. Our nightmare began. The London Beth Din, the
> Court of the Chief Rabbi, told my wife that, as she was 'insincere at the
> moment of conversion,' they would not recognise it, a conversion that
> had occurred five years before they met her. There was no explanation, no
> appeal, just an edict from upon high.
>
> Fortunately, we discovered the astonishing Rabbi Jonathan Wittenberg,
> who welcomed us into the New North London Masorti community. Here
> we rebuilt our traditional Jewish life. Eighteen years on, I am a *shammes* in
> shul, my wife helps run the children's services, my children attend and
> teach at the cheder, and we maintain a kosher home.
>
> Four years ago, we tried to send our daughter to JFS, where my wife is
> head of English, and where I was a pupil. My daughter was denied a place.
> Our attempts to talk to the Chief Rabbi and the Beth Din, in private, met a
> wall of silence ... At every stage, our desire for compromise and dialogue
> has been met with silence and contempt.
>
> We now find ourselves ranged against the full force of the Office of the
> Chief Rabbi, with the formidable resources and finances it can muster. It begs
> the question: why is the Chief Rabbi prepared to spend hundreds of thousands
> of pounds to stop two Jewish children from getting a Jewish education?

Support we have received from across all sections of the community proves that this is not a battle about Orthodoxy; it is a simple matter of right and wrong. I cannot stand by and let this unjust situation continue, and I urge all right-minded Jews to join us in this battle for justice, and to unite rather than divide the community.[45]

* * *   * * *   * * *

The Chief Rabbi's response to the Court of Appeal was immediate – and combative. 'The principles underlying membership of the Jewish faith,' he declared on the afternoon of the judgment, 'have been maintained consistently throughout Judaism's long history, as has our duty to educate our children in the principles and practice of the faith itself. These principles have nothing to do with race and everything to do with religion. Ethnicity is irrelevant to Jewish identity, according to Jewish law.

'Education has been the crucible of Judaism throughout the millennia, and the development of Jewish faith schools is one of Anglo-Jewry's greatest achievements. I have advised the leadership of JFS, the United Synagogue and the Board of Deputies, on behalf of our community, that they have my full personal support and encouragement to use the necessary avenues available to them to maintain our historic rights to be true to our faith and a blessing to others, regardless of their faith.'[46]

Expanding on his statement a week later, the Chief Rabbi wrote:

The learned judges who ruled that the admission procedures of the JFS were in breach of the Race Relations Act clearly did not wish to claim that Judaism is racist. Yet, by one of the great ironies of our time, a law, intended to protect Jews from racism, has now been used against them.

Since the days of Abraham and Moses, Jews have been commanded to educate their children and thus hand on their faith across the generations. We are the people who predicated our survival on education, the first in history to create a universal system of schooling. Our citadels are schools; our heroes, teachers; and our passion, education and the life of the mind. We believe in teaching our children to be active citizens, honouring the law of the land, contributing to the wider society and the common good.

Jews have been in Britain for 353 years, and the JFS has been in existence since 1732. In all those years the same principle has applied, as it has applied throughout Jewish history. We extend Jewish education to Jews, that is, those born of Jewish mothers or those who have converted according to the standards of the religious authority to which the school belongs. This is a religious, not a racial, test and it applies to all Jewish schools, Orthodox and non-Orthodox alike.

Now, an English court has declared this rule racist, and since this is an essential element of Jewish law, it is in effect declaring Judaism racist. In seeking to compel a Jewish school to admit a child that it does not consider to be Jewish, the courts are in effect using the power of civil law to force a Jewish school to change its religious character.

The immediate result of the ruling will be to plunge all Jewish schools into confusion, whichever section of the community they seek to serve. Furthermore, if Jewish schools are compelled by English law to impose a test of religious practice instead of the existing test of membership of the Jewish faith, they will no longer be able to teach the Jewish faith to those who have little or no experience of practising it.

We must now work together as a community to ensure that the Jewish educational system – a source of pride to Jews and Britain alike – is not now put at risk. The implications of this ruling are vast and affect us all.

To be told now that Judaism is racist, when Jews have been in the forefront of the fight against racism in this country, is distressing. To confuse religion and race is a mistake. To use anti-racist legislation to deprive Jews of their right to religious self-governance is a bad ruling, at a bad time. We respect it, but we must join together to challenge it, for the sake of Jews and Judaism, and for the sake of Britain as the fair and decent country we know it to be.[47]

On behalf of the United Synagogue, its president, Simon Hochhauser, asserted: 'The US and other communities under the Chief Rabbinate are unshakeably committed to inclusive Orthodoxy. We are open to all Jews, observant and non-observant, who are willing to respect the religious principles on which our synagogues and schools are based.

Considerable confusion exists about Orthodox schools generally – JFS specifically – and this has been heightened by the recent court case. Certain facts should therefore be made clear. The first is that the religious identity and policy of JFS has not changed in recent years ... What has changed is not admission criteria, or Orthodox attitudes to non-halachic conversions, but the simple fact that JFS is no longer under- but oversubscribed – a tribute to its excellence. Under those circumstances, it would be absurd to favour children who are not halachically Jewish over those who are: absurd because JFS was, is and will continue to be an Orthodox school.[48]

All of us within the United Synagogue take with full seriousness the sense of disappointment on the part of children who find themselves excluded because of a non-halachic conversion. But nowhere in the world are non-halachic conversions recognised as valid by Orthodox authorities. The non-Orthodox world displays similar distinctions, and every movement practises some form of exclusion. The only form of conversion universally recognised is an Orthodox one.

Ironically, the court ruling is an open invitation for our schools to be less rather than more inclusive, since it insists that the criteria of admission be based on religious practice. The community should therefore be assured that all of us – the Chief Rabbi, dayanim and rabbanim, United Synagogue lay leaders, school governors and head teachers – have decided that the principle of inclusivity remains central to our philosophy of Judaism. We will therefore set the religious practice bar as low as possible, with the aim of excluding as few as possible.'[49]

Reacting to the judgment, E told the *Jewish Chronicle*: 'We are delighted and relieved that this most unpleasant wrong has been corrected by the three Appeal Court judges, and that justice is starting to be done. It is a great shame that my son and I had to pursue this case through the courts. We would have much preferred to reach a fair settlement with the school to revise its policy for the benefit of the whole Jewish community. Unfortunately, that has not been possible.'[50]

Under the banner headline, 'Top London Jewish school "unlawfully racist" in landmark ruling,' the *Evening Standard* quoted E's solicitor, John Halford: 'JFS admits the children of atheist or practising Christian parents whose mothers happened to be born Jewish, but denies entry to children like M who practise Judaism, but whose mothers' conversions are not recognised by the Office of the Chief Rabbi. The ending of this practice, which has caused great distress to many families, is long overdue.

'The school's governors now stand at a crossroads. They should do what the law demands, admitting immediately and devising inclusive admissions criteria that are fair to all who want their children to have a Jewish education. We have never sought to interfere with the right of Orthodox Jews to define for their own religious purposes whom they do or do not recognise as Jewish. However, it is unlawful for a child's ethnic origins to be used as the criterion for entry to a school. Such a practice is even more unacceptable in the case of a comprehensive school funded by the taxpayer.'[51]

For the Liberals, Rich declared: 'Liberal Judaism is not opposed to the United Synagogue or to faith schools, but it welcomes the decision because it believes that it is not proper for the State-funded JFS to decide its admissions on the basis of the status of the mother of a prospective pupil, and particularly by reference to only one British Jewish religious authority, the Office of the Chief Rabbi.

'Liberal Judaism has long argued that it is preferable for the State not to involve itself with the private concerns of religion. But when, at the State's expense, a religious group practises discrimination even within that sect itself, it may well be time for the State to act. Liberal Judaism would hope that, even at the last minute, a chastened Jewish community might put its own house in order.'[52]

Addressing a meeting of the United Synagogue Rabbinical Council, Finchley's Ephraim Mirvis stated that he and his colleagues were 'deeply concerned' over the possible consequences of the court ruling on Jewish schools. He had himself been chairman of governors of a Jewish school when he had 'inherited a situation.' The previous authorities, he said, 'had accepted children who were not halachically Jewish.

'Huge pressure had been brought upon the governors and they just buckled under for the sake of *shalom* in the community, and they said: "Let's be kind to this family and let's accept the children." I saw these children on a daily basis at school, bright kids, lovely kids. We had *shacharit* every morning, we couldn't include the boys in the minyan, we couldn't call them up to the Torah. Although they were the best Hebrew readers, they were unable to lead the service. They were ostracised within our school. It was all so very wrong, it should never have been that way.'

At 16, said Mirvis, the older boy started to date a girl from a respected family in the community, embarking on a serious relationship which lasted for years. The boy 'adamantly refused to convert according to halachah' and the situation produced a rift within the girl's family. 'We brought this about – and that's not what Jewish schools have been created for.

'The court has now decided that what will determine admission to our schools will not be halachah but rather practice. The Jewishness of the person will be determined by the level of practice within that family. I must tell you, it is an abhorrent mindset for us to adopt. It is the very antithesis of what we are all about. It's not for us to play God, to give the future children of our congregants, members of our community, marks out of ten as far as what they do or what they don't. The outcome will be that some Jewish children will lose out by being denied school places. Instead, we will have non-halachic Jews coming into our system, and the very ethos of our schools will be threatened.'[53]

Days later, the Chief Rabbi issued admission guidelines to Jewish schools in the wake of the ruling. New entry rules, he said, based on Jewish practice, should be 'as inclusive as possible – inclusive rather than exclusive. They should reflect the rabbinic principle that the world stands on three things: *Torah* (Jewish study and knowledge), *avodah* (the life of religious observance and prayer) and *gemilut chasadim* (acts of kindness and social responsibility).

'Evidence of practice in any one of these areas should normally be considered as positive evidence of religious commitment. Otherwise, schools risk denying the opportunity for an Orthodox Jewish religious education to many children who would greatly benefit from it.'

Schools, the Chief Rabbi stressed, would be free to devise their own entry policies, but they would not be able to ask whether a child is halachically Jewish. The new practice criteria would make no distinction between Orthodox and Progressive families; nor would schools be able to turn down the children of non-Orthodox converts if they met the entry standards. But admitting children to school under these rules 'will not mean recognition of their Jewish status.'[54]

As the 2009–10 school year approached, a 'radical shake-up' of the admissions system was announced, with a warning that 'children who fail to go to synagogue over the High Holy-days may miss out on a place at a Jewish school next year.' New rules published by the JFS, and followed by other Jewish secondary schools, allowed for the allocation of places on the basis of points scored for synagogue attendance and other observance. Parents also needed a certificate signed by their rabbi or other community official testifying to religious practice, mirroring the procedure in some Catholic schools.

Under the revised JFS system, children had to score a minimum of three points to gain priority in the competition for places. Attending synagogue at least twice a month, plus the High Holy-days and at least one day of Sukkot, scored three points. Children who were present on all the High Holy-days or, alternatively, at least four times, scored two points, and less frequent visitors none. Crucially, the entry rules made no distinction between Orthodox and non-Orthodox synagogues.

Children who had attended a Jewish primary school or cheder, or who had had a Jewish tutor for at least two years, gained one point, as did a child who had volunteered (or whose parent had done so) in any Jewish communal, charitable or welfare activity.

Kett pointed out that the school had introduced the changes 'only because it is advised that legally it has no option,'[55] a view confirmed by United Synagogue chief executive Jeremy Jacobs, who added: 'While the legal process continues, we have been working feverishly to develop robust, clear and fair rules to enable a seamless process at synagogues during the very busy *yomin noraim* [High Holy-day] period.'[56]

Picking up on the United Synagogue's – and the Chief Rabbi's – adoption of the term 'inclusive Orthodoxy' in connection with the revised admission policy, *Jewish Tribune* columnist Ben Yitzchok remarked: 'I wonder how many new words and phrases have crept into Anglo-Jewish phraseology in recent years.

'One expression which springs to mind is "inclusive Orthodoxy," which Dr Simon Hochhauser has used … The president doesn't say how low the "practice bar" will be set. Does it mean three-times-a-year Reform temple attendance? Or a contribution to the UJIA? Membership of a Jewish sports club? "Conversion" to Judaism by criteria which are not recognised by the London *Beis Din*? Tell us, Mr President, where does the US set its "practice bar"?

'Please, Mr President, reread the [1995 *Jewish Tribune*] statement by the Chief Rabbi and explain in unambiguous terms where you detect a reference to "inclusive Orthodoxy" or to "a practice bar as low as possible." He [the Chief Rabbi] clearly writes about the need to believe in *Torah min hashomayim* and makes no reference to this new terminology of "inclusive Orthodoxy." So who and what has changed?'[57]

Decrying the 'robustness' of the rules, Ben Yitzchok later described them as 'a sheer and utter mockery of basic Jewish values which must be resisted by all means.'[58]

Equally scathing was Geoffrey Alderman, his JC counterpart, who declared: 'I have read few documents in the field of Anglo-Jewish history more miserable in tone and more immature in content than the "Certificate of Religious Practice" which is now required from all parents who wish their children to be considered for admission to the JFS in 2010.'

The requirements, he asserted, 'lack any semblance of religious depth. Nothing about keeping kosher. Nothing about knowledge of synagogue ritual. A "synagogue"-attending "Jew for Jesus" could pass this "religious practice" test with flying colours.'[59]

Days earlier, it became known that the JFS had accepted the child of a non-Orthodox-converted mother as a first-year pupil, despite its previous rejection of such children. The child was among three hundred eleven-year-olds entering the school in the 2009–10 academic year.

Kett, however, declined to concede any U-turn or to say whether the decision had been taken as a result of the Court of Appeal ruling. He remarked: 'The school does not comment on individual applicants or students. The admissions for September 2009 were dealt with under the old admissions policy and the offer process predated the court decision. The school was over-subscribed with applicants who were confirmed as Jewish by the Office of the Chief Rabbi.'

But Kett did reveal that forty-three appeals had been heard on behalf of children initially turned down, with three places awarded by an appeals panel.[60] A spokesman for Brent Council, the school's local authority, said:

'All appeals must be heard by a panel independent of the school. Any decision made by the independent panel must be implemented.'

In contrast, another United Synagogue-sponsored school, King Solomon High, admitted that for several years it had accepted the children of non-Orthodox converts because there were insufficient pupils qualifying under the Beth Din's definition.[61]

'Under the pressure of an Appeal Court ruling,' wrote Alderman of these developments, 'Lord Sacks has decreed that the rules of entry into the JFS previously sanctioned by him must be set aside, and in their place new rules must be substituted which disregard entirely the status of the applicant's mother – or father – and which focus instead upon what he is pleased to call religious practice ...

'If Chief Rabbi Professor Lord Sacks and his dayanim are prepared, now, to concede that the admission of children to the JFS and recognition of the Jewish status of those children are two completely different things, why in heaven's name did they not pronounce thus a decade and more ago, thus preventing a great deal of human misery and saving the United Synagogue a great deal of money into the bargain?'[62]

* * *   * * *   * * *

In a judgment on costs, delivered on 14 October, 2009, two weeks before it began hearing a substantive appeal against the Appeal Court's ruling, the newly constituted Supreme Court of the United Kingdom made a dramatic – and unexpected – revelation, received with the barest of news coverage in the Jewish (or national) press:

> On 31 July, 2009, the House of Lords refused an application by the governing body [of the JFS] and its independent admission appeal panel for a continuation of the stay of that part of the order of the Court of Appeal directing JFS to reconsider M's admission, with the result that M was offered a place at JFS starting in the academic year 2009–10. He has now been admitted to the school, and JFS accepts that he and any siblings of his will stay there regardless of the decision on its appeal.[63]

Alderman – once again – was considerably more voluble than his news-gathering colleagues. 'Mark those words,' he wrote: '"*he and any of his siblings.*"

> So M and his family have won, no matter what the outcome of the Supreme Court's legal protestations. That being the case, we do need to ask why so much money is being spent trying to convince the Supreme Court that

the Court of Appeal erred in condemning as a breach of the 1976 Act the inquiry into M's matrilineal antecedents that resulted in the original rejection of this child's JFS application.

The answer seems to be that the JFS governors, the United Synagogue and the Chief Rabbi all resent, deeply and sincerely no doubt, the accusation that they are racists, no better (it might be said) than the vilest thug who finds himself in the dock for uttering crude anti-black or even anti-Jewish epithets. I do understand this resentment. But I have little, if any, sympathy with it.

In his statement of the grounds upon which JFS wished to overturn the judgment of the Court of Appeal, David Pannick, QC, admitted that M would be regarded as Jewish by a Jewish school that applied criteria used by Reform, Masorti or Liberal Judaism but not by Orthodox Jews.

But what Lord Pannick could not then have known was that Dinah Rose, QC, representing M's father, was about to present the Supreme Court with a letter, signed by Chief Rabbi Sacks himself, personally, in 1994, certifying that the St Albans Masorti synagogue 'constitutes a congregation of persons professing the Jewish religion.'[64]

Unless the Chief Rabbi believes that there is more than one authentic 'Jewish religion' (and if he does, no doubt he will share this fascinating belief with the rest of us), the words he used fifteen years ago can only mean that he, for his part, accepts that Masorti Judaism constitutes merely an acceptable variant of the Judaism he practises – rather like Lubavitch Chasidim, for instance. And if Masorti Judaism is just an acceptable variant of Orthodoxy, then a person accepted as Jewish by its rabbis must surely be Jewish.

In other words, what was really on trial at the Supreme Court was Lord Sacks' policy of 'inclusivism,' the policy he proclaimed so loudly and eloquently fifteen years ago but has since abandoned.[65]

* * *   * * *   * * *

For three days in October 2009, before Lord Phillips, president of the Supreme Court, and eight fellow law lords, several of Britain's leading silks argued the appeal – brought by the governing body of the JFS – against the unanimous finding of Sedley, Smith and Rimer.[66] Six weeks later, dismissing the appeal by a majority vote, Phillips introduced his court's 91-page judgment with the opening verses of Deuteronomy, chapter seven, including the injunction relating to the 'seven nations greater and mightier' than the Israelites: 'Neither shalt thou make marriages with them; thy daughter thou shalt not give unto his son, nor his daughter shalt thou take unto thy son.'

It is a fundamental tenet of Judaism, or the Jewish religion [said Phillips], that the covenant at Sinai was made with all the Jewish people, both those then alive and future generations. It is also a fundamental tenet of the Jewish religion, derived from the third and fourth verses that I have quoted, that the child of a Jewish mother is automatically and inalienably Jewish. I shall describe this as the 'matrilineal test.' It is the primary test applied by those who practise or believe in the Jewish religion for deciding whether someone is Jewish. They have always recognised, however, an alternative way in which someone can become Jewish, which is by conversion.[67]

Outlining the background to the case, the judge noted: 'The requirements for conversion of the recently formed denominations are less exacting than those of Orthodox Jews. Lord Jonathan Sacks, Chief Rabbi of the United Hebrew Congregation of the Commonwealth and leader of the Orthodox Jews in this country, issued a paper about conversion, through his office ("the OCR"), on 8 July, 2005.

'In it he stated that conversion was "irreducibly religious." He commented: "Converting to Judaism is a serious undertaking, because Judaism is not a mere creed. It involves a distinctive, detailed way of life. When people ask me why conversion to Judaism takes so long, I ask them to consider other cases of changed identity. How long does it take for a Briton to become an Italian, not just legally but linguistically, culturally, behaviourally? It takes time."'

Phillips continued: 'A Jew by conversion is a Jew for all purposes. Thus, descent by the maternal line from a woman who has become a Jew by conversion will satisfy the matrilineal test.'[68]

Of the issues at the centre of the case, the judge remarked: 'JFS is an outstanding school. For many years, far more children have wished to go there than there have been places in the school. In these circumstances it has been the policy of the school to give preference to those whose status as Jews is recognised by the OCR – that is, to children whose mothers satisfy the matrilineal test or who are Jews by conversion by Orthodox standards.

'The issue raised by this appeal is whether this policy has resulted in an infringement of section 1 of the Race Relations Act 1976 ("the 1976 Act").[69]

While the court has appreciated the high standard of the advocacy addressed to it, it has not welcomed being required to resolve this dispute. The dissatisfaction of E and M has not been with the policy of JFS in giving preference in admission to Jews, but with the application of

Orthodox standards of conversion which has led to the OCR declining to recognise M as a Jew.

Yet this appeal necessarily raises the broader issue of whether, by giving preference to those with Jewish status, JFS is, and for many years has been, in breach of section 1 of the 1976 Act. The implications of that question extend to other Jewish faith schools, and the resolution of the bone of contention between the parties risks upsetting a policy of admission to Jewish schools that, over many years, has not been considered to be open to objection.[70]

This demonstrates that there may well be a defect in our law of discrimination.[71] In contrast to the law in many countries, where English law forbids direct discrimination it provides no defence of justification. It is not easy to envisage justification for discriminating *against* a minority racial group. Such discrimination is almost inevitably the result of irrational prejudice or ill-will.

But it is possible to envisage circumstances where giving preference to a minority racial group will be justified. Giving preference to cater for the special needs of a minority will not normally involve any prejudice or ill-will towards the majority. Yet a policy which directly favours one racial group will be held to constitute racial discrimination against all who are not members of that group ...

Nothing that I say in this judgment should be read as giving rise to criticism on moral grounds of the admissions policy of JFS in particular or the policies of Jewish faith schools in general, let alone as suggesting that these policies are 'racist' as that word is generally understood.[72]

Explaining its judgment, the Supreme Court noted that the simple legal question to be determined was whether, in being denied admission to the JFS, M was disadvantaged on grounds of his ethnic origins, or his lack thereof.[73]

The reason that M was denied admission to JFS was because of his mother's ethnic origins, which were not halachically Jewish. She was not descended in the matrilineal line from the original Jewish people. There can be no doubt that the Jewish people are an ethnic group within the meaning of the 1976 Act.

While JFS and the OCR would have overlooked this fact if M's mother had herself undergone an approved course of Orthodox conversion, this could not alter the fundamental nature of the test being applied. If M's mother herself was of the requisite ethnic origins in her matrilineal line, no conversion requirement would be imposed. It could not be said that M was adversely treated because of his religious beliefs. JFS and the OCR were indifferent to these and focused solely upon whether M satisfied the test of matrilineal descent ...[74]

The reason for the refusal to admit M to JFS was his lack of the requisite ethnic origins: the absence of a matrilineal connection to Orthodox Judaism.[75] M's ethnic origins encompass, among other things, his paternal Jewish lineage and his descent from an Italian Roman Catholic mother. In denying M admission on the basis that he lacks a matrilineal Orthodox Jewish antecedent, JFS discriminated against him on grounds of his ethnic origins ...[76]

The fact that a decision to discriminate on racial grounds is based upon a devout, venerable and sincerely held religious belief or conviction cannot inoculate or excuse such conduct from liability under the 1976 Act.[77]

On the issue of direct discrimination, the decision of the court was by a majority of five (Lord Phillips, Lady Hale, Lord Mance, Lord Kerr and Lord Clarke) to four (Lord Hope, Lord Rodger, Lord Walker and Lord Brown). The majority held that the JFS had directly discriminated against M on grounds of his ethnic origins.

Hope and Walker, in the minority, would have dismissed the appeal on the ground that the JFS had indirectly discriminated against M, having failed to demonstrate that its policy was proportionate. Rodger and Brown would have allowed the school's appeal in its entirety.

Disputing the court's finding of both direct and indirect discrimination, Rodger contended: 'The decision of the majority means that there can in future be no Jewish faith schools which give preference to children because they are Jewish according to Jewish religious law and belief.

If the majority are right, expressions of sympathy for the governors of the school seem rather out of place, since they are doing exactly what the Race Relations Act exists to forbid: they are refusing to admit children to their school on racial grounds. That is what the court's decision means. And, if that decision is correct, why should Parliament amend the Race Relations Act to allow them to do so? Instead, Jewish schools will be forced to apply a concocted test for deciding who is to be admitted. That test might appeal to this secular court, but it has no basis whatever in 3,500 years of Jewish law and teaching.

The majority's decision leads to such extraordinary results, and produces such manifest discrimination against Jewish schools in comparison with other faith schools, that one can't help feeling that something has gone wrong.

The crux of the matter is whether, as the majority hold, the governors actually treated M less favourably on grounds of his ethnic origins. They say the governors did so, but for a *bona fide* religious motive. If that is really the position, then, as Lord Pannick, QC, was the first to accept on their behalf, what the governors did was unlawful and their *bona fide* religious motive could not make the slightest difference.

But to reduce the religious element in the actions of those concerned to the status of a mere motive is to misrepresent what they were doing. The reality is that the Office of the Chief Rabbi, when deciding whether or not to confirm that someone is of Jewish status, gives its ruling on religious grounds. Similarly, so far as the oversubscription criteria are concerned, the governors consider or refuse to consider children for admission on the same religious grounds. The only question is whether, when they do so, they are *ipso facto* considering or refusing to consider children for admission on racial grounds.

Lady Hale says that M was rejected because of his mother's ethnic origins, which were Italian and Roman Catholic. I respectfully disagree. His mother could have been as Italian in origin as Sophia Loren, and as Roman Catholic as the Pope, for all that the governors cared: the only thing that mattered was that she had not converted to Judaism under Orthodox auspices.

It was her resulting non-Jewish religious status in the Chief Rabbi's eyes, not the fact that her ethnic origins were Italian and Roman Catholic, which meant that M was not considered for admission. The governors automatically rejected M because he was descended from a woman whose religious status as a Jew was not recognised by the Orthodox Chief Rabbi; they did not reject him because he was descended from a woman whose ethnic origins were Italian and Roman Catholic.[78]

'So far as indirect discrimination is concerned,' Rodger argued, 'I agree with Lord Brown and, indeed, with [Mr Justice] Munby. The aim of the school, to instil Jewish values into children who are Jewish in the eyes of Orthodoxy, is legitimate. And, from the standpoint of an Orthodox school, instilling Jewish values into children whom Orthodoxy does not regard as Jewish, at the expense of children whom Orthodoxy does regard as Jewish, would make no sense.

'That is plainly why the school's oversubscription policy allows only for the admission of children recognised as Jewish by the Office of the Chief Rabbi. I cannot see how a court could hold that this policy is a disproportionate means of achieving the school's legitimate aim.'[79]

Earlier, relating his court's judgment to the JFS admission criteria – the 'concocted test,' as Rodger put it – introduced after the Court of Appeal ruling, Lord Phillips noted: 'Concern has been expressed that the majority decision will compel Jewish faith schools to admit children whom the Jewish religion does not recognise as being Jewish – that is, children who are not descended from Jews by the maternal line. It is not clear that this is so.

'As a result of the decision of the Court of Appeal, the JFS has published a new admission policy for admission in September 2010. This applies a test of religious practice, including "synagogue attendance, Jewish education and/or family communal activity." As matrilineal descent or conversion is the requirement for membership of the Jewish faith according to the law of that faith, those who satisfy a practice test are likely to satisfy this requirement.

'Thus, instead of applying the matrilineal descent test by way of direct discrimination, the school will be applying a test that will indirectly discriminate in favour of those who satisfy the matrilineal descent test. It is not clear that the school will now be faced with applications from those who do not satisfy the test.'[80]

On the question of costs, the Supreme Court unanimously allowed, in part, the United Synagogue's appeal. The US was ordered to pay 20 per cent of E's costs from the Court of Appeal, but not those incurred in the High Court. The 20 per cent of E's costs in the High Court previously allocated to the US was transferred to the JFS, in addition to the 50 per cent it had earlier been ordered to pay.[81]

In a statement from his office within minutes of the ruling, the Chief Rabbi commented: 'The closeness of the court's judgment indicates how complex this case was, in both English law and debated issues of Jewish identity. I welcome the judges' vindication of the good faith in which the United Synagogue, the London Beth Din and our office have acted.[82]

'I likewise welcome the suggestion of the president of the Supreme Court that the issue at stake in this case may merit legislative remedy. However, these matters require careful reflection and consultation, and instant reactions would be inappropriate. Our office will be working closely together with the schools, the United Synagogue, the Board of Deputies and other interested parties to consider the implications of the verdict before making a full response.'[83]

Whether full or partial, instant or delayed, within twenty-four hours Sacks appeared to have reversed his view on 'inappropriate' reactions. 'The judges, without exception,' he wrote on the morrow of the result, 'were emphatic in denying that racism played any part in this case.

> The most important outcome is a point made, one way or another,
> by eight of the nine judges, that there may be something wrong with

race relations legislation as it stands, and that what this case calls for is legislative remedy.

The judges had no doubt that the school acted on religious principle, according to Jewish law. As one judge put it, 'Jewish law has enabled the Jewish people and the Jewish religion to survive throughout centuries of discrimination and persecution. The world would undoubtedly be a poorer place if they had not.'

To understand the case we must rid ourselves of the confusion with which it has been surrounded. Many people think it was about conversion. It was not. The court would have applied the same principle, with the same result, had the child's mother not converted at all.

Many think it was about Jewish Orthodoxy versus Progressive denominations. Again it was not. The court's ruling applies to all Jewish denominations, Orthodox, Reform, Liberal and Masorti. It applies to the new progressive school, JCoSS [the Jewish Community Secondary School],[84] as well as to the JFS. The judges were quite explicit about this point.

This case had nothing to do with denominations or conversions. It focused on one simple fact: that Jewish identity is – conversions aside – conferred by birth, by the mother, or in the case of Liberal Judaism, by the father if the mother is not Jewish. Any discrimination, regardless of motive, between Jew and non-Jew, unless specifically exempted in law, has now been held to contravene the 1976 Race Relations Act.

This cannot be what the framers of that legislation intended. Among other things, they intended to protect the Jewish community against anti-Semitism, the world's oldest and most devastating hatred. They certainly did not intend that the law should be used, as it was in this case, to adjudicate a dispute between Jew and Jew on a matter of Jewish law. Nor did they intend to circumscribe the freedom of Jews in Britain to practise their religion and educate their children in their faith.

You do not have to be an expert in jurisprudence to realise that, as one of the judges put it, the court's decision 'leads to such extraordinary results, and produces such manifest discrimination against Jewish schools in comparison with other faith schools, that one can't help feeling that something has gone wrong.'

So we must now work with Parliament and the Equality and Human Rights Commission to do what several of the judges advise – namely, to seek legislative remedy. In doing so, we will find support from across the political community. We must proceed together as a community, using the principle that 'on matters that affect us regardless of our religious differences, we will work together regardless of our religious differences.'

Good will eventually come from this case, but first there is work to be done, for the sake of British justice and religious freedom, for the sake of our children and our faith.[85]

The path towards a legislative remedy was, however, less smooth than Sacks would have wished. Blocking a cross-communal front, 'regardless of our religious differences,' was a demand from the Reform, Liberal and Masorti movements that their converts be accepted into mainstream Orthodox schools as a condition of non-Orthodox support for any amendment to the Equality Bill then before Parliament.

In anticipation of an adverse ruling from the Supreme Court, Jonathan Arkush, senior vice-president of the Board of Deputies, had earlier stated that the Board was exploring the possibility of a change in the Bill – 'a simple amendment, in line with other faith schools, that would effectively reverse the judgment. Just as Protestant and Catholic schools may lawfully give preference to Protestant and Catholic pupils, so Jewish schools must have the right to give preference to Jewish pupils.'

Responding to this proposal, Bayfield commented: 'We are in favour of legislation to remove the operation of the Race Relations Act for determining Jewish status in any area. But we could support such a change in the law only if, in the area of schools, there is no going back to the status quo ante. All State-funded Jewish schools should be open, on an equal basis, to all Jewish children whose status is determined by any denomination under the auspices of the Board of Deputies.'

For Masorti, Wittenberg said that his movement would similarly support a legal change 'so long as we receive written undertakings that it will not be used simply to return school-admission policies to the status quo ante. We will favour a cross-communal policy for the purposes of access to State-funded schools – and to all the charitable services offered by the community – in which anyone is regarded as Jewish who is accepted as such by any synagogue body forming part of the Board of Deputies.'

The Liberals expressed opposition to legislation that would prejudice non-Orthodox converts, or potential pupils on grounds of descent. 'We will not support moves to allow State-aided Jewish faith schools to discriminate against children on the basis of biology,' said Rich.

As for the Equality and Human Rights Commission – which had welcomed the Supreme Court judgment, and whose help the Chief Rabbi was also pursuing – a spokesman remarked that, while it was 'seeking to strengthen religious freedom and protection' in the Equality Bill and other proposed laws, 'we believe that the current Race Relations Act and future Equality Bill strike the correct balance. We do not feel that an exemption should be included to permit faith schools to discriminate on grounds of ethnic origin.'[86]

In the face of these reservations, the Board of Deputies and its Orthodox partners soon dropped their initial plans to press for an amendment to the law. Vivian Wineman, the Board's president, announced 'widespread agreement' that it was better not to go immediately for legislative change. Although the proposed amendment was 'neat,' he said, 'we didn't know how it would work out or whether it would have unintended consequences.'

Consultations with synagogue and other leaders had made it clear that 'the vast majority of the community would rather see how the Supreme Court judgment impacts on their activities and then consider what kind of amendment we need rather than rush into it. Everyone felt it sensible to wait.'

While the United Synagogue lay leadership backed the decision, its Rabbinical Council issued a defiant challenge. Following a crisis meeting headed by Schochet, the rabbis declared:

> We are deeply appreciative of the huge amount of effort and resource which has been expended to date in defence of the Orthodox community's right to determine priority right of admission to its Jewish day schools on the singular criteria [sic] of halachic status. However, we are deeply concerned to learn that a change in legislation is not being actively pursued.
>
> While we appreciate that the outcome may be unpredictable, we feel that in looking to preserve Jewish integrity, every possible effort must be exerted. It is deeply regrettable that we should be seen surrendering rather than actively and aggressively pursuing every avenue available to us, regardless of how remote the chances.
>
> Furthermore, we reject the non-Orthodox movements' holding us to ransom in this matter by agreeing to a change of legislation only on condition that we do not revert to the status quo ante. It is untenable that a movement that has been around little more than 100 years should seek to impose its standards on a community that has remained faithful to the tenets of Jewish tradition for nearly 3,500 years. It is unacceptable and unconscionable that we should yield to that sort of pressure.
>
> As rabbis, we are guarantors for the Jewish future and share in the responsibility of ensuring that we will have Jewish grandchildren. To that end, it is in our paramount interest to ensure that every halachically Jewish child, regardless of observance level, is given an opportunity for Jewish education, and that his or her place not be compromised by those who do not fall into that bracket.[87]

Differences among the US Rabbinical Council emerged within days, when its joint vice-chairmen – Borehamwood and Elstree's Naftali Brawer and Hampstead's Michael Harris, neither of whom was present at the meeting – described the Council's challenge as 'bombastic and aggressive.'

Calling for 'realism and a willingness to compromise on the part of the Orthodox community,' the two maintained: 'The only plausible way forward is for all denominations to work together for a change in the law on the understanding that, in future, priority places at Jewish schools will be offered to anyone deemed Jewish by the rabbinic authority of any mainstream Jewish denomination – Orthodox, Masorti, Reform or Liberal …

'Cross-communal efforts towards a change in the law require a process of healing in the aftermath of the pain, anguish and frustration felt on all sides of the debate about school admissions … Just as we are hurt by disparaging descriptions of Orthodoxy by the non-Orthodox, so the non-Orthodox are rightly offended by intemperate language. It is surely possible – and desperately necessary – for UK Jewish denominations and their spokespersons to articulate even the deepest disagreements in a spirit of communal *darchei shalom*.'[88]

For its part, the Chief Rabbi's office limited itself to a one-line statement that Lord Sacks was 'giving consideration to what the next step will be.'[89]

* * *   * * *   * * *

Censuring the Orthodox sector's handling of the case – rejected, in the final analysis, by ten (out of thirteen) of the most senior judges in the land – the *Jerusalem Post* asserted: 'As Jewish civilisation hopefully pursues a golden mean to the identity conundrum, it is unfortunate that Sacks and his dayanim painted M's family into a corner, forcing them to seek a solution in the British courts. Could not a more humane and politic alternative have been found?

'The larger lesson here is that when Orthodoxy is accepted by the State as the authorised expression of Judaism, it ought to exhibit greater humility and tolerance towards other Jews … The Orthodox have every right to set standards for their stream, but when their clergy are called upon to act in a fiduciary capacity for the entire community, they need to show greater forbearance and love.'[90]

'Once again,' wrote Daniella Peled in *Haaretz*, 'the Anglo-Jewish establishment has scored a spectacular own goal, this time over the Jewish Free School's admission criteria.

> Does it make sense, at a time when the community in England is shrinking, to reject people who want to be Jewish? Yes, apparently, believes the United

Synagogue, whose head, the recently ennobled Rabbi Jonathan Sacks, thought it suitable to pursue this case to legal extremis, at a reported cost of one million pounds ...

This is not an issue that British judges ever wanted to address. This is simply an example of the peevish arrogance of a Jewish establishment that seems irresistibly attracted to zero-sum games ... And now, despite some creeping *Schadenfreude* from a few Liberal and Reform quarters, even those who opposed United Synagogue policy are keeping quiet over the affair.

It's clear that the whole sorry mess has emphatically not been good for the Jews. It seems impossible to find even an Orthodox establishment figure who isn't privately groaning over the behaviour of the US, the Chief Rabbi, and the school. 'It all could have been avoided if the United Synagogue had not opened this can of worms,' sighs one senior community figure. 'Insane and indefensible,' says another ...

Lacking the confidence of the American community, and the nonchalant identity of Israeli Jews, Anglo-Jewry once again has wasted its resources, not least the patience of its constituents. From the increasingly ultra-Orthodox United Synagogue to its misguided lay leadership, from the poor child who wanted to study at JFS to the school itself – this has been a game, doomed from the start, in which there are no winners.[91]

The *Jewish Chronicle* voiced similar concerns:

Parliament never meant, in the Race Relations Act, to ban Jewish faith schools from deciding to admit pupils on grounds of Jewish law ... The blame lies not with the government, but with the United Synagogue and its associated parties, which doggedly pursued the case to the bitter end. It is difficult to imagine a more self-defeating waste of time, energy, money – hundreds of thousands of pounds frittered away on legal fees – and good will. The child in question is now at the school; a solution was available if the US were not determined to fight for the sake of fighting. As it is, all they have achieved is to establish in law that it is up to the State to define the nature of Judaism – about as far from a welcome result as it is possible to imagine.[92]

9

The Dynamic of Renewal

'I call to our educators: let us see how we can make the whole of Anglo-Jewish education greater than the sum of its constituent parts.' [1]

Weeks before the Supreme Court's hearing of the JFS appeal, Rabbi Jeffrey Cohen – since his retirement, in 2006, emeritus minister of Stanmore Synagogue – came out openly for an easing of the London Beth Din's policy on conversion. Participating in a *Jewish Chronicle*-sponsored Rosh Hashanah symposium, he revealed that he had been asking the dayanim for forty years to review the process.

'The Chief Rabbi, who has spoken about our having to be more inclusive, needs to do a lot of hard talking to his Beth Din if that is what he really means. We as a Jewish community are in an emergency situation, with assimilation in a number of areas, with all the problems facing Israel, with a threat to our survival.'

The original Shulchan Aruch (code of Jewish law), said Cohen, showed that conversion could be 'such a simple thing. According to Rabbi Joseph Karo, its compiler, if someone comes to be converted, you circumcise him and you dip him in the mikveh. You tell him some of the light precepts of Judaism and some of the more weighty precepts of Judaism. But you don't overdo it.

'That is what he said, you don't overdo it. You ask: "Why do you want to become a Jew? Don't you know how oppressed we Jews are today?" Then you say to him: "The reason why we are oppressed is because, if God gave us all the reward in this world for being his chosen people, the enjoyment of it might send us astray. Therefore God keeps it for the future." Why do we do this? In order, says the Shulchan Aruch, not to deter him. It then states: "If he says, 'I understand that and I accept it,' you accept him."' [2]

Referring to children barred entry to Jewish schools because the Orthodox authorities did not consider them Jewish, Cohen said: 'This is an opportunity for us to reflect on, and take great pride in, the Jewish schools we have in this country. We have schools catering for the right wing, and we have the Jewish Community Secondary School. JFS is a gem ...

'The conversion process should be made easier. There should be halachic solutions to enable these children to be regarded as full Jews. It is vital that our schools should be open to every child who wants a Jewish education.'[3]

* * *   * * *   * * *

Years before Cohen's call – in fact, within months of Sacks' installation – the problems of conversion, and their impact on school entry, had featured notably on the Chief Rabbinical agenda, following the report of an inquiry into Jewish education headed by communal activist Fred Worms and involving all religious streams within Anglo-Jewry. Declaring that 'the key to Anglo-Jewry's survival lies in education,' Worms had spelled out the challenges:

'Intermarriage is rife. A large proportion of Jews have lost interest in their heritage. The number of one-parent families is increasing, and there are more children with problematical halachic provenance. Sixty per cent of our teenagers have opted out by not attending either Hebrew classes or Jewish schools after their bar/batmitzvah. By the time they are seventeen, only 10 per cent will have stayed the course. It is not surprising that many of our youngsters grow up Jewishly illiterate.'[4]

Commenting on the findings, Sacks wrote: 'We stand at a critical moment in the history of Anglo-Jewry. We are losing four thousand Jews each year. But at the same time we have a unique opportunity to create a dynamic of Jewish renewal. We have come late – but not too late – to the realisation that Jewish education holds the key to the vitality of our community, intellectually, spiritually and even demographically. Those who know, grow; those for whom Judaism and Jewish identity are a closed book gradually drift away.

'We must move Jewish education to the highest place on the communal agenda. Above all, we must create a genuinely national structure that allows us to use our limited resources to the maximum effort. The single most striking finding to emerge is the sheer fragmentation of Anglo-Jewish education as presently constituted ... The time has come for us to pool our resources and labour together.'[5]

Explaining its rationale, Worms' report declared:

The Anglo-Jewish community survives by transmitting a vibrant sense of commitment and Jewish identity to its young people. The problem is that the process is faltering. Almost two-thirds of young Jews are missing from the annual statistics of synagogue marriages. Surveys of religious belief show that a substantial fraction of the community, probably the majority, have very limited faith in the essential spiritual and ethical tenets of Judaism.

Research on Jewish education, at least prior to the 1980s, casts doubt on the capacity of Jewish schools to enhance the religious beliefs and values of their pupils. At the same time, and perhaps by way of explanation, the cultural environment grows increasingly liberal and pluralistic, underlying the voluntary nature of religious identification and encouraging individual choice of lifestyle.

These trends have serious implications for the very survival of Anglo-Jewry, but at the same time they contain the seeds of a communal response. Recognition of recent demographic changes has created an unprecedented determination to revitalise the community, to encourage collaboration and synergy, and to develop the community's latent human resources – all essential features of the Chief Rabbi's call for a 'Decade of Renewal.'[6]

'It is now generally recognised within the community,' the report concluded, 'that something has to be done as a matter of urgency to resolve these problems ... In the context of a contracting and more interdependent community, both economics and logic point to the need for some kind of communal forum to encourage and facilitate educational collaboration and planning.

'There remains an urgent need for a single communal body capable of taking an overwiew of the whole system. Such a body might be called the National Council for Jewish Education (NCJE) ... As a first step, it is proposed that the Jewish Educational Development Trust [established by Jakobovits in 1971][7] should take the initiative, together with the Office of the Chief Rabbi, to set up the NCJE. In time, this will ensure that vital communal developments are evaluated, managed and funded. An essential priority would be to examine and carry forward the proposals arising from this review.'[8]

* * *   * * *   * * *

As events transpired, it was Jewish Continuity – initially, at least – that emerged as the 'single communal body.' Many of its problems have been examined here, but in the area of schooling others remain to be discussed, particularly in light of the growing non-Orthodox involvement in Jewish schools and the increase in applications from 'children with problematical halachic provenance.'

This rise, wrote sociologist Rona Hart, was attributable in part to responses from many parents to a weakening of Jewish identity, and to the accompanying loss of communal affiliation and the decline in religious practice. Such parents were 'searching for ways to maintain and cultivate their children's identities and turning to the Jewish school for reinforcement.' In the British context, reflecting the shift to multiculturalism, this ethos 'legitimises cultural heterogeneity, maintaining that individuals and groups can simultaneously hold their ethnic affiliation and develop national loyalties within a national space.'[9]

Following the creation of Jewish Continuity, the attempted evolution of an inclusivist educational and inspection policy for Anglo-Jewish schools drew in both the new organisation and the Board of Deputies. Continuity launched its campaign with full-page advertisements in the JC, depicting the community's decline, through intermarriage, with an image of young Jews at the edge of a precipice.[10]

Continuity announced commitments to major educational initiatives, both formal and informal, a substantial component of which was the establishment of a research and quality development unit in Jewish education. Further support was to be made through an open competitive scheme of grant awards, to be allocated twice yearly to Jewish schools and educational bodies.

Alongside this, substantial funds went towards the creation of an educational foundation to replace the London Board. The first strategic plan for the new Agency for Jewish Education proposed the development of an inspection service – including the preparation of Jewish schools for Section 13 Ofsted inspection[11] – and the formulation of an agreed syllabus for religious education.

Educationist Judy Keiner, who was involved in the process, noted at the time[12] that 'a third major Jewish communal body came to take an increasingly proactive role with Jewish schools in response to the emergence of the Ofsted system – the education committee of the Board of Deputies.

> Over the years [wrote Keiner], the Board's education function has been primarily that of representing Judaism and Jewish educational concerns to the non-Jewish educational world – for example, developing training and curricular materials about Judaism for non-Jewish schools. It has also had an important role in negotiating with examination bodies and local authorities over the observance of the holy days for Jewish candidates and teachers. In practice, all its materials and pronouncements can be seen to contain no element which represents interpretations of Judaism and Jewish practice other than the Orthodox.

With the advent of the national curriculum, with its extensive programme of consultation at the development stage of the proposed curricula, the Board of Deputies came into increasing prominence on the national educational scene, as the Department of Education's first port of call for consultation with the Jewish community. As the religious-education initiatives grew in prominence, the Board began to play a major role as the effective sole representative of Judaism on the national-curriculum development body responsible for outlining model religious-education syllabuses.

Once the Ofsted system of training inspectors had been established, claimed Keiner, the Board of Deputies 'set out an initiative to influence and co-ordinate the selection of inspectors for Jewish schools in general, and of Section 13 inspections in particular. It started with the more traditional method of forming an invited working group drawn exclusively from educationists who were members of the Orthodox community and within the United Synagogue's sphere of influence.[13]

'It also advertised in the *Jewish Chronicle*, asking any Jews who had qualified in Ofsted training to contact the Board in order to register as qualified inspectors with Jewish status. As a result of its group meetings, the Board of Deputies evolved an ambitious programme which could be seen as amounting to a major, if inexplicit, challenge to the two Jewish foundation bodies in seeking to become the most influential body in relation to quality control of Jewish schools.

It emerged that a more subtle process of religious vetting would be involved in the Board of Deputies' proposal to establish a register of qualified inspectors with Jewish status. At a meeting of the Association of Governors of Orthodox Jewish Schools, in April 1994, the director of education commented that 'Ofsted inspection will be able to do for schools what heads and governors have wanted for years.'[14]

He outlined the Board's intention to establish a training programme for inspectors of Jewish schools which, he hoped, would be the sole validated route recognised by Ofsted of such schools. He envisaged that the religious credentials of inspectors to be involved in Jewish school inspections would be subject as part of this process to approval by the senior judge of the United Synagogue's ecclesiastical court, the London Beth Din.

The newly established Ofsted bureaucracy appeared to be as eager to embrace the Board's initiative as the Board itself was to establish it. Faced with the prospect of including inspections of up to a quarter of the existing Jewish voluntary-aided schools in the first year of its operations, Ofsted's then chief executive established contacts with the Office of the Chief Rabbi and the Board of Deputies, and was prepared to offer accelerated access to Ofsted training – for which there was a substantial waiting-list – to candidates approved by the Board.

The Board subsequently obtained funding from Jewish Continuity of over £310,000 to develop a framework for Section 13 inspections of Jewish schools, designed to parallel the published framework for Ofsted's Section 9 inspections.[15]

In July 1995, it issued the first draft of a detailed framework, called Pikuach ('Inspection'), in which it adopted a novel approach to the interpretation of the legal responsibilities for Jewish religious education. The proposals were sent in confidential draft form to the head teachers of all Jewish schools, with a covering letter stating that head teachers were to have 'ownership' of the proposals, although a wider process of consultation would be involved.

The proposals, inter alia, required inspectors to take into account 'the levels of Jewish commitment among the communal groups served by the school' and 'any other relevant influences on pupils' behaviour and Jewish values which are at play in the wider community and the school environment.' As these proposals came to fruition, wrote Keiner, they were challenged by new developments which had threatened the credibility, and even the existence, both of Ofsted and of Jewish Continuity.

'Continuity became a subject of intense controversy inside and outside the Jewish community. A major television documentary made by the BBC, as part of its prestigious prime-time Everyman series, portrayed it as an almost sinister body bent on promoting Jewish separatism, inspired by advertising which had sought to sensationalise Jewish outmarriage.

'More sustained and damaging controversy bubbled up repeatedly within the Jewish community, focusing on the incompatibility of its claims to be a cross-community body, while quietly ensuring that all its major decisions and recipients were within the United Synagogue or other Orthodox orbit. It is not clear whether senior policy-makers at Ofsted were aware of the fact that Board of Deputies educational initiatives were effectively becoming enmeshed within the "turf wars" among the various Jewish communal and professional organisations involved with education.

'Senior Ofsted officials continued to appear at Board-organised events related to the development of Pikuach, notably a consultative conference held to discuss its third draft, in November 1995, at which the president of Board of Deputies referred to its claims to "work across communal boundaries and reach across the divisions," and to its "vibrant and proactive role in enhancing Jewish education." Thus, from having previously been an organisation confined largely to advocacy of Judaism and Jewish educational roles to the wider world, the Board was now claiming a central, perhaps the central, role in promoting Jewish education in Britain.

'In March 1996, the [Wagner] review into Jewish Continuity proposed to remedy the situation by reconstituting the organisation as a genuinely cross-communal initiative. It remains to be seen [concluded Keiner] whether this can be achieved in a situation where Orthodox participants will accept only the legitimacy of their own authorities within any cross-communal initiative.'

* * *   * * *   * * *

In fact, within thirty months, Jewish Continuity ceased to exist, having been swallowed up by the newly formed United Jewish Israel Appeal. But inclusivist initiatives did begin to emerge, among them proposals to build – several years down the line – London Jewry's first cross-community schools, both primary and secondary.

Nor were non-Orthodox projects ruled out of court. From a total grant allocation of £1 million, during the two years of life left to Continuity, £50,000 went to the Reform Synagogues of Great Britain; £24,000 to the Union of Liberal and Progressive Synagogues; £28,000 to them jointly;[16] and £26,000 to Masorti. The role of Jewish Continuity's newly established (if controversial) 'independent' allocations board – it was quick to point out – was 'to ensure that proposals from all sections of the community are treated fairly and objectively.'[17]

The first of the cross-communal schools were primaries – Clore Shalom in Shenley, Hertfordshire (1999), and Clore Tikva, in Redbridge, Essex (2000), both established with help from the Clore Foundation. The former, a voluntary-aided school situated in the appropriately named Hugo Gryn Way, gained support from the Reform, Liberal and Masorti movements and, in particular, the Centre for Jewish Education of Leo Baeck College. In its own words, it 'exemplifies an open, pluralist and inclusive Jewish environment and respects the wide variety of Jewish beliefs, customs and practices of the families of the school.'[18]

A Pikuach inspection report noted that 'Clore Shalom's provision for its pupils' spiritual, moral and cultural development is outstanding. The pupils really care about each other and the school community as a whole. A major emphasis is placed on helping pupils to feel secure in their spiritual and religious growth, with Jewish values at the core.'[19]

Like its partner in Shenley, Clore Tikva 'nurtures a love for learning where pluralist Jewish values and respect for others and ourselves are at the heart of a warm, caring community.'[20] It, too, received high praise from Ofsted: 'Pupils' spiritual, moral, social and cultural development is outstanding. Pupils have an excellent understanding of their own culture, but also are very well informed about those of others.'[21]

Orthodox reaction to Anglo-Jewry's first cross-communal high school, the £50-million Jewish Community Secondary School (known popularly as JCoSS) – located in Barnet, and functioning from 2010 – told a different story. Planned to cater for the needs of the 'entire Jewish community' (as its founders declared), it faced controversy from its earliest planning stages in 2002, initially on grounds of alleged over-provision and perceived competition, and later on religious grounds.

Objections were raised to the building of a Jewish secondary school in addition to the burgeoning Yavneh College[22] in Borehamwood, which opened in 2006 and which, with the proposed JCoSS, would bring to six the number of mainstream Jewish secondary schools in Greater London. Addressing these and other concerns, the cross-community organisers stated: 'JCoSS will need to find its own answers to some of the challenging questions we face, but in doing so we will be able to learn from the best practice of those that have gone before.

'JCoSS will extend the choice of a Jewish education to all Jews, whatever their background, affiliation, status and practice. Broad and inclusive in outlook, it will promote diversity within and beyond the Jewish community. If you want to be part of the JCoSS community and consider yourself Jewish, then we welcome you …

'We are often asked how it can be possible to create a genuinely cross-community school, and how we will deal with difficult issues such as teaching Jewish studies or managing different levels of observance. In fact, while JCoSS will be the first cross-community Jewish secondary school in Britain, most Jewish schools outside the United Kingdom are cross-communal, while already there are a number of primary schools in the UK with which we share our approach.'[23]

'Our approach,' however, offended Orthodox sensibilities. This was despite (or perhaps because of) the self-proclaimed 'vision' of a 2008 Jewish Schools Commission, headed by Wagner, that 'Jewish schools, collectively, should reflect the religious diversity of the community, and thus provide the opportunity for every Jewish child who wishes to attend a Jewish school to do so. Jewish schools should seek to meet the educational needs of every child, enabling them to develop their potential to the full.'[24]

One of the concerns examined by the Commission, and expressed by the Orthodox, was the potential shift in demand from existing schools to JCoSS, which would 'seek to attract pupils from across the community, including the non-affiliated. It will accept as Jewish anyone who is acceptable for membership of any of the synagogal organisations.

'Those responsible for the development of JCoSS believe, on the basis of their market research, that their more pluralistic approach will attract significant numbers who would not wish to attend the existing secondary schools. In this way, they will – they argue – broaden the market for Jewish secondary education. However, they also accept that their school will be attractive to some who might otherwise have attended one of the existing schools.'[25]

Placing these developments within their pragmatic context, David Graham, director of social and demographic research at the Institute for Jewish Policy Research, commented: 'This reflects an inevitable process. As the community becomes more diverse religiously, it makes sense that education provision will become more diverse.'[26]

Wagner, meanwhile, predicted an expansion in numbers as well as diversity. Echoing Hart's assessment, he asserted: 'People are worried about the secular assimilationist forces at work and are looking to Jewish schools to foster an identity. Even though the Jewish population is shrinking, the percentage of parents choosing Jewish schools is rising. Almost 60 per cent of non-charedi children in London – a record figure – are due to enrol in Jewish primary and secondary schools. If these schools continue to maintain high academic standards, and people continue to worry about assimilation, the percentages could go up further.'[27]

The UJIA's director of educational leadership, Alastair Falk – formerly head of two Orthodox schools, the Independent Jewish Day School[28] in Hendon and Redbridge's King Solomon High[29] – remarked of his newly adopted cross-communal role: 'We exist to help schools come up with Jewish education that fits their ethos. We work with all sorts of Jewish schools – primary and secondary, Orthodox, non-Orthodox and cross-communal – offering advice and assistance to meet their particular needs.'[30]

In broadening its appeal and desired intake, JCoSS chair of governors Michael Grabiner was unambiguous on his (and its) approach. The school, he declared,

> will respect all Jewish students, regardless of their background, affiliation or practice. That is why it is called a cross-community school. While

completely understanding that JCoSS will not be for everyone, we are determined that no one should be excluded on the grounds of how they practise their Judaism. This principle applies equally from Orthodox to secular. Hence our innovative Jewish education programme, which will be text-based and will value and encourage debate.

We will provide kosher food, and the school will close in time for children to be home for Shabbat. We will close the school for lessons on all yomtovim, but provide optional activities for those who observe one day yomtov on Pesach, Sukkot and Shavuot. We practise what we preach, with a chair of governors from the Reform movement, a head teacher from a United synagogue, and Masorti, Liberal and unaffiliated members on the governing body.[31]

The school's head teacher-designate, Jeremy Stowe-Lindner,[32] was equally upbeat: 'There are some excellent Jewish schools in the UK, but all are Orthodox. For the very first time, we will be offering a truly inclusive Jewish secondary school with an open-door policy.

'Every family who considers themselves to be Jewish is welcome. Our innovative, exciting Jewish education programme will reflect the variety and vibrancy of our community. We are not just going to accept our differences as Jews in a modern British society, but we will teach our students about them. We will equip them with the knowledge and confidence to make their own choices.'

JCoSS, he said – adapting a well-known advertising slogan – would do 'exactly what it says on the tin. We are striving to achieve an educational standard that will put us among the top 10 per cent of schools in the first year. Our criteria have always looked to include, not exclude, Jewish children. What is key to us is that our school reflects the entire community.'

Offering places to children who identified themselves as Jewish regardless of practice or affiliation, Stowe-Lindner estimated, would result in 'at least half the pupil population coming from families who identify with the mainstream Orthodox communities.' Synagogue attendance was not necessarily a condition of entry, but in lieu of this, evidence of two out of three other commitments – shul membership, formal Jewish education, or a parent or child's charitable activity – was required instead.

'People say they have been waiting for this – a school not tied to any denomination. We will keep Shabbat and kashrut, and the full range of young Jews will therefore be able come to the school. Nothing connected with our faith should be turned into anything negative. If you make prayers or the wearing of kippot compulsory, it is inevitable that this will encourage teenage rebellion. Everything we do will be designed to welcome all Jews, whatever their backgrounds, beliefs or abilities.'[33]

As the opening date for JCoSS drew near, the centrist-Orthodox establishment began to amplify its disapproval of the school and its ethos. Although United Synagogue chief executive Jeremy Jacobs and joint-treasurer Russell Tenzer attended the ground-breaking ceremony, ministers at the 2009 US rabbinical conference – two of whom, Mill Hill's Yitzchok Schochet and Golders Green's Harvey Belovski, were soon to be tipped as possible frontrunners in the Chief Rabbinical succession stakes[34] – expressed concern at the school's likely impact on the mainstream community.

Schochet, chairman of the US Rabbinical Council, gained support from 'the whole spectrum' of his colleagues for the view that JCoSS 'does not represent the ethos of the United Synagogue and, as such, is not an option for anyone seeking to give their child a Jewish education in keeping with that ethos. We recognise the need to do more to promote the many wonderful Orthodox Jewish schools in our community.'

Another conference participant observed that JCoSS 'is not an Orthodox school but is trying to attract Orthodox children. If United Synagogue members decide to send their children to a non-Orthodox school, obviously we will not be happy. One of the things that rabbis are keen to avoid is bad feeling that might drive people into the arms of the school. That's why we want to play it low-key.'[35]

Despite this assertion, the US rabbinate intensified its opposition, while simultaneously adopting a fatalistic approach. Its stance, in public at least, was to recognise – as Belovski put it[36] – that 'numerous children from US-type homes will attend JCoSS. However the Orthodox rabbinate might prefer the world to look, we will support and nurture the Jewish lives of our communities' children, irrespective of the educational choices made for them by their parents.

> It is no secret [declared Belovski] that, in a rare display of virtual unanimity, United Synagogue rabbis have strongly opposed formal involvement with JCoSS. Yet this has no bearing on our commitment to our children in the school. There is a spirited and evolving debate about how to achieve this: some will run out-of-school programming; others are grappling with alternatives to support JCoSS pupils. And it is with deep sadness that we currently feel unable to work within JCoSS: this painful decision is informed by real concern for our children expressed in the context of legitimate anxieties about its identity.

Unfortunately, behind the happy 'cross-communal' picture painted by the JCoSS website and cautiously worded literature, there lies a confused ideology that conflicts squarely with basic Orthodox principles. I am certain that JCoSS will indeed try to teach its pupils 'to understand and respect all the mainstream Jewish traditions.' This inclusivism may even succeed at a practical level: the school intends its kitchens to be kosher and its weekend programmes to be Shabbat-observant, even if it cannot commit to closing on second-day yomtov.

But ideologically this descends into pluralistic incoherence. Presumably, pupils will be taught that some believe the Torah to be the unmediated word of God, while others think that it was authored by human beings; that some consider traditional Shabbat restrictions to be optional, but others consider them absolutely binding; that while the Torah itself expressly forbids certain types of relationships, some movements consider them to be valid life-options.

And while this dissent is simply a statement of fact, the ethos of JCoSS demands that each of these contradictory options is taught as equally legitimate. Apart from the obvious fact that children need certainty, a sense of imperative and firm ideas to help them build a meaningful connection to their faith, this type of pluralism is theologically untenable from an Orthodox perspective.

A school whose raison d'être is the validation of conflicting stances on key issues of belief and practice must be considered at best non-Orthodox; in reality it is, theologically, completely and irreconcilably at odds with Orthodoxy. The somewhat clumsy phrase 'pan-non-Orthodox' is a more theologically accurate description of JCoSS than 'cross-communal.'

I understand the motivation of JCoSS's founders. The educational world is dominated by Orthodoxy: in varying degrees, the non-Orthodox denominations disagree with Orthodox beliefs and practices, and most acutely with its definition of Jewishness. Why shouldn't they create a school that incorporates their brands of Judaism? Actually, JCoSS acknowledges that, in the event of over-subscription, it will prioritise those 'who are not considered to be halachically Jewish by ... all other Jewish schools' – that is, children considered Jewish only by the non-Orthodox.[37]

I respect their objectives, albeit tempered by genuine concern for the children of US communities; but I challenge the founders of JCoSS to reciprocate that respect by abandoning the term 'cross-communal' in favour of a more candid representation of their school's ideology. Potential parents should recognise that they may be inadvertently depriving their children of their Torah heritage.

'Unsurprisingly,' Belovski concluded, 'JCoSS has provoked an identity crisis for the United Synagogue. The US has always been good at asserting what it isn't (too frum, too Zionist), but imprecise when stating what it actually stands for. Are we too afraid of the consequences to admit that even the welcoming, inclusivist version of Orthodoxy that we champion has hard edges?

'Sometimes it is necessary to state the obvious: pluralism and Orthodoxy are antithetical. As the Chief Rabbi has written: "Pluralism is no more tolerant than Orthodoxy … Each represents a way of viewing the relationship between belief and truth, and each excludes the other."

'We need not be scared of this truth, nor be anything other than respectful of others, such as the founders of JCoSS, who advocate pluralism. But failing to articulate the unbridgeable gulf between Orthodoxy and pluralism misrepresents both ideologies and creates false hope for a unified Jewry. In fact, I believe that it hinders cross-communal co-operation in those areas where it is possible.'

* * *   * * *   * * *

An earlier obstacle to cross-communal co-operation 'where it is possible' arose in 1995, four years into Sacks' Chief Rabbinate, when the London Beth Din voiced objections to the participation of Orthodox rabbis in the annual Limmud educational conference.

Founded in 1980 as a non-denominational – indeed, pluralistic – event, the flagship five-day gathering regularly attracted hundreds of participants from across (and outside) the religious spectrum and, before his appointment as Chief Rabbi, had been attended by Sacks himself. In 1988, as principal of Jews' College, he had delivered an address at Limmud in Oxford on 'The future of Jewish peoplehood,'[38] while United Synagogue president Sidney Frosh had participated in a panel discussion, on 'Lay leadership in Jewish education,' with Reform vice-president Julian Levy and the director of Jakobovits' Jewish Educational Development Trust, Simon Caplan.[39]

Limmud's top billing in 1995, in advance of the Beth Din's intervention, had been widely trumpeted as the strictly Orthodox Adin Steinsaltz, world renowned as a talmudist and philosopher. In what was described as 'a showdown between the Chief Rabbi and the Beth Din,'[40] Sacks immediately responded by 'overriding the objections of his own rabbinical court to clear the way for Orthodox rabbis to take part in the conference,' at which non-Orthodox rabbis were also scheduled to appear.

Publicly acknowledging for the first time its opposition to Orthodox rabbinical participation in Limmud, the Beth Din had announced: 'It is the opinion of the dayanim that, in view of the fact that the Limmud conference has been politicised in a way damaging both to Orthodoxy and to its original educational objectives, Orthodox rabbis ought not to attend. We have made our views known to the members of the rabbinate.'

Sacks' office reacted by stressing that the Beth Din had given 'no ruling on this matter,' that the Chief Rabbi 'maintains his long-standing position that Orthodox rabbis' participation is a matter of individual conscience,' and that he had expressed the hope that Limmud could remain 'a non-political and uncontroversial environment.'

While the dayanim upheld their opposition, they avoided an open conflict with Sacks by conceding that their objections 'do not constitute a formal ruling.' Despite this, at least one United Synagogue rabbi – Schochet – indicated that, 'after pondering my position all week,' he was pulling out of the conference 'on the orders of the dayanim.' Dayan Ivan Binstock countered that 'he must have misunderstood,' but Schochet insisted he had had 'no choice,' asserting that the Beth Din's view 'was expressed to me as an official ruling.'

Official or not, the dayanim's view appeared to have triumphed: only one United Synagogue minister, Hampstead's Michael Harris, participated in the conference. Steinsaltz withdrew days before its opening, stating through an aide that he had 'been forced to cancel all travel plans abroad to devote his energies to a new initiative to reinvigorate Jewish learning in the USSR.' Steinsaltz himself told Limmud: 'I understand that an element of controversy has attached itself to the event. This is certainly regrettable, as *limmud Torah* [Torah learning] must remain above partisan beliefs.'

'We share that belief,' the conference organisers responded. 'Limmud will continue working for the promotion of Jewish education for all of British Jewry.'[41] But this reassurance was of little avail. While Orthodox lay support mushroomed over the years, that of Orthodox rabbis largely disintegrated.

'This is a pity,' bemoaned the JC, 'not least because their presence would have enriched the content of the diverse seminars. It is to be hoped that, at next year's Limmud, rabbis of all synagogal groupings will – if only, to use the Chief Rabbi's phrase, in an individual rather than an organisational capacity – join in an educational enterprise which surely no Jew in search of learning need fear, and from which all, equally, can benefit.'[42]

Backing for this view came from Jeffrey Cohen – then still at Stanmore – in a Shabbat sermon, when he described the Limmud controversy as 'just one facet of a bitter struggle within Orthodoxy for possession of the religious middle ground, traditionally occupied by the rank-and-file of Anglo-Jewry.

> These are people who wish to have a Judaism that does not divorce them either from fellow Jews or from wider society and culture. They seek to be part of an Orthodox tradition that is tolerant and open-minded, prepared to enter into dialogue with all who believe that Judaism is worth preserving, even if they seem to be preserving it along non-traditional lines.
>
> Debate cannot be stifled. And if we believe that our Torah is *morashah kehilat Ya'akov* – an inheritance for the entire community of Jacob – then we have a duty to show all Jews that we care for them and their spiritual welfare; that we will go almost anywhere to bring the authentic message of Torah to them; and that we will leave no stone unturned to find courageous solutions to problems which obstruct the synthesis of Judaism with modern living.
>
> The victory for Torah will be won by peaceful means, by dialogue and persuasion, not by divisiveness and separatism; by outreach, not by withdrawal; by realising that fraternisation and debate with the non-Orthodox do not, in any way, imply legitimisation ...
>
> In the absence of considered argument and debate, authoritarian prohibitions or condemnations are counter-productive. They convince both the thinking people and the waverers that one has no answers, that one cannot defend one's entrenched position, and that one fears the moral superiority or philosophy of the opposition.
>
> Orthodoxy has to have confidence in itself, or it is lost. It has to have rabbis who have a broad-minded Jewish and general cultural knowledge as well as being halachic specialists, so that they can articulate effectively its principles and philosophies, and demonstrate their continuous relevance. It has to be prepared to defend its patch at any time and in any place.

The notion, said Cohen, 'that we are granting legitimisation by fraternising with those who do not sympathise with Orthodox principles, or by going to teach and to promote our values in a place where there is a plurality of opinion, is untenable. That is the sure way to hand the Progressive movement its greatest victory and to ensure that we polarise into two camps. The Orthodox centre would then be divided up, unequally, between the strictly Orthodox and the Progressives, with the lion's share going inevitably to the latter.

'The battle for the centre ground of the Orthodox community is, I believe, just such a situation, which calls for a total reappraisal of our traditional position in relation to religious dialogue, and the "setting aside" of some of our entrenched and manifestly ineffective positions. It certainly calls for us to avoid squandering such a heaven-sent opportunity as that offered by Limmud to promote our Orthodox philosophy and to bring hundreds of disciples to a greater awareness, love and knowledge of Torah.'[43]

10

Rites and Wrongs

*'What, then, should we hope to achieve? ... An Anglo-Jewry in which we do not pretend
that all is right with our community so long as there are groups who feel neglected,
and there are groups who feel neglected: women, the young, intellectuals ...'* [1]

In relation to their place in the community, the word 'women' appeared
only once in the Chief Rabbi's installation address. But its inclusion,
albeit that once, was significant: it indicated Sacks' readiness – indeed,
his determination – to tackle head-on some of the most 'exclusivist,' if
not intractable, issues on the Orthodox agenda. Nor was this the first
Chief Rabbinical engagement in the growing campaign – particularly
among feminist groups across the Jewish world – for an enhanced role in
synagogue and communal life [2] and for the resolution of personal-status
problems that had blighted women's lives for centuries.

The women of the United Synagogue had waited until the mid-1970s
before launching their battle. Their champion was none other than Amélie
Jakobovits, wife of the then Chief Rabbi and president of the Association of
United Synagogue Ladies' Guilds. Addressing the association's first biennial
meeting, in response to a resolution seeking the inclusion of women on
synagogue boards of management, she declared: 'I feel passionately that
women should have a strong liaison with men in running synagogues,
particularly in anything to do with education.'

Some months later, her husband appeared to give an unqualified nod
to the idea of women sitting on synagogue boards, following a call to this
effect at a provincial councils conference in Leeds. He would be 'only too
happy,' he said, to sponsor a working session on the subject of women's
representation on such bodies.

Responding, under pressure, to calls for 'positive action' on the issue,
he subsequently issued a statement asserting that 'the religious community
and its organisations can only benefit from the increased participation of
our womenfolk in their deliberations and activities. At present, neither
at local nor at communal level are sufficient opportunities afforded for
women to make their full contribution, thus recognising the role of our
womenfolk within the organised structure of our community and its

effort to give a more dynamic response to current challenges.'

Jakobovits pointed out, however, that the halachah on women's participation prohibited the election of women as honorary officers or officiants, and that they had 'an active, but not a passive, elective right – that is, they may elect to office but may not themselves be elected. They may be appointed or nominated to synagogue boards and councils – either by women of the congregation or by the local ladies' guild or other local women's organisations – and they may exercise full membership rights.'

A later demand that women be allowed to serve on the boards of management and councils of Orthodox synagogues was carried, by an overwhelming majority, at a nationwide meeting of the League of Jewish Women. With only four opposing votes among more than 200 women present, the meeting approved a resolution that 'urges the United Synagogue and other Orthodox synagogal bodies to allow those women who are full members in their own right and wish to play a fuller part in the life of the synagogue to serve on boards of management and councils.'

Nothing more was heard for two years, but when Jakobovits did return to the subject, he dashed the campaigners' hopes with a declaration that 'women cannot be elected to serve on boards of management of synagogues under the aegis of the United Synagogue, nor its council.' The US president, Salmond Levin, told the council that he had received a letter from the Chief Rabbi relating to a clause (41b) in the Charity Commissioners' scheme for the United Synagogue which laid down its working constitution.

'I reaffirm,' Jakobovits had stated, 'that, in accordance with the ruling given by my predecessor [Israel Brodie] on 9 January, 1951, Clause 41b cannot be amended.' The clause noted that 'a female member shall not be eligible for election, or hold office as an honorary officer of the US, or serve as a member of the council or of the executive committee of the US, or of the finance committee, or as an honorary officer of any synagogue of the US, or serve on the board of management of such synagogue.'

Seeking to clarify the position, the Chief Rabbi's office issued a statement late in 1977 in which Jakobovits suggested an alternative proposal – designated by the US council as Clause 41c, and welcomed by the Association of United Synagogue Ladies' Guilds – to transfer the general functions of a congregation in the spheres of education, youth, cultural and other activities from boards of management to newly formed synagogue councils. On these councils, both male and female members would be eligible to serve.

'I would not regard the election of women to the proposed councils as infringing the halachah,' Jakobovits declared. 'Accordingly, while I myself feel that, in the relationship between the proposed new council and the board of management, their respective jurisdictions and control over finances have yet to be defined with sufficient clarity, I have no objection to the proposal on religious grounds.'

Clause 41c, however, never materialised. It was rejected by the US council on the grounds that such lower councils 'would prejudice the present functions of boards of management, which, in any case, are free to set up committees covering the subjects with which the proposed councils would deal.'

Little more was heard on the issue until 1986, when the Chief Rabbi and Beth Din were warned by Levin's successor, Victor Lucas, that 'the search for a formula to enable women to play a more active role in Orthodox Judaism cannot be postponed indefinitely.'

Lucas told the US ladies' guilds that 'a route must be found within the halachah for what will undoubtedly prove, when resolved, a boon to the traditional community.' In response, Jakobovits reaffirmed that halachic requirements excluded women's eligibility to serve as honorary officers – 'which is neither sought nor constitutionally admissible' – and a formal role in decision-making as congregational representatives.

'To that latter end,' said the Chief Rabbi, 'several options are open: 1. To restrict their membership of synagogue-sponsored governing bodies to consultative or observer status. 2. To set up councils of management in each individual congregation to discuss all relevant matters and to decide, by vote if necessary, on recommendations to be put to boards of management. 3. To devise technical safeguards which will ensure their full participation short of vesting formal decision-making in women representatives, in whatever way they are elected or appointed … This method will also enable specific interests of and by women to be ascertained and pursued collectively.'

The chairman of the guilds' association, Ann Harris – wife of then St John's Wood minister Rabbi Cyril Harris[3] – described the proposals as 'disappointing and tortuous.' The women's campaign, she said, 'is by no means a bid for a takeover, or even equality, since no religious rights are requested, just parity in non-religious decision-making. I ask the following question to US council members: "Are you happy that your own synagogues work so well that you can afford to disenfranchise half the workforce?"'

Jakobovits responded: 'It is no good asking for halachic guidance and then, when it is received, arguing: "Yes, but we cannot accept it, unless we know the sources," or "We need a change in traditional attitudes to the halachah." If the halachah is to be our guide, then we need to change our attitudes to conform to it.

'As has been made clear, it is perfectly compatible with the halachah for women to "have an influence on decision-making" – as demanded by the Association of United Synagogue Ladies' Guilds – and the manner in which this can operate has now been spelled out in some detail. This advance should be acknowledged as well as encouraged, and any attempt to belittle or negate its significance can only prove counter-productive, increasing resistance, scepticism and resentment.

'If what the women want is full participation, they can and will have everything. If what they want is equal rights in a spurious quest for "women's liberty," they will have nothing. This distinction is all-important. The contribution of our women to enriching and intensifying our communal life can be invaluable. The anaemia so widespread in our community badly needs the injection of their energy and their vision.

'What the halachah requires even more urgently than circumscribing the role of women on boards and committees is to insist on retaining the uniqueness of the services rendered to Judaism and the Jewish people by men and women, respectively. If by opening up our institutional leadership ranks to women we would lose or weaken their primary commitment to securing stable marriages, building happy homes and raising intensely Jewish children,[4] the sacrifice of further eroding the strength of Jewish family life would not be worth the gain in improving the management of communal affairs.'[5]

*   *   *   *   *   *   *   *   *

Other women's issues confronting the Orthodox community had perplexed the Chief Rabbinate in the period preceding Sacks' election. Discussing, after his retirement, the growing calls for action to alleviate the plight of the *agunah*, the 'chained wife' refused a Jewish divorce (*get*) by her recalcitrant husband, Jakobovits referred to amendments to the Family Law Act being considered by British parliamentarians.

'The amelioration of the *agunah* problem,' he wrote, 'is for me a deeply personal commitment. On the last day of his life, nearly fifty years ago, my father told me that he had had a disturbed night. Visions of pleading *agunot*, whom he could not help, would not let him sleep. He was then a dayan of the London Beth Din, having previously been head of Berlin's communal Beth Din. To show how rabbis agonise over the problem, I related this story to Lord Mackay when he became Lord Chancellor in 1987. The story registered. He reminded me of it in later deliberations on the *get* amendment to the Family Law Bill.'[6]

Over the years, a number of attempts were made to alleviate the plight of the *agunah* – and, rarely, of the male victim, the *agun* – including a proposal in the 1950s to insert into the *ketubah* a clause empowering the Beth Din to obtain a monetary sum from the recalcitrant party by way of compensation.

Halachic objections were raised to this and other suggestions, although a pre-nuptial agreement brokered by the London Beth Din shortly after Sacks' installation – by which the husband undertook, following the civil divorce, to maintain his wife until he had written a valid *get* – was thought to have satisfied Jewish law. Subsequent cases, however, revealed a number of loopholes, while, additionally, the strictly Orthodox rabbinate was reluctant to co-operate. Pre-existing *agunot*, for whom halachic advances had come too late, were meanwhile left in limbo.

Alongside several unresolved *agunah* issues, the question of women's participation in synagogue services, and of women's prayer groups, also captured Jakobovits' attention, following the import from North America of so-called Rosh Chodesh groups within the feminist movement.

In the spring of 1990, he received a *cri de coeur* from 'an Orthodox woman now living in Jerusalem,' educated at Jewish schools in London and, at the time of writing, 'in a modern-day predicament, functioning as a person with a limited role and responsibility within traditional Judaism … It is important [she declared] for Rabbi Jakobovits to recognise that, by asking for a women's prayer group, women are challenging the status quo. The fact that they want it to be legitimised by him shows their concern that if there is to be a new perspective, it be within the bounds of halachah.'[7]

'You want equality in ritual practices,'[8] the Chief Rabbi replied. 'I do not believe Jewish religious observances are meant to serve as demonstrations, as protests for "symbolic reforms," nor even as palliatives to mollify emotional hunger …

> Could it be that the tasks and mitzvot specifically assigned to women give you no pride and self-fulfilment, parallel to, and compensating for, the specific duties incumbent upon men? Quite frankly, I see this as a psychological problem rather than as a religious challenge. There is a sense of frustration which you seek to turn into the norm when in fact it is the exception. Were this women's quest for male functions to succeed, we would be promoting inequality, since the women would assume male as well as female roles, while the men would be prevented by nature from assuming such a dual role.
>
> The damage which the resultant inequality has already done to the fabric of society, and particularly to the hitherto almost impregnable stability of the Jewish home, is incalculable … My charge, as a rabbi, is

to counter these trends and to rebuild the confidence of every Jew and every Jewess in the indispensable contribution of each to the continuity of Jewish life and to the consummation of the Jewish purpose in history. I admit it is not easy to withstand the pressures of current fads. But has not the Jewish fortitude in resisting these pressures always been the chief factor in our survival?[9]

A decade before those words were written, and well before he publicly acknowledged women as 'a neglected group,' Sacks discussed their role in Judaism in a contribution to the book *Man, Woman and Priesthood*, published in 1978 by the Society for Promoting Christian Knowledge. In it, he concluded: 'Judaism accepts the idea of roles in religious life which may be of the utmost importance without their being chosen. It is only in this context that the distinct roles of men and women can be understood.

Although the role of the woman is closely related to the home and the family, it is neither limited to it, nor is it something outside the concern of the man. More importantly, it should be clear that the home is far from being of limited, minor significance to Judaism. It is, in fact, the locus of many of its most important religious activities and has, historically, been the crux of its survival.

The fact that women are exempted from some of the commandments does not mean that they are excluded from them. The exemption was intended to leave them free to pursue their role. And the domains that they have made their own are far more significant than those they have not. Their most conspicuous absence – from the conducting of services in the synagogue – is largely to be understood in terms of the different worlds of prayer that men and women inhabit in Judaism. The commandments, the *mitzvot*, serve to sanctify even the simplest and most inconspicuous aspects of daily life for the Jew. And in this women have a part to play at least as great as, probably greater than, men's.

Liberation can be understood in two ways. It can be freedom from something or freedom to do something. The religious Jew or Jewess does not find his or her role as something from which to seek liberation. From the outside, it can seem a burden, a constraint. From within, lived, affirmed, it can itself seem the greatest liberation. The freedom to be what one was chosen for. The freedom of knowing that one's life has a meaning beyond one's own arbitrary choices. The freedom that comes from knowing that the world is God's question, and one's life is the answer.[10]

* * *   * * *   * * *

Within six months of his installation, Sacks launched the first plank of his Decade of Jewish Renewal – a major review of women's place in Anglo-Jewry. Asserting that 'there is no doubt that women have borne the brunt of immense changes' in both secular society and the Jewish community, he declared: 'If ever there was a Jewish challenge, this is it.'

But, he warned, there was no place in its resolution for 'pressure-group politics. That is not a Jewish way of dealing with human problems, and no one has gained. It has to flow from Jewish, not secular, values; it has to be set in motion at a rabbinic level; and it has to be led by a woman. Most importantly, it has to be conducted in continuous partnership with halachic authorities to replace confrontation with true dialogue and mutual understanding.'

The two individuals whom he saw as 'essential to its success,' said the Chief Rabbi, were Rosalind Preston, 'one of the most distinguished women ever to have graced Anglo-Jewry,'[11] and the Beth Din's Chanoch Ehrentreu, 'our most authoritative halachist. Together, they will ensure that the project achieves its three essential aims: to listen to the concerns of women throughout the community; to draw up appropriate modes of response; and to ensure that the process is guided throughout by the values and principles of Jewish law.

'What will be its outcome? That is impossible to predict. But of this I am confident: that from here on, women will have an address for their concerns. The project will, of course, be criticised – by the liberals for proposing too little, too late; and by the conservatives for proposing too much, too soon. But it will be recognised by the vast majority of the community for what it is: a giant first step towards Jewish renewal.'[12]

In the run-up to the review's publication, some two years later, one of the issues destined to feature prominently in its findings[13] – women's prayer groups – returned to the communal arena in controversial fashion. Amid murmurings and agitation for women-only services on synagogue premises, Sacks laid down the law, circumscribing their activities within strict halachic boundaries.

'Women,' he told them, 'are neither obligated to pray with a minyan, nor do they constitute one. To this day, a congregation is defined by the presence of ten men, and a woman may not serve as the leader of public prayer. This has been an unbroken tradition since the days of Moses, and it is axiomatic to Jewish law ...

'Against this background, the question of women's prayer groups is a simple one. Women may pray privately alone or together, and there is no distinction in Jewish law between the two. Their gathering does not count as a congregation. They are therefore forbidden to say any text requiring a minyan. This includes *borchu, kaddish, kedushah,* and the repetition of the *Amidah.*

> In a private responsum delivered by his grandson, the late Rabbi Moshe Feinstein wrote that 'if there is a group of righteous women whose intention is purely for the sake of Heaven, without intending to undermine God's Torah or Jewish practice, then, of course, why prevent them from praying together?'
>
> My predecessor, Lord Jakobovits, gave a similar answer to a group of students [at Cambridge, in 1989].[14] In these circumstances, and in non-synagogue contexts – homes, schools, seminaries, and student societies – women's prayer groups are permitted. But the synagogue stands firmly in another tradition. It is the place of congregational rather than private prayer. Symbolically and halachically, the synagogue is a *mikdash me'at,* a miniature Temple. Its very name, *bet haknesset,* means 'home of the congregation.'
>
> Though individuals may pray in the synagogue if no minyan is available, a shul remains the place of collective worship. Allowing women's services in the synagogue would blur the critical distinction between private and public prayer by housing the former in a place dedicated to the latter.
>
> In the Jewish past, when women prayed privately, they did so in private contexts. When they came to the synagogue, they prayed as part of the congregation. To locate private prayer in a congregational environment would be divisive and infringe several of the rules governing synagogue custom. When we attend a shul, we do so with a specific purpose: to join our prayers to those of the community. We worship not as individuals but as a 'congregation of Israel' standing collectively before God.
>
> So, within the synagogue complex, women-only services are not permitted. The only exception is that women who meet for other purposes, such as study, may begin or end their meetings with prayer, so long as they have the permission of the rabbi, at a time other than when the congregation is praying, and do not make use of a Sefer Torah.[15]

Of this statement, and its application to previous rulings, the *Jewish Chronicle* later pointed out that Sacks had omitted the second part of Feinstein's endorsement, which read: 'And they [women] may also read from the Torah Scroll, provided that they take care not to do it in such a way that one might erroneously believe it to be a public reading.' Sacks had also neglected to add (said the paper) that Jakobovits, in sanctioning the Cambridge women's prayer group, had approved their use of a Sefer Torah.[16]

> Unfortunately, the Chief Rabbi has declined various requests to endorse the use of a Sefer Torah in prayer meetings of the sort initiated, outside synagogal premises, by the Stanmore Women's Tefillah Group … There may be other – political, rather than halachic – reasons why Rabbi Sacks would oppose the use of a Sefer Torah even in such circumstances. But, if not, it would seem especially timely for him to follow his predecessor and others in lending his imprimatur to such non-synagogue prayer gatherings. Far from bowing to 'pressure,' this would help obviate the need for Orthodox women's groups to look elsewhere for further spiritual fulfilment which, in a genuine 'decade of renewal,' can and should be provided under the umbrella of the United Synagogue.[17]

Prompting this call was an announcement that, with the approval of its spiritual leader, Rabbi Michael (Mickey) Rosen, the independent Yakar synagogue in Hendon had sanctioned the holding of a women-only prayer service, with the use of a Sefer Torah, to celebrate Rosh Chodesh – a move Sacks had immediately condemned.

Sharon Lee, joint organiser of the proposed service and a co-founder of the Stanmore group – the first to be established, loosely, within the United Synagogue[18] – explained that the women would be reading and learning from the scroll and that none would be called up. She described the Chief Rabbi's ban on using a Sefer Torah as 'very distressing and alarming, an erosion of women's rights within the halachah.

'The Chief Rabbi is attempting to put constraints where, to our knowledge, no halachic authority has ever put them before. Women have been told by him that he is opening doors and not closing any. Now the doors are shutting in our faces.'

Doreen Fine, another Stanmore co-founder, said: 'If the Chief Rabbi is unable to support this service, it will be the last opportunity to further his support for women's tefillah groups.'

The women were referring to a statement from the Chief Rabbi's office, in response to their planned service, that it would 'affect future progress on the involvement of women in the United Synagogue. Using a Sefer Torah goes beyond the limits placed by Rabbi Sacks on women's services. Unless we maintain these parameters, it will undermine achievements thus far.'

In a second statement, highlighting his various initiatives on women's issues, Sacks added: 'I am gravely concerned that these rulings are being challenged in some cases by the very women who have addressed inquiries to me. I will not be a party to such controversies, which mar and deface our religious life. A rejection of those rulings involves forfeiting my authority and approval.'

Commenting on the Chief Rabbi's ban, Rosen declared: 'There are those women who wish to develop and grow in the world of Torah and who, without a sense of tokenism or defiance, want to express their learning and love of Torah by reading from it. This view has a legitimate place in halachah, and Yakar seeks to encourage, and not reject, women's quest to learn.

'For the last generation, Anglo-Jewry has seen its more creative men and women opt out of the community, and denying women what is a legitimate halachic position sends out all the wrong signals and encourages that exodus.'[19]

Despite the ban, and the continuing controversy, the service went ahead, attended by more than one hundred women. 'It looked like any other women's gathering in any United synagogue,' reported journalist Valerie Monchi. 'But Sunday's event at Yakar marked an historic milestone in Anglo-Jewry – the first-ever Orthodox women-only service to use a Sefer Torah.

> The much-awaited moment finally arrived. With little ceremony, two women made their way towards the Ark and opened it. The Sefer Torah was handed over to [the officiant], who carried it down the aisle to allow the women to kiss it with their prayer books. The first of four women who were to read from the scroll was ready to begin. But before proceeding, she wanted to recite *shehecheyanu*, the prayer to sanctify all things new. She was obviously nervous, but sang her rather short Torah portion with confidence. Complete silence hovered over the room. Even the baby sitting on the lap of one of the women kept quiet.[20]

Weeks after the service, Preston published her report, writing in the preface that the review had 'provoked a variety of responses – surprise that the Chief Rabbi's first major initiative on taking office was to focus on women's concerns; scepticism that it would be yet another exercise in futility; approval that the invitation extended to Jewish women of all affililiations; and, above all, hope that the vital issues concerning women and halachah would be addressed anew.

'As a result of the long process of investigation, exploration, discussion and debate, the agenda of women's concerns has been brought to the forefront of the community consciousness. Individual women have responded in their thousands, seizing this unique opportunity to explore their own hopes and expectations, concerns and fears, not just for themselves, their immediate families and their local communities, but also out of a strong desire to safeguard and strengthen the well-being of Jewish life in this country – to guarantee Jewish continuity.'

Would the review, Preston asked, 'carry forward and build on the prodigious endeavours and wide-ranging consultations undertaken by many outstanding British Jewish women during previous decades?' Declaring that the report was 'now handed to Chief Rabbi Dr Jonathan Sacks for his consideration, and, in turn, to the entire community,' she answered her own rhetoric with a quotation from Proverbs (3:27): 'Do not withhold good from those who deserve it, when it is in your power to act.'[21]

Sacks responded through an interview in The Independent, which described him as 'a scholar with an awkward manner of speaking, interrupted by sudden rushes of passion.'

> We wanted an opportunity [he told journalist Andrew Brown] genuinely to move away from the confrontation which has characterised the conflicts in other faiths, and towards co-operation. Feminism, both as an ideology and as an economic fact, poses problems for all religions. We are walking a tightrope. The question is: 'Can you hold things together?' We had a certain image of the Jewish woman as a mother. And now we have a generation of Jewish women with huge educational attainments.
>
> We had to learn that there is a huge tension between the roles these women are allotted in the outside world and the roles open to them in, for example, synagogue management. It is an article of Orthodox faith that men and women cannot pray together. The women have their own partitioned balcony from which they may watch the men at prayer. We hope that equality in power will compensate for difference at prayer.
>
> Traditional Jewish life in Eastern Europe was very matriarchal; that is certainly how I remember my grandmother in the East End, too. But once the Orthodox community became anglicised, once we had escaped into the open society, we started building these huge cathedral-type structures, and a lot of the women began to feel excluded.

The answer the Chief Rabbi favoured, Brown quoted him as saying, 'is not to abolish the segregation between sexes in worship, but to try to find prayers and rituals that can be used by women alone to celebrate events that are special to their lives. An advantage of a faith which is something like four thousand years old is that you can usually discover resources

within the tradition for anything. We have been here before ... and we
have all the freedom we need.

'Religious law is like the grammar of a language. Any language is
governed by such rules, otherwise it ceases to be a language. But within
them, you can say many different sentences and write many different
books. Historically speaking, Jews throughout the world and throughout
the centuries, though bound by the same rules, have written many different
books. So we have the resources today to write a book that women will
read and say: "This is my story."'[22]

* * *   * * *   * * *

'My story,' as described by Judy Goodkin and Judith Citron in the
introductory section of the review,[23] began with 'The Early Years' and the
birth of a child. The opening paragraphs typified the concerns expressed
by the participating women — over a range of issues — throughout the
lengthy investigation:

> 'I really wanted to say something after my baby was delivered, but I
> didn't even know if such a *berachah* [blessing] existed.' A large number of
> affiliated women countrywide reported in the meetings a profound wish
> to express thanks to God at key events in their life and the lives of their
> families. Yet many were unclear about the mechanisms for giving thanks
> following the birth of a baby. From the range of views canvassed, it
> would appear that *birchat hagomel* is the best-known thanksgiving formula
> of a number of options available to women at this time. While several
> other prayers do exist, they occupy a position of relative obscurity, with
> many women remaining completely unaware of the alternatives open
> to them.
>
> Yet, despite many women's familiarity with *birchat hagomel*, there
> was deep dissatisfaction over the use of an all-purpose thanksgiving
> benediction, not on the grounds of its content but chiefly by virtue of
> the company it keeps. *Gomel*, the traditional expression of gratitude for
> deliverance from life-threatening circumstances, may be applied by those
> who have survived road accidents, crossed the sea or wilderness, or been
> released from prison.
>
> Given that maternal mortality during childbirth is a relatively rare
> event in late twentieth-century medicine, women consider *gomel* too blunt
> an instrument to convey adequately their sense of joy and wonder at the
> emergence of a new life.

Across a clutch of concerns in 'the early years' – single parenthood, working mothers, schooling, children's synagogue services, sex education, children with disabilities, eating disorders, barmitzvah/batmitzvah – women reported insufficient provision, inadequate advice, isolation and disadvantage on a Jewish and communal level. As the life cycle progressed towards 'stepping out,' university, marriage and divorce, death and bereavement, the problems accumulated and became ever-more acute.

On specifically religious issues, the review reflected the increasing fragmentation of Anglo-Jewry in the communal arena. The synagogue-affiliated sector, it confirmed, was 'simultaneously shrinking and polarising.' Membership has declined by 25 per cent in one generation, with a gradual shift from the central Orthodox to the Progressive and, to a lesser extent, the strictly Orthodox wings.

> Many Jewish women are dissatisfied with synagogue services and find them 'inappropriate to their needs.' Almost half the respondents (45 per cent)[24] said that they had *never* attended a synagogue which they found acceptable from the point of view of a woman. This percentage was much lower for members of Progressive synagogues (23 per cent), and higher in the central Orthodox sector (56 per cent) and among the unaffiliated (69 per cent).
>
> Those attending United synagogues and other central-Orthodox synagogues were not only less likely to have found a satisfactory synagogue, but even those who had found one often found it in the Progressive sector; about 40 per cent of 'satisfied' Orthodox members came into this category. In contrast, members of Progressive synagogues invariably found satisfaction within their own synagogal grouping.
>
> An attempt was made to analyse the causes of dissatisfaction. Predictably, there was a high level of agreement with statements endorsing women's *equal rights* with regard to representation, visual access, and 'ownership' of the synagogue ... In general, concern over equal rights did not seem to discourage women from attending synagogue – that is, frequent attenders were no less concerned about these matters than those who stayed away. The factors that were most closely associated with attendance or non-attendance related to the perceived *ethos* of the synagogue – its spirituality, openness to outsiders, and willingness to provide explanations.

On attitudes towards rabbis, the review noted that these were 'generally positive as far as their treatment of women was concerned ... However, evidence suggests that rabbis, at least in the Orthodox sector, are not very effective as agents of communal development. This may have implications for the way in which women's concerns about the ethos of the synagogue are addressed.'

As for the various batei din, wrote the reviewers, their ratings by women who had dealt with them 'suggest that they are reasonably efficient, but sometimes lacking in courtesy and sensitivity to the needs of women. There is evidence that some of the criticisms levelled against the Beth Din may be coloured by dissatisfaction with the outcome or ruling, and that those with direct experience are less critical than those who are affected indirectly.

'The London Beth Din received poorer ratings than other batei din on measures of courtesy and sensitivity, but it was seen by some women as making an effort to improve the quality of its service and to address difficult problems in a sympathetic manner.'[25]

Overall, the review published fourteen 'findings' and 108 'recommendations,' among which were the following:

B1: Alternative forms of service are wanted by many women on Shabbat and festival mornings: alternative minyanim; explanatory services; briefer services followed by learning opportunities.

B2: There is a need for enhanced and upgraded ceremonies, and positive acknowledgement of a batmitzvah celebrant, agreed by the Chief Rabbi and acceptable to all rabbis, to ensure that all girls have the same opportunities and achieve a real sense of belonging.

B9: In the absence of men, or in the presence of men who are not members of their household, or who may not wish or be able to perform the mitzvah, women's obligations require clarification regarding *kiddush*, *zimmum*, *havdalah*, *bensching gomel*, *birchat habanim*, and *hamotzi*.

C1: The United Synagogue is currently addressing the issue of women in management within its constituent synagogues. [Changes to the by-laws, allowing limited women's participation on the US council and boards of management, were passed early in 1994 and strengthened in 1996.[26]] However, in the regions, each Orthodox synagogue operates under its own rules. There are also widespread variations and inconsistencies in regard to women's rights to membership and election to councils which cause much concern and dissatisfaction.

C2: The seating arrangement most favoured by women who wish to move away from the gallery setting is that of men and women sitting on the same level, separated by a *mechitzah* running down the length of the synagogue.

C3: There is a need for clear definition of the term '*mechitzah*' and classification of its purpose.

D1: The review process created an opportunity for women across the community, regardless of age, religious affiliation and marital status, for an excellent cross-fertilisation of ideas and expertise and an increased sense of understanding and mutual respect.

F5: While there is a need for basic/practical shiurim for women, there is also a need for shiurim which will help women grapple with issues that are directed specifically at women's concerns – for example, the obligation of a woman to perform mitzvot and to study Torah, women in the synagogue, etc.

G6: It should be remembered that contact with a Beth Din usually occurs at a highly charged emotional time in a person's life.

H8: It is recognised that, in certain cases, get or chalitzah is withheld until there has been substantial payment of money or until unacceptable conditions have been agreed upon.

H12: It has been revealed that there are many cases of considerable distress resulting from the status of mamzer being perpetuated through the generations, the outcome of an agunah being left with no option other than to make a subsequent union outside Orthodoxy. The present situation relating to agunot has, particularly over the past two decades, resulted in the birth of thousands of children halachically deemed mamzerim.[27]

A separate report to the Chief Rabbi from the review's get and agunah working party proposed twelve wide-ranging recommendations, but noted that, 'since writing our original report, we have been encouraged to learn that several are in the process of implementation by the London Beth Din ... We warmly endorse the proposed changes, which we believe will help to alleviate the problems of get for future generations.'[28]

To widespread acclaim, as copies of the review took their 'giant first step,' Sacks called on 'all communal bodies to investigate ways of implementing its recommendations. The review,' he said, 'must not gather dust on its shelf. In no area will it be left without implementation.'[29]

* * *　* * *　* * *

Confounding that claim, Women in the Jewish Community had a chequered history. Eight months after its release, 'signs emerged of hold-ups in implementing aspects of the review.' Among key elements involved were the pre-nuptial agreement proposed by the Chief Rabbi a year earlier, and a call for guidance on when women were permitted to recite kaddish.

The Chief Rabbi's office, reported the JC,[30] 'is understood to have urged women who were involved in the review to refrain from any action which might complicate "sensitive, behind-the-scenes" negotiations on ways to apply its recommendations.' Jonathan Kestenbaum, the office's executive director, stated: 'The review has placed before Anglo-Jewry an extensive agenda. Much of this is being closely considered and, indeed, implemented. A considerable amount remains to be carefully reflected upon by a range of institutions throughout the community.'

But, the paper noted, 'concern appears to be mounting among members of the Jewish Women's Network that nothing has happened since the review was published.'

In 1996, controversially calling on the Chief Rabbi to retire, Stanley Kalms wrote: 'He [Sacks] stood for the total equality of women, but this issue was deliberately rolled away with a long-drawn-out commission, ably attempted by Rosalind Preston but ultimately largely pigeon-holed.'[31] A distinguished United Synagogue executive later commented that the review had 'produced virtually nothing in the long term, and certainly nothing of significance.'[32]

Fifteen years after its publication, Preston revealed that she had been asked on numerous occasions, 'What happened to your report and its many recommendations?' As a result, she wrote,

> in 2008 I approached the Board of Deputies with a view to revisiting the work we had carried out a decade and a half earlier. It soon became apparent that we had to broaden the scope of our original project, reaching out not just to those women who contributed to the ideas in our 1994 report and whose lives had now moved on, but to a whole new generation of younger Jews.
>
> The intervening fifteen years had seen many changes in family structure and attitudes to personal relationships, in the economic climate, and, above all, in the ways in which we communicate through new technologies. How had these changes impacted on women's lives, on their approaches to their Judaism, and on their sense of Jewish heritage? How had they influenced women's perception of community?

The outcome of Preston's approach was a second review, *Connection, Continuity and Community: British Jewish Women Speak Out*,[33] 'one of the most exciting elements of which was our online survey. Through this survey, along with our focus and discussion groups, website, questionnaires and face-to-face meetings, we elicited the views of almost one thousand Jewish women. We decided to let the women speak for themselves.

'We believe the report represents the authentic voice of female Jewry in Britain today. Women are very articulate about their desire for a cohesive, dynamic, inclusive community. We sincerely hope they will be listened to and that the leadership of the community, across the religious spectrum, will heed their concerns and their hopes.'[34]

In its opening section, the 2009 review listed as its main themes 'inclusion and exclusion, engagement and disengagement, enfranchisement and disenfranchisement.'

> There appears to be something of a reality gap between the ways in which Jews today live (and will increasingly live) their diverse lives and the ways in which the leaders of institutional Judaism would ideally wish they might live their lives.
>
> Women are very articulate about this reality gap. On the one hand, they talk about what they regard as the perceived norm of the Jewish community – a stereotypically married, heterosexual, halachically Jewish couple with children. On the other, they describe through their personal experiences and observations a scenario which contradicts this stereotype. This inevitably raises questions about what is the family norm within Jewish communal life – or if there can any longer be a predominant norm – and the extent to which the community organises communal and spiritual life to reflect the current demographics …
>
> Women are very clear about the benefits of an inclusive community. There is a strong sense that the leadership of the community must acknowledge and accommodate the changes in the structure of family life. There is also a huge feeling of dissatisfaction among singles which crosses all religious boundaries. Women in mainstream Orthodoxy express their frustration about what they see as archaic and inconsistent attitudes towards women's participation in synagogal leadership and spiritual life.[35]

The report continued: 'We cannot afford to be exclusive. The arithmetic is not difficult. The genetic pool of born-Jews is very small. Unless we effectively engage those already-affiliated Jews and embrace others who feel, for whatever reason, disconnected from communal life, we will see an unconscious drift away from Jewish heritage and an inevitable demographic downward spiral.

'However, a vibrant community is about more than numbers. It is about the quality of engagement with the community. We need to invest in a professional approach to seek out and meet the needs of all members of the community …[36]

> Leadership in Orthodox Jewry remains an anachronism. The community is brimming with dynamic, able women whose business and management

skills are acknowledged and rewarded within their secular lives, but who cannot receive proper recognition within the community simply because of their sex. It is the community's loss that these women's abilities are not effectively utilised.

Unless women are offered opportunities to lead the community on an equal footing with men, the gap between their secular and their communal lives will become unbridgeable. Young women have no desire to sustain another generation of tea-makers. They will find other, more productive outlets for their talents, potentially outside of the Jewish community.

Women's participation in spiritual life is often a rabbinic lottery within mainstream Orthodox Jewry. There is a lack of coherence about policy and its implementation which needs to be addressed.

If men's halachic role underpins their relationship with synagogue life, it is not surprising that, without such underpinning, women in many communities feel disenfranchised. Enlightened attitudes towards female participation can greatly enhance how connected women feel towards their Judaism, and more importantly, the extent to which they can, in turn, inspire and enable their children to connect with their Jewish heritage.[37]

On the question of Jewish education for women and girls, the report was equally forceful: 'Disempowered Jewish mothers disempower their daughters. Unless we find the means to empower women through knowledge, there is a real danger that the community will atrophy. We cannot afford to create another generation of ill-educated and consequently disenfranchised women who will, in turn, pass on to their own daughters – and their sons – an ever-growing sense of disconnection. This is not what women want for themselves, their children or the community.

'It is time women's desire for learning was taken seriously. Jewish women celebrate their educational achievements in the secular world, where their levels of academic attainment exceed those in the wider community. It is therefore deeply disheartening that so many respondents feel frustrated by the learning opportunities currently available, especially within mainstream Orthodox Jewry.

'With women playing the pivotal role in securing the future of the next generation of Jews, it is shortsighted to deny them equal access to all aspects of study. Educational opportunity is not simply about how much is on offer, but about what is on offer and how, when and where it is delivered.

'We need first-class responsive teachers who can meet women's educational ambitions. We should aim to produce not just learned individuals, but more high-calibre women educators as role models. We have to satisfy this thirst for unbounded knowledge.'[38]

Introducing the report of the Agunah Group, which she headed, Judge Dawn Freedman disclosed that around 220 Jewish bills of divorce (*gittin*) were delivered each year in Britain, though national trends suggested that the figure did not reflect the number of divorces between Jewish couples.

Recommendations in the 1994 review report, she said, had brought 'many positive outcomes.' It had raised awareness of the issue of *agunim* and *agunot* in the community, and the batei din had become 'more determined' in dealing with recalcitrant spouses. Additionally, women 'befrienders' had been introduced at the London Beth Din.

The Divorce (Religious Marriages) Act 2002 had allowed judges discretion to postpone a decree absolute until both parties had fulfilled their religious obligations. Even though few applications had been reported, it was thought to have proved 'a useful incentive' in encouraging spouses to deliver or receive a *get*. At the same time, the United Synagogue had amended its by-laws to provide for the effective ostracism of recalcitrant husbands, and that approach had been adopted informally by other synagogal bodies.

Freedman noted that 'the Chief Rabbi's pre-nuptial agreement, while not enforceable under English civil law, remains a helpful educational tool, even though many couples are reluctant to discuss divorce on the threshold of their marriage.' The family law group of the Board of Deputies, whose report was due in 2012, would be giving evidence to the Law Commission exploring the possibility of legislation that would make pre-nuptial agreements legally enforceable.

'However,' the judge stressed, 'challenges remain. Neither the current legislation nor synagogue policies will necessarily be able to deal with the most recalcitrant spouses. More fundamentally, although rabbis and academics worldwide have put forward possible halachic solutions, none has been found to be acceptable globally.

'We are optimistic that dayanim, rabbis and academics will continue to work to secure a resolution. Meantime, our immediate objective is to put forward a twofold action plan which we hope will encourage people, especially young Jews, to understand the significance of *get* and find practical ways to address the problems and alleviate the distress that unresolved *get*-related issues cause.'[39]

* * *   * * *   * * *

'Jewish women have spoken out,' the working party declared in delivering its report. 'The voices you have heard are those of spiritual and lay leaders, professionals, community activists and academics, as well as hundreds of women from across the religious spectrum with diverse religious outlooks.

> All of them were motivated to articulate their hopes and concerns about the future well-being of the British Jewish community. They illustrate the perceived gulf between women's achievements and aspirations in secular life and their Jewish communal and spiritual experience. Women highlight the fact that we may have become complacent about what it means to be truly inclusive. They prioritise the need to recognise and embrace new family structures.
>
> Women pinpoint high-calibre education delivered by charismatic educators as the key to our future. They note the critical link between knowledge, connection and continuity. Women recognise that if we do not empower them with learning and understanding, they will not be able to empower and inspire their daughters and their sons.
>
> Above all, women acknowledge the importance of community. However, they identify the need to rethink our assumptions about how we define 'community' and the ways in which we connect with it. Although women express many deeply held frustrations and disappointments, there is a real sense that, by listening and responding to what they have to say, we will secure a dynamic and vibrant future for Jews in Britain.[40]

The Stanmore Discords

'*We can prove the Torah's greatness only by inspiration, not by negation.*'[1]

Commenting, some ten weeks before the appointment of Jonathan Sacks, on a declaration from the Union of Liberal and Progressive Synagogues (ULPS) that 'the Chief Rabbi to be elected has no authority over our own rabbis or lay people, nor does he represent us or speak on our behalf,'[2] the *Jewish Chronicle* contended:

> There is nothing new in the statement from the ULPS disavowing the authority of the Chief Rabbi – any Chief Rabbi – over its members. Indeed, it is difficult to imagine a situation in which the incumbent would be regarded as a spiritual guide to it, or its members as a natural flock for him. The same would apply to almost all the Reform movement … Masorti has placed itself outside the United Synagogue mainstream by its rejection of the classic Orthodox understanding of Revelation.
>
> Thus, it is essentially that collectivity known as the United Synagogue, and those many mainstream traditional congregations in the regions and a number overseas, which regard the Chief Rabbi as their guide and mentor. It is from their strength, which is predominant in Anglo-Jewish life, that he draws his. Lord Jakobovits has put his own special stamp on the Chief Rabbinate to the extent that the global perception of him is that of sole spiritual leader of the Anglo-Jewish community.

But, the paper added a few lines later,

> there is a crying need for a restatement of the philosophy of what we call United Synagogue Judaism. The intense interest in the fate of mainstream religious thinking was amply demonstrated by the massive attendance at the 'Traditional Alternatives' conference in London earlier this year. However, the US, both in its lay leadership and its rabbinate, failed miserably, with one or two honourable exceptions, to pick up the ball and run with it.
>
> There is a perception of a rabbinate always looking over its shoulder

lest it fall foul of the Right. The US takes pride in a Beth Din which, whatever the truth, is perceived as being unbending in its approach to the interpretation of Jewish religious law. It has taken on a life of its own, outside its traditional role as 'Court of the Chief Rabbi.'

What is to be the relationship between the two? This question should be addressed before the mantle of the Chief Rabbinate is placed upon other shoulders. That consideration could well dictate the character of the successful candidate. So, too, could his approach to working with other segments of the community which do not share his religious outlook but which share a common interest in defending Anglo-Jewry against its enemies and in uniting its strength in support of Israel and local causes.

There probably does not exist one man who embodies all those merits which the position demands. But the minimum that can be asked is that his deep religious conviction should be allied with a vision of a revitalised United Synagogue community and an ability to translate that vision into a sense of purpose for a community which so often seems to be without one.[3]

Central to an assessment of the Sacks Chief Rabbinate is a resolution of the fundamental questions posed above – the nature of his relationship with the Beth Din and 'his approach to working with other segments of the community which do not share his religious outlook.' The first became evident only after 'the mantle of the Chief Rabbinate' was placed upon his shoulders; the second, however, seemed mapped out in advance – though, as these chapters have demonstrated, it was increasingly confounded as his incumbency progressed.

In the summer of 2003, the two questions again received a simultaneous (and very public) response, and the patience of the 'kingmaker' – as Alderman labelled Kalms[4] – finally evaporated, with yet another call on Sacks to resign.

Attending the *aufruf* of David Ward, his granddaughter Paula's husband-to-be, Louis Jacobs was barred by the London Beth Din from being called up to the Sabbath reading of the Torah at the Bournemouth Hebrew Congregation, a synagogue under the Chief Rabbi's authority. The minister, Lionel Rosenfeld – who had been instructed by the dayanim to operate the ban – had offered Jacobs the honour of opening the ark, but this was not taken up.

Commenting on reports that he was responsible for the incident, Rosenfeld wrote later to Ward: 'What happened has been very upsetting, not only for me but also for the community. I have refrained from giving any explanations, but since you have asked me, let me tell you that I did not approach the Beth Din on this issue. I did discuss it with a rabbinical colleague who, some days later, informed me that he had spoken to the dayanim – which I had not requested him to do. The rest you know.

'Since then, I have had some very upsetting letters and e-mails, and the saga continues. I did not contact the Beth Din "on behalf of the family," as was reported.[5] The last thing I wanted was to bring any unpleasantness to what was going to be a beautiful Shabbat.' Rosenfeld told Ward that it had indeed been 'a lovely Shabbat, and I know very well that Paula's family enjoyed it.'[6]

A spokesman for Sacks' office told the *Jewish Chronicle*: 'It is not the policy for synagogues under the Chief Rabbi's jurisdiction to call up non-Orthodox rabbis. We are comfortable that the protocols of the Stanmore Accords have been complied with. The accords state that there is "no expectation that non-Orthodox ministers will participate in Orthodox services."'[7]

The clause in the accords relevant to the episode – open to varying interpretations, but evidently operated by the Beth Din with its 'unbending approach' – included the stipulation: 'Orthodox bodies do not invite Reform, Liberal and Masorti rabbis and ministers to speak at or participate in services under Orthodox auspices.' Considerable debate was occasioned, both in and outside Bournemouth, over the precise meaning of 'invite' and 'participate in.'

The accords, as we have seen, emerged from the ruins of the Consultative and Liaison Committees established in an effort to defuse intra-communal tensions, and disbanded in 1997 following the Gryn debacle. Repeated and clandestine attempts during Jakobovits' Chief Rabbinate 'to encourage respect and tolerance' had failed, however, to prevent the ULPS declaration, although Liberal leaders were later to assert that Sacks' appointment 'seemed to herald a new era for Anglo-Jewry and hold out the possibility of some kind of rapprochement with Progressive Jews.' Indeed, they recalled, Sacks had lectured at the Leo Baeck College in the 1970s and had invited Reform and Liberal figures to his induction service.[8]

But neither of these perceived manifestations of partnership was quite what it seemed. The Leo Baeck 'lectureship' – the description of which was itself disputed – had occurred in 1974 when, it was reported, 'Mr Jonathan Sacks, a part-time lecturer in philosophy at Jews' College, has started teaching concurrently at the Leo Baeck College, a training institute for Reform and Liberal rabbis and teachers.

Announcing Mr Sacks' appointment, the Leo Baeck newsletter welcomed 'the opportunity of introducing one of the thoughtful young traditionalists of Anglo-Jewish life to our students and faculty.' A Cambridge graduate and former lecturer in philosophy at Middlesex Polytechnic, Mr Sacks is at present studying for his rabbinical diploma at Jews' College, as well as lecturing as a graduate assistant in rabbinics and Jewish thought.

At the Leo Baeck College, he teaches Talmud. Rabbi Nachum L. Rabinovitch, principal of Jews' College, declined to confirm whether Mr Sacks had taken up the appointment at the Leo Baeck with his consent. He said that Mr Sacks' engagement 'does not call for any comment.' Mr Sacks stated that he had accepted the Leo Baeck College appointment because he was 'concerned that there should be no barriers to Jewish learning.'[9]

Two years later, recording that 'semichah diplomas have been awarded by Jews' College to Mr Jonathan Sacks and the Rev J. Grunewald,' the *Jewish Chronicle* had added: 'Rabbi Sacks, a Cambridge philosophy graduate, has lectured on his subject both at Jews' College and the Leo Baeck College.'[10] The report provoked a forceful rebuttal from the newly ordained Sacks:

Orthodoxy cannot, in principle, accept Reform as a valid interpretation of Judaism. The acceptance of traditional Jewish law as authoritative is the criterion which must always stand in the way of formal recognition of Reform Judaism. On the other hand, a Reform Jew is a Jew, like any other, and with him as an individual the Orthodox may legitimately seek to communicate and to share the values of our religious heritage.

It follows that, while an Orthodox Jew may, and should, try to open the world of Jewish learning to his fellow Jew, whatever his degree of commitment, he cannot and may not do so as a formal member of an institution which rejects the axiom of his faith – the sanctity of Jewish law.

I mention this because you reported in your news columns that as well as teaching at Jews' College, I had been a lecturer at Leo Baeck. This is not true. Two years ago, I agreed privately to learn with some individuals who were studying at Leo Baeck College, as part of the general obligation that I felt – to spread Jewish knowledge to whoever wishes to learn.

There was no lectureship. I was at no time a member of the teaching faculty of the college. And when, a short time later, a report appeared in the *Jewish Chronicle* that I had been appointed to a lectureship, this misconstruction of a private relationship forced me immediately to discontinue.

Apart from wishing to set the record straight, I must add my personal conviction that confusing the area of informal willingness to share traditional learning with that of formal recognition of Reform Judaism does great harm to the cause of Jewish unity.[11]

Not so, retorted Rabbi David Goldberg, of the Liberal Jewish Synagogue. 'We all tend to put a favourable gloss on our pasts, and Rabbi Jonathan Sacks is no exception. My own recollection – as a member of the Leo Baeck College academic committee – of his connection with the college differs significantly from his.

> It is indeed true that two years ago certain faculty and students of the college wished to benefit from the then Mr Sacks' ability by engaging him, on a stipend, to give lessons in Talmud, and for a time these took place. However, when it was reported to the academic committee that, in order to preserve the purity of his 'Orthodox' reputation, Mr Sacks could not be seen in the environment of the college, and likewise would have to explain away his association with Progressive students by the tortuous kind of justification displayed in his letter, we reluctantly decided that the arrangement could not continue.
>
> Leo Baeck College is a respected institute of higher learning, and scholars of even more distinguished reputation than Rabbi Sacks, and with just as traditional a background, are happy openly to acknowledge their links with the college. It was this factor, not a *Jewish Chronicle* report, that led the college – rather than Mr Sacks – to discontinue an association which might have benefited both.
>
> All of which is a great pity. Anglo-Jewry is not so rich in students committed to the preservation and transmission of our heritage that it can allow academic co-operation to founder on bigoted, and largely meaningless, definitions of what does and doesn't constitute a 'valid interpretation' of Judaism.[12]

Shortly after this spat, Sacks teamed up with Leo Baeck lecturers Rabbi Jonathan Magonet and Dr Hyam Maccoby – as well as with Rabbis Louis Jacobs, Abraham Levy, Jeremy Rosen and Shmuel Lew – for a Union of Jewish Students nationwide project, 'Chapter and Verse.' The cross-communal team, described as 'the best Jewish speakers in the country,' had 'offered to talk about the things which really inspire them – those ideas, words and passages which interest them more than all others.' Sacks' subject was 'Halachah: The Rabbinic Legal System,' while Jacobs spoke on 'Texts from the Talmud.'[13]

Armed with his semichah, Sacks was fifteen months later appointed to the pulpit of the Golders Green Synagogue, succeeding the acting minister,

Dayan Morris Swift, who had held the fort since the death, in December 1976, of Rabbi Eugene Newman.

Commenting on the novice's unopposed election by members of the congregation, JC columnist Ben Azai (who in due course was to declare himself as Chaim Bermant) wrote: 'I worry for Rabbi Jonathan Sacks, a bright young man, who is to succeed to the pulpit at Golders Green under the surveillance of an emeritus minister [the Rev Isaac Livingstone[14]] and at least one dayan. Looking around his congregation, he might well come to the conclusion that he will be more engaged in seeing parishioners off to the next world than in making them comfortable in this. Can't we use his talents better?'[15]

But, looking around his congregation, Sacks clearly thought differently – at least for a while. Delivering his installation sermon in the presence of Jakobovits, the new minister set out his stall. 'In the Golders Green area,' he said, 'there are left and right wings of Judaism, with the United Synagogue in the centre. The synagogue must rise above these polarities and must go out to the uncommitted. It should no longer stand half-way. We must lead and welcome those who have not yet found their spiritual home.'[16]

This approach was emphasised when, addressing a meeting of the London Society of Jews and Christians, he responded to a call from Canon Peter Schneider – consultant to the Archbishops of Canterbury and York on interfaith relations – for religious dialogue that would move away from intolerance. 'Judaism,' declared Sacks, 'welcomes pluralism and co-existence.'[17]

That the synagogue had to rise about politics as well as polarities was demonstrated one Shabbat morning when United Synagogue secretary Nathan Rubin, a member of Sacks' congregation, walked out of the service 'after what he considered to be an "offensive" sermon from the minister.'[18] In the course of his address, Sacks had referred to the JC's report of a US council meeting at which joint treasurer Mark Kleiner had criticised some of its ministers 'for complaining about, and vilifying, the United Synagogue.'

Reacting to Rubin's walk-out, Sacks claimed that his theme had been 'to refute any suggestion that ministers are not deeply committed to the United Synagogue and are, in fact, striving to improve their contribution.' When asked to comment, Rubin retorted: 'My clear impression of Rabbi Sacks' remarks was that before a layman – under the guise of the treasurer – criticised the ministry, the United Synagogue should put its own house in order. I'm fed up with Rabbi Sacks' continuous use of the pulpit to attack the US. He appears to have a phobia about it.'

Sacks, reported the JC, remained mystified. 'Any suggestion that I attacked the United Synagogue is absolutely against the grain,' he said. 'I made no express statement above the fact that rabbis should have faith in the US and themselves.'

Rushing to Sacks' defence, US stalwart Rudolph Stern told the paper: 'What in fact Mr Rubin has done... is to provide in full measure the answer as to why the ministerial pulpits throughout the country cannot be filled. He obviously would have liked Rabbi Sacks to behave like a meek, obedient servant who is all things to all men, and even if there are problems that the rabbi is deeply concerned with, he had better ignore them and sweep them under the carpet. In other words, he wants mediocre performers.

'Mr Rubin apparently does not comprehend that the United Synagogue ought to consider itself fortunate to get someone of Rabbi Sacks' stature, who is endowed with great intellectual powers, piety, learning and, above all, humility. Without men of his calibre, the United Synagogue will slide down a slippery slope.'[19]

Within two years – perhaps belatedly taking Bermant's advice about 'using his talents better' – Sacks vacated his Golders Green pulpit and, shortly after, became minister at Marble Arch, combining the post with his recently acquired principalship of Jews' College, and its Jakobovits Chair. Remarked Marble Arch ex-warden Louis Mintz: 'We are delighted he is coming. For how long it will last, I don't know.'[20]

* * *   * * *   * * *

Days after his induction, in September 1991, the new Chief Rabbi joined in a BBC Radio 4 panel discussion with novelist Howard Jacobson, journalist Melanie Philips, and Yakar's Michael Rosen. A fifth participant, Raymond Goldman, executive director of the Reform Synagogues of Great Britain, was selected by the BBC after Sacks had indicated, through his spokesman Jonathan Kestenbaum, that he 'would not take part if a Reform rabbi were on the panel.' It would be 'undignified,' explained Kestenbaum, 'for two rabbis to argue on air. It is the Chief Rabbi's policy to enter into discussions with all Jews on an individual basis.'

Sacks' action prompted a furious response from John Rayner, chairman of the Council of Reform and Liberal Rabbis. 'It is quite outrageous, preposterous and inexcusable,' he said, 'that Rabbi Sacks refused a public debate with non-Orthodox rabbis.' And, while softening his tone in a subsequent statement, he spelled out yet further grievances:

I have nothing but the highest regard and friendliest feelings for the new Chief Rabbi of the United Hebrew Congregations, and I have more than once conveyed to him the warmest good wishes of the Council of Reform and Liberal Rabbis, and their readiness to co-operate with him for the good of the community. It is all the more regrettable that he should have insulted the Council by not inviting its chairman to his installation, and by refusing, as a matter of policy, to participate in any public discussion with any of its members.

No one asks an Orthodox rabbi to express views inconsistent with Orthodoxy, or not to argue the case for Orthodoxy as vigorously as he may wish. But to refuse to engage in public discussion with those qualified to expound other points of view can only be regarded as intolerance.

The time has come to drop the bully-boy tactics which the Orthodox Establishment has so long practised towards the Progressives. Surely we should be able to rise above such pettiness and behave like mature adults in a democratic society. If Chief Rabbi Sacks were to inaugurate such an era of glasnost in Anglo-Jewry, he would earn the gratitude of the entire community, except for an extremist fringe, and greatly enhance respect for Judaism, not least Orthodox Judaism.[21]

In March 1994, Ernest Hornung, a member of Cardiff's New Synagogue (Reform), was refused an aliyah in the neighbouring United Synagogue (Orthodox) at the barmitzvah of his grandson.[22] Sacks subsequently issued a ruling that 'membership of a Reform congregation is not in itself a reason to prevent a person being called up in an Orthodox synagogue, provided that the person is halachically Jewish.'[23]

This provoked a sharp response from a coalition of dayanim, eliciting what amounted to a Chief Rabbinical volte-face. A statement from the group – Lichtenstein, Krausz and Toledano, of the Federation, Manchester and Sephardi batei din; Dunner, of the UOHC; and Rakow, of Gateshead – spoke of 'a worrying erosion' in the nature of Orthodox–Reform relations, and added:

We have been given an explicit assurance [by the Chief Rabbi] that communal policies regarding formal association with, or acceptance of, adherents to non-Orthodox movements – which we consider to be detrimental to both the character and the ethos of an Orthodox community – are to be determined on a local level. The prerogative of determining such policies is to remain, therefore, with local rabbinic authority, with a view to the preservation and enhancement of the Orthodox nature of the particular community. We welcome this assurance that there has been no new acceptance of non-Orthodox ideologies, nor any attempt to confer a degree of legitimacy upon them.[24]

Later that year, following a two-thirds majority vote by another Cardiff Orthodox congregation to alter its constitution, Rakow and Dunner, with Rabbi Shamai Zahn of Sunderland, 'defied the Chief Rabbi by instructing the Penylan Synagogue that changing its constitution to allow members of the Reform movement an aliyah is against halachah.'[25]

In mid-1995, the London Beth Din 'reacted strongly'[26] to a Shabbat-morning aliyah granted to Maidenhead (Reform) Synagogue's Rabbi Jonathan Romain at the South Hampstead (United) Synagogue. Ehrentreu told the *Jewish Tribune* that the London Beth Din had 'always held that it is absolutely forbidden to call up non-Orthodox (Masorti, Reform or Liberal) ministers in synagogues under its aegis.'

This ruling, he added, would 'continue to apply, and was fully consistent with a well-known *teshuvah* [responsum] of the late Rabbi Moshe Feinstein. This was a separate issue from that of calling up ordinary members of non-Orthodox congregations.'

The *Tribune* reported that 'the anxiety expressed in rabbinical circles when news of the South Hampstead call-up became known was compounded by the fact that Chief Rabbi Dr Jonathan Sacks was present in the synagogue at the time. Rabbi Sacks had apparently not been consulted about the aliyah and did not know that it was taking place until Dr Romain was actually on the *bimah* and was reciting the *berochoh*. Dr Romain was not called up with the title "*horav*."'

On the involvement of South Hampstead's minister, the paper asserted: 'The decision to call up Dr Romain was made by Rabbi Shlomo Levin, who subsequently said that he was unaware at the time that the calling up of Reform ministers to the Torah was prohibited by the London Beis Din and that, had he known this, he would not have done so.

'He also emphasised that he would not repeat this in the future. Nevertheless, Rabbi Levin did not consider that, in the circumstances in question, the decision to call up Dr Romain was inherently wrong.'

I took a view [said Levin] that a Reform minister is fundamentally a Jew and that it would be appropriate to show a public gesture of tolerance. I appreciate that it may be somewhat difficult for the charedi community to accept, but it should be understood that in South Hampstead I am operating in a specialised environment and many of our members were originally completely outside the community. The call-up of Dr Romain should not be seen as an implied recognition of the Reform, against whom

I take an extremely strong line. But Reform has to be fought on issues and not personalities.[27]

* * *   * * *   * * *

In his statement following the Gryn affair, and the formulation of the Stanmore Accords after a protracted period of difficult negotiations, the Chief Rabbi declared: 'On matters which touch on religious differences, we agree to differ, but with courtesy. Absence of recognition does not imply absence of respect. Think twice before condemning a fellow Jew.'

Largely absent from his statements and actions during his Chief Rabbinate, however, has been any manifestation of this appeal to 'think twice' before condemning the non-Orthodox, or of exerting influence over his Beth Din to 'exercise charity in interpretation.' Alongside the major disputes hitherto explored was a succession of other issues touching on intra-communal relations.

By early 2001, barely two years after the accords were signed, it had become abundantly clear that all was not well on the intra-communal front. Concerns over the Chief Rabbi's participation in a national ceremony to mark Holocaust Memorial Day were met by a hastily convened meeting, under Board of Deputies auspices, to thrash out issues that had built up over time.

Opening the meeting, attended by representatives of the United Synagogue, the non-Orthodox movements and the Board, and presided over by Tabachnik, Bayfield referred to 'two significant areas of difficulty' – halachic and status issues and the institution of the Chief Rabbinate, both of which 'could undermine the positive achievements of the past few years.' Issues related to 'representation, visibility and communication' had marred Holocaust Memorial Day and the commemoration of the millennium by faith communities.

Middleburgh commented that it was 'not just a question of the institution of the Chief Rabbinate: the individual and the office have become virtually inseparable. It is the office-holder who has disenfranchised the non-Orthodox communities and given out misleading information about them.'

Bayfield pointed out that the Chief Rabbi had often laid great stress on all Jews constituting a single people and 'on what a good example the British Jewish community could provide to the world. I believe the Chief Rabbi genuinely wants this but recognises that there might be pressures on him.'

Sheldon, who had succeeded Elkan Levy as United Synagogue president, said that he recognised that 'the man cannot be separated from the office' and that, 'despite the power of that office, the Chief Rabbi is not always in a position to confront all the pressures upon him. I believe him to be an inclusivist at heart, but unable to move forward as much as he might personally want.'

The Chief Rabbi, said Sheldon, was often called upon because of 'his exceptional communication skills' and was widely perceived by the outside world as the religious head of British Jewry. 'If this perception were undermined, the entire community might lose, because there is little doubt that the Chief Rabbi does an admirable job in representing the entire Jewish community in wider society.'

Sheldon noted that participants in the Consultative Committee had had no discussions with Sacks since the Gryn Affair and suggested that 'it might be helpful for this group to open up discussions with the Chief Rabbi on an informal basis.' Board vice-president Jo Wagerman added that 'it might be wise to attempt to raise with the Chief Rabbi the contradiction which many feel between his strong public messages of inclusiveness and his actions.' Masorti chairman Paul Shrank, confirming that there had been no meetings with Sacks, said that he had 'no sense of knowing whether the Chief Rabbi is, in practice, prepared to do anything to promote greater inclusivity.'

Sheldon concluded the proceedings by suggesting an informal meeting at the Chief Rabbi's home. Adopting the proposal, the participants stipulated that, while they would be prepared to accept a one-off meeting there, 'if further meetings are envisaged, they should be on neutral territory.'[28]

During the year that elapsed before the meeting was held, Wittenberg presented a paper – *Where It Hurts* – to a gathering of the Consultative Committee, attended by, among others, Sheldon and US chief executive Rabbi Saul Zneimer. Wittenberg described the document as 'not a personal or a Masorti view, but a summary of material I have received. These are areas where differences in policy regarding issues of personal status are felt to hurt. This "hurt" refers to the feelings of the individuals, their families, and often the communities and the rabbis concerned.'

Covering issues as diverse as education, students, and death, the main thrust of the paper was on conversion and marriage. Of the former, Wittenberg wrote: 'The non-recognition of converts hurts them, their children and the movements to which they belong. It is also especially painful in the case of adopted children. The adopting parents have usually suffered and hoped for years to have children. Now they have the issue of the status of the children they adopt.'

Describing the question of non-US marriages as 'very sore,' Wittenberg asserted that 'the rhetoric of non-recognition of Liberal, Reform and Masorti marriages hurts greatly. This may be done by inference or through what is not said, but it spreads unwarranted fear. Suggestions that there may be problems, sometimes even hints about the "illegitimacy" of future children, feel like scare tactics.'[29]

Aimed at discussing these issues directly with the Chief Rabbi, the planned meeting was eventually hosted by Sacks and attended by Sheldon, Freedman and Shrank. The principal matter discussed was that of representation, about which Sacks declared there had been 'significant changes.' He referred to the appointment of Friedlander as a full president of the Council of Christians and Jews; to his own association with Progressive rabbis at the Union of Jewish Students' conference; and to other occasions where non-Orthodox rabbis had been 'in attendance.' He had also offered, he said, to take with him 'a Progressive representative' to official meetings with government ministers.

Shrank retorted that, so far as Masorti was concerned, the Chief Rabbi did not represent them, a position shared by the other non-Orthodox bodies. This, replied Sacks, was 'an important issue' and it seemed opportune, therefore, to reconvene the Liaison Committee. As for the Consultative Committee, he said, its function involved 'inter-synagogal matters' and it did not have the remit enjoyed by the former Consultative Committee for Jewish–Christian Relations, which he offered to revive.

Freedman expressed disappointment that the Stanmore Accords had been 'disregarded' over Orthodox rabbinic representation on the Consultative Committee. The United Synagogue, in parallel with the other parties to the accords, had agreed to observe their provisions, but events had 'proved otherwise.' Why, he inquired, if the accords allowed for an halachically acceptable Reform, Liberal or Masorti Jew to be called up at an Orthodox service, did this not also apply to a rabbi or minister? Describing this as 'a complex question,' the Chief Rabbi declined to elaborate.

Shrank asked Sacks whether he had seen Wittenberg's *Where It Hurts*, to which he replied in the negative. Having then read it, he remarked that most of the issues were 'halachic matters not for discussion' and, on being told by Shrank of a 'whispering campaign' against Masorti marriages, said that any such instances should be referred to him.[30]

Summing up their hour-long discussion, Freedman wrote later: 'The meeting was cordial, and the only reason I was not disappointed by the outcome was that I had no expectations of change.'[31]

This view was vindicated by a number of subsequent incidents, including a Masorti member being denied the *haftarah* (prophetical portion) at his son-in-law's *aufruf* in the Western Marble Arch Synagogue; a scribe's refusal to write a *ketubah* for a Masorti marriage; and the censorship of a eulogy at the Orthodox funeral of a 101-year-old woman, omitting any reference to the New London Synagogue which she had long attended.

Commenting on these episodes, and on the vicissitudes of the Stanmore agreement since its inception, Shrank provided a revealing insight:

> I signed the statement with some mixed feelings. There were forceful voices in Masorti which suggested that we should not be a party to this agreement, because it meant we would have to be less assertive in public and we would have to accept the United Synagogue conventions, which did not satisfy all our complaints about discriminatory practices. I felt, however, that it was important for the whole community that we should be part of the effort to achieve harmony, and that we would always regret it if we had not tried.
>
> I also felt that, over time, the establishment of personal relationships and dialogue, particularly between rabbis, would led to a softening of those things which were causing us pain ... After a time, it became obvious that the United Synagogue had no intention of moving on any of these issues, and when I had a private meeting with the Chief Rabbi, in the company of US president Peter Sheldon and the then ULPS chairman Jeromé Freedman, Rabbi Sacks contemptuously dismissed the issues we raised and said that the reason for denying aliyot to Rabbi Jacobs was 'halachic.' So much for the dignity of difference ...
>
> The dialogue with the United Synagogue has been a dialogue of the deaf, and the spirit in which we signed the Stanmore Accords has been dissipated ... There is no prospect of an end to the vicious discrimination which occurs in this community, so I see little point in continuing the façade of dialogue. Masorti should return to asserting its position vigorously and not hesitate to publicise those incidents that cause so much hurt to our members. I do not regret signing the Stanmore Accords, but I must now admit that, unfortunately, they were an experiment which has failed.[32]

For the Liberals, Goldberg commented: 'The Stanmore Accords are not worth the paper they were written on. The establishment United Synagogue, haemorrhaging members and no longer capable of even maintaining a college for the training of its rabbis, nevertheless has learnt from the British establishment the trick of appearing to concede in order to keep things as they are ...

'In return for crumbs from the United Synagogue table, the right of the Chief Rabbi to speak on behalf of all Jews goes unchallenged, even though his organisation now represents a minority in Anglo-Jewry. Having survived from the Gryn Affair to the Jacobs Affair Mark II, it is now time for all the parties involved to give a decent burial to the accords.'[33]

Brichto concurred: 'The Jacobs incident must be the testing ground for the continuation of the Stanmore Accords. If neither the Chief Rabbi of the United Synagogue nor its lay leaders can reverse this decision, the accords will only amount to the cowardly agreement of the Jewish community to give assent to the unacceptable moral blindness of the Beth Din in whatever direction it decides to take. The accords will then become no more than a treaty of surrender.'[34]

With such views, the Chief Rabbi – not unnaturally – begged to differ. Appearing on BBC Radio 4, he was asked by presenter Roger Bolton: 'You wrote recently that Judaism remains as quarrelsome as ever. There have been serious internal divisions within the community during your period in office. Do you have to learn to live with that?'

Sacks replied: 'We can be argumentative, but we do so with mutual respect. Three years ago, we set out a series of protocols, the Stanmore Accords, which got all the different groups within the community to agree to work together. The two basic principles were that on anything that affects Jews regardless of their religious beliefs, we will work together regardless of our religious beliefs; and that wherever our religious differences are relevant, we will agree to respect those differences. That, I think, is a good way forward – and it's worked.'[35]

The most telling of the responses to Jacobs Mark II came from the 'kingmaker' himself, in his second call on Sacks to step down from office. Reviewing the Chief Rabbi's recent record, Kalms wrote:

> He has no plans for another Traditional Alternatives-style conference to keep open the doors of our faith to the widest circle. The row over Rabbi Dr Louis Jacobs shows only too well that one step forward has been followed by two steps back. In the middle ground between the fundamentalist right and radical left, the Chief Rabbi is like a shuttlecock. Inclusivism, the theme of his original manifesto, is but a distant memory.
>
> It has not been a good two years for the Chief Rabbi. He has been marginally unfortunate and, I suppose, paraphrasing Napoleon, we could mutter under our breath: 'We need a lucky Chief Rabbi.' Instead, we seem to have a Duke of York.
>
> What we have missed is sufficient evidence of a deep, unstoppable

passion to fight the good fight, to give 110 per cent. In a global society rocked by the potential clash of civilisations, the Chief Rabbi adopts a policy of 'wait-and-see' instead of setting out his stall clearly and without ambivalence.

For all his difficulties, the Chief Rabbi remains gifted both as an orator and thinker. He would do well to consider throwing off the chains of office and giving himself the freedom and independence that would allow his undoubted talents to be expressed to the full. He would be a formidable exponent of Jewish ideals and would attract many supporters.

I am aware that his praetorian guard will immediately rally to his side and try to persuade him to stay on as Chief Rabbi, but even they, I suspect, will be acting out of loyalty rather than conviction. In this dangerous time for world Jewry, can we afford a low-key leadership?[36]

No sooner was Kalms' piece in print than, as predicted, the 'praetorian guard' rallied to Sacks' side. 'It is not surprising,' wrote Radlett minister Gideon Sylvester,

that over the last few months a number of criticisms have appeared in this newspaper condemning the work of the Chief Rabbi. While it is undoubtedly true that he has made mistakes, these polemics have failed to credit some real achievements … Jewish tradition recognises that even our leaders may make mistakes, but where they recognise them and correct them, their leadership remains not just undiminished, but greater. The Chief Rabbi has discovered that trying to please the entire community all of the time does not work. Stanley Kalms may be correct to identify the problems associated with endless attempts at consensus and compromise. But as the Chief Rabbi emerges as his own man, implementing his own philosophy, we will be the beneficiaries.[37]

* * *   * * *   * * *

Whether or not it worked – as Sacks had confidently suggested – the Stanmore agreement survived, but after two further years of wrangling the non-Orthodox parties began a process of serious reconsideration.

In the aftermath of the signing, they had had positive expectations, summed up by Shrank in a report to the Masorti council in 2002. 'We believed,' he wrote, 'that the accords had met with the approval of the Chief Rabbi, the London Beth Din, and the body of United Synagogue rabbis. We also believed that the US accepted that the Consultative Committee would act as a serious forum to debate the issues dividing us, with a willingness to make an attempt to resolve these issues, and that the Chief Rabbi would occasionally attend meetings of the committee.

'But two things happened immediately. First, we were told that the meetings of the Consultative Committee had to be kept confidential, with secrecy extending to the location of the meetings and the names of the representatives. The lay leadership of the US did not, as yet, have the full support of their rabbanim and were nervous about the reaction of Orthodoxy in Israel if the contents of our meetings were made public. In effect, we were warned that any leakage could cause the collapse of the Consultative Committee. Secondly, it was suggested that since we would be meeting as the Consultative Committee, the tripartite group [of the non-Orthodox] should be disbanded, having served its purpose.'

Following the signing, Shrank conceded, the committee had met on a regular basis and had proved to be 'a considerable factor in the lowering of communal tension.' But, three years on, he had formed negative perceptions of where they stood now.

> The United Synagogue [he declared] has no intention of making any move to alter its position on the *Where It Hurts* issues, though it is content to carry on meeting. The Reform see some purpose in meeting, but the ULPS has virtually given up: Progressive rabbis at present are no longer attending.
>
> Rabbi Sacks has no real intention of sharing representation. His offer at our meeting to reconstitute the Liaison Committee is seen as an attempt to emasculate the Consultative Committee. There continue to be occasions where Masorti representation is denied (for example, the UJIA conference) or excluded by omission (the Israel rally).
>
> We have interpreted the Stanmore Accords as a mutually agreed 'gagging' agreement, and this has led to a sense of frustration as our grievances continue to be unaddressed.[38]

Reporting to the Masorti council some four years later, Shrank's successor, Michael Gluckman, asserted that 'little has changed. There is still no rabbinic representation from the United Synagogue and, while Liberal Judaism now sends a rabbi, the idea of Rabbi Sacks attending has not been aired.

'Many non-contentious issues have been discussed to a degree that – as I have often complained in committee – are a diversion from the true purpose of the group: to tackle issues that divide us. We have pressed the United Synagogue on some of those issues, but no progress has been made since we raised them in 2002. The main item of contention under discussion was the denial of an aliyah to Rabbi Jacobs in 2003.

'We need to know whether the United Synagogue still stands by Annexe 1 [Conventions of Orthodox communities as adopted by the United Synagogue]; why the US has not kept to its side of the agreement by ensuring that a rabbinic representative attends the meetings; and why it maintains its insistence on secrecy, when we would prefer to see full transparency and open debate.

'If the United Synagogue cannot answer these points to our satisfaction, it is they who will be abrogating the accords. Carrying on with the meetings would then become questionable.'[39]

In January 2008, leaders of the Reform, Liberal and Masorti movements called for a 'rethink' of the agreement, having sought 'greater focus on trying to resolve problems that stem from issues over Jewish status,' and having encountered 'little leeway on this' within the United Synagogue.[40] Bayfield asserted: 'I think the Stanmore Accords have reached the end of their useful life, and a new initiative is in the making by the Reform, Liberal and Masorti movements.

'The agreement promised something significant and, under the Chief Rabbi's "one people" agenda, was successful at first. But the United Synagogue's stultified, defensive and increasingly reactive preoccupation with the right-wing sector of the community over the past several years has changed the name of the game. What is unclear is whether Jonathan Sacks is the prisoner or the leader of this process.'[41]

As the months wore on, the accords began to look increasingly threatened. Without so much as mentioning Stanmore by name, and eschewing any direct reference to the Chief Rabbinate or the United Synagogue, the religious and lay leaders of Liberal, Masorti and Reform Judaism – embracing, as they put it, 'around a third of British Jewry' – launched 'a major shift in the way in which the various synagogue movements representing the UK's quarter of a million-strong Jewish community behave towards each other.'

The initiative, they announced, 'is in part prompted by growing Jewish fundamentalism, which is exclusive and judgmental. The Jewish community cannot afford to divide against itself, and we call for a new voice that is open, tolerant, collaborative and respectful.'[42] In what they described as 'A Statement on Communal Collaboration,' they laid out their aims:

Pluralism means living creatively with diversity. It is based on treating other groups and their philosophies with respect, while maintaining the right to uphold the value of one's own position. Diversity is a reality within the British Jewish community; true pluralism is, as yet, not. We believe that British Jewry both needs and deserves better.

Wisdom dictates that our small community (267,000, and shrinking inexorably at the rate of 1 per cent each year) is best served by a leadership which embraces the values of pluralism and acts accordingly. Pragmatically, we cannot afford to duplicate the use of resources or waste them on denominational competition. If the Jewish community is to be renewed, it is manifestly obvious that we have to plan and work together. We acknowledge the challenges faced by the British Jewish community in terms of resources, and commit ourselves to avoiding destructive competition and needless duplication.

Perhaps the most inspiring example of pluralism to benefit our community is Limmud, which began in Britain and has spread throughout the Jewish world. A key feature of its success is that it welcomes both teachers and students from all the movements within Judaism today, and from none. But there are also other examples of respectful and creative cross-communal partnership, such as the UJIA and Jewish Care. These organisations model how we should behave towards one another.

Respect for those who hold different positions from ourselves must begin with our leaders. We therefore resolve to treat one another accordingly, honouring the titles and status of rabbis and teachers and instructing our communities to do likewise.

Such respect is no less the due of every individual, especially at sensitive times in the life cycle, including marriage, the celebration of namings, brit and bnei mitzvah, as well as during illness and after death. Whereas we acknowledge that there are significant differences between the movements on questions of personal status, we undertake to do our utmost to negotiate them in a spirit of respect for the dignity of each individual as created in the image of God. Whether at the chuppah or the cemetery, we resolve to work together as co-operatively as possible and to seek ways to prevent individuals from suffering because of the differences between our movements.

The values of pluralism must also influence the way in which we develop our institutions. We have every right to seek to further the goals of our own movements. But at the same time we recognise that there are many situations in which it is better to share than to squander limited financial and human resources on replication and competition. We resolve to bear this reality in mind at all times, and, even as we pursue our own objectives, to have as our primary aim the overall good of the whole community.

Pluralism is not the same as spineless acquiescence. Debate, even to the extent of impassioned argument, is not only legitimate in Judaism, it has always been considered a positive value, so long as it is for the sake of Heaven. We therefore encourage informed and creative dialogue and disagreement. But we undertake to do our best never to let this descend to the delegitimisation of the rights of others to hold to the integrity of their positions.

No less important than being able to disagree with dignity is our ability to agree, and to be seen to agree in public, so as to demonstrate leadership and solidarity on issues of vital and universal moral importance. These include opposition to racism and anti-Semitism, public stances regarding Israel, support of interfaith initiatives, campaigns for justice, welfare, charity and the environment. We should not rely on external organisations to add us to their list of sponsors one at a time, but should be prepared, in appropriate contexts, to articulate Judaism's prophetic vision and values openly together.

We believe that synagogue organisations need to model a pluralist manner of co-operative working in Britain, remembering the message of the Midrash that the Second Temple was destroyed on account of *sinat chinam*, causeless hatred between factions. Co-operation for the sake of Heaven, *l'shem shamayim*, is a profound religious value.

There are many ways in which we differ. We have different approaches to that vast and distinctive Jewish inheritance – the halachic tradition. We use different prayer books, and our styles of services are different. We feel ourselves to be heirs to different Jewish cultural expressions (Ashkenazi, Sephardi, German, Eastern European, and American). These differences should be seen to add to the richness and diversity from which Jews of different tastes and temperaments can choose.

Discussing the possible 'areas for co-operation,' the leaders declared: 'For this to succeed, we must move beyond just talking and look where we can truly work together and demonstrate our commitment to these ideals. Such areas are many, but they would include schools, students and young adults, and Jewish ethics.'

On the question of schools, 'we believe that this is one of the areas where there is a widespread consensus, namely, that one of the best ways of ensuring Jewish survival, the transmission of Judaism and a knowledgeable and committed Jewish community of the future is through Jewish day schools for all who seek such an education.'

Of students and young adults, they asserted: 'Most of these form one constituency and do not like to be "classified." They are our future, and supporting and nurturing them through this formative stage in their lives is critical. By working together, we can avoid wasteful duplication and finance a well-resourced programme which responds to their needs.'

In the area of Jewish ethics, the statement declared: 'Judaism taught the world that God is the embodiment of the ethical and commands ethical action, the pursuit of justice and righteousness. We are committed to a Jewish ethical response to the cutting-edge issues of our day – the environment, human rights, business ethics, medical ethics, development, the eradication of poverty. We know that no religious tradition contains all wisdom or possesses all the answers. We cannot repair the world on our own. We stress learning from others, working with others, networking, and partnership in advocacy.'

Their document, the leaders concluded, 'is not just a statement of principle, however important the principle. It is a commitment to work together for the sake of the Jewish community, the future of Judaism in Britain. We have a responsibility to come together and demonstrate that we can truly work together.'[43]

Not all in the Progressive movement saw it that way. Dismissing the statement, Richard Buckley, a leading figure in the Bristol and West Progressive Jewish Congregation, argued: 'My biggest objection to these proposals is that they exhibit a degree of insecurity or uncertainty about the legitimacy of Progressive Judaism. They suggest that in some way we need Orthodoxy's approbation.

'I fundamentally disagree with this. Liberal, Reform and Masorti Judaism is as authentic as the form of Judaism practised by the Orthodox, arguably more so in some respects. We can stand on our own feet as the equal of any other form of Judaism and we shouldn't be ashamed to do so.'

Reflecting a wide cross-section of Progressive opinion, Buckley declared of the Stanmore Accords: 'They were negotiated by the great and the good of British Jewry and have no relevance whatever to ordinary Jews. My understanding has always been that they were entered into by the Orthodox in a cynical attempt to try to repair the image of the United Synagogue following the damage caused to it by the Chief Rabbi's extraordinary and offensive comments about Rabbi Gryn, and that they had no real intention of allowing the accords to change anything.'[44]

For Reform, Bayfield described the collaboration statement as 'a watershed in British Jewish history.' Warning of the consequences of 'the process of *charedi*-isation' in Anglo-Jewry, he declared: 'It is the inexorable rise and rise of the influence of the fundamentalists within the United Synagogue that is decisive and presents the US with a challenge, not the collaboration of Liberal, Masorti and Reform ... British Jewry will be at the forefront of religious thinking and social action in the years ahead. It will not retreat into fundamentalist irrelevance.'[45]

On the future of the accords, in light of the statement and his perception of the United Synagogue's direction and focus, Bayfield was sceptical about their long-term viability:

> The Consultative Committee [he said] will meet in due course to discuss our proposals. We shall want to continue meeting, though probably with three people representing Reform, Liberal and Masorti rather than nine. And we want the United Synagogue to field a senior rabbi, as it was supposed to do under the Stanmore agreement but never consistently did.
>
> In a nutshell, we are saying that the United Synagogue has changed its focus. Fifteen years ago, when Jonathan Sacks wrote *One People?*, the agenda was about keeping the Jewish people together by whatever devices were necessary. Today, the US is focused entirely on the needs of the traditionally observant community. It lives in constant fear of having its authority questioned by the far right, which is why it has become more and more l'chumreh [strict] on kashrut, conversion and schools admissions.
>
> We are saying that 80 per cent of the community will not respond to charedi Judaism. Will the United Synagogue join us in a more inclusive, pluralistic approach to the diverse needs of that 80 per cent? If 'yes,' fine. If, as we suspect, the answer is 'no,' we will get on with providing the leadership, the initiatives, the thinking and the programmes that are needed. Ultimately, this is about not writing off the mainstream of the community and not settling for just a charedi rump in the year 2050.[46]

In support of this view, an unnamed 'source close to the group behind the document' told the JC: 'The Chief Rabbi and the United Synagogue have to face up to the consequence of having moved from being the de facto leadership of the whole of the community to having become the vehicle for the fundamentalist revival.'

Asked if he expected the United Synagogue to sign up to the new platform, he said: 'On balance, sadly, no. But we would love to be proved wrong.' He explained that it had been decided to publicise the statement rather than circulate it privately because 'otherwise we will have another umpteen years of frustration and inertia.'[47]

Sharing Bayfield's concerns about the 'charedi-isation' of Anglo-Jewry, emeritus minister Jeffrey Cohen described his experiences while working within the United Synagogue. 'About fifteen years ago,' he recalled in 2009, 'I went to America and saw women's tefillah groups and other experimental services. I came back and I spoke to my community [Stanmore] about how wonderful this was.

> Lord Jakobovits, to whom I was very close, said to me: 'Jeffrey, I am going to advise you as a friend. Don't try to found a Modern Orthodox movement in Britain because you will fail. Why? Because the charedim are in the ascendancy. They are getting numerically stronger, they have the passion, and they are going to take over. I can only hope that, once they are in a seat of power, they will moderate their position.'
>
> He was right – but we have yet to see any evidence of them moderating their position. However, I still entertain the hope that Modern Orthodoxy will get a bit more confidence, that rabbis in Britain and America will not be looking over their right shoulder all the time, but will provide a modern approach to Jewish life.[48]

Commenting on Bayfield's pessimistic view of the accords' future, Elkan Levy, who had steered the negotiations a decade earlier, laid what he termed 'their possible abandonment' firmly at the door of the non-Orthodox movements. 'They have,' he contended, 'unreasonable expectations of what is possible within Orthodox Judaism. Their ignorance of Orthodoxy is very deep and very real, summed up by the Liberal woman rabbi who was convinced that, within ten years, the United Synagogue, too, would have women rabbis.'

The Gryn controversy that had led to the accords was, said Levy, 'a tacit admission by the Reform that the Chief Rabbinate somehow encompassed them, that Sacks' presence at the funeral would have lent credence to the religious nature of the ceremony. This itself is strange: if, as they maintain, they are a self-confident and self-sufficient communion, why did they crave the presence of a religious leader whose authority, they say, means nothing to them?'[49]

Backing Levy's contention that the non-Orthodox had 'unreasonable expectations of what is possible within Orthodox Judaism,' the JC remarked: 'Some Orthodox readers will struggle to get past even the first word [of the collaboration statement]. That is because the joint declaration begins with the dreaded p-word – "pluralism." Indeed, the very mention of the bogey term, even if not intended to be provocative, may prove hard for the Orthodox establishment to swallow.'[50]

That this assessment bore weight was signified the following week by incoming US president Simon Hochhauser: 'Recognising our boundaries,' he declared, 'on Jewish education and halachah we agree to differ, with respect and dignity.'[51] Preceding his comment was the release of a 'United

Synagogue Manifesto' – presented by Hochhauser and his fellow officers
– which declared that the US

> is a family of communities dedicated to vibrant Jewish life and Torah
> values. It has, at its core, the ethos of kol Yisrael arevim ze ba'zeh – every Jew
> has an equal responsibility to his or her fellow Jew, regardless of religious
> observance ... The past three years have seen a major transformation of
> the United Synagogue towards an open, transparent organisation capable
> of passionate open debate and the adoption of change. This environment
> augurs well for the next three years.[52]

As events showed, abandonment of the accords was not immediately
on the communal agenda. The Consultative Committee met in December
2008 and unanimously agreed 'to renew their commitment to work
together for the sake of the Jewish community and the future of Judaism
in Britain.' Six weeks later, and ten years after the accords first appeared,
the successors of the original signatories reaffirmed and republished their
aims – which, they emphasised, 'still hold true today.'[53]

Welcoming the move, Wittenberg maintained: 'Through our continuing
commitment to the Stanmore Accords, the Masorti, Liberal and Reform
movements recognise that, despite significantly differing views, the
religious movements in Britain must work together in the interests of the
community as a whole.

'Pragmatically, we cannot afford to duplicate the use of resources or
waste them on denominational competition. If the Jewish community is
to be renewed, it is manifestly obvious that we have to plan and work
together. No issue is harder to grapple with than status, and we are pleased
to see the reconfirmation on the position on marriages contained within
the accords."[54]

Despite his earlier reservations, Hochhauser observed that, 'by
reaffirming the Stanmore Accords, we are demonstrating our commitment
to working closely with other movements within the Jewish community for
the benefit of all of our members and of the community as a whole. There
are many areas on which we can co-operate while respecting our religious
differences. It is extremely positive that the different religious movements
are so enthusiastic to work closely together to ensure communal harmony
going forward.'[55]

On this, Bayfield commented: 'The president of the United Synagogue
is clearly responding to the "challenge" of the statement of collaboration
between Reform, Liberal and Masorti by taking the Consultative Committee
forward. We have now, for the first time, a senior Orthodox rabbi – Michael

Harris, joint vice-chairman of the United Synagogue Rabbinical Council –
at our meetings,[56] and they have gone public, as manifested in the report
of the first meeting of the revamped group. One suspects, however, that Dr
Hochhauser is leading on his own and does not have the full support of
everyone within the United Synagogue. Why he is responding in this way
is unclear.' And, Bayfield added – echoing Mintz's remark at Marble Arch,
years earlier, and presaging the JFS outcome, months later – 'how long the
period of openness will last, who knows?'[57]

The Mirage of Unity

*'We are more deeply divided than at almost any time in our history.
Israel is divided. We in the diaspora are divided. A few years ago, Jewish thinkers
asked the question: "Will there be one Jewish people in the year 2000?"
Today there are already many prepared to give the answer "No."'* [1]

Enveloping the British Chief Rabbinate over the past 150 years has been the vulnerability of its occupants as the forces of reason took on the fortress of faith. While, historiographically, much is made of divisions within Orthodox ranks over the policies and posturing of the communal grandees and their ecclesiastical heads,[2] scant attention has been paid to non-Orthodox attitudes to the Chief Rabbinate in its institutional guise, aspects of the religious divide that were to become increasingly dominant as twentieth-century Anglo-Jewry assumed function and form.[3]

The early decades, it is true, evinced signs of promise. Despite varying degrees of opposition to the ritual 'modifications' of the West London Synagogue, relations between the Orthodox and Reformers softened considerably over the course of Nathan Adler's incumbency. 'The strong feelings which were evoked fifty years ago against the Reform Movement,' declared a *Jewish Chronicle* supplement in 1892, 'have long since died a natural death. For many years past, the closest domestic ties by marriage, and the growth of general enlightenment and forbearance, have combined to reunite the two sections of the community into one; one for all practical purposes of communal action and religious sympathy despite the deviations in external forms of public worship.'[4]

That the two sections were 'reunited into one' was clearly an expression both of journalistic hyperbole and of wishful thinking, but co-operation had reached a close enough point by Adler's death in 1890 to prompt six of their 'influential members' to suggest taking steps 'with the object of uniting the entire Anglo-Jewish Community under one Spiritual Chief.'[5] In a letter to Lord Rothschild, president of the United Synagogue, signed by (among others) Samuel Montagu, MP, acting president of the Federation of Synagogues, and Sir Philip Magnus, a council member of the West London Synagogue, they wrote:

There is now abundant evidence of the existence of a widespread desire for (a) a comprehension of the English Jews under the guidance of one presiding Chief Rabbi, who shall be the Chief Spiritual adviser of all the Jews residing in the British Empire; and (b) a certain latitude to individual congregations within well-defined limits to vary the present order of Divine Service in some details.

It may be useful to point out that though there are some differences of outward practice and of ritual observance between sections of Jews, differences which may perhaps be the outcome of their surroundings, the main principles of the Creed of all are not merely similar but identical, and that the brotherhood of Israel is far stronger than any divergence of liturgy or rite.

We, the undersigned, acting entirely without any representative authority, submit to you that the time has now arrived when you can usefully invite 1. The Spanish and Portuguese Synagogue; 2. The Federation of Synagogues, whose acting President is one of the signatories of this letter; 3. The West London Synagogue of British Jews, of the Council of which some of us are members; 4. The other Metropolitan and the Provincial Synagogues to join with 5. The United Synagogue, of which you are the President, in the election of a consultative Committee, who shall endeavour to formulate a plan of comprehension of the Jews of the British Empire.[6]

The first of the three bases for such 'comprehension' – the second and third dealt with modes of ritual service – proposed that 'the Chief Rabbi shall be the Spiritual head of the whole of the Jews of the British Empire, but in respect to the Portuguese and West London Congregations in a consultative capacity only, such congregations respectively retaining their autonomy.'[7] At a related meeting the following day, a memorial signed by 472 members of the United Synagogue was adopted urging, inter alia, that the US constitution 'be so amended as to render possible the admission of the West London Synagogue of British Jews as a constituent synagogue.'[8]

A fortnight later (6 May, 1890), the United Synagogue council authorised Rothschild 'to invite representatives from the Metropolitan and Provincial Synagogues to consider in conjunction with the Honorary Officers of the United Synagogue the proposals contained in the letters addressed to the President in reference to the appointment of Chief Rabbi.'

The West London Synagogue and Federation of Synagogues were among those subsequently invited by Rothschild 'to elect gentlemen to represent them at the Conference which I propose summoning to give effect to this resolution.'[9] The West London's response, preceded by a 'long and animated'[10] debate within its council, represents the first overt indication of Reform's historical, and ultimately unyielding, opposition to the Chief Rabbinate as an institution. At the council,

> a proposal was made by the chairman, Sir Julian Goldsmid, to return a courteous negative to the invitation of the President of the United Synagogue; to this proposal an amendment was moved by Mr L. Schloss accepting the invitation, but limiting very greatly the powers of any delegates who might be appointed ... A very strong feeling was shown by both parties to preserve the autonomy of the congregation.
>
> Eventually, the resolution of Sir Julian Goldsmid that the invitation of Lord Rothschild should be declined was carried by a narrow majority of three – twelve votes to nine. The majority included the chairman of the council, the three wardens, and the two treasurers. The ministers attended the meeting to express their views, and two of them (the Rev Prof Marks and the Rev Isidore Harris) recommended that the invitation should not be accepted. Prof Marks, in a very earnest speech, stated that if the suggestions contained in the letter signed by three of his congregants were carried into effect, he would have no alternative but to retire from his ministrations.

Immediately thereafter, as the conference was later informed,[11] Goldsmid wrote to Rothschild:

> We wish to acknowledge with much satisfaction both the courtesy shown in this invitation and the desire for closer relations between our body and the constituents of the United Synagogue. At the same time, it appears to the great majority of the members of this Congregation that the principle upon which it has been founded must, of necessity, prevent its being represented at a meeting intended to prepare the way for the election of a new Chief Rabbi, as the congregation has uniformly declined to accept the spiritual authority of such an officer, however personally distinguished.[12]

'The union of the three joint sections of the community under one spiritual direction,' editorialised the *Jewish Chronicle* after the deliberations,

> would have been an epoch-making event that would for all time have marked the conference as a memorable occasion in the annals of Anglo-Jewish history. But the idea was slain at the moment of its birth, and the authors of its being could have derived little satisfaction from its reception

by two of the three sections of the community.[13] Clearly the time was not ripe for the practical realisation of the project. It is as well, however, that it should have been made manifest that some leading members of all three sections are favourable to a more complete union than that which exists.[14]

As events were to demonstrate in the decades, and Chief Rabbinates, that followed, no time was ripe – or could be – for a realisation of the project.

* * *   * * *   * * *

The election of 1913 was an altogether more divisive, and bitter, affair. By then there was no hint, let alone talk, of Reform representation in the cumbersome and drawn-out process. The differences occurred in the Orthodox arena, with the Federation of Synagogues withdrawing from the Chief Rabbinical conference following a dispute over the number of delegates, its 6,500-strong membership having received twenty-eight votes against the 314 allotted to the 5,412 members of the United Synagogue. 'The [Federation] Board,' wrote its secretary, Joseph Blank, to his US counterpart,

> cannot give its adhesion to a scheme which practically secures to the United Synagogue, representing as it does only about one-sixteenth of the Jews of the United Kingdom, the election or dismissal of the Chief Rabbi ... [E]very argument advanced by the Federation is strengthened by the action of the Council of the United Synagogue. The Board has only to repeat (a) that the Federation cannot therefore share in the responsibility of an election in which it has practically no voice, and (b) trusts that after the United Synagogue has made its choice of a Chief Rabbi, the Federation will be able to accept him.[15]

That the Chief Rabbinate itself was dispensable after the 'religious dictatorship' of the Adlers was a view expressed – not without support – by communal activist Redcliffe Salaman, an eminent geneticist and future member of Jews' College council, who was to cross swords with more than one Chief Rabbi over the years.[16] 'Our late Chiefs and their system,' he declared during the campaign, 'destroyed the independence and sapped the virility of the Jewish rabbinate. Before we find a new Chief, we must find ourselves.

'We must allow each congregation to feel once more its own

independence and responsibility. Natural selection, so long restrained, once more at work, will soon evolve for us a suitable minister. To appoint any of the impossible candidates before the community is not only to court disaster but to ensure it. We must have a ten years' breathing-space. In that time, we shall have regained our self-respect. We shall have found a fitting title for our chief, a rational name for his kingdom.'[17]

Representing the views of the immigrant community, the Association for Furthering Traditional Judaism in Great Britain told the selection committee that there was 'no room for a Chief Rabbi who could be the ecclesiastical chief of all the other rabbis in the kingdom. Their experience of other countries showed that where a Chief Rabbi existed, Orthodox Judaism completely disappeared. They were entirely opposed to the appointment of a Chief Rabbi, but would withhold their objections for the sake of peace.'[18]

No such inhibitions were displayed, however, by the turncoat Joseph Hochman who, while still ministering at the time to the New West End Synagogue, 'constantly and consistently pleaded for a postponement of the appointment of a Chief Rabbi, pending the consideration of the communal organisation of Anglo-Jewry:

> No Rabbi of commanding importance has been presented to the community, and nowhere is there a Rabbi who exercises the authority which Anglo-Jewry would entrust to its Chief Rabbi. The prestige of the community has not suffered through the absence of a Chief Rabbi. The vigour of the community has benefited by the increased sense of responsibility which the absence has fostered, and before the appointment of a Chief Rabbi we should secure such rearrangement of communal organisation and congregational responsibility as will enable us to maintain this vigour, and teach us to look to ourselves for our security. It were better to change the Act of Parliament than to shelter behind it against the demands of changing circumstance.[19]

Most forthright among the critics were Harry Sacher and Leon Simon, joint editors of The Zionist, a Manchester-based journal which, throughout the campaign, railed against 'the dangers of Chief Rabbinism,' expressing the hope that 'out of the dissatisfaction created by the Chief Rabbi on the one hand, and the "foreign Rabbis" on the other, there will grow a movement towards a real orthodoxy – an orthodoxy thoroughly true to Jewish tradition, and especially to the tradition of Jewish learning, but free from the excrescences of traditionalism.'[20]

As the intra-Orthodox wrangling intensified, so, too, did calls for the abolition of the Chief Rabbinate. 'It is common ground,' *The Zionist* declared, 'that the late Dr Adler made the Chief Rabbinate the present thing which nobody ventures to approve. The plain truth of the matter is that the Chief Rabbinate in England is so utterly unjustifiable that it would collapse if exposed to the fresh air of scientific curiosity.'[21] The leader-writers added in a subsequent issue:

> Since the Jews of the British Empire are to be given the sort of 'Chief' Rabbi that Lord Rothschild likes, it is necessary to see what Lord Rothschild's taste is. The aim of the Jewish community, he told the Conference, is to anglicise the foreign Jewish immigrants, and the function of the 'Chief' Rabbi is to assist and direct the process of anglicisation.
>
> That is the naked truth, and it explains why a great many Jews in this country have no excessive respect for the Anglo-Jewish community and would like to see the 'Chief' Rabbinate abolished. They believe that the business of a healthy Jewish community and of a Jewish Rabbi ought to be not to anglicise but to judaise, and to judaise not only immigrants from abroad but also the native born ...
>
> It is pleasant to be a Pope-maker, and a tame Pope may be so useful. But Lord Rothschild, Mr Jessel and Mr Felix Davis[22] may give; it rests with ourselves to decide whether we shall take. Whichever be the obscure person 'trained in an English University' who is made 'Chief' Rabbi, it may be safely said that the fiction of his ecclesiastical sovereignty over the British Empire will be blown to pieces pretty quickly.
>
> A Pope has as much place in Judaism as has the Trinity, and the Jews of England will not suffer its perpetuation. Those Jews who are determined to have no part or lot in the Jewish Papacy must take steps to make their repudiation of it too emphatic and too concrete to be misunderstood or ignored.[23]

With the election on 16 February, 1913, of Joseph Herman Hertz, who trounced Moses Hyamson by 298 votes to 39, *The Zionist* – speaking, arguably, for the silent majority of Anglo-Jewry – delivered its final verdict on the 'Jewish Papacy':

> It is obvious that the new 'Chief' Rabbi cannot be accepted by a very considerable section of the community. But the dissentient element will not be able simply to disregard him and go their own way. Invested as he is with an authority based on Act of Parliament, and backed by the financial power of the house of Rothschild, he will be bound, even in spite of himself, to run counter in many ways to those who feel themselves

compelled to deny his right to pose as the spiritual leader of the Jews of the British Empire.

Thus it is inevitable that for some time to come much effort must be wasted in internecine strife which might have gone into the channel of constructive work. In saying this, we are casting no reflection on the particular Rabbi who has been chosen. There is no occasion here for personal criticism. We object not to this or that 'Chief' Rabbi, but to the 'Chief' Rabbinate itself … As things are at present, the 'Chief Rabbinate of the United Hebrew Congregations of the British Empire' is just a sham, and not even an angel from heaven could occupy the position without retarding Jewish progress.[24]

* * *   * * *   * * *

No 'angel from heaven' himself, Hertz was nevertheless well equipped to straddle the worlds of 'East' and 'West' that his predecessor had addressed in his parting message. 'Forget not moderation,' the incoming Chief Rabbi urged the fractious elements of his adopted community. 'We simply cannot succeed without sympathetic understanding and co-operation. Tower-builders, even when such are labouring for the greater glory of God, must understand one another. Confusion of tongues can wreck any scheme.'[25]

Weeks before these words were uttered, on the eve of the electoral college's vote, Hertz had received a glowing endorsement from Solomon Schechter,[26] writing from New York as head of the Jewish Theological Seminary – though another, less than flattering, encomium was allowed to gather dust.[27] The 'best school' to nurture Hertz's qualities of mind and leadership, Schechter had asserted, was

the London Chief Rabbinate, with its wide possibilities and manifold problems and variety of opinions, in which he would be compelled to bring some harmony and unity … [U]nless you have a man of his oratory, able to present the ideas and ideals of ancient Judaism in an intelligent and lucid manner, and even to enlist modernity itself in the defence of Conservatism, Traditional Judaism will soon be a matter of the past.

It is not a question of denouncing Radicalism, which is out of date, but of giving Conservative Judaism a fair chance by explaining and interpreting it in such a manner as to awaken the sympathies and arouse the loyalty and devotion of the congregation to our great heritage. And I thoroughly believe that Dr Hertz is the man able to accomplish this great task.[28]

By the time Schechter wrote this, the Conservative Judaism espoused by his Seminary had veered several degrees to the left of that which, two decades earlier, Hertz had imbibed at the feet of its founders, and yet several degrees further from that of the 'progressive conservatism' upon which his legacy came to rest. Indeed, it was the differing interpretations of 'Conservative' and 'Traditional' that were to fuel many of the controversies of his Chief Rabbinate, and of those that followed over the succeeding century.

Significantly, however – for the first and last time during the 'internecine strife' foreshadowed by *The Zionist* – Hertz reserved his fiercest armoury for his battle with the Liberals, maintaining a degree of 'clerical unity'[29] with the West Londoners, and even speaking on their premises, until Abramsky's arrival ended the fraternisation.

In relation to this dual approach, the ritual and theological differences between the Progressive movements – highlighted by Claude Montefiore in his strictures against Reform – became increasingly evident, and the Chief Rabbi's responses markedly selective. In denouncing Upper Berkeley Street for opening its pulpit to the Liberals' Israel Mattuck, the *Jewish Chronicle* gave voice to the thinking behind Hertz's stand:

> It is surely a glaring inconsistency for the synagogue to invite a minister of the 'Liberal' Synagogue to teach Judaism according to the lights of the congregation of which he is the spiritual head, and which he himself has shown to be so palpably opposed to the faith for which Berkeley Street stands ...
>
> To the plain man, the invitation to Rabbi Mattuck reads, and can only read, like an intimation that notwithstanding all that has been proclaimed as the attitude of 'Liberal' Judaism, no 'fundamental' differences subsist between the real opinions of Berkeley Street and the teachings of the 'Liberal' congregation. Since the very gravest differences do in fact exist, nobody who cares an iota for the sheer decencies, not to say the mere honesty, of religious belief can regard that as other than a serious matter.
>
> There is no question here of broadmindedness or toleration; it is a matter of clear understanding and of knowing just where we stand in these vital matters. If there are 'fundamental differences' between the 'Liberal' congregation and the remainder of the community, then it is useless, and worse, to pretend that they are not fundamental, and represent merely shades of the same religious colour ...
>
> Much of the weakness of our community in the past has been the habit of make-believe and of self-confusion on religious matters, which has tended to tarnish the clarity of its outlook in regard to so much with which it is concerned.[30]

Hertz acknowledged as much when, justifying his presence in 1934 at the opening of the West London Synagogue extension, he declared that he was 'the last person in the world to minimise the significance of religious difference in Jewry.' But, he told the gathering,

> far more calamitous than religious difference in Jewry is religious indifference. The erection and dedication of a building such as this, intended primarily for school purposes, means a determination on the part of the West London Synagogue of British Jews to provide the only adequate safeguard against religious indifference – a more intensive and extensive system of Jewish religious education that will bring all the children and adolescents within the sphere of your influence to the living fountains of Jewish inspiration and faith.[31]

This was, however, the last such declaration of Chief Rabbinical support. Hertz's subsequent brush with the Liberals over the appointment of a marriage secretary, and his humiliating capitulation to Robert Waley Cohen, marked the end of his flirtation with Reform and the onset of a war against the wider non-Orthodox movement that has continued unabated to the present day. The hostilities were intensified after calls for closer ties between the Liberals and Reformers led, for brief periods at least (1936–37 and 1981–87), to mutual proposals for a full-scale merger.[32]

* * *   * * *   * * *

Events led, too, to further question-marks over the authority and viability of the Chief Rabbinate. With the halachic validity of Liberal marriages challenged again, during the interregnum following Hertz's death,[33] 'the traditional structure of Anglo-Jewry behind its impressive façade,' wrote Cecil Roth, 'has suddenly shown such fissures and weaknesses that a catastrophic collapse, within a very short period, seems likely. That the two characteristic historical institutions of the community [the Board of Deputies and the Chief Rabbinate] should be menaced at the same time is perhaps more significant than purely coincidental.'

Referring, tangentially, to the Federation of Synagogue's earlier detachment from the Chief Rabbinical election process, Roth predicted, with uncanny accuracy:

> If no satisfactory arrangement can be reached between the United Synagogue and the Federation – and I am afraid that there can be no satisfactory compromise short of capitulation on the part of the former

body – there can be little doubt that the latter will refuse to recognise the authority of the new Chief Rabbi when he is appointed, and will elevate their own Principal Rabbi into an anti-Pope.

If there are two Chief Rabbis, there can be no logical reason why there should not be three, or four: and I foresee the emergence of Chief Rabbis in the major provincial centres, as well as, of course, a Chief Rabbi of the Union of Orthodox Hebrew Congregations, which has already declared its neutrality (or, as it is better to term it, non-belligerency) in a conflict the outcome of which it will not recognise.

As for the Liberals, whose number and organisation have very much increased in the last generation, they were willing to acquiesce, however reluctantly, in the institution of the Chief Rabbinate as formally representing the community, so long as a certain degree of tolerance was maintained. But it is too much to expect them to maintain this attitude now that they have been declared by the Chief Rabbinate, *sede vacante*, to be entirely outside the bounds of Judaism.

Thus extremes are meeting; and it may be questioned whether a Chief Rabbinate so diminished, and so rivalled, will be a Chief Rabbinate at all. It will add to the variety and interest of Anglo-Jewish life, of course, and, after all, people may be right when they say that the entire conception of a Chief Rabbi is somewhat new and alien to Judaism.[34]

By the time of Israel Brodie's departure from the post, some twenty years later, Roth's forecast had been all but realised. The two decades had seen, in the words of another observer,[35] 'a new realignment: a coalition between the supporters of the Chief Rabbinate and the ultra-Orthodox who suddenly sprang to the defence of an office the jurisdiction of which they themselves never recognised.'[36]

The Federation's 'anti-Pope,' Eliezer Kirzner, was appointed, with the title of Rav Rashi, and an 'understanding' reached – though speedily unhinged – with the incoming Chief Rabbi, Jakobovits, 'to ensure the closest and most effective co-operation between us,' to 'give full and unqualified recognition to each other's rabbinic rulings,' and 'to restore the solidarity of Orthodox Judaism as a constructive force to inspire and uplift the Anglo-Jewish community.'[37]

Commenting on reports to this effect – that Britain's 'Jews may get two Chief Rabbis' – the Liberals' Sidney Brichto riposted:

There are very substantial sections of Anglo-Jewry which, on principle, won't have one Chief Rabbi, still less two. Liberal Synagogues, as only one example, do not believe in a religious hierarchy by appointment. All matters of religious policy are decided by a conference of rabbis in which the knowledge and vision of the individual rabbi, and not his office, determine the respect and authority he will win for himself. It is our firm conviction that the non-acceptance of any rabbi as 'Chief' is in keeping with the religiously democratic spirit of the Jewish religion.[38]

Earlier, Brichto had commented: 'For our purpose, personalities are of no concern. It would make no difference to us if the title of Chief Rabbi were held by the most brilliant, excellent, saintly, kindly, competent Jew in the world ...

'We do not accept a form of Judaism in which there is an inseparable gulf between the religious and lay leaders in belief and practice. Anglo-Jewry must hear that we believe in a form of Judaism in which all may participate with full honesty. We believe in the equality of all rabbis and we reject the idea of a Chief Rabbinate as the sole source of religious authority.'[39]

For the Reform movement, one of its senior ministers, Ignaz Maybaum, wrote of the Chief Rabbinate:

[T]his office is not based on a true conception of Judaism, but is in fact a product of assimilation to the Christian concept of hierarchical organisation ... The rabbis of Anglo-Jewry who are under the jurisdiction and supervision of a Chief Rabbi are no longer free.

Why should young men choose the rabbinical profession under such undignified conditions? These conditions make a rabbi a minor official, a *mesharet* of a *mesharet* – and *mesharet* means servant in the most derogatory sense ...

The jurisdiction of the Chief Rabbi is also responsible for the present sterility of Anglo-Jewish public life. The best brains and the finest characters turn with disgust from Anglo-Jewish public life. The office of the Chief Rabbi must disappear from the scene or be changed into an honorary position, with a new occupant, say, every third year.[40]

Rejecting an approach by the newly elected Jakobovits to bring the New London Synagogue under the jurisdiction of the Chief Rabbinate, Louis Jacobs declared:

I was brought up, by pious rabbis of the old school, to believe that the Chief Rabbinate, of very recent origin, is an example of *chukkat hagoy* [Gentile practice], and further experience and study have convinced me that in this they were right. It is not only that the idea of a superior rabbi is unknown in Judaism and involves the abdication by the subordinate rabbi of the responsibilities conferred on him by his *semichah*.

The office of chief rabbi in Anglo-Jewry is modelled on that of bishop and archbishop in the Christian Church, which, in turn, is based on belief in the apostolic succession. Thus, unlike the wearing of the clerical collar and canonicals, the institution has strong doctrinal overtones. It is not for us to cast stones at those who see fit to recognise the office, but for ourselves we prefer to abide by Jewish tradition.[41]

When pondering whether to accept the position, Jakobovits himself appears to have had doubts over its status in Judaism. 'At my yeshivah,' he wrote, 'the whole concept of the Chief Rabbinate had run counter to all my teachers' principles. For them, the leading rabbi of an area had to be the one whose rabbinic skills were the most prodigious. The idea that a lay-appointed rabbi could be empowered to lay down the law to dayanim and every type of rabbi and minister under his jurisdiction had no traditional basis in halachah ...

'In the end, the decisive judgment came from my father-in-law, Rabbi Elie Munk, in Paris. He asserted – perhaps ruled is the better word – that morally I was duty-bound to accept the challenge and had no right to refuse it, lest the office fall into the wrong hands.'[42]

Jakobovits' Chief Rabbinate, punctuated by fiery – and self-admittedly futile – attempts to reconcile the opposing factions, ultimately led to the spurning of the 'hand in friendship'[43] he had once extended. 'The obsession with communal unity,' he declared on his retirement, 'is a peculiarly Anglo-Jewish trait. It does not feature in such a form among American or European Jews – and certainly not in Israel.

'It is time we shifted our concern from form to substance: how to live as fuller and better Jews, rather than how to gloss over differences and proclaim a unity which turns out to be a mirage.'[44]

13

The Pull of Pluralism

'What, then, should we hope to achieve? An Anglo-Jewry in which we reach out in love and with respect to every Jew.' [1]

At the heart of a lengthy and acrimonious dispute in the early 1970s over the religious status of the Progressives at the Board of Deputies[2] lay the role within the Board of the Chief Rabbi of the United Hebrew Congregations, and the Haham of the Spanish and Portuguese Jews' Congregation.

Clause 43 of the Deputies' constitution – stating that the Board 'shall be guided on religious matters' by these two ecclesiastical heads – was a source of long-standing concern to the Reform and Liberal movements, which had sought a similar role for their own religious leaders, and which had threatened on several occasions to leave the Board if this was not effected. The dispute was settled at a meeting of deputies on 24 October, 1971, when – by 228 votes to seven – they voted to amend the clause, requiring the Board henceforth 'to consult with those designated by such groups and congregations as their respective religious leaders on religious matters in any matter whatsoever concerning them.'[3]

In protest, the Union of Orthodox Hebrew Congregations left the Board, never to return, and the Federation of Synagogues absented itself for two years. However, under pressure from a growing number of right-wingers within the United Synagogue, a campaign in 1984 succeeded in introducing a 'code of practice' into the renumbered Clause 74, making it mandatory for the Board 'to follow the guidance of its ecclesiastical authorities, and to support such guidance in all ways possible and with all due speed.'

The code allowed for groups and organisations not under the jurisdiction of the ecclesiastical authorities 'to be notified in writing of any action the Board intends to take in accordance with the guidance of those authorities.' But the Progressives failed in committee to add a stipulation that, 'in the absence of a consensus, the Board must inform those seeking its advice or opinion that a minority view is held by some sections of the community.' The Reformers were nonplussed. 'What is the use of consultations,' they asked of their own position, 'if the guidance of the ecclesiastical authorities is mandatory?'[4]

That very point was taken up by Jack Wolkind, former chairman of a Board of Deputies working party which, a decade earlier, had recommended fundamental changes in its structure and administration. Delivering a public lecture in London,[5] he commented on the Clause 74 ambiguities:

> The clause stipulates that, in religious matters, the Board shall be guided by the ecclesiastical authorities, who, for this purpose, are the Chief Rabbi and the religious head of the Sephardi community. I have some doubt as to whether the words 'shall be guided by' can be read as a mandatory duty to act in accordance with the advice of the ecclesiastical authorities.
>
> Nor do I understand what seems to me to have been a contradictory line taken in past years, as illustrated by this extract from a letter written by the Board's then president in 1971: 'We have always assumed that the words "the Board shall be guided on religious matters... by the ecclesiastical authorities" are mandatory and mean, *inter alia*, that the Board cannot act contrarily to the guidance it receives from the ecclesiastical authorities.' However, the letter goes on: 'The Board must always reserve the right to decide for itself what course it should take in the light of that guidance.'
>
> I find it difficult to read those two extracts without coming upon an apparent contradiction. If the Board regards the acceptance of what is described as 'guidance' as being mandatory, how can it at the same time reserve the right to decide what course to take in the light of that guidance?
>
> Moreover, if, as claimed by the Orthodox representatives, the acceptance of the guidance of the ecclesiastical authorities is mandatory on the Board of Deputies, what meaning is to be given to the requirement, in the same clause of the Board's constitution, to consult those designated by the Progressive movement? What is the worth and significance of any such consultation?
>
> And why was it necessary to raise the issue in this manner, when it must have been known that to do so was to run the risk of causing a major rift in the Board and, thereby, in the Jewish community? That such a rift was averted should make us all the more vigilant to ensure that the risk is not taken again.
>
> We can do without these potentially explosive issues: the community faces enough problems without striving to manufacture new ones. I see no reason why the Progressives should not have been allowed the opportunity of expressing what, inevitably at present, would be – and

would be seen to be – a minority opinion, and clearly stated as such.

I know this solution was rejected by some of my good friends in the Orthodox community. In the first issue of the United Synagogue's new magazine, The Path, Sidney Frosh, a respected honorary officer, wrote: 'Can one imagine the credence that would be given to representations by the Board which were accompanied by comments that there are those who disagree with the views being proposed? It is our view that, under such circumstances, the representations would have very little credibility.'[6]

I regret I cannot accept that view. The expression of a minority view does not weaken or denigrate a majority view. A decision of, say, the Court of Appeal is no less binding because one of the justices expresses a minority view; nor does a minority dissenting view among, say, members of a Royal Commission downgrade the authority of the majority view. What these expressions of minority opinion do, however, is to make clear that there is another opinion.

The view was expressed in some quarters during the Clause 74 incident that it might be better if the Board were relieved of its duty of having to consider matters of a religious nature. This, I believe, merits further consideration. One might ask, perhaps, whether there is a case for disestablishment.

In a civilised society, it ought to be possible to differ without either party abusively questioning the sincerity of the other. Whenever this happens, it is not only painful, but it does considerable harm to the Jewish community. Of course there are fundamental differences between the Orthodox and Progressives, but do they have to be accompanied by sour, bitter and abusive comments?

Some suggest that, in matters of principle, there is no room for compromise, though I have doubts about this. We are not being asked to accept views and practices that are contrary to our strongly held principles; but we should, and must, be asked to respect the sincerity of those who hold those views and who follow those practices – and, moreover, to work for the good of the community with all others, whatever their religious convictions.

* * *   * * *   * * *

At the outset of Nathan Adler's Chief Rabbinate, in 1845, the climate allowed for an overarching religious leader of Anglo-Jewry. The community's response to the problem of religious authority in a secular society, writes Stephen Sharot, 'was to substitute the authority of a religious office – the Chief Rabbinate – for the authority of the Shulchan Aruch,' then reigning supreme over the Jewries of Eastern Europe. 'The traditional rabbi's authority rested on the recognition of his superior knowledge of the religious law. The English Chief Rabbi's authority depended on his occupying that office.'[7] As the *Jewish Chronicle* put it:

> It matters little whether the [ritual] alterations introduced by the Chief Rabbi are an improvement (as we think they are) or not; it is enough for us that *he* has authorised them, and our duty is to obey. The most Rev the Chief Rabbi should be invested with the authority due to his high office, with all the confidence due to his commanding position … By this means [the paper added a fortnight later] we shall secure all the great and noble advantages to be obtained by numbers having a unity of purpose; and the strength which is too often wasted in petty rivalries … will be increased tenfold by such co-operation. [8]

In England, Sharot maintains, 'the leaders of the community had no legal authority to enforce sanctions, and a primary concern was the maintenance of some sort of coherent group life. The emergence of a Chief Rabbinate was, in part, a response to this situation, since it served as a centripetal institution for a community whose association-based organisation was potentially liable to schism … [The] upper-class acculturated lay leaders mixed socially with Anglicans, and they were concerned that Anglo-Jewry should have a religious head who would occupy a position of authority somewhat parallel to that of the Archbishop of Canterbury in the Anglican Chuch.'[9]

The hitherto decentralised character of Anglo-Jewish life, asserts Endelman, proved an obstacle to the solution of such communal problems as the relief of poverty, the removal of civil disabilities, and the provision of religious facilities. To meet these needs, London's Jewish elite – the two hundred or so banking and mercantile families who dominated the organisational life of Anglo-Jewry as a whole – created a number of institutions to provide the community with some centralised direction, the most influential being the Chief Rabbinate.

'Despite the absence of doctrinal or ritual rigour in the Judaism of the London notables, they did not as a group show any enthusiasm for a liberal form of worship and belief. Most of them were members of Orthodox congregations, whose services, while doctrinally unreformed, were nevertheless decorous and dignified. Many served as officers of the United Synagogue; few were attracted to Reform Judaism.'[10]

The then editor of the *Jewish Chronicle*, Michael Henry, summarised Anglo-Jewry in similar terms:

The Judaism of England is at one and the same time conservative (we mean in a religious, not a political, sense) and enlightened. The Judaism of England is an intelligent Orthodoxy. Our doctrines and practices do not partake of the latitudinarianism, the indifference, the bigotry, the fanaticism, the atheistical philosophy, the sensational rush after the *chukkat hagoyim* which characterise – we had almost said stigmatise – the Judaism of certain countries other than our own … In England, Jews may be relied on for the championship of the true principles of their faith against radical innovation and neo-philosophy, on the one hand, and against the apprehension of ignorant fanaticism, on the other hand.[11]

Discussing Adler's influence on this 'conservative and enlightened' community, Norman Cohen – a close associate of later Chief Rabbis – argues that 'it may seem paradoxical, but it is not improbable, that his high rabbinic standing owed something to the fact that the Chief Rabbi exercised only limited functions – the exercise of judicial powers in purely religious matters, where there was no clash of jurisdiction with the secular courts … The popular acceptance of the Chief Rabbi as a sort of Jewish Archbishop of Canterbury is not, therefore, without good historical grounds. It undoubtedly fostered the conception that the Chief Rabbinate was an ecclesiastical rather than a halachic eminence.

The Chief Rabbinate, as an institution, gained prestige from this development, although its effect on the internal development of traditional Judaism in Great Britain is more doubtful … The [Chief] Rabbi was easily able to keep all the reins of halachic control firmly in his own hands. The reins, after all, were few, and the steeds far from frisky.

Thus was born the Anglo-Jewish minister of the old school, never more than a satellite of the Chief Rabbi. It was a development which suited its contemporaries very well, but they regarded as Orthodoxy what was, in truth, only an Anglo-Jewish mutation, and this was to create many problems when its unreality was unsympathetically exposed by more lettered immigrants.

To the layman with a sound Jewish knowledge, a rabbi is an authority to whom he appeals on doubtful points; but to the ordinary Anglo-Jewish layman, the Chief Rabbi became not so much a decisor in matters of halachah as the virtual embodiment of the halachah … The complete ascendancy of the Chief Rabbi within the Jewish community further strengthened his standing in the non-Jewish world. He was without a rival as the representative of the Jewish faith.

But, adds Cohen, 'nobody could possibly have envisaged the fantastic growth in the size of Anglo-Jewry, and the consequent responsibilities of the Chief Rabbi ...'[12]

* * *   * * *   * * *

That the steeds were 'far from frisky' is amply illustrated in an appeal to the United Synagogue – and through it, implicitly, to the Chief Rabbinate – published as the Progressives advanced rapidly at the turn of the century. Jews' College, not for the first or last time in its precarious history, was in dire financial straits, the ministry was understaffed and overstretched, and, in the words of 'Historicus' (a distraught pamphleteer within the London community), 'it cannot be maintained that its success leaves nothing to be desired.'[13]

If Judaism was to thrive in the future, he wrote, 'if we are to do our duty to the coming generation, it is our most essential obligation to provide, as generously and as thoroughly as our means will permit, for the training and equipment of those who are to preach the tenets of our faith hereafter. Nothing should be allowed to stand in the way of that duty.

> At the present moment, English Judaism lies in the melting-pot. Many dissolvent forces are at work, and for years to come there is likely to be a determined struggle between those who would preserve the material in its ancient form (though, maybe, burnished and tempered by the fire through which it has passed) and those who would transform it into quite another shape. What will be the result? That depends upon ourselves – upon the efforts we make to produce men of the highest calibre as champions of our side.
>
> Our present ministers are a capable body of men, imbued with a high sense of their obligations towards the community; but they were trained to cope with far less rigorous conditions than those which now prevail. It is only within the last two or three years that Reform has made any real progress in this country, but it is now making up for lost time. Unless some extraordinary counter-effort is made, its inroads upon Orthodoxy will become more and more effective every year, and none the less effective because indirect.
>
> Well, we of the present generation must do the best we can, fortified by whatever spiritual armour we can command, to resist at once the attack and the invitation. But what of the next generation? It is they who will have to determine the crisis one way or the other. How are we helping them to arrive at a decision?

> We shall be playing into the hands of the Radical Reform if we ensure
> that our future religious leaders shall be provided with a minimum of
> equipment, and if we continue in our refusal to hold out any inducements
> by which the best intellects in the community might be moved to enter
> the ministry.[14]

The appeal fell, however, upon an uncompromising leadership. At the
ministers' conference in 1911 – feisty if not frisky – the Rev Joseph F.
Stern, describing the Chief Rabbinate as 'an autocracy,' suggested replacing
it by an ecclesiastical board, and was duly ignored by the lay hierarchy.

A year on, the United Synagogue honorary officers rejected a proposal
from their clergy, led by the New West End's Joseph Hochman, to form a
central consistory of some twenty ministers and preachers to assist the new
Chief Rabbi in settling questions 'heretofore decided by the Chief Rabbi on
his own authority.' And in the immediate run-up to the Chief Rabbinical
election, in January 1913, the standing committee of the Conference of
Anglo-Jewish Ministers unsuccessfully sought a postponement of the
poll so that a deputation might convey its views to the Chief Rabbinate
Conference on the candidature of Hertz.

When this was refused, the ministers fired a protest to the Jewish
press, with a copy to the Chief Rabbinate Conference, expressing 'our
strong feeling that in no other religious denomination would there have
been possible the contemplation of an appointment of this character
without regard to the opinions and the special knowledge of those most
immediately concerned ...

'Our contention is that the recommendation of the election of the
Rev Dr Hertz as the final conclusion of the Selection Committee is one
that, to our great regret, we cannot bring ourselves to regard as a suitable
solution. It is our opinion it should be a sine qua non that the Chief
Rabbi should possess qualifications of outstanding eminence, and we
cannot persuade ourselves that these are possessed by the recommended
candidate.'[15]

Decades later, soon after his installation, Jakobovits felt compelled to
acknowledge: 'I believe that the Chief Rabbinate, for good reasons that
applied 150 years ago but that no longer apply in our society, inevitably
helped to stunt the growth of a dynamic and enterprising ministry that
could assume real leadership of the communities in their charge.

'If a man is told that he can never make any religious decisions; that
he cannot participate in formulating religious policies; that he must refer
every major problem he faces to some office in Adler House [the home of
the Chief Rabbinate], you cannot expect him to develop initiative, to have

a broad vision, to arise and assume the responsibilities of leadership.'[16]

Despite the relentless battle fought against the Liberals by the incoming Hertz, the inter-war years – contends sociologist Barry Kosmin – provided 'the golden age of homogeneity, unity and communal bliss' in Anglo-Jewry.[17] These years, he suggests, 'saw a favourable scenario from the viewpoint of community unifiers or homogenisers.

'The integration of the children of the immigrants into the "native Orthodoxy" of the United Synagogue was made possible by that body's financial and administrative resources, combined with the still-dominant social prestige of those who led it. The process of anglicisation and homogenisation was evident in the doubling of the size of the US to fifty synagogues by 1939.'

In 1943, commenting on this support for the United Synagogue, the religiously right-wing Solomon Schonfeld, head of the Union of Orthodox Hebrew Congregations and Hertz's son-in-law, noted that the 'vast majority of Jews in Britain and the British Dominions subscribe to Traditional Judaism, if only with lukewarm interest. They pay allegiance to one central Chief Rabbinate and to the general principles of Orthodox Judaism.'[18]

By the end of the Second World War, however, that scenario had changed, with Jakobovits ascribing the altered atmosphere and direction largely to wartime conditions. Addressing a conference on 'Jewish Life in Britain,' in 1977, he declared: 'The fairly homogeneous, almost monolithic, character of Anglo-Jewry was long ago transferred into a pluralistic society, especially with the heavy refugee influx before, during and after the war.

'The cohesion of "mainstream Judaism" as the broad heartland encompassing the vast majority of "average" Anglo-Jews has been preserved until more recent times. But, during the past fifteen years, this pattern has changed quite radically, and with increasing speed, as the centrifugal forces have gained momentum.'[19]

Explaining the pull of pluralism, Kosmin writes: 'Such a process is inevitable among free citizens in an open society. Jewish homogeneity was an artificial device and a reflection of Jewish subordination in society. Since British Jewry is not a closed society – a classical ghetto – and not separated from the outside world by ritual rules, and since there is neither compulsory segregation, nor social control even along the lines of the Sephardi *mahamad* of the seventeenth century, fissiparous tendencies are to be expected.'[20]

It became clear over time that the Chief Rabbinate's influence was diminishing – and its approach counter-productive – as its constituency waned, and as those of the opposition (to both the left and the right) rapidly grew. With each new movement came the need for a redistribution of authority, and for a broader recognition of the nature of pluralism. In the course of the nineteenth century, noted Alderman during the Masorti controversy of 1995,

> a group of synagogues in Britain decided to elect for themselves a 'Chief Rabbi.' This they were perfectly entitled to do. What they were not entitled to do – and what Mr Gladstone's government, in 1870, prevented them from doing – was to have this person designated, by statute, as 'the Chief Rabbi.' Nonetheless, they and their heirs have done their utmost to hoodwink both Anglo-Jewry and the non-Jewish world into believing that the Jews of Britain have one, supreme ecclesiastical head.
>
> There is not, and never has been, any such office. The authority of the Chief Rabbinate of the United Hebrew Congregations is not recognised by the Spanish and Portuguese Congregation, nor by the Federation of Synagogues, the Union of Orthodox Hebrew Congregations, the Reform Synagogues of Great Britain, the Union of Liberal and Progressive Synagogues, or the Association of Masorti Synagogues, all of which possess their own ecclesiastical authorities.
>
> There are Anglo-Jewish views, but there is no Anglo-Jewish view. This plurality is well recognised by Her Majesty's government, and official consultations with 'Anglo-Jewry' typically involve, on the Anglo-Jewish side, a variety of individual organisations.'[21]

Earlier, Alderman had written: 'The notion that the Chief Rabbi of the United Synagogue – who is, additionally, the Chief Rabbi of the United Hebrew Congregations of the Commonwealth – is also, somehow, the Chief Rabbi of all the Jewish communities of the United Kingdom, is now no longer tenable. The process by which this state of affairs has come to pass encompasses much of the communal history of the Jewish communities of Great Britain over the past fifty or so years.

> British Jewry has always been obsessed by the contemplation of its public image. It has liked to appear united (more especially when it has been very disunited), and it has an aversion to washing its dirty linen in public, preferring sometimes not to wash the linen at all. The existence of a 'Chief Rabbi' has served a most useful purpose in convincing the outside world that British Jewry is a happy monolith, and that diversity exists only within an overarching identity of interests ...
>
> It is, in fact, a waste of communal energies to try and force the religious pluralism which the Jewish communities of Britain now exhibit into a mould fashioned with reference to the concept of a Chief Rabbinate. To

make such an attempt is not merely wasteful, but counter-productive into the bargain.

To insist, through sustaining the notion of a Chief Rabbinate, that unity – and, more particularly, religious unity – is alive and well is perfectly in order only so long as that unity is a tangible reality. When it is not, those who sustain such a notion are defending an empty folly. What is more, they are bound to be found out.[22]

Even the notion of the Chief Rabbi's sovereignty hovering over 'the United Hebrew Congregations of the Commonwealth' was hotly disputed. Former Bayswater and Hampstead minister Raymond Apple – writing as senior rabbi of the Great Synagogue, Sydney – declared in the aftermath of the Masorti dispute: 'There is not one congregation anywhere in Australia which owes any constitutional allegiance to the Chief Rabbi's office.

'Yes, there was a time when the emergent congregations in this continent automatically deferred to the diktat of London. But Australian Jewry has now outgrown its colonial cringe and is not beholden to anyone. We greatly respect Dr Sacks, as we did his predecessor, Lord Jakobovits. But we control our own destiny and are not under the Chief Rabbi's aegis – or jurisdiction, or authority, whatever word you choose.'[23]

Within Chief Rabbinical jurisdiction, 'the diktat of London' received a further rebuff from former US honorary officer Raymond Cannon. Addressing 'some of the serious issues raised by the Chief Rabbi's intemperate attack on the Masorti movement,' he wrote:

> The manifestly inept advice Rabbi Sacks must have received inevitably casts doubt on the judgment of the coterie to whom he presumably defers. Another consequence of his diatribe, which identifies him with a particular brand of Judaism, means that he can no longer claim to represent, or speak authoritatively on behalf of, the Anglo-Jewish community.
>
> There is here an abdication of leadership, compounded by a disinclination – itself a glaring form of weakness – not only to share a platform with Masorti, but to engage in serious public debate with any group of Jews deemed untouchable. Sadly, the Chief Rabbi has alienated many of those who originally supported his appointment, and we are left to speculate whether he has been unduly influenced by, or even become a prisoner of, creeping religious fundamentalism which regards inclusivism as an anathema.[24]

Richard Loftus, another influential figure in the Orthodox community, elected to differ. 'We have been blessed,' he asserted, 'with a Chief Rabbi of great intellect, energy and vision, who has the courage to address the issues of the day. His leadership alone gives us the opportunity to reverse the decline of the past forty years and to breathe new life into the young and those who have lost touch with Jewish traditions and spiritual values.

'Doing nothing and saying nothing is the easy way to be popular, but ultimately achieves nothing. Those on both the left and the right of the community who focus solely on their own narrow self-interests should realise that they are sowing the seeds of our self-destruction.'[25]

* * *   * * *   * * *

The progression of events, reactions and ramifications traced over the pages of this volume – and of its prequel – leaves little doubt that, in today's world, the Chief Rabbinate has run its course, and that an alternative form of leadership is called for which recognises both the plurality of the community and the application of inclusivism in deed as well as word. In so doing, Anglo-Jewry's movers and shakers, to whom the 'Jewish Papacy' is largely anachronistic, might well heed the advice of a far-sighted observer commenting, a century ago, on factional strife. Writing during the Chief Rabbinical interregnum following Hermann Adler's demise,[26] he noted that,

> to all outward appearance, Anglo-Jewry has not changed an atom through the absence of this functionary ... The idea that the failure to find a Chief Rabbi will be disastrous deserves to be analysed a little more closely. Disastrous to whom? Of course to the candidates who are not successful; but then we are presumably dealing with a serious subject. Apart from these victims, it is not so easy to locate the expected calamity. Shall we say, to the community as a whole?
>
> A cry is raised in some quarters that the unity and solidarity of the community are in danger. Unity and solidarity: nice names to play with; but do they stand for anything that the community really wants, that it could not perfectly dispense with?
>
> If they stand for the state of things which prevailed under the rule of the late Chief Rabbi – well, it has already been established that the community, as such, has been at least no worse off since it has been left to its own devices; and what it could do during those twelve months it can surely go on doing for an indefinite period longer.
>
> So long as the community is free from scandals, it may be said to have as much 'unity' and 'solidarity' as it requires; and to judge from

experience, it is more likely to enjoy this freedom without a Chief
Rabbi than with one.[27]

The point is worth reinforcing. One hundred years on, despite what
Kalms calls 'the sticking-plaster that holds the community together,' Anglo-
Jewry is more fragmented and disputatious than ever. In a polarising
world, the Jews of Britain – steadily shrinking in number and affiliation –
have little to celebrate. Few see signs of unity, let alone uniformity; many
(if not most) regard the Chief Rabbinate as divisive, and would not miss
it should it cease to exist.

Nathan Adler's incumbency peaked with Orthodox rebellion, while
his son saw the 'old paths' wither away. Hertz failed to halt the Liberal
advance; Brodie the emergence of Masorti; and Jakobovits the crumbling
of his 'bridges of understanding.'[28] As we have seen, Sacks opened his Chief
Rabbinate with a clarion response to the 'challenge' posed by the Kalms
review. 'Now,' he declared, 'is a time for religious leadership if ever there
was one; and we must not be found wanting.' In recent years, however,
his 'Coalition for Peace in the Community' has largely battled itself – and
inclusivism – out of the picture.

In this context, a close (though not uncritical) supporter of Sacks –
a former top executive of the United Synagogue – contends: 'Externally,
Sacks' record as Chief Rabbi is superb, having raised the prestige of the
Chief Rabbinate, Anglo-Jewry and himself to great heights in the eyes of
the Gentile world. Within the Jewish community, however, his record is not
good, partly because he fails to understand how his statements and actions
impact on ordinary people, and partly because he lacks the courage and
drive to take a stand on anything in which he really believes. He lacks the
backbone to make a decision and stick to it, and this is glaringly obvious
behind his public presence and the glamour of his speeches.'[29]

In similar vein, *The Independent* commented in a profile marking the Chief
Rabbi's first ten years in office: 'If Dr Sacks is lauded as a thoughtful and
devoted leader by the wider community, he is a prophet with significantly
less honour among his own people. The *Jewish Chronicle* is currently running
an Internet poll on the question "Have Jonathan Sacks' first ten years as
Chief Rabbi been a success?" Voting is still going on, but at one point
yesterday a resounding 71 per cent had voted "No" …

> From the outset, the paradox was that a man trained in the philosophical
> tradition of suspecting everything had taken on the job of a spokesman
> for an institutional tradition that meant, in the discourse of his university
> peers, defending the rationally indefensible. 'From the beginning,' says

one who knows him well, 'it induced in him a kind of intellectual schizophrenia. He was the wrong man for the job' ...

In an attempt to modernise the role of women in Orthodoxy, he set up the equivalent of a Jewish royal commission. Two years later, it reported with recommendations for sweeping changes in social and religious rules, which included a Jewish singles dating agency, reform of the divorce system, and changes to prayer ceremonies and rituals to make them more relevant to the spiritual needs of women worshippers. But the main recommendations were, in the words of one critic, 'lobbed into the long grass.' Many of Dr Sacks' most ardent admirers became disillusioned ... Critics saw a terrible inevitability in it all.

'The previous Chief Rabbi had believed it all unquestioningly,' said one insider. 'But Jonathan's Western education set up a tension for him. His trouble is that he has never known quite where to position himself between the diehard traditionalists and an openness to modernity.'[30]

The Jewish Quarterly wrote at the height of the Gryn controversy: 'For a Chief Rabbi whose primary concern has been a lofty concept called Jewish Continuity (the organisational version of which was a financial disaster), Jonathan Sacks has managed to create a good deal of discord in the Anglo-Jewish community.

His tenure has been marred by acrimonious controversy and divisive politics. Yet, at the same time, he has succeeded in cultivating an image of the freethinking philosopher-rabbi, and his many books on political and social issues attest to his active interest in the world at large. Lately this image has been questioned: while an editorial in *The Times* described Sacks as being on a par with such great Jewish minds as Freud and Einstein, a *Guardian* columnist denounced him as a 'fundamentalist.'

Who is the man in the midst of all this controversy? Should he be accused of cowardice, for ingratiating himself to a religious leader more Orthodox than himself, who does not even recognise the office of the Chief Rabbi? Or should he be admired for his strength and resilience in dealing with a splintered and angry community? Is he a true leader, or does he occupy a post many believe is a superfluous relic of the past? And is there a link between Sacks the religious figure and Sacks the author of his latest book, *The Politics of Hope*?[31]

The United Hebrew Congregations, of which the Chief Rabbi is the titular head though not 'his own man,' now constitute less than one-half of the community in nominal terms, and far less in terms of Orthodox allegiance.[32] No other synagogal movement accepts his jurisdiction, and many have called for the abolition of his office. His authority is undermined by his own Beth Din, and his mistakes have been acknowledged both by himself and by his own rabbis. His 'kingmaker' and former patron twice urged him to resign, while many of his supporters – and not a few of his opponents – credit him more as a writer and orator than for his communal input. Under a new leadership structure, things can only get better.

* * *   * * *   * * *

A disestablished Rabbinate – designated as 'a,' not 'the,' by the 1870 Jewish United Synagogues Act – and a similarly constructed Board of Deputies could pave the way for the elevation of an alternative figure as the recognised leader of a pluralistic Anglo-Jewry. As has been widely acknowledged, references to an 'Anglo-Jewish community' are no longer appropriate. Scholars talk of 'a series of communities,' 'a community of communities,' and 'a loosely knit complex of separate communities,'[33] of an Anglo-Jewry steadily splintering because 'Chief Rabbis Brodie, Jakobovits and Sacks, despite professions of "inclusivism" and denunciations of fractious behaviour, attacked liberal forms of Judaism in terms that encouraged polarisation.'[34] The plural term 'communities,' observes Kosmin,

> is increasingly a much more accurate description of the sociological reality than is the singular noun … Their own nuclear family, their own particular synagogue, their own suburb or town, is the setting in which the individual Jew or Jewess defines and plays out his or her ethnic and religious role. Moreover, the organisational structure of British Jewry is essentially pluralistic, and most of the power, finance and decision-making process in communal affairs lies at the local level. As a result, national and even regional bodies are usually merely confederations with representative rather than executive functions.[35]

Norman Cohen told the first conference on 'Jewish Life in Modern Britain,' in 1962, that 'the basic fact of religious life in Anglo-Jewry is that the great bulk of the community has only the slightest concern with Judaism … There is, at first sight, an impressive façade of institutional religion. But, behind it all, the amount of apathy is not to be underestimated.'[36]

The historical record demonstrates that religious observance has become more relaxed with each passing generation and that, whether or not they belonged to a nominally Orthodox congregation, many –

perhaps most – were not Orthodox in either practice or belief. A large number who remained members of congregations acknowledging the Chief Rabbi's authority did so because 'convenience, habit, family tradition, and indifference (as well as the wish to hold on to accumulated burial rights and to be buried near family) were stronger than religious consistency.'[37]

In modern times, asserts Alderman, 'belief in God has never been an essential prerequisite of Jewishness. Synagogue membership is, and always has been, an optional extra. But the broad message of recent survey evidence is, unmistakably, that for most British Jews, ritual practice and religious observance are a means of affirming their *ethnic* identity as Jews, rather than an expression of purely religious faith. With the exception of the deeply devout, ethnic identity is much stronger within Anglo-Jewry than religious commitment, and it is the former, not the latter, which appears to motivate religious observance.'[38]

British Jewry, Alderman notes further, is both contracting and 'outgrowing the norms that it has inherited from a more elitist and centripetal age ... As it becomes more pluralistic in a religious sense, its members have become less willing to acquiesce in a situation in which the representative communal bodies fail to embody and effect this diversity to the full ...

'There are many challenges facing the Jews of Britain [and] none is more pressing than the need to construct a new institutional framework that will reflect this diversity, and allow for its expression and articulation in an atmosphere that is at once as free from internal oppression as it ought to be from external threat.'[39]

*   *   *   *   *   *   *   *   *

Underlining the ethnic component in religious observance and 'the tension between the Orthodox stance of the United Synagogue and the non-Orthodox practice of the majority of its members,' sociologist Stephen Miller told a 1992 conference on 'Jewish Identities in the New Europe': 'To some extent this inconsistency is resolving itself by a process of realignment. Younger members of the traditional (non-Orthodox) Jewish community are joining Progressive synagogues in greater numbers, while the proportion of younger United Synagogue members who are strictly Orthodox is rising.

'But there remain large numbers of traditional Jews who show no sign of shifting their affiliation and seem to be increasing their involvement in synagogue life.' For these members, the synagogue 'is becoming less of a religious institution and more of a focus for the expression of ethnic identification ... seen by some purely as an ethnic club.'[40]

Addressing the same forum, Sacks agreed that, 'in Britain, significant numbers of young Jews now see their identity in essentially ethnic terms. For them, Jewish belonging is a matter of mixing with other Jews, supporting Israel, and fighting anti-Semitism; it has no especially religious connotation.'[41] And Alderman told the conference: 'Self-styled "secular" Jews have, in effect, adopted a purely ethnic form of identity.'[42]

A 2001 survey of London and South-East Jews found that, with regard to Jewish practice, 11 per cent were 'non-practising' ('secular' or 'cultural') and 22 per cent 'just Jewish.' In religious outlook, 25 per cent regarded themselves as 'secular,' and 33 per cent as 'somewhat secular.'[43]

Writing four years earlier, communal commentator Gerald Jacobs put it this way: 'For many, Jewish identity has little or nothing to do with religious observance. The proud-of-his-roots, bagel-eating, klezmer-playing, Woody Allen-watching secular Jew is now a distinctive part of the London landscape as he (and she) has been for a long time in New York.'[44]

On the gradual change in Anglo-Jewry's self-perception, Board of Deputies demographer Marlena Schmool writes: 'British Jewry has historically seen itself as a community with a "religious" rather than "ethnic" identity ... However, within the Jewish community, attitudes are on the move.

> While the long-standing communal view of the ethnic question [in the national census] has been negative, in recent years there have been perceptible shifts in attitude. Since the 1991 census, the opposition of the Jewish establishment has been weakening, in part reflecting the changing experiences and ages of those now in opinion-forming positions ... They are also a generation that has come to maturity in a multicultural society ...
>
> The resulting awareness has, I submit, permitted an ethnic/religious/cultural freedom not allowed to earlier generations ... To set out in print the case for 'Jewish ethnicity' may be an example of either stating the obvious or taking the argument too far. Nevertheless, I have come, through my work and study as a communal researcher, to support the case strongly.[45]

Translated into practicalities, into facts, figures and characteristics relating to the United Synagogue's core constituents – those who 'paid allegiance to one central Chief Rabbinate,' as Schonfeld had called them

– Kalms' *A Time for Change* spelled out, in statistics compiled by Miller and Schmool, the results of what it termed 'the structural weakness of the United Synagogue' and 'its failure to relate to its mission.'[46]

> It had been thought [wrote Kalms] that the very strength of the United Synagogue lay in its historic lack of ideology. It was an 'umbrella' organisation. But lack of ideology is not the same as lack of mission. The traditional United Synagogue had a clear message, affectionately summed up in the phrase *minhag Anglia*,[47] a celebration of the twofold blessing of being Jewish and British.
>
> There was in *minhag Anglia* much to be admired. Tolerance and moderation – treasured values that deserve a home in contemporary society. Also integration – the challenge and the tension of living with at least one foot in the modern, secular, Western world. This was part of the social glue that bound, and still binds, most of the membership of the United Synagogue together.
>
> At the same time, *minhag Anglia* stood for ways whose time has long past, and whose continued hold on the organisation alienates thousands of bystanders – irregular members and potential members – who want something different. Many do not want the pomp and ceremony, the imitation of the Church, the habits and customs that lead to the atmosphere of the 'club.' The non-participative services, the proliferation of by-laws, the rule of dominating personalities, the cold, reserved English environment, the narrow focus on the politics of the synagogue as distinct from the development of community – these are aspects of the United Synagogue that no longer win it friends or members ...
>
> Arresting the decline in membership and reasserting the vitality of Jewish community life within the context of the United Synagogue has to be the clarion call for the organisation and its goal for the next ten years. To do it, we recommend that the United Synagogue looks to what was traditionally its greatest strength – not the negative quality of being non-ideological, but rather its positive face as an inclusivist organisation.
>
> As Chief Rabbi Dr Sacks defined it in his Jakobovits Chair lecture of 1989: 'What, then, is the task of the United Synagogue? The answer consists of two words – 'including Jews.' The task of the United Synagogue is to make as many Jews as possible feel included, not excluded, by Judaism.[48]

If the principle of including Jews within tradition were accepted as the goal of the United Synagogue, Kalms argued, 'it should apply at all levels within the organisation. This means that inclusivist attitudes should have at least a vote, if not a veto, in the development of policy, including religious policy ...

'We need to develop rabbinic leadership confident enough in its learning to find a way to help the lay leadership to include and not exclude Jews ... It should, for example, be inconceivable for an organisation such as the United Synagogue, dedicated to including Jews, to espouse positions on halachic matters which are exclusivist, if viable inclusivist halachic options are available.'[49]

Since the appearance of the Kalms report, however – despite its radical recommendations for revival and regeneration – affiliation to mainstream Orthodoxy within Anglo-Jewry continued to drop rapidly, losing 31.1 per cent of its support between 1990 and 2005–06.[50] The greatest beneficiary was Masorti, up 63.3 per cent in the same period, and 43.2 per cent in the later years. Membership of the Union of Orthodox Hebrew Congregations (UOHC) rose by 51.4 per cent, while both Reform (-3.5 per cent) and Liberals (-5.5 per cent) showed increasing losses, and the Sephardim (+3.5 per cent) a latter-day gain.

Overall, the share of mainstream Orthodoxy in synagogue membership fell during those fifteen years from 66 to 55 per cent, with increases for the UOHC (up from 6 per cent to 10.5 per cent), Reform (17 per cent to 20 per cent), Liberals (7 per cent to 8 per cent), and Masorti (1 per cent to 2.5 per cent).

In Greater London alone, mainstream Orthodoxy accounted for less than half of membership (49.5 per cent), with Reform attracting 19.9 per cent, the UOHC 12.4 per cent, Liberals 9.9 per cent, and the Sephardim and Masorti (combined because of the small number of synagogues) 8.4 per cent.[51] The continued slump in male membership of centrist Orthodox congregations,[52] as embodied in the United Synagogue, clearly questioned the efficacy of the Chief Rabbi's exhortation as expressed in his Jakobovits Chair lecture.

The statistics thrown up by Miller and Schmool in *A Time for Change*, as a result of quantitative research questionnaires, showed that the religious observance of United Synagogue members – representing 'the way you live in Jewish terms' – could be broken down as follows: non-religious ('secular Jew'), 4 per cent; 'just Jewish,' 16 per cent; Progressive Jew, 3 per cent; traditional ('not strictly Orthodox'), 67 per cent; strictly Orthodox (Sabbath observant), 10 per cent. 'Weak observers' thus accounted for 23 per cent of the total; of the 'traditional' respondents, 88 per cent admitted to travelling by car on Shabbat, and 95 per cent to switching on lights.

On religious beliefs, the survey found that around 50 per cent of the respondents appeared to have 'some degree of faith in God.' It was consistent with the findings, the report added, that 'a feeling of belonging, rather than a belief in God, is the driving force behind synagogue attendance and other forms of involvement.'

The 'strictly Orthodox' had 'consistent and high ratings on all three dimensions – belief, practice and ethnicity.' The 'traditional' group were 'very strongly identified in an ethnic sense, observe a common set of key, family-oriented practices (with little variation), but have moderate to low levels of religious beliefs.'

The 'weak observers' resembled traditional Jews 'in having relatively low levels of belief and in being strongly identified in an ethnic sense, though not quite as strongly as the traditional group. They are, however, far less observant and far more individualistic in their religious practices.' Their observance was 'more closely related to strength of identity than to belief, but that identity is less family-oriented and more global in nature.'[53]

What would happen, asked Kalms, if the United Synagogue and the Judaism it represented did not exist? 'Our research suggests that something like 10 per cent of its members – those who identify themselves as "strictly Orthodox" – would join synagogues to the right of the United Synagogue. The remaining 90 per cent, the "traditional" and "non-Orthodox," would either join the Masorti, Reform or Liberal movements or would not join a synagogue at all. Anglo-Jewry as a traditional and relatively Orthodox community would disintegrate. Many Jews would be lost to Judaism, and many more would be lost to Orthodoxy.'[54]

The 2009 women's review, *Connection, Continuity and Community*, spoke out forcefully in response to Kalms' rhetoric on the dangers facing the United Synagogue and 'the Judaism it represents.'

> There is an urgent need [the survey found] for the leadership of synagogues in particular, and of the community in general, to acknowledge and respond to the increasingly diverse needs and expectations of the Jewish population. We are likely to witness a shift away from communities based on highly structured institutions to more relaxed networks, where social exchanges rather than physical edifices become the primary route through which people connect with their Jewish heritage.
>
> This does not necessarily imply the demise of conventional synagogue-centred activity, but it does require rethinking how we facilitate the business of connection for the coming generations. Most of all, we have to recognise that the desire to connect may be motivated by ethnic rather than religious considerations.

One of the highlights of the review programme was the focus groups, which provided an opportunity for women across the communal spectrum to have a chance to talk to, and learn from, each other. These exchanges are incredibly valuable; they should be a regular feature of Jewish communal life.

There is huge scope for the community to work together, and many successful models of it are doing just that: from the Board of Deputies to women's organisations such as the League of Jewish Women, and educational initiatives like Limmud.

Intra-communal respect must be a priority. Rabbis and community leaders need to think carefully about the effects of their pronouncements both locally and nationally, and the impact these have on their own and other communities, on their ability to work together, and on their regard for each other. Hostility between different congregations is self-defeating.

Moreover, faced with falling numbers, communities must consider regrouping rather than clinging to the vestiges of the past. Where congregations work together, everyone benefits, regardless of their 'brand' of Judaism.[55]

* * *   * * *   * * *

Reflecting, and reacting to, the changing face of British Jewry – and its increasingly recognised ethnic and pluralistic complexion as 'a community of communities' – the Institute for Jewish Policy Research (JPR) in 1998 established a Commission on Representation of the Interests of the British Jewish Community.

'The pace of this change,' it noted, 'has placed considerable strain on the historic central representative structures – the Board of Deputies of British Jews and the Chief Rabbinate. Questions have been raised as to why Jewish representative institutions have been unable to defuse tensions and resolve disputes that frequently surface in the public sphere.'[56]

Representation of the community, the Commission declared after its two-year investigation, 'must be seen as multifaceted. There is no one best way, nor is one overarching organisation or leader able, to speak on behalf of the entire community.[57]

There has been a persistent and increasing grumble of complaint that the Chief Rabbinate and the Board of Deputies are unrepresentative and ineffectual. These institutions are being buffeted by the winds of pluralism.

Vocal and variegated interest groups, ranging from the strictly

Orthodox to the Progressive, claim either that the Chief Rabbinate fails to speak for them or that it fails to bridge divisions between communal factions. Many in the middle ground are exasperated that diverse religious groups within the British family refuse even to talk to each other on a public platform …

It was concerns such as these that prompted the present attempt to re-examine how the Jewish community pursues its interests in the wider world through its representational activity. However, the Commission has been mindful of the limitations on such an exercise.

In particular, it would not be appropriate for it to address, nor could it hope to resolve, the fundamental divisions between different sections of the community, to say nothing of the current lack of dialogue between them. Instead, the Commission has wrestled with the core conundrum: how can a community with so many variegated and sometimes disputatious interest groups support its representative structures?

Exploring the difficulties associated with religious representation, the report quoted the professional head of one religious institution: 'It is neither desirable nor possible to have one religious voice. There needs to be a reconstituted, non-ecclesiastical Board of Deputies which should act in a politically astute manner – even on religious issues – to support other parts of the community.'

The strictly Orthodox groups, however – which (it will be recalled) walked out of the Board of Deputies in 1971 and never returned – were satisfied with diverse representation. One associated official stated: 'We don't need the Board of Deputies to have our voice more legitimately or effectively heard. When we need to, we can have the ear of the government without any intermediary.'[58]

From a government official came the view that, on the religious front, 'we know that if you deal with the Chief Rabbi, you must consult with the Reform and Liberals as well. We are sensitive to that. We also recognise that there isn't one definitive, authoritative voice in these matters.'[59]

Many of those interviewed affirmed that Sacks had 'a high media profile' and was seen by most outsiders as 'the face of the community.' Commenting on this view, the broadcast media and religion correspondents noted: 'The Chief Rabbi is regarded as a primary news source and spokesperson on issues and affairs relating to British Jewry. He is a known entity, especially for the media, and what happens to him is of news interest.' Individual correspondents, however, generally felt that 'he represents only part of British Jewry.'[60]

This was supported by a Progressive lay leader in relation to the Chief

Rabbi's role within the Board of Deputies – despite the 'solution' reached during the Clause 43 dispute. 'All of us in the non-Orthodox sector,' he said, 'are delegitimised by having only two ecclesiastical authorities [the Chief Rabbi and the Spanish and Portuguese religious head] ... An overarching structure such as the Board should not be the exclusive means of representing Liberal Jewish interests.'

Nor were the Progressives alone in expressing doubts about the Board's links with 'certain religious authorities.' One charedi leader argued: 'Where there is a shared ideology, or where there are common interests, we don't mind working together. But we don't want to have official relations with an official Reform representative or with someone from the Reform clergy.

'In these and other matters, we would not ask the Board of Deputies to represent our interests. In each case, we prefer to do it on our own. If the Board were a totally secular organisation, yes – that would be a different matter. If everyone in the community sent lay representatives, we could sit around the same table. As it is structured now, however, we cannot. We have to be absolutely certain that our interests are being heard.'[61]

While advancing no leadership solutions of its own, the Commission offered alternatives based on its nationwide consultations. 'In looking at ways respondents and interviewees believed that representation should be carried out, we were open to ideas for radical, far-reaching proposals for overall reform.' These included holding an annual 'national issues' conference, forming a Jewish Community Relations Council, and creating a Jewish civil service. A senior figure in defence work stated: 'What is needed is some sort of council that would unite the agencies, the Board of Deputies and the various religious groupings, without too much bureaucracy behind it.'

The Progressives proposed 'a central address, a single, effective and neutral place for contact and consultation' – an idea not rejected by the strictly Orthodox. A charedi spokesman said: 'I am convinced that that kind of organisation could work for the entire community – from the strictly Orthodox to the Reform – on common interests such as anti-Semitism, shechitah, bioethical issues, Kosovo. The fact is, you need people to come together on critical issues when the occasion warrants it.'

A social-welfare representative recommended appointing an individual – 'one of the great and the good' – to preside over an organisation made up of communal heads, to discuss strategies and common interests and concerns. 'It would be more of a consultative, professional and representative body.'

The Conference of Presidents of Major American Jewish Organisations, commented the JPR Commission, 'is similar to this proposal. A leading Sephardi rabbi suggested that, since we have much to learn from the vibrancy of the American Jewish community, such a model might be appropriate for the United Kingdom.'[62]

Given an appropriate figure of stature and authority, sadly lacking in this postmodern setting, a disestablished Board of Deputies might have been the natural source from which to find an overarching leader of Anglo-Jewry's 'community of communities.' But the reservations voiced at both ends of the polarising spectrum preclude any such possibility within the foreseeable future.

In line with many of the JPR recommendations, perhaps it will fall to the cross-communal, if amorphous, Jewish Leadership Council – established three years after the Commission's report[63] and drawing on representatives from both Orthodox and Reform 'to strengthen the major institutions of British Jewry, to promote co-operation between them, and to help the leadership of our community articulate a confident and compelling narrative of mainstream Jewish life in the United Kingdom'[64] – to find another way, another time.

* * *   * * *   * * *

Welcoming the Chief Rabbi on the day of his installation – 1 September, 1991 – *The Observer* observed, in an unsigned profile widely believed to have been written by Chaim Bermant:

> Rabbi Sacks starts with an immense disadvantage, for he has excited only hope. He is a native born and bred, with British attitudes and British ways, even to the point of being an Arsenal supporter (though the day he made the fact known, Arsenal lost 6–2 to Manchester United) ... Widely admired in the Jewish world, his Reith lectures last year earned him a national reputation, and no Chief Rabbi in British history will assume office with such a burden of expectations.
>
> But more than that, if Jakobovits began as Chief Rabbi in unpromising circumstances, he triumphed over his handicaps, gave Jewish teaching a new relevance not only to the life of the community but to the life of the nation, and gave his office a standing and eminence it had not previously enjoyed. His very achievements have thus, in a sense, added to the burdens of his successor, for he will be a hard act to follow ...
>
> Sacks is less emotional than Jakobovits, more subtle, more cerebral, more philosophic, and – being a trained logician – he has great, perhaps

even excessive, faith in the powers of argument. His handicaps are outweighed by his advantages. He has all the gifts necessary to make him the greatest Chief Rabbi the country has had. But if he should falter in his purpose and fail in his aim, he will almost certainly be the last.[65]

Notes

PREFACE

[1] Jonathan Sacks, *A Decade of Jewish Renewal*, Address Delivered on his Installation as Chief Rabbi of the United Hebrew Congregations of the Commonwealth, St John's Wood Synagogue, London, 1 September, 1991 (London: Office of the Chief Rabbi, 1991), p.1.

[2] Meir Persoff, *Faith Against Reason: Religious Reform and the British Chief Rabbinate, 1840–1990*, London and Portland, OR: Vallentine Mitchell, 2008.

[3] Stanley Kalms (chairman), *A Time for Change: United Synagogue Review*, London: Stanley Kalms Foundation, 1992.

[4] *Faith Against Reason*, p. 390, and Jonathan Sacks, 'The Challenge,' in *A Time for Renewal* (London: Office of the Chief Rabbi, 1992), pp.20-21.

[5] *A Time for Change*, p.1.

[6] At the time of his statement, Leibler was vice-president of the World Jewish Congress and chairman of the Australian Institute of Jewish Affairs, and had served three terms as president of the Executive Council of Australian Jewry. A prolific writer on matters of Jewish concern, now living in Jerusalem, he is widely acknowledged as one of the founders of the international protest movement on behalf of Soviet Jews.

[7] Isi Leibler, *Jewish Religious Extremism: A Threat to the Future of the Jewish People*, New York: World Jewish Congress–Australian Institute of Jewish Affairs, 1991.

[8] Ibid, p.3.

[9] Ibid, p.45.

[10] Ibid, pp.44-45.

[11] Ibid, pp.3-4.

[12] See particularly the references in chapters 11-13 below.

[13] On the Chief Rabbi's peerage, see chapter 1 and chapter 7, note 12, below.

[14] 'A need to lead,' *Jewish Chronicle*, 14 March, 1997, p.32.

[15] Ibid, 26 January, 1996, p.26.

[16] Lord Kalms to this writer, 17 June, 2008. See chapter 1 below.

[17] David Goodman (Office of the Chief Rabbi) to this writer, 23 November, 2009. In a further communication (7 December) – following an hour-long telephone conversation between this writer and a former aide to the Chief Rabbi, and subsequent calls from that intermediary and from the Chief Rabbi himself (2-3 December) – his office wrote that 'having reflected on your most recent request, he confirms his decision not to respond to the issues you raised.'

[18] Endelman is William Haber Professor of Modern Jewish History at the University of Michigan, and author of *The Jews of Britain, 1656 to 2000* (Berkeley: University of California Press, 2002); *The Jews of Georgian England, 1714–1830: Tradition and Change in a Liberal Society* (Ann Arbor: University of Michigan Press, 1999); and *Radical Assimilation in English Jewish History, 1656–1945* (Bloomington: Indiana University Press, 1990).

[19] *Faith Against Reason*, pp.xxv-xxvii.

[20] Todd M. Endelman, *British Jewry and the Jewish Historiographical Mainstream*.

[21] *Whatever Happened To British Jewish Studies?*, 15–16 July, 2008, Parkes Institute for the Study of Jewish/non-Jewish Relations, University of Southampton, supported by the Ian Karten Charitable Trust and the journal *Jewish Culture and History* (London: Vallentine Mitchell).

[22] Miri Freud-Kandel, *Orthodox Judaism in Britain Since 1913* (London and Portland OR: Vallentine Mitchell, 2006), pp.63, 108-109.

[23] Endelman, *British Jewry and the Jewish Historiographical Mainstream*, pp.10-12.

[24] Ibid, p.13. An admirable example of this approach is Liesbeth Schimmel, *Towards a Future of Sincerity*

and Harmony: Dutch Jews and the Appeal of Reform Judaism (MA thesis, University of Utrecht, 2007), which discusses, *inter alia*, the rise of Reform Judaism in Britain within a wider European context.

[25] The situation in the United States became clouded with the intervention of Israel's Chief Rabbinate in the conversion process (*Jewish News*, New Jersey, 6 March, 2008, op-ed; *Jewish Week*, New York, 30 April, 2008, p.1). On the desirability of instituting a Chief Rabbinate in the United States, see chapter 13, note 62, below.

[26] See chapter 8 below.

[27] Neutral Citation Number: [2008] EWHC 1535/1536 (Admin), judgment handed down 3 July, 2008, paragraphs 36-46 (London: Royal Courts of Justice, 2008), pp.12-14.

[28] David Golinkin, '"Who is a Jew?" once again,' in the *Jerusalem Post Magazine*, 25 July, 2008, p.10. Two months later, Israeli Attorney-General Menachem Mazuz 'called on the High Court of Justice to accept a petition by a Danish-born convert to Judaism demanding that it overrule rabbinical court decisions nullifying the conversions, including hers, made by special courts headed by Rabbi Chaim Druckman.' In response, 'Kiryat Ono Chief Rabbi Ratzon Arussi, one of ten rabbis elected [on 23 September, 2008] to the Council of the Chief Rabbinate, charged that the Attorney-General's legal opinion was a blatant example of illegitimate, secular intervention in a purely religious matter ... "The proper forum for debate and decision-making is within the Chief Rabbinate Council," Arussi said' (*Jerusalem Post*, 25 September, 2008, pp.1, 9). On Druckman, see Matthew Wagner, 'Rabbi Chaim Druckman: The "darling" of religious Zionism' ('People of the Year') in the *Jerusalem Post Magazine*, 26 September, 2008, p.21.

[29] Oxford: Clarendon Press, 1992; new and expanded edition, 1998.

[30] Boston: Academic Studies Press, 2008.

CHAPTER 1

[1] Jonathan Sacks, *A Decade of Jewish Renewal*, Address Delivered on his Installation as Chief Rabbi of the United Hebrew Congregations of the Commonwealth, St John's Wood Synagogue, London, 1 September, 1991 (London: Office of the Chief Rabbi, 1991), p.1.

[2] 'Kalms urges Chief Rabbi to retire,' letter to the *Jewish Chronicle*, 26 January, 1996, p.26. For communal reaction, see Interlude: *From First to Second*, below.

[3] *Jewish Chronicle*, 12 January, 1996, p.29.

[4] Lord Kalms to this writer, 17 June, 2008. Kalms was created a life peer as Baron Kalms, of Edgware in the London Borough of Barnet, in 2004. Like his protégé, he received his secondary education at Christ's College, Finchley. Christ's has its roots in two different schools: Chapel Street School (later Alder School), founded in 1842, and Finchley Hall School, established in 1857 by the Rev Thomas Reader White, Rector of Finchley, and renamed Christ's College three years later. See also notes 15 and 83 below.

[5] *United Synagogue Review: A Time for Change*, Stanley Kalms, chairman; London: Stanley Kalms Foundation, September 1992, pp.85, 94.

[6] 'About the London Beth Din (Court of the Chief Rabbi),' London: United Synagogue, 2010. At the time of writing, the dayanim were Menachem Gelley – who succeeded Chanoch Hacohen Ehrentreu as Rosh Beth Din (presiding dayan) in 2007 – Yonason Abraham, Ivan Binstock and Shmuel Simons.

[7] *United Synagogue Review*, p.87.

[8] The extended family included Moses Hirsh Segal, rabbi of Oxford from 1902–09 and later lecturer in Hebrew, then professor, at the Hebrew University of Jerusalem; Professor Lord Samuel Segal (1902–85), surgeon and politician; Professor Judah Benzion Segal (1912–2003), Orientalist and educationist; Professor Oliver Sacks (b. 1933), neurologist; and Abba Eban (Aubrey Solomon) (1915–2002), Israeli politician and diplomat.

[9] *Jewish Chronicle*, 18 September, 2009, p.6. References to Sacks' childhood and to his family's debt

to British life, tradition and culture featured in his maiden speech in the House of Lords on 26 November, 2009.

[10] Sacks, *A Decade of Jewish Renewal*, p.2.

[11] Jonathan Sacks, *Celebrating Life: Finding Happiness in Unexpected Places* (London: Fount-HarperCollins, 2000), p.xiv.

[12] Jonathan Sacks, 'Diary of a Chief Rabbi,' Rosh Hashanah 5760, *Jewish Telegraph*, 29 September, 1999. For an expansion of these sentiments, see the conclusion to chapter 5 below.

[13] Jonathan Sacks, *Community of Faith* (London: Peter Halban, 1995), p.140.

[14] Ibid, pp.140-141.

[15] '... a name no sectarian Orthodox Jew would dare repeat' – Geoffrey Alderman, *Modern British Jewry* (new edition, Oxford: Clarendon Press, 1998), p.392. Appearing on BBC Radio 5, Sacks was confronted with the following comment by presenter Simon Mayo: 'Many people would be surprised to learn, as indeed I was, as I was reading about you, to discover that you went to a Church of England primary school and to Christ's Church, Finchley, high school.' Sacks replied: 'Christ's College.' Mayo: 'Christ's College, Finchley, I beg your pardon. I should, ah, many people would see that as a surprising education for a future Chief Rabbi.' Sacks: 'Well, I wouldn't advise it as the best possible cv for the job, but I have got to say that I will never cease to be grateful to those schools. They were Christian schools which, because they had a respect for their own faith, had a respect for our faith as Jewish pupils. I think it helped me feel very warmly towards people of other faiths. And I have to say that the respect they had for us was a tremendous boost. So there you are, you can become Chief Rabbi from all sorts of backgrounds, and I will never cease to be grateful to those schools' ('Simon Mayo Show,' BBC Radio 5 Live, 31 August, 2001).

[16] Chaim Bermant, *Lord Jakobovits: The Authorized Biography of the Chief Rabbi* (London: Weidenfeld and Nicolson, 1990), p.203. An unsigned profile in *The Observer* (1 September, 1991) described Sacks in similar terms: 'He is eloquent, witty, and carries his great learning lightly ... He lacks the restless energies and demonic drive of his predecessor and, for all his cheerful bonhomie, is happier among books than among people, and is unsure how he will face up to the social demands of the office. He is, however, no sluggard. At one time, he seemed to hold more jobs than Cardinal Wolsey ... He prefers to be overloaded than underloaded and thrives on the principle that time somehow expands with the extent of one's responsibilities.' The article noted that Sacks met his wife, Elaine, 'an attractive and rather demure young blonde with pre-Raphaelite looks, when she was a radiographer at Addenbrooke's Hospital, Cambridge. They married when he was 22, and he barely recalls a time when he wasn't married. They have three children.'

[17] During this period, Sacks recalls, 'I taught at Middlesex Polytechnic (now University) for a few years. In those days, I think it had the biggest philosophy department in Britain.' Among the faculty was David Conway, who would later have Sacks as his rabbi. (On Conway, see chapter 7 below.)

[18] Julian Baggini, 'My Philosophy: Jonathan Sacks,' the Chief Rabbi in conversation with the editor of *The Philosophers' Magazine* (London: Philosophy Press), No. 44, March 2009, pp.120-126.

[19] Sacks to Jacobs, Gonville and Caius College, Cambridge, 6 November, 1967 (Jacobs Papers, London).

[20] Sacks, *Celebrating Life*, pp.159-160.

[21] Jonathan Sacks, *Radical Then, Radical Now: The Legacy of the World's Oldest Religion* (London: HarperCollins, 2001), p.211.

[22] Ibid, pp.216-217.

[23] Sacks, *Community of Faith*, p.142.

[24] Sacks to this writer, 3 December, 2009. *Yoreh Deah* ('Teaching Knowledge'), the second section of the *Shulchan Aruch* ('Arranged Table'), dealing with complex issues requiring rabbinic decisions.

[25] 'Path of Life,' the opening section of the *Shulchan Aruch*, covering the laws of Sabbath and the festivals, prayer, and general religious duties.

[26] The Jews' College *semichah* of both candidates is recorded in the 120th annual report of the College (5737–1977), p.xiii. A fellow ordinand at Etz Chaim yeshivah was Shlomo Levin, who subsequently became minister of the South Hampstead (United) Synagogue; a third student at the time was the future Dayan Ivan Binstock. On Sacks' period at Jews' College, see his 'A close-knit

academic community, with a clear sense of its role. Reflections of a semichah candidate' (*Jewish Chronicle*, Jews' College Supplement, 3 September, 1976, p.ii). On Levin, see chapter 11 below.

[27] Sacks to the JC, 30 October, 1976 (*Jewish Chronicle* Archives).

[28] The episode is recounted in *Faith Against Reason*, pp.283-301.

[29] Jonathan Sacks, *Traditional Alternatives: Orthodoxy and the Future of the Jewish People* (London: Jews' College Publications, 1989), pp.6-7. Sacks stood down as principal of Jews' College soon after this was written, having held the post (together with his earlier appointment to the Sir Immanuel [later Lord] Jakobovits Chair in Contemporary Jewish Thought and Literature) since 1984 (see *Jews' College Annual Report* 5743–1983, p.viii; and *Jews' College Annual Report* 5744–1984, p.vi). A lengthier account by Sacks of the College's history, philosophy, role and 'vision' appears in 'Jews' College: the way ahead. A story of self-discovery' (*Jewish Chronicle*, 26 October, 1984, p.43). See also his article, 'Jews' College in Crisis: Commitment to the Community' (ibid, 30 November, 1979, p.21).

[30] Professor Nehama Leibowitz (1905–97), winner of the Israel Prize in education, wrote a widely circulated series on *Studies in the Weekly Torah Portion* and provided a correspondence course in Bible, using her popular *gilyonot* (worksheets), for more than thirty years. The review to which Sacks refers appeared in the *Jewish Chronicle*, 19 November, 1973, and discussed Leibowitz's *Studies in the Book of Genesis*, translated and adapted from the Hebrew by Aryeh Newman (Jerusalem: Alpha Press, 1972).

[31] The Documentary Hypothesis: 'that there are four documents of diverse ages to be detected in the Pentateuch, put together by a series of redactors ... The conclusion that the Pentateuch is, in part at least, post-Mosaic, and that it is a composite work, is accepted by every Bible scholar of note today who "plays the game" – that is, who does not dismiss the scholarly enterprise itself as erroneous. This is based on the strongest evidence and is extremely unlikely to be overthrown' (Louis Jacobs, 'Reflections on a Controversy,' in *Quest* 1, ed., Jonathan Stone, London: Paul Hamlyn, 1965, p.5).

[32] Responding from Emmanuel College, Cambridge, the following week (*Jewish Chronicle*, 26 January, 1973, p.25), Newman wrote, *inter alia*: 'I am not surprised that the reviewer ... regards the questions of authorship, and the detecting of sources and literary strata, as the only kind of biblical scholarship worthy of the name. This, I am aware, seems to figure as a major ingredient of the learned reviewer's message to the Anglo-Jewish community. But to maintain that this constitutes "scholarship as it is nowadays understood" is far from the ideal of objectivity that Rabbi Jacobs calls for.'

[33] Sacks to Jacobs, 19 January, 1973 (Jacobs Papers, London).

[34] Sacks to Jacobs, 26 January, 1973 (ibid).

[35] Oxford University Press for the Littman Library of Jewish Civilization, 1984.

[36] *Jewish Chronicle*, 2 November, 1984, pp.24-25.

[37] Among the contributors to the debate were Rabbi Thomas Salamon, Hertsmere Progressive Synagogue, London (ibid, 23 November, 1984, p.23); Professor T. A. Kletz, University of Technology, Loughborough; Rabbi D. Cohn-Sherbok, Director for the Study of Religion and Society, University of Kent, Canterbury; Rev Chaim N. Ingram, Minister/Reader, United Hebrew Congregation, Newcastle upon Tyne; Rabbi Isaac Newman, Co-ordinator of Hebrew Studies, Middlesex Polytechnic, Trent Park; Dr Joseph Udelson, Associate Professor of History, Tennessee State University (ibid, 30 November, 1984, p.19); Rabbi Arye Forta, Lubavitch; Dr Tali Loewenthal, Lubavitch; Rabbi Alan A. Kimche, Ner Yisrael Congregation, London; Salmond S. Levin, former president, United Synagogue, London (ibid, 7 December, 1984, p.23); Rabbi Dr J. Immanuel Schochet, Professor of Philosophy, Humber College, Toronto; Rabbi Zalman I. Posner, Congregation Shearith Israel, Nashville, Tennessee; Rev M. Plaskow, Woodside Park Synagogue, London; Rabbi E. Gastwirth, Salford; Dayan Dr S. Herman, London (ibid, 14 December, 1984, p.17).

[38] Ibid, 16 November, 1984, p.25.

[39] S. B. Lieberman to his friend Rabbi Aharon (whom he does not identify further), 3 November, 1984. Translation by Benjamin Balint.

[40] Assigned to a labour squad, Lieberman had been shunted between six concentration camps before ending up in Theresienstadt, near Prague. He did not speak of his Holocaust experiences until the last years of his life, when he confided them verbally to his son, Rabbi Yitzchak Meir Lieberman, who committed the account to his computer.

[41] Obituary of Kahana, *Jewish Chronicle*, 21 July, 1978, p.20.

[42] Lloyd P. Gartner to this writer, 26 October, 2009. Gartner was a frequent guest at the home of Simche and Chava (née Klajman) Lieberman while a research student in England in 1952. Of Abramsky's involvement, Gartner records: 'Simche's unfavourable view of the situation at Windermere was put in a lengthy letter he wrote in Hebrew to Dayan Yechezkel Abramsky, an outstanding rabbinic scholar and exceptional personality. Seventeen boys signed the letter, explaining their dissatisfaction with the educational programme. The letter opened with a witty, meaningful pun – "Tuesday, *Chayyei Tsorah* [life of woe]," instead of "*Chayyei Sarah* [life of Sarah]," the Torah portion read in the synagogue that week. It received Dayan Abramsky's serious attention and he took the long train journey to Windermere, where he met and spoke with Simche and others in the group. It was agreed that they could move to London and study at the small Etz Chaim yeshivah, where the dayan was a key figure. Simche moved to the metropolis, but did not stay long at Etz Chaim, which had few full-time students. His uncle was urging him to go to America, where he could study Talmud at the Isaac Elchanan Yeshivah under the renowned Rabbi Joseph Soloveichik. Dayan Abramsky also advised him to go, but Simche chose instead to study at the growing yeshivah of Gateshead.' On the Ger (Gur) Chasidic dynasty, including a passage on Lieberman, see Harry Rabinowicz, *A World Apart: The Story of the Chasidim in Britain* (London and Portland OR: Vallentine Mitchell, 1997), pp.187-194.

[43] *Jewish Chronicle*, 8 February, 1985, p.1.

[44] Ibid, 15 February, 1985, p.5.

[45] Ibid, 22 February, 1985, p.6.

[46] Ibid, 1 March, 1985, p.4.

[47] *Hundred & Fifteenth Annual Report*, 2 July, 1972 (London: Jews' College, 1972), p.xii.

[48] From a letter sent by Jakobovits to Dr Tuvia Preschel, of New York, who then disclosed its contents to Lieberman.

[49] *Jewish Chronicle*, 15 February, 1985, p.5.

[50] Ibid, 1 March, 1985, p.4.

[51] Lieberman to Geoffrey Alderman, 5 March, 1985. Alderman (see note 61 below) was involved in the negotiations over Lieberman's redundancy settlement. See note 60 below on the events leading up to the settlement.

[52] *Jewish Chronicle*, 7 August, 2009, p.38

[53] Ibid, 5 July, 1985, p.8.

[54] *One Hundred and Twenty-Eighth Annual Report*, 5745–1985 (London: Jews' College, 1985), p.5.

[55] Ibid, pp.7-8.

[56] 'Tension has been mounting since the introduction by Rabbi Sacks of a BA course' (*Jewish Chronicle*, 8 February, 1985, p.1).

[57] *One Hundred and Twenty-Eighth Annual Report*, pp.9-10.

[58] Jews' College changed its name to the London School of Jewish Studies (LSJS) in July 1998. Writing in March 1999 as LSJS president, Sacks asserted: 'The London School carries with it … the best of the College's traditions of the past, together with a fresh new focus on Anglo-Jewry's emerging agenda of Jewish renewal' (*Report 5756–5758/1996–1998*, London: LSJS, 1999, p.5). Wikipedia notes: 'In 1998, the University of London announced that it would be terminating the "Associated Institute" status that the College and three other small institutions enjoyed. Jews' College was forced to seek an academic partner within the University in order to be able to continue its degree programmes. Without the freedom to determine its own curriculum and the financial security that came from student-fee income, it became increasingly difficult for the College to survive in its previous form. Rabbinic training was also uneconomic as many able students looked to the Torah centres of Israel and America for their education and as the number of available rabbinic posts in the UK decreased. In 2002, the School of Oriental and African Studies (SOAS) decided to terminate its relationship with LSJS, precipitating a crisis which was nearly fatal.' The LSJS website (2010) declares that its mission is 'to inspire our community with a lifelong love of Jewish learning and practice by being a vibrant modern Orthodox centre of Jewish scholarship and teaching. Our mission involves eight principal commitments: 1. To educate adults by increasing their Jewish knowledge, improving their textual skills and building their confidence as independent learners. 2. To encourage all our students to pass on their knowledge both at home and within their own communities. 3. To develop a faculty

of outstanding educators who teach with respect, openness, intellectual rigour and creativity. 4. To study with *yirat shamayim*, a profound reverence for God, in order to strengthen character, guide actions and elevate lives. 5. To exchange ideas at the highest level through academic research and the advanced study of traditional Jewish texts. 6. To promote the full participation of women in Jewish learning. 7. To deepen our community's understanding and love for Israel. 8. To examine critical issues facing modern society in order to develop a Jewish response and to promote social action.'

[59] Lieberman died in Israel on 28 June, 2009, aged 79.

[60] A Deed of Submission dated 13 May, 1985, and signed by Lieberman (on the one side), and Jakobovits, Kalms and Sacks – 'acting for and on behalf of, and with the authority of, the honorary officers and council of the said College' – (on the other), agreed, *inter alia:* '1. To refer for determination by arbitration and adjudication (by a Beth Din referred to hereafter as "the Beth Din") all claims which the aforementioned Rabbi Simche Lieberman makes against the aforementioned College, and the award of the said Beth Din shall be binding upon the parties, who hereby specifically agree to accept and perform such award forthwith. 2. The expenses incurred by the Beth Din shall be apportioned by the Beth Din in whatever manner seems to the Beth Din to be appropriate, and the Beth Din shall make such orders in respect of costs incurred by the parties hereto as it think fits.' Those sitting on the Beth Din – the proceedings of which were to be held in London (though never took place) – were named as Rabbi Benzion Blau, of London N16, and Rabbis Kreiswirth and Lieberman, of Antwerp.

[61] *The Times*, 27 July, 2009, p.46. On further background to Lieberman's dismissal, see Geoffrey Alderman, *Albert Road: An Everyday Story of Jewish Folk* (Egham: Royal Holloway & Bedford New College, 1990), reproduced in Alderman, *Controversy and Crisis* (Boston: Academic Studies Press, 2008), pp.30-36. See also Lieberman's obituary in the *Jewish Chronicle* (7 August, 2009, p.38); Aron Freedman and Meir Salasnik, 'A Tribute on Shabbat Nachamu, the "Sabbath of Consolation,"' in *The Arch: Newsletter of the Western Marble Arch Synagogue, London* (11 Av, 5769–1 August, 2009), p.1; and Lloyd P. Gartner, *Simche Bunim Lieberman*, address to the Jewish Historical Society of England, Israel branch, 7 February, 2010.

[62] On Sacks' ministry at Golders Green, see chapter 11 below.

[63] Sacks, *Community of Faith*, p.143.

[64] 'Jewish World,' Greater London Radio, 24 September, 1989.

[65] On earlier Federation responses to the Chief Rabbinical election process, see chapter 12 below.

[66] On the possible candidacy of Rabbi Cyril Harris, see chapter 10, note 3, below.

[67] *The Daily Telegraph*, February 26, 1990.

[68] *Jewish Chronicle*, 2 March, 1990, p.1.

[69] 'Whose Chief Rabbi? – Elena Lappin talks to Jonathan Sacks about politics and hope,' in *The Jewish Quarterly*, Vol. 44, No. 2 (166), summer 1997, pp.5-6. Elaborating on this theme, Sacks told BBC Radio's Pam Rose: 'I never dreamt of becoming a rabbi. I sort of fell into it. When I was a student, I had all sorts of dreams, maybe being an academic, or a barrister, or an economist, but I thought that my generation, which was by and large the first generation of people I knew who went to university – I was the first person in my family to go to university – was going to be an educated generation, but none of my contemporaries was going into the rabbinate, and at the end of the day I thought, well, if nobody else is doing it, then perhaps ... ('Good Morning Sunday,' BBC Radio 2, 2 September, 2001). Two days earlier, asked whether he was surprised to have been offered the job, Sacks told BBC Radio's Simon Mayo: 'I was very relaxed about it. If the offer came, I thought, it is a challenge you can't say no to.' Mayo: 'Was it something you allowed yourself to aspire to?' Sacks: 'Not really. I just know I share a rabbinate with a tremendous bunch of dedicated people, and there were many people I would have been happy to serve with, and I am delighted that they have served with me. So, I was very easy about it. But once the offer came, I couldn't possibly say no' ('Simon Mayo Show,' BBC Radio 5 Live, 31 August, 2001).

[70] Sacks, *Traditional Alternatives*, pp.1, 9.

[71] 'The State of Orthodoxy,' a symposium occupying an entire edition of *Tradition* (Vol. 20, No. 1, spring 1982, New York: Rabbinical Council of America), introduced by then editor Walter Wurzburger thus: 'In recent years, the vigor as well as the image of Orthodoxy has been completely revitalised.

Gone are the predictions of the inevitable demise of what was widely dismissed as an obsolete movement that could not cope with the challenges of the "open society." Orthodoxy has made such a remarkable recovery that its new self-confidence has regrettably generated in some quarters a deplorable sense of smugness and, occasionally, has given rise to a spirit of "triumphalism."' The symposium was discussed by Sacks in 'Modern Orthodoxy in Crisis,' in L'Eylah, Vol. 2, No. 7, spring 5744–1984, pp.20-25.

[72] Kalms to Jakobovits, 28 September, 1988 (Jakobovits Papers, London).

[73] 'Speculation about the next Chief Rabbi has been rife in the community for some time, although no clear favourite has yet emerged. Names mentioned include … Rabbi Dr Reuven Bulka, who has been brought over from Canada to give a lecture in London tomorrow night, organised by the United Synagogue' (Jewish Chronicle, 28 October, 1998, p.1). On speculation over Sacks' successor, see chapter 9 below.

[74] Sacks, Traditional Alternatives, p.1.

[75] Bulka's wife, Naomi (who died in 2001), was a daughter of the Chief Rabbi's brother, George (1921–2009), and Sessi Jakobovits, of Montreal.

[76] Jewish Chronicle, 26 May, 1989, pp.8-9.

[77] Ibid, p.8.

[78] Ibid, 1 September, 1989, p.1.

[79] Ibid, 8 September, 1989, p.12.

[80] One Hundred and Thirty-First Annual Report, 5748–1988 (London: Jews' College, 1988), p.5.

[81] Ibid, p.7.

[82] One Hundred and Thirty-Second Annual Report, 5749–1989 (London: Jews' College, 1989), pp.7-8.

[83] Kalms to Jakobovits, 9 May, 1988 (Jakobovits Papers, London). Kalms preceded this comment by thanking Jakobovits for quoting Sacks during a House of Lords debate on the Education Reform Bill, held the previous week. The Chief Rabbi had said (3 May, 1988): 'If we consider religious faith and precept as the spiritual lifeblood of the nation and all its citizens, then effective religious instruction can no more be administered by and to persons of a different faith than can a blood transfusion be safely given without first ensuring blood-group compatibility. Indiscriminate mixing of blood can prove dangerous, and so can the mixing of faiths in education. I should like to apply that in practice from a Jewish perspective. I shall do so by quoting from a "Thought for the Day" talk on Radio 4 given last Thursday by my learned colleague, Rabbi Jonathan Sacks, principal of Jews' College. He described how he was raised at a primary school which was devoutly C of E and where Jewish boys had their separate Jewish assemblies. He said: "The effect of this schooling on our Jewish identity was curious. It made us, of course, acutely aware that we were different. But because those around us were taking their religion seriously, it made us consider our Judaism seriously too." Then he added: "So it isn't so strange that all this produced a rabbi. From living with those who valued their traditions, I learned to cherish my own." Continuing, he said: "What brought this to mind was the report… called 'Crisis in Religious Education,' in which two Newcastle teachers complained that children in today's schools are losing the chance to grow up as practising Christians. They might, I think, have gone further still; for if Christianity suffers, so, in a curious way, does every other faith as well." He continued: "It happens with the best of intentions. How else, in a multicultural society, should we promote tolerance than by teaching children something about every religious group with which they are likely to come into contact; a touch of Christianity; a dash of Judaism; a slice of Islam; and so on through a fruit cocktail of world faiths. But the whole that emerges can be less than the sum of its parts. For it misses out on the most crucial element of all: the fact that, for each of us, there is usually only one faith that resonates with personal meaning: the faith of our community, our culture, our family, our past. In trying to teach all faiths, it's possible that we succeed in teaching none." Finally, he concluded: "From schools that had confidence in their Christianity, I learned an answering pride in my Jewishness; and I discovered that those who best appreciate other faiths are those who treasure their own. Might not teaching children their own traditions do more for tolerance, and for faith, than teaching them everyone else's?"' (Hansard, 4 May, 1988, reproduced with the permission of the Controller of Her Majesty's Stationery Office on behalf of Parliament).

[84] Jakobovits to Kalms, 17 June, 1988 (Jakobovits Papers, London).

[85] Kalms to Jakobovits, 18 July, 1988 (ibid).

[86] Kalms to Jakobovits, 28 September, 1988 (ibid).

[87] Kalms to Jakobovits, 30 September, 1988 (ibid).

[88] Jakobovits to Kalms, 30 September, 1988 (ibid).

[89] One Hundred and Thirty-Third Annual Report, 5750–1990 (London: Jews' College, 1990), p.6.

[90] Jewish Chronicle, 6 April, 1990, p.48.

[91] Ibid, 2 March, 1990, p.24.

[92] David Englander, 'Integrated But Insecure: A Portrait of Anglo-Jewry at the Close of the Twentieth Century,' in The Growth of Religious Diversity: Britain From 1945, Vol. I. – Traditions, ed., Gerald Parsons (Routledge, in association with the Open University, 1993), pp.124-125.

[93] On Paula Cohen, see M. Ish-Horowicz, 'The Case of Mrs Paula Cohen and her Children,' in The Jewish Law Annual 11 (1994), pp.171-194.

[94] 'Rabbis, old and new,' leading article, Jewish Chronicle, 30 August, 1991, p.16.

[95] Immanuel Jakobovits, Address Delivered at the Installation of Rabbi Dr Jonathan Sacks as Chief Rabbi of the United Hebrew Congregations of the Commonwealth (London: Office of the Chief Rabbi, 1991), pp.2-3. The service, held on 1 September, 1991, at the St John's Wood Synagogue, London, was conducted by Dayan Chanoch Ehrentreu, Dayan Gabriel Krausz, Rabbi Lionel Cofnas, Rabbi Alan Plancey, Rev Simon Hass and Rev Lionel Rosenfeld (Order of Service at the Installation of Rabbi Dr Jonathan Sacks as Chief Rabbi of the United Hebrew Congregations of the Commonwealth, London: Office of the Chief Rabbi, 1991, pp.1-28).

[96] Sacks, A Decade of Jewish Renewal, p.9.

CHAPTER 2

[1] Jonathan Sacks, A Decade of Jewish Renewal, p.4.

[2] Jonathan Sacks, A Time For Renewal: A Rabbinic Response to the Kalms Report, 'A Time For Change' (London: Office of the Chief Rabbi, 1992), pp.6-7.

[3] Bye Laws of the Constituent Synagogues (London: United Synagogue, November 1881), pp.xix-xx.

[4] Ibid, pp.xi-xii.

[5] Laws of the Congregation of the Great Synagogue, Duke's Place (London: J. Wertheimer and Co., 5623–1863), p.v.

[6] On the cherem, its consequences and its revocation by the Sephardi authorities, see the prologue and chapter 1 of Faith Against Reason.

[7] 'Hambro' Synagogue: Extract from the Introduction to the Edition of the Laws Published in 5605–1844,' in Bye Laws of the Constituent Synagogues, pp.vii-viii.

[8] Adler, Laws and Regulations for all the Synagogues in the British Empire (London: John Wertheimer and Co., 5607–1847).

[9] Laws of the Congregation of the Great Synagogue, Duke's Place, p.xiii.

[10] An Act for confirming a Scheme of the Charity Commissioners for the Jewish United Synagogues [33 & 34 Vict., Ch. cxvi], 14 July, 1870, p.2. Alderman points out (Modern British Jewry, Oxford: Clarendon Press, 1992, pp.88-89): 'The United Synagogue scheme, as originally drafted, had spoken of "the Chief Rabbi," under whose authority and control all religious matters were to fall. Gladstone's Liberal Government objected to the legislative underpinning of ecclesiastical jurisdiction in this way: the clause had to be modified. Nathan Adler did not therefore become, by the authority of statute law, "the Chief Rabbi," a British equivalent, so to speak, of a Continental Landesrabbiner. But he did become, under the scheme scheduled to the Act, "a Chief Rabbi."' Joseph Jacobs writes (Jewish Encyclopedia, Vol. 5, New York: Funk and Wagnalls, 1925, p.172): 'In the charter [of the United Synagogue] an attempt was made to give the Chief Rabbi autocratic powers over the doctrines to be taught in the Jewish communities throughout the British Empire. But Parliament, which had recently disestablished the Irish Church, did not feel disposed to establish the Jewish Synagogue, and the clause was stricken out.'

The United Synagogue's *Deed of Foundation and Trust* states (Clause 2): 'One of the objects of the Institution called the United Synagogue shall be the contributing with other bodies to the maintenance of the Chief Rabbi, and of the Ecclesiastical Board; and the Scheme shall be read and construed as if, in the fifth clause thereof, the words "the maintenance of the Chief Rabbi, and of the Ecclesiastical Board," were substituted for the words "the maintenance of a Chief Rabbi and of other Ecclesiastical persons."' The Deed granted the Chief Rabbi powers of supervision and control over forms of worship, religious observances, and religious administration (Clause 3); and over the appointment of preachers, readers and 'others performing religious duties,' who required the Chief Rabbi's certification 'under his hand that he is a fit and proper person to perform the same' (Clauses 7 and 9). Clause 11 stipulated that 'Any synagogue to be hereafter erected and founded under the sixty-fourth clause of the Scheme shall previously to, and as a condition of, its admission as a constituent synagogue be consecrated by or with the sanction of the Chief Rabbi' (*Recorded Minutes of the First Meeting of Elected Members of the Vestry of the United Synagogue*, London, 11 January, 1871, pp.1-7; and *Deed of Foundation and Trust*, signed, sealed and delivered by Sir Anthony de Rothschild, Baronet; Lionel Louis Cohen; Sampson Lucas; Solomon Schloss; and Assur Henry Moses, in the presence of Algernon E. Sydney, Solicitor, 46 Finsbury Circus, London, EC, 13 January, 1871, pp.1-4). On the development of the role and powers of the Chief Rabbinate, see Stephen Sharot, 'Religious Change in Native Orthodoxy in London, 1870–1914: Rabbinate and Clergy,' in the *Jewish Journal of Sociology*, Vol. XV, No. 2, December 1973 (London: William Heinemann), pp.167-176; A Special Correspondent, 'The British Chief Rabbinate,' in the *Jewish Monthly*, No. 2, May 1947, pp.23-33; and 'Resolutions on Matters Relating to the Office of the Chief Rabbi, passed at Meetings of the Several Metropolitan and Provincial Congregations' (in February 1843), *Voice of Jacob*, 3 March, 1843, pp.121-123.

[11] Maurice Simon, *Jewish Religious Conflicts* (London: Hutchinson's University Library, 1950), p.118.

[12] Ibid, p.120.

[13] Michael Leigh, 'Reform Judaism in Britain (1840–1970),' in *Reform Judaism*, ed., Dow Marmur (London: Reform Synagogues of Great Britain, 1970), p.21.

[14] Moses Gaster, *History of the Ancient Synagogue of the Spanish and Portuguese Jews* (London: privately published, 5661–1901), p.171. The petition was submitted to the *mahamad* (Elders) of Bevis Marks on 4 December, 1836, by a small number of members, who were opposed by the majority of the congregation, fearful of 'a demand for radical reform.' This latter view prevailed – 'and the Elders concurred with them entirely.'

[15] *Forms of Prayer, used in the West London Synagogue of British Jews, with an English Translation. Volume I – Daily and Sabbath Prayers*, ed., D. W. Marks (London: Wertheimer and Co., 1841). Of the liturgy contained therein, Marks wrote in his introduction: 'Many portions of the common ritual, by their holy dignified tenor, afford every Israelite the opportunity of joining cordially in the worship of his brethren wherever he meets them in the house of prayer, and thus form a valuable bond of union amongst all Hebrew congregations. These sublime portions we trust we shall be found to have carefully preserved; and we hope to have strengthened rather than weakened the bond of union which they constitute, by blending in our ritual the varying form of the Portuguese [Sephardi] and German [Ashkenazi] Liturgies, and striving to give, on all occasions, the preference to the superiority of intrinsic merit alone' (ibid, p.x).

[16] Minutes of the inaugural meeting 'of those who finally organised the reformed congregation' – twenty-four members of the Bevis Marks and Great Synagogues – held at the Bedford Hotel, Russell Square, London, on 15 April, 1840, and cited in the *Jewish Chronicle*, 29 January, 1892, p.17.

[17] Morris Joseph, 'The English Reform Movement,' letter to the *Jewish Chronicle*, 14 May, 1909, p.12. See also Liesbeth Schimmel, *Towards a Future of Sincerity and Harmony: Dutch Jews and the Appeal of Reform Judaism* (MA thesis, University of Utrecht, 2007), pp.45-47.

[18] Immanuel Jakobovits, 'The Evolution of the British Rabbinate Since 1845,' in *The Timely and The Timeless* (London: Vallentine Mitchell, 1977), p.269. On similar lines, John Shaftesley writes: 'The forms of religious controversy in Anglo-Jewry have been more often administrative or personal than theological, and they have arisen chiefly out of the structure of the community: a voluntary establishment whose religious head, to most of the Jews and to the outside world, has been the Chief Rabbi. Each Chief Rabbi has had his authority conferred on him, by the terms of his appointment,

by the majority of the Orthodox community; and each had to contend with challenges to that authority, some of them along uncannily parallel lines' ('Religious Controversies,' in *A Century of Anglo-Jewish Life, 1870–1970*, ed., Salmond S. Levin, London: United Synagogue, 1970, p.93).

[19] Jonathan Sacks, *Community of Faith* (London: Peter Halban, 1995), pp.80-83.

[20] Ibid, p.109-110. On Hirsch, see *Faith Against Reason*, pp.xix, 4-6.

[21] *Faith Against Reason*, chapter 4.

[22] Cecil Roth, *History of the Great Synagogue, 1690–1940* (London: Edward Goldston & Son, 1950), pp.256-258.

[23] James Picciotto, *Sketches of Anglo-Jewish History* (first published in the *Jewish Chronicle*, 1872–75; published in book form, London, 1875; reissued, ed., Israel Finestein, London: Soncino Press, 1956), pp.379-380.

[24] Roth, in his preface to Barnett's history of the congregation (see note 25), writes: 'At all times of communal strife, it persisted in observing a benevolent neutrality between the warring communal organisations, whether East or West, "Right" or "Left" of it, without surrendering or imperilling its own conservative independence' (p.xiv). Roth authored *Records of the Western Synagogue, 1761–1932* (London: Edward Goldston, 1932), to which is appended a reprint of Matthias Levy's *The Western Synagogue: some materials for its history*, originally published in 1897.

[25] Arthur Barnett, *The Western Synagogue Through Two Centuries, 1761–1961* (London: Vallentine Mitchell, 1961), pp.177-178. On the Western's opposition to the cherem and to the Chief Rabbinate's edict that it be proclaimed by 'the secretaries of the principal Metropolitan Synagogues … from their respective reading desks,' see *Faith Against Reason*, pp.16-17.

[26] Aubrey Newman, *The United Synagogue 1870–1970* (London: Routledge & Kegan Paul, 1977), p.56.

[27] – temporarily, it might be added.

[28] Israel Finestein, *Anglo-Jewry in Changing Times* (London: Vallentine Mitchell, 1999), p.17.

[29] Todd M. Endelman, *The Jews of Britain 1656 to 2000* (Berkeley: University of California Press, 2002), p.120.

[30] Lloyd P. Gartner, *The Jewish Immigrant in England, 1870–1914* (London: George Allen & Unwin, 1960), p.15.

[31] Bernard Homa, *Orthodoxy in Anglo-Jewry 1880–1940* (London: Jewish Historical Society of England, 1969), p.7.

[32] Geoffrey Alderman, *Modern British Jewry* (Oxford: Clarendon Press, 1992), p.151.

[33] Minutes of the United Synagogue council, 18 February, 1890, quoted in Gartner, op. cit., p.204. The meeting was reported in the *Jewish Chronicle*, 21 February, 1890, pp.8-9.

[34] Homa, op. cit., p.10.

[35] Gartner, op. cit., pp.191, 207.

[36] 'On the motion [before the United Synagogue council] of Mr A. H. Jessel, KC, who referred to his eminent qualities, Rabbi Avigdor Chaikin was unanimously elected a Dayan, it being understood that he should continue as Minister of the Federation of Synagogues' (*Jewish Chronicle*, 10 November, 1911, p.27).

[37] Newman, op. cit., p.93. On the circumstances leading to Chaikin's appointment, see Alderman, *The Federation of Synagogues 1887–1987* (London: Federation of Synagogues, 1987), pp.35-41; and the *Jewish Chronicle*, 22 June, 1928, p.11.

[38] On the establishment of the Union of Orthodox Hebrew Congregations, see *Faith Against Reason*, pp.227-228.

[39] Newman, op. cit., pp.107, 109.

[40] 'Progressive conservatism – the synthesis of the best citizenship and the broadest humanitarianism with the warmth and colour, the depth and discipline of the olden Jewish life' (J. H. Hertz, *Opening Address by the Chief Rabbi*, Conference of Anglo-Jewish Preachers, London: Oxford University Press, 1923, p.19).

[41] *Bye-Laws Made by the Council of the United Synagogue* (London, United Synagogue, July 1936), p.i. Ironically, as described in *Faith Against Reason* (p.303), this paragraph was invoked by the rebellious honorary officers of the New West End Synagogue in 1964 in their attempt to reinstate Louis Jacobs as minister of the congregation, following the Chief Rabbi's refusal to grant a ministerial certificate.

[42] Aaron Sorasky, *Melech Beyofyo* [*A King in His Glory*], Vol. I (Jerusalem: privately published, 2004), p.393.

[43] Jakobovits, 'The Evolution of the British Rabbinate Since 1845,' p.271.

[44] For an elaboration of this view, see Jonathan A. Romain, 'The establishment of the Reform Beth Din in 1948: a barometer of religious trends in Anglo-Jewry,' in *Jewish Historical Studies*, Vol. XXXIII (London: Jewish Historical Society of England, 1995), pp.249-262; the same writer's *The Reform Beth Din: The Formation and Development of the Rabbinical Court of the Reform Synagogues of Great Britain, 1935–1965*, PhD dissertation, University of Leicester, 1990; and Michael Curtis, 'The Beth Din of the Reform Synagogues of Great Britain,' in Dow Marmur (ed.), *Reform Judaism: Essays on Reform Judaism in Britain* (London: Reform Synagogues of Great Britain, 1973), pp.129-139. Adath marriage certification dates back to 1919 (Homa, op. cit., p.28), and its rival Beth Din to 1935, following Abramsky's appointment to the London Beth Din (*Jewish Chronicle*, 4 January, 1935, p.10). The Federation of Synagogues' Beth Din was established on 25 August, 1959 (Alderman, *The Federation of Synagogues, 1887–1987*, p.98), and that of the Liberals – its Rabbinic Conference – in April 1966. British Masorti's Beth Din is under the umbrella of the European Masorti Beth Din, affiliated to the Conservatives' Rabbinical Assembly.

[45] 'About the London Beth Din (Court of the Chief Rabbi),' United Synagogue website, 2010.

[46] David Philipson, *The Reform Movement in Judaism*, new edn. (New York: Macmillan, 1931), pp.353-358.

[47] Then denoting 'Orthodox.' On Solomon Schechter's use of the term, see chapter 12 below.

[48] Claude G. Montefiore, *Outlines of Liberal Judaism* (London: Macmillan, 1912), p.284. On equating the terms 'Conservative' and 'Orthodox' Judaism, see Montefiore's introduction to *Outlines*, p.8, and his Jewish Religious Union sermon, 'Religious Differences and Religious Agreements' (quoted in *Faith Against Reason*, pp.137-138).

[49] The first home of the Orthodox-orientated Jews' College, where in 1863 Joseph won the Judith Lady Montefiore award, 'the most valuable of all the scholarships within the gift of the College' (Albert M. Hyamson, *Jews' College London, 1855–1955*, London: Jews' College, 1955, pp.29-30). See also Isidore Harris, *Jews' College Jubilee Volume* (London: Luzac, 1906), pp.clxxxviii, cxciii.

[50] Morris Joseph, *Judaism as Creed and Life* (London: George Routledge and Sons, 1903), pp.33-34.

[51] On Joseph Hochman, see *Faith Against Reason*, chapter 9, and chapter 12 below in relation to his opposition to the Chief Rabbinate as an institution.

[52] For an unparalleled insight into Jacobs' early life and yeshivah training, see Elliot Joe Cosgrove, *Teyku: The Insoluble Contradictions in the Life and Thought of Louis Jacobs* (PhD dissertation, University of Chicago, 2008), pp.10-50. See also Cosgrove's memorial tributes to Jacobs delivered (23 July, 2006) following his death, and to mark his first *yahrzeit* (20 June, 2007).

[53] Louis Jacobs, *Helping With Inquiries: An Autobiography* (London: Vallentine Mitchell, 1989), pp.78, 80.

[54] An early manifestation of Jacobs' reformist tendencies appears in 'Organic Growth vs. Petrification' (*The Jewish Spectator*, Vol. XVII, No. 10, New York, November, 1952, pp.9-11), regarding an attempt by the Manchester Association of Rabbis and Ministers, headed by the Communal Rabbi, Dr Alexander Altmann, to implement changes in the liturgy and ritual, as a means of improving synagogue decorum. Responding to a protest by what he describes as 'a small but highly vociferous group calling itself "The Committee To Fight Reform," the members of which were well-known zealots in the Manchester community,' Jacobs (then 'Rov' – his terminology – of Manchester's Central Synagogue and a member of the Association) writes: 'This Manchester episode is symptomatic of two trends in Orthodoxy today. The point at issue is this: can there be change in Judaism, or does loyalty to Orthodoxy commit us to a petrification of our religious life? ... The way of the moderate traditionalist can never be without difficulties. But moderation and tolerance are needed today in the religious life of Jews as never before, and those who are prepared to tread the middle path and to face the vituperations of the extremists on either side are performing a notable service to the cause of Judaism.'

[55] Louis Jacobs, *We Have Reason to Believe* (London: Vallentine Mitchell, 1957), p.11.

[56] 'A Retrospect of the "Jacobs Affair,"' in ibid, fifth expanded edition (London and Portland OR: Vallentine Mitchell, 2004), pp.viii-ix.

[57] See *Faith Against Reason*, pp.302-317. The undercurrents of the Jacobs Affair are fully explored in Miri J. Freud-Kandel, *Orthodox Judaism in Britain Since 1913* (Vallentine Mitchell, 2006), pp.123-157; and Benjamin J. Elton, *Britain's Chief Rabbis and the Religious Character of Anglo-Jewry, 1880–1970* (Manchester University Press, 2010). A Conservative viewpoint is supplied by Sefton Temkin, 'A Crisis in Anglo-Jewry,' in *Conservative Judaism*, Vol. XVIII, No. 1, ed., Samuel H. Dresner (Rabbinical Assembly, New York, fall 1963), pp.18-34; an Orthodox perspective by Norman Cohen, 'The Religious Crisis in Anglo-Jewry,' in *Tradition*, Vol. 8, No. 2, ed., Walter S. Wurzburger (Rabbinical Council of America, New York, 1966), pp.40-57; and a Reform overview by Ignaz Maybaum, 'The Jacobs Affair,' in *Quest* 1, ed., Jonathan Stone (Paul Hamlyn, London, September 1965), pp.80-83. Jacobs provides detailed discussions in 'Reflections on a Controversy,' in *Quest* 1, pp.4-5; the Epilogue to *We Have Reason to Believe*, third edition (1965), pp.138-151; the 'Retrospect' to the fifth edition (2004), pp.viii-xvi; *Helping With Inquiries: An Autobiography* (Vallentine Mitchell, London, 1989), pp.134-222; and *Beyond Reasonable Doubt* (Littman Library of Jewish Civilization, London, 1999) pp.1-30. On the twenty-fifth anniversary of the Jews' College controversy, he examined 'its contemporary relevance and long-term repercussions' in 'For the Sake of Heaven' (*Jewish Chronicle*, 19 December, 1986, pp.22-23). A *Jewish Chronicle* insider's view is in William Frankel, *Tea With Einstein And Other Memories* (Halban, London, in association with the European Jewish Publication Society, 2006), pp.157-171.

[58] Isidore Epstein, *The Place of Halachah in Jewish Life and Thought*, Paris: Conference of European Rabbis, 1961; reproduced in Israel Brodie, *Statement by the Very Rev the Chief Rabbi, Dr Israel Brodie* (London: United Synagogue, 1964), p.6.

CHAPTER 3

[1] Jonathan Sacks, *A Decade of Jewish Renewal*, p.10.

[2] Published in 1995 by Jason Aronson, of Northvale, New Jersey, the book was the North American version of *Traditional Alternatives: Orthodoxy and the Future of the Jewish People*.

[3] Jonathan Sacks, *Arguments for the Sake of Heaven*, p.ix.

[4] Ibid, pp.206-207.

[5] Ibid, p.215.

[6] *Orthodoxy Confronts Modernity*, ed., Jonathan Sacks (Hoboken, NJ: Ktav, in association with Jews' College, 1991), p.8.

[7] Jonathan Sacks, 'On the Definition of a "Good Jew,"' in *L'Eylah*, Vol. I, No. 3, spring 5737–1977 (A. Melinek, chairman of editorial board, London: Office of the Chief Rabbi), pp.29-31. At the time of writing, Sacks was lecturer in philosophy and rabbinics at Jews' College.

[8] Jonathan Sacks, *Tradition in an Untraditional Age* (London: Vallentine Mitchell, 1990), p.133. The book is dedicated to Louis Mintz – 'tireless fighter for the cause of Jewish unity' – who was instrumental in the sale of the redundant St John's Wood (United) Synagogue building to Louis Jacobs' New London Synagogue in 1964 (see *Faith Against Reason*, chapter 16).

[9] Jonathan Sacks, *One People? Tradition, Modernity, and Jewish Unity* (London: Littman Library of Jewish Civilization, 1993), pp.117, 148, 151.

[10] Ibid, p.151.

[11] Ibid, pp.215-216.

[12] Ibid, p.217.

[13] Ibid, pp.222, 226-227.

[14] Stefan Reif, 'Dilemma of Dr Jonathan and Rabbi Sacks,' in the *Jewish Chronicle*, 30 April, 1993, p.15. Reif was director of the Taylor-Schechter Genizah Research Unit at Cambridge University Library.

[15] Ephraim Borowski, 'The Jewish People,' in *Le'ela*, No. 36, September 1993 (London: Office of the Chief Rabbi and Jews' College), pp.44-45. Borowski was head of the department of philosophy at Glasgow University, and honorary secretary of the Glasgow Jewish Representative Council.

[16] As described in a *Jewish Chronicle* leading article, 'Just Jews,' 2 October, 1987, p.24.

[17] Immanuel Jakobovits, *Preserving The Oneness Of The Jewish People: Orthodox–Progressive divisions and discussions on marriage, divorce and conversion – can a permanent schism be averted?* Lecture to the Jewish Marriage Council, Royal Society of Medicine, London, 14 December, 1987 (London: Office of the Chief Rabbi, 1988), p.13.

[18] Sidney Brichto, 'Halachah with Humility,' in the *Jewish Chronicle*, 2 October, 1987, p.29. On the background to this article, see *Faith Against Reason*, pp. 365-371, 377. Writing then in a personal capacity, as he did with his review of *One People?*, Brichto was executive vice-president and director of the Union of Liberal and Progressive Synagogues from 1964–89, and subsequently, until his death in 2009, senior vice-president.

[19] Sacks to Brichto, 4 March, 1990 (Brichto Papers, London).

[20] 'Sidney Brichto, 'The Need for Bridge-Building: Centrist Orthodoxy and Jewish Status,' in *Judaism Today*, No. 3, winter 1995–96 (London: Assembly of Masorti Synagogues), pp.13-14. The subject resurfaced in correspondence between Brichto and Jakobovits in 1997, when the Liberal leader drew the Emeritus Chief Rabbi's attention (25 April, 1997) to their exchange of views arising from the 'Halachah with Humility' proposals ten years earlier. 'While much water has flowed down the Thames since then,' Jakobovits replied (30 April, 1997), 'I think some of our deliberations, and perhaps even suggestions, are still as relevant now as they were then ... I know I was thinking at the time of the pre-war German model in which my father and [the Reform] Leo Baeck were rabbinical colleagues serving the same community, and in which all Beth Din matters were left to be administered by the Orthodox Beth Din serving the entire community. I know this model was certainly discussed between us ... I will now consider whether, and in what form, I could best use the experience of that period to promote some progress now.' Brichto commented (30 April, 1997): 'I appreciate the matter is so terribly complicated, but the attempt to resolve these issues would in itself reveal good will and a common purpose, two factors so sadly lacking among our present religious leadership.' Jakobovits responded (1 May, 1997): 'I still think the idea is worth pursuing, yet am not sure who are to be the *dramatis personae* in the next act.' Taking up this point, Brichto wrote (7 May, 1997): 'I would imagine that ultimately the key actors would need to be the active leaders of the religious communities, but I see no reason why some of us could not meet without the pressures of office, time and publicity to see what we could come up with. If between us we saw something remotely feasible, we could submit it to the community as a blue (discussion) paper for consideration.' Jakobovits expressed agreement (13 May, 1997), adding that 'the idea of some new understanding does bear further exploration. For my part, I shall keep my eyes and ears open for any opportunity to encourage the search' (Brichto Papers, London). Once again, 'the search' came to nothing: thirty months after these lines were written, Jakobovits died (31 October, 1999) and was buried in Jerusalem.

[21] Sidney Brichto, 'Liberal welcome for Sacks' "inclusivism,"' in the *Jewish Chronicle*, 7 May, 1993, p.15.

[22] Dow Marmur, 'How Sacks Shuts Us Out,' in *Manna*, No. 41, autumn 1993 (London: Sternberg Centre for Judaism and Manor House Society), pp.2-3.

[23] Reif, op. cit.

[24] Borowski, op. cit.

[25] Editorial, *L'Eylah*, No. 21, Pesach 5746–April 1986 (editor-in-chief, Jonathan Sacks, London: Office of the Chief Rabbi and Jews' College), p.2.

[26] *Jewish Chronicle*, 19 May, 1989, p.29.

[27] Ibid, 26 May, 1989, p.8.

[28] Jonathan Sacks, 'The Way Forward,' in ibid, 29 September, 1989, p.73.

[29] 'Sacks to stress unity,' interview with Bernard Josephs, in ibid, 2 March, 1990, p.6.

[30] 'Chief Rabbi Sacks: The Need For Change,' leading article, *Manna*, No. 33, autumn 1991, p.1.

[31] Stanley Kalms, *A Time for Change*, p.263. Emphasis as in *A Time for Renewal*, p.14.

[32] *A Time for Renewal*, pp.14-15. Sacks presented an early version of his vision for the United Synagogue in 'The Search for Ideology,' published in *L'Eylah*, Vol. 1, No. 9, spring 5740–1980 (pp.6-13), while he was minister of the Golders Green Synagogue. He followed this up with 'Ideology and Tolerance,' in *L'Eylah*, Vol. 2, No. 1, spring 5741–1981 (pp.19-28).

[33] Geoffrey Alderman, *Modern British Jewry*, new edition (Oxford: Clarendon Press, 1998), pp.392-393.

[34] 'Stage one' was Sacks' launch of his 'Women in the Jewish Community' initiative, on which see chapter 10 below.

[35] Sacks, *Studies in Renewal*: 1. *From Integration to Survival to Continuity*; 2. *The Crisis of Continuity*; 3. *The Secret of Jewish Continuity*; 4. *Rethinking Priorities*; 5. *From Jewish Continuity to Jewish Continuity* (London: Office of the Chief Rabbi, June–October 1993). The studies were subsequently reworked into Jonathan Sacks, *Will We Have Jewish Grandchildren?* (London: Vallentine Mitchell, 1994).

[36] *Studies in Renewal* 1, p.1.

[37] Ibid, pp.2-3. One 'squall' developed in 1992 over what Sacks described as 'the novel attempt to express community – the Walkabout' (*Studies in Renewal* 1, p.2), when the Jewish Lesbian and Gay Helpline was banned from participating in the event.

[38] *Studies in Renewal* 5, pp.3-4, 6-7.

[39] *Change in Continuity: Report of the Review into Jewish Continuity*, Leslie Wagner, chairman (London: Jewish Continuity, 1996), p.3.

[40] Ibid, p.4.

[41] *Jewish Chronicle*, 28 April, 1995, p.29.

[42] *Change in Continuity*, p.4.

[43] Ibid, p.58, quoting a Jewish Continuity press release of 25 May, 1994.

[44] Ibid, p.4.

[45] *Jewish Tribune*, 12 January, 1995, p.5.

[46] *Jewish Chronicle*, 20 January, 1995, p.20.

[47] *Change in Continuity*, p.15.

[48] See chapter 9 below.

[49] 'Step forward,' *Jewish Chronicle*, 14 April, 1995, p.26.

[50] 'The Future Must Embrace Us And Them,' leading article, *Manna*, No. 49, autumn 1995, p.1.

[51] Chief executive's report to Reform Movement board meeting, 22 January, 1996. Board Minutes, RSGB, November 1995–January 1997.

[52] Chief executive's report to Reform Movement board meeting, 18 March, 1996. Ibid.

[53] *Jewish Chronicle*, 21 June, 1996, p.8.

[54] *Change in Continuity*, p.i.

[55] The Spiro Ark, launched originally as the Spiro Institute by Nitza and Robin Spiro, 'uses innovative teaching methods in order to encourage a learning community.' It provides Hebrew and Yiddish courses, cultural activities, and international Jewish heritage tours.

[56] *Change in Continuity*, pp.32-38

[57] *Jewish Chronicle*, 21 June, 1996, p.1. Ratification of the merger followed five months later (ibid, 15 November, 1996, p.2).

[58] Ibid, 22 March, 1996, p.17.

[59] Ibid, 26 September, 1997, p.27.

[60] Ibid, 3 October, 1997, p.2.

[61] Ibid, 18 September, 1998, p.42.

CHAPTER 4

[1] Jonathan Sacks, *A Decade of Jewish Renewal*, p.11.

[2] Minutes of meeting of the Board of Deputies, London (item 7), 2 July, 1967, LMA/ACC/3121/A042.

[3] Chaim Bermant, Jakobovits' 'authorised' biographer, in the *Jewish Chronicle*, 31 December, 1993, p.19.

[4] Minutes of meeting of the Chief Rabbinate Council, London, 17 July, 1977, p.3.

[5] *Jewish Chronicle*, 30 September, 1983, p.1

[6] The issue of non-Orthodox conversions surfaced many years later, in the context of a High Court case – and subsequent appeals – over 'the propriety and legality of the criteria governing admission to the JFS school in London.' For a full discussion, see chapter 8 below.

[7] 'Louis Jacobs and the Beth Din,' letter from Judge Alan Lipfriend (chairman, New London Synagogue) and Anthony Tibber and Gerald Kirsh (joint chairmen, New North London Synagogue), *Jewish Chronicle*, 7 October, 1983, p.18.

[8] Letter from the Hon. Ewen E. S. Montagu, ibid. On Montagu's clash with the dayanim during the 1962 Jews' College crisis, see *Faith Against Reason*, pp.295-298; and for a contrasting account of Abramsky's involvement in the dispute, and in Jacobs' proposed ministry of Brondesbury Synagogue in 1949, see ibid, pp.287-288.

[9] Letter to the *Jewish Chronicle*, 7 October, 1983, p.18.

[10] Ibid, 14 October, 1983, p.1. For further background to the controversy, see *Faith Against Reason*, pp.337-339.

[11] *New North London Synagogue Magazine*, Rosh Hashanah issue, September 2009, p.8. Ivor Jacobs told this writer (27 September, 2009) that his account was based on conversations with his father.

[12] Sacks to the Board of Deputies, 11 January, 1994; Jakobovits to the president of the Board of Deputies, 24 September, 1981.

[13] *Jewish Chronicle*, 17 December, 1993, p.11.

[14] Ibid, 31 December, 1993, p.19.

[15] Letter from Jeremy Freedman, ibid, 7 January, 1994, p.16.

[16] Ibid, 31 December, 1993, p.19.

[17] Ibid, 14 January, 1994, p.20.

[18] Letter from C. Goldbaum, *Jewish Tribune*, 22 December, 1994, p.4

[19] *Jewish Chronicle*, 2 December, 1994, p.1.

[20] 'Rabbis strip mask from Masorti group,' *Jewish Tribune*, 22 December, 1994, p.1.

[21] *Jewish Chronicle*, 23 December, 1994, p.1.

[22] Letter from B. Seitler, *Jewish Tribune*, 22 December, 1994, p.4

[23] *Jewish Chronicle*, 6 January, 1995, p.9.

[24] Jacobs to Sacks, 23 February, 1994, LMA/ACC/2805/008/003/026/003.

[25] *Jewish Tribune*, 22 December, 1994, p.4

[26] *Statement on Masorti Marriages*, signed by Rabbi Dr Louis Jacobs, Rabbi Jonathan Wittenberg and Rabbi Chaim Weiner, London: Assembly of Masorti Synagogues, January 1995. The statement appeared in Masorti publications and as a paid advertisement in the national Jewish press. Later that year, the movement's approach to conversions was examined by Wittenberg in 'The Significance of Motivation in the Halachah of Conversion' (*Judaism Today*, No. 3, winter 1995-96, pp.19-23), of particular relevance to the JFS case discussed in chapter 8 below.

[27] Lind to Sacks, 21 June, 1996, LMA/ACC/2805/008/003/026/003.

[28] Sacks to Lind, 26 September, 1996, ibid.

[29] Lind to Sacks, 9 October, 1996, ibid.

[30] Laurie Rosenberg (executive director, Office of the Chief Rabbi) to Lind, 13 October, 1996, ibid.

[31] 'Family quarrels,' *Jewish Chronicle*, 16 December, 1994, p.22.

[32] Ibid, 13 January, 1995, p.1.

[33] As reported in the *Jewish Chronicle*, 13 January, 1995, p.1.

[34] Ibid, p.22.

[35] Simon Rocker, 'Chief Rabbi denounces Masorti as "dishonest and dangerous,"' ibid, p.1.

[36] Weeks earlier, in a letter to the *Jewish Tribune* referring to the United Synagogue's 1994 decision to admit women to its council and local boards of management (on which see chapter 10 below), Lichtenstein had written: 'I advised him [the Chief Rabbi] of my opinion that the halochoh forbade women to serve on the US council.' And a week before Sacks' article appeared, *Tribune* columnist Ben Yitzchok commented: 'I cannot recall a period when there has been so wide a gulf between the establishment Rabbinate on one side and a growing number of leading and distinguished Rabbonim on the other' (*Jewish Tribune*, 5 January, 1995, p.4).

[37] 'The Torah Challenge' (*Jewish Tribune*, 12 January, 1995, p.5), reprinted the following week in the *Jewish Chronicle* (20 January, 1995, p.26) under the heading 'The importance of being Orthodox.'

[38] On a contrasting view of Hertz, see chapter 13 below.

[39] Reluctant to refer to the *Jewish Chronicle* by name in the anti-JC Adath mouthpiece, Sacks was alluding to 'The Origin of Torah,' his review of Jacobs' *A Tree of Life* in the JC, 2 November, 1984, pp.24-25 (see chapter 1 above). In February 1995, days after Sacks' *Jewish Tribune* and *Jewish Chronicle* articles, Rabbi Yitzchok Schochet, minister of the Mill Hill (United) Synagogue, lectured to his congregation on 'Torah from Heaven,' provoking a lengthy commentary from Jacobs (based on a transcript provided by Schochet), in the introduction to which he wrote: 'I would not have thought it necessary to offer this response were it not that, so far as I can tell, Rabbi Schochet speaks for all his Orthodox colleagues, including, it would seem, the Chief Rabbi. I challenge the Chief Rabbi to state clearly and unambiguously that he believes Moses to have written every word of the Chumash at the dictation of God, and that he rejects totally all modern biblical scholarship, not only the Documentary Hypothesis' (*Masortimatters*, March 1995, pp.1-4, London: Assembly of Masorti Synagogues). Sacks' response appeared in *Le'Ela*, No. 40, September 1995 (London: Office of the Chief Rabbi and Jews' College), pp.10-15, in the form of extracts from his *Crisis and Covenant: Jewish Thought After the Holocaust* (Manchester: University Press, 1992), chapters 7 and 8.

[40] Statement from David Walsh (chairman) and Rabbi Tony Bayfield (chief executive), Reform Synagogues of Great Britain.

[41] An earlier debate on the Board of Deputies' ecclesiastical authorities is discussed in *Faith Against Reason*, pp.352-356, and in chapter 13 below.

[42] Statement from Eldred Tabachnik, president of the Board of Deputies.

[43] Statement from Dr Michael J. Sinclair, chairman of Jewish Continuity. All the comments appeared in the *Jewish Chronicle*, 20 January, 1995, p.26.

[44] Jonathan Wittenberg, 'More Questions than Answers,' ibid, p.27.

[45] Harry Freedman (development director, Association of Masorti Synagogues), *Masortimatters*, March 1995, pp.8-9.

[46] 'After the Storm,' leading article, *Jewish Chronicle*, 20 January, 1995, p.22.

[47] 'Politics of Contempt,' leading article, ibid, 13 January, 1995, p.22. The impact of Sacks' attack on public perceptions of the Chief Rabbbinate, and on the extent of its writ, is discussed by Geoffrey Alderman in 'The Chief Rabbinate: An Excursion into Myth-Making' (*Judaism Today*, No. 3, winter 1995–96, pp.36-41).

[48] 'Chief extends olive branch amid fury at Masorti attack,' *Jewish Chronicle*, 20 January, 1995, p.1.

[49] Sacks, 'Community and Conflict,' in ibid, pp.24-25.

[50] 'Whose Chief Rabbi? – Elena Lappin talks to Jonathan Sacks about politics and hope,' *The Jewish Quarterly*, Vol. 44, No. 2 (166), summer 1997, pp.6-7.

[51] The wording on non-Orthodox marriages in Annexe 1 of the 1998 Stanmore Accords, renewed in 2009 (see chapters 6 and 11 below) – 'Where a marriage could have been solemnised in an Orthodox synagogue but the parties marry under Reform, Liberal or Masorti auspices ...' – left the validity of such marriages open to question.

[52] London Family I to this writer, 22 December, 2009. Names supplied.

[53] London Family II to this writer, 8 December, 2009. Names supplied.

[54] Tony Sacker, chairperson, Rosita Rosenberg, director, Union of Liberal and Progressive Synagogues; Rabbi Marcia Plumb, acting chairperson, ULPS Rabbinic Conference, *Jewish Chronicle*, 27 January, 1995, p.22.

[55] Eldred Tabachnik, president, Board of Deputies; Sir Trevor Chinn, president, Joint Israel Appeal; Michael Levy, chairman, Jewish Care; Dr Michael Sinclair, chairman, Jewish Continuity; Lord Young, chairman, Central Council for Jewish Community Service, ibid.

[56] Ibid, 20 January, 1995, p.22.

[57] Leading article, ibid, 24 February, 1995, p.26.

[58] Ibid, p.60.

[59] Ibid, 3 March, 1995, p.68.

[60] 'Unity – We Can Grasp It,' leading article, *Manna*, No. 47, spring 1995, p.1.

[61] *Jewish Chronicle*, 7 April, 1995, p.17.

[62] Ibid, 31 March, 1995, p.64.

[63] Ibid, 7 April, 1995, p.32.

[64] 'Sacks softens line on "doubting" believers,' ibid, 24 March, 1995, p.1.

[65] Ibid, pp.33.

[66] Ibid, 31 March, 1995, p.28.

[67] 'The United Synagogue: Ignoring The Real Issues,' *Jewish Review*, Vol. 15, No. 4, September 1995, p.2.

[68] 'To Right The Wrongs,' *Jewish Tribune*, 26 October, 1995, p.4.

[69] 'The Future Must Embrace Us And Them,' leading article, *Manna*, No. 49, autumn 1995, p.3.

[70] *Jewish Chronicle*, 13 October, 1995, p.1.

[71] Ibid.

[72] 'Thought for the Day,' BBC Radio 4, 19 September, 2007.

[73] Jonathan Sacks, *Letters to the Next Generation* (London: Office of the Chief Rabbi, 2009), pp.25, 5.

CHAPTER 5

[1] Jonathan Sacks, *A Decade of Jewish Renewal*, p.13.

[2] *The Independent*, 20 August, 1996.

[3] Gerald Jacobs, 'Who'd want to be Chief Rabbi?', *New Statesman*, 27 June, 1997, p.35.

[4] *Jewish Chronicle*, 23 August, 1996, p.1.

[5] Ibid, 30 August, 1996, p.22.

[6] Jackie Tabick, 'Rabbi Hugo Gryn,' *hesped* (eulogy) delivered at the Golders Green Cemetery, Hoop Lane, London, 21 August, 1996.

[7] *Jewish Chronicle*, 30 August, 1996, p.1.

[8] Ibid, 23 August, 1996, p.14.

[9] Ibid, 30 August, 1996, p.1.

[10] Ibid. On the Consultative Committee, and on similar reactions involving it, see chapters 6 and 11 below.

[11] *Jewish Chronicle*, 6 September, 1996, p.36.

[12] The Chief Rabbi adopted such an arrangement when attending the funeral of Linda Bayfield, wife of Tony Bayfield, at Reform's Hoop Lane cemetery in 2003. He was also present at Louis Jacobs' funeral at Cheshunt cemetery in 2006. The *Jewish Chronicle* noted in its obituary of Linda Bayfield (1 August, 2003, p.17): 'She and her husband ... maintained a personal relationship with Chief Rabbi Dr Jonathan Sacks and Elaine Sacks over many years, the Chief Rabbi and Rabbi Bayfield having been at Cambridge at the same time.' See *A History in our Time: Rabbis and Teachers Buried at Hoop Lane Cemetery*, compiled by Jon Epstein and David Jacobs (London: Leo Baeck College, 2006), p.9 (Linda Bayfield), p.15 (Hugo Gryn). Among others buried at Hoop Lane were Leo Baeck and Morris Joseph.

[13] Friedlander to Sacks, 22 August, 1996, LMA/ACC/2805/008/003/026/003.

[14] Sacks to Friedlander, 2 September, 1996, ibid.

[15] LMA/ACC/2805/008/003/026/003.

[16] Chief executive's report to the Reform Movement board meeting, 9 September, 1996. Board Minutes, Reform Synagogues of Great Britain, November 1995–January 1997.

[17] *Jewish Chronicle*, 30 August, 1996, p.1.

[18] Chief executive's report to the Reform Movement board meeting, 20 November, 1996. Board Minutes, Reform Synagogues of Great Britain, November 1995–January 1997.

[19] Ibid.

[20] Jackie Tabick, Kol Nidre sermon, West London Synagogue of British Jews, 22 September, 1996.

[21] 'Anglo-Jewry Demands Honesty,' leading article, *Manna*, No. 55, spring 1997, p.1.

[22] *Jewish Chronicle*, 17 January, 1997, p.1.

[23] *Jewish Tribune* columnist Ben Yitzchok, 16 January, 1997, p.4.

[24] Ruth Gledhill, 'Orthodox Jews urge Sacks to boycott memorial for Gryn,' *The Times*, 18 January, 1997.

[25] 'A Brother's Hand: The Chief Rabbi is right to attend the Gryn memorial,' ibid.

[26] *Jewish Chronicle*, 24 January, 1997, p.13.

[27] Ibid, 31 January, 1997, p.1.

[28] Padwa to Sacks, erev Rosh Chodesh Shevat 5757 [8 January, 1997], from the Office of the Rabbinate of the Union of Orthodox Hebrew Congregations, 140 Stamford Hill, London N16. The letter was addressed to 'His Honour, Rabbi Jonathan Sacks, *shlita* [may he live long and happily, amen!], Chief Rabbi.'

[29] Office of the Rabbinate of the UOHC, 23 January, 1997, LMA/ACC/2805/008/011/005/003.

[30] United Synagogue, 29 January, 1997, ibid.

[31] Chief Rabbi Dr Jonathan Sacks, *If This Is A Man*, address at the Board of Deputies-sponsored memorial meeting for Rabbi Hugo Gryn, Congress House, London, 20 February, 1997, LMA/ACC/2805/008/003/026/002.

[32] *Jewish Chronicle*, 28 February, 1997, p.13; 14 March, 1997, p.6.

[33] Chief Rabbi Jonathan Henry Sacks (Plaintiff) and (1) The Jewish Chronicle Newspaper Limited; (2) Edward Temko (Defendants), Order for an Injunction. Case No.: 1997 S. No. 226, in the High Court of Justice, Queen's Bench Division, before Mr Justice Astill, Wednesday, 12 February, 1997.

[34] This writer participated in the all-night meeting of JC staff and lawyers on 10-11 February, 1997.

[35] Dovid Stern, *Jewish Tribune*, 20 March, 1997, p.1.

[36] Memorandum from Charles Corman (Titmuss Sainer Dechert) to Chief Rabbi Jonathan Sacks, 4 March, 1997, LMA/ACC/2805/008/003/026/002.

[37] Matthew Norman, *The Guardian*, 4 March, 1997.

[38] *Evening Standard*, 4 March, 1997.

[39] The Chief Rabbi's article appeared contemporaneously with the abridged letter in the JC of 14 March, 1997.

[40] Draft terms of settlement, Corman to Sacks, 24 February, 1997, LMA/ACC/2805/008/003/026/002. The final version of the settlement was dated 28 February, 1997, and was communicated by Corman to Temko and to Maddie Mogford, of Crockers – the *Jewish Chronicle's* solicitors – on 3 March, 1997.

[41] *Jewish Chronicle*, 14 March, 1997, p.6. The 'three brief passages of a personal nature' – in fact there were more – explained the Chief Rabbi's absence from the funeral and the memorial service and related to his opposition to affording any form of recognition to the Reform movement ('that fraudulent sect'), or to 'Mr' Hugo Gryn's role in it (describing him as *oso ho'ish*, 'that man') – passages that were clearly 'central to the letter's contents.' At one point in the letter, excluded from the published text, Sacks wrote that 'all the pressure – and it was great – was on me to go to the funeral and the memorial service. And to that I said, absolutely no.' On further background to the cuts, see Geoffrey Alderman, 'That Letter: Rabbinical Politics and Jewish Management,' in *Judaism Today*, No. 8 (winter 1997–98), pp.40-43; and the same writer's 'When a kindness becomes a betrayal,' in the *Times Higher Education Supplement*, 14 February, 1997.

[42] *Jewish Chronicle*, 14 March, 1997, pp.2, 3.

[43] 'A need to lead,' ibid, pp.1, 32.

[44] Proverbs 27:5-6.

[45] Sacks adds, in his unexpurgated letter, 'but rather – on the contrary – opposition to it.' In the event, as his memorial address indicated, he referred to 'our religious differences' rather than to 'opposition.'

[46] Translation as agreed between the parties and as published in the JC, 14 March, 1997, pp.2, 6. Several versions of the translation were prepared and considered (LMA/ACC/2805/008/003/026/002).

[47] *Jewish Chronicle*, 14 March, 1997, p.3.

[48] Letter from Neville Sassienie (chairman, RSGB), Rabbi Tony Bayfield (chief executive), Rabbi Daniel Smith (chairman, RSGB Assembly of Rabbis), 12 March, 1997 (Reform Judaism Archives).

[49] Of the leak, Alderman writes: 'By January 1997, the Union of Orthodox Hebrew Congregations

placed little trust in Dr Sacks. He professed one set of beliefs, but seemed to practise something quite different. The Union Rabbinate was at the end of its tether. Its public statement of 23 January condemned Dr Sacks' decision to attend the memorial meeting for Rabbi Gryn, a decision it publicly branded as a *chillul Hashem*. Yet even at this stage, some within the Union were prepared to give Dr Sacks the benefit of the doubt: after all, he had assured the Union Rabbinate, in writing, that he would use his presence at the meeting to demonstrate his opposition to the Reform movement. Only after the meeting, at which he had delivered a speech very different from that which he had led the Union Rabbinate to expect, was the decision taken to leak his four-page letter. Although written to Dayan Padwa, the letter was in fact a response to one that the Dayan had written on behalf of the entire Union Rabbinate. Contrary to the impression given by Dr Sacks in his response published in the JC on 14 March, it was in no sense "sent to the Dayan for his eyes only," a personal letter from one rabbi to another. The identity of the person who faxed the letter to the JC is known to this writer – and beyond. It was leaked, from within the world of the Union of Orthodox Hebrew Congregations, quite simply to teach Dr Sacks a lesson he would never forget' (Geoffrey Alderman, 'That Letter,' in op. cit., p.41).

[50] The name was misspelt as 'Calman' in the paper.

[51] Ian Burrell, 'Leaked letter widens schism in Jewry,' *The Independent*, 15 March, 1997.

[52] 'To Unite The Jews,' leading article, *The Times*, 15 March, 1997.

[53] 14 March, 1997, LMA/ACC/2805/008/011/005/003.

[54] Statement from the Reform Synagogues of Great Britain, signed by Sassienie, Bayfield and Smith, 14 March, 1997 (Reform Judaism Archives).

[55] Deborah Leipziger, Jewish Telegraphic Agency, 21 March, 1997.

[56] Eldred Tabachnik, QC, statement to the Board of Deputies of British Jews, Newcastle Civic Centre, 16 March, 1997.

[57] Ismar Schorsch, 'Chancellor's Parashah Commentary,' 5 April, 1997, New York: Jewish Theological Seminary of America, Department of Community Development. The language used by Schorsch in his denunciation is a good deal stronger than that conveyed in these brief extracts. Subsequently chancellor emeritus of the JTS and Rabbi Herman Abramovitz Professor of Jewish History, Schorsch retired as chancellor in 2006, having served in the post for twenty years.

[58] Letter from Chief Rabbi Dr Jonathan Sacks, Office of the Chief Rabbi, 14 March, 1997, embargoed until Shabbat, 15 March, LMA/ACC/2805/008/011/005/002.

[59] 'Questions & Answers,' Office of the Chief Rabbi, ibid.

[60] On the presence of Chief Rabbi Hermann Adler and his dayanim at the funeral and West London memorial service of the Rev David Woolf Marks, see *Faith Against Reason*, pp.138-139; and of Chief Rabbi Joseph Herman Hertz, Haham Moses Gaster, the Federation of Synagogues' chief minister, Rabbi Moshe Avigdor Chaikin, and the dayanim of the London Beth Din at the funeral and West London memorial service of the cremated Rev Morris Joseph, ibid, p.113.

[61] 'Whose Chief Rabbi? – Elena Lappin talks to Jonathan Sacks about politics and hope,' in *The Jewish Quarterly*, summer 1997, p.10. The interview (pp.5-11) took place, at Sacks' St John's Wood residence, in March 1997, days after the publication of his letter to Padwa. In her introduction, Lappin wrote: 'The Chief Rabbi's Office asked me twice to submit a list of questions prior to the interview, and twice I refused. Rabbi Jonathan Sacks is, understandably, a bit nervous about speaking to the Jewish press ... The Chief Rabbi, when he enters the room, is smart-looking, cautiously friendly, and – very nervous, at least in the beginning. After listening to my explanation as to why I wouldn't "give away" my questions – I want us to have a natural conversation, not a stilted exchange – Rabbi Sacks answers everything, even those questions he describes as "offensive"' (ibid, p.5).

[62] Maureen Lipman Rosenthal, 'The posthumous trial of Hugo Gryn,' letter to the *Jewish Chronicle*, 28 March, 1997, p.31.

[63] Geoffrey D. Paul, 'How the Chief can patch up his umbrella,' in ibid, p.29.

[64] Ibid, 21 March, 1997, p.1.

[65] Ibid.

[66] Ibid, 14 March, 1997, p.3.

[67] Ibid, 21 March, 1997, p.1.

[68] Statement by the president of the United Synagogue and chairman of the Rabbinical Council of the US, 14 March, 1997, LMA/ACC/2805/008/003/026/002.

[69] *Jewish Chronicle*, 'A need to lead,' 14 March, 1997, p.32.

[70] 'The Politics of Hope?', leading article, *Judaism Today*, No. 7, spring 1997, pp.2-3.

[71] 'Anglo-Jewry Demands Honesty,' op. cit.

[72] *Jewish Chronicle*, 18 September, 2009, New Year Supplement, p.5.

[73] Hugo Gryn with Naomi Gryn, *Chasing Shadows: Memories of a Vanished World*, London: Viking, 2000.

[74] Aloma Halter, 'Out of the Shadows,' *Jerusalem Post Magazine*, 13 April, 2001, pp.11, 13.

[75] 'The moral maze of life and death,' *Daily Telegraph*, 11 March, 2000.

[76] Naomi Gryn, 'Days of Awe,' *The Jewish Quarterly*, spring 2003, p.13.

[77] Halter, 'Out of the Shadows,' pp.10-13.

[78] Jonathan Sacks, *Celebrating Life: Finding Happiness in Unexpected Places*, London: Fount, 2000.

[79] 'Staying sane in troubled times,' ibid, p.3.

[80] Ruth Gledhill, 'Foreword,' ibid, pp.xi-xii.

[81] 'Good Morning Sunday,' BBC Radio 2, 2 September, 2001.

[82] Sacks provides a further insight into coping with difficulties in the opening section of *Covenant & Conversation: Genesis – The Book of Beginnings* (Jerusalem: Maggid Books and the Orthodox Union, 2009): 'Time and again, in the midst of troubled times or facing difficult decisions, I've found the words of the weekly *parashah* giving me guidance – or conversely, the events themselves granting me deeper insight into the Torah text. For that is what "Torah" means: teaching, instruction, guidance ... One of the things that gives us the courage and wisdom to chart our way through the wilderness of life is knowing that we are not alone, that God goes before us in a pillar of cloud and fire, signalling the way. The way He does so for us is through the words of the Torah, to which every Jewish life is a commentary, and each of us has our own annotation to write' (pp.2-3). Writing in 2009, in the context of the weekly portion of *Vayeshev*, the Chief Rabbi cautioned: 'Only do those things by which you would not be embarrassed if they were published on the front page of tomorrow's newspaper' (Chief Rabbi Lord Sacks, 'Standards in Public Life,' *Daf Hashavua*, Vol. 22, No. 9, 12 December, 2009 [London: United Synagogue], p.3). The quotation appears as one of the epigraphs at the opening of this book.

[83] 'Faith: the undiscovered country,' *Celebrating Life*, p.191.

CHAPTER 6

[1] Jonathan Sacks, *A Decade of Jewish Renewal*, pp.10-11.

[2] *Jewish Chronicle*, 21 March, 1997, p.1.

[3] 'Need for tolerance,' ibid, p.28.

[4] *See Faith Against Reason*, chapter 19. Participating in the *Jewish Chronicle* symposium which included Naomi Gryn's recollection of the Padwa-letter episode (chapter 5 above), Rabbi Jeffrey Cohen said of the Consultative Committee: 'In Lord Jakobovits' time, the committee met at his home every three months. It contained representatives of the Orthodox community and the Reform and the Liberals, the Sephardim and the Board of Deputies. And this is a measure of Lord Jakobovits: the chairman of the Consultative Committee was always one of the Progressive, Liberal or Reform rabbis. Rabbi Hugo Gryn occupied the chairmanship for many years' (*Jewish Chronicle*, 18 September, 2009, New Year Supplement, p.5). On Jeffrey Cohen, Limmud, and the conversions issue, see chapter 9 below.

[5] *Jewish Chronicle*, 16 May, 1997, p.1.

[6] Lawrence Rigal and Rosita Rosenberg, *Liberal Judaism: The First Hundred Years*, London: Liberal Judaism, 2004, pp.170, 175.

[7] Paragraph 13.3, Reform Movement Board report to the RSGB Council, 15 December, 1996, Board Minutes, Reform Synagogues of Great Britain, November 1995–January 1997.

[8] *Jewish Chronicle*, 28 March, 1997, p.30.

[9] Ibid.

[10] Ibid, 21 March, 1997, p.29.

[11] AMB [Tony Bayfield], *Preliminary Thoughts on the Present Crisis*, 18 March, 1997 (Reform Judaism Archives).

[12] Freedman to Bayfield, 20 March, 1997 (Jacobs Papers, London).

[13] Bayfield to Middleburgh, 18 March, 1997 (Reform Judaism Archives).

[14] Bayfield to Peter Levy, 19 March, 1997 (ibid).

[15] Bayfield to Harry Freedman, 24 March, 1997 (ibid).

[16] Bayfield in conversation with this writer, 23 July, 2008.

[17] 'Lionel Swift, son of the late Rabbi Harris Swift, is a barrister who has been a Queen's Counsel since 1975 and a Recorder of the Crown Court since 1979. Among his various appointments, he served as a Junior Counsellor to the Treasury in Probate Matters and has published a book on Criminal Procedure' – bibliographical note introducing Swift's 'The Chief Rabbi: An Appreciation,' in *Tradition and Transition: Essays Presented to Chief Rabbi Sir Immanuel Jakobovits to Celebrate Twenty Years in Office*, ed., Jonathan Sacks (London: Jews' College Publications, 1986), p.vii. On Harris Swift (then minister of London's Western Synagogue) and his brother, Dayan Morris Swift, see *Faith Against Reason*, p.280.

[18] *Jewish Chronicle*, 16 May, 1997, p.1

[19] Bayfield to Swift, 1 April, 1997 (Reform Judaism Archives).

[20] Ibid.

[21] Bayfield to Sassienie and David Walsh, 24 March, 1997 (ibid).

[22] Tony Bayfield, 'Fundamentalism and Reform Judaism in the 1990s,' Manchester Festival of Reform Judaism, 22 June, 1997 (ibid).

[23] Neville Sassienie, Jeromé Freedman, Ivor Jacobs and Alex Sklan to Elkan Levy, 12 May, 1997 (ibid).

[24] United Synagogue chief executive Jonathan Lew to Bayfield, 19 May, 1997 (Jacobs Papers, London).

[25] Sassienie, Freedman, Jacobs and Sklan to Tabachnik, 2 May, 1997 (Reform Judaism Archives).

[26] *RSGB/ULPS/Masorti–US Meeting: An Aide Memoir*, London, May 1997 (Jacobs Papers, London).

[27] 'Notes of a meeting of the RSGB/ULPS/Masorti Group,' 13 June, 1997 (ibid).

[28] For an expansion of this issue, see Interlude below.

[29] 'Notes of a meeting of the "Preparatory Group,"' 7 July, 1997 (Jacobs Papers, London).

[30] Harry Freedman to Alex Sklan and Ivor Jacobs, 8 July, 1997 (ibid).

[31] Jacobs, Sklan and Freedman 'to all members of the ULPS/RSGB/AMS Group,' 13 July, 1997; copy to Lionel Swift (ibid).

[32] Described by the Liberal participants as 'frustrating approaches to the United Synagogue.' Rigal and Rosenberg, op. cit., p.175.

[33] Memorandum from Alex Sklan, 29 July, 1998 (Jacobs Papers, London).

[34] John Rayner to Sidney Brichto, 16 June, 1998 (Brichto Papers, London).

[35] The accords were signed at Levy's home, additionally by Sassienie (Reform), Jeromé Freedman (ULPS), and Sklan and Paul Shrank (AMS).

[36] *Jewish Chronicle*, 13 November, 1998, p.1.

[37] Ibid.

[38] Ibid, 6 November, 1998, p.1.

[39] 'Brave, Bright Future,' leading article, *Manna*, No. 62, winter 1999, p.1.

[40] *Jewish Chronicle*, 20 November, 1998, p.2.

[41] Ibid, 13 November, 1998, p.1.

[42] Ibid, p.30.

[43] Ibid, 20 November, 1998, p.20.

INTERLUDE

[1] Jonathan Sacks, *A Decade of Jewish Renewal*, p.13.

[2] Extracted from Jonathan Sacks, *From Renewal to Responsibility* (London: Office of the Chief Rabbi, 2001), pp.i, 3-31.

[3] 'Silver lining,' leading article, *Jewish Chronicle*, 2 February, 1996, p.26.

[4] 'Chief Rabbi's Role in Anglo-Jewry,' ibid, 2 February, 1996, pp.26-27; 9 February, 1996, p.24.

[5] On a later use of this phrase, arousing further conflict within the community, see chapter 9 below.

[6] On women's issues, see chapter 10 below.

[7] Communal activist Fred Worms was the chairman of *Securing our Future: An Inquiry into Jewish Education in the United Kingdom* (London: Jewish Educational Development Trust, 1992), initiated by Sacks (see chapter 9 below).

[8] Author, historian and Holocaust scholar Dr Ronnie S. Landau was education director of the Spiro Institute for the Study of Jewish History and Culture.

[9] On Limmud, and the controversy surrounding it, see chapter 9 below.

[10] *Jewish Chronicle*, 2 February, 1996, p.26.

[11] Chaim Bermant, 'Sacking Sacks will give bigots bigger say,' ibid, p.27.

[12] Stanley Kalms, 'On the Right Track: The Chief Rabbi's First Ten Years,' ibid, 31 August, 2001, pp.28-29. In an editorial on the article, and on Sacks' record, the JC wrote: 'His first ten years have been marked by major successes. He, more than anyone, helped put "Jewish continuity" – learning, outreach, investment in youth programmes – high on the Anglo-Jewish agenda ... There were, of course, failures as well – his handling of relations with non-Orthodox leaders and synagogal movements, for instance, and of the role of women in religious and communal life – where his rhetoric of inclusivity and change raised expectations, and his actions dashed them. Perhaps unsurprisingly, Rabbi Sacks enters his second decade apparently reluctant to tackle these most difficult of communal challenges ... As a Jewish voice in modern Britain's national conversation, he has few peers. It is a role in which he clearly revels. Sir Stanley Kalms – an early supporter, later critic, and now a renewed admirer of Rabbi Sacks – rightly suggested that this wider ministry is one in which the community can and should take enormous pride. He was equally right to suggest that key inconsistencies of Rabbi Sacks' first decade in office – the more difficult business of defining the meaning of inclusiveness, tolerance and "modern Orthodoxy" within the Jewish community – are yet to be clarified and resolved' ('Sacks' Second Decade,' ibid, 7 September, 2001, p.34).

[13] Ibid, 'Chief Rabbinical Change,' 2 November, 2001, p.28.

[14] Clifford Longley, *Daily Telegraph*, 12 February, 1999.

[15] Letter from Neville Sassienie (chairman, RSGB), Jeromé Freedman (chairman, ULPS), Ivor Jacobs and Alex Sklan (joint chairmen, AMS) to the Bishop of Oxford, 12 May, 1997 (Jacobs Papers, London).

[16] *Jewish Chronicle*, 12 February, 1999, p.68.

[17] This situation now prevails, with three further Jewish presidents – Sephardi, Masorti and Liberal – added in February 2009. At the time of writing, the following presidents were in office: The Most Rev and Rt Hon Rowan Williams, Archbishop of Canterbury; Lord Sacks; Rt Rev Cormac Murphy O'Connor, Cardinal Archbishop of Westminster; Rabbi Dr Abraham Levy, Spanish and Portuguese Sephardi Congregations; Rt Rev Gregorios, Archbishop of Thyateira and Great Britain; Rabbi Dr Tony Bayfield, head of the Movement for Reform Judaism; Commissioner Elizabeth Matear, Moderator of the Free Church Group; Rabbi Danny Rich, chief executive of Liberal Judaism; Rt Rev David Lunan, Moderator of the General Assembly of the Church of Scotland; Rabbi Jonathan Wittenberg, senior rabbi of the Assembly of Masorti Synagogues.

[18] *Jewish Chronicle*, 19 February, 1999, p.68.

[19] Ibid.

[20] Ibid, 2 November, 2001, p.68.

[21] Ibid, p.28.

[22] *Daily Telegraph*, 12 February, 1999.

CHAPTER 7

[1] Jonathan Sacks, *A Decade of Jewish Renewal*, p.8.
[2] Chaim Bermant, 'Wrong time, place, words and audience,' *Jewish Chronicle*, 20 January, 1995, p.23.
[3] Ibid, 13 January, 1995, p.22.
[4] Ibid, 20 January, 1995, p.22.
[5] Jonathan Sacks, *Faith in the Future*, London: Darton, Longman and Todd, 1995.
[6] Ibid, p.vii.
[7] Ibid, pp.x-xi.
[8] 'Is Faith Enough?', *Jewish Chronicle*, 10 March, 1995, p.27.
[9] Leading article, ibid, p.24.
[10] Jonathan Sacks, *The Politics of Hope*, London: Jonathan Cape, 1997 (hardback); London: Vintage, 2000 (paperback).
[11] 'Whose Chief Rabbi? – Elena Lappin talks to Jonathan Sacks about politics and hope,' in *The Jewish Quarterly*, Vol. 44, No. 2 (166), summer 1997, p.6. Supporting this view, Masorti asserted: 'British Jews have problems relating to a spiritual head who is a man of ideas. Despite the hype in *The Times*, his book, *The Politics of Hope*, has set forth an incisive historical analysis of why society has plunged into the chaotic mess it now finds itself. Not everyone will agree with everything he writes, but the fact that a Jew basing himself on Jewish sources has the ability to present such a blueprint to British society is remarkable in itself ... One repeated criticism is that he has been Chief Rabbi to the goyim and not to the Jews. Indeed, in his book he comes over as the quintessential Englishman, a fact welcomed by a multi-cultural British establishment and *The Times*. Yet the obverse is that a parochial Jewish community has never welcomed intellectuals, and those who have the insight to utilise the Torah as their base for universal redemption even more so' ('The Politics of Hope?', leading article, *Judaism Today*, No. 7, spring 1997, ed., Colin Shindler, London: Assembly of Masorti Synagogues, p.3).
[12] Gordon Brown, foreword to *The Politics of Hope*, pp.ix, xii, August 2000. Brown became Prime Minister in 2007, some two years before the Chief Rabbi took his seat as a peer, on 27 October, 2009, assuming the title Baron Sacks, of Aldgate in the City of London, with the sponsorship of Baron Winston of Hammersmith (Professor Robert Winston) and the former Archbishop of Canterbury, Baron Carey of Clifton.
[13] Sub-titled *How to Avoid the Clash of Civilizations* (London and New York: Continuum, first edition, 2002).
[14] Publisher's jacket description of the book's theme.
[15] 'Enlarged by diversity,' *Jewish Chronicle*, 6 September, 2002, New Year Section, pp.vi, viii, ix, x.
[16] Ibid, 27 September 2002, p.1; 4 October, 2002, p.2.
[17] Edited transcript of sermon delivered at the Whitefield Hebrew Congregation, Shemini Atseret 5763 (28 September, 2002).
[18] *Jewish Chronicle*, paid advertisement, 18 October, 2002, p.8.
[19] Ibid, paid advertisement, 25 October, 2002, p.4.
[20] 'Here I must make an autobiographical admission. I am not a liberal Jew. My faith is orthodox. I am used to being called, by my liberal colleagues, a fundamentalist, and it is precisely here that contemporary challenge is most acute. The revivals in most of the world's faiths in recent decades have been at the conservative rather than liberal end of the spectrum. The power of conservative religious movements has been precisely the fact that they represent protests against, rather than accommodations to, late modernity ... It is religion not so much in its modern but in its counter-modern guise that has won adherents in today's world, and it is here that the struggle for tolerance, co-existence and non-violence must be fought' (*The Dignity of Difference*, p.18).
[21] London: Office of the Chief Rabbi, October 2002; quoted in the *Jewish Chronicle*, 25 October, 2002, p.35.

[22] Ibid, 8 November, 2002, p.1.

[23] Ibid, 1 November, 2002, p.3.

[24] Ibid.

[25] Chambers Global (Guide to the World's Leading Lawyers), ed., Edward Shum, London: Chambers & Partners, 2009. Alan Sacks (b. London, 1956) is the third of the four brothers.

[26] Jewish Chronicle, 15 November, 2002, p.28.

[27] Irving Jacobs (b. London, 1938) was dean of Jews' College from 1984–90 and principal until his retirement in 1993, having taught Bible, Midrash and Jewish liturgy for many years. He was the first incumbent of the Sir Israel Brodie Chair in Bible Studies.

[28] Jewish Chronicle, 1 November, 2002, p.30.

[29] At the time of these comments, Conway (b. London, 1947) was head of the School of Philosophy and Religious Studies at Middlesex Polytechnic (later University). He subsequently became professor, and then emeritus professor, before moving to Roehampton University as a senior research fellow in theology and religious studies.

[30] Jewish Chronicle, 30 August, 1991, p.17.

[31] 'Unity – We Can Grasp It,' leading article, Manna, No. 47, spring 1995, p.1.

[32] 'Mainstream Judaism, Not Fundamentalist Judaism,' leading article, Manna, No. 101, autumn 2008, p.1.

[33] A rabbinical graduate of Leo Baeck College, London (1980), and a qualified psychoanalytic psychotherapist, Cooper pursued a dual career, combining rabbinic work with a therapy practice and an increasing involvement in written projects. He served as director of education at the Finchley Reform Synagogue from 1982–86 and joined its first rabbinic team in 1989.

[34] Jewish Chronicle, 8 November, 2002, p.32.

[35] Williams, then holding the posts of Archbishop of Wales and Bishop of Monmouth, reviewed the book for the Jewish Chronicle (20 September, 2002, p.30). For a Catholic perspective, see Fred Dallmayr, 'The Dignity of Difference: A Salute to Jonathan Sacks,' in Millennium: Journal of International Studies (London School of Economics), Vol. 33, No. 2, March 2004, pp.397-405; reprinted in Dallmayr, Small Wonder: Global Power And Its Discontents (Rowman & Littlefield, 2005), pp. 209-217.

[36] Leading article, The Guardian, 19 November, 2002.

[37] Referring to this aspect of the interview, the Daily Telegraph's religion correspondent, Jonathan Petre, wrote (28 August, 2002): 'Dr Sacks is used to diplomatic minefields. Since becoming Chief Rabbi eleven years ago, he has had the unenviable task of trying to heal the rifts of a Jewish community deeply split between Liberal and Orthodox wings. Regarded as a figure of impressive intellect and moral authority who can speak to both Jews and non-Jews – his contributions to national debate have won him a wide range of admirers – he has often had to walk a diplomatic tightrope to keep the peace within his own fractious constituency. His latest comments on the Middle East, though hardly earth-shattering, are certain to fuel distrust among ultra-Orthodox Jews, many of whom are suspicious of his secular education. Almost as controversial with some will be his decision to make his views known in The Guardian, a newspaper regarded as hopelessly anti-Israeli in the Jewish community. His views will be welcomed, however, by liberal Jews, who have been disappointed by his reluctance to follow the lead of his predecessor, the late Lord Jakobovits, who angered many on the Right with his criticism of Israeli policy. Dr Sacks, 54, is one of a handful of spiritual leaders who are as well known outside their religious communities as within them, and he has become a media favourite. He has written widely on issues from consumerism to the family, and his admirers include Tony Blair and Gordon Brown, who provided the foreword to one of his major works, The Politics of Hope ... His latest comments on the Middle East will provoke a mere ripple in comparison [with the Gryn episode], but the controversy demonstrates once again what a delicate path he has to tread.'

[38] The Guardian, 27 August, 2002.

[39] 'Sacks and Salvation: England's Chief Rabbi claims that Jews don't hold the monopoly on truth,' Jewish Week, New York, 27 September, 2002.

[40] Continuum advertisement, Jewish Chronicle Literary Supplement, 21 February, 2003, p.vii.

[41] Jonathan Sacks, The Dignity of Difference (London and New York: Continuum, revised edition, 2003), p.vii.

[42] Among the 'redrafted' passages are the following ('O' relates to the first [original] edition, 2002; 'R' to the revised edition, 2003) – O: 'Here I have not hesitated to be radical and I have deliberately chosen to express that radicalism in religious terms' [p.17]; R: 'Here I have not hesitated to return to the very sources of Western monotheism to ask what God wants of us' [p.17]; O: 'Judaism, Christianity and Islam are religions of revelation – faiths in which God speaks and we attempt to listen' [p.19]; R: Deleted. O: 'The glory of the created world is its astonishing multiplicity: the thousands of different languages ... the hundreds of faiths, the proliferation of cultures ... in most of which ... we will hear the voice of God' [p.21]; R: 'The glory of the created world is its astonishing multiplicity: the thousands of different languages ... the proliferation of cultures ... in most of which ... we will hear the voice of wisdom' [pp.20-21]; O: 'God has created many cultures, civilisations, and faiths, but only one world' [p.23]; R: 'There are many cultures, civilisations and faiths, but God has given us only one world ...' [p.23]; O: 'Judaism is a particularist monotheism. It believes in one God but not in one religion, one culture, one truth. *The God of Abraham is the God of all mankind, but the faith of Abraham is not the faith of all mankind*' [pp.52-53]; R: 'Judaism ... believes in one God but not in one exclusive path to salvation. *The God of the Israelites is the God of all mankind, but the demands made of the Israelites are not asked of all mankind*' [p.52]; O: 'The radical transcendence of God in the Hebrew Bible means nothing more or less than that *there is a difference between God and religion*. God is universal, religions are particular ... In the course of history, God has spoken to mankind in many languages: through Judaism to Jews, Christianity to Christians, Islam to Moslems' [p.55]; R: 'The radical transcendence of God in the Hebrew Bible means that the Infinite lies beyond our finite understanding ... As Jews we believe that God has made a covenant with a singular people, but that does not exclude the possibility of other peoples, cultures and faiths finding their own relationship with God within the shared frame of the Noahide laws' [p.55]; O: '... no one creed has a monopoly on spiritual truth ...' [p.62]; R: Deleted; O: 'In heaven there is truth; on earth there are truths. Therefore, each culture has something to contribute' [p.64-65]; R: 'Each culture has something to contribute to the totality of human wisdom' [p.64]; O: 'The way I have discovered ... is that the truth at the beating heart of monotheism is that God is greater than religion; that He is only partially comprehended by any faith. He is my God, but also your God. He is on my side, but also on your side. He exists not only in my faith, but also in yours' [p.65]; R: 'The way I have discovered ... is that the truth at the beating heart of monotheism is that God transcends the particularities of culture and the limits of human understanding. He is my God, but also the God of all mankind, even of those whose customs and way of life are unlike mine' [p.65].

[43] Ruben occupied the post of director of Jews' College (renamed the London School of Jewish Studies) from 2000–02. He then became director of New York University in London, and Professor of Philosophy at Birkbeck College, University of London.

[44] *Jewish Chronicle*, 28 February, 2003, p.31.

[45] Tony Bayfield, 'Faith in a Time of Uncertainty: Or, Un-certainty is the way forward for the faiths.' Cardiff Adult Education Centre, City Church, Cardiff, 29 October, 2009, pp.1-7.

[46] In the subsequent publication of this lecture, Sacks noted that, following the book's first appearance, 'I put all the sources in a 100-page footnote to this highly controversial paragraph in *The Dignity of Difference* on our website (http://www.chiefrabbi.org/).'

[47] New York, Carnegie Council for Ethics in International Affairs, 1 May, 2003. Founded by Andrew Carnegie in 1914, the Council 'is an independent, non-profit, educational institution serving international-affairs professionals, teachers and students, and the attentive public. As a non-partisan organisation, it does not have a legislative or policy agenda. Since its inception, it has focused on the enduring importance of ethical values in international relations. Then, as now, it aspires to be a worldwide "voice for ethics," providing a home for discussions that go beyond the political efficacy and economic efficiency of policies to issues of right and wrong, discussions which might not otherwise take place. The Council takes a pluralistic approach to ethics.'

[48] *Jewish Chronicle*, 25 October, 2002, p.32. Addressing the Oxford Union in March 2010, Sacks admitted publicly for the first time that he would have had to resign had he not amended *The Dignity of Difference* (ibid, 19 March, 2010, p.8).

CHAPTER 8

[1] Jonathan Sacks, *A Decade of Jewish Renewal*, p.11.

[2] Gerry Black, J.F.S.: *The History of the Jews' Free School, London, Since 1732*, (London: Tymsder Publishing, 1998), pp.1, 34-35, 38-39, 80-83, 214-215. See also Mr Justice Munby's judgment referred to in note 14 below.

[3] Jaclyn Chernett to members of the Masorti Assembly of Synagogues executive, 18 February, 1986 (Jacobs Papers, London).

[4] 'Statement by the JFS Comprehensive School' (ibid).

[5] Jaclyn Chernett to Jo Wagerman, 25 February, 1986 (ibid). Attached to Chernett's letters was a document to parents of potential pupils, headed 'Transfer of pupils from primary to secondary school,' requesting that they bring 'a copy of your ketubah [to the interview] as proof that the candidate for admission is Jewish.'

[6] Chernett to the London Board of Jewish Religious Education, 5 March, 1986 (ibid).

[7] Nathan Rubin to Chernett, 3 April, 1986 (ibid).

[8] Wagerman to 'Parents,' 'date as postmark' (ibid).

[9] 'A wedding of more than usual communal and rabbinic interest will take place at the New London Synagogue on November 14 [1967]. The bridal couple are Mr Ivor Jacobs, [eldest] son of Dr and Mrs Louis Jacobs, and Tirza, [younger] daughter of Rabbi and Mrs Alexander Carlebach, formerly of Belfast, now of Jerusalem ... The young couple have known each other for many years. They first met when they were both attending Jewish Youth Study Groups' (*Jewish Chronicle*, 20 October, 1967, p.9; see also ibid, 2 September, 1966, p.10, and 24 November, 1967, p.9).

[10] Jacobs to Wagerman, 17 March, 1986 (Jacobs Papers, London).

[11] Wagerman to Jacobs, 19 March, 1986 (ibid).

[12] Jacobs to Jakobovits, 27 March, 1986 (ibid).

[13] Shimon D. Cohen to Jacobs, 2 April, 1986, and 18 March, 1986 (ibid).

[14] R [E] v the Governing Body of JFS and the Admissions Panel of JFS, case no. CO/7896/2007; R [E] v Office of the Schools Adjudicator, case no. CO/11587/2007, Royal Courts of Justice, before Mr Justice Munby, 4-7 March 2008; judgment handed down 3 July 2008. London: Royal Courts of Justice, 2008. Crown Copyright ©, reproduced by permission.

[15] The case of Family S is outlined in ibid, paragraphs 47-55. As in the case of Family L, it featured a woman (Miss B as she was then) who was converted in Israel, on 21 June, 1990, and married Mr S, in Israel, in October 1990. In November 1994, the parents applied for their son to be admitted to the JFS and were told that 'the conversion of the mother ... is not recognised by the London Beth Din.' The parents appealed, but the Beth Din continued to question the validity of the conversion.

[16] Ibid, paragraph 60. Subsequent numbering in these notes refers to paragraphs in the official transcript.

[17] Ibid, 34, 35.

[18] Ibid, 1, 2.

[19] Ibid, 78, 79.

[20] Ibid, 31.

[21] Ibid, 18.

[22] Ibid, 22.

[23] Ibid, 23.

[24] Ibid, 24.

[25] Ibid, 20, 21.

[26] Ibid, 26, 27.

[27] Ibid, 92.

[28] Ibid, 101.

[29] *Jewish Chronicle*, 4 July, 2008, p.1.

[30] Ibid, 18 July, 2008, p.4.

[31] Ibid, 27 February, 2009, p.3.

[32] Ibid, 3 July, 2009, p.1.

[33] England and Wales Court of Appeal (Civil Division) Decisions: Neutral Citation Number [2009] EWCA Civ 626. Case No.1 C1/2008/2187 and No.2 C1/2008/2188, London, 12-14 May, 2009. Judgment handed down 25 June, 2009. Crown Copyright ©, reproduced by permission.

[34] Ibid, paragraphs 3, 4. Subsequent numbering in these notes refers to paragraphs in the official transcript.

[35] Ibid, 5.

[36] R [E] v the Governing Body of JFS and the Admissions Panel of JFS, case no. CO/7896/2007, 167-168.

[37] England and Wales Court of Appeal (Civil Division) Decisions, 21-23.

[38] Ibid, 29, 31.

[39] Ibid, 32, 33, 39.

[40] Formulation contained in the Race Relations Act 1976, 'introduced ... in order to give effect to the Equal Treatment Directive 2000/43/EC' [ibid, 40].

[41] Ibid, 43-46.

[42] Ibid, 48, 49.

[43] The 'interested parties,' apart from Mr and Mrs L, were the Secretary of State for Children, Families and Schools, the London Borough of Brent, and (in one of the two cases) the Office of the Schools Adjudicator. Mr L was present in person but made no submissions; the others did not attend and were not represented.

[44] R [E] v the Governing Body of JFS and the Admissions Panel of JFS, case no. CO/7896/2007, 36-46.

[45] *Jewish Chronicle*, 3 July, 2009, p.3

[46] 'A Statement from the Chief Rabbi, Sir Jonathan Sacks,' 25 June, 2009, London: Office of the Chief Rabbi.

[47] *Jewish Chronicle*, 3 July, 2009, p.2.

[48] 'JFS aims to develop thoughtful, respectful, responsible and caring young citizens who have a strong sense of identity with Judaism and Israel' (*The JC Guide to Schools*, Vol. 1, 2010, pp.36-37).

[49] *Jewish Chronicle*, 7 August, 2009, p.27.

[50] Ibid, 3 July, 2009, p.4.

[51] *Evening Standard*, 25 June, 2009.

[52] *Jewish Chronicle*, 3 July, 2009, p.2.

[53] Ibid, 17 July, 2009, p.2.

[54] Ibid, 7 August, 2009, p.1.

[55] Ibid, 4 September, 2009, p.1.

[56] Ibid, 11 September, 2009, p.38.

[57] *Jewish Tribune*, 20 August, 2009, p.14

[58] Ibid, 10 September, 2009, p.14.

[59] *Jewish Chronicle*, 11 September, 2009, p.39.

[60] Reporting that, with 300 first-year places available, the JFS was 'heavily over-subscribed' for 2009–10, the JC noted: 'Jewish primary-school heads have voiced dismay that their pupils are not being given priority at JFS' (ibid, 2 October, 2009, p.9). In a leading article, the paper commented: 'Parents who send their sons and daughters to Jewish primary schools have every reason to expect that it is not a one-way commitment. Yet children who attended United Synagogue schools have been forced to continue their education at secular comprehensives after being denied places at JFS and other Jewish secondary schools. In the event, the opening of a cross-communal secondary school, JCoSS, in Barnet in 2010 should create sufficient places to ensure against repetition of the problem. But that will be scant consolation for those who feel that the system has failed them so miserably this year' ('Failed by schools,' ibid, p.28).

[61] 'JFS in entry U-turn: Child of non-Orthodox convert admitted,' ibid, 11 September, 2009, p.1.

[62] Ibid, p.39.

[63] Judgment [2009] UKSC1, p.4, para.4 (London: The Supreme Court), 2009. On appeal from: [2009] EWCA Civ. 626, [2009] EWCA Civ. 681. R (on the application of E) (respondent) v Governing Body of JFS and the Admissions Appeal Panel of JFS (Appellants) and others; R (on the application of E) (respondent) v Governing Body of JFS and the Admissions Appeal Panel of JFS (United Synagogue) and others (appellants). Before Lord Hope of Craighead (Deputy President), Baroness Hale of Richmond, Lord Brown of Eaton-under-Heywood. Heard on 1 October, 2009; judgment delivered 14 October, 2009. Crown Copyright ©, reproduced by permission.

[64] Referred to in chapter 4 above.

[65] Geoffrey Alderman, 'JFS is inclusive – exclusively so,' *Jewish Chronicle*, 6 November, 2009, p.33.

[66] R (on the application of E) (Respondent) v Governing Body of JFS and the Admissions Appeal Panel of JFS (Appellants) and others; R (on the application of E) (Respondent) v Governing Body of JFS and the Admissions Appeal Panel of JFS and others (United Synagogue) (Appellants), before Lord Phillips, President, Lord Hope, Deputy President, Lord Rodger, Lord Walker, Lady Hale, Lord Brown, Lord Mance, Lord Kerr, Lord Clarke. Heard on 27–29 October, 2009; judgment given on 16 December, 2009. The Supreme Court, London, Michaelmas Term [2009] UKSC 15; on appeal from [2009] EWCA Civ 626. Crown Copyright ©, reproduced by permission.

[67] Ibid, paragraph 2. Subsequent numbering in these notes refers to paragraphs in the official transcript.

[68] Ibid, 4.

[69] Ibid, 5.

[70] Ibid, 8.

[71] See Leslie Wagner, 'Yet another defect in UK law,' *Jerusalem Post*, 17 December, 2009, p.16.

[72] R (on the application of E), Supreme Court, London, 9.

[73] Ibid, 9, 54, 124, 156.

[74] Ibid, 66, 67.

[75] Ibid, 112.

[76] Ibid, 121, 122.

[77] Ibid, 35, 92, 113, 119, 120.

[78] Ibid, 225-228.

[79] Ibid, 233.

[80] Ibid, 50.

[81] Ibid, 217.

[82] The 'vindication' to which the Chief Rabbi referred was summarised by Lord Kerr in the following passage: 'One can have sympathy with the school authorities in their wish to pursue what must have seemed to them an entirely legitimate religious objective. It is plain that the Chief Rabbi and the governors of JFS are entirely free from any moral blame. That they have fallen foul of the 1976 Act does not involve any reprehensible conduct on their part, for it is accepted on all sides that they acted on sincerely and conscientiously held beliefs. Their motives are unimpeachable. The breach of the legislation arises because of the breadth of its reach. The grounds on which the rejection of M was made may well be considered perfectly reasonable in the religious context, but it is because they amount to ethnic grounds under the legislation that a finding against the school became, in my opinion, inescapable' (ibid, 124).

[83] 'Statement from the Chief Rabbi Lord Sacks on Supreme Court judgment,' Office of the Chief Rabbi, 16 December, 2009.

[84] On JCoSS, see chapter 9 below.

[85] Lord Sacks, 'We will find the legislative remedy to this verdict,' Office of the Chief Rabbi, 17 December, 2009.

[86] 'Convert challenge to Chief after JFS: Liberal, Masorti, Reform demand denominational parity with Orthodox,' *Jewish Chronicle*, 25 December, 2009, p.1.

[87] 'JFS fight collapses as Board retreats,' ibid, 8 January, 2010, pp.1, 4.

[88] Ibid, 15 January, 2010, p.30. The two rabbis' declaration immediately sparked further dissension within the Council as senior ministers dug in their heels against concessions to the non-Orthodox.

Writing to their lay leaders, Schochet and thirteen of his colleagues said that they were 'troubled' by the position adopted by Brawer and Harris, and that the original statement reflected the 'overwhelming majority of the US rabbinate.' The signatories included four past chairmen of the Council – Yisroel Fine, Mordechai Ginsbury, Ephraim Mirvis and Meir Salasnik – and nine other executive members (ibid, 22 January, 2010, p.8).

[89] Ibid, 8 January, 2010, p.4.

[90] '"E" versus JFS,' leading article, *Jerusalem Post*, 18 December, 2009, p.13.

[91] Daniella Peled, 'Anglo-Jewry defeats itself,' *Haaretz* (English edition), 25 December, 2009, p.B4.

[92] 'Unintended law,' leading article, *Jewish Chronicle*, 18 December, 2009, p.36. 'Had the Board of Deputies pursued a change in equality legislation without consensus,' commented the paper's leader-writer three weeks later, 'we would doubtless have been treated to painful scenes in the House of Lords, with Jewish peers from across the religious map confronting each other, and the community thrown into near-schism. But it is too early to say that this affair is over. United Synagogue rabbis are furious at what they see as a "surrender" to the Supreme Court judgment, and may well not accept that the law should stay as it is now. Many others in the community are uncomfortable with a court wading into Jewish identity. And we still do not know the full implications of the ruling. The JFS saga has a long way to run' ('JFS affair not over,' ibid, 8 January, 2010, p.32). *Guardian* journalist Jonathan Freedland, writing in the same issue of the JC, added: 'There are victims of this fiasco: the children denied a Jewish education, the good causes deprived of cash diverted into legal bills, and the good name of British Jewry itself. And there are culprits. Some want to blame the Supreme Court justices, but that is a delusion. Those who led our community into this dead end have to admit their own responsibility. Among them are the governors of JFS, the United Synagogue, the Office of the Chief Rabbi, and the Chief Rabbi himself. Not one of them called a halt to this madness, when it was utterly obvious to anyone who cared to look that it was going to end in disaster … If such a monumental error of judgment happened in any other area, the demand for accountability would be swift and ruthless. If a government minister or a corporate chief executive were guilty of an equivalent failure – one that incurred a massive loss of cash and reputation and was equally avoidable – he would surely pay with his job. Yet for some reason no one says this in our community. We act as if our misfortunes fall out of the sky, nothing to do with us, and as if our leaders were protected by divine mandate, so that even to question them constituted an act of heresy. But they are all too human – and they must be held to account' ('JFS: Why are no heads rolling?', ibid, p.33).

CHAPTER 9

[1] Jonathan Sacks, *A Decade of Jewish Renewal*, p.11.

[2] *Yoreh Deah*, chapter 268.

[3] *Jewish Chronicle*, 18 September, 2009, p.6; New Year Supplement, pp.2-5.

[4] *Securing our Future: An Inquiry into Jewish Education in the United Kingdom* (Fred Worms, chairman; London: Jewish Educational Development Trust, 1992), p.iii-iv.

[5] Ibid, pp.i-ii.

[6] Ibid, p.1.

[7] On the evolution of the JEDT, see Yaacov Lehman, *Let My People Know: Proposals for the Development of Jewish Education*, London: Office of the Chief Rabbi, 5732–1971.

[8] *Securing our Future*, pp.43-44.

[9] Rona Hart, *Jewish Continuity: The Demographic Crisis and Jewish Renewal Efforts* (paper presented at a conference in honour of Professor Na'ama Sabar Ben-Yehoshua, Tel Aviv, December 2007), pp.8-9. Reprinted in Ben-Yehoshua, *Jewish Education: A Global Perspective*, Tel Aviv: School of Education, Tel Aviv University, 2010.

[10] The campaign attracted considerable adverse publicity, as typified by these comments from Dr Richard Marran, of London (*Jewish Chronicle*, 20 January, 1995, p.23): 'Chief Rabbi Jonathan Sacks

admits that Jewish Continuity – his creation – is concerned only with educational programmes, built on strictly Orthodox principles. This is not, however, how Jewish Continuity has been representing itself since its inception. Indeed, it has spent large sums of donors' money suggesting that it is genuinely interested in pluralism, indulging in crass PR sloganising and manipulating unsophisticated imagery in order to impress the uninformed and to scare the unwary. It all seems predicated on the assumption that British Jewry is unintelligent and gullible. Any community-wide funding body which, while suggesting cross-denominationalism, keeps its real agenda pretty well hidden – and tries to create a monopoly for itself – deserves to be well and truly shunned. What is desperately needed is an educational initiative which is prepared seriously to come to terms with the reality of Jewish diversity, and is manifestly independent of a Chief Rabbinate that presides, counter-productively, over the most reactionary Jewish community in the world.' A number of Continuity-related letters along similar lines, in response to Sacks' attack on Masorti (see chapter 4), appeared alongside Marran's remarks, including one from Rabbi David Soetendorp, chairman of the Reform Synagogues' Assembly of Rabbis.

[11] Schools inspection aimed at 'contributing to the community's spiritual, moral, mental and physical development by securing primary and secondary education' (Section 13, Education Act 1996), and 'ensuring that functions relating to the provision of education are exercised with a view to promoting high standards' (Section 13a). Ofsted – Office for Standards in Education.

[12] Judy Keiner, 'Opening up Jewish Education to Inspection: the Impact of the Ofsted Inspection System in England,' in *Education Policy Analysis Archives*, Vol. 4, No. 5, 25 March, 1996, College of Education, Arizona State University.

[13] Keiner cites minutes of a meeting of the Association of Governors of Orthodox Jewish Schools, 23 January, 1994 (notes of presentation by Syma Weinberg, of Jewish Continuity).

[14] Keiner writes in a footnote: 'Presentation by Mr Laurie Rosenberg, director of education of the Board of Deputies, 24 April, 1994, meeting of the Association of Governors of Orthodox Jewish Schools.'

[15] Inspections under Section 9 of the Education Act 1992. Initially, through Section 9, and then Section 10 of the School Inspections Act 1996, primary, secondary and special schools were inspected in a four-yearly and subsequently six-yearly cycle. These periods have since been varied further.

[16] Leo Baeck College Partners in Leadership (£23,000), and the Centre for Jewish Education (£5,184).

[17] *Change in Continuity*, pp. 89-92.

[18] Clore Shalom School prospectus, 2009–10.

[19] Pikuach inspection carried out under Section 48 of the Education Act 2005, 13–14 December, 2006.

[20] Clore Tikva School prospectus, 2009–10.

[21] Ofsted inspection carried out under Section 5 of the Education Act 2005, 19–20 June, 2007.

[22] 'As a modern Orthodox school, [Yavneh's] aim is to produce young people who are proud of their Jewish heritage, confident in their religious practice, and equipped with the academic qualifications and wider key skills necessary for success in today's employment market' (*The JC Guide to Schools*, Vol. 1, 2010, p.37).

[23] 'Our ethos,' JCoSS website, August 2009.

[24] *The Future of Jewish Schools: The Commission on Jewish Schools* (chairman, Leslie Wagner), London: Jewish Leadership Council, 2008, p.6.

[25] Ibid, p.19. Commenting on his Commission's report in an interview with the *Jewish Chronicle* (18 July, 2008, p.6), Wagner noted: 'We haven't gone into the issue of halachic and non-halachic Jews.'

[26] Quoted in Nathan Jeffay, 'A lesson in history,' in *The JC Guide to Schools*, Vol. 1, 2010, p.8

[27] Ibid.

[28] 'The Independent Jewish Day School prepares pupils to live as modern Orthodox Zionist Jews, participating in every aspect of modern life and drawing direction from a thorough understanding of Jewish principles and practice' (ibid, p.40)

[29] 'King Solomon High is a modern Orthodox school which teaches Torah values, community and

tzedakah [charity], has Israel at its heart, and is a special community in which to be educated' (ibid, p.37).

[30] Quoted in James Martin, 'Carry on teaching,' in ibid, p.10.

[31] 'JCoSS News,' No. 2, summer 2009, supplement to the *Jewish Chronicle*, 15 May, 2009, p.3. Brought up in a United Synagogue household, Grabiner joined Finchley Reform Synagogue in 1987 and was treasurer of the Reform movement from 2002–05 and chair from 2005–08. His other posts included the vice-chairmanship of the World Union for Progressive Judaism and membership of the Jewish Community Day Schools advisory board.

[32] Aged 35 when appointed, Leeds-born Stowe-Lindner was deputy head teacher and religious-education master at Swakeleys Secondary School, Hillingdon. A member of both Hendon (United) Synagogue and North Western Reform Synagogue, he says: 'Half my family are frum and the other half are anglicised, so I was brought up as a mix of the two. You can't get more JCoSS than that' (*Jewish Chronicle*, 11 September, 2009, p.C3).

[33] 'JCoSS News,' No. 2, p.4; *Jewish Chronicle*, 11 September, 2009, p.C3; ibid, 18 September, 2009, p.C3.

[34] The notional launch of the Chief Rabbinical stakes came during the 5770 (2009) High Holy-day period: 'While the Chief Rabbi prepares to don his ermine next month, speculation is growing over who is likely to succeed him as mainstream Orthodoxy's spiritual supremo. The soon-to-be Lord Sacks of Aldgate is due to retire in three and a half years, on reaching 65. But whereas he was tipped for the top job long before he was chosen, seasoned rabbi-watchers are finding it hard this time to name a frontrunner. Home-based pulpiteers that could be in the frame are Rabbis Naftali Brawer, of Borehamwood, and Harvey Belovski, of Golders Green, while Mill Hill's media-savvy Rabbi Yitzchok Schochet may have his backers. Another potential candidate is former Barnet Synagogue minister Shaul Robinson, who landed a prime post at one of New York's best-known congregations, Lincoln Square, four years ago. Also being talked about is Rabbi Yaakov Kermaier, who did a tour of duty in Hong Kong, which, as a former Commonwealth colony, falls within the province of the Chief Rabbinate. He now leads New York's Fifth Avenue Synagogue [served by Jakobovits from January 1959 to April 1967].' Simon Rocker, 'The Chief Rabbi's Successor,' *Jewish Chronicle*, 25 September, 2009, p.35.

[35] Ibid, 15 May, 2009, p.C1.

[36] Ibid, 25 June, 2009, p.29.

[37] In the run-up to its September 2010 opening, the JCoSS admissions criteria were as follows: 'If the school is oversubscribed, JCoSS's proposed admissions policy will give priority (in the order shown) to: (i) children who would benefit from use of the Special Resource Provision, or who have other special needs which would benefit from attending JCoSS; ii) Jewish children who would not be eligible (in the first instance) for admission to any other Jewish secondary school; (iii) children who have a sibling at the school; (iv) children attending existing inclusive Jewish primary schools. In the event of a further tie-break being needed, this is likely to be based on distance from the school. This admissions policy will be reviewed regularly by the Governors once JCoSS opens to ensure that it is working fairly in practice' (JCoSS website, August 2009).

[38] In a light-hearted reference to Sacks and Limmud, JC columnist and comment editor Miriam Shaviv wrote (*Jewish Chronicle*, 1 August, 2008, p.25): 'Chief Rabbi Jonathan Sacks: "Hashem [God], protect my family and me – especially my son-in-law who is involved with Limmud. Forgive me my sins, and get the Beth Din off my back – and off my books. Make the Jews love me as much as the goyim [Gentiles] do. And by Jews I mean the Orthodox, of course."' Shaviv was mimicking Barack Obama's plea to God deposited in Jerusalem's Western (Wailing) Wall and subsequently removed (by a yeshivah student, who later apologised) and published in the Israeli daily, *Maariv* (25 July, 2008, p.1). Written on the letterhead of the King David Hotel, where he was staying, Obama's note read: 'Lord – protect my family and me. Forgive me my sins, and help me guard against pride and despair. Give me the wisdom to do what is right and just. And make me an instrument of your will.'

[39] *Jewish Chronicle*, 15 January, 1988, p.10.

[40] Ibid, 8 December, 1995, p.1.

[41] Ibid, 29 December, 1995, p.40.

[42] Ibid, p.18.

[43] 'The Limmud Controversy,' sermon delivered at the Stanmore Synagogue, London, 19 January, 1996, in Jeffrey M. Cohen, *Issues of the Day* (London: Genesia Publications, 1999), pp.158-162.

CHAPTER 10

[1] Jonathan Sacks, *A Decade of Jewish Renewal*, p.12.

[2] On women's attachment to synagogue life in the nineteenth century, see Michael Clark, *Albion and Jerusalem: The Anglo-Jewish Community in the Post-Emancipation Era, 1858–1887* (Oxford: University Press, 2009), pp.201-203. Todd M. Endelman writes of this period: 'The wives and daughters of communal magnates appear to have been more concerned [than their husbands] with spiritual matters – a dramatic reversal of traditional gender roles within Jewish family life, and a clear indication of the impact of Protestant habits on Anglo-Judaism' ('Communal Solidarity Among the Jewish Elite of Victorian London,' in *Victorian Studies*, 28:3, Indiana: University Press, spring 1985, p.501).

[3] On Cyril Harris (1936–2005) – subsequently Chief Rabbi of South Africa – The Times wrote (19 September, 2005): 'After training at Jews' College, Harris served suburban congregations in the London area, in Kenton and Edgware, before moving to the prestige pulpit of St John's Wood in 1979. For five years, from 1966 to 1971, he also served as senior Jewish chaplain to HM Forces. For three years, Harris swapped canonicals for jeans and sweater as a full-time student chaplain. Everywhere he attracted attention by his handsome profile and his charismatic, and at times fiery, preaching style. He drew less favourable notice when his short fuse exploded into a major public row with the popular Reform rabbi, Hugo Gryn, in a Radio 4 broadcast. The two men began to trade insults, with Harris held to have been the more offensive. He dismissed Gryn as having little Jewish religious knowledge and accused most of his non-Orthodox colleagues of "not knowing an aleph from a swastika." The national storm that followed had blown itself out by the time Chief Rabbi Lord Jakobovits announced his impending retirement in 1990. Harris, by now in Johannesburg, was considered papable, and his name was put forward for the succession to Jakobovits in competition with that of Rabbi Jonathan Sacks. However, Sacks appeared to be the preferred candidate, and Harris withdrew his name before the final decision was announced. Given the unique chance to make history that awaited him in South Africa, that move proved providential.'

[4] 'In addition to their capacity as bearers of children, women are frequently their nurturers,' writes Kim Knott in 'Women and Religion in Post-War Britain' (in *The Growth of Religious Diversity: Britain From 1945*, Vol. II – Issues, ed., Gerald Parsons, London: Routledge, in association with the Open University, 1994, pp.204-206). 'In relation to the continuity of religious traditions, there is hardly a more important role ... This has special meaning in Judaism, where a child's identity as a Jew is determined by his or her mother's Jewishness ... In Islam and Judaism, the major religious responsibilities occur within the family group and are located in the domestic sphere.'

[5] For a fuller account of the early campaign, see Meir Persoff, *Immanuel Jakobovits: a Prophet in Israel* (Vallentine Mitchell: London and Portland OR, 2002), pp.227-232, from which these introductory paragraphs are adapted.

[6] Lord Jakobovits, 'The Tortuous Path to Relief for *Agunot*,' Jewish Chronicle, 26 July, 1996, p.21.

[7] Immanuel Jakobovits, *Dear Chief Rabbi* (ed., Jeffrey M. Cohen, Hoboken, NJ: Ktav, 1995), pp.84-85.

[8] Knott writes (op. cit., pp.206, 216-217): 'In Orthodox synagogues, women do not have ritual responsibilities. Orthodox Judaism does not allow women to become rabbis; it operates with the idea that, in Judaism, women are equal but different. Their authority lies in a different sphere to that of men – the home – and in the synagogue they are of secondary importance. The rabbi, cantor and those who make up the minyan are all men, and this seems unlikely to change. However, women in the Reform, Liberal and Progressive traditions have been training for the rabbinate at Leo Baeck College since the mid-1970s. By 1989, ten women had been ordained. Julia [now Lady] Neuberger,

a British female rabbi, supported her Anglican sisters with the following statement made in an article in *The Times* (8 March, 1987): "Let it be understood that women will no longer be silent. We wish to minister alongside men, to the needs of Jews and Christians irrespective of sex. In the nonconformist churches, it has happened for years. In Progressive Judaism, we have been around for fifteen years. The earth has not opened up, nor the heavens caved in. Our congregations have not diminished, nor have those in our care perished."'

[9] *Dear Chief Rabbi*, pp.87-88.

[10] Jonathan Sacks, 'The Role of Women in Judaism,' in *Man, Woman, and Priesthood*, ed., Peter Moore (London: SPCK, 1978), pp.27-44.

[11] Rosalind Preston OBE (b. 1935) is described in the *Jewish Year Book* as a 'professional volunteer,' a trustee of the Jewish Volunteering Network, former vice-president of the Board of Deputies, and active in several communal, inter-faith and Zionist organisations.

[12] Jonathan Sacks, 'Casting Off Mediocrity: Women in the Decade of Jewish Renewal,' *Jewish Chronicle*, 6 March, 1992, p.17.

[13] Judy Goodkin and Judith Citron, *Women in the Jewish Community: Review and Recommendations* (London: Office of the Chief Rabbi, 1994), pp.32-34.

[14] In the autumn of 1989, the synagogue secretary of Cambridge University Jewish Society sought Jakobovits' advice on the feasibility of organising a women's prayer group, and added: 'It has been suggested to me that, with regard to the use of a Sefer Torah, there could be a problem relating to the *halochos* of *niddah* (laws of impurity). Is there any truth in this? Are there any problems with using a Sefer Torah?' Jakobovits replied, *inter alia*: 'In principle, there is no objection to women organising a prayer group on the lines described in your letter … On the question of women using a Sefer Torah, the consideration you mention can be disregarded. But since the usual Torah blessings cannot be recited, they might as well use a Chumash for Torah readings' (*Dear Chief Rabbi*, pp.90-91).

[15] 'Private Concerns: Chief Rabbi Dr Jonathan Sacks sets out his rulings on the question of women-only services and the principle of collective, public worship,' *Jewish Chronicle*, 12 February, 1993, p.13.

[16] As note 14 suggests, this assertion was somewhat disingenuous.

[17] 'Politics and halachah,' leading article, *Jewish Chronicle*, 18 February, 1994, p.18.

[18] On the attitude of Stanmore's Rabbi Jeffrey Cohen to women's tefillah groups, see chapter 11 below.

[19] *Jewish Chronicle*, 11 February, 1994, p.1; 18 February, 1994, p.1.

[20] 'Worshippers shrug off controversy over decision to ignore Chief Rabbi's ban,' ibid, 18 March, 1994, pp.1, 12.

[21] Rosalind Preston, 'Foreword,' in *Women in the Jewish Community: Review and Recommendations*, pp.i, iii.

[22] Andrew Brown, 'Orthodox Feminists Awake,' *The Independent*, 30 June, 1994.

[23] *Women in the Jewish Community: Review and Recommendations*, p.1.

[24] The findings of a postal survey of 1,350 British Jewish women are discussed in Marlena Schmool and Stephen Miller, *Women in the Jewish Community: Survey Report* (London: Office of the Chief Rabbi, 1994), pp.i-xix, 1-144, plus three appendices spanning a further seventy pages.

[25] *Women in the Jewish Community: Review and Recommendations*, pp.106-107.

[26] See Simon Rocker's interview with Sacks, 'New role for women in United Synagogue' (*Jewish Chronicle*, 4 February, 1994, p.18), and leading article, 'The battle goes on' (ibid, 11 February, 1994, p.18).

[27] *Women in the Jewish Community: Review and Recommendations*, pp.R1-R13.

[28] Ibid, pp.93-95.

[29] *Jewish Chronicle*, 1 July, 1994, p.1.

[30] Ibid, 23 December, 1994, p.40.

[31] Ibid, 26 January, 1996, p.26.

[32] United Synagogue executive to this writer, 26 August, 2008.

[33] Tobe Aleksander, *Connection, Continuity and Community: British Jewish Women Speak Out* (London: Women's Review Task Force, 2009). The review was prepared in association with the Board of Deputies.

[34] Ibid, p.3.

[35] Ibid, p.6.
[36] Ibid, p.7.
[37] Ibid, pp.11-12.
[38] Ibid, pp.17-18.
[39] Ibid, p.24.
[40] Ibid, p.27.

CHAPTER 11

[1] Jonathan Sacks, *A Decade of Jewish Renewal*, p.9.

[2] Harold Sanderson and Rosita Rosenberg, 'Statement on the Appointment of the Chief Rabbi of the United Hebrew Congregations,' Union of Liberal and Progressive Synagogues, London, 14 December, 1989 (Brichto Papers, London). Sanderson was the chairman, and Rosenberg the director, of the Union. See *Faith Against Reason*, p.373.

[3] *Jewish Chronicle*, 22 December, 1989, p.20.

[4] Geoffrey Alderman, 'Public matters need a public airing,' in ibid, 2 January, 2004, p.19.

[5] The JC (15 August, 2003, p.1) reported that 'the Rev Rosenfeld said he had approached the London Beth Din on behalf of the family three weeks before the call-up. He was told of the Beth Din decision while in America.'

[6] Rosenfeld to Ward, 18 September, 2003 (Jacobs Papers, London). Ward's family were prominent members of the Bournemouth Hebrew Congregation.

[7] *Jewish Chronicle*, 1 August, 2003, p.11.

[8] Lawrence Rigal and Rosita Rosenberg, *Liberal Judaism: The First Hundred Years* (London: Liberal Judaism–Union of Liberal and Progressive Synagogues, 2004), p.173.

[9] *Jewish Chronicle*, 29 November, 1974, p.9.

[10] Ibid, 5 November, 1976, p.6.

[11] Jonathan Sacks, 'Reform not valid,' letter to the JC, 26 November, 1976, p.22.

[12] David J. Goldberg, ibid, 3 December, 1976, p.22.

[13] '*Chapter and Verse*: A Union of Jewish Students Educational Project,' London: UJS, spring term 1977 (Jacobs Papers, London). 'For most of us,' declared the Union, 'the real sources of Judaism are closed books. This project is designed to open them.' At the time of the series, Sacks (misspelt in the UJS literature as 'Sachs') was teaching Jewish philosophy and Talmud at Jews' College, before becoming principal in 1984; Magonet, who had qualified as a medical doctor and then gained a PhD after studies in Jerusalem and Heidelberg, taught Bible at Leo Baeck and later paralleled Sacks as principal there. Jacobs – 'an eminent and controversial Jewish thinker' – was listed as 'a former lecturer at Jews' College, now minister of the New London Synagogue and lecturer at Leo Baeck.'

[14] On Isaac Livingstone, see *Jewish Chronicle*, 28 September, 1979, p.28.

[15] Ibid, 2 June, 1978, pp.5, 18.

[16] Ibid, 22 September, 1978, p.6.

[17] Ibid, 7 March, 1980, p.9.

[18] Ibid, 11 July, 1980, p.7.

[19] Ibid, 18 July, 1980, p.18.

[20] Ibid, 5 August, 1983, p.28.

[21] John M. Rayner, ibid, 20 September, 1991, p.14. A mini-controversy broke out in the JC following publication in the same issue (p.16) of an 'Open Letter' by Goldberg – 'No time like the present' – highly critical of Sacks' installation address and of his declared policies. A week later (ibid, 27 September, 1991, p.5), under the heading 'Give Sacks a chance,' the paper reported Progressive lay and rabbinical officials dissociating themselves from Goldberg's remarks; and in the issue of 4 October, 1991 (p.14), Goldberg moderated his approach.

[22] Ibid, 11 March, 1994, p.13.

[23] Ibid, 27 May, 1994, p.13.

[24] Ibid.

[25] Ibid, 23 December, 1994, p.40.

[26] 'Rabbonim reiterate: Aliyos to Reform are forbidden,' *Jewish Tribune*, 15 June, 1995, p.1.

[27] Ibid, p.2.

[28] Neville Nagler (director-general, Board of Deputies), 'Note of a meeting held at the Board of Deputies of British Jews, 22 March, 2001' (Jacobs Papers, London).

[29] Jonathan Wittenberg, *Where It Hurts: Paper for the Cross-Communal Consultative Committee*, 18 December, 2001 (ibid).

[30] Jeromé Freedman and Paul Shrank, 'Notes of meeting held at 85 Hamilton Terrace, 20 February, 2002' (ibid).

[31] Ibid.

[32] *Jewish Chronicle*, 15 August, 2003, p.18.

[33] Ibid, 22 August, 2003, p.20.

[34] Ibid, 29 August, 2003, p.18.

[35] The Chief Rabbi in conversation with 'Sunday' presenter Roger Bolton, BBC Radio 4, 9 September, 2001.

[36] Stanley Kalms, 'Time for the Chief Rabbi to step down?', *Jewish Chronicle*, 19 December, 2003, p.20.

[37] Gideon Sylvester, 'Tough at the top,' ibid, 2 January, 2004, p.20.

[38] Paul Shrank, 'Report on the Stanmore Accords,' May 2002 (Jacobs Papers, London).

[39] Michael Gluckman, 'Stanmore Accords Discussion Document,' March 2006 (ibid).

[40] *Jewish Chronicle*, 11 January, 2008, p.7.

[41] Bayfield in conversation with this writer, 23 July, 2008.

[42] RSGB news release, 12 September, 2008.

[43] *A Statement on Communal Collaboration*, signed by Nigel Cole, chair, Liberal Judaism; Michael Gluckman, executive director, Assembly of Masorti Synagogues; Stephen Moss, chair, Movement for Reform Judaism; Rabbi Dr Tony Bayfield, head, Movement for Reform Judaism; Rabbi Danny Rich, chief executive, Liberal Judaism; Rabbi Jonathan Wittenberg, senior rabbi, Assembly of Masorti Synagogues (London, 4 September, 2008). An announcement preceding publication of the statement gave Reform representation at 20 per cent, Liberal at 8 per cent, and Masorti at 6 per cent of British Jewry. It added: 'The three movements span from the progressive to the traditional, both in their practices and in their attitudes to Jewish law.'

[44] Richard Buckley, 'Should we co-operate?', in *Alonim*, newsletter of the Bristol and West Progressive Jewish Congregation, November–December 2008, pp.10-11.

[45] 'Mainstream Judaism, Not Fundamentalist Judaism,' leading article, *Manna*, No. 101, autumn 2008, p. 1.

[46] Bayfield to this writer, 9 September, 2008.

[47] *Jewish Chronicle*, 12 September, 2008, p.1.

[48] Ibid, 18 September, 2009, New Year Supplement, p.5.

[49] Levy to this writer, 10 September, 2008. In response to Bayfield's comment on the absence of a United Synagogue rabbinical representative on the Consultative Committee for much of the decade, Levy admitted that 'it was a real mistake on my part not to ensure that a US rabbi was appointed to the committee. Having Malcolm Weisman [the non-rabbinical religious adviser to the small communities] as the US representative – in the capacity of so-called "Orthodox rabbinic leader" – was a way for the Chief Rabbi to avoid the issue.' Weisman's role on the committee came under fire at the 'informal meeting' held at Sacks' home in February 2002, when 'Paul Shrank and Jeromé Freedman were both disappointed that there was no US rabbinic representative on the committee, Malcolm Weisman only representing Jonathan Sacks and not being an employee of the US' (from notes compiled by Freedman and Shrank). Following the Reform-Liberal-Masorti statement, United Synagogue president Simon Hochhauser reaffirmed 'our commitment that the US will include a senior rabbi at all meetings' (*Jewish Chronicle*, 19 September, 2008, p.39).

[50] 'Trouble with unity,' leading article, ibid, 12 September, 2008, p.40.

[51] Ibid, 19 September, 2008, p.39.

[52] *United Synagogue Manifesto 2008*, presented by Simon Hochhauser, president-elect; Keith Barnett, Steve

Pack, Peter Zinkin, vice-presidents-elect; Steve Fenton, Geoff Hartnell, Russell Tenzer, treasurers-elect.
[53] The signatories, with Hochhauser, were Bill Benjamin and Jeremy Kelly, co-chairmen of the
Assembly of Masorti Synagogues, and Cole and Moss for, respectively, the Liberals and Reform. The
renewed accords, sealed in February 2009, followed a meeting of the Community Consultative
Committee on 18 December, 2008.
[54] *Jewish Chronicle*, 20 February, 2009, p.C1. The convention on non-Orthodox marriages (Annexe
1.3) was unchanged from that agreed in the original Stanmore Accords.
[55] *Jewish Chronicle*, 20 February, 2009, p.C1.
[56] Harris attended the 18 December, 2008, meeting, the first time the CCC had convened for more
than a year. The atmosphere was described by Wittenberg as 'very positive-spirited and relaxed'
(ibid, 26 December, 2008, p.4).
[57] Bayfield to this writer, 4 March, 2009.

CHAPTER 12

[1] Jonathan Sacks, *A Decade of Jewish Renewal*, p.6.
[2] See, in particular, Aubrey Newman, *The United Synagogue, 1870–1970* (London: Routledge & Kegan
Paul, 1976), pp.89-102; Miri Freud-Kandel, *Orthodox Judaism in Britain Since 1913* (London and Portland
OR: Vallentine Mitchell, 2006) pp.42-51; Benjamin J. Elton, *Britain's Chief Rabbis: The Jewish response to
modernity and the remoulding of tradition* (PhD dissertation, University of London, 2007); David Englander,
'Anglicized Not Anglican: Jews and Judaism In Victorian Britain,' in *Religion in Victorian Britain*, I. –
Traditions, ed., Gerald Parsons (Manchester and New York: Manchester University Press, 1988),
pp.235-273; Daniel Gutwein, *The Divided Elite: Economics, Politics and Anglo-Jewry 1882–1917* (Leiden: E. J.
Brill, 1992), pp.235-240; Eugene C. Black, *The Social Politics of Anglo-Jewry 1880–1920* (Oxford: Basil
Blackwell, 1988), pp.50-66; Stuart A. Cohen, *English Zionists and British Jews* (Princeton NJ: Princeton
University Press, 1982), p.141.
[3] While sketching some of the disputes between their movements and the six Chief Rabbis since
1845, even the 'official' accounts of Reform and Liberal Judaism in Britain offer little insight into
their views on the conception of a Chief Rabbinate. The main historical works are Anne J. Kershen
and Jonathan A. Romain, *Tradition and Change: A History of Reform Judaism in Britain 1840–1995* (London:
Vallentine Mitchell, 1995), and Lawrence Rigal and Rosita Rosenberg, *Liberal Judaism: The First Hundred
Years* (London: Liberal Judaism, 2004). See also John D. Rayner, 'Nonconformism in Anglo-Jewry,' in
The Jewish Quarterly, Vol. 46, No. 4 (176), winter 1999–2000, pp.55-59.
[4] 'History of the Reform Movement,' in *Supplement to the Jewish Chronicle*, 29 January, 1892, p.20.
[5] *Jewish Chronicle*, 25 April, 1890, p.9. Among the rank and file, however, not all supported 'uniting
the entire Anglo-Jewish community under one Spiritual Chief,' and in the years leading up to this
proposal, dissident voices were seldom silenced. During one bitter exchange in the *Jewish Chronicle*,
headed 'Ecclesiastical administration of the Jewish community,' 'T' wrote (1 August, 1879, p.5):
'I believe the whole ecclesiastical government of our community to be "out of joint." We are
living under a hierarchy equally despotic as the papacy.' Earlier comments by 'T,' and others, had
prompted 'Z' to remark: '[They] seem to me to have reached the borderline where criticism ends
and scurrility begins. That, under cover of a regard for ecclesiastical authority, they are adapted to
bring ecclesiastical authority into contempt, and to give pain to some of the most honoured and
honourable men in the community, may be asserted with absolute confidence' (ibid, 25 July, 1879,
p.5).
[6] *Jewish Chronicle*, 9 May, 1890, p.9. The other signatories to the letter, dated 22 April, 1890, were F.
D. Mocatta, Alfred L. Cohen, Herbert G. Lousada and Alfred H. Beddington.
[7] Ibid.
[8] Ibid, 25 April, 1890, p.9.
[9] Ibid, 23 May, 1890, p.6.

[10] Ibid, 13 June, 1890, p.11.

[11] Ibid, 25 July, 1890, p.20.

[12] Appended to this letter was the text of a resolution 'that the Congregation, whilst desiring to maintain and, if possible, to strengthen the cordial relations now happily subsisting between it and the United Synagogue, cannot be represented by delegates at a Conference which is called to consider the conditions of the appointment of a Chief Rabbi.'

[13] The invitation was also rejected by the Spanish and Portuguese Jews' Congregation at Bevis Marks (City of London); Bryanstone Street (Central London); and Manchester – from each of which 'No official reply has been received'; Ramsgate ('No reply'); and the Manchester Congregation of British Jews ('Decline to send a delegate'), Jewish Chronicle, 25 July, 1890, p.18, quoting the official list of delegates to the conference.

[14] Ibid, 1 August, 1890, p.9.

[15] Letter dated 30 May, 1912, from Joseph Blank to Philip Ornstein, secretary of the United Synagogue, Jewish Chronicle, 7 June, 1912, p.14. In his reply, dated 4 June, 5672–1912, Ornstein wrote: 'The choice of the Chief Rabbi is not vested in the United Synagogue. The large number of synagogues throughout the British dominions which have not shirked the responsibility of taking part in the Election is sufficient evidence to refute this allegation' (ibid).

[16] On Redcliffe Nathan Salaman, see Faith Against Reason, pp.267-270; Jewish Chronicle, 17 June, 1955, p.12; James W. Parkes, 'Redcliffe Nathan Salaman,' memorial address delivered before the Jewish Historical Society of England, 26 October, 1955, in Transactions of the Jewish Historical Society of England, Vol. XVIII, London, 1953–1955, pp.296-298; George H. Fried, Encyclopaedia Judaica, Vol. 14 (Keter, Jerusalem, 1972), pp.670-671; Redcliffe N. Salaman, Whither Lucien Wolf's Anglo-Jewish Community? The Lucien Wolf Memorial Lecture, 1953 (London: Jewish Historical Society of England, 1954); Todd M. Endelman, 'Practices of a Low Anthropologic Level: A Shechitah Controversy of the 1950s,' in Food in the Migrant Experience, ed., Anne J. Kershen (Ashgate Publishing, 2002), pp.77-97.

[17] Jewish Chronicle, 28 June, 1912, p.15.

[18] Newman, op. cit., p.98, and the same writer's Chief Rabbi Dr Joseph H. Hertz, C.H. (London: United Synagogue, 1972), pp.4-5, citing minutes of the United Synagogue council, 13 March, 1912, LMA/ACC2712/1/143.

[19] Joseph Hochman, 'The Chief Rabbinate,' unsigned editorial in The Jewish Review, Vol. III, No. 17 (ed., Norman Bentwich and Joseph Hochman, London: George Routledge and Sons, January 1913), p.382. Similar sentiments were expressed in Vol. III, No. 18 (March 1913), p.465, and Vol. IV, No. 23 (January–February 1914), pp.381-384. On Hochman, see Faith Against Reason, chapter 9.

[20] 'The Rabbinical Conference,' unsigned editorial in The Zionist [formerly The Zionist Banner], Vol. 2, No. 1, April 1911–5671, pp.1-2. London-born Harry Sacher (1881–1971), a prominent lawyer, was for several years on the editorial board of the Manchester Guardian and, with Simon (later Sir Leon), belonged to the Manchester Zionist Circle headed by Chaim Weizmann. Southampton-born Simon (1881–1965), the son of a rabbi, was a civil servant and writer.

[21] The Zionist, Vol. 2, No. 8, November 1911–5672, p.122.

[22] President and vice-presidents, respectively, of the United Synagogue.

[23] The Zionist, Vol. 2, No. 10, January 1912–5672, pp.153-154.

[24] Ibid, Vol. 3, No. 9, February 1913–5673, pp. 129-130.

[25] The Installation Sermon of the Very Rev Dr Joseph Herman Hertz, Chief Rabbi of the United Hebrew Congregations of the British Empire (London: United Synagogue, 1913), p.19.

[26] Romanian-born Schechter (1847–1915) was Claude Montefiore's private tutor in rabbinics and, in 1890, became lecturer (and later reader) in rabbinics at Cambridge University. From 1898–1902 he was professor of Hebrew at University College London, before succeeding Sabato Morais as president of the Jewish Theological Seminary of America. His many publications included Studies in Judaism and Some Aspects of Rabbinic Theology. Although Jessel commended Schechter to his colleagues as 'one of the leading living Rabbis,' whose position 'is unassailable, and [whose] orthodoxy is unquestioned,' he is generally regarded as the founder of Conservative Judaism as it is known today.

[27] See chapter 13 below.

[28] Letter from Solomon Schechter to Albert H. Jessel, chairman of the Chief Rabbinical Selection

Committee, 31 January, 1913, *Jewish Chronicle*, 14 February, 1913, p.13.

[29] Kershen and Romain, op. cit., p.123.

[30] 'An Inconsistent Invitation,' *Jewish Chronicle*, 23 January, 1920, p.7.

[31] Ibid, 1 June, 1934, p.10.

[32] See Kershen and Romain, op. cit., pp.156-158, 310-316.

[33] *Faith Against Reason*, chapter 13.

[34] Cecil Roth, 'The Collapse of English Jewry,' in *The Jewish Monthly*, No. 4 (London: Anglo-Jewish Association, July 1947), pp.11-17.

[35] 'The Making of a Chief Rabbi,' unsigned article in *the jew: Quest 2* (London: Cornmarket Press, 1967), p.11.

[36] This was demonstrated, for example, by a leading article in the *Jewish Tribune* (11 November, 1966, p.4): 'British Jewry, despite all the undermining which it has been forced to witness in recent years, is basically loyal and devoted to its [Chief] Rabbinate. There is no doubt whatever that a concerted and resolute effort by the Rabbinate will produce a change in atmosphere in the whole of the community which will not only promote greater harmony and understanding but also generate a new spirit necessary to give the newly elected Chief Rabbi [Jakobovits] a fair chance to succeed in his aims.' Noting this support, Jacobs' successor at the New West End Synagogue, Chaim Pearl, wrote at the time, after assuming the pulpit of the Conservative Synagogue of Riverdale, New York: 'The right-wing Union [of Orthodox Hebrew Congregations] is a self-contained *kehillah*. They add to the religious and educational strength of the community. They do not show any penchant just now for power politics and, if anything, they are likely to be secret if not open supporters of the new incumbent, whose origins and background are similar to their own' (Pearl, 'About "Chief Rabbis,"' *The Jewish Spectator*, New York, January 1967, p.22).

[37] '"Understanding" with the Rav Rashi-Elect of the Federation of Synagogues,' in Immanuel Jakobovits, *Prelude to Service* (London: Office of the Chief Rabbi, Adar II 5727–April 1967), pp.29-30.

[38] Letter from Sidney Brichto, executive vice-president, Union of Liberal and Progressive Synagogues, to *The Observer*, 12 February, 1967.

[39] Brichto, 'What is wrong with the Chief Rabbinate?', in *Liberal Jewish Monthly* (London: ULPS, May 1965), pp.101-104.

[40] Ignaz Maybaum, *The Office of a Chief Rabbi* (London: Reform Synagogues of Great Britain, 1964), p.13.

[41] Louis Jacobs, letter to the *Jewish Chronicle*, 7 April, 1967, p.6.

[42] Jakobovits, 'Fragments from an Unpublished Autobiography,' in Meir Persoff, *Immanuel Jakobovits: a Prophet in Israel*, London and Portland OR: Vallentine Mitchell, 2002, p.115.

[43] Jakobovits, 'The major tasks ahead,' letter to the *Jewish Chronicle*, 16 December, 1966, p.6.

[44] Jakobovits, 'Putting stability before "mirage" of unity,' in ibid, 10 January, 1997, p.23.

CHAPTER 13

[1] Jonathan Sacks, *A Decade of Jewish Renewal*, p.12.

[2] See *Faith Against Reason*, chapter 18. Full accounts of the dispute are in Abba Bornstein and Bernard Homa, *Tell It In Gath: British Jewry and Clause 43 – The Inside Story* (published privately, London, 1972), for the Orthodox; and, for the Progressives, Harold Langdon, 'The Place of Reform in Anglo-Jewry Today,' in *A Genuine Search*, ed., Dow Marmur (London: Reform Synagogues of Great Britain, 1979), pp.239-255.

[3] *Jewish Chronicle*, 29 October, 1971, p.6.

[4] Ibid, 21 December, 1984, p.4

[5] Jack Wolkind, *London and its Jewish Community*, annual West Central Lecture delivered at University College London, 13 June, 1985 (London: West Central Counselling and Community Research,

1985), pp. 1-26. Wolkind (1920–97) was chief executive, and former town clerk, of Tower Hamlets and an adviser to the London Boroughs Association and the Association of Metropolitan Authorities. In 1974, he headed a working party set up by Lord Fisher of Camden, the Board of Deputies' president, to recommend changes in its structure and administration. His committee members included Harold Langdon, Sidney Frosh and Louis Mintz, each of whom played a significant role in the communal controversies of the Brodie and Jakobovits Chief Rabbinates.

[6] Sidney Frosh, 'Clause 74 And All That,' in *Hamesilah* [The Path], Pesach 5745 (London: United Synagogue, 1985), pp. 24-25. Frosh was president of the United Synagogue.

[7] Stephen Sharot, 'Religious Change in Native Orthodoxy in London, 1870–1914: Rabbinate and Clergy,' in the *Jewish Journal of Sociology*, Vol. XV, No. 2 (London: William Heinemann, December 1973), p. 168.

[8] *Jewish Chronicle*, 13 November, 1846, p. 22; ibid, 27 November, 1846, p. 29.

[9] Sharot, op. cit., pp. 168, 171.

[10] Todd M. Endelman, 'Communal Solidarity Among the Jewish Elite of Victorian London,' in *Victorian Studies*, 28:3, Indiana: University Press, spring 1985, pp. 494, 502.

[11] Michael Henry, 'The Synagogue Question,' *Jewish Chronicle*, 23 February, 1872, p. 9. On Henry, see David Cesarani, *The Jewish Chronicle and Anglo-Jewry, 1841–1991* (Cambridge: University Press, 1994), pp. 50-60.

[12] Norman Cohen, 'Non-Religious Factors in the Emergence of the Chief Rabbinate,' in *Transactions of the Jewish Historical Society of England*, Vol. XXI (London, 1968), pp. 304-313.

[13] 'Historicus,' *Ministers in the Making: Jews' College, the Synagogue, and the Community* (privately published, London, 1910), p. 4.

[14] Ibid, pp. 25-26.

[15] *Second Conference of Anglo-Jewish Ministers*, report, London, 1911; *Jewish Chronicle*, 19 January, 1912, p. 22; ibid, 7 February, 1913, p. 30. The letter was signed by A. A. Green, president; M. Abrahams, vice-president; Michael Adler, treasurer; J. F. Stern and S. Levy, honorary secretaries; and G. J. Emanuel, past president.

[16] Immanuel Jakobovits, *Looking Ahead*, an address to the lay leaders of the United Synagogue, 26 November, 1967 (London: United Synagogue, 1967), p. 8.

[17] Barry A. Kosmin, 'Localism and Pluralism in British Jewry, 1900–80,' in *Transactions of the Jewish Historical Society of England*, Vol. XXVIII (London, 1982), p. 113.

[18] Solomon Schonfeld, *Jewish Religious Education: A Guide and Handbook* (London: National Council for Jewish Religious Education, 1943), p. 34.

[19] Immanuel Jakobovits, 'An Analysis of Religious Versus Secularist Trends in Anglo-Jewry,' in *Jewish Life in Britain, 1962–1977*, ed., Sonia L. Lipman and Vivian D. Lipman (New York and London: K. G. Saur, 1981), pp. 40-41.

[20] Kosmin, 'Localism and Pluralism,' p. 115.

[21] Geoffrey Alderman, letter to the *Jewish Chronicle*, 31 March, 1995, p. 28.

[22] Alderman, 'The British Chief Rabbinate: a Most Peculiar Practice,' in *European Judaism*, Vol. 23, No. 2, autumn 1990, p. 53. Alderman also touches on this theme in 'Power, Authority and Status in British Jewry: The Chief Rabbinate and Shechitah,' in *Outsiders and Outcasts: Essays in Honour of William J. Fishman*, eds., G. Alderman and C. Holmes (London: Duckworth, 1993), pp. 12-31; *Anglo-Jewry: A Suitable Case for Treatment*, Egham: Royal Holloway & Bedford New College, 1990, pp. 1-41; 'The defence of shechitah: Anglo-Jewry and the "humane conditions" regulations of 1990,' in *new community* 21(1), January 1995, pp. 79-93; 'The Disunited Synagogue: Public Quarrels, Fragmentation and Disarray,' in *Judaism Today*, No. 4, spring 1996, London: Assembly of Masorti Synagogues.

[23] Raymond Apple, letter to the *Jewish Chronicle*, 7 April, 1995, p. 32.

[24] Raymond Cannon, letter to ibid, 10 February, 1995, p. 20.

[25] Richard Loftus, in a letter published immediately below Cannon's.

[26] Hermann Adler died in July 1911, and Hertz was not elected until February 1913.

[27] 'The Chief Rabbinate – And After': 'M.S.', *The Zionist*, Vol. 3, No. 3, August 1912, pp. 38-39.

[28] The phrase was first used by Jakobovits in a pre-Chief Rabbinical letter to the Progressive journal *Pointer* (London: Union of Liberal and Progressive Synagogues, spring 1967), p. 4.

[29] United Synagogue lay executive in conversation with this writer, 26 August, 2008.

[30] Paul Vallely (religious-affairs and associate editor of *The Independent*), 'Jonathan Sacks: Defender of the Faith,' 8 September 2001, Comment Section, p.5.

[31] 'Whose Chief Rabbi? – Elena Lappin talks to Jonathan Sacks about politics and hope,' *The Jewish Quarterly*, Vol. 44, No. 2 (166), summer 1997, p.5.

[32] As recently as 1979 – some fifteen years after the establishment of the New London Synagogue, with the Liberals, Reform and Union of Orthodox Hebrew Congregations making similarly significant advances, and in the face of Jakobovits' own contemporaneous anxieties (see the Epilogue to *Faith Against Reason*, pp.383-386) – Sharot nevertheless felt able to assert: 'The "Central Orthodox" position, as exemplified by the United Synagogue, remains the dominant one in London Jewry, and there is no sign that this is likely to change in the near future' ('Reform and Liberal Judaism in London: 1840–1940,' in *Jewish Social Studies*, Vol. XLI, New York: Conference on Jewish Social Studies, 1979, p.225). Only two years earlier, however, Jakobovits had declared: 'The Anglo-Jewish predilection for the middle of the road, under the umbrella of moderation, is bound to be squeezed into gradual disappearance by the converging pressures of intensified commitment from the right and of rampant secularisation – sometimes via various progressive half-way houses – from the left' (Jakobovits, 'An Analysis,' p.44). Statistics on synagogue membership adduced in the preface to *Faith Against Reason*, the views of former 'Central Orthodox' worshippers – and of Kalms himself – cited in *A Time for Change*, and the sequence of events described throughout this book all demonstrate the fallacy of Sharot's prognostication, if by 'near future' is meant the rising generation.

[33] Alderman, *Modern British Jewry*, p.378; Israel Finestein, 'A Community of Paradox: Office, Authority and Ideas in the Changing Governance of Anglo-Jewry,' in *Jewish Centers and Peripheries: Europe Between America and Israel Fifty Years After World War II*, ed., Selwyn Ilan Troen (New Brunswick, NJ: Transaction Publishers, 1998), p.155; Kosmin, 'Localism and Pluralism,' p.120.

[34] Todd M. Endelman, *The Jews of Britain 1656 to 2000* (Berkeley: University of California Press, 2002), p.252.

[35] Barry A. Kosmin, 'The case for the local perspective in the study of contemporary British Jewry,' in *Jewish Life in Britain, 1962–1977*, pp.83-84.

[36] Norman Cohen, 'Trends in Anglo-Jewish Religious Life,' in *Jewish Life in Modern Britain* (ed., Julius Gould and Shaul Esh (London: Routledge & Kegan Paul, 1964), p.42.

[37] Endelman, op. cit., pp.249, 254.

[38] Alderman, *Modern British Jewry*, p.389; and 'British Jewry: The Disintegration of a Community,' in *Continuity, Commitment, and Survival* (Westport: Praeger, 2003), reprinted in *Controversy and Crisis* (Boston: Academic Studies Press, 2008), p.334.

[39] *Modern British Jewry*, pp.374, 378.

[40] Stephen H. Miller, 'Religious Practice and Jewish Identity in a Sample of London Jews,' in *Jewish Identities in the New Europe*, ed., Jonathan Webber (London and Washington: Littman Library of Jewish Civilization, for the Oxford Centre for Hebrew and Jewish Studies, 1994), p.203. At the time of writing these comments, presented to a conference held in July 1992 at the Oxford Centre's Yarnton Manor, Miller was Dean of the School of Social Sciences at City University, London, and actively involved in social research on the Anglo-Jewish community.

[41] Jonathan Sacks, 'From Integration to Survival to Continuity,' in ibid, p.111.

[42] Geoffrey Alderman, 'British Jewry: Religious Community or Ethnic Minority?', in ibid, p.192.

[43] Harriet Becher, Stanley Waterman, Barry Kosmin, Katarina Thomson, *A Portrait of Jews in London and the South-East: A Community Study* (London: Institute for Jewish Policy Research, May 2003), tables 2.9 and 2.11. See also *Long-term Planning for British Jewry: Final Report and Recommendations* (London: Institute for Jewish Policy Research, Report No. 5, 2003), pp.57-67

[44] Gerald Jacobs, 'Who'd want to be Chief Rabbi?', *New Statesman*, 27 June, 1997, p.36.

[45] Marlena Schmool, 'The Ethnic Question on the British Census: A Jewish Perspective,' *Patterns of Prejudice*, Vol. 32, No. 2, 1998 (London: Sage Publications), pp.65-71. Schmool, executive director of the Board of Deputies' community research unit, notes that she is 'not writing as an official spokeswoman for British Jewry but rather as a researcher involved with the daily practicalities of research.'

[46] Kalms, *A Time for Change*, p.36.

[47] On the evolution and nature of the concept, see *Minhag Anglia: The English Usage*, on Oz Torah, the website of Raymond Apple (http://www.oztorah.com).

[48] *A Time for Change*, p.37.

[49] Ibid, pp.39-40.

[50] *Faith Against Reason*, p.xviii.

[51] Rona Hart and Edward Kafka, *Trends in British Synagogue Membership, 1990–2005/06* (London: Board of Deputies of British Jews, 2006), pp.19-23.

[52] Male membership of the United Synagogue fell 12.1 per cent from 22,761 in 1992 to 20,004 in 2006, though this was offset by a rise in female members from 16,851 to 19,907, bringing the respective totals to 39,612 and 39,911 (Research and Development Executive, United Synagogue Community Division, 2007).

[53] *A Time for Change*, pp.240-244.

[54] Ibid, p.41.

[55] *Connection, Continuity and Community: British Jewish Women Speak Out* (London: Women's Review Task Force, 2009), pp.21, 23.

[56] *A Community of Communities: Report of the Commission on Representation of the Interests of the British Jewish Community* (London: Institute for Jewish Policy Research, 31 March, 2000), p.1.

[57] Ibid, p.4.

[58] Ibid, p.28.

[59] Ibid, p.30.

[60] Ibid, p.36.

[61] Ibid, p.37.

[62] Ibid, p.39. A 2009 survey within American Jewry, rejecting the notion of a Chief Rabbinate, lent support for such a model. From Orthodox to Reconstructionist, and beyond, those interviewed spoke with one voice ('Should the United States Have a Chief Rabbi?', *Moment*, Vol. 14, No. 1, January/February 2009, pp.26-27): 'The idea of a Chief Rabbi is an illusion of a unified community. Where the office exists, no one is satisfied,' said Modern Orthodox Rabbi Yitz (Irving) Greenberg, of New York. 'England's distinguished Chief Rabbi has won national recognition as a spiritual leader, but, hobbled by Orthodox disrespect for liberal Jews and pressured by the charedim, he has alienated Masorti and Reform Jews.' Rabbi Joseph Maroof, of Rockville's Magen David Sephardi congregation, asserted: 'A Chief Rabbinate can unify the practice and standards of an observant, homogeneous Jewish community. In pluralistic and multidenominational settings, it would be divisive and ineffective, exacerbating the tensions that already plague American Jewish life.' Rabbi Julie Schonfeld, of the Conservatives' Rabbinical Assembly, maintained that 'the institution of one Chief Rabbi would stifle rather than spur Jewish involvement.' According to Rabbi Aaron Panken, vice-president of Hebrew Union College (Reform), 'one need only look to the countries in which Chief Rabbis operate today to see the pain and suffering possible with an American Chief Rabbinate.' Reconstructionist Rabbi Fred Scherlinder Dobb, of Bethesda's Adat Shalom Congregation, declared: 'A Chief Rabbinate works miserably in Israel, where unelected ultra-rabbis have lately exercised capricious leadership. It works tolerably in Europe and elsewhere, where wise and good men occupy untenable positions, representing only those Jews within their orbits. An inclusive, pluralistic rabbis' group, with rotating leadership, should guide but not govern.'

[63] Surveying the impact of the report ten years on, Dr Winston Pickett, former JPR director of external relations – who helped to oversee its production – wrote: 'The final publication of the report seemed to have landed less with a bang and more with a thud, prefacing its findings with ten high-minded principles for representation, and ending with three recommendations that were rich in detail but thin on prescription. For Stephen Chelms, the only member of the charedi community on the Commission, the report's impact was minimal. "I think it's safe to say it didn't simply land on rocky soil, it landed on concrete," he said. "When working with the voluntary sector, change from the outside is virtually impossible." But another member of the Commission, Maurice Helfgott, says that it was the catalyst for deep changes in Anglo-Jewry, not least the creation of the Jewish Leadership Council and the London Jewish Forum – an observation corroborated by Adrian Cohen, then a lawyer and former chair of the Union of Jewish Students and now chairman of the

LJF itself. Following publication, Helfgott gave a report on the Commission's findings to a group of forty up-and-coming executives and Jewish professionals known as the "Cavendish Group." A key member of the group, which included political consultant and public-relations specialist Jon Mendelsohn, philanthropist Trevor Pears, lawyer James Libson and communal activist Lisa Ronson, was Douglas Krikler, who is now chief executive of UJIA. "It may not have been a road map, but the report definitely influenced a group of key people who were engaged in finding ways to best bring the community forward," says Krikler, noting that the ad hoc Cavendish Group had now morphed into a semi-official "new leadership network" which acts as a conduit to the Jewish Leadership Council, and can also be seen as a response to the report's call for more leadership development' ('So is your voice being heard yet?', *Jewish Chronicle*, 1 January, 2010, p.6).

[64] Jewish Leadership Council website, 2010. Among the Council's members in early 2010 were Simon Hochhauser (president, United Synagogue); Stephen Moss (chair, Movement for Reform Judaism); Lucian Hudson (chairman, Liberal Judaism); Robert Yentob (Spanish and Portuguese Jews' Congregation); Vivian Wineman (president, Board of Deputies of British Jews); and Brian Kerner (co-chair, Cross-Communal Group). On the establishment of the Council – originally designated as the Jewish Community Leadership Council, and restructured in 2006 – see the *Jewish Chronicle*, 24 October, 2003, p.3, and 3 March, 2006, p.3.

[65] 'The native and the wanderer,' *The Observer*, 1 September, 1991.

Bibliography

Act for confirming a Scheme of the Charity Commissioners for the Jewish United Synagogues [33 & 34 Vict., Ch. cxvi], 14 July, 1870.

Adler, N. M., *Laws and Regulations for all the Synagogues in the British Empire*, London: John Wertheimer and Co., 5607–1847.

Alderman, Geoffrey, *The Federation of Synagogues 1887–1987*, London: Federation of Synagogues, 1987.

Alderman, Geoffrey, *Anglo-Jewry: A Suitable Case for Treatment* (and appendix, *Albert Road: An Everyday Story of Jewish Folk*), Egham: Royal Holloway & Bedford New College, 1990.

Alderman, Geoffrey, 'The British Chief Rabbinate: a Most Peculiar Practice,' *European Judaism*, Vol. 23, No. 2, 1990.

Alderman, Geoffrey, *Modern British Jewry*, Oxford: Clarendon Press, 1992; new edition, 1998.

Alderman, Geoffrey, 'Power, Authority and Status in British Jewry: The Chief Rabbinate and Shechitah,' in *Outsiders and Outcasts: Essays in Honour of William J. Fishman*, eds., G. Alderman and C. Holmes, London: Duckworth, 1993.

Alderman, Geoffrey, 'The defence of shechitah: Anglo-Jewry and the "humane conditions" regulations of 1990,' *new community* 21(1), January 1995.

Alderman, Geoffrey, 'The Chief Rabbinate: An Excursion into Myth-Making,' *Judaism Today*, No. 3, London: Assembly of Masorti Synagogues, winter 1995–96.

Alderman, Geoffrey, 'The Disunited Synagogue: Public Quarrels, Fragmentation and Disarray,' *Judaism Today*, No. 4, London: Assembly of Masorti Synagogues, spring 1996.

Alderman, Geoffrey, 'British Jewry: The Disintegration of a Community,' in *Continuity, Commitment, and Survival*, Westport: Praeger, 2003.

Alderman, Geoffrey, *Controversy and Crisis: Studies in the History of the Jews in Modern Britain*, Boston: Academic Studies Press, 2008.

Aleksander, Tobe, *Connection, Continuity and Community: British Jewish Women Speak Out*, London: Women's Review Task Force, 2009.

A Special Correspondent, 'The British Chief Rabbinate,' *The Jewish Monthly*, No. 2, London: Anglo-Jewish Association, May 1947.

Baggini, Julian, 'My Philosophy: Jonathan Sacks,' *The Philosophers' Magazine*, London: Philosophy Press, No. 44, March 2009.

Barnett, Arthur, *The Western Synagogue Through Two Centuries, 1761–1961*, London: Vallentine Mitchell, 1961.

Becher, Harriet, Stanley Waterman, Barry Kosmin, Katarina Thomson, *A Portrait of Jews in London and the South-East: A Community Study*, London: Institute for Jewish Policy Research, May 2003.

Bermant, Chaim, *Lord Jakobovits: The Authorized Biography of the Chief Rabbi*, London: Weidenfeld and Nicolson, 1990.

Black, Eugene C., *The Social Politics of Anglo-Jewry 1880–1920*, Oxford: Basil Blackwell, 1988.

Black, Gerry, *J.F.S.: The History of the Jews' Free School, London, Since 1732*, London: Tymsder Publishing, 1998.

Blackburn, David, et al., *A Community of Communities: Report of the Commission on Representation of the Interests of the British Jewish Community*, London: Institute for Jewish Policy Research, 2000.

Bornstein, Abba, and Homa, Bernard, *Tell It In Gath: British Jewry and Clause 43 – The Inside Story*, London: privately published, 1972.

Borowski, Ephraim, 'The Jewish People,' *Le'ela*, No. 36, London: Office of the Chief Rabbi and Jews' College, September 1993.

Brichto, Sidney, 'What is wrong with the Chief Rabbinate?', *Liberal Jewish Monthly*, London: Union of Liberal and Progressive Synagogues, May 1965.

Brichto, Sidney, 'Halachah with Humility,' *Jewish Chronicle*, 2 October, 1987.

Bye Laws of the Constituent Synagogues, London: United Synagogue, November 1881.
Bye-Laws Made by the Council of the United Synagogue, London, United Synagogue, July 1936.

Clark, Michael, *Albion and Jerusalem: The Anglo-Jewish Community in the Post-Emancipation Era, 1858–1887*, Oxford: University Press, 2009.
Cohen, Jeffrey M., *Issues of the Day*, London: Genesia Publications, 1999.
Cohen, Norman. 'Trends in Anglo-Jewish Religious Life,' in *Jewish Life in Modern Britain*, ed., Julius Gould and Shaul Esh, London: Routledge & Kegan Paul, 1964.
Cohen, Norman, 'The Religious Crisis in Anglo-Jewry,' in *Tradition*, Vol. 8, No. 2, ed., Walter S. Wurzburger, Rabbinical Council of America, New York, 1966.
Cohen, Norman, 'Non-Religious Factors in the Emergence of the Chief Rabbinate,' in *Transactions of the Jewish Historical Society of England*, Vol. XXI, 1968.
Cohen, Stuart A., *English Zionists and British Jews*, Princeton NJ: Princeton University Press, 1982.
Cole, Nigel, et al., *A Statement on Communal Collaboration*, London: Liberal Judaism, Assembly of Masorti Synagogues, Movement for Reform Judaism, September 2008.
Cosgrove, Elliot Joe, *Teyku: The Insoluble Contradictions in the Life and Thought of Louis Jacobs*, PhD dissertation, University of Chicago, 2008.
Curtis, Michael, 'The Beth Din of the Reform Synagogues of Great Britain,' in Dow Marmur (ed.), *Reform Judaism: Essays on Reform Judaism in Britain*, London: Reform Synagogues of Great Britain, 1973.

Dallmayr, Fred, 'The Dignity of Difference: A Salute to Jonathan Sacks,' *Millennium: Journal of International Studies*, Vol. 33, No. 2, London: London School of Economics, March 2004.

Elton, Benjamin J., *Britain's Chief Rabbis and the Religious Character of Anglo-Jewry, 1880–1970*, Manchester: Manchester University Press, 2010.
Endelman, Todd M., *The Jews of Britain 1656 to 2000*, Berkeley: University of California Press, 2002.
Endelman, Todd M., *British Jewry and the Jewish Historiographical Mainstream*, Southampton: Parkes Institute for the Study of Jewish/non-Jewish Relations, 2008.
Endelman, Todd M., 'Communal Solidarity Among the Jewish Elite of Victorian London,' *Victorian Studies*, 28:3, Indiana: University Press, spring 1985.
England and Wales Court of Appeal (Civil Division) Decisions: Neutral Citation Number [2009] EWCA Civ 626. Case No.1 C1/2008/2187 and No.2 C1/2008/2188, London, 12–14 May, 2009. Judgment handed down 25 June, 2009. London: Court of Appeal, 2009.
Englander, David, 'Anglicized Not Anglican: Jews and Judaism in Victorian Britain,' in *Religion in Victorian Britain, I. – Traditions*, ed., Gerald Parsons, Manchester: University Press, 1988.
Englander, David, 'Integrated But Insecure: A Portrait of Anglo-Jewry at the Close of the Twentieth Century,' in *The Growth of Religious Diversity: Britain From 1945, Vol. I. – Traditions*, ed., Gerald Parsons, London: Routledge, in association with the Open University, 1993.
Epstein, Jon, and Jacobs, David, *A History in our Time: Rabbis and Teachers Buried at Hoop Lane Cemetery*, London: Leo Baeck College, 2006.
Epstein, Isidore, *The Place of Halachah in Jewish Life and Thought*, Paris: Conference of European Rabbis, 1961; reproduced (in part) in Israel Brodie, *Statement by the Very Rev. the Chief Rabbi, Dr Israel Brodie*, London: United Synagogue, 1964.

Finestein, Israel, 'A Community of Paradox: Office, Authority and Ideas in the Changing Governance of Anglo-Jewry,' in *Jewish Centers and Peripheries: Europe Between America and Israel Fifty Years After World War II*, ed., Selwyn Ilan Troen, New Brunswick, NJ: Transaction Publishers, 1998.
Finestein, Israel, *Anglo-Jewry in Changing Times*, London and Portland OR: Vallentine Mitchell, 1999.
Freud-Kandel, Miri, *Orthodox Judaism in Britain Since 1913*, London and Portland OR: Vallentine Mitchell, 2006.

Friedman, Manis, et al., 'Ask the Rabbis: Should the U.S. Have a Chief Rabbi?', Moment, January–February 2009.

Frosh, Sidney, 'Clause 74 And All That,' in Hamesilah [The Path], No. 1, London: United Synagogue, 1985.

Gartner, Lloyd P., The Jewish Immigrant in England, 1870–1914, London: George Allen & Unwin, 1960.

Gartner, Lloyd P., Simche Bunim Lieberman, address to the Jewish Historical Society of England, Israel branch, 2010.

Gaster, Moses, History of the Ancient Synagogue of the Spanish and Portuguese Jews, London: privately published, 5661–1901.

Golinkin, David, '"Who is a Jew?" once again,' Jerusalem Post, 25 July, 2008.

Goodkin, Judy, and Citron, Judith, Women in the Jewish Community: Review and Recommendations, London: Women in the Community [Office of the Chief Rabbi], 1994.

Greenberg, Eric J., 'Sacks and Salvation: England's Chief Rabbi Claims That Jews Don't Hold the Monopoly on Truth,' Jewish Week, New York, 27 September, 2002.

Gryn, Hugo, with Naomi Gryn, Chasing Shadows: Memories of a Vanished World, London: Viking, 2000.

Gutwein, Daniel, The Divided Elite: Economics, Politics and Anglo-Jewry 1882–1917, Leiden: Brill, 1992.

Halter, Aloma, 'Out of the Shadows,' Jerusalem Post, magazine section, 13 April, 2001.

Harris, Isidore, Jews' College Jubilee Volume, London: Luzac, 1906.

Hart, Rona, Edward Kafka, Trends in British Synagogue Membership, 1990–2005/06, London: Board of Deputies of British Jews, 2006.

Hart, Rona, Jewish Continuity: The Demographic Crisis and Jewish Renewal Efforts (paper presented at a conference in honour of Professor Na'ama Sabar Ben-Yehoshua, Tel Aviv, December 2007); reprinted in Ben-Yehoshua, Jewish Education: A Global Perspective, Tel Aviv: School of Education, Tel Aviv University, 2010.

Hertz, Joseph H., The Installation Sermon of the Very Rev. Dr Joseph Herman Hertz, Chief Rabbi of the United Hebrew Congregations of the British Empire, London: United Synagogue, 1913.

Hertz, Joseph Herman, Opening Address by the Chief Rabbi, Conference of Anglo-Jewish Preachers, London: Oxford University Press, 1923.

'Historicus,' Ministers in the Making: Jews' College, the Synagogue and the Community, London: privately published, 1910.

Hochman, Joseph, 'The Chief Rabbinate,' The Jewish Review, Vol. III, No. 17, London: George Routledge and Sons, January 1913.

Homa, Bernard, Orthodoxy in Anglo-Jewry 1880–1940, London: Jewish Historical Society of England, 1969.

Hyamson, Albert M., Jews' College London, 1855–1955, London: Jews' College, 1955.

Ish-Horowicz, M., 'The Case of Mrs Paula Cohen and her Children,' in The Jewish Law Annual , No. 11, 1994.

Jacobs, Gerald, 'Who'd want to be Chief Rabbi?', New Statesman, 27 June, 1997.

Jacobs, Louis, 'Organic Growth vs. Petrification,' The Jewish Spectator, Vol. XVII, No. 10, New York, November 1952.

Jacobs, Louis, We Have Reason to Believe, first edition, London: Vallentine Mitchell, 1957.

Jacobs, Louis, 'Reflections on a Controversy,' in Quest 1, ed., Jonathan Stone, London: Paul Hamlyn, 1965.

Jacobs, Louis, A Tree of Life: Diversity, Flexibility, and Creativity in Jewish Law, Oxford: University Press, for the Littman Library of Jewish Civilization, 1984.

Jacobs, Louis, *Helping With Inquiries: An Autobiography*, London: Vallentine Mitchell, 1989.

Jacobs, Louis, Wittenberg, Jonathan, Weiner, Chaim, *Statement on Masorti Marriages*, London: Assembly of Masorti Synagogues, January 1995.

Jacobs, Louis, 'A Retrospect of the "Jacobs Affair,"' in *We Have Reason to Believe*, fifth expanded edition, London and Portland OR: Vallentine Mitchell, 2004.

Jakobovits, Immanuel, 'The Evolution of the British Rabbinate Since 1845,' in *The Timely and The Timeless*, London: Vallentine Mitchell, 1977.

Jakobovits, Immanuel, 'An Analysis of Religious Versus Secularist Trends in Anglo-Jewry, Especially During the Past Fifteen Years,' in *Jewish Life in Britain, 1962–1977*, ed., Sonia L. Lipman and Vivian D. Lipman, New York/Munich/London/Paris: K. G. Saur, 1981.

Jakobovits, Immanuel, *Preserving the Oneness of the Jewish People: Orthodox–Progressive divisions and discussions on marriage, divorce and conversion – can a permanent schism be averted?* London: Office of the Chief Rabbi, 1988.

Jakobovits, Immanuel, *Address Delivered at the Installation of Rabbi Dr Jonathan Sacks as Chief Rabbi of the United Hebrew Congregations of the Commonwealth*, London: Office of the Chief Rabbi, 1991.

Jakobovits, Immanuel, *Dear Chief Rabbi*, ed., Jeffrey M. Cohen, Hoboken, NJ: Ktav, 1995.

Jakobovits, Immanuel, 'The Tortuous Path to Relief for *Agunot*,' *Jewish Chronicle*, 26 July, 1996.

Jakobovits, Immanuel, 'Fragments from an Unpublished Autobiography,' in Meir Persoff, *Immanuel Jakobovits: a Prophet in Israel*, London and Portland OR: Vallentine Mitchell, 2002.

Joseph, Morris, *Judaism as Creed and Life*, London: George Routledge and Sons, 1903.

Joseph, Morris, 'The English Reform Movement,' *Jewish Chronicle*, 14 May, 1909.

Kalms, Stanley (chairman), *A Time for Change: United Synagogue Review*, London: Stanley Kalms Foundation, 1992.

Kalms, Stanley, 'On the Right Track: The Chief Rabbi's First Ten Years,' *Jewish Chronicle*, 31 August, 2001.

Keiner, Judy, 'Opening up Jewish Education to Inspection: the Impact of the Ofsted Inspection System in England,' in *Education Policy Analysis Archives*, Vol. 4, No. 5, Arizona: State University, College of Education, March 1996.

Kershen, Anne J. (ed.), *RSGB/ULPS: 150 Years of Progressive Judaism in Britain, 1840–1990*, London: London Museum of Jewish Life, 1990.

Kershen, Anne J., and Romain, Jonathan A., *Tradition and Change: A History of Reform Judaism in Britain, 1840–1994*, London: Vallentine Mitchell, 1995.

Kosmin, Barry A., 'The case for the local perspective in the study of contemporary British Jewry,' in *Jewish Life in Britain, 1962–1977*, ed., Julius Gould and Shaul Esh, London: Routledge & Kegan Paul, 1964.

Kosmin, Barry A., 'Localism and Pluralism in British Jewry, 1900–80,' in *Transactions of the Jewish Historical Society of England*, Vol. XXVIII, London, 1982.

Langdon, Harold S., 'The Place of Reform in Anglo-Jewry Today,' in *A Genuine Search*, ed., Dow Marmur, London: Reform Synagogues of Great Britain, 1979.

Lappin, Elena, 'Whose Chief Rabbi?', in *The Jewish Quarterly*, Vol. 44, No. 2 (166), summer 1997.

Laws of the Congregation of the Great Synagogue, Duke's Place, London: J. Wertheimer and Co., 1863.

Lehman, Yaacov, *Let My People Know: Proposals for the Development of Jewish Education*, London: Office of the Chief Rabbi, 5732–1971.

Leibler, Isi, *Jewish Religious Extremism: A Threat to the Future of the Jewish People*, New York: World Jewish Congress–Australian Institute of Jewish Affairs, 1991.

Leigh, Michael, 'Reform Judaism in Britain (1840–1970),' in *Reform Judaism*, ed., Dow Marmur, London: Reform Synagogues of Great Britain, 1970.

Long-term Planning for British Jewry: Final Report and Recommendations, London: Institute for Jewish Policy Research, Report No. 5, 2003.

Marks, D.W. (ed.), *Forms of Prayer, used in the West London Synagogue of British Jews, with an English Translation. Volume I – Daily and Sabbath Prayers*, London: Wertheimer and Co., 1841.

Marmur, Dow (ed.), *Reform Judaism: Essays on Reform Judaism in Britain*, London: Reform Synagogues of Great Britain, 1973.

Marmur, Dow (ed.), *A Genuine Search*, London: Reform Synagogues of Great Britain, 1979.

Marsden, Norman (comp.), *Register of Research in Jewish Studies in Great Britain*, Oxford: Oxford Centre for Postgraduate Hebrew Studies and British Association for Jewish Studies, 1975.

Maybaum, Ignaz, *The Office of a Chief Rabbi*, London: Reform Synagogues of Great Britain, 1964.

Miller, Stephen H., 'Religious Practice and Jewish Identity in a Sample of London Jews,' in *Jewish Identities in the New Europe*, ed., Jonathan Webber, London and Washington: Littman Library of Jewish Civilization, for the Oxford Centre for Hebrew and Jewish Studies, 1994.

Montefiore, Claude G., *Outlines of Liberal Judaism*, London: Macmillan, 1912.

Newman, Aubrey, *Chief Rabbi Dr Joseph H. Hertz, C.H.*, London: United Synagogue, 1972.

Newman, Aubrey, *The United Synagogue 1870–1970*, London: Routledge & Kegan Paul, 1977.

Paul, Geoffrey, 'How the Chief can patch up his umbrella,' *Jewish Chronicle*, 28 March, 1997.

Pearl, Chaim, 'About "Chief Rabbis,"' *The Jewish Spectator*, New York, January 1967.

Peled, Daniella, 'Anglo-Jewry defeats itself,' *Haaretz* (English edition), 25 December, 2009.

Persoff, Meir, *Immanuel Jakobovits: a Prophet in Israel*, London and Portland OR: Vallentine Mitchell, 2002.

Persoff, Meir, *Faith Against Reason: Religious Reform and the British Chief Rabbinate, 1840–1990*, London and Portland OR: Vallentine Mitchell, 2008.

Philipson, David, *The Reform Movement in Judaism*, revised edition, New York: Macmillan, 1931.

Picciotto, James, *Sketches of Anglo-Jewish History*, first published in the *Jewish Chronicle*, 1872–1875; published in book form, London, 1875; reissued, ed., Israel Finestein, London: Soncino Press, 1956.

R [E] v the Governing Body of JFS and the Admissions Panel of JFS, case no. CO/7896/2007; R [E] v Office of the Schools Adjudicator, case no. CO/11587/2007. Before Mr Justice Munby; judgment given on 3 July, 2008. London: Royal Courts of Justice, 2008.

R (on the application of E) (Respondent) v Governing Body of JFS and the Admissions Appeal Panel of JFS (Appellants) and others; R (on the application of E) (respondent) v Governing Body of JFS and the Admissions Appeal Panel of JFS (United Synagogue) and others (appellants). Judgment [2009] UKSC1. On appeal from: [2009] EWCA Civ. 626, [2009] EWCA Civ. 681. Before Lord Hope of Craighead (Deputy President), Baroness Hale of Richmond, Lord Brown of Eaton-under-Heywood. Heard on 1 October, 2009; judgment given on 14 October, 2009. London: The Supreme Court, 2009.

R (on the application of E) (Respondent) v Governing Body of JFS and the Admissions Appeal Panel of JFS (Appellants) and others; R (on the application of E) (Respondent) v Governing Body of JFS and the Admissions Appeal Panel of JFS and others (United Synagogue) (Appellants). Before Lord Phillips (President), Lord Hope (Deputy President), Lord Rodger, Lord Walker, Lady Hale, Lord Brown, Lord Mance, Lord Kerr, Lord Clarke. UKSC 15. On appeal from [2009] EWCA Civ 626. Heard on 27, 28 and 29 October, 2009; judgment given on 16 December, 2009. London: The Supreme Court, 2009.

Rayner, John D., 'Nonconformism in Anglo-Jewry,' *The Jewish Quarterly*, Vol. 46, No. 4 (176), winter 1999–2000.

Recorded Minutes of the First Meeting of Elected Members of the Vestry of the United Synagogue, London: United Synagogue, 11 January, 1871.

Reif, Stefan, 'Dilemma of Dr Jonathan and Rabbi Sacks,' *Jewish Chronicle*, 30 April, 1993.

'Resolutions on Matters Relating to the Office of the Chief Rabbi, passed at Meetings of the Several

Metropolitan and Provincial Congregations, the Great Synagogue, London, 19 and 21 February, 1843,'*Voice of Jacob*, 3 March, 1843.

Rigal, Lawrence, and Rosenberg, Rosita, *Liberal Judaism: The First Hundred Years*, London: Liberal Judaism, 2004.

Romain, Jonathan A., *The Reform Beth Din: The Formation and Development of the Rabbinical Court of the Reform Synagogues of Great Britain, 1935–1965*, PhD dissertation, University of Leicester, 1990.

Romain, Jonathan A., *Faith and Practice: A Guide to Reform Judaism Today*, London: Reform Synagogues of Great Britain, 1991.

Romain, Jonathan A., 'The establishment of the Reform Beth Din in 1948: a barometer of religious trends in Anglo-Jewry,' *Jewish Historical Studies*, Vol. XXXIII, London: Jewish Historical Society of England, 1995.

Roth, Cecil, *Records of the Western Synagogue, 1761–1932*, London: Edward Goldston, 1932.

Roth, Cecil, 'The Collapse of English Jewry,' *The Jewish Monthly*, No. 4, London: Anglo-Jewish Association, July 1947.

Roth, Cecil, *History of the Great Synagogue, 1690–1940*, London: Edward Goldston & Son, 1950.

Sacks, Jonathan, 'A close-knit academic community, with a clear sense of its role. Reflections of a semichah candidate,' *Jewish Chronicle*, Jews' College Supplement, 3 September, 1976.

Sacks, Jonathan, 'The Role of Women in Judaism,' in *Man, Woman, and Priesthood*, ed., Peter Moore, London: SPCK, 1978.

Sacks, Jonathan, 'Jews' College in Crisis: Commitment to the Community,' *Jewish Chronicle*, 30 November, 1979.

Sacks, Jonathan, 'Jews' College: the way ahead. A story of self-discovery,' *Jewish Chronicle*, 26 October, 1984.

Sacks, Jonathan, 'The Origin of Torah,' *Jewish Chronicle*, 2 November, 1984.

Sacks, Jonathan, *Traditional Alternatives: Orthodoxy and the Future of the Jewish People*, London: Jews' College Publications, 1989; published as *Arguments for the Sake of Heaven*, Northvale, NJ: Jason Aronson, 1995.

Sacks, Jonathan, *Tradition in an Untraditional Age*, London: Vallentine Mitchell, 1990.

Sacks, Jonathan (ed.), *Orthodoxy Confronts Modernity*, Hoboken, NJ: Ktav, 1991.

Sacks, Jonathan, *A Decade of Jewish Renewal*, Address Delivered on his Installation as Chief Rabbi of the United Hebrew Congregations of the Commonwealth, St John's Wood Synagogue, London, 1 September, 1991, London: Office of the Chief Rabbi, 1991.

Sacks, Jonathan, *A Time for Renewal: A Rabbinic Response to the Kalms Report, 'A Time for Change*, London: Office of the Chief Rabbi, 1992.

Sacks, Jonathan, *Crisis and Covenant: Jewish Thought After the Holocaust*, Manchester: University Press, 1992.

Sacks, Jonathan, 'Casting Off Mediocrity: Women in the Decade of Jewish Renewal,' *Jewish Chronicle*, 6 March, 1992.

Sacks, Jonathan, *One People? Tradition, Modernity, and Jewish Unity*, London: Littman Library of Jewish Civilization, 1993.

Sacks, Jonathan, *Studies in Renewal: 1. From Integration to Survival to Continuity; 2. The Crisis of Continuity; 3. The Secret of Jewish Continuity; 4. Rethinking Priorities; 5. From Jewish Continuity to Jewish Continuity*, London: Office of the Chief Rabbi, June–October 1993.

Sacks, Jonathan, *Will We Have Jewish Grandchildren? Jewish Continuity and How to Achieve It*, London: Vallentine Mitchell, 1994.

Sacks, Jonathan, *Community of Faith*, London: Peter Halban, 1995.

Sacks, Jonathan, *Celebrating Life: Finding Happiness in Unexpected Places*, London: Fount-HarperCollins, 2000.

Sacks, Jonathan, *From Renewal to Responsibility*, London: Office of the Chief Rabbi, 2001.

Sacks, Jonathan, *Radical Then, Radical Now: The Legacy of the World's Oldest Religion*, London: HarperCollins, 2001.

Sacks, Jonathan, *The Dignity of Difference: How to Avoid the Clash of Civilizations*, first edition, London and New York: Continuum, 2002; revised edition with new preface, 2003.

Sacks, Jonathan, *Covenant & Conversation: Genesis – The Book of Beginnings*, Jerusalem: Maggid Books and the Orthodox Union, 2009.

Sacks, Jonathan, 'Standards in Public Life,' in *Daf Hashavua*, Vol. 22, No. 9, December 2009, London: United Synagogue.

Schimmel, Liesbeth, *Towards a Future of Sincerity and Harmony: Dutch Jews and the Appeal of Reform Judaism*, MA thesis, University of Utrecht, 2007.

Schmool, Marlena, 'Register of Social Research on the Anglo-Jewish Community, 1987–88,' *Jewish Journal of Sociology*, Vol. XXX, No. 1, June 1988.

Schmool, Marlena, and Miller, Stephen, *Women in the Jewish Community: Survey Report*, London: Women in the Community [Office of the Chief Rabbi], 1994.

Schmool, Marlena, 'The Ethnic Question on the British Census: A Jewish Perspective,' *Patterns of Prejudice*, Vol. 32, No. 2, London: Sage Publications, 1998.

Schonfeld, Solomon, *Jewish Religious Education: A Guide and Handbook*, London: National Council for Jewish Religious Education, 1943.

Shaftesley, John M., 'Religious Controversies,' in *A Century of Anglo-Jewish Life, 1870–1970*, ed., Salmond S. Levin, London: United Synagogue, 1970.

Sharot, Stephen, 'Religious Change in Native Orthodoxy in London, 1870–1914: Rabbinate and Clergy,' *Jewish Journal of Sociology*, Vol. XV, No. 2, London: William Heinemann, December 1973.

Sharot, Stephen, 'Reform and Liberal Judaism in London: 1840–1940,' *Jewish Social Studies*, Vol. XLI, New York: Conference on Jewish Social Studies, 1979.

Simon, Maurice, *Jewish Religious Conflicts*, London: Hutchinson's University Library, 1950.

Sorasky, Aaron, *Melech Beyofyo [A King in His Glory]*, Jerusalem: privately published, 2004.

Stanmore Accords, signed by the lay leaders of the United Synagogue, Reform Synagogues of Great Britain, Union of Liberal and Progressive Synagogues, and Assembly of Masorti Synagogues, Stanmore, Middlesex, November 1998–Cheshvan 5759, London: United Synagogue, 1998; renewed 2009.

Vallely, Paul, 'Jonathan Sacks: Defender of the Faith,' *The Independent*, London, 8 September, 2001.

Wagner, Leslie (chairman), *Change in Continuity: Report of the Review into Jewish Continuity*, London: Jewish Continuity, 1996.

Wagner, Leslie (chairman), *The Future of Jewish Schools: The Commission on Jewish Schools*, London: Jewish Leadership Council, 2008.

Wagner, Matthew, 'Rabbi Chaim Druckman: The "darling" of religious Zionism' ('People of the Year'), *Jerusalem Post*, 26 September, 2008.

Webber, Jonathan (ed.), *Jewish Identities in the New Europe*, London: Littman Library of Jewish Civilization, 1994.

Wittenberg, Jonathan, 'The Significance of Motivation in the Halachah of Conversion,' *Judaism Today*, No. 3, London: Assembly of Masorti Synagogues, winter 1995–96.

Wolkind, Jack, *London and its Jewish Community*, annual West Central Lecture delivered at University College London, 13 June, 1985, London: West Central Counselling and Community Research, 1985.

Worms, Fred (chairman), *Securing our Future: An Inquiry into Jewish Education in the United Kingdom*, London: Jewish Educational Development Trust, 1992.

London Metropolitan Archives (40 Northampton Road, London EC1R 0HB) houses the papers of, among other institutions, the Board of Deputies of British Jews (ACC/3121), United Synagogue (ACC/2712), Office of the Chief Rabbi (ACC/2805), London Beth Din (ACC/3400), Kashrus Commission (ACC/2980), Federation of Synagogues (ACC/2893), Western Synagogue (ACC/2911), Liberal Jewish Synagogue (ACC/3529), West London Synagogue (ACC/2886), Westminster Synagogue (LMA/4071), London School of Jewish Studies, formerly Jews' College (LMA/4180), Jewish Memorial Council (ACC/2999).

The Archive and Manuscript Collections of the Hartley Library, University of Southampton (Highfield, Southampton SO9 5NH), include the papers of C. J. Goldsmid-Montefiore (MS 108), Lord Swaythling (MS 117), Selig Brodetsky (MS 119), Michael Adler (MS 125), Laski family (MS 134), West London Synagogue (MS 140), Bernard Homa (MS 141), London Board of Shechita (MS 142), P. Goldberg (MS 148), New London Synagogue (MS 149), Machzike Hadath Congregation (MS 151), Cecil Roth (MS 156), Jewish Religious Education Board (MS 157), H. F. Reinhart (MS 171), J. H. Hertz (MS 175), Solomon Schonfeld (MS 183), Adolf Büchler (MS 186), Salis Daiches (MS 189), Victor Schonfeld (MS 192), Israel Brodie (MS 206), *Jewish Chronicle* (MS 225), J. M. Shaftesley (MS 230), V. D. Lipman (MS 245), Van der Zyl family (MS 297).

The Special Collections of the Mocatta Library at University College London (140 Hampstead Road, London NW1 2BX) include books, manuscripts and papers of Frederic David Mocatta, Hermann Gollancz, Israel Abrahams, Lucien Wolf, Moses Montefiore and Moses Gaster.

The Archives in the Special Collection of the Jewish Theological Seminary of America Library (3080 Broadway at 122nd Street, New York, NY 10027-4649) contain personal papers of Nathan Marcus Adler (boxes 5-1 to 5-4), Hermann Adler (3-1 to 3-3) and Marcus Nathan Adler (4-1). Earlier and later Adler material is in boxes 1 and 2; papers relating to Morris Joseph, Albert H. Jessel and Albert M. Hyamson are in box 3; to Moses Montefiore, Judith, Lady Montefiore, Claude G. Montefiore, Cecil Roth and Redcliffe Nathan Salaman, in box 4; to Isidore Spielmann, in box 5. Boxes 6 to 17 include a wealth of material from organisations across the Anglo-Jewish spectrum.

For further study, the reader is directed to the Bibliography in *Faith Against Reason: Religious Reform and the British Chief Rabbinate, 1840–1990*, pp.449-464.

Index

Abraham, Yonason, 173, 318

Abrahams, M., 355

Abramsky, Yechezkel, 15, 30, 40-41, 68, 288, 321

Adler, Hermann, xi, xvii, 39, 186, 286, 303-304, 335

Adler, Michael, 355

Adler, Nathan Marcus, xi, 9, 34, 36, 38, 57, 187, 281, 295, 297, 304

Agunah/Agunot, 24, 240 seq., 251, 255

Alderman, Geoffrey, 208-209, 258, 301, 307-308, 319, 324, 335

Altmann, Alexander, 327

Ansell, Anthony, 86

Apple, Raymond, 302, 357

Archbishop of Canterbury, 163, 165, 296-297, 338, 340

Archbishop of Westminster, 163

Arkush, Jonathan, 217

Arussi, Ratzon, 318

Association for Furthering Traditional Judaism, 285

Association of Masorti Synagogues, 69, 118, 140, 191, 227

Association of United Synagogue Ladies' Guilds, 237-238

Australia, 79, 302

Baeck, Leo, 91, 118, 329

Balint, Benjamin, 320

Bard, Julia, 150

Barnett, Arthur, 38

Bayfield, Linda, 333

Bayfield, Tony, 61, 66, 85, 93, 95, 117, 126-128, 130-131, 164-165, 181, 193, 217, 266, 276-277, 338

Belovski, Harvey, 231-233, 347

Ben Azai (Chaim Bermant), 262

Ben Yitzchok, 208, 331

Berger, Isaac, 67

Berlin, Naftali Yehuda Zvi, 183

Bermant, Chaim, 6, 28, 70, 158, 167, 315

Bevis Marks Synagogue, 325

Binstock, Ivan, 173, 234, 318-319

Blair, Tony, 102

Blank, Joseph, 284

Bleich, David, 159

Board of Deputies, xviii, 65, 77-78, 84, 96, 99, 111, 116, 128, 140, 187, 218, 224-227, 266, 293 seq., 312 seq.

Bolton, Roger, 270

Borowski, Ephraim, 52, 328

Boteach, Shmuel, 86

Bournemouth Hebrew Congregation, 258

Bradfield, Gabrielle, 153

Brawer, Naftali, 219, 347

Brent Council, 208

Brichto, Sidney, 49-51, 55, 136, 188, 270, 290-291, 329

Brodie, Israel, xii, 42, 56, 188, 290, 304, 306

Brodie, Yehuda, 71, 86

Brown, Andrew, 247

Brown, Gordon, 170, 339

Brown, Lord, 213-214

Buckley, Richard, 276

Bulka, Naomi, 323

Bulka, Reuven, 23-24

Cambridge University, 6-7, 9, 48, 167, 260

Cannon, Raymond, 302

Caplan, Simon, 233

Cardiff New Synagogue, 264

Carlebach, Alexander, 342

Carnegie Council, 182, 341

Carr, Marcus, 67

Cavendish Group, 358

Chaikin, Moshe Avigdor, 39-40, 326, 335

Chazan, Yossi, 171-172

Chelms, Stephen, 357

Chernett, Jaclyn, 188

Chief Rabbinate, xi, xvi, 3, 21, 35, 116, 120, 128, 131, 133-134, 157, 166, 258, 281, 284 seq., 297 seq., 312 seq.

Chinn, Sir Trevor, 130

Christ's College, 6

Citron, Judith, 248

Clarke, Lord, 213

Clause 43/74 (Board of Deputies), 293-294, 314

Clore Shalom School, 227

Clore Tikva School, 227-228

Cofnas, Lionel, 324

Cohen, Adrian, 357

Cohen, Arnold, 22

Cohen, Jeffrey, 221, 234-236, 277-278, 336

Cohen, Norman, 297, 306

Cohen, Shimon, 191
Cohn-Sherbok, Dan, 320
Commission on Representation, 312 seq.
Connection, Continuity and Community (women's report, 2009), 252-256, 311-312
Conrad, A., 102
Consultative Committee, 93, 126-129, 134, 136, 140-141, 259, 267-268, 271-272, 277, 279-280
Conversion, xix, 41, 49, 51, 69, 72, 76, 81, 188-189, 191 seq., 208-209, 211-215, 221-222, 267, 277
Conway, David, 176-177, 319, 340
Conway, Joy, 150
Cooper, Howard, 178, 340
Corman, Charles, 334
Corob, Sidney, 151
Cosgrove, Elliot Joe, 327
Council of Christians and Jews, 106, 134, 162 seq., 268
Court of Appeal (UK), 196 seq., 215

Davis, Felix, 286
de Lange, John, 157
de Lange, Nicholas, 24
de Rothschild, Baron Lionel, 187
de Rothschild, Sir Anthony, 187
Decade of Jewish Renewal, xvii, 50, 56, 145-147, 168, 223, 243
Divorce, 41, 49, 240, 251, 255
Dobb, Fred Scherlinder, 357
Documentary Hypothesis, 10, 320
Druckman, Chaim, xx, 318
Dunner, J. H., 173, 264

Eban, Abba, 318
Edward VII, xi
Ehrenkranz, Joseph, 180
Ehrentreu, Chanoch, 17, 172-173, 243, 265, 324
Ellenson, David, 180
Elyashiv, Yosef Sholom, 174
Emanuel, G. J., 355
Endelman, Todd M., xvii, 38, 296, 317
Englander, David, 28
Epstein, Isidore, 43-44
Etz Chaim yeshivah, 9, 15

Falk, Alastair, 229
Federation of Synagogues, 22, 39, 62, 75, 142, 282, 284, 289-290
Feinstein, Moshe, 244, 265
Feldman, Emmanuel, 159

Fine, Doreen, 245
Fine, Yisroel, 117, 345
Finestein, Israel, 38, 151
Forta, Arye, 320
Freedland, Jonathan, 179, 345
Freedman, Harry, 86, 125-126, 129, 134, 268, 293
Freedman, Judge Dawn, 255
Frei, David, 195
Friedlander, Albert, 93, 165, 172, 268
Fromson, I., 154
Frosh, Sidney, 21-22, 160, 233, 295
Frumkin, Arye Leib, 4
Frumkin, Eliyahu Ephraim, 6

Gainsford, Sir Ian, 155
Gartner, Lloyd P., 16, 321
Gaster, Moses, 335
Gastwirth, E., 320
Gateshead, 15, 173
Gee, George, 22, 92
Gelley, Menachem, 173, 193, 209, 318
Ger Chasidim, 16
Ginsbury, Mordechai, 345
Gladstone, W. E., 301, 324
Gledhill, Ruth, 123-124, 168
Gluckman, Michael, 193, 272-273
Goldberg, David J., 149, 261, 269-270, 350
Goldblatt, S., 154
Golders Green Synagogue, 21, 158, 261-263
Goldman, Raymond, 86, 188, 263
Goldsmid, Sir Julian, 283
Golinkin, David, 318
Goodkin, Judy, 248
Goodman, David, 317
Grabiner, Michael, 229-230, 347
Graham, David, 229
Great Synagogue, xi, 5, 33-34
Greek Orthodox Archbishop of Great Britain, 163
Green, A. A., 355
Greenbat, Alan, 92, 94
Greenberg, Yitz (Irving), 357
Gross, Michael, 156, 174
Grunewald, Ya'akov, 9, 260
Gryn, Hugo, 91 seq., 126, 136, 138, 164, 227, 259, 266, 278, 305, 336, 348
Gryn, David, 94
Gryn, Jackie, 93-94, 100, 109
Gryn, Naomi, 121-123
Guttentag, Jonathan, 71, 172

Hale, Lady, 213-214

Halford, John, 205
Halpern, Elchonon, 175
Halter, Aloma, 121
Hambro' Synagogue, 33
Hamburg, 34-35
Hamburger, Sir Sidney, 154
Handler, Arieh, 90
Harries, Bishop Richard, 163
Harris, Ann, 239
Harris, Cyril, 239, 348
Harris, Isidore, 283
Harris, Lester, 174
Harris, Michael, 219, 234, 279
Harris, Simon, 85
Hart, Rona, 223, 229
Hartman, David, 159-160
Hass, Simon, 324
Hebrew Union College, 41, 91
Heine, Heinrich, 185
Helfgott, Maurice, 357
Henry, Michael, 296
Herman, S., 320
Hertz, Joseph Herman, xi, 40, 56, 76, 80, 286
    seq., 299-300, 326, 335
Hillman, Shmuel Yitzchak, 39-40
Hirsch, Samson Raphael, 36, 132, 183
Hirschell, Solomon, 33
'Historicus,' 298
Hochhauser, Simon, 204, 208, 278-279, 358
Hochman, Joseph, 42, 285, 299
Holocaust, xi, 20, 31, 48, 96-97, 108, 111,
    116, 122, 266
Holy Blossom Temple (Toronto), 51
Hope, Lord, 213
Hornung, Ernest, 264
Hudson, Lucian, 358
Huller, Sidney, 71
Huntington, Samuel, 182, 184
Hyamson, Moses, 286
Hyman, Geoffrey, 16

Inclusivism, xii, xvii, 1-2, 4, 36, 46, 47-49,
    51-52, 55-56, 60, 62, 77-79, 87-88, 210,
    224, 228-231, 253, 270
Independent Jewish Day School, 229
Ingram, Chaim N., 320
Institute for Jewish Policy Research, 229, 312
    seq.
Israel (State of), xix, xx, 4, 7-8, 48, 122, 147,
    175, 179, 200, 220, 281, 318, 340

Jackson, Edward, 73
Jacobs Affair, xii, 9, 12, 67

Jacobs, Cyril, 153
Jacobs, Gerald, 308
Jacobs, Irving, 16, 176, 340
Jacobs, Ivor, 69, 127, 190-191, 342
Jacobs, Jeremy, 231
Jacobs, Joseph, 324
Jacobs, Louis, 7, 10, 12-14, 42-43, 67, 70, 72,
    74, 88-90, 190, 258, 261, 291-292, 327,
    332
Jacobs, Paula, 190-191, 258-259
Jacobs, Tirza, 190, 342
Jacobsohn, Israel, 34
Jacobson, Howard, 263
Jakobovits, (Lady) Amélie, 159, 237
Jakobovits, George, 323
Jakobovits, Immanuel, xii, 17, 20-21, 24-31,
    49, 67, 69, 93, 147, 160, 164, 237 seq.,
    257, 278, 290, 292, 299-300, 304, 306,
    329
JCoSS (Jewish Community Secondary School),
    228 seq., 347
Jessel, Albert H., 286, 326
Jewish Chronicle, 74, 84, 91, 101, 103-104, 125,
    142-143, 148, 165, 167-169, 185-186,
    257-258, 281
Jewish Continuity, 56 seq., 77, 224 seq.
Jewish Educational Development Trust, 24,
    159, 233
Jewish Gay and Lesbian Helpline, 78, 330
Jewish Religious Union, 41
Jewish Theological Seminary of America, 111,
    287, 335
Jewish Tribune, 59, 61, 75, 79, 84, 86, 89
Jewish United Synagogues Act (1870), 34,
    306
Jewish Women's Network, 252
Jews' College, 9, 15-20, 25-28, 31, 169, 259
Jews' Free School (JFS), xiii, 187 seq.
Joint Israel Appeal, 59-60, 63, 65, 77, 84
Joseph, Morris, 35, 42

Kahana, Kopul, 16
Kalman, Matthew, 110
Kalms, Lord (Stanley), xvii, 1, 16-17, 20, 23-
    28, 55, 148 seq., 158 seq., 186, 252, 258,
    270-271, 304, 309-311
Karo, Joseph, 221
Keiner, Judy, 224-227
Kermaier, Yaakov, 347
Kerner, Brian, 65, 358
Kerr, Lord, 213, 344
Kestenbaum, Jonathan, 70, 92, 252, 263
Kett, Russell, 196, 207-208

Kimche, Alan A., 320
King Solomon High School, 209, 229
Kirsh, Gerald, 331
Kirzner, Eliezer, 290
Kleiner, Mark, 262
Kletz, T. A., 320
Kopelowitz, Lionel, 156, 164
Kosmin, Barry, 300
Krausz, Gabriel, 264, 324
Krikler, Douglas, 358

Landau, Ronnie, 152
Lappin, Elena, 113, 335
Leadership, xv-xvi, 1, 28-31, 84, 104, 109,
    112, 115, 117-120, 127-130, 169, 174,
    176-177, 253, 295 seq., 203-304, 312
    seq.
League of Jewish Women, 238
Lee, Sharon, 245
Leibler, Isi, xv-xvi, 317
Leibowitz, Nehama, 10, 320
Leo Baeck College, 227, 259-261
Levin, Salmond S., 22, 238, 320
Levin, Shlomo, 265-266, 319
Levine, Frank, 9
Levy, Abraham, 70, 92, 261, 338
Levy, Elkan, 95, 117, 125-126, 133-136, 141,
    266, 278, 351
Levy, Julian, 233
Levy, Peter, 129
Levy, S., 355
Lew, Jonathan, 126, 134-135
Lew, Shmuel, 261
Liberal/Progressives, xvii, 28, 36, 41-42, 46,
    49, 50-52, 54-55, 62-63, 66, 84, 93, 97,
    105, 119, 125, 129, 132, 139-140, 162,
    164-165, 177, 188, 192, 205-206, 210,
    217, 227, 257, 259, 261, 263, 268, 273,
    288, 290-291, 293, 298-299, 301, 307,
    311, 314
Libson, James, 358
Lichtenstein, Yisroel, 75, 96, 264, 331
Lieberman, Simche Bunim, 15-21, 25, 27, 91
Lieberman, Yitzchak Meir, 320
Lightman, David, 200, 202
Lightman, Kate, 200, 202
Limmud, 233 seq., 274, 312
Lind, Eleanor, 73-74, 82
Linden, Tom, 199
Lipfriend, Alan, 331
Lipman, Maureen, 114
Livingstone, Isaac, 262
Loewenthal, Tali, 320

Loftus, Richard, 302-303
London Beth Din, xvi, xix, 2-4, 41, 49, 67, 72,
    76, 140-142, 189, 193, 200, 202, 215,
    233-234, 241, 250, 258
London Board of Jewish Religious Education,
    189, 224
London School of Jewish Studies (formerly
    Jews' College), 321-322
London Society of Christians and Jews, 262
London University, 6-7
Longley, Clifford, 163-166, 168
Loren, Sophia, 214
Lucas, Victor, 22, 239
Lyon, Hart, 33

Maccoby, Hyam, 261
Machzike Hadath, 39
Mackay, Lord, 240
Magnus, Sir Philip, 281
Magonet, Jonathan, 261, 350
Maidenhead Synagogue, 265
Maimonides, Moses, 36, 56, 143, 167
Mance, Lord, 213
Manchester, 71, 74, 174
Mandla v Dowell-Lee, 198
Manna, 54, 61, 85, 89, 119, 141, 177-178
Marble Arch Synagogue, 21, 263
Marks, Clive, 58, 61, 151
Marks, David Woolf, 283, 325, 335
Marmur, Dow, 51-52
Maroof, Joseph, 357
Marran, Richard, 345
Marriage, 41, 49, 52, 67-74, 76, 79, 81-83,
    90, 140, 267-268, 279, 289
Masorti Beth Din, 193
Masorti, xii, xvii, xx, 46, 49-50, 52, 59-63,
    67, 69 seq., 80, 82-83, 86-90, 105, 118-
    119, 125, 129, 132, 139-140, 164, 188,
    191, 210, 217, 227, 258-259, 268, 271-
    273, 301, 311
Mattuck, Israel, 288
Maybaum, Ignaz, 291
Mayo, Simon, 319, 322
Mendelsohn, Jon, 358
Middleburgh, Charles, 127, 129, 141-142,
    164-165, 266
Miller, Stephen, 307, 309-310, 356
Millett, Sir Peter, 59, 93, 151
Minhag Anglia, 76, 309, 357
Mintz, Louis, 263, 280, 328
Mirvis, Ephraim, 206, 345
Moderator of the Free Church Federal Council,
    163

Moderator of the General Assembly of the Church of Scotland, 163
Monchi, Valerie, 246
Montagu, Ewen, 68
Montagu, Lily, 41, 91
Montagu, Sir Samuel, 281
Montefiore, Claude, 41, 288, 353
Montefiore, Sir Moses, 57, 187
Moss, Stephen, 358
Munby, Mr Justice, 191 seq., 214
Munk, Elie, 292
Muswell Hill Synagogue, 70

New London Synagogue, 67, 72-73, 191, 291, 299
New North London Synagogue, 202
New Synagogue, 33
New West End Synagogue, 43, 285
Newman, Arye, 320
Newman, Aubrey, 38
Newman, Eugene, 262
Newman, Isaac, 320
Norman, Matthew, 102

Obama, Barack, 347
Ofsted, 224-227, 346
Oldham, Peter, 194-195
Ordman, Nosson, 9
Oxford University, 6

Padwa, Chenoch Dov, 91, 98, 102, 108, 112
Padwa, Rena, 121
Pale of Settlement, 39
Panken, Aaron, 357
Pannick, Lord, 197, 199, 210, 214
Paul, Geoffrey, 115
Pears, Trevor, 358
Peled, Daniella, 219-220
Philips, Melanie, 263
Phillips, Lord, 210 seq.
Picciotto, James, 37
Pickett, Winston, 357
Pikuach, 226-228
Plancey, Alan, 72, 324
Plaskow, M., 320
Pluralism, xii, xvii, 1, 4, 23, 26, 39, 47, 52-54, 65, 88, 105, 137, 169, 179-182, 229-231, 233, 235, 273 seq., 278, 300, 306 seq.
Posner, Zalman I., 320
Preston, Rosalind, 243, 246 seq., 252-253

Rabbinic Hebrew, 15, 91, 98, 103-104, 108, 115

Rabin, Yitzhak, 109
Rabinovitch, Nachum L., 9, 260
Race Relations Act (1976), 192 seq., 211 seq.
Rakow, B., 173-174, 264
Rayner, John, 136, 263-264
Reform Synagogues of Great Britain, 95-96, 109-110, 128, 140, 191, 227
Reform, xvii, 24, 28, 34-37, 41-42, 46, 49-52, 54, 66, 77, 93, 95, 97, 105, 107, 109-110, 115, 125, 127-129, 132, 139-140, 164-165, 188, 191, 210, 217, 227, 259, 263, 268, 273, 291, 297, 301, 311
Reif, Stefan, 52, 328
Rich, Danny, 193, 205, 217, 338
Rimer, Lord Justice, 196, 210
Robinson, Shaul, 347
Rodger, Lord, 213-214
Romain, Jonathan, 109-110, 265-266
Ronson, Lisa, 358
Rose, Dinah, 197-199, 210
Rose, Pam, 322
Roseman, N. S., 154
Rosen, David, 172
Rosen, Kopul, 172
Rosen, Michael (Mickey), 245-246, 263
Rosenberg, David, 150
Rosenberg, Laurie, 346
Rosenberg, Rosita, 134
Rosenfeld, Lionel, 258-259, 324
Rosenthal, Jack, 114
Rosenthal, Joel H., 182
Rosh Chodesh prayer groups, 78, 241, 243 seq., 277-278
Roth, Cecil, 37, 289, 326,
Rothschild, Lord, 281-283, 286
Rowe, J., 154
Ruben, David-Hillel, 181, 341
Rubin, Nathan, 189, 262

Sacher, Harry, 285, 353
Sacks, Alan, 175, 340
Sacks, Elaine, 92, 94, 162, 319
Sacks, Jonathan, on A Tree of Life, 12; birth and childhood, 4 seq.; Board of Deputies, 3-4; Celebrating Life, 123-124; Chief Rabbinical appointment, 22-23, 322; 'Coalition for Peace,' 116-117, 121, 125 seq., 138, 304; coping with difficulties, 123-124, 336; Court of Appeal judgment, 203-204; Decade of Jewish Renewal, 145-147; Decade of Jewish Responsibility, 145, 147-148; 'diplomatic minefields,' 340; diversity, 8; 'Dr Jonathan and Rabbi Sacks,'

48; education, 222, 323; enigma, xii; *Faith in the Future*, 168; Golders Green Synagogue, 21, 261-263; Hugo Gryn, 91 seq., 99-102; inclusivism, 1, 36, 46-48, 56; induction, 29-31; Israeli policy, 179, 340; Jakobovits Chair (Jews' College), 320; *Jewish Chronicle*, 91 seq.; Jewish Continuity, 56 seq.; Jewish Darwinism, 57; Leo Baeck College, 259-261; Limmud, 233 seq.; Marble Arch Synagogue, 21, 263 Masorti, 75 seq.; *One People?*, 47-52; peerage, xvii, 4, 318-319, 339; philosophy, 6-9, 104, 305, 315; popularity, 304 seq.; Reith lectures, 22, 31, 169; *semichah*, 9, 260-261; Stanmore Accords, 143, 270; Supreme Court judgment, 215-217; *The Dignity of Difference*, viii, 171 seq., 339, 341; *The Politics of Hope*, 170-171, 305; tradition as argument, 45-46, 53; Traditional Alternatives, 23, 46; United Synagogue, 6, 9, 21; women's status, 242 seq.

Sacks, Louis, 4-5, 124
Sacks, Louise (Libby), 4-5, 124
Sacks, Oliver, 318
Safed, 21
Saideman, Seymour G., 149
Salaman, Redcliffe, 284-285
Salamon, Thomas, 320
Salasnik, Meir, 345
Salomon, Gotthold, 34
Sassienie, Neville, 126-127
Schechter, Solomon, 287, 353
Schiff, David Tevele, 33
Schloss, L. 283
Schmool, Marlene, 308-310, 356
Schneider, Peter, 262
Schochet, J. Immanuel, 320
Schochet, Yitzchok, 97, 218, 231, 234, 332
Schonfeld, Julie, 357
Schonfeld, Solomon, 40, 300, 308
Schorsch, Ismar, 111, 335
Schwalbe, A., 154
Scruton, Roger, 7
Sedley, Lord Justice (Sir Stephen), 196 seq., 210
Seesen (Hanover), 34
Segal, Hirsch, 318
Segal, Judah Benzion, 318
Segal, Samuel, 318
Shack, Jonathan, 156
Shaftesley, John, 325
Sharot, Stephen, 295-296, 356
Shaviv, Miriam, 347

Sheldon, Peter, 174, 266-268
Shindler, Julian, 70-73
Shrank, Paul, 267-269, 271-272
Shulchan Aruch, 221, 295
Silver, Yehuda, 71
Simon, Leon, 285, 353
Simon, Malcolm, 86
Simons, Shmuel, 318
Sinclair, Michael, 58
Six-Day War, 8
Sklan, Alex, 127, 135-136, 138
Smith, Lady Justice, 196, 210
Solomon, Norman, 169
Solomons, Stanley, 68
Soloveichik, Joseph, 321
South Hampstead Synagogue, 265-266
Spanish and Portuguese Jews' Congregation/Sephardim, 79, 88, 92, 261, 275, 282, 293-294, 301, 310, 314-315, 325, 335, 338, 357
St Albans Synagogue, 69
St Mary's Primary School, 6
Stanmore Accords, 138 seq., 259, 266, 268 seq., 279
Statement on Communal Collaboration, 273 seq.
Steinsaltz, Adin, 233-234
Stern, Joseph F., 299, 355
Stern, Rudolph, 263
Sternberg, Sir Sigmund, 130, 132
Stowe-Lindner, Jeremy, 230-231, 347
Supreme Court (UK), 209 seq.
Swift, Harris, 337
Swift, Lionel, 130-132, 135-136, 337
Swift, Morris, 68-69, 261
Sylvester, Gideon, 271

Tabachnik, Eldred, 111, 117, 133, 266
Tabick, Jackie, 92, 95, 111, 123, 126
Temko, Edward (Ned), 101-102
Tenzer, Russell, 231
Theresienstadt, 15, 91
Tibber, Anthony, 331
Tiefenbrun, Natan, 154
Titmuss Sainer Dechert, 101
Toledano, Pinchas, 264
Torah min hashamayim, 10 seq., 42-44, 71, 75-76, 88, 208, 257
Traditional Alternatives, 23, 28, 31, 46, 53, 167, 257, 270
Trilling, Lionel, 7
Tripartite Group, 130, 133-135, 272

Udelson, Joseph, 320

Ultra-Orthodoxy, xii-xiii, xv, 24, 26, 39-41, 56, 71, 75, 88, 96-99, 132, 142, 175, 235, 273, 276, 300, 307, 311, 313-314
Union of Jewish Students, 261, 268
Union of Liberal and Progressive Synagogues, 84, 140, 227, 257
Union of Orthodox Hebrew Congregations (Adath), 40, 62, 98, 102, 108, 142, 173, 293, 310, 354
United Jewish Israel Appeal, 66, 227, 229, 274
United Synagogue Rabbinical Council, 98-99, 117, 206, 218-219, 231, 279, 344-345
United Synagogue, xvi, xviii, 1, 3, 9, 33-34, 55, 99, 112, 116, 140, 159-160, 174, 188, 204, 215, 231, 249, 257, 268, 272, 282, 284, 293, 325

van der Zyl, Werner, 91
Vital, David, 52

Wagerman, Jo, 189-190, 267
Wagner, Leslie, 59 seq., 157, 227-229, 346
Waley Cohen, Robert, 289
Walker, Lord, 213
Wall, Alan K., 156
Ward, David, 258
Wasserstein, Bernard, 97
Weinberg, Syma, 346

Weiner, Chaim, 85
Weisman, Malcolm, 165, 351
West London Synagogue, xvii, 35, 42, 59, 91, 93, 114, 281-282, 288-289
Western Marble Arch Synagogue, 269
Western Synagogue, 38
Westheim, Osher, 71
Williams, Bernard, 7
Williams, Rowan, 179, 340
Wineman, Vivian, 218, 358
Wise, Isaac Mayer, 41
Wittenberg, Jonathan, 71, 82-83, 202, 217, 267-268, 279
Wolf, William, 93
Wolfe, Joy, 154
Wolkind, Jack, 294-295, 355
Women in the Jewish Community, 246 seq.
Women's status, 75, 232 seq., 248 seq.
Woolf, Lord, 151
Worms, Fred, 150, 222
Wurzburger, Walter, 322

Yakar, 85, 245-246
Yavneh College, 228
Yentob, Robert, 358

Zahn, Shammai, 265
Ziff, Michael, 66
Zneimer, Saul, 267

Also by Meir Persoff

The Running Stag: The Stamps and Postal History of Israel (1973)

Immanuel Jakobovits: a Prophet in Israel (2002)

Faith Against Reason: Religious Reform and the British Chief Rabbinate,
1840–1990 (2008)

Lightning Source UK Ltd.
Milton Keynes UK
01 June 2010

154956UK00001B/32/P